The Renewal
of Sunday Worship

THE COMPLETE LIBRARY
OF
CHRISTIAN WORSHIP

THE COMPLETE LIBRARY
OF
CHRISTIAN WORSHIP

Volume 3, The Renewal of Sunday Worship

ROBERT E. WEBBER, EDITOR

HENDRICKSON
PUBLISHERS

The Complete Library of Christian Worship, Vol. 3, The Renewal of Sunday Worship.

Hendrickson Publishers, Inc.
P. O. Box 3473
Peabody, Massachusetts 01961–3473

Printed in the United States of America

Hendrickson Publishers' edition
ISBN 1–56563–187–0
Hendrickson edition published by arrangement with Star Song Publishing Group, a division of
Jubilee Communications, Inc.
2325 Crestmoor, Nashville, Tennessee 37215.

CONTENTS

110764

List of Illustrations and Tables

Tables

Board of Editorial Consultants

The Board of Editorial Consultants is made up of leaders in worship renewal from major Christian denominations. They have functioned as advisors, often through letter and telephone. Every attempt has been made to include material on worship representing the whole church. For this reason, different viewpoints are presented without any attempt to express a particular point of view or bias. A special word of thanks is due to the executive and consulting editors for their helpful input. Their ideas, suggestions and contributions have strengthened the *Complete Library of Christian Worship*. Omissions and weaknesses in all seven volumes are the sole responsibility of the compiler and editor.

Betty Carr Pulkingham
Community of Celebration, Aliquippa, Pennsylvania

John Rempel
Manhattan Mennonite Fellowship, New York, New York

James Rosenthal
Anglican Consultative Council, London, UK

Donald Saliers
Candler School of Theology, Atlanta, Georgia

Frank C. Senn
Immanuel Lutheran Church (ELCA), Evanston, Illinois

Robert Shaper
Fuller Theological Seminary, Pasadena, California

Dan Sharp
St. Andrews Presbyterian Church, Newport, California

Stephen Shoemaker
Broadway Baptist Church, Dallas, Texas

Ron Sprunger
Ashland Theological Seminary, Ashland, Ohio

Gilbert W. Stafford
Anderson University, Anderson, Indiana

Howard Stevenson
Evangelical Free Church, Fullerton, California

Sonja M. Stewart
Western Theology Seminary, Holland, Michigan

Thomas Troeger
Iliff School of Theology, Denver, Colorado

Terry Howard Wardle
Simpson Graduate School, Reading, California

Keith Watkins
Christian Theological Seminary, Indianapolis, Indiana

John Weborg
North Park Theological Seminary, Chicago, Illinois

John Westerhoff, III
Duke University, Durham, North Carolina

James F. White
Notre Dame University, Notre Dame, Indiana

Susan J. White
Westcott House, Cambridge, England

James Wilde
Oregon Catholic Press, Portland, Oregon

Gregory Wilde
University of Notre Dame, Notre Dame, Indiana

Benjamin Williams
Antiochian Orthodox Church, Archdiocese of North America, Draper, Utah

William Willimon
Duke University Chapel, Durham, North Carolina

Contributing Editors

Jean Ackerman
Diocese of Memphis, Memphis, Tennessee

Doug Adams
Pacific School of Religion, Graduate Theological Union, Berkeley, California

Marlin Adrian
Wheaton College, Wheaton, Illinois

J. Neil Alexander
General Theological Seminary, New York City, New York

Patrick H. Alexander
Hendrickson Publishers, Peabody, Massachusetts

Ronald Allen
Western Theological Seminary, Portland, Oregon

Ronald J. Allen
Christian Theological Seminary, Indianapolis, Indiana

Timothy Allen
Evangelical Free Church, Naperville, Illinois

Lora Allison
Celebration Ministries, La Porte, Texas

Chester Alwes
University of Illinois, Champaign-Urbana, Illinois

Patti Amsden
Son-Life Church, Collinsville, Illinois

Rubén P. Armendáriz
McCormick Theological Seminary, Chicago, Illinois

Anton Armstrong
St. Olaf College, Northfield, Minnesota

Kerchal Armstrong
Faith Missionary Church, Indianapolis, Indiana

Brent Assink
Calvary CRC, Minneapolis, Minnesota

Diane S. George Ayer
Canadian Theological Seminary, Regina, Saskatchewan, Canada

Edith Bajema
Grand Rapids, Michigan

John D. Baker
Druid Hills Baptist Church, Atlanta, Georgia

Judith Wall Baker
Atlanta, Georgia

Randall Bane
Kansas City, Missouri

Henry Baron
Calvin College, Grand Rapids, Michigan

Christine A. Chakoian
Fourth Presbyterian Church, Chicago, Illinois

Bryan Chapell
Covenant Theological Seminary, St. Louis, Missouri

Nancy Chinn
San Francisco, California

John J. Chisum
Integrity Music, Mobile, Alabama

LeRoy Christoffels
Trinity CRC, Artesia, California

William Cieslak
Franciscan School of Theology, Berkeley, California

Donald L. Clapper
Pine Street Presbyterian Church, Harrisburg, Pennsylvania

Karen Clarke
Mercy Hospital, Pittsburgh, Pennsylvania

Philip K. Clemens
College Mennonite Church, Goshen, Indiana

Arthur G. Clyde
United Church Board for Homeland Ministries, Cleveland, Ohio

William B. Coker
Ashbury College, Wilmore, Kentucky

Ruth Collenridge
Womens Aglow International, Seattle, Washington

Mary Collins
The Catholic University of America, Washington, D.C.

Patrick Collins
***Modern Liturgy**, San Jose, California*

Philip W. Comfort
Tyndale Press, Carol Stream, Illinois

Bernard Cooke
The Liturgical Press, Collegeville, Minnesota

Gilbert Cope
New Westminster Dictionary of Liturgy and Worship

Robert Copeland
Geneva College, Beaver Falls, Pennsylvania

Judson Cornwall
Fountain Gate Ministries, Plano, Texas

Melva Costen
Interdenominational Center, Atlanta, Georgia

David Cottrill
Wright Air Force Base, Kettering, Ohio.

Harvey Cox
Harvard Divinity School, Boston, Massachusetts

J. D. Crichton
Retired Parish Priest, UK

Daniel A. Csanyi
Little Flower Church, South Bend, Indiana

Robert D. Culver
Grace Theological Seminary, Winona Lake, Indiana

G. J. Cuming
Kings College, London, UK

Joe Cunningham
Trinity Lutheran Church, Davenport, Iowa

Stephen Cushman
Wheaton College, Wheaton, Illinois

Jerald Daffe
Lee College, Cleveland, Tennessee

Harold Daniels
Presbyterian Church USA, Louisville, Kentucky

Randall E. Davey
Fairview Church of the Nazarene, Fairview, Pennsylvania

Robert E. Davis
Temple Bible College, Cincinnati, Ohio.

Pam de Boom
Christ Community Reformed Church, Clifton Park, New York

Sandra DeGidio
Lecturer/Writer, Crystal Lake, Illinois

Carolyn Deitering
Diocese of Tucson, Tucson, Arizona

Cynthia De Jong
Calvin College, Grand Rapids, Michigan

Carla De Sola
The Liturgical Dance Company, New York, New York

Alan F. Detscher
Secretariat for the Liturgy, Washington, D.C.

John Dettoni
Fuller Theological Seminary, Pasadena, California

William De Vries
First Christian Reformed Church, Detroit, Michigan.

Dennis C. Dickerson
Historiographer, African Methodist Episcopal Church, Williamstown, Massachusetts

David J. Diephouse
Calvin College, Grand Rapids, Michigan

John Dillenberger
Graduate Theological Union, Berkeley, California

Thomas Dipko
Board of Homeland Ministries, Cleveland, Ohio

Susan Jorgensen
Spiritual Life Center, Burlington, Connecticut

Thomas Kane
Weston School of Theology, Cambridge, Massachusetts

Catherine Kapikian
Wesley Theological Seminary, Washington, D.C.

Angela Kauffman
ACTA Publications, Chicago, Illinois

David Kauffman
ACTA Publications, Chicago, Illinois

Aidan Kavanagh
Divinity School, Yale, New Haven, Connecticut

Ralph A. Keifer
St. Mary's Seminary and University, Baltimore, Maryland

Duane Kelderman
Neland Avenue Christian Reformed Curch, Grand Rapids, Michigan

Jeff Kemper
Mt. St. Mary's Seminary, Cincinnati, Ohio

Graham Kendrick
Make Way Music, Pevensey, East Sussex, UK

Joseph Kennan
Philadelphia, Pennsylvania

LeRoy E. Kennell
Christ Community Mennonite Church, Schaumburg, Illinois

Jeffrey Keyes
St. Edward's Parish, Newark, California

Jeannie Kienzle
Grace—St. Luke's Episcopal Church, Memphis, Tennessee

Martha Ann Kirk
Incarnate Word, San Antonio, Texas

Marlene Kropf
Mennonite Board of Congregational Ministries, Elkhart, Indiana

Jill Knuth
· *Bethany Lutheran Church, Menlo Park, California*

Theresa Koernke
Washington Theological Union, Silver Spring, Maryland

Rex A. Koivisto
Multnomah School of the Bible, Portland, Oregon

David T. Koyzis
Redeemer College, Ancaster, Ontario, Canada

Tom Kraeuter
Outreach Ministries, Hillsboro, Missouri

Carolyn Krantz
Diocese of Lafayette, Lafayette, Louisiana

Eleanor Kreider
London Mennonite Center, Manchester, UK

Catherine Krier
Christ on the Mountain Porish, Lakewood, Colorado

John M. Kubiniec
Office of Liturgy, Rochester, New York

Ron Kydd
Central Pentecostal College, Keene, Ontario, Canada

Clements E. Lamberth
Church of the Covenant, Washington, Pennsylvania

John R. Landgraf
Midwest Commission on the Ministry, ABC Clergy

Craig Brian Larson
***Leadership**, Carol Stream, Illinois*

Jan Larson
Archdiocese of Seattle, Seattle, Washington

Lloyd Larson
Church of God, Anderson, Indiana

Lizette Larson-Miller
Loyola Marymount College, Los Angeles, California.

Gordon Lathrop
The Lutheran Theological Seminary, Philadelphia, Pennsylvania

Michael Lawler
Creighton University, Omaha, Nebraska

Katherine Lawrence
Bethany Theological Seminary, Lombard, Illinois

Cathy Lee
Corinthians VI, Australia

Janice E. Leonard
Laudemont Ministries, Arlington Heights, Illinois

John Brooks Leonard
Center for Pastoral Liturgy, Notre Dame University, Notre Dame, Indiana

Richard C. Leonard
Laudemont Ministries, Arlington Heights, Illinois

Curtis Lewis
Western Oaks Nazarene Church, Oklahoma City, Oklahoma

Todd Lewis
Biola University, La Mirada, California

Gary Liddle
Evangel College, Springfield, Missouri

Boyd Lien
Memorial Drive Presbyterian Church, Houston, Texas

List of Cooperating Publishers

Book Publishers

Abbott-Martyn Press
2325 Crestmoor Road
Nashville, TN 37215

Abingdon Press
201 8th Avenue South
Nashville, TN 37202

Agape
Hope Publishing
Carol Stream, IL 60187

Alba House
2187 Victory Boulevard
Staten Island, NY 10314

**American Choral
Directors Association**
502 Southwest 38th
Lawton, Oklahoma 73505

**Asian Institute for
Liturgy & Music**
P.O. Box 3167
Manila 1099 Philippines

Augsburg/Fortress Press
426 S. Fifth Street
Box 1209
Minneapolis, MN 55440

Ave Maria Press
Notre Dame, IN 46556

Baker Book House
P.O. Box 6287
Grand Rapids, MI 49516-6287

Beacon Hill Press
Box 419527
Kansas City, MO 64141

Bethany House Publishers
6820 Auto Club Road
Minneapolis, MN 55438

The Brethren Press
1451 Dundee Avenue
Elgin, IL 60120

Bridge Publishing, Inc.
200 Hamilton Blvd.
South Plainfield, NJ 07080

Broadman Press
127 Ninth Avenue, North
Nashville, TN 37234

C.S.S. Publishing Company
628 South Main Street
Lima, OH 45804

Cathedral Music Press
P.O. Box 66
Pacific, MO 63069

**Catholic Book
Publishing Company**
257 W. 17th Street
New York, NY 10011

CBP Press
Box 179
St. Louis, MO 63166

Celebration
P.O. Box 309
Aliquippa, PA 15001

Channing L. Bete Company
South Deerfield, MA 01373

Choristers Guild
2834 W. Kingsley Road
Garland, TX 75041

Christian Literature Crusade
701 Pennsylvania Avenue
Box 1449
Ft. Washington, PA 19034

Christian Publications
3825 Hartzdale Drive
Camp Hill, PA 17011

**The Church
Hymnal Corporation**
800 Second Avenue
New York, NY 10017

The Columba Press
93 Merise
Mount Merrion
Blackrock, Dublin

Concordia Publishing House
3558 S. Jefferson Avenue
St. Louis, MO 63118

Covenant Publications
3200 West Foster Avenue
Chicago, IL 60625

Cowley Publications
980 Memorial Drive
Cambridge, MA 02138

CRC Publications
2850 Kalamazoo SE
Grand Rapids, MI 49560

**Creative Communications
for The Parish**
10300 Watson Road
St. Louis, MO 63127

**Crossroad Publishing
Company**
575 Lexington Avenue
New York, NY 10022

Crossroad/Continuum
370 Lexington Avenue
New York, NY 10017

Dominion Press
7112 Burns Street
Ft. Worth, TX 76118

Duke Univesity Press
Box 6697 College Station
Durham, NC 27708

Faith and Life Press
724 Main Street
Box 347
Newton, KS 67114

The Faith Press, Ltd.
7 Tufton Street
Westminster, S.W. 1
England

Fleming H. Revell Company
184 Central Avenue
Old Tappen, N.J. 07675

Folk Music Ministry
P.O. Box 3443
Annapolis, MD 21403

Franciscan Communications
1229 South Santee Street
Los Angeles, CA 90015

Georgetown University Press
111 Intercultural Center
Washington, D.C. 20057

GIA Publications
7404 S. Mason Avenue
Chicago, IL 60638

Great Commission Publications
7401 Old York Road
Philadelphia, PA 19126

Grove Books
Bramcote Notts
England

Harper & Row Publishers
Icehouse One-401
151 Union Street
San Francisco, CA 94111-1299

Harvard University Press
79 Garden Street
Cambridge, MA 02138

Harvest Publications
Baptist General Conference
2002 S. Arlington Heights Road
Arlington Heights, IL 60005

Hendrickson Publishers, Inc.
P.O. Box 3473
Peabody, MA 01961-3473

Herald Press
616 Walnut Avenue
Scottdale, PA 15683

Hinshaw Music Incorporated
P.O. Box 470
Chapel Hill, NC 27514

Holt, Rinehart & Winston
111 5th Avenue
New York, NY 10175

Hope Publishing Company
Carol Stream, IL 60188

Hymn Society of America
Texas Christian University
P.O. Box 30854
Ft. Worth, TX 76129

Indiana University Press
10th & Morton
Bloomington, IN 47405

Integrity Music
P.O. Box 16813
Mobile, AL 36616

J.S. Paluch Company, Inc.
3825 Willow Road
P.O. Box 2703
Schiller Park, IL 60176

**The Jewish Publication
Society of America**
1930 Chestnut Street
Philadelphia, PA 19103

Judson Press
P.O. Box 851
Valley Forge, PA 19482-0851

**Light and Life Publishing
Company**
P.O. Box 26421
Minneapolis, MN 55426

Liguori Publications
One Liguori Drive
Liguori, MO 63057

Lillenas Publishing Company
Box 419527
Kansas City, MO 64141

The Liturgical Conference
1017 Twelfth Street, N.W.
Washington, D.C. 20005-4091

The Liturgical Press
St. John's Abbey
Collegeville, MN 56321

Liturgy Training Publications
1800 North Heritage Avenue
Chicago, IL 60622-1101

**Macmillan Publishing
Company**
866 Third Avenue
New York, NY 10022

Maranatha! Music
25411 Cabot Road
Suite 203
Laguna Hills, CA 92653

Mel Bay Publications
Pacific, MO 63969-0066

Meriwether Publishing, Ltd.
885 Elkton Drive
Colorado Springs, CO 80907

Michael Glazier, Inc.
1723 Delaware Avenue
Wilmington, Delaware 19806

Morehouse-Barlow
78 Danbury Road
Wilton, CT 06897

Multnomah Press
10209 SE Division Street
Portland, OR 97266

**National Association
of Pastoral Musicians**
25 Sheridan Street, NW
Washington, DC 20011

NavPress
P.O. Box 6000
Colorado Springs, CO 80934

New Skete
Cambridge, NY 12816

**North American
Liturgical Resources**
1802 N. 23rd Avenue
Phoenix, AZ 85029

Oxford University Press
16-00 Pollitt Drive
Fair Lawn, NJ 07410

The Pastoral Press
225 Sheridan Street, NW
Washington, D.C. 20011

Paulist Press
997 McArthur Boulevard
Mahwah, NJ 07430

The Pilgrim Press
132 West 31st Street
New York, NY 10001

Psalmist Resources
9820 E. Watson Road
St. Louis, MO 63126

Pueblo Publishing Company
100 West 32nd Street
New York, NY 1001-3210

Regal Books
A Division of Gospel Light
Publications
Ventura, CA 93006

Resource Publications, Inc.
160 E. Virginia Street #290
San Jose, CA 95112

The Scarecrow Press
52 Liberty Street
Box 416
Metuchen, NJ 08840

Schocken Books
62 Cooper Square
New York, NY 10003

**Schuyler Institute for
Worship & The Arts**
2757 Melandy Drive, Suite 15
San Carlos, CA 94070

SCM Press Ltd.
c/o Trinity Press International
3725 Chestnut Street
Philadelphia, PA 19104

Servant Publications
P.O. Box 8617
Petersham, MA 01366-0545

The Sharing Company
P.O. Box 2224
Austin, TX 78768-2224

Sheed & Ward
115 E. Armour Boulevard
P.O. Box 414292
Kansas City, MO 64141-0281

Shofar Publications, Inc
P.O. Box 88711
Carol Stream, IL 60188

SPCK
Holy Trinity Church
Marylebone Road
London, N.W. 4D4

St. Anthony Messenger Press
1615 Republic Street
Cincinnati, OH 45210

St. Bede's Publications
P.O. Box 545
Petersham, MA 01366-0545

St. Mary's Press
Terrace Heights
Winona, MN 55987

St. Vladimir Seminary Press
575 Scarsdale Road
Crestwood, NY 10707-1699

Thomas Nelson Publishers
P.O. Box 141000
Nashville, TN 37214

Twenty Third Publications
P.O. Box 180
Mystic, CT 06355

Tyndale House Publishers
351 Executive Drive
Carol Stream, IL 60188

United Church of Christ
Office of Church Life and
  Leadership
700 Prospect
Cleveland, OH 44115

United Church Press
132 West 31st Street
New York, NY 10001

**The United Methodist
Publishing House**
P.O. Box 801
Nashville, TN 37202

**United States
Catholic Conference**
Office of Publishing and
  Promotion Services
1312 Massachusetts Avenue, NW
Washington, DC 20005-4105

University of California Press
1010 Westward Blvd.
Los Angeles, CA 90024

**University of Notre
Dame Press**
Notre Dame, IN 46556

The Upper Room
1908 Grand Avenue
P.O. Box 189
Nashville, TN 37202

Victory House Publishers
P.O. Box 700238
Tulsa, OK 74170

Westminster John Knox Press
100 Witherspoon Street
Louisville, KY 40202-1396

**William B. Eerdmans
Publishing Company**
255 Jefferson S.E.
Grand Rapids, MI 49503

**William C. Brown
Publishing Company**
2460 Kerper Boulevard
P.O. Box 539
Dubuque, IA 52001

William H. Sadlier, Inc.
11 Park Place
New York, NY 10007

Winston Press
P.O. Box 1630
Hagerstown, MD 21741

Word Books
Tower-Williams Square
5221 N. O'Conner Blvd. Suite
  1000
Irving, TX 75039

**World Council of
Churches Publications**
P.O. Box 66
150 Route de Ferney
1211 Geneva 20, Switzerland

**World Library
Publications, Inc.**
3815 N. Willow Road
P.O. Box 2701
Schiller Park, IL 60176

**The World
Publishing Company**
Meridian Books
110 E. 59th Street
New York, NY 10022

Yale University Press
302 Temple Street
New Haven, CN 06510

Zion Fellowship
236 Gorham Street
Canadagina, NY 14424

**Zondervan Publishing
Company**
1415 Lake Drive S.E.
Grand Rapids, MI 49506

PERIODICAL PUBLISHERS

The American Center for Church Music Newsletter
3339 Burbank Drive
Ann Arbor, MI 48105

American Organist
475 Riverside Drive, Suite 1260
New York, NY 10115

ARTS: The Arts in Religious and Theological Studies
United Theological Seminary of the Twin Cities
3000 5th Street, NW
New Brighton, MN 55112

Arts Advocate
The United Church of Christ Fellowship in the Arts
73 S. Palvuse
Walla Walla, WA 99362

The Choral Journal
American Choral Directors Association
P.O. Box 6310
Lawton, OK 73506

Choristers Guild Letters
2834 W. Kingsley Road
Garland, TX 75041

Christians in the Visual Arts
(newsletter)
P.O. Box 10247
Arlington, VA 22210

Church Music Quarterly
Royal School of Church Music
Addington Palace
Croyden, England CR9 5AD

The Church Musician
Southern Baptist Convention
127 9th Avenue N.
Nashville, TN 37234

Contemporary Christian Music
CCM Publications
P.O. Box 6300
Laguna Hills, CA 92654

Diapason
380 E. Northwest Highway
Des Plaines, IL 60016

Doxology
Journal of the Order of St. Luke in the United Methodist Church

1872 Sweet Home Road
Buffalo, NY 14221

Environment and Art Letter
Liturgy Training Publications
1800 N. Hermitage Avenue
Chicago, IL 60622

GIA Quarterly
7404 S. Mason Avenue
Chicago, IL 60638

Grace Notes
Association of Lutheran Church Musicians
4807 Idaho Circle
Ames, IA 50010

The Hymn
Hymn Society of the United States and Canada
P.O. Box 30854
Fort Worth, TX 76129

Journal
Sacred Dance Guild
Joyce Smillie, Resource Director
10 Edge Court
Woodbury, CT 06798

Journal of Ritual Studies
Department of Religious Studies
University of Pittsburgh
Pittsburgh, PA 15260

Let the People Worship
Schuyler Institute for Worship and the Arts
2757 Melendy Drive, Suite 15
San Carlos, CA 94070

Liturgy
The Liturgical Conference
8750 Georgia Avenue, S., Suite 123
Silver Spring, MD 20910

Liturgy 90
Liturgy Training Publications
1800 N. Hermitage Avenue
Chicago, IL 60622

Modern Liturgy
Resource Publications
160 E. Virginia Street, Suite 290
San Jose, CA 95112

Music in Worship
Selah Publishing Company
P.O. Box 103
Accord, NY 12404

Newsnotes
The Fellowship of United Methodists in Worship, Music, and Other Arts
P.O. Box 54367
Atlanta, GA 30308

Pastoral Music
225 Sheridian Street, NW
Washington, D.C. 20011

PRISM
Yale Institute of Sacred Music
409 Prospect Street
New Haven, CT 06510

The Psalmist
9820 E. Watson Road
St. Louis, MO 63124

Reformed Liturgy and Music
Worship and Ministry Unit
100 Witherspoon Street
Louisville, KY 40202

Reformed Music Journal
Brookside Publishing
3911 Mt. Lehman Road
Abbotsford, BC V2S 6A9

Reformed Worship
CRC Publications
2850 Kalamazoo Avenue, SE
Grand Rapids, MI 49560

Rite Reasons
Biblical Horizons
P.O. Box 1096
Niceville, FL 32588

St. Vladimirs Theological Quarterly
757 Scarsdale Road
Crestwood, NY 10707

Studia Liturgica
Department of Theology
University of Notre Dame
Notre Dame, IN 46556

Today's Liturgy
Oregon Catholic Press
5536 NE Hassalo
Portland, OR 97213

Worship
The Liturgical Press
St. John's Abbey
Collegeville, MN 56321

Worship Leader
CCM Communications, Inc.
107 Kenner Avenue
Nashville, TN 37205

Worship Today
600 Rinehard Road
Lake Mary, FL 32746

Preface to Volume 3

Volume 3 of *The Complete Library of Christian Worship* is distinctly different than the two preceding volumes.

Both *Biblical Foundations of Christian Worship* (Volume 1) and *Twenty Centuries of Christian Worship* (Volume 2) present the basic biblical and historical material a person needs in order to *understand* worship. This volume, *The Renewing of Sunday Worship,* moves the reader from the more theoretical to the more practical realm. Its intent is to take the fruit of biblical and historical scholarship and show how it may be implemented in the renewal of worship.

In the preparation of this volume, I have been keenly aware that true worship cannot take place without the presence and empowerment of the Holy Spirit. I have struggled with the fear that some will assume that worship renewal will happen if their church follows this or that order or this or that resource. Obviously having the right resource will not bring worship renewal. So why worry about order, resources, or planning? Why not just let the Holy Spirit lead?

That question cannot be answered fully in a preface. But a perspective can be given that will point toward an answer. It is this: the Holy Spirit works in and through our planning, and the Holy Spirit has given the church rich insights and resources throughout the history of its worship. From the beginning God has provided the church with individuals gifted for various ministries, including the direction of worship. Sensitive to the Spirit, attentive to Scripture, and exercising their gifts, Christians have always developed, and just as often reformed, patterns and texts of worship. Consequently, this volume simply puts the resources that God has given the church at your fingertips.

Use these resources prayerfully. Leave plenty of space open in your worship for the work of the Spirit, and plan with a heart and mind that is open and sensitive to how the resources of the past and the present may be adapted and put to good use in your worship.

Robert E. Webber, Editor

Introduction

The *Complete Library of Christian Worship* has been designed to meet a need in the church. Christian leaders and congregations are becoming increasingly interested in the subjects of worship and worship renewal in the local church. Often, however, they lack adequate biblical and historical perspective or the necessary materials and resources to engage in the renewal process.

To fulfill the demand for worship resources, publishing houses, particularly those of specific denominations, have been producing materials for the local church. While these materials may find use within the constituency of a particular denomination, only a few break across denominational barriers and become known throughout the church at large.

The Complete Library of Christian Worship draws from more than one hundred publishing houses and the major Christian denominations of the world in order to bring those resources together in a seven-volume work and make them readily available to all.

The purpose of this introductory material is to acquaint the reader with *The Complete Library of Christian Worship* and to help him or her to use its information and resources in the local church. First, the reader needs to have some sense of the scope of worship studies and renewal that are addressed by *The Complete Library of Christian Worship* (see section 101 below). Second, it is important to learn how to use the *Library* (see section 102). Finally, there is a need to understand the precise content of Volume 3, *The Renewal of Sunday Worship*.

These three introductory entries are a key to the whole concept of the *Library,* a concept that brings together instruction in worship and vital resources for use in worship. The *Library* also directs the reader to a vast array of books, audio tapes, videotapes, model services, and resources in music and the arts. It seeks to provide direction and inspiration for everything the church does in worship.

101 • INTRODUCTION TO *THE COMPLETE LIBRARY OF CHRISTIAN WORSHIP*

The word *library* implies a collection of resources, together with a system of organization that makes them accessible to the user. Specifically, *The Complete Library of Christian Worship* is a comprehensive compilation of information pertaining to the worship of the Christian church. It draws from a large pool of scholars and practitioners in the field, and from more than two thousand books and media resources in print.

The purpose of *The Complete Library of Christian Worship* is to make biblical, historical, and contemporary resources on worship available to pastors, music ministers, worship committees, and the motivated individual worshiper. The *Library* contains biblical and historical information on all aspects of worship and numerous resource materials, as well as suggested resource books, audio tapes, and video instructional material for every worship act in the local church.

The twentieth century, more than any century in the history of Christianity, has been the century for research and study in the origins, history, theology, and practice of Christian worship. Consequently there are seven broad areas in which worship studies are taking place. These are:

1. the biblical foundations of worship;
2. historical and theological development;
3. resources for worship and preaching;
4. resources for music and the arts in worship;
5. resources for the services of the Christian year;
6. resources for sacraments, ordinances, and other sacred acts; and
7. resources for worship and related ministries.

The Complete Library of Christian Worship is organized around these seven areas of worship renewal. In these seven volumes one will find a wide variety of resources for every worship act in the church, and a select but broad bibliography for additional resources.

102 • HOW TO USE *THE COMPLETE LIBRARY OF CHRISTIAN WORSHIP*

The Complete Library of Christian Worship differs from an encyclopedia, which is often organized alphabetically, with information about a particular subject scattered throughout the book. The *Library* does not follow this pattern, because it is a work that intends to educate as well as to provide resources. Consequently, all the material in the *Library* is organized under a particular theme or issue of worship.

The difference between the *Library* and an encyclopedia may be illustrated by examining the topic of environmental art in worship. Some of the themes essential to environmental art are banners, candles, stained glass windows, lighting, pulpit hangings, table coverings, and Communion ware. In a typical encyclopedia these entries would be scattered in the B, C, J, L, P, and T sections. Although this is not a problem for people who know what environmental art is, and what needs to be addressed in environmental art, it is a problem for the person whose knowledge about the subject is limited. For this reason *The Complete Library of Christian Worship* has been organized—like a textbook—into chapters dealing with particular issues. Therefore, all the matters dealing with environmental art may be found under the chapter on environmental art (see Volume 4, *Music and the Arts in Christian Worship*). In this way a reader becomes educated on environmental art while at the same time having the advantage of encyclopedia information on the various matters pertaining to this aspect of worship.

Therefore, the first unique feature of *The Complete Library of Christian Worship* is that each volume can be read and studied like a book.

The second unique feature of the *Library* is that the materials have been organized to follow the actual *sequence in which worship happens.*

For example, Volume 1, *The Biblical Foundations of Christian Worship,* looks at the roots of Christian worship in the biblical tradition, while Volume 2, *Twenty Centuries of Christian Worship,* presents the development of various historical models of worship along with an examination of the theology of worship. Next, Volumes 3 through 7 provide resources for the various acts of worship: Volume 3, *The Renewal of Sunday Worship,* provides resources for the various parts of worship; Volume 4, *Music and the Arts in Christian Worship,* presents resources from music and the arts for the different aspects of worship. Volume 5, *The Services of the Christian Year,* branches out to the services of Advent, Christmas, Epiphany, Lent, Holy Week, Easter, and Pentecost, providing resources for those special services that celebrate the saving acts of God in Jesus Christ. Volume 6, *The Sacred Actions of Christian Worship,* deals with communion, baptism, funerals, weddings, and other special or occasional acts or worship. Finally, Volume 7, *The Ministries of Christian Worship* deals with evangelism, spirituality, education, social action, children's worship, and other matters impacted by Christian celebration.

Each volume contains an alphabetical index to the material in the book. This index makes desired information readily available for the reader.

The resources in these volumes are intended for use in every denomination and among all groups of Christians: liturgical, traditional Protestant, those using creative styles, and those in the "praise and worship" tradition. Resources from each of these communities may be found in the various volumes.

It is difficult to find material from the "free" churches (those not following a historic order of worship) and from the charismatic traditions. These communities function with an oral tradition of worship, and therefore do not preserve their material through written texts. Nevertheless, a considerable amount of information has been gathered from these oral traditions. Recently, leaders in these communities have been teaching their worship practices through audio tapes and videotapes. Information on the availability of these materials has been included in the appropriate volumes.

The written texts have been the easiest to obtain. Because of this, *The Complete Library of Christian Worship* may give the appearance of favoring liturgical worship. Due to the very nature of written texts, the appearance of a strong liturgical bent in unavoidable. Nevertheless the goal of the *Library* is not to make free churches liturgical. Rather, it is to expand the perspective of Christians across a wide range of worship traditions. In this way, liturgical resources may serve as guides and sources of inspiration and creativity for free churches, while insights from free traditions may also enrich the practices and understanding of the more liturgical communities.

In sum, the way to use *The Complete Library of Christian Worship* is as follows:

1. *Read each volume as you would read a book.* Each volume is full of biblical, historical, and theological information—a veritable feast for the curious, and for all worshipers motivated to expand their horizons.
2. *Use the alphabetical index for quick and easy access to a particular aspect of worship.* The index for each volume is as thorough as the listings for an encyclopedia.
3. *For further information and resources, order books and materials listed in the bibliography of resources.* Addresses of publishers may be found in your library's copy of *Books in Print.*
4. *Adapt the liturgical materials to the setting and worship style of your congregation.* The worship materials in *The Complete Library of Christian Worship* have been intentionally published without adaptation. Most pastors, worship ministers, and worship committee members are capable of adapting the material to a style suitable to their congregations, with effective results.

103 • INTRODUCTION TO VOLUME 3: *THE RENEWAL OF SUNDAY WORSHIP*

The Renewal of Sunday Worship introduces the reader to a number of resources that will be immediately useful in the task of thinking through worship renewal and in leading the congregation in renewal worship.

Part 1 invites the reader to take in the scope of worship in more than fifty major Christian denominations in North America. Here the reader may glean insights from the Eastern Orthodox, Roman Catholic, traditional Protestant, restorationist, Holiness, Pentecostal, evangelical, and charismatic communities of worship.

Part 2, "Introducing Worship Renewal," acquaints the reader with this important development. It presents a strong case for the need of revitalized worship and explores how different traditions have adapted to innovations.

Part 3 examines patterns of worship. Since all worshiping communities follow the basic historic pattern of coming into God's presence (Entrance), hearing God speak (Service of the Word), celebrating at God's table (Service of Communion or Eucharist), and sending the people forth (Service of Dismissal), resources representing the various traditions have been included.

Part 4 contains material on preaching; it is designed primarily for the minister or preacher. Here the sermon writer will find a brief history of preaching, insights into the different styles of preaching, and some directions for sermon delivery in worship.

Part 5 will be of particular interest and value to worship planners and leaders. Here they will find directions and helpful ideas that run the gamut from the liturgical to praise-and-worship traditions.

In addition, we have provided an artist's rendering of many historic symbols of Trinity. Feel free to use these illustrations as clip art for bulletins and other church publications. Permission to reproduce them for use within the congregation is granted.

We encourage readers to put what they learn here into practice. Our main intent is to present resources and directions that have an immediate and practical use by those who plan and lead worship.

PART ONE

Worship among the Churches

❦ ONE ❦

Worship Renewal among the Contemporary Churches

This chapter explores worship renewal in the major denominations and Christian fellowships in North America. While there is a considerable amount of diversity from one denomination to the next, these articles reveal a surprising consensus on worship that is emerging in many Western churches. First, there is a remarkable agreement among churches on the need for renewal. Even the most liturgically conservative denominations see the need for reviving worship in a contemporary cultural context. Second, in many cases, churches that study their roots—either denominational or early Christian or both—often rediscover traditions that bring fullness and integrity to worship. Ancient liturgical forms are being adapted and used in very different settings. Third, the praise-and-worship movement is supplying material for renewal in just as many churches. Some are even finding that denominational traditions and more contemporary forms of worship are not necessarily incompatible.

---

104 • ADVENTIST CHURCHES

The sabbatarian worship of the Seventh-day Adventist churches follows in the free church tradition of worship and, aside from its distinctive Sabbath observance, is similar to that of many other evangelical churches. The church is likewise undergoing efforts at renewal that has grown out of the work of several Adventist professors in the 1970s and 1980s.

Like other evangelicals, Adventists view the Bible as the propositional source for their understanding of a theology of worship. The first great scriptural truth in Genesis 1, which presents God as Creator and human beings as creatures, has far-reaching implications for both the notion and the expression of worship.

Adventists hold that their view of the intimate connection between Creation, the Sabbath, and worship is consistent with the opening passages of Scripture. Rather than being tied exclusively to Israelite custom, this connection contains real history and has experiential implications for preserving the universal Creator-creature relationship for all humankind. Instead of identifying a place for his crea-

tures to worship, God set aside time, abstract as it is, as a suitable symbol of the intangibility as well as the crucial subtlety of worship.

Adventists stress that worship is the natural response of intelligent human beings once they realize they are in the presence of God. Theoretically they see worship as capable of expression in a number of forms. Though early Adventists drew significantly on the emotionally inclined Methodist tradition of the mid-nineteenth century, the liturgical emphasis of the 1940s left the church generally suspicious and resistant to any change that involves emotionalism. This is particularly true of the North American church, which has historically set the standard for the rest of the world's Adventists.

The form that public worship takes has been under the scrutiny of propositional truth from the earliest days of the denomination. Early conflicts over charismatic manifestations also contributed to a reluctance to move too far into a more emotionally expressive form of worship. At the same time, Adventist roots in the radical Reformations have kept their worshipers, as a rule, from becoming involved in the more formalized liturgical renewal movement.

Renewal or change for Adventists could better be described as fresh than different. In order to be characterized as Adventist, renewal must remain in the tradition of worship expression that concedes to a biblical balance of awe, respect, and reason. The same battle over boredom, sameness, and relevance waged in other evangelical communities today with regard to worship is also being fought in Adventism.

In the 1980s the church experienced the phenomenon of the "Celebration" movement, which was dedicated to more inspiring, interactive, and emotionally expressive worship. This movement has made worship an issue that will undoubtedly last throughout the 1990s. Largely because of this movement, Adventists have written more and generally paid more attention to worship during the last decade than at any other time in their 130-year history.

Parameters for Adventist Worship Renewal

The parameters for worship renewal are set by Adventist understanding of biblical principles of worship as led by the Holy Spirit. These principles are commonly held to be: (1) The object of our worship is always whatever (or whomever) we deem to be of most value to us. (2) The worship of God is not a shared worship, i.e., God must be the only object of our worship. (3) Worship is open to all who recognize they are in the presence of God. (4) Worship carries with it a genuineness that gains its integrity through a consistent life worthy of its calling in the gospel. (5) Worship transcends the single act as expressed in formal settings (such as church) and is demonstrated in the wholeness of daily life. We do not respond in part to the work of Christ for us—we commit ourselves totally to him. This is "our reasonable service" (Rom. 12:1-2, KJV). (6) Worship professes our belief that God really is present with us. (7) Unity in Christ is seen in the diversity of his people, which allows for various expressions that match these diversities.

Thus, Adventism has within its confessional framework the capability of renewal based on biblical principles and an openness to change of expression. Worship is like the new birth experience in that it does not entail simply a one-time action but allows for daily renewal in relationship as the believer grows in understanding, appreciation, and victory in Christ.

During the last two decades of this century, Adventist leadership has supported serious efforts at worship in the form of creative worship. Elements of drama, choral reading, group prayer, extended congregational singing (with emphasis on praising), reader's theater, more creative responsive readings, and general celebration of God's bestowing of spiritual gifts within the congregation are fresh elements for most Adventists.

Worship renewal in Adventism is not accidental. Serious work to this end has been underway since the 1980s. Material produced by denominational leadership in conjunction with teachers and ministers in the local churches is expressing greater concern for more spontaneity and an expression that appreciates the affective needs of worshipers. An increasing awareness and acceptance of the principles explicated by the church growth movement in neo-evangelicalism has also been instrumental in this change of worship emphasis. Christians are diverse, and growth results in part from recognizing and appreciating diversity of expression in worship. Furthermore, a growing recognition of the alarming number of Adventists who leave the church claiming boredom and irrelevance in worship is causing concern among informed church leaders.

The renewal movement is actively promoted in mainline church periodicals such as *Collegiate Quarterly, Adult Sabbath School Lesson Quarterly, Celebration Magazine, The Adventist Review,* and *Ministry.* In addition to these sources, helpful materials designed to stimulate creative worship are being published under the auspices of Church Ministries Departments of the North American Division headquartered in Maryland and the Pacific Union Conference in Southern California. These calls for renewal are ongoing and provide hope for Adventists who are convinced that traditional worship needs help or who feel the inadequacy of their own corporate worship experience.

Adventist Order of Worship

A traditional order of worship is suggested but not prescribed by the Adventist *Church Manual.* Each local church sets its own standard within the limits of Adventist notions of worship as conditioned by sociological factors such as congregational size and sophistication. A comparison of a traditional and a creative worship service would typically look like this:

Traditional (Longer Form)	Creative
Organ Prelude	Organ Prelude
Announcements	Choir Enters
Introit	Choral Musical Praise
Choir and Ministers Enter	Announcements
[Overheads]	Pastoral Welcome
Doxology	Congregational Response
Invocation	(shaking hands,
Scripture Reading	hugging, greeting of
Hymn of Praise	friends and visitors)
Pastoral Prayer	Congregational Praise
Singing	Choir Anthem
Anthem or Special Music	Offering
Offering	Congregational Singing
Singing	[Dramatic Sketch]
Hymn of Consecration	Sermon
Sermon	Benediction
Benediction	Organ Postlude
Congregation stands or sits	
for silent prayer	
Organ Postlude	

Commentary

In those services where the Lord's Supper is observed (quarterly), the order is changed to include time for the sacramental elements of unleavened bread and unfermented wine.

Announcements. Some Adventist worship leaders insist that announcements should precede worship. Others include the announcements in the service because the greatest number is present at worship services and the work of the church is not incompatible with the worship of God. Most churches include relevant announcements in a church bulletin and announce only events or needs of a more pastoral nature.

Hymns. The choice of hymns varies by congregation. Many ministers of music feel the burden of teaching hymnody to the congregation and periodically introduce new hymns found in the _Seventh-Day Adventist Hymnal_ (1985). The standard of inclusion for hymns in these hymnals has been scriptural and doctrinal soundness and suitability for congregational singing. Adventist congregations are encouraged but not required to use the official hymnal.

Hymn singing in contemporary Adventist churches influenced by the creative worship movement involves a decided emphasis on praise. Overhead projectors are sometimes used to set the words in a place where the congregation can avoid having their heads buried in a hymnal. Contemporary Adventist churches include more hymn singing. This is interspersed through the service in most cases. The Celebration churches incorporate a greater selection of musical instruments, the most prominent of which are drums and electric guitars.

Prayer. In Adventist renewal, prayer receives more emphasis and is less traditional. This may vary from a couple praying alternately in the pulpit to the "Garden of Prayer" practiced in an increasing number of Adventist churches. The latter is a contemporary version of the _season of prayer,_ which was traditionally confined to times of church gathering other than the worship hour on Saturday morning. In Adventist churches that engage in the Garden of Prayer the worship leader invites worshipers with specific needs or burdens to come forward and gather around the rostrum. The pastoral staff is present to counsel or comfort and lay on hands. The Garden of Prayer typically lasts around ten to fifteen minutes.

Offering. Ordinarily a musical offertory accompanies the taking of the offering. In traditional Adventist worship settings organist, pianist, or an occasional special music group plays the offertory. Offering is considered a significant element in Adventist worship.

Special Music. Usually special music indicates a choir anthem or guest group or soloist. Occasionally, taped accompaniment is used with vocal solo or duet, but not all worship committees accept this practice.

Larger Adventist churches typically demonstrate accomplished musicianship. The church has nearly a dozen liberal arts colleges and two universities (Andrews and La Sierra) in North America, with accomplished musicians offering degrees in music. This long-standing emphasis on music is reflected in virtually all Adventist churches. Celebration churches maintain this standard of musicianship, but choose nontraditional music partly due to their view on relevance, singability, and the notion that worship primarily involves praising. These churches actively seek singable, simple, praise music.

Sermon. For the most part Adventist preaching is in the tradition of evangelical Protestantism. Since the appearance of *Ministry* magazine (1928) and the introduction of formal ministerial training (1932) that led to the establishment of the Seventh-day Adventist Theological Seminary (1937), an increasing number of Adventist ministers are seminary-trained. This training has insisted on biblical, Christ-centered preaching. Adventist worship typically sees the sermon as the center of worship in that it purports to bring the worshiper into contact with the objective Word of God.

Benediction. Most Adventists close the worship service with a benediction immediately following the sermon, and a musical postlude brings formal worship to an end. In many congregations the benediction is actually a closing prayer rather than an act or pronouncement of blessing.

Contemporary Alternatives. Most renewal in Adventist worship simply emphasizes or alters one or more of these worship elements. In general an ambience of informality, expectancy, and spontaneity accompanies the congregation dedicated to creative worship.

Churches involved in creative worship will lengthen the time for singing, for example, or change the kind of hymns, usually employing more praise choruses. Some contemporary worship leaders will stress the importance of experiential elements, such as prayer, by including a Garden of Prayer. More Adventist churches are including a greeting time in their worship services where people are free to roam the sanctuary hugging friends and greeting visitors with warm handshakes and words.

The past decade has seen more use of drama in the worship service. While this seldom involves full-fledged theatrical productions in church, it may involve responsive readings and the use of several readers as in reader's theater. Short drama sketches designed to stimulate interest in the subject of the sermon are especially appreciated by younger worshipers. Drama groups such as *Reflections* (Campion Academy, Loveland, Colorado), *Destiny* (Southern College, Collegedale, Tennessee), and *The Destination Players* (La Sierra University, Riverside, California) are well known through their efforts to bring relevance and interest to Adventist worship.

Special Worship Events. Thanksgiving pageants filling the entire worship hour, complete with native Americans and children dressed as pilgrims, are not unusual. Such events are generally followed by community action, e.g., collecting and distributing food for the poor. Easter, Christmas, and other holidays also provide opportunities for such variations that suggest human service as the natural outgrowth of divine worship. In some churches, occasional liturgical presentations feature participants of all ages. These usually involve readings of various kinds from Scripture, theologians, sociologists, or relevant political or religious leaders that engender a Christian awareness of world needs such as the environment, hunger, secularism, or apocalypticism. Usually such specialized worship services are confined to Adventist educational centers. As a rule, Adventists are very open to variation in worship on special occasions.

The Future of Adventist Worship Renewal

Although interest in worship has always been an Adventist concern, renewal began in earnest with the publishing of Norval F. Pease's book *And Worship Him* (Nashville: Southern Publishing Association, 1967). Pease called for a formal recognition and evaluation of worship as something Adventists had seriously neglected. Pease's seminary classes in worship served to motivate his students to plan their worship services intelligently. His legacy was carried on by C. Raymond Holmes, also an Andrews University professor, who published *Sing a New Song* (Berrien Springs, Mich.: Andrews University Press, 1984) which, though in the legacy of Pease, stimulated more interest in creative worship.

Worship workshops and seminars are becoming more common among Adventists. An international worship conference held in Portland, Oregon, in 1989 launched a new emphasis on the importance of worship for the Adventist Christian. This stimulated a second similar conference in 1993 at Riverside, California. These conferences featured both Adventist and evangelical worship leaders in workshops and plenary sessions covering the spectrum of worship philosophy and form. Banner making, calligraphy, drama, order, praise, and music were among the topics of discussion and examination.

The issue of worship has been identified by many Adventists as the issue for the 1990s. It is a topic whose time has come in Adventist churches.

Church leadership has been progressive and supportive of the creative worship movement, a fact that most pastors and lay leaders find encouraging.

Adventists frequently refer to Revelation 14:7 as their mandate for existence: "Fear God and give him glory, for the hour of his judgment has come: and worship him who made heaven and earth, the sea and the fountains of water"(KJV). Hence worship is an integral part of their confessional identity and will continue to stimulate discussion and the integration of creative forms.

Ed Zackrison

105 ❖ AFRICAN METHODIST EPISCOPAL CHURCHES

African Methodist Episcopal worship is grounded in the traditions of John Wesley and Richard Allen, founder of the African Methodist Episcopal Church in 1797. Worship is African, liturgical, kerygmatic, charismatic, and democratic. Its special emphases are on preaching and participation, with focus on the altar call.

Transplanted Africans in America, under the leadership of Richard Allen, shaped Wesleyan worship with the ardor of their African tradition. Like their African forebears, they worship with body, mind, and soul. The genius of the black church is worship. Worship is the heart of the black church. The black church was born out of the need to commune with God.

African Methodism is a part of the larger Methodist tradition, and Richard Allen, founding the African Methodist Church in 1797, preserved many of the elements of the Wesleyan tradition. Thus one aspect of African Methodist worship is the _liturgical_. The _Book of Discipline_ of the AME Church states that the order of service must have such unity as to insure that all members of their church will feel at home in an AME church.

The consequent emphasis upon maintaining standards of liturgical orthodoxy has been strengthened by the order of service for African Methodists found in the _Hymnal_, the _Book of Discipline_, and the _Book of Worship_.

The Centrality of Proclamation. The _kerygmatic_ dimension of AME worship stresses the proclamation of the Word as the basis of worship. In the beginning, Allen turned to Methodism in part because of the exciting preaching that was understandable to the common person. Allen states,

> I was confident that there was no religious sect or denomination that would suit the capacity of the colored people as well as the Methodist; for the plain and simple gospel, [so that] the unlearned can understand, and the learned are sure to understand; for all other denominations preach so high-flown that [many] were not able to comprehend their doctrine. (_Life Experience and Gospel Labors_ [Nashville: African Methodist Episcopal Church Publishing House, 1990], 19.)

When this kerygma is combined with black self-expression, then Pentecost occurs within the black worship context.

The Pentecostal Influence. Yet another quality of African Methodist worship is its _charismatic_ nature. In this form of worship, the release of the spirit brings the liturgy to life and gives it power. The older Pentecostal movement of the late nineteenth century emerged out of John Wesley's search for spiritual perfection, which was carried a step further by contemporary Pentecostals with their stress on glossolalia.

The charismatic style of worship is much more emotion-oriented than the liturgical emphasis upon order and decorum. C. Eric Lincoln points out that AME neo-Pentecostalism combines deep Pentecostal spiritual piety and the AME tradition (C. Eric and Lawrence Lincoln, _The Black Church in the African American Experience_ [Durham, N.C.: Duke University Press, 1990], 385).

This form of worship has brought forth an emerging tension in the denomination as African Methodists seek to understand the proper role of the Holy Spirit in worship and ministry.

The Altar Call. Amidst this diversity, there is one common thread running through all African Methodist worship traditions, a thread that traces back to an incident at Saint George's Methodist Church in 1787. There two worshipers, Richard Allen and Absalom Jones, were pulled off their knees while praying—an act that so outraged Allen that he and the other African-Americans "all went out of the church in a body, and they were no more plagued with us in the church" (Allen, _Life Experiences and Gospel Labors,_ 16).

Since then, when African Methodists gather for

prayer at the altar, they reestablish a connection with the past in the midst of the contemporary worship experience. The altar call is a liturgical re-creation of that event at Saint George's Methodist Church and a means of *democratizing* the worship experience.

It is a form of active participation that signifies that all Christians have the obligation to pray, and that congregants do not need the minister to pray on their behalf. African Methodist ministers generally call the congregants to prayer by exhorting them to consider the importance and necessity of prayer.

Due to the incident at St. George's there is an almost mystical significance surrounding the *altar* and *altar call* within African Methodism.

Individuals come and kneel at the altar, praying as long as they please. Usually, they line up along the walls, or down the middle of the aisle, waiting for their turn to kneel at the mercy seat. There is no rush placed on this part of the service, and it lasts as long as necessary. Everyone must be given the opportunity to pray, an opportunity denied Allen by his fellow Christians.

When one prays at the altar, one joins millions of African Methodists who kneel every Sunday, all over the world. And when one prays at the altar, one joins millions of African Methodists who have prayed at this and other altars for more than two hundred years. For it is through worship that blacks are able to achieve true self-consciousness, wholeness, and liberation.

Kenneth Hill

106 ◆ AFRICAN METHODIST EPISCOPAL ZION CHURCHES

Zion Methodism adheres to the traditional American Methodist liturgy adapted by Francis Asbury. Although its basic ritual pattern has remained unchanged, renewal is having an effect on observance of the Christian year and on music and spirituality.

Traditional. The African Methodist Episcopal Zion Church, over the course of two centuries, has resisted expansion or revision of its worship pattern under the influence of the broad range of possibilities in worship today. There is a tenacious will to retain a staid, European-style African-American church: orthodox, quiet, and reserved.

The rituals of Zion Methodism continue to be the 1792 form of Methodist liturgy revised by Francis Asbury. This continuum of worship experience makes Zion Methodism the purest form of Methodist worship. This is seen not as a hindrance to true worship, but it does maintain constancy throughout the denomination.

New Elements in Worship. An earnest effort has been made during the past ten years to make Zion Methodism more liturgically oriented. A resolution calling for the use of the Christian church year across the denomination was adopted in 1992. A similar resolution was adopted in 1988 to revise and enlarge the hymnal to coincide with the church's bicentennial celebration in 1996.

The sacrament of the Lord's Supper remains the highlight of AME Zion worship. It is not a memorial; rather it is a celebration, as John Williamson Nevin stated, of the mystical presence of Christ. The sanctuary is transformed to demonstrate a different type of worship experience and expression. Everything done points to the belief that the congregation is enacting a tradition of praise and thanksgiving for Christ's act of at-one-ment.

Traditions such as the kiss of peace and the charismatic praise songs are all but nonexistent in Zion Methodism. There is, in the orthodox mind of Zion, a resistance to clapping (which is deemed applause) in worship. This resistance is fading with the demand for upbeat modern gospel music from both clergy and laity alike. This movement has accompanied the emergence of far more forms of expression in worship than have been historic to Zion Methodism.

Praise and Song. The reality of Zion, in spite of the orthodox hierarchy, is that its main area of strength has been expressive forms of praise. These include the continuation of the common meter form of singing and praise devotional services. The more animated style of the processional "strut" of gospel choirs and the emotional expression now being found throughout Zion are simply the rediscovery of its true worship roots.

Traditionalists, including the present writer, guard against worship being turned into an entertainment hour by maintaining the regular order of worship of Zion Methodism. We have used material in the proposed *Book of Worship for African-Methodists,* developed by this writer, to provide variety without loss of order. This work includes and fosters more congregational participation through congregational calls to worship, congregational invocations, and congregational seasonal prayers.

Zion Methodists generally have no desire to discontinue the use of the King James Version of the Bible from the pulpit, although other versions are read and are in the pews. Nor do they feel the need to tamper with the Order of Worship or the wording of the rituals. Continuing their heritage as singers of hymns and appreciators of anthems and spirituals, they are making room for gospel music also to take its place in worship. They intend to maintain the tradition of their founders and allow the inclusion of other forms of worship that do not hinder proper reverence in the sanctuary at worship.

Music has been the driving force that has challenged orthodoxy in Zion. The needs of worship for today's congregation require more than meditations from the pulpit and anthems from the choir. There is a need, encouraged by societal pressures, for more vibrant expressiveness in what is said and done in worship. It seems that where orthodox practice prevails, one finds a declining membership. Where tradition is flexible, one finds the growth of members seeking diverse expression.

African-American Concerns. Ethnic pride in the nineties has greatly increased the desire for a more African-American emphasis in worship. Clerical garb with kente stoles, the use of drums and tambourines, the celebration of historic events and persons, such as Kwanzaa and Malcolm X, which were all but taboo in Zion ten years ago, are taking place regularly. This renewal has brought about a new zeal for capturing the spirit and the accompanying spiritual power of our foreparents that enabled them to overcome difficult times. The hopes of integration and civil rights have not been realized and the people have sought to return to their roots.

Unfortunately, Zion Methodism has not rethought the architecture of the churches being designed and built. Their buildings remain geared only to worship. Development of facilities that are both multipurpose and practical for daily use has not yet caught fire. They need to move from a praying people to a viable force in local communities addressing the needs of the whole person. This can only take place when their churches become the hub of community life and activity as they were before 1960.

Andrew Foster

107 • AMERICAN BAPTIST CHURCHES IN THE USA

Worship in the Baptist groups organized just after the American Revolutionary War was subsequently shaped by the revivalist tradition. More recently, the pedagogical model of worship has prevailed. In the future, American Baptist worship will likely be influenced by liturgical and inclusive styles as well as by charismatic worship practices.

Worship in a Diverse and Congregational Denomination

Two realities that shape any attempt at generalization about American Baptist churches make it difficult to characterize worship in the American Baptist Churches/USA. First is the fundamental principle of the autonomy of local congregations in matters of governance and practice. Thus the worship practices of each church are created out of its own traditions, needs, and expectations. The one exception is the practice of believer's baptism and the observance of the Lord's Supper as ordinances, not as sacraments.

A second reality of life within the ABC/USA as a denomination is a self-conscious and experienced diversity. A 1991 Biennial Statement of Concern stated that

> as American Baptists we affirm that God through Jesus Christ calls us to be . . . an inclusive people who, gifted by a plurality of backgrounds, find unity in diversity and diversity in unity, who embrace a pluralism of race, ethnicity, gender, and theology, who represent individual differences of conviction, and who bring the free church tradition to cooperative and ecumenical Christianity.

Worship practices vary widely according to the tradition of ethnic groups; and denominational statistics for 1990 show that of a total resident membership of 1.2 million in 5,739 churches, 39 percent are African-American, 0.5 percent are Asian American, 57.7 percent are White (Anglo) Americans, 2.4 percent are Hispanic, 0.1 percent are Native Americans, and 0.3 percent are other ethnic and language groups. Theological diversity likewise is a major factor in varieties of worship styles.

Thus worship practices of the churches of ABC/USA can be characterized first of all as diverse and varied. In the November 1990 issue of the denominational magazine, _The American Baptist,_ a survey of services of worship in the churches in the East

Bay Area of San Francisco, California, revealed a spectrum of worship styles from formal to spontaneous and of worship orders from those that are liturgical or in some way traditional to innovative designs that vary weekly.

The Centrality of Worship in Congregational Gatherings

Within this diversity, however, a second generalization must focus on the centrality of worship to the life of the gathered people. The 1987 document on denominational identity affirms that as American Baptists, "we are . . . a worshiping people, who regularly gather to praise God, who receive nourishment by communion with the Risen Christ, who share an open and public confession of faith, and who believe that private worship brings vitality to corporate celebration."

A survey conducted by the editors of *The American Baptist* in 1990 shows that 90 percent or more of the respondents rated the following elements as essential or important in worship: preaching (95 percent), giving of tithes and offerings (93 percent), Communion (90 percent), congregational singing (90 percent), music (90 percent), Scripture readings (83 percent), prayers by the worship leader (83 percent), silent prayers (67 percent), altar call or invitation to faith (63 percent), and prayers by the congregation (58 percent).

Worship Renewal

There is an increasing interest in worship renewal. Several areas of concern need to be addressed. One is the limited preparation most American Baptist clergy have had in the field of worship studies, often completing seminary training with little or minimal preparation in the field of worship.

Another is the limited number of printed resources for worship. The most recent denominational hymnbook, *Hymnbook for Christian Worship,* was published in 1970, and there are no current plans to issue a new one. Ernst Skoglund's *A Manual of Worship,* published in 1968 by the denominational publishers Judson Press, had only limited acceptance. No similar American Baptist worship book has been published subsequently, but Judson Press has issued Garth House's *Litanies for All Occasions* (1989) and Roy Pearson's *Prayers for All Occasions: For Pastors and Lay Leaders* (1990).

However, although no formal denominational documents have been issued with regard to worship

renewal, there are signs of hope. For example, in the 1980s one denominational program, in identifying the marks of growing and caring churches, only belatedly admitted worship to the list. But in June 1991, the governing body of the denomination voted to embark upon a program entitled "ABC 2000: Renewed for Mission," which lists worship first among three foci for renewal. This movement of the place of worship from a peripheral position in the 1980s to a central place for the 1990s is visible evidence of movement in a positive direction.

Another such sign is the organization in 1989 of the American Baptist Fellowship for Liturgical Renewal. Under the leadership of Ronal and Inga Freyer Nicholas this small but growing group publishes an occasional paper called *Liturgy and Life* and in 1992 led a "Retreat on Worship," as a retreat and workshop at the American Baptist Assembly at Green Lake, Wisconsin, the national conference center. Reclaiming the heritage of liturgical worship that is part of Baptist history is a priority, along with the development of a holistic approach to worship renewal with a recognition of the need for varieties of structures and style in the expression of the Christian story.

Most encouraging of all is the number of individual pastors and many congregations who have sought worship renewal through greater awareness of the church calendar, through greater use of responsive readings, litanies, and unison prayers, through the introduction of drama, liturgical dance, choral reading groups, and contemporary music forms for congregations and choirs. A number of American Baptist clergy have been influenced by the biblical storytelling movement, bringing creative approaches into preaching. Worship in regional and national gatherings as well as in local congregations reflects these trends toward renewal.

Despite the limited formal evidence, there is nevertheless a sense among many American Baptists that the decade of the 1990s will be a time of significant worship renewal.

Jeannette F. Scholer

108 ✦ ANGLICAN/EPISCOPAL CHURCHES

Anglican/Episcopal worship has always been guided by The Book of Common Prayer. The Revised Rites of 1976 introduced the liturgical forms and styles of renewal. Many _churches have also incorporated charismatic elements of worship._

"In Corporate Worship, we unite ourselves with others to acknowledge the holiness of God, to hear God's Word, to offer prayer, and to celebrate the sacraments." So the catechism in the 1979 _Book of Common Prayer_ in the United States describes worship.

This prayer book definition emerges from the historical context of an English-speaking liturgy handed down from Thomas Cranmer in the first English prayer book (1549). Yet it looks beyond to the present era of liturgical renewal and experimentation.

Anglicans for the last ten years have sought to define, through a great deal of study and "trial use," the role of liturgy in the life of a church whose historical identity is reflected in its worship. Throughout the Anglican Communion there is also a felt need for understanding liturgical inculturation alongside renewal.

Variety and Unity in Worship. The worship experience in an Anglican or Episcopal church can vary. One Anglican may worship with such catholic expressions of worship and ceremony as incense, holy water, genuflections, signs of the cross, and the

Three Interwoven Circles. _The three interwoven circles of equal size is an ancient symbol expressing both the unity and the equality of the Trinity._

echoing of plain chant. Another may experience instead the stark simplicity of a New England colonial, low church, evangelical congregation where the Holy Communion is celebrated at a small table located underneath a central pulpit. The real unity of worship within Anglicanism comes through _The Book of Common Prayer._ Recent versions of the prayer book in various parts of the Communion offer that same sense of unity that was evident at the time of Archbishop Cranmer's first English Prayer Book while introducing new tones of joy and resurrection.

Renewal of Worship. Today, renewal movements such as Faith Alive, Cursillo (Little Journey with Christ), and Happenings bring with them new musical expressions, mostly informal in nature, which participants seek to bring into the worship experience of their own parish (often, however, not without controversy). There is also a move to reclaim such historical features of Anglican worship as the ministry of healing, complete with anointing and laying on of hands. Local parish churches, now as always, may offer a healing service within the context of a celebration of Holy Communion, giving special emphasis to intercessory prayer.

Anglican/Episcopal churches are seeking a renewed liturgical vision drawing priest and people close through the experience of corporate worship. Instructed Eucharists, training classes, books on liturgy, and worship committees are all now part of the norm of local parish life. Studying the Sunday Bible Propers (the lessons appointed for the day) in the three year lectionary cycle helps bring Anglicans into an ecumenical stance with other Christians. Such an exposure to Scripture gives worship new meaning and vitality.

Eucharist in Worship. The American prayer book sees the Holy Eucharist as "the principal act of Christian worship on the Lord's Day and other feasts." The rite used by Anglicans/Episcopalians generally follows the Roman and Lutheran liturgies with an entrance song of praise, the "Gloria in Excelsis." During the seasons of Advent and Lent, however, the Kyrie ("Lord Have Mercy") or the Trisagion is sung. Most churches offer services in modern and traditional language rites, faithfully following the church year.

It is likely that Episcopalians hear more Scripture on Sundays than any other Christian denomination. Readings from the Old and New Testaments, Psalms, and Gospels follow the prayer of the day. After a homily, creed, and prayers, the faithful exchange a sign of peace, moving into the celebration of the Eucharist by offering bread and wine, themselves, their souls and bodies as the liturgy says. Money offerings are made as well.

As the great thanksgiving unfolds the dramatic story of redemption, the celebrant offers the bread and wine to become the body and blood of our Lord Jesus Christ, through the power of the Holy Spirit, given for the faithful. The Lord's Prayer and the breaking of the bread lead to the moment when all believers who are present share in the bread and wine. During this time, music associated with renewal can be incorporated effectively. Praise music, Taizé chants, silence, and instrumental music have all become part of this reflective time.

Styles of Worship. Various styles of Eucharistic celebrations on a given Sunday in a large parish church may include an 8:00 A.M. celebration of Communion with a short sermon, usually no music, and a small congregation. That same parish at 9:00 A.M. might have a Family Eucharist which would incorporate the use of a children's choir, instruments, varying musical styles, and a sense of informality.

More formal would be the next service, the 11:00 A.M. Solemn Eucharist, featuring a full choir, the great anthems, an occasional swing of the incense pot, and sprinkling of holy water. This last service would also include the use of traditional hymns and chanting of Psalms.

It would not be surprising for that same church to gather on an evening for a very informal house Mass or a Table celebration, where there would be hand-clapping, choruses, raising of hands in praise, and prayer. The celebration possibly might even include dance.

Where Are They? The substance of renewal in Anglican worship is reflected in prayer books from all over the world. The new prayer book of the church in Australia finds worship to be "the highest activity of the human spirit," while from another continent, the new prayer book of the church of the Province of Southern Africa calls upon the people of God to clothe the liturgy "with the devotion of heart and mind" so that worship may release "into the world with its needs and its pains, its sorrows and its hope, an influence for healing and wholeness which we shall never fully comprehend." This is the substance of renewal in Anglican worship.

Committed Anglicans have testified that God is doing a new thing in their lives. Certainly it is true that liturgical Christians will indeed be well prepared to cry "Holy, Holy, Holy" as they approach the throne of God, because their cry on earth has been united with the whole company of heaven in that proclamation of praise to almighty God in their liturgy.

James Rosenthal

109 • ASSEMBLIES OF GOD CHURCHES

The activity of the Holy Spirit is central to worship in Assemblies of God churches. The presence of the Spirit is experienced in prayer, praise, singing, and the operation of the gifts of the Spirit. The praise-and-worship style appeals to many who are dissatisfied with traditional forms of worship.

The Ideal of Worship

Perhaps the best way to describe worship in the Assemblies of God would be to focus initially on the ideal of that event among believers and congregations. "Pentecostal" worship centers on the immanent work of the Holy Spirit within the worshiping community.

Tracing patterns from the Gospels, the book of Acts (2:42-47), and certain Epistles, this approach seeks *interaction with* rather than simply *learning about* God. Spirit-baptized believers, in gathering, ought to experience the Spirit's presence corporately in prayer, praise, singing, testimony, and the operation of the charismata (1 Cor. 12, 14). Petitionary prayers for the sick and needy and the proclamation of the Word will exalt Christ and build up the church in love and power to the glory of God the Father. In this dynamic atmosphere, miracles, healings from sicknesses, conversions of unbelievers who are present, and deliverances from satanic oppression and chemical addictions can be normal and not unusual.

Given this ideal, Pentecostals often view the liturgical structures of the historic churches as hindrances to following the Spirit's directives, discouraging the spontaneity that characterized the worship of the first-century church (1 Cor. 14:26). Not surprisingly, the church year is generally ignored, with the exceptions of Christmas, Easter, and Pentecost. Neither has the denomination authorized a commission on worship or recommended an order of service, and few congregations provide their members with printed copies of the order of worship. Such outlines are usually reserved for the worship leader(s), pianist, and organist.

Nevertheless, church services have become increasingly predictable while achieving various levels of success in modeling the ideal. Despite important distinctives, the overall pattern of worship in the Assemblies of God reveals that it did not emerge in a vacuum. The frontier revivalism of the Methodists, Baptists, and the Disciples of Christ created the general backdrop for Pentecostalism. In particular, however, it was the spirituality of the revivalistic holiness movement with its Wesleyan and Reformed components that shaped the Assemblies of God when it was organized in 1914. This spirituality emphasizes sanctification (understood as the deeper life in Christ), music, preaching, and spontaneity.

Worship Elements and Practices

Through the years, Sunday morning services have come to include the following elements, although not necessarily in this precise sequence: (1) invocation, (2) congregational singing (gospel songs and/or hymns as well as choruses), (3) pastoral prayer (with the congregation often praying vocally in concert), (4) announcements, (5) greeting of visitors, (6) collection of tithes and offerings, (7) special music (choir and/or vocal or instrumental solo), (8) sermon (preceded by the reading of the biblical text and prayer), (9) altar call response (occasionally), and (10) benediction. Old Testament motifs appear frequently and involve the use of church orchestras, clapping of hands, and lifting hands in prayer and praise.

Anointing the sick with oil and having the elders of the church pray for them (James 5:14-16) has also characterized Assemblies of God churches, despite a declining emphasis on faith healing. Holy Communion, usually celebrated once a month, is interpreted according to the Zwinglian notion of the Lord's Supper, although the Reformed conception of the "Real Presence" (the spiritual as opposed to the physical presence of Christ) is found occasionally. Baptism by immersion (in a specially constructed tank on the platform) for new believers occurs infrequently during Sunday evening services.

Contemporary variations of this configuration include the preference for singing choruses (with the congregation standing) as the words are shown on a screen from an overhead projector, reflecting the influence of the charismatic movement. In many congregations, this has virtually replaced the use of the Assemblies of God's *Hymns of Glorious Praise* (1969) or other hymnals. Instead of one song leader, a worship team of several singers (each with a microphone) may together lead the congregation. In some churches, "singing in tongues" (glossolalia) and/or "dancing in the Spirit" (sometimes choreographed) are encouraged, although the latter remains especially controversial.

The Role of the Charismata

What makes the order of Assemblies of God services different from those of other evangelical churches is the role of the charismata in the service. Despite the paucity of denominational materials on worship, much has been written on those distinctive pneumatological perspectives that strongly relate to it.

The nine gifts of the Spirit (1 Cor. 12:8-10) have at times been divided into three categories. Gifts of revelation include the word of wisdom, the word of knowledge, and the discerning of spirits; gifts of power are those of faith, miracles, and healings; while gifts of utterance include prophecy, tongues, and interpretation.

This last group plays a vital role in a congregation's striving to experience the ideal of Pentecostal worship. A word of prophecy (1 Cor. 14:1-5) may offer encouragement or comfort to the congregation from the Lord through a member of the worshiping community. Incidentally, preaching is considered to be generically prophetic. A message in tongues (glossolalia) also has potential for similar prophetic function, but only if followed by an interpretation (1 Cor. 14:6-19).

If the vocal gifts are manifested, they should occur at convenient pauses in the order of worship to complement rather than distract from the theme of the service; in some instances, however, they may redirect the focus as the Spirit leads. This sense of divine guidance is often referred to as the "flow" of the Spirit.

Providing an opportunity for response, altar calls allow time at the end of the service for those who wish to be converted, rededicate their lives to Christ, receive prayer for healing, or simply spend time alone in personal meditation. The posture for this may be either standing or kneeling.

Whether a local congregation moves toward the

ideal in worship or more closely parallels the patterns of non-Pentecostal evangelical churches is strongly influenced by the pastor, who is the principal worship leader. Although the apostle Paul indicated that the distribution of the charismata are sovereignly dispensed by the Holy Spirit (1 Cor. 12:7, 11), if the pastor has not been used in a vocal utterance or is hesitant about such manifestations, then the church services that he or she directs will probably not model the uniqueness of Pentecostal worship.

Undoubtedly, the tension between the de facto liturgical structure of worship in the Assemblies of God and the ideal of allowing the Spirit to enrich congregational worship with the spiritual gifts will long continue to challenge worship leaders.

Gary B. McGee

110 • BAPTIST (EVANGELICAL DENOMINATIONS & INDEPENDENT BAPTIST CHURCHES)

The worship of the Independent and Evangelical Baptist groups traditionally features strong preaching, gospel music, and invitations. New emphases include thematic planning, a wide variety of music styles, and greater congregational participation in prayer and in the use of the senses.

Independent and smaller Evangelical Baptist groups have historically worshiped in the traditional evangelical style, including preaching of the Word of God, congregational singing, choir specials, an offering, and an invitation to accept Jesus as personal Savior. In many of our churches, this structure remains the normal experience.

Increasingly we are realizing that Christians in worship need to experience the presence of God and respond by offering praise and adoration in this presence. If we are merely spectators we will probably miss this vital encounter with our Lord. Carefully planned services motivate the congregation, choir, and worship leaders to respond to and communicate with God during the service.

——————— **Varied Worship Styles** ———————

Independent and Evangelical Baptist churches draw from a vast and diverse background of Christian traditions both liturgical and nonliturgical, Catholic and Protestant, traditional evangelical, and Pentecostal. We have learned that sometimes people experience intimacy with the Lord best within the familiar contexts of their first Christian worship styles.

However, sometimes the opposite is true. For example, a person raised as a Southern Baptist may feel much closer to God drawing from the quietness and private prayers of the Catholic or Anglican tradition. Conversely, a person coming from a Catholic tradition may feel profound freedom in experiencing God's presence without the historical practices of the Roman Church or even the necessity of a priest to lead her in worship. Our goal in planning worship is to assist people to worship, not to make them conform to a single worship style. We want to discover and employ structures that help worshipers communicate with God.

Many of our congregations plan worship, therefore, around a specific truth or theme. Ideally, services will be planned out by the pastor, musicians, and others many months in advance. The truth, stated in one sentence and written down, becomes the organizing factor as the service is planned.

Music in Worship. Music plays a significant role in our corporate worship. We strongly emphasize congregational singing, often using four or five hymns in their entirety. The choir may prompt the congregation to worship by singing choral works, responses, and calls to praise. Musical styles include a significant variety of contemporary and classical, while the hymns range from unpublished original hymns through praise songs to traditional hymns of the fifteenth to eighteenth century.

We are committed to singing the Scriptures. Congregations and choirs usually sing the Psalms, using traditional metrical hymn tunes as well as four-part Anglican style chants. Since the chant melodies are simple and repetitive, they help make the singing of Scripture an expression of our hearts.

The Place of Scripture and Prayer. Scripture is read as the drama that it is. Some congregations may use two or three readers, or the choir may lead responsive readings. Both Old and New Testament lessons are chosen to emphasize the truth around which the service is designed and to reinforce the idea to be presented in the homily.

Prayers take several forms in our services. In bidding prayer we pay attention to specific needs in the world, our community, or our church. Written prayers from prayer books may be read by the entire congregation. The emphasis is on prompting the congregation to pray rather than praying on behalf of the congregation.

Communion. Though we do not hold uniform theologies about Communion, our common agreement is that during Communion we experience the personal presence of God. We see the bread and juice as set apart for a holy purpose. For all of us they are at least symbols of Jesus' sacrifice. For some of us they are even more. Some congregations use portions of _The Book of Common Prayer_ for this portion of the service.

Celebration of Holy Communion is often quiet and somber—a time for reflection, confession, and prayer. We invite people to come forward and receive the elements individually, as groups of close friends and as families. Sometimes following the words of institution, the elements are blessed at the table, and people come to the altar and take them without further contact by worship leaders. Sometimes they are served individually by elders as worshipers come forward. The elders and pastors may also pray for individuals and anoint with oil as a symbol of the healing power of the Holy Spirit if desired.

However, since our practice of Communion is almost always central to a response to God in our services, it is not always quiet and reflective. Sometimes the congregation and choir sing historic joyful hymns of praise to God using a full organ with choral descants. Often the choir sings the Gloria as a call to Communion.

Proclamation and Response. Proclamation of the Word is included in each service. Program notes in the bulletin prepare worshipers to anticipate the truth around which worship will be centered. From time to time we employ drama such as reader's theater to proclaim the gospel. We also follow the seasons of the Christian year to a great extent, celebrating many of the historical feast days of the church.

Every service calls the worshipers to respond to God in a manner appropriate to our focus for the day—coming forward for prayer by others, focusing upon one particular truth throughout the following week, celebrating the confidence that we have been forgiven.

The use of all our senses in worship is evoked through symbols. Processions, crosses, banners, candles, colors, original bulletin covers, art, altar cloths, ballrooms, aroma of fresh bread baking, ashes, oil, startling sounds, confusion, varied physical arrangements of the sanctuary—all, used sparingly, become symbols to help us focus on specific truths.

Focus. In order to focus during corporate worship on encountering God's love together, we deal with agenda items such as announcements either before or following the service. Once the service has begun, we talk primarily to God, not to each other.

If worshipers can enter into this kind of focus, we can later draw great strength from God as we recall, in the midst of our hectic schedules, these moments of encounter. Leaders and planners of worship are encouraged to labor and discover ways of making each service personally meaningful to those whom we lead in worship.

Larry D. Ellis

III • BAPTIST GENERAL CONFERENCE CHURCHES

Worship in the Baptist General Conference follows the historic free church tradition, with, however, a contemporary flair. While there is no particular pattern evident among all the churches, there is a strong influence from the praise-and-worship style and a concern to establish seekers services. Some churches are finding ways to enhance the celebration of the Lord's Supper.

The Baptist General Conference, a denomination of more than one thousand churches in the USA, also has an autonomous Canadian counterpart and more than one thousand churches in other nations of the world. The member churches are strongly autonomous, so they are free to establish their own form of government, hire the pastor of their own choice, and decide just how much to involve the local church in the affairs and goals of the denomination.

Organized more than one hundred years ago, this denomination sprang from the desire of Swedish Baptist congregations to accomplish things that no one congregation could ever hope to do on its own. The independence of each church is actually one of the strengths of the worldwide mission of the denomination.

Varied Worship Styles

Given this background, it is impossible to pinpoint a definitive "worship style" common to all our churches. Not only does worship vary with the cultures of North America, but also with local leadership. Although our tradition is pietistic, with strong emphasis on the Word and on service to humankind, the range of worship styles today is wide.

One evidence of this is the choice not to produce a denominational hymnal, but rather to make congregations aware of the outstanding materials already available.

In many new congregations the tendency is toward the praise model of the charismatics. There is much singing, mostly of newer praise-and-worship songs sprinkled with an occasional hymn, and led by a "worship team," including singers and instrumentalists—a couple of keyboard players and a rhythm section, or perhaps just a synthesizer and guitars. Hand-clapping seems more "planned" on certain songs, not as free as in a charismatic gathering.

This singing leads to a message from the Word of God, with emphasis on its relevance to current events and the problems of contemporary lifestyle. Although a personal response is called for and even specifically suggested, it is not usually given as a public "altar call." Rather, the preacher makes it clear that questions will be welcomed at any time during the week.

Evangelism and Worship. It is common for regular attenders and guests alike to participate in Bible study and in building relationships during a second hour, perhaps after the worship service. Often this is followed by a lunch especially prepared for guests. The byword of this worship style is evangelism, with emphasis on personal lifestyle on Monday through Saturday as well as the corporate experience on Sunday. Activities associated with the liturgical tradition, such as the kiss of peace, would be hinted at in a time of greeting and handshaking. There is little emphasis on space and form, vestments, and so on.

A potential weakness of this style is the lack of regular observance of the Lord's Table. The fear is that guests will be embarrassed. The Communion service is therefore held at other times—perhaps Sunday evening or Wednesday. There are, however, many congregations included in this worship style who do observe the Lord's Table at every Sunday morning gathering.

Some of these congregations are quite creative in the use of drama, Scripture readings/litanies, and other texts, adapting resources from the charismatic tradition rather than drawing literally from liturgical practice.

Joy in Worship. The norm for public worship in the Baptist General Conference is along the lines of typical free tradition churches in the evangelical mainstream. But this is with a contemporary flair, not an early American flair! There is a great joy and exuberance, not silent sobriety. The Word of God is supreme, the active participation of individuals is facilitated, and the ordinances are encouraged and understood. Here is a possible order of worship for many of our churches:

A Possible Worship Service Plan

Prelude by musicians
Scripture Call to Worship
Hymn of Adoration
Recognizing God's Presence (invocation)
Greetings ("The Kiss")
Singing: worship and praise songs
Scripture (responsive reading, or creative)
Choir
Congregational singing
Sermon (including reading of text and prayer)
Song(s) of response: solo, congregation
Offering
Church Life; Opportunities (announcements)
Dismissal and Benediction

Although the "pastoral prayer" is often added to a Scripture reading, the present trend is towards continuity between Scripture and music. Music includes both traditional hymnody and anthem material as well as contemporary songs and worship choruses. There is a growing hunger for serious singing, emphasizing giving due praise to God, with fewer songs of testimony or personal walk such as the "old-time gospel songs."

The Lord's Table is observed by most congregations at the conclusion of the service, after a shortened sermon. There is great interest, however, in taking much more time at the Table. Many churches are designing the opening part of the hour or taking the entire service—morning or evening—to dwell on Christ's work and life.

Fresh Openness in Worship. Even in more traditional congregations there is just as much freedom to raise or clap hands as in new ones. There is an openness to creativity and freshness. Many of the things said about the newer congregations could be repeated here. This sense of joy and freedom springs from a trend toward personal involvement in worship and a desire to make the Sunday worship service dynamic and fulfilling, with an understanding that the object or focus of all is God.

Toward this end, Bethel College and Seminary has been instrumental in providing solid teaching on music and worship. Also, for a period of three years there was a full-time Director of Worship Resources who was available for teaching and interaction with any BGC church.

Perhaps for these two reasons, along with the strong commitment of national and district leadership, worship is an ongoing "hot" topic in the Baptist General Conference. There is a growing understanding that even the goals of global evangelism and social concern find root in the concept and practice of true worship.

There is a strong consciousness of the need to understand worship in Spirit and in truth. Worship is not a fad, and the people who attend BGC churches would much rather do it than merely discuss it. The great freedom and autonomy of BGC churches continue to encourage a nationwide surge of creativity and diversity in worship.

Timothy Mayfield

112 ✦ BRETHREN (PLYMOUTH) ASSEMBLIES

Brethren worship does not rely on clerical leadership. Rather, persons from within the assembled group, spontaneously moved by the Holy Spirit, lead worshipers through an experience of both Word and Table.

────────── **History** ──────────

The Plymouth Brethren are an independent evangelical movement that originated in the early nineteenth century. Weary of religious strife, clericalism, and the spiritual dryness of the Established church and the narrow attitudes of existing nonconformist churches, Christians from various groups began meeting informally for Communion, prayer, and Bible teaching. Shortly before and after 1830 centers were established in Dublin, Plymouth, and Bristol. From these beginnings the movement grew rapidly.

Their original principle of union was the believ-

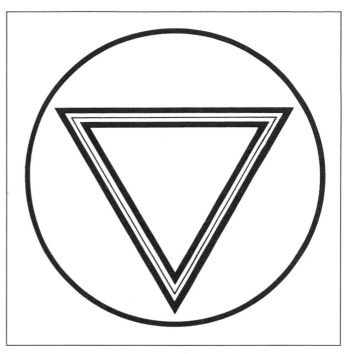

**The Equilateral Triangle.** One of the oldest symbols of the Trinity. The equal side and angles carry the idea of unity. They combine to form not three figures, but one. Thus the equality of the three distinct sides and angles express three persons, and the oneness of the figure expresses the unity of the Divine Essence.

er's love of Jesus rather than oneness of judgment on minor things. Doctrinal differences and the question of church discipline, however, eventually split the movement in 1848. One group, known as "Exclusive," departed from the open pattern of worship, accepting only their own members to Communion. The other group, the "Open" Brethren, retained the original pattern of worship and welcome all professing Christians to the Lord's Table. While differences on admission to Communion exist between the two groups, the pattern of worship for both has remained basically the same and continues to be a central distinctive of Brethren churches.

────── **The Centrality of the Lord's Table** ──────

The central focus of corporate worship is the Lord's Table, which is observed each Sunday. The Table, which holds the elements of bread and wine, is centrally located. Typically the service begins with a hymn, usually spontaneously given out. Customarily this hymn will set the theme for the entire service and is developed by other hymns and prayers and the reading of Scripture, which may or may not be expounded upon.

These flow out of individual silent reflection and prayer. In the silence of personal worship the Holy Spirit leads certain ones to share audibly. There is no reliance upon clerical leadership. Each one is encouraged to be personally led of the Holy Spirit in their private and public participation. The Holy Spirit takes the Word presented in the hymns, prayers, and Scripture publicly shared or privately reflected upon to lead the worshiper in remembrance of the Lord.

As the service progresses, one is led of the Spirit to give thanks for the broken body of Christ whereupon the loaf is broken, passed, and taken by those participating. Following this, another is led to give thanks for the shed blood, and the cup is then passed to all and taken. The service normally is concluded with either a hymn or prayer.

Traditionally for the Brethren, worship has consisted of thanksgiving and praise and the act of remembering the Lord in the breaking of bread. The object and subject of worship is the Lord himself, symbolically present in the elements of bread and wine. While some Brethren Assemblies limit the subject of worship to only the Lord's death, in many others the whole life of Christ is remembered: his coming, living, dying, rising, ascending, interceding, coming again, and reigning.

Principles of Worship

At least three leading principles underlie Brethren worship. First, worship is fundamentally a spiritual exercise that is dependent upon the leading of the Holy Spirit. Therefore it is believed there is no need for liturgical directions; the Holy Spirit is competent to lead. Second, it is believed that worship is the prerogative of all believers as individual priests before God. Therefore there is no need for clerical leadership. And third, corporate worship flows out of the silence of private worship. True worship means quiet waiting on the Spirit of God. As worship rises in the quietness of each heart, the Holy Spirit moves and leads certain ones to momentarily break the silence with a hymn, prayer, Scripture reading, or personal word of thanksgiving or praise. Such audible contributions supplement the silent worship.

New Elements of Worship

Although this pattern of worship has characterized Brethren throughout their more than a century-and-a-half history, new elements have been introduced along the way. Initially, no musical instrument was used during the service. All singing was done a cappella. Today many Assemblies (especially among the Open Brethren) employ the use of organs and pianos, and some have introduced additional instruments such as the guitar.

Hymns used within the "Breaking of Bread" service (the name commonly given to their time of worship) generally have been limited to the Brethren's own collections and are little known outside the movement. The hymns themselves were selected with the Lord's Table in view and are limited in range. Because of the morbid and pedestrian nature of many, in recent years other additional hymnals and praise choruses have been introduced. While some continue to resist these innovations, many have enthusiastically welcomed them.

As noted above, the Breaking of Bread service is intentionally unstructured, that is, a predetermined theme is not given nor is the service conducted from up front, but is led by the congregation as the Spirit leads. This continues to be the general practice of most Assemblies. However, some Assemblies have begun to introduce one or both of these practices. Objections have been raised, however, that the introduction of a set theme or a worship leader derogates from the role of the Holy Spirit and unduly infringes upon the right of the individual worshiper as a believer-priest to be led of the Holy Spirit in their manner of participation.

While other tensions exist within the context of Brethren worship, one needs mentioning here. It has been the position of the Brethren since the beginning that during the corporate worship meeting women are not permitted to participate verbally except to join in corporate hymn singing. While this remains the dominant position both of the Exclusive and Open Brethren, recently this has been challenged by certain Open groups. The issue is especially sensitive and in cases has led to division.

In spite of the open and spontaneous nature of the Breaking of Bread service, Brethren worship has often been accused, even within their own ranks, of being solemn and gloomy with hymns sung like a funeral dirge. Those situations where the subject of worship is limited to Christ's death tend more to exhibit this quality, though it certainly is not limited to them. Since there is an awareness of this (particularly among Open Assemblies), efforts are being made to recapture the vitality and vibrancy of their worship by encouraging thanksgiving and praise and introducing new and more robust hymns and songs. Still the basic principles remain the same: Spirit dependent, congregationally led, and spontaneous.

Christopher Mitchell

113 ✦ CALVARY CHAPEL

Calvary Chapel is representative of the newer independent churches characterized by lively, young congregations and free worship.

Almost a quarter century has elapsed since the first "Jesus People" began to populate the pews at Calvary Chapel to hear pastor Chuck Smith. Raised in a variety of religious backgrounds and emerging from lifestyles that involved everything from LSD to Eastern religions and free love, these new believers expressed their faith in ways that were consistent with their culture rather than the language of the church. Through Calvary Chapel they found love, life, and learning in the things of Christ. Over the past two and a half decades, the numbers of those touched by this church have grown as has the number of Calvary Chapels that have now been planted across the United States.

Worship at Calvary Chapel has not changed significantly during this time. The emphasis is still on intimacy in worship, contemporary praise, and straight to-the-point Bible teaching. The songs used include a blending of contemporary choruses and older hymns. While some services may use a large worship team, at other times the music may come from a single guitar or keyboard and a singer. The service simply flows as people are lead to sing, share, pray, read Scripture, and hear the Word taught. During the many services held at the Costa Mesa church, the music styles vary from night to night. Sunday services remain quite consistent and revolve around the teaching ministry of the pastor.

According to John Wickham of Calvary Chapel in Costa Mesa, the best word to describe their worship is *open*. Just as Mary sat at Jesus' feet while Martha prepared the meal, the church takes time to sit at his feet, clear their minds of things of the world, and commune with him. Usually weekly worship alternates between contemporary worship of hymns and choruses with teaching and two or three hymns with time given for baby dedications and other ministries.

While Calvary Chapel does encourage the gifts and ministries of the Holy Spirit, it is not in a strict sense charismatic. As people have come and continue to worship, receive feeding from the Word, and become mature in Christ through the ministry of Calvary Chapel, the church has felt no need for change in its structure of worship.

Randolph W. Sly

114 ✦ CHARISMATIC CHURCHES

Any Christian congregation open to the practice of the New Testament charismata in its worship, especially tongues, interpretation, prophecy, the word of knowledge, and the word of wisdom, is often described as a "charismatic" church. These phenomena, however, are not the dominant element of charismatic worship, which is more accurately described as worship based on praise in the presence of the Lord. It is often said that informality in worship and a continual openness to the direction of the Holy Spirit are the hallmarks of a charismatic church, but the degree of informality and spontaneity varies greatly from fellowship to fellowship.

The Charismatic Spectrum

The spectrum of charismatic churches is a broad one and may even be expanded to incorporate congregations which are part of historic denominations, including those which follow a prescribed liturgy. Some churches belonging to the Pentecostal denominations are also more charismatic in flavor than traditionally pentecostal. The more specifically "charismatic" churches fall into several recognizable categories:

Restoration or "revival" churches (not to be confused with the restoration movement of the 1800s, which produced the Christian or Disciples churches) include many whose roots go back to the Latter Rain Revival of the late 1940s in North America. Such churches emphasize the presence of God in the assembly and tend to downplay eschatology. The "tabernacle of David" theology taught in many of these churches results in an identification of the worshiping church as spiritual "Zion."

Faith churches are likely to view worship as the celebration of the believer's victory, in the Lord, over economic pressures, illness, or demonic influences. The leadership of these churches is usually influenced by Kenneth Hagin, Kenneth Copeland, or another of the well-known "faith" teachers. Other churches, not "faith" churches in this sense but like them, focus on deliverance ministry.

Vineyard churches are networked through the ministry of John Wimber and those associated with him in what originated as a "signs and wonders" outreach. Inner healing and community are priorities of Vineyard churches. The Vineyard movement produces much of its own music and worship materials.

Covenant churches focus on the family structure of the church and the spiritual responsibilities of family heads. These churches (not to be confused with the Evangelical Covenant Church) are often influenced by the Christian Reconstruction movement (better known in Reformed circles). The covenant churches, many of them associated with the ministry of Charles Simpson, have a historic relationship with Integrity Music, a leading producer and distributor of new praise-and-worship music.

Similar influences are at work in **kingdom** churches, which celebrate the present dominion of the Lord and thus hold a nonfuturistic eschatology.

Fivefold Ministry churches emphasize church structure, in particular the ministry gifts listed in Ephesians 4:11; these congregations tend to be networked through those exercising the gift of apostleship.

The New Testament churches have some traits in common with the Fivefold Ministry churches and stress the role and responsibility of elders in the local church.

These and other influences tend to crossbreed within the charismatic community and are likely to be found to some degree in any congregation. It is probably impossible to conceive a *generic* charismatic church. Although astute leadership often strikes an intelligent balance of emphases, generally one strain of influence predominates.

Despite these distinctions, there is a general similarity of worship across the charismatic continuum. Charismatic congregations of all varieties are networked through worship conferences, traveling ministry seminars, music media, and well-known personalities—a whole new worship industry. Trends originating in one band of the spectrum can spread quickly to others, on a selective church-by-church basis. The following discussion deals with some of the themes and emphases that influence the panorama of charismatic worship.

Praise and Worship: The "Manifest Presence" of God

The praise-and-worship format is virtually universal in charismatic circles and has migrated into evangelical and "mainstream" congregations as well. This style is adaptable to wide variation in liturgical practice and theological coloration. In charismatic churches, the service begins with an extended period (generally 15–45 minutes) of sequenced choruses led by a worship leader, usually backed by a team of instrumentalists and singers. Music usually starts with up-tempo songs, or psalms such as, "I will enter his gates with thanksgiving in my heart, I will enter his courts with praise . . ." (Ps. 100). Similar songs follow without pause, inviting the congregation to gather in the praise of the Lord and celebrating his greatness. Before long, however, these opening songs phase into a group of mid-tempo choruses, and finally into the more intense moments of adoration characterized by ballad-like choruses, such as "Alleluia!" or "I Love You, Lord," or the majestic "I Exalt Thee!" In some congregations, these two moods of worship are separated by other material, such as the pastor's greeting and announcements.

The congregation is encouraged to participate thoroughly in all aspects of the service, worshiping not only in song but through clapping, raising the hands, or dancing. Depending on local practice, the song sequence may be interrupted at strategic points by a word of prophecy or other utterance under the movement of the Spirit, or the "song of the Lord" may break out in spontaneous praise in both tongues and the vernacular. The goal is that worshipers might "enter into" the presence of the Lord.

Theologically, the distinctive feature of the praise-and-worship tradition, as found in charismatic churches, is its emphasis on the "manifest presence of God" experienced by believers during times of corporate worship. The belief that God "inhabits the praises" (Hebrew *tĕhillah*) of his people, drawn primarily from Psalm 22:3, is taken seriously and experienced in a way not unlike that in which sacramentally oriented Christians experience the doctrine of the transubstantiation of the elements of the Eucharist. That is, God is omnipresent, but at certain times in worship, as the congregation enters into the "high praises of God" (Ps. 149:6, NASB), he becomes *especially* present.

This "manifest presence" is often compared to the "glory of the LORD" that filled the temple of Solomon (2 Chron. 5:13-14) to the point that "the priests could not perform their service." It is in this atmosphere that the *charismata* or giftings of the Lord are often released. Just as many people, throughout the history of the church, have experienced physical and spiritual healing while partaking of the symbols of the Lord's body and blood at the table of Christ, so today worshipers testify to special manifestations of the Holy Spirit in worship, as God is enthroned on the praises of his people.

The Tabernacle Model of Worship

Though all four elements of the basic early church model of worship (*entrance, Word, Table, dismissal*) have their place in charismatic worship, the time of praise and worship generally focuses on the "entrance" aspect. That is, the "worship" time is concentrated in the beginning of the Sunday morning gathering (though it may recur as an "afterglow" at the end of the service, or as a response to the sermon). The entrance itself, as described above, takes the form of the joyous celebration of worshipers gathering in praise of their God. However, as the mood intensifies, and the congregation "enters into" the Lord's presence, the flow of worship approximates the movement from the outer court of the sanctuary into the inner court, and finally into the Holy of Holies, the presence of God himself. As one chorus expresses it,

> Take me past the outer courts,
> And through the holy place,
> Past the brazen altar;
> Lord, I want to see your face.
> Pass me by the crowds of people,
> The priests who sing their praise;
> I hunger and thirst for your righteousness,
> And it's only found one place.
> So take me in to the Holy of Holies,
> Take me in by the blood of the Lamb;
> So take me in to the Holy of Holies,
> Take the coal, cleanse my lips, here I am.
> (Dave Browning, "Take Me In")

In this way the architecture of the Old Testament tabernacle and temple are taken as a model for the progression of worship. The pattern of outer court and altar, sanctuary, and Holy of Holies also serves as an instructional paradigm for personal growth in Christian commitment and spirituality.

The Davidic Model: Psalmic Worship

Another model influencing charismatic worship has been the Davidic or psalmic style, which may be traced to the Latter Rain Revival that began early in 1948 in North Battleford, Saskatchewan. A number of Pentecostal believers, hungry for a fresh move of God, gathered at a Christian school to fast and pray. The resulting revival brought new insights into worship, especially the concept of the restoration of the tabernacle of David. Students of the Bible have always been aware that King David, upon recovering the ark of God from the Philistines, placed it in an open tent in the city of Zion instead of returning it to the tabernacle of Moses in Gibeon. The significance of this, however, went virtually unrecognized until the Latter Rain movement.

Davidic worship was seen as foreshadowing New Testament worship, for two reasons. First, unlike previous Israelite worship, it was carried on directly before the ark, the visible representation of God's presence. The New Testament makes clear that in the crucifixion of Christ the veil of the sanctuary has been stripped away, revealing God's glory to his people (Matt. 27:51; Rev. 11:19). Second, it employed the New Testament sacrifice of praise (Heb. 13:15), rather than animal sacrifices such as were still being offered on the altar at Moses' tabernacle. God's promise to restore the fallen booth of David—recorded in Amos 9:11-12 and quoted by James in Acts 15:16 in connection with the entrance of Gentiles into the covenant in the last days—seemed to confirm the idea that the Davidic worship of Zion was God's pattern for worship in the church.

This Davidic worship was marked by festive celebration and the outbreak of prophetic song. Many of the psalms contain words spoken by the Lord himself; these, it was thought, could well have come through the prophetic anointing upon David or the other musicians he had appointed to worship and prophesy continually before the ark (1 Chron. 16:4-7; 25:1-31). This anointing was also understood to include prophecy upon instruments and the "song of the Lord," or free-flowing, spontaneous praise, equated with the "selah" that appears frequently in the psalms. (*Selah* may be related to the verb *salal,* used of "lifting up" a song in Ps. 68:4.) This spontaneous song was seen as equivalent to "singing in the Spirit" (1 Cor. 14:15; Col. 3:16), a phenomenon that had reappeared during the Pentecostal revivals but had not been regularly practiced. Spoken prophecy was accepted in Pentecostal churches, and praise was sung to instrumental accompaniment, but the idea of prophesying upon an instrument alone, or of regular praise to the Lord in spontaneous song, was new.

Other celebrative aspects of Davidic worship, such as organized dance (not the individual "dancing in the Spirit" already familiar to many Pentecostals), represented a breakthrough in the worship of these groups. As revolutionary as was the concept of psalmic worship, it began to appear in the "restoration" churches that emerged from the Latter Rain Revival and eventually came to impact the charismatic community as a whole.

One vehicle through which the "tabernacle of David" concept has been propagated has been the International Worship Symposium, which originated in a 1978 music ministers' conference in Oakland, California, organized by Barry Griffing (later joined by Steve Griffing, Larry Dempsey, and David Fischer as Symposium directors). By 1980, the Worship Symposium had introduced banners carried in festive procession, on the basis of Psalm 68:24-26. Processions, the use of banners, and festive dance (already in use in varying degree within the historic denominations) were a departure for Pentecostal worshipers and an approach toward the incorporation of the fine arts into emerging charismatic worship, the aim being to "make his praise glorious" (cf. Ps. 66:2).

Many churches, while not completely accepting the Davidic restoration theology, have adopted elements of psalmic worship. The movement is propagated through worship conferences and dance workshops; a midwestern ministry, Pazaz, produces streamers, banners, flags, dance costumes, and instructional materials for festive worship. Every year, thousands of North American Christians gather in Jerusalem with other believers from around the world, to celebrate the Feast of Tabernacles in music, dance, and pageantry.

Traditional Influences and Convergence Worship

The specific musical expressions of charismatic worship range from the traditional to the contemporary. The maturing of the charismatic church has brought a deepened appreciation for the great hymnody of the faith. A significant number of churches are finding it quite natural to incorporate some of the older hymns into their worship life, just as the more "mainstream" or standard evangelical churches are finding a new release in worship by blending appropriate worship choruses with their hymn singing.

The new phenomenon of "convergence worship" creates a blend of charismatic praise and worship with historic liturgy. Whereas charismatic congregations have tended to concentrate on the Entrance as the heightened time of worship, many are now giving renewed attention to the service of the Word and of the Lord's Table as elements that come within the framework of worship. The Lord's Supper, especially, is being celebrated with greater ceremony and festivity, without the loss of the Spirit-led spontaneity and intensity that characterize the entrance.

With respect to the service of the Word, recent years have seen an increased interest in doctrinal instruction and exegesis, as leaders of charismatic congregations have made a serious effort to impact their constituents with the core principles of Christian faith and practice. Scandal among some of its more highly visible figures has brought about a sober self-assessment within this tradition and a strong move toward the lifestyle of holiness, unity, doctrinal integrity, and stability.

Freedom, Order, and Government

The balance of freedom and order in the charismatic churches is a matter determined largely by the pastor or eldership of the individual congregation. Most of these churches do not follow the pattern of some older denominations, which practice democratic rule or government by committee. Neither do most of these churches practice total autocracy. The general pattern of leadership is that of an "elder among elders," one pastoral elder taking the lead in decision-making and church government. Often, during an invitational moment toward the end of the Sunday morning service, the elders as a group will be called upon for specific ministry to the congregation, such as counseling or prayer for the sick. Other functions of the eldership and the diaconate in this tradition include involvement in the general ministries and helps that facilitate the weekly business and activities of the church and the service of the Lord's Table.

Churches of the charismatic tradition have seen significant growth in the last decade, due perhaps to what John Naisbitt, in his best-seller *Megatrends,* referred to as the need for "high touch" in our "high tech" society. People are hungry for an experience to accompany their theology. With much variation in style and expression, charismatic Christians join with those in liturgical churches, who celebrate Christ with historic ceremony and a belief in his special presence in the Eucharist; with their creative and contemporary evangelical brethren, who utilize the praise-and-worship style and a more relational approach to teaching and preaching; and with more traditional evangelicals, who emphasize evangelism and discipleship, with stress on family life and church activities. In short, charismatic churches embrace much of the experience and truth known to their Christian brothers and sisters universally; increasingly, they emphasize a lifestyle of worship, both individual and corporate, as well as the foundational doctrines of the inerrant Word of God.

John Chisum
Janice and Richard Leonard
Randolph W. Sly

115 ◆ CHRISTIAN CHURCH (DISCIPLES OF CHRIST)

The worship of the Christian Church (Disciples of Christ) is rooted in a Reformed tradition that has historically maintained both Word and sacrament. Worship is celebrated by an "ordained laity," seeks to involve the people as participants, and draws from a variety of sources developed by Catholic, evangelical, and charismatic communities.

The Christian Church (Disciples of Christ) is rooted in the Reformed tradition, influenced both by the Presbyterian and Congregational branches. It was founded in the early nineteenth century as part of an effort to overcome the denominational barriers dividing American Protestants.

—— The Eucharist and the Lay Eldership ——

Since its origins the liturgical practice of this church has been marked by three characteristics:

First, the Sunday service is always eucharistic. Disciples worship is typical of Protestantism in its strong emphasis upon preaching and congregational singing. Yet Disciples differ from many other churches in always celebrating the Lord's Supper during the regular Sunday services.

Second, the leaders at the table are elders elected by the congregation. Earlier in Disciples history, these elders were understood to be the congrega-

tion's ministers and were ordained locally. Later, a settled, ordained pastorate also developed and the ministerial character of the eldership diminished. Even so, elders have continued to offer the Communion prayers.

Third, the eucharistic prayers ordinarily are composed by these elders. Usually each elder develops a new prayer for each occasion at which he or she presides. Although the prayers differ widely, they usually include thankful remembrance of Jesus' sacrifice and the acknowledgment of our need for forgiveness.

At its best, worship among Disciples appeals both to the mind and to the heart. Strong preaching and deeply introspective meditation during Communion are consistently present in congregations of this tradition.

Worship of this type is also subject to problems. Because the elders are not educated in the church's theological tradition, and because there are few manuals to guide them in the preparation of prayers, idiosyncratic ideas about the meaning of the Eucharist frequently are stated in the prayers.

A second problem is triviality. When offered by a well-prepared leader, free prayer deals with the major themes of the faith and the central concerns of life. When preparation is inadequate and habitual patterns of speech are used, these prayers easily lose their connections with faith and life.

—— Reforming Eucharistic Practice ——

For many Disciples renewal in worship begins with efforts to reform their eucharistic practice. One criterion being used for such reforms is that they should adhere to the Disciples tradition of celebrating the Lord's Supper every Sunday, under local leaders, using extemporaneous prayer. Another criterion is that these celebrations should be shaped by the emerging ecumenical consensus concerning the meaning of the Eucharist.

As these criteria are used, the following trends can be seen. First, in many congregations the order of the Sunday service is being changed. Early in the twentieth century, the practice arose of conducting Communion early in the service and preaching the sermon near the end. Now these two elements are being reversed so that the actions at the Table are the culmination of the service.

The pastor of the congregation is becoming more prominent as leader. Elders continue to preside and offer the Communion prayers. But now the pastor joins them, offering the invitation to Communion, speaking the biblical words of institution for breaking the bread, and perhaps offering one of the Communion prayers. Elders and pastors together constitute the spiritual leadership of the congregation.

Reform also focuses upon the form and content of the Communion prayers. Recent Disciples publications outline principles to be followed and offer models for study by elders and pastors. An example of these publications is *Thankful Praise: A Resource for Christian Worship* (1987). This book recommends one pattern for the Sunday service. It affirms traditional values of Disciples liturgical practice but also recommends that this practice be made more consistent with the emerging ecumenical consensus.

Previous to the publication of this book, Disciples borrowed materials from other churches but with little impact upon the form and intentions of their own Communion service. Disciples eucharistic practice departed more and more from that of other churches. "The most immediate result of *Thankful Praise*," says Gerard Moore in a dissertation at Catholic University, "is that it has placed Disciples worship firmly within the great tradition of eucharistic worship" (p. 142).

——— Differing Paths to Renewal ———

Renewal of worship among Disciples congregations also deals with hymnody, the celebrative style, and the involvement of the congregation. There is a growing restiveness concerning traditional hymnody. Musicians and congregants are searching for a style of congregational song that is emotionally warm and theologically strong.

Like other Protestant churches, Disciples have experienced a period of increased propriety and diminished energy. In response, interest is increasing in services that provide interactions among the congregants while still preserving a basic orderliness. The leadership responsibilities of the members are being brought into the service, and pastors are less dominant in leading than once was the case.

Not all Disciples are persuaded by the approach to renewal described above. Instead, they are drawn toward a more evangelical approach. These congregations continue the emphasis upon Communion every Sunday, the presidency of elders from the congregation, and extemporaneous prayer. They differ from other Disciples in liturgical style, espe-

cially music, and theological emphases. Gospel songs, both traditional and contemporary, predominate. The theological emphasis tends to be upon the experience of salvation expressed in ways similar to other evangelical Protestant churches.

Under the leadership of their Division of Homeland Ministries, Disciples have developed print and electronic materials to assist congregations and pastors in the renewal of worship. These publications focus upon the work of elders, congregational approaches to the renewal of worship, and the continuing education of pastors as worship planners and leaders.

In addition, a growing body of scholarly literature has developed that presents and interprets the Disciples liturgical experience. Among these works are several books and essays by Keith Watkins, including *The Breaking of Bread (1969), The Feast of Joy* (1977), and *Patterns of Prayer* (1991). Other publications with important essays about Disciples worship are: *People of the Chalice* by Colbert S. Cartwright (1987); *Classic Themes of Disciples Theology,* edited by Kenneth Lawrence (1986); *Interpreting Disciples,* edited by L. Dale Richesin and Larry D. Bouchard (1987); and *Case Study of Mainstream Protestantism: the Disciples Relation to American Culture, 1880–1989,* edited by D. Newel Williams (1991).

Keith Watkins

116 • CHRISTIAN CHURCHES (INDEPENDENT) & INSTRUMENTAL CHURCHES OF CHRIST

Christian churches generally follow the free-worship tradition in its nineteenth-century evangelical form, featuring gospel songs, informal structure, and evangelistic sermons with invitations. Unlike most other free churches, however, they celebrate the Lord's Supper weekly. In recent years, some churches have been influenced by liturgical and praise-and-worship practices.

In the United States alone there are some 1.5 million members of the Christian Church/Church of Christ, yet in some ways the group is unknown and difficult to identify. The churches go by different titles, the most common being Christian Church (Church of Christ) or Church of Christ (Instrumental). The group has no denominational headquarters or central governing body to officially recognize a congregation, so many divergent viewpoints and worship practices are represented. The churches do not form a denomination or even an association, but constitute a "brotherhood" of mutually cooperating independent churches sharing a basic ideal. They attempt to give up all sectarian labels and call themselves "Christian" in a generic sense; it is their nondenominational plea to restore New Testament Christianity.

Through the years there have come to be three major identifiable branches of what is called the Restoration movement: Churches of Christ (noninstrumental), fully autonomous conservative evangelical churches known for their rejection of mechanical musical instruments in the worship service; the Christian Church (Disciples of Christ), whose leadership adopted a fully denominational position involved in ecumenism; and the centrist branch, Christian churches, which remain independent, and Churches of Christ, which choose to allow the use of musical instruments in worship.

Christian churches tend to be conservative and broadly evangelical. They reject written creeds and historically have had little association with other evangelicals, though in recent years they are moving more into the evangelical mainstream.

There are some elements of worship practice that all of the congregations of the Christian churches and Churches of Christ have in common: They all insist on following biblical examples as much as possible, seeking to find ways to apply the principles to contemporary culture; virtually all of the churches baptize adults by immersion; nearly all celebrate the Lord's Supper (as a memorial) weekly; and certainly all have a substantial place given for a preached message. Most of the churches are of the free worship tradition following the evangelical model of the nineteenth century: use of gospel songs, informal structure, and evangelistic sermon with invitation.

——————— An Order of Worship ———————

Here is a typical order of worship and its terminology from a Christian Church or Church of Christ dating from any time between 1920 and 1980, before recent experimentation in worship renewal began.

Organ Prelude. Originally people were in quiet meditation during the prelude, but in most churches now they visit quietly during this time. The music is either classical music or an arrangement of a hymn or gospel song.

Call to Worship. Usually either a few verses from a psalm or a congregational hymn; choir processional in some churches.

Invocation. Offered by minister or appointed layman, extemporaneous.

Hymns. One to three congregational songs, consisting of chosen stanzas of hymns or gospel songs, led by a volunteer male song leader; the organ is the principle instrument for musical accompaniment, with help from the piano.

Prayer Hymn. A more meditative hymn; one or two stanzas.

Prayer. Sometimes silent meditation precedes the minister or an elder voicing pastoral prayer concerns of the congregation; in many churches the organ plays softly under the prayer.

Communion Hymn. One or two stanzas of a hymn, announced by the song leader but sung without his direction; the men who will distribute the elements gather and proceed to the front during the singing.

Communion Meditation. A two- to five-minute meditative thought, presented by one of the elders; either original material or read from his own source; prayer by two elders—one for each element—or a combined prayer by one elder.

Lord's Supper. Also called Communion or the Lord's Table; passed by deacons and other men to the congregation; individual cups and unleavened bread squares are most common. Open Communion policy, although many churches specify that it is open to immersed believers.

Offertory Prayer. After the men serving Communion return to the front, one of them offers a prayer for the offering; sometimes a stewardship meditation by the minister is inserted before this.

Offering. The men again pass trays through the congregation while the organ and piano play an uplifting song arrangement.

Scripture Reading. The text for the sermon; usually a few verses from the New Testament.

Special Music. Either a solo, lately often with prerecorded accompaniment tracks, or the choir serving as proclaimers of truth, preparing the hearts of the congregation to hear the message.

Morning Message. Sometimes called the sermon, lasting from twenty to thirty minutes and always concluding with an invitation for people to come to the front pew.

Invitation Hymn. People stand and sing a gospel song, always one verse beyond the last response to the invitation.

Baptismal Service. Those who respond to the invitation are introduced to the congregation, asked to confess, "I believe that Jesus is the Christ, the Son of the living God," and are immersed.

Announcements. Free and informal, often allowing members to speak.

Benediction. Extemporaneous summarizing prayer, usually offered by one of the men called upon by the minister, and not uncommonly by any visiting Christian minister or elder from another congregation who is in attendance that day.

———— Diversifying Practice ————

Within the last decade, worship practices have diversified within the Christian churches. Some are more formal, but virtually none adhere to the church calendar. Some are mildly charismatic and sing worship choruses and praise music for forty minutes or more. Many of the churches lately are taking the lead of the recent evangelism model of Willow Creek Community Church, holding seeker services on Sunday mornings or Saturday evenings, with less congregational singing and informal but very polished performance of a presentation of the basics of Christianity for the unchurched of the community.

Many of the Christian churches look to the Southeast Christian Church in Louisville, Kentucky, as an example for their worship services. Several thousand people attend Southeast each weekend in multiple services, and they are attracted by the smoothly flowing song service that incorporates about twelve minutes of congregational singing, involving a conscious balance between choruses and hymns, computer-projected on a large screen. Transitions enable the songs to flow smoothly from one to the other, with an additional twelve minutes of other elements of the service interspersed—such elements as Scripture reading, prayer, "Congrega-

tion-Greet-One-Another" time, baptisms (of those who responded at earlier services, slice-of-life dramatic sketches, announcements, meditations, and musical performances—one to three special selections each week. The Communion portion of the service consists of a brief introduction and prayer and about a six-minute time of passing trays and partaking. The message is thirty minutes long (for radio play), and the invitation time often involves singing two or three hymns or choruses while people are responding. The entire service is precision-timed to be done in less than seventy minutes and is built around the theme of the sermon. Wednesday evenings the church has "Celebration," which involves more praise choruses and deeper instruction for the Christian members of the church.

As society has been changing, the style of the service has shifted among Christian churches and Churches of Christ. Yet a simple, informal service with a twofold emphasis on the Lord's Table and evangelism continues to be the guiding principal of worship.

Ken Read

117 ◆ CHRISTIAN AND MISSIONARY ALLIANCE CHURCHES

Worship in the Christian and Missionary Alliance Church is rooted in the evangelical style of the sermon-oriented, invitation-focused service. More recently the trend has been toward the praise-and-worship tradition, with much greater emphasis upon music, the arts, and physical participation through dancing, clapping, and hand raising.

The father of the Christian and Missionary Alliance, Albert Barnes Simpson, possessed a deep love for God and undying concern for lost people that issued in a movement that has, since its origins in 1887, prioritized the personal nature of faith in Jesus Christ. For people of the Alliance, true belief is more than adherence to correct doctrine. Christian faith involves a personal relationship with the resurrected Christ. This intimate encounter begins at new birth and deepens with the subsequent and ongoing work of the Holy Spirit.

———— Rapid Growth ————

For one hundred years the C&MA has sent men and women around the globe with the message of salvation. As a result, overseas membership has

The Triangle and Circle Interwoven. *This ancient symbol of the Trinity features a full circle, which represents eternity, interwoven with the equilateral triangle, which represents the idea of eternity of the Three Persons and of the Divine Essence.*

grown to more than 2 million. The Alliance is also one of the fastest growing denominations in North America. Through evangelism and church planting, its membership has doubled in a decade.

Yet along with the impressive growth, the C&MA has problems similar to those of other evangelical denominations. In its zeal for world missions, the Alliance has at times fallen into task orientation. This has given some the impression that people are saved to participate in a cause, rather than to have a personal relationship with the living Lord. Second, many of the thousands of new believers rapidly ushered into the denomination's fellowship do not understand nor have as yet embraced the "deeper life" experience of the Holy Spirit. Finally, numerous local churches are experiencing a lifelessness in worship that creates a funereal atmosphere rather than a sense of celebration. This has contributed to the rapid decline and death of some congregations. It is within this context that worship renewal in the C&MA has taken root.

A More Participatory Style

The most significant change in worship has been a shift away from the sermon-dominated service. Rooted in the nineteenth-century evangelistic model, most local churches of the Alliance have been pulpit-focused and corporately passive. In recent years, numerous congregations have moved to a more inclusive and participatory style. The sermon, while still held in high esteem, is not the primary focus of worship. Instead it is one of many forms used to usher worshipers into the presence of God.

Music has played a significant role in Alliance worship, and until recently, the dominant expression was the hymn. While biblically based, Alliance hymnology does not represent the style of music that appeals to most contemporary worshipers. More recently, many congregations have begun to include Scripture songs and choruses in the worship service. Along with the new songs have come more instruments, such as guitars, drums, and synthesizers. In some settings, worship teams with singers and instrumentalists have replaced the traditional choir and organ. Some congregations have started to use banners and drama, introducing the arts into the worship experience.

Another significant shift has occurred in regard to body language and worship. For several decades, hand raising and clapping were seen by many people as signs of imbalance, reflecting unwelcome influence from the charismatic movement. But more and more people of the Alliance are engaging the whole person in the act of worship. Numerous pastors have recaptured the biblical postures of worship and sensitively introduced them to people in their congregations.

Another major change centers on the celebration of the Lord's Supper. Many congregations seemed to focus so much on the death of Christ that Communion seemed almost dull and lifeless. A shift has occurred in some churches, in which the focus is instead on the presence of the living Christ in the midst of the sacrament. Worshipers are encouraged to bring their needs to the Lord. In several churches, ministry teams pray for people as they return from the Table. The emphasis is upon the present Christ, ready and able to meet worshipers in the midst of the sacrament.

Sources of Renewal

The impetus for these changes has come, first of all, from the Alliance Theological Seminary, which experienced worship renewal over a five-year period that influenced more than four hundred students. Many of these men and women would later 🙐

serve as pastors and missionaries within the denomination.

Second, the denomination's publication of *Exalt Him: Designing Dynamic Worship Services* was well received and initiated numerous seminars on worship renewal across the U.S. Third, personnel at the denomination's National Office of Church Growth saw a critical need for worship renewal. Through their publications, special conferences, and seminars, denominational leaders were encouraged to embrace a new understanding of worship.

Fourth, Dr. Robert Webber's lectures at ATS had a positive impact on some people's understanding of the Lord's Supper. Fifth, on the West Coast particularly, the Vineyard movement and Fuller Theological Seminary have had a limited affect on worship practices.

Sixth, like most denominations, the C&MA has indeed experienced a degree of influence from the charismatic movement. Finally, expressions of worship used within the many ethnic congregations of the denomination have opened the North American church to forms of worship previously disregarded.

What has been the response to renewal within the Christian and Missionary Alliance? One segment of the denomination has opposed change in worship. Both nontraditional and liturgical expressions of worship are seen as a threat to the movement. Others have naively embraced worship renewal as the answer to all of their problems. In an effort to bring in change, everything traditional has been cast aside and that which is popular and contemporary embraced. Unfortunately, deeper hindrances to growth are ignored.

A third posture toward worship renewal focuses on the desire to please God and lead worshipers into his glorious presence. Only those forms of worship renewal that glorify God, are Christ-centered, edify believers, and appeal to visitors are embraced. This approach appears to predominate, which bodes well for the future of the Christian and Missionary Alliance.

Terry Wardle

118 • CHRISTIAN REFORMED CHURCHES

Worship in the Christian Reformed Church centers on the sermon but also emphasizes metrical psalms and the participation of families in worship. Worship renewal draws from Catholic, evangelical, and charismatic sources. There is a growing concern to celebrate Communion more frequently and to incorporate praise music at appropriate places in worship.

The Christian Reformed Church (CRC) began in 1857 as a small group of Dutch immigrants with a worship style inherited from the sixteenth-century Dutch Reformed leader Peter Datheen. Today there are approximately 300,000 members in 900 congregations. The psalter, to which were appended the required liturgical forms for the sacraments, was the effective worship book for these churches. The Dutch *Genevan Psalter* was used until 1914, when the 1912 Psalter was adopted.

The CRC has never officially adopted any one form of worship. Considerable discretion has always been left to the elders of each congregation. Yet for the first hundred years the structure of worship was relatively uniform. An attempt to reform and standardize the liturgy in 1928 met with stiff resistance. The first major change in the content of worship was the move from singing only metrical psalms to the acceptance of hymns, which began with the first edition of the *Psalter Hymnal* in 1934.

A new approach to structuring public worship can be traced to the work of a standing liturgical committee appointed in 1964. Their major 1968 Report (*Acts of Synod 1968,* 134–198) was deeply reflective of both historic Christian worship and the principles of Reformed worship. Their work stands within the broader liturgical renewal movement in mainline Protestantism following Vatican II.

More recently, the growing ethnic and cultural diversity within the CRC has resulted in increasing influence from evangelical and charismatic traditions. On any given Sunday, sixteen different languages are used in CRC worship services; after English, Korean, and Spanish are most heard. About 14 percent of congregations can be considered multicultural and/or multiethnic.

——— Traditional Worship Patterns ———

The traditional emphasis of all CRC worship has been exegetical preaching, with a practice of annually preaching through the Heidelberg Catechism as a means of covering the basics of Christian doctrine. Church order requires two services each Sunday. The second service originated as a catechism teaching service and until recently was similar in structure to the morning service.

The order of worship inherited from the sixteenth century is still used in some congregations:

(Organ Prelude)
Votum (Psalm 124:8) or Invocation
Salutation
Hymn
The Law (a reading of the Decalogue in the
    morning service; the Apostles' Creed in the
    second service)
Offering
Hymn
Congregational Prayer
Hymn
Scripture
Sermon
Prayer
Hymn
Doxology
Benediction
(Organ Postlude)

In this traditional style of worship, the minister was the only worship leader, and all action took place from the pulpit. The people's actions were limited to congregational singing. Gradually, the role of the people has expanded to include choirs, responsive reading of Scripture, and prayers led by someone other than the minister.

———— Liturgical Renewal ————

The 1968 Report made recommendations for change based on the understanding that a basic dialogic shape has been discernable throughout the history of the church: "Worship in God's covenant community is a meeting between a Person and persons, as it had been from the beginning." The Report presented to Synod three complete models for morning worship. Synod subsequently adopted several complete services for the Word and sacraments. The following order is now typical of much CRC worship:

The Opening
Organ Prelude
Minister: Call to Worship (opening sentences)
Minister: Greeting from God

Confession and Assurance
Minister: The Call to Confession
All: The Confession (_said or sung_)
Minister: The Declaration of Pardon
All: The Response (_Gloria Patri, or another hymn of praise_)
Minister: The Dedication (_reading of the Decalogue or some other scriptural passage_)
All: Hymn
[_When baptism is celebrated, it usually comes at this point or is interwoven with the confession and assurance._]

Proclamation of the Word
Minister or other member: Prayer for Illumination
(_spoken, or sung by all_)
Minister or other member: Scripture lesson(s)
Minister: Sermon
Minister: Prayer

The Response
All: Hymn
All: Creed (Apostles' or Nicene)
[_always recited when the Lord's Supper is celebrated_]
Minister or other member: Prayer
Offering
[_When the Lord's Supper is celebrated it is placed here after a doxology is sung_]

The Dismissal
All: Hymn (Doxology)
Minister: Benediction
Organ Postlude

The liturgical renewal encouraged by the 1968 Report has continued to spread. Triennial denomination-wide conferences on liturgy and music began in 1979. In 1985 a denominational office of music and liturgy was established, which in 1986 began publishing _Reformed Worship,_ a quarterly journal designed to give practical assistance in planning, structuring, and conducting worship. In 1990, 87 percent of churches had worship committees.

A major revision of the _Psalter Hymnal_ (1987) significantly influenced worship, since it included a virtually new metrical psalter and a great variety of styles, including both historic and contemporary hymnody, songs from many ethnic traditions, Scripture choruses, and children's songs. Also included in the hymnal were newly edited liturgical forms and, for the first time, complete services for the Word and sacraments.

Liturgical renewal in the CRC is most evident in a more careful ordering of the acts of worship to reflect a dialogic structure, in greater lay participation, and more frequent celebrations of the Lord's Supper. Most congregations are beginning to observe the church year and use banners and other visual arts. In 1990 about 25 percent were following the *Common Lectionary* for part of the year. A few ministers still wear a black Genevan gown (without the white tabs); very few have begun to wear vestments. Anthem choirs are now common, with a few beginning to function as service choirs singing each week. Drama and dance are rare in all but a few congregations.

Worship leadership is increasingly diverse, with lay members involved in leading prayers and sometimes in service as liturgists for complete sections of the service. In a few congregations the minister only preaches; the rest of the service is lead by lay members—especially men, but increasingly women and youth as well.

Most worship in the CRC stands somewhere between the two outlines given above. Those congregations influenced by the 1968 report, follow the direction of liturgical renewal as seen also in mainline Protestant denominations. Meanwhile, other congregations have been strongly influenced by both the evangelical and charismatic traditions. The increasing cultural and ethnic diversity has also encouraged diversity in worship styles. The praise-and-worship tradition is growing rapidly.

The Table

CRC congregations traditionally celebrated the Lord's Supper four times per year, the minimum required. A "Preparatory Exhortation" was read the preceding week. The traditional forms, one translated from sixteenth-century documents and two adopted in 1964, are lengthy and didactic.

With growing desire for more frequent celebration of the Lord's Supper, the traditional forms have been supplemented by complete services of the Word and sacraments (1981), including seasonal variants based on the principles and structure outlined in the 1968 report.

While parts of the service are outlined but not prescribed, several components of the Lord's Supper form "should be read in their entirety and not changed in any way." Those components include the Introduction, the beginning of the Prayer of Thanksgiving (with variants possible thereafter), the Institution, the Memorial, the Preparation of the Elements, and the Communion. The Prayer of Thanksgiving ends with a song, most typically "Holy, Holy, Holy," but with seasonal variants. As part of the Thanksgiving after Communion, Psalm 103 is usually said or sung. *Reformed Worship* also publishes complete services of word and sacraments as resources.

By 1990, 11 percent of CRC congregations celebrated the Lord's Supper the minimum four times per year; 67 percent observed the sacrament from five to seven times, 18 percent eight to twelve times, and 4 percent more than once per month. A couple of churches celebrate weekly.

Although a few congregations come forward to receive the elements, most partake in the pews. Some churches serve both wine and grape juice, others just grape juice. Congregational singing is gradually replacing organ music during the distribution of the elements.

Admittance to the Table is by public profession of faith, most commonly by young people in their upper teens. At issue currently is the relationship between profession of faith and admittance to the Table for younger children, who increasingly are seeking admittance to the Table.

Traditionally, the Table was guarded by elders who interviewed visitors before the service. But in recent decades it has become the general practice to issue an invitation from the pulpit to all who are members of a Christian church and desire to live a Christian life. A record of their participation is still commonly sent to their home congregation.

Preaching, Psalmody, and Family Participation

The second service is often similar to morning worship but is more informal. It is common for worship to begin with an opening song service followed by congregational prayer requests. The pattern roughly follows the morning structure, with a time of praise and song, the sermon, and the response of prayer and offering. The best attendance at this second service is found in the most traditional congregations and in those exploring the praise-and-worship style, especially when accompanied by strong exegetical preaching.

The historic emphasis on preaching is still reflected in the course requirements for the pastoral ministry. The denominational seminary, Calvin Theological Seminary (Grand Rapids, Michigan), has a strong academic program of systematic and historical theology but offers no courses in worship.

One of the strong features of Christian Reformed worship is a continuing tradition of vigorous and lively congregational singing. Only metrical psalms were sung in worship until publication of the first edition of the *Psalter Hymnal* in 1934. After that, hymn singing virtually replaced psalm singing in many congregations. In churches influenced by charismatic traditions, even historic hymnody has given way to a predominance of contemporary popular choruses. Recently, especially in churches beginning to follow the lectionary, there is a return to psalmody.

Another characteristic of CRC worship is the strong tradition of faithful attendance by complete families. Attendance does not change significantly on Easter Sunday, for example. In the last ten years, many churches have instituted children's bulletins and a children's message, often with the children coming forward. During the 1980s many congregations began "Worship Center" programs in which young children meet for their own worship experience during part or all of the regular service.

The sacrament of baptism always takes place in public worship, at the front of the church. In large churches, infant baptism is celebrated monthly, with children being brought usually within the first three months after birth.

Emily Brink

119 • CHURCH OF THE BRETHREN

Worship in the Brethren churches, influenced by Anabaptist and Pietist traditions, rejects formal liturgy in favor of "free worship." The emphasis in the past and now is on community, the Word, singing, and occasional services that combine the Agape feast and footwashing. Recently some churches have been influenced by either the liturgical movement or the more informal approach of the praise-and-worship tradition.

History and Principles of Worship

The Brethren were born out of the Anabaptist movement and radical Pietism in seventeenth- and eighteenth-century Germany, when small groups of people began meeting for Bible study, discussion, singing, and prayer. A 175-year-old description lifts up several aspects of worship still important in Brethren practice:

They gather about a long table, a hymn is sung. . . . The sisters on one side, the brethren on the other, arise and wash one another's feet. Then they eat the Lord's Supper, pass the kiss of charity with the right hand of fellowship, partake of the holy Communion, sing a hymn and go out. (Martin Grove Brumbaugh, *A History of the German Baptist Brethren in Europe and America* [Mount Morris, Ill.: Brethren Publishing House, 1899], 156.)

Singing, praying, observing the ordinances, sharing together, and lay leadership are still major principles in Brethren worship. The sense of freedom in worship valued by Brethren emphasizes the inseparable relationship between God's love for us and our love for one another; between personal faith and the corporate gathering of the faith community. For Brethren sacramental acts that embody Christ's presence are truly sacramental if they point to Christ's presence in life, where two or three are gathered in his name.

"Sign Acts" or Ordinances

Brethren name the "sign acts" as ordinances, several of which play an important role in worship, even if not celebrated every Sunday. They include baptism, love feast, anointing, the holy kiss, and laying on of hands.

Believer's baptism is practiced by immersing three times forward. Baptism for Brethren is not only the beginning of faithfulness in the church but the beginning of ministry.

Through the church's history the love feast has been central to the worship life of a congregation even though celebrated by most churches only one or two times a year, usually on a Sunday evening. The service has four parts: a self-examination service, feetwashing, a simple agape meal, and Communion. In addition many congregations celebrate Eucharist or Communion as a shortened form of love feast that can be a part of Sunday morning worship.

Another ordinance observed by the Brethren is anointing, as described in James 5:14-16. The service might be held at a hospital bed before surgery or when one is very sick, or in the church for various types of healing (physical, spiritual, relational). Hands are laid on the head of the one anointed and brief prayers are offered.

Free Ministry

Worshiping together in homes, simple meeting-houses, and steepled churches, the Brethren Church for years was led through "free ministry." Four to six male ministers served a congregation free of pay while also working at secular jobs. During worship, these men sat behind a wooden table, with the elder-in-charge seated at the head. He would begin the worship with a welcome and then to his colleagues would say, "Be free, Brethren," or "I extend the liberty." This was an invitation for one of them to preach.

Thus, the form and structure of Brethren worship has varied from east to west, from congregation to congregation, from Sunday to Sunday. Occasionally today's congregations will incorporate elements of more liturgical worship such as affirmations of faith, bidding prayers, the *Gloria Patri,* and doxology. Special moments with the children and the sharing of congregational joys and concerns are a part of many worship services.

If liturgy indeed is the work of the people, then the people need to do their work—preparing and enacting, bringing freedom of the Spirit into an ordered structure. Present-day pastors, many of whom are seminary graduates, strive toward a better balance between order and spontaneity, structure and freedom. A new edition of the *Pastor's Manual,* which provides orders of worship services and rituals harmonious with church polity, came out in 1992. The denominational headquarters provides other worship resources upon request.

Brethren have long believed that liturgy as worship and liturgy as service belong together. Dale Brown, professor at Bethany Theological Seminary, says that "this double meaning [of liturgy] should remain basic to an understanding of the Brethren. We are a people for whom all of life . . . is sacred [or sacramental]" ("A People without a Liturgy?" *Brethren Life and Thought* 31 [Winter 1986]: 24).

Brethren Worship in the Future

The primary concerns for worship in the future are inclusion, involvement, and liberation. There undoubtedly will be "greater diversity, freedom and participation with careful attention . . . to language [of worship], roles/participation [in the assembly], [and matters of liturgical] form" (Jimmy R. Ross, "The Road Ahead," *Brethren Life and Thought* 31 [Winter 1986]: 33). Leadership and participation will be shared on an equal basis between sisters and brothers, clergy and laity, children, youth, and adults of varying cultures and ethnicity.

Singing will continue to be the most important part of worship, almost the liturgy itself. In addition to the a cappella congregational singing that is such a rich part of the heritage, today's churches also may use the organ or piano, choir, or a song leader. Types of music used run the gamut from German chorales to gospel songs, from Catholic liturgical pieces to praise music and scriptural songs. Brethren make a special effort to provide the denomination with musical resources that reflect the unique church worship heritage. The year nineteen ninety-two brought together the strong musical traditions of three peace churches, Church of the Brethren, Mennonite Church, and General Conference Mennonites, in a joint hymnal.

Worship courses are required as a part of seminary education. Students plan and lead worship that has been carefully thought through and is ready for critical feedback. Thematic worship and biblical preaching are emphasized. Models of lay worship committees are studied. Use of the lectionary during parts of the church year is encouraged. Inclusive human language is required and a widening of the images of God is modeled. The importance of music as an aid to worship and an act of worship is demonstrated.

Yet, the heartbeat of Brethren worship is not in structure but in community, "the love we have for each other and the commonality we have in God as God's children. Worship creates community. When Brethren together praise God and witness to the love of Jesus Christ, they build up the church in one accord" (Nancy Rosenberger Faus, "Pictures of Brethren at Worship," *Brethren Life and Thought* 31 [Winter 1986]: 23). The church is built up by praising God and, in word and act, showing forth the love of Jesus Christ.

Nancy Rosenberger Faus

120 • CHURCH OF GOD (ANDERSON, INDIANA)

Worship in the Church of God draws on both the holiness and ecumenical traditions. There is a strong emphasis on the "altar call" for conversion and the use of the "public altar" during congregational prayer for healing of relationships and emotions. Currently worship is being influenced by both the praise-and-worship movement and liturgical renewal.

The Church of God (Anderson, Indiana) conceives of itself not as a holiness denomination, but as a movement with a double concern for holiness of life and Christian unity. This dual concern is manifested in a broad spectrum of worship modes that include both the meditative and the overtly expressive, both the use of the hymn book alone and the use of words on a screen alone, both camp-meeting style services with a strong "altar call" and more polished services typical of mainline Protestantism.

A Singing People

From its beginning in the early 1880s, the people of the Church of God "Reformation Movement" (an in-house self-reference) have been a singing people. The movement's founder, Daniel S. Warner, was himself a songwriter and poet.

The church's newest hymnal, _Worship the Lord: Hymnal of the Church of God_ (1989), and the hymnal companion (1990) reflect the fact that congregational singing continues to be the primary means by which the church expresses itself in worship. Of the 734 items in the new hymnal, 638 are hymns and gospel songs, 125 more than in the immediately preceding _Hymnal of the Church of God_ published in 1971. The new hymnal contains a wide variety of musical styles. Even within one service it is not at all unusual for the range of selections drawn from it to include classical hymnody, camp meeting songs, praise choruses, Church of God heritage music, and choral responses.

In small congregations the song director is usually the worship leader. A service without congregational singing would be highly unusual. The raising of one hand during the singing of hymns and songs is widely practiced. While the lifting of both hands in adoration and praise is practiced in some congregations, it is the exception to the rule. The raising of one hand is more a testimony to others than an expression of adoration to God. It is a way of saying, "This song expresses my own personal experience."

The movement's strong emphasis on singing is evidenced by the fact that more often than not the second staff person in larger churches is a minister of music. The Church of God has produced such widely known vocalists as Sandi Patti, Bill and Gloria Gaither, and Doug Oldham.

The ordained ministry of the Church of God has always been racially and ethnically diverse and has included both men and women. Thus, one generally finds a strong sensitivity to race and gender in worship life. With over 20 percent of its congregations predominantly black, it is not unusual to find a great appreciation for traditional black worship modes even in non-black churches. The new hymnal includes songs especially close to the black tradition. Spanish translations for some songs are also included. And in most hymns inclusive language is used in reference to humankind.

Altar Response

Preaching continues to be the focal point of Sunday services with a strong emphasis on the importance of personal response to the Word and Spirit. Worshipers may be called to an "altar response" as well as being challenged to be "doers of the Word."

The term _altar response_ refers to coming forward to kneel at the altar rail in front of the pulpit. The rail is usually called the altar because it is the designated place where people offer themselves to God and where God's work of redemption, infilling, sanctification, healing, encouragement, and help is accomplished in the lives of those who respond in faith. It is the recognized place—though certainly not the only place—for divine-human transactions. While many black congregations do not have kneeling rails, believers are nevertheless urged to come forward for prayer especially at the close of the service.

In the Church of God one often hears about "the altars being filled" or about "not much altar work being done," the first used to express gratitude for evidence that God is at work and the latter expressing concern about the spiritual state of the church. This way of speaking grows out of the conviction that true worship should lead to change in those present—either in the initial conversion of sinners or in the ongoing "conversions" of believers.

A new and related phenomenon now appearing

in more and more congregations is the use of the "public altar," i.e., the kneeling rail, during the congregational or pastoral prayer. People are invited to come forward to bring their burdens, petitions, intercessions, and thanksgivings. Sometimes acts of reconciliation occur, special dedication prayers are offered, and anointing with oil in connection with prayers for the sick takes place. In some congregations, worshipers are invited to be anointed on behalf of others who because of sickness are absent from the service. Sometimes people even experience initial conversion at this time.

Recent Trends

Increasing attention is being given to the Lord's Table both architecturally and liturgically. While the most typical design is for a central pulpit with a Communion Table in front of it, many churches now have the pulpit off center with the Table central.

More important, however, is the increased interest in greater frequency of participation in the Lord's Supper. Traditionally, Anglo congregations have participated in the Supper only two or three times in the course of a year—on Maundy Thursday in connection with feetwashing, on World Wide Communion Sunday, and on New Year's Eve. Black congregations have tended to participate quarterly. Some congregations, however, now participate once a month. The number of items pertaining directly to the Supper has increased from six in the old hymnal to fourteen in the new.

One of the most significant changes reflected in the new hymnal is the new openness to the use of corporate affirmations of faith. Historically, the movement has persistently resisted the use of creeds. However, in *Worship the Lord,* three creeds appear—modern Protestant, Anabaptist, and ancient (the Nicene in its Western form). While it would be highly unusual for a congregation to use any one of these on a regular basis, one does find congregations that now use them as resources for worship in much the same way that hymns or responsive readings are used.

Education for Worship

The Board of Christian Education of the Church of God has had a staff person with the worship portfolio for several decades. That portfolio has

Two Interwoven Triangles. The combination of two equilateral triangles with one apex downward and another upward is an ancient symbol of the Trinity. The six-pointed star that forms is a symbol of Creation and expresses the triune God who created the heavens and the earth.

been upgraded more recently with the appointment of a person who has done graduate work in the field of worship.

The church's seminary, Anderson University School of Theology, requires a basic course in the theology and leadership of worship. Students are introduced to a wide spectrum of Christian worship traditions, are encouraged to give serious consideration to the place of the Lord's Supper in corporate worship and are provided with the opportunity to think theologically about the nature of Christian worship.

In the seminary chapel, the common lectionary is used, the passing of the peace is a regular component of worship, the use of the corporate "amen" at the end of prayers is encouraged, and participation in the Lord's Supper usually takes place once a month. The influence of the seminary's curricular emphasis on worship and its introduction of new practices into chapel worship can be seen in changes that are beginning to take place in churches where the pastoral leadership is from the seminary.

Gilbert W. Stafford

121 ✦ CHURCH OF GOD (CLEVELAND, TENNESSEE)

Worship in the Church of God, Cleveland, has long included elements of renewal such as lay participation, warm personal appeal, and energetic singing. New to the church, on the other hand, are some of the elements of liturgical worship. As in all such processes, new practices have replaced some older traditions.

Like most other denominations headquartered within the United States, the Church of God, Cleveland, has been impacted by worship renewal. However, the specific attention to this renewal came much later than in many other denominations. It was not until 1983 that the church began a three-year emphasis on worship, culminating in the celebration of its centennial.

This delay in worship renewal emphasis can be traced to a variety of factors. All of them are directly related to the Pentecostal style of worship. When seen as a whole, these factors tended to cause both clergy and laity to ignore the movement since they were already practicing many of its suggestions for renewal. There was a sense of waiting for others to catch up.

First, the norm of enthusiastic, often emotional, participation already provided a personal, relevant approach to worship while maintaining the corporate nature of the church.

Second, most Churches of God already involved considerable numbers of lay people, both men and women, in the leadership as well as overall participation in worship. They led the congregation in singing, read Scripture, and prayed for the needs of the gathered body of believers.

Third, the renewal movement's emphasis on creativity again came as preaching to the converted. The inclusion of common or folk instruments such as guitars, accordions, tambourines, and various wind instruments had been a part of Church of God worship since the beginning of the century. Choruses and testimonial songs were used not only in the annual camp meetings, but were a vital part of the Sunday and weekday church music. Moreover, there was a constant stream of new musical literature being made available through the annual camp meeting songbooks.

Fourth, the freedom and change offered by worship renewal had been a reality for decades in the denomination. The free style of worship without a written liturgy, always open to the "leading of the Holy Spirit," allowed the order of service to be changed instantly. In many cases, in fact, there was not thought of a prescribed order of service.

Renewal cannot be seen uniformly throughout the Church of God, Cleveland. Some congregations have been dramatically affected while many others continue relatively unchanged. Some of the changes have come because of the rising economic and educational status of the constituency. Also, as the church growth movement has spawned larger congregations than ever before, it has out of necessity brought some changes in worship.

Even before the Church of God began to experience the expanded impact of worship renewal, a new hymnal, _Hymns of the Spirit,_ was printed (late in the 1960s). The intention was to include some of the newer literature by denominational writers, as well as selected older hymns of the church in general, plus provide _sine resoibsuve_ Scripture readings. It received mixed reception and even now, over twenty years after its release, it is being outsold by the much older _Church Hymnal._

There are some definite signs of worship renewal in the Church of God. A number of them reflect a swing toward the more liturgical aspects of worship. Many congregations have adopted a standardized order of service with printed bulletins that even list the sermon title. The order of service may include a thematically developed program reflected in every segment of the service. A very few churches have also made banners and use them in selected processionals as art of a special worship emphasis.

The basic gestures of worship such as uplifted hands are still practiced. Applause has become widespread and, as a result, in many congregations the use of "Amen" and "Hallelujah" has diminished. Standing for prayer has overtaken the previously common practice of kneeling.

Lively, energetic singing is still a part of the congregational music. But many of the old testimonial songs are being replaced by Scripture songs and other choruses that emphasize other dimensions of worship. Where the old hymns and songs have been completely replaced, the result has been a young generation who are totally unfamiliar with the songs their parents knew by heart.

Other evidence of the impact of worship renewal includes a marked increase in the number of sermons on worship, frequent articles on worship in denominational periodicals, conferences on worship, classes on the subject in academic institutions, several books on the topic, and more frequent celebration of Communion.

All of this has brought new issues regarding the management of time to the Church of God. How can there be sufficient time for an extended praise and prayer time geared for worship? Should congregations move to a seventy-five or ninety minute morning worship? How will the Sunday school hour be maintained? Or is it necessary to shorten the sermon to fulfill other needs of worship? These and other questions comprise the current phase of renewal among Churches of God.

Jerald Daffe

122 ◆ Church of God in Christ

The Church of God in Christ is of Pentecostal origin. Worshipers bring their life experiences before God and open themselves to the power of the Spirit. Spontaneous expressions of praise such as shouting, dancing, and clapping are encouraged. Yet there is also an order and discipline that checks abuses of that freedom.

The Church of God in Christ (COGIC) emerged out of the Pentecostal revivals at the Azusa Street Mission in Los Angeles in the first decade of the twentieth century. Originally the Pentecostal revivals were racially integrated, but groups soon formed along racial lines, reflecting the reality of a segregated society. Founded by Bishop C. H. Mason, the COGIC became the spiritual home for many black Pentecostals. While COGIC members of African heritage take pride in their African roots, the church understands itself as an expression of an orthodox Pentecostalism that transcends racial and ethnic barriers.

A Passionate Activity. The theological essence of Sunday morning worship in the COGIC is an affirmation of the moving power of God and the blessing received through giving God praise. Psalm 100 serves as a reference for corporate worship. It declares that one should make a joyful noise, sing, and give God praise and thanksgiving. Worship is a passionate activity for those in the COGIC, not a passive event. The whole body is actively engaged in giving service through worship.

The believer's life circumstances are closely integrated with the worship experience. The saints are encouraged to petition God for their needs at worship. They cry out before God and tell him all their troubles. A people so emotionally and physically involved give free expression to their powerful feelings.

Open to the Unscheduled. It is Church of God in Christ tradition to allow the unique, unscheduled, strange, and wonderful things of the Spirit to happen during worship. Specifically, the Pentecostal worship service is free-flowing and people are uninhibited. Shouting, dancing in the Spirit, and hand clapping, all of which the Scriptures encourage, are customary manifestations of spirit and praise. The free operation of the Spirit in worship is foundational to the COGIC experience. Even the pastor is prompted to defer to a lay person rejoicing in the Spirit.

To the uninitiated such services may seem disorderly, but that is a misconception. The often strange and spontaneous aspects of worship are not without parameters. The COGIC takes seriously Paul's admonitions to order and discipline in 1 Corinthians 14, which place constraints on potential abusers of the freedoms associated with Pentecostal worship.

The pastor has the final word about who is anointed to lead the worship and for how long. The pastor administers the necessary checks and the balances during the worship. Should anyone "get in self," that is, get out of the inspiration and will of God, the pastor can stop the rejoicing, prophesying, or whatever is going on. In response to any abuse of the spirit the pastor will quickly state, "the spirit is subject to the prophet." Hence, worship in the COGIC is filled with enthusiasm, but it is properly balanced.

Music and expressions of praise set the stage for the coming of the preached Word. Contrary to popular opinion, the minister does not hold the center position in the service; rather, the Word of God does. When the minister stands behind the sacred desk he brings a highly expressive message of hope. His preaching is usually accompanied with singing, prayer, often rejoicing and praise, and he normally sits down to the sounds of rejoicing. A minister in the COGIC works unusually hard during the Sunday morning worship service. Surrendering to and being led of the Spirit means total commitment to the movement of God.

Changing Package, Unchanging Content. A trend toward a more polished and sophisticated approach to worship has occurred over the years. For example, one will not find many churches engaging in the once common testimony service on Sunday mornings. Church buildings were once mostly storefronts. But attractive new edifices have arisen, and with them have come robed choirs, seminary-trained ministers, and professional people filling the pews.

Yet while the package in which worship takes place has changed, the content of the worship remains true to the foundations of traditional Pentecostal worship. The order of worship in the largest and finest COGIC congregations is usually opening prayer, Scripture reading, announcements, choir selections, offering, and the morning sermon with intermittent clapping of hands, shouting, spiritual dancing, and the working of the gifts of the Spirit. Amidst developing forms, the worship maintains spontaneity.

The Social Dimension. As with the Acts community, there is a social dimension important to worship in the COGIC. Daily prayer is still practiced in many local congregations. This kind of frequent interaction is a social opportunity particularly valuable for many of the elderly and working poor.

Sunday morning worship is a social event. Everyone is expected to be there. There is an emotional investment associated with the worship service and people come looking for the dividends. The gathering of the body of believers means that person-to-person contact is going to happen, which is essential to the Pentecostal worship experience. The church worships collectively, touching one another and then touching God.

Worship in the COGIC is a source of spiritual renewal, though not in a classic mystical tradition. The practical aspect of worship is manifest as people leave their anxieties, pains, and frustrations on the altar. The impact of the experience is then expressed through individual witnessing. The saints can leave worship saying, "I know I've been touched by the Lord."

David A. Hall

123 • CHURCH OF THE NAZARENE

Although rooted in the Holiness tradition, Nazarene worship has been influenced in its historical development by the revivalistic approach to worship. Revivalism has been directed toward both initial salvation and complete sanctification.

Recently Nazarene worship has been moving in two directions: one segment of the church is seeking to redeem its Wesleyan and Anglican roots while another segment is striving to displace the revivalistic form with a praise-and-worship style.

Revolution has recently come to corporate worship in the American Holiness Movement. Historically, John Wesley and some of his American interpreters shaped the theology of the movement and nineteenth-century revivalism shaped its corporate worship. But lately, many have come to believe that the revivalist influence is as much a liability to the Wesleyan heritage as it is an asset. Corporate worship patterns developed under the influence of nineteenth-century revivalism provide a very effective vehicle for proclaiming the Wesleyan doctrine of entire sanctification as an instantaneously granted "second work of grace." But they are severely limited with respect to the other critical point in the Wesleyan understanding of Christian perfection, the point of encouraging and developing growth in grace.

Increasingly, it is being recognized that corporate worship must move beyond a solely evangelistic aim and express the basic Christian disposition to adore and praise God, to learn of God, and to learn of life in God.

—— The Camp Meeting Model ——

Many, however, encouraged by the administrative leadership within the movement and by its corps of itinerant evangelists, retain and promote as the ideal for corporate worship a stereotype of the late nineteenth-century camp meeting service. The features of such worship include: spirited singing of gospel songs; fervent, spontaneous prayers said aloud by many; shouts of "Amen," "Hallelujah," and so on; spontaneous personal testimony; excited preaching that need not hew closely to the biblical text; and "altar services" in which the mourners' bench is lined with sobbing penitents seeking either justification or entire sanctification.

The liveliness of such services is almost always attributed to the presence of the Holy Spirit, who is there, it is believed, to help people distinguish clearly between sanctity and sinfulness, to determine which class they belong to, and to act accordingly.

This boisterous ideal has tended to shut out sustained contemplation of either the divine or human nature and generally it has inhibited nurture. And, admittedly, it has tended to be susceptible to sheer emotionalism. The standard of this model is applied even to sacramental services, which are evaluated in terms of degrees of overt emotional demonstration. The safeguards against evaluating all things by emotional criteria alone are putatively located in the ultimate authority of Scripture and in rather rigorous behavioral codes. But it is true that one would seldom hear commended as a model a service characterized by a quiet, thoughtful, generally unemotional spirit.

Traditional Patterns

Up until the mid-1960s the pattern of Sunday morning corporate worship varied little from congregation to congregation across the Holiness movement. That pattern is still common: opening hymn (choir and minister already in place); gospel song; pastoral prayer; announcements and offering (piano or organ offertory); choir number; gospel song; "special" music; sermon; benediction. Only one biblical passage would be read—the sermon text, immediately prior to the sermon. The pastoral prayer would be spontaneous or extemporaneous. "Read prayers" would have been considered quite inappropriate. The benediction would, more often than not, be an extension of the sermon—recapitulation, additional material, or suggested application. Seldom was it Trinitarian or even biblical; almost never was there an ascription in place of a benediction.

Processionals and recessionals were a rarity, but not unknown. However, they were simply matters of getting a choir into and out of the loft and served no liturgical function. Preludes were understood to be mood setters, but usually accompanied much socializing in the pews. The idea of silence in the moments before a service was considered to be of secondary importance, and might even be opposed. Hospitality came first and hence, socializing.

Universally until the 1960s, and still quite commonly thereafter, the Sunday evening service was constructed of the same elements as that of Sunday morning, with some exceptions: the gospel songs were chosen for their liveliness and their evangelistic content, there would often be more in the way of "special" music, and the sermon would almost invariably lead to an altar call, a call to conversion or to entire sanctification.

The heart of this model, the lively fervor or "excitement" described as the "presence of the Holy Spirit," has remained the desideratum for the past 125 years. But since the 1960s, the means of achieving or sustaining it have changed. As the movement has become increasingly middle class, the older practices of spontaneous shouting, testifying, and praying aloud simultaneously have been curtailed. As a result, much of the "burden" for maintaining the desideratum has fallen on music, and music has also been assigned the task of mood control.

Consequently, in many places, direct congregational participation is reduced to the singing of choruses and snippets of hymns and gospel songs surrounded by elements of performance and entertainment in which members of the congregation are mere spectators. The song leader has become a sort of emcee, responsible for keeping up "a good spirit" with a line of pious commentary, observation, and introductions. The use of lush stereo tapes in the accompaniment of local musicians furthers the mood of performance and entertainment.

A Place for Adoration

While very few in the Holiness movement would want to discard evangelism as an essential purpose of corporate worship, the dominance of the evangelistic model has met with increasing resistance. In many places there is a revolutionary concern to make a place for adoration, contemplation, and nurture. This concern, often only dimly perceived and poorly articulated, has not yet universally removed evangelism from its place of priority, but it has in some places and is showing signs of doing so quite widely.

Here the historical tendency of the Holiness movement to reject out of hand any worship patterns and perspectives other than its own (even failing to recognize its indebtedness to Methodism and Anglicanism) has generally left it without the basic experiences and perspectives that would permit and encourage careful discussion of change. On the one hand, it has been sharply critical of the freedom of the Pentecostals, and, on the other hand, it has declared the traditional forms to be "cold, dead, and formal." Even where it has retained older rituals, as in baptism and the Lord's Supper, it has developed a studied offhandedness in celebrating them, for the worst of all sins in public worship is "formalism."

— The Quest for Contemporary Appeal —

So it is that two distinct new approaches to worship have been developed, in addition to the older pattern and its modern mutation, already noted. Perhaps most common are those approaches for which the word *contemporary* holds high value, and which are concerned primarily with psychological or aesthetic satisfaction. The language and experience of the social sciences and the entertainment industry are given high credence. The patterns chosen are those of the gospel sing or those of the televangelists, in which the aim appears to be an emotional tone—a sense of having "gotten in touch with God" or a sense of having "refocused life," not usually evangelism. The music, especially, is turned toward self-affirmation.

In these patterns, the choir will often begin the service with a rousing contemporary chorus of praise which often repeats a biblical verse and in which the congregation will be asked to join on a second go-round. This will be followed by an informal word of greeting from the pastor or the song leader and often an invitation to "turn around and shake hands with those near you." Then will come another chorus or a gospel song, or even one of the livelier hymns, followed by yet another chorus or gospel song, a "prayer chorus" and "prayer time."

"Prayer time," which is usually directed by the pastor against a background of "mood music" is principally given over to petitions, most of them having to do with physical and emotional health and material desires. It is usually closed with the choir or the choir and congregation singing a chorus.

The mood then rapidly shifts as visitors are greeted, announcements are made, and various activities are vigorously promoted. The offering is then taken as an offertory is either played or sung. The offertory prayer is quite informal. It is always spontaneous and is usually prayed by one of the ushers. This is usually followed by a "choir special," which, in turn, is followed by a chorus or a verse or two of a hymn or gospel song by the congregation. If the offertory music was instrumental, there will now usually be a vocal "special."

Then comes the sermon, almost always delivered in conversational tones. While there is some tendency now among those following this model to attempt to fit the music to the theme of the sermon, ordinarily it will not show any clear relationship. In fact, ordinarily the text will not be known until the pastor reads it as a preface to his sermon. The service is closed according to the pattern set much earlier, but the aim will not be clearly evangelistic. There is often no clear aim beyond the psychological one of feeling affirmed.

—— Recovery of Historic Traditions ——

At the same time some are reaching back to the Methodist and Anglican roots of the Holiness movement and seeking to reclaim more traditional forms of worship. These give high credence to the language and experience of the historic traditions. They choose patterns that aim at recognition of the sovereign God and at thanksgiving for the redemption brought to us, in our unworthiness, by Christ. They emphasize the dialogical character of worship, with the use of spoken and sung response to Scripture reading, to prayer, to the sermon, and to the offering.

Especially noteworthy is the increasing use of the lectionary for both public reading of Scripture and sermon text, of the Lord's Prayer, and of congregational response to prayer and Scripture reading. All of this, in turn, has led to more careful observance of the high holy days in the liturgical year besides Christmas and Easter. It has also led to a redirecting of the role of music—from mood-setter and means of personal testimony to a form of active participation in worship itself.

The order of service itself is essentially a simplified form of the older Anglican service of Morning Prayer with sermon. Also characteristic is a return to more frequent celebration of the Lord's Supper. The ritual followed here is usually a simplified version of that devised for the American Methodists by John Wesley, with strong emphasis on penitence now being replaced by an emphasis on solemn celebration and thanksgiving. For all of this, the twentieth-century hymnody of the Holiness movement has proven inadequate, so it is quite common to find bulletin inserts containing older hymns, especially those of Charles Wesley.

Almost all of the major Holiness denominations are currently creating new hymnals. This is being done with careful attention to "what the people [seem to] want," and only minimal consultation with theologians and biblical scholars. This very deliberate policy can only strengthen the so-called contemporary style of worship and further move the unique theological and experiential identity of the Holiness movement in a mainline evangelical direction. On the other hand, the publication of the Wesleys' hymns and worship aids point to a reviving of the liturgical spirit that gave birth to Wesleyanism.

The Holiness movement has not been self-critical or reflective concerning its patterns of worship, and has therefore not established worship commissions or even mandated courses in corporate worship for its clergy. And, at the moment, the signs of change are to be seen in local congregations, not denominational offices or schools.

Paul Bassett

124 • Churches of Christ (Non-Instrumental)

Historically, the Churches of Christ have stressed observance of forms and orders of worship that adhere strictly to New Testament practices. A recent renewal movement has brought innovation and greater diversity to worship in an effort to involve the emotions and to bring about a genuine encounter with God.

Churches of Christ, which are numerically strongest in the southern "Bible Belt" of the United States, grow out of the nineteenth-century American Restoration movement. A key component in the theology of this movement has been a deep conviction that the Bible is the absolute, infallible Word of God and that the New Testament provides the model for Christian worship. Thomas Campbell, one of the early fathers of the Restoration movement, popularized a slogan which became a motto for congregations in the Restoration tradition: "Where the Scriptures speak, we speak; where they are silent, we are silent."

This theological foundation has determined much of the form of worship in Churches of Christ for the past century. It explains, for example, why Churches of Christ have rejected instrumental music in public assemblies, and rely, instead, only upon a cappella singing.

— Correct Form vs. Heartfelt Encounter —

Traditionally, Churches of Christ have focused on order and form in public assemblies. They have emphasized five acts of worship: a cappella singing, praying, weekly observance of the Lord's Supper, giving, and preaching (or study of Scripture).

Throughout most of the twentieth century, Churches of Christ have given detailed attention to the "what" and the "how" of worship. They wanted to be certain they were doing worship correctly, according to God's pattern.

Churches of Christ that are trying to renew worship argue that worship which focuses almost entirely on "correct form" but puts little emphasis on encountering God in worship has become rote, cold, boring, and too predictable. Renewing congregations feel that there must be more focus on the "why" of worship and on a heartfelt encounter with the living God who is present among his assembled people.

Prior to the 1990s there was a high degree of uniformity of worship in Churches of Christ. A vacationing member could attend a service in Dallas, Los Angeles, Nashville, Miami, or New York and know exactly what to expect. The diversity which now characterizes Churches of Christ has created a tension among many of its congregations. Congregations fearful of change maintain that much of what is occurring in worship renewal is a liberal departure from biblical patterns. Many other congregations are pursuing worship renewal with the conviction that it is actually more in keeping with scriptural principles and less tied to tradition. They also believe that the old forms and styles of worship no longer connect with the unchurched community in an effective manner.

—————— Features of Renewal ——————

One change occurring in renewing churches is that much more planning is going into worship. Worship committees and worship teams, unheard of in previous decades, are becoming increasingly common in renewing congregations.

Preaching remains a vital part of the Sunday morning assembly. Expository preaching is the order of the day in most renewing churches. However, these congregations do not believe preaching should be the "main event," where one "star" shines on stage and the majority of worshipers sit passively and listen. There is more emphasis on the participation and interaction of worshipers.

It is not unusual for renewing congregations to hire worship leaders who are trained in music. These congregations tend to sing more contemporary songs and hymns drawn from Scripture, especially the Psalms. They sing more hymns of praise directed to God—songs that have a vertical focus rather than a horizontal focus. New songs are often displayed on overhead projectors or made available in song sheets or supplemental songbooks. More variety characterizes the order of worship, and in many congregations, worship lasts longer than the traditional one hour.

In more traditional Churches of Christ, one would not expect the lifting of hands in praise, kneeling in prayer, or the use of drama or choral groups to teach a lesson. Nor would one expect to hear personal testimonies, corporate confessions, responsive readings of Scripture, hand-clapping during songs, and robust ''Amens'' scattered throughout the service. Traditional Churches of Christ have de-emphasized the place of emotion in worship. These expressions of worship are not widespread even among renewing Churches of Christ. However, they are not unusual, nor are they discouraged. Renewing churches believe that unity and diversity can coexist. They teach that the church can be faithful to Scripture and, at the same time, allow freedom and diversity.

A Renewing Congregation

One congregation in Abilene, Texas, serves as an illustration of the types of changes occurring in worship renewal in Churches of Christ. They have moved Bible School to Sunday evening and have devoted two hours to worship on Sunday morning. Their service looks like this:

9:00 A.M.—''Family Worship''
The entire family is together for the praise assembly. The congregation sings both traditional hymns and contemporary praise hymns (using overhead projector). Occasionally a choral group will sing to help the congregation learn new songs. Scripture readings (some responsive) and prayers also included in this period. This segment is God-directed, upbeat, emotional, and optimistic.

9:30 A.M.—''Ministry of the Word''
While the minister preaches to the adults, the children go to their own assembly.

10:00 A.M.—''Family Fellowship''
Children return from Children's Church. The offering is taken and announcements are made during this period. About fifteen minutes is given for a variety of concerns. Two elders go to a designated room and make themselves available to anyone who wants to talk to a shepherd. Two of the elders' wives do the same thing in another room. Others may go to the fellowship hall for coffee and conversation. A quartet begins singing at the front of the auditorium when it is time to reassemble.

10:30 A.M.—''Bread and Cup''
A great amount of attention is given to the Lord's Supper. This segment includes prayers, Scripture reading, a time of meditation, singing, and readings from sources that help worshipers focus on the Lord's death, burial, and resurrection. One of the shepherds concludes the morning worship with a blessing (usually a brief reading from Scripture with little or no commentary), and the congregation says, ''Amen.''

Churches of Christ are nondenominational. The autonomous nature of each congregation makes it unlikely that there will ever be universal agreement among Churches of Christ concerning the style and form of Christian worship. However, the renewal movement is strong among many congregations, and it is expected to grow over the foreseeable future.

Dan Dozier

125 • CONGREGATIONAL CHURCHES

Congregational Church worship, while based on sixteenth-century traditions and influenced by a late nineteenth-century pattern, remains at the discretion of each congregation. The twentieth century has introduced new elements of worship. Nevertheless, there is a broad similarity of worship patterns from church to church.

Basic Forms. Freedom from imposed forms of worship and ''man-made ceremonies'' was the goal of sixteenth-century Congregational leaders like John

Greenwood, Henry Barrow, and John Penry. But this freedom did not mean chaos. William Ames spoke for all when he wrote in his *Marrow of Theology* (1620): "Public worship, which is to be celebrated most solemnly, necessarily requires Scripture reading, meditation, prayer, holy discourse, and contemplation of the works of God wherein . . . worship may become truly effective in us." Ames's book was required reading for ministerial students in North America for more than a century. The worship he described first appeared in print in John à Lasco's 1555 order for the worship of the church he served in London under royal charter.

When the first International Congregational Council assembled in London in 1891, the order of worship was invocation, hymn, Scripture reading, prayer, hymn, sermon, hymn, benediction. This order has remained a basic pattern for twentieth-century Congregational churches. At the same time, the twentieth century has brought change in Congregational worship through the advent of radio and television broadcasting, centralization/ecumenism, developments in church architecture, and the reentry of drama and dance into worship.

Broadcasting. Charles E. Fuller's "Old Fashioned Revival Hour" was the most widely heard radiocast of its kind from 1930 to 1950. The format consisted of song, Scripture, response-letter reading, sermon, and prayer. (Fuller had pastored Baptist churches, but later became associated with Lake Avenue Congregational Church in Pasadena, California.) Television brought more fundamental changes. Churches that telecast their services had to reconfigure their chancel area for visual effect. An early example is the Oneonta Congregational Church of South Pasadena, California, which in 1950 dedicated a house of worship with an enlarged chancel with space for a sizable choir. Churches elsewhere made similar adjustments for television ministry. The order of service was also affected by the time constraints of broadcasting, especially with regard to extemporaneous prayer and sermon length.

Centralization/Ecumenism. The centralization of Congregational Church agencies for mission, publications, education, and other work that occurred in the United States in the period 1936–1957 also affected the worship of the churches. In 1938 the General Council of the Congregational Christian Churches installed a Minister of the General Council. Few realized the scope and implications of this

assumption of ecclesiastical authority that had hitherto been centered solely in each local church. A decade later, in 1948, the Minister of the General Council would take part with ecclesiastical dignitaries the world over in the establishment of the World Council of Churches. As a result of this ecumenical exposure, a steady stream of experimental worship materials flowed from denominational sources into local churches, youth conferences, and the like, leading to a greater diversity of worship within Congregationalism.

Church Architecture. In the twentieth century, the classic, sometimes stark "meeting house" style of Congregational Church architecture has given way to new forms. Economic factors, plus the strength and flexibility of modern building materials, have led Congregational churches in North America to create buildings adaptable to multiple use. As a result, the fixed pews of older churches have been replaced by flexible seating arrangements, with implications for worship style. Similar developments have occurred in Great Britain, where Congregational churches erected since World War II have enlarged space around the pulpit and Communion Table and a more intimate size (150–200 people). Worship in these new structures has returned to the "family gathering" of early Congregational structures in Britain and New England. The new prominence of the Communion Table in some churches signifies the renewed emphasis on the service of the Lord's Table.

Reentry of Drama and Dance. Around 1950, English Congregationalists began to publish a series of booklets on worship renewal, including material on Christian drama. When the International Congregational Council met in Hartford in 1958, both drama and choreography were used in worship. The role of these worship arts varies from congregation to congregation, with some churches having an outstanding ministry in this area. Plymouth Congregational Church of suburban Minneapolis, for example, erected a fine arts center in 1968 with a well-equipped two-hundred-seat theater; the First Congregational Church of Los Angeles has created a series of Sunday afternoon dramas enlisting Hollywood talent.

Dance in Congregational worship was pioneered by Margaret Palmer Fiske in Hanover, New Hampshire, in the 1940s, and on the west coast by Helen L. Gray in 1948 at South Pasadena, California. In

The Trefoil. The trefoil, which contains three lobes of equal size that combine to make one figure, is an ancient symbol of the Trinity. It is a modification of the three interlaced circles.

1958 the Sacred Dance Guild was founded in Boston by a group of ministers' wives and education directors; by 1991 the Guild enrolled 770. Distinctive of the dance is the development of multigenerational dance choirs including adults, teenagers, and children. Worship dance in Congregationalism has not been limited to formal liturgy; periodic regional workshops held by Guild chapters span liturgical, educational, and evangelistic applications of the movement arts. In some instances, one finds clapping or lifting of the hands in Congregational churches.

Sunday Worship. Each Congregational church is free to allow its own style and order of worship, and each minister is free to direct worship according to his or her own insights, subject to review by the congregation. It is striking, however, that despite this freedom there is an underlying unity and similarity of worship across Congregationalism. In the Congregationalist view, there is no authoritative liturgy, since the New Testament does not specify any order of service. The alternative to such a traditional liturgy is worship with simplicity, attention to Christian experience, and dignity, with all done "in a fitting and orderly way" (1 Cor. 14:40). Within these guidelines there is wide scope for creativity in Congregational Christian worship.

The following are the orders of service from a smaller congregation, Mayflower Congregational Church of Laguna Hills, California, and from the larger (more than one thousand members) Oneonta Congregational Church of South Pasadena, in November 1991:

Mayflower Congregational Church	Oneonta Congregational Church
Organ Prelude	Organ Prelude
Choral Introit	Choral Introit and Call to Worship
Pastor's Welcome and Announcements	Processional Hymn
Hymn	Invocation and Lord's Prayer
Invocation	Gloria Patri
Responsive Reading	Church Concerns
Duet Scripture Reading	Call to Prayer
Call to Prayer	Morning Prayer with Choral Response
Lord's Prayer	Offertory
Tithes and Offerings, with Offertory Prayer	Doxology and Prayer of Dedication
Offertory (Solo)	Hymn
Doxology	Scripture Lesson
Informal Greeting	Sermon
Sermon	Prayer of Ascription
Hymn	Hymn
Benediction with Choral Response	Benediction and Choral Response
Organ Postlude	Organ Postlude

Henry David Gray

126 ✦ EASTERN ORTHODOX CHURCHES

Absolutely central to Orthodox worship is its concern to remain faithful to apostolic Christianity and its worship. Consequently, renewal in Orthodox worship always seeks to incarnate the old into the new situation of history and culture. Some Orthodox churches incorporate praise-and-worship music during the reception of bread and wine.

Within the past decade a great many things have been happening in the worship of the Eastern Orthodox church. The majority of these changes have been generated within the liturgical tradition, as a natural flowering or fulfillment of the church's experience of itself in the twentieth century, rather than resulting from external pressures or sources.

It has been said that the Orthodox church only

changes to remain the same, and while that may sound like a contradiction, it captures two fundamental truths. The first is an absolute commitment to remain true to that which has been taught from the beginning, that which constituted the faith and practice of the early Christian church. The second truth is the commitment to incarnate that faith and practice in a manner that makes it relevant to today's Christian.

Origins of Orthodox Liturgical Worship

A commitment to be true to that which has been taught from the beginning requires asking not just what was done in the beginning, but what were its origins? Just where did Christian worship "come from"? The apostolic church did not create a new form of church worship *ex nihilo*. Rather, early Christian worship was a continuity of Jewish synagogue and temple worship practices, to which was added that which was both unique and fulfillment, the Eucharist—the body and blood of Jesus Christ.

As one contemporary liturgical scholar has stated, "the structure of Christian worship originates in the worship of Judaism, primarily in its synagogue variation. Hebrew worship can be definitely characterized as a liturgy of time; it is set up in relation to the daily, weekly, and yearly cycles." The product of this liturgy of time is the liturgical year, the weekly and daily cycles of worship and the lexical approach to Scripture reading.

Liturgical scholars are in agreement that the earliest Christian worship was composed of two parts: synaxis and Eucharist. The synaxis, or gathering, is that portion of the church's worship that begins with the literal gathering of the people of God to worship, and is both part of and preparation for the second portion, the Eucharist or Holy Communion. While the Eastern Orthodox church is a "sacramental" body, it does not hold to the view that the Eucharist is the sole sacrament but rather affirms a sacramental view of life. Thus the gathering for worship is the first sacrament to be experienced in worship that consummates with the reception of the ultimate sacrament.

The earliest structure of the synaxis parallels the synagogue service: opening greeting, psalmody, lesson, and sermon. From the temple worship of Judaism came additional forms of worship such as icons, vestments, incense, singing, and altar. The Eucharist was added to these Jewish forms, and the Divine Liturgy of the Eastern Orthodox church still follows this pattern until today. Building upon this core, elements of beauty, antiphonal singing, and ceremonial action were added to show forth the glory of the kingdom as the liturgy flowered during the first few centuries. Yet, it remained true to the fundamental structure that constituted the worship of the early Christian church.

The Orthodox understanding of worship is based upon two elements: liturgy and the kingdom of God. Liturgy literally means the "work of the people," and all the people must work together to accomplish this thing called worship. In Orthodox tradition, the Eucharist may not be celebrated by clergy alone; it requires the presence of the people, who cocelebrate as members of the royal priesthood of believers. The second element is the simple acknowledgment that worship of God must occur in the place of God, that is in the kingdom.

Worship as Ascent

The almost universally celebrated liturgical form within the Eastern Orthodox church today is called the Divine Liturgy of St. John Chrysostom, which represents the consummation of the liturgical period of the first centuries. Like all other Eastern liturgies, it is characterized by ascent—worship as ascent to the kingdom of God. A recent author summarizes thus: "The Orthodox liturgy begins with the solemn doxology: 'Blessed is the Kingdom of the Father, the Son and the Holy Spirit, now and ever and unto ages of ages.' From the beginning the destination is announced: the journey is to the Kingdom. This is where we are going—and not symbolically, but really" (Alexander Schmemann, *For the Life of the World* [Crestwood, N.Y.: St. Vladimir's Seminary Press, 1973], 29). The kingdom is the goal and the end of all our desires and interests, of our whole life. It is the supreme and ultimate value of all that exists. This understanding and the "Amen" of the people to the doxology is in fact the first act of liturgy. It is also critical to full comprehension of both liturgical worship and the Divine Liturgy of the Eastern Orthodox church.

The doxology is followed by the Great Litany, an antiphonally chanted series of prayers and petitions. The litany is followed by the Antiphons and the Entrance, the coming of the celebrants to the altar. Both of these components have their roots in early Christian practice. The antiphons are the remnants of the singing of psalms by the faithful as they awaited the arrival of the clergy. The Entrance is the direct descendent of that arrival, the clergy entering the church carrying the Gospel and the sacred vessels to the altar. The Entrance into the sanctuary takes place with the prayer "grant that the holy angels may enter with us, to serve and glorify Your goodness with us." This is the first formal step in ascending from this world, in entering into the kingdom within the communion of the saints. The singing of the Thrice-Holy Hymn [*Trisagion*], among the oldest hymns in Christendom, immediately follows. Then comes the epistle and Gospel readings and finally the sermon, which concludes the Liturgy of the Word, the parallel to the synaxis of the synagogue.

———— Focused on the Eucharist ————

All of the foregoing may be seen as preparation for the ultimate purpose of the Divine Liturgy: participation in the Eucharist. A reading of the apostolic Fathers makes it quite apparent that the early church was a eucharistic community. As St. Ignatius said, the Eucharist is "the medicine of immortality, the antidote against death, and everlasting life in Jesus Christ." This conviction still animates the Divine Liturgy and constitutes the sacramental conviction of Orthodox Christians. The Eucharist is the body and blood of Jesus Christ and provides spiritual nurture and life.

The balance of the liturgy is ascent, an actualization of the kingdom and participation in its gifts. It is the worshiping assembly being taken up into the company of the saints gathered round the heavenly altar. Thus the altar is not a place where a new sacrifice is offered, but where we may participate in the eternal sacrifice of Jesus Christ.

———— Discovery as Renewal ————

Little if any "renewal" is going on within the Eastern Orthodox church if by renewal we mean restoring something to its former state, for, as we have seen, it has hardly changed from the beginning. Nor is there renewal as a result of contemporary or innovative processes being imported from without.

On the other hand, a very real renewal is occurring in terms of recognition, understanding, and participation. This is the case because historically the Orthodox church has suffered from a handicap the churches of the West never really experienced. From the time of the Ottoman conquest in the fifteenth century, almost all of the Orthodox church (except in Russia) fell under the oppression of Islam. The Bolshevik revolution resulted in similar oppression and persecution for the Orthodox churches of Russia and Eastern Europe. The result in those countries was the closure of churches, seminaries, and monasteries, with the consequent impact upon faith and practice. The establishment of Orthodox Christianity in North America paralleled the arrival of immigrants from the Old World. These immigrants were typically uneducated and spoke little if any English. While the importation of ethnic priests assured the establishment and continuity of the Orthodox faith, it also assured a ghetto mentality with a very low level of liturgical understanding.

In North America the Orthodox church has transcended its identity crisis and is recognizing the rich liturgical heritage it possesses. The single most important contribution to this process is the increasing use of English for most, if not all, liturgical worship. Few third- or fourth-generation children of immigrant families speak the old language; thus the use of English is designed to include these newer worshipers as well as make liturgical worship accessible to English-speaking people not of Orthodox heritage. The value of this process is further confirmed by the thousands of Protestants who have converted to Orthodox Christianity in the past few years.

In Eastern Europe and Russia, a similar rediscovery is taking place as the faithful, whose religious practice had been suppressed for so long, are recovering their churches and monasteries, and reclaiming their faith and its practice in an environment of personal freedom.

— Characteristics of Orthodox Worship —

The worship of the Eastern Orthodox church is, as we have seen, an unbroken historical continuity, a commitment to that which has been taught and practiced from the beginning. For Western Christians, that means an unsullied liturgical treasure that truly shows forth historical Christian worship practices.

While Orthodox worship is both liturgical and sacramental, it can be characterized by one word: *mystery.* We ascend to the kingdom to partake of the divine mysteries, that we may be spiritually nurtured and return to the world to incarnate that of which we have partaken. Equally significant, Eastern Orthodox worship is holistic. It addresses the whole person: body, soul, and spirit. We are created as psychosomatic beings, and worship must address all aspects of our being, including all of our senses. Thus in Orthodox worship sight, smell, hearing, taste, and touch are all addressed.

The iconography of Orthodox churches not only creates a holy atmosphere, but evokes deep spiritual meaning and states a theological understanding that we are all created in the icon (image) of God. Jesus Christ is the image of the Father, and his redemptive work consists in renewing the image of God, which was distorted by sin. Thus Jesus Christ is at the heart of all iconography.

Further, the entire service is sung or chanted, and involves the people as well as the clergy in the very act of worship. While the clergy are understood to be the celebrants, it is also understood that the laity cocelebrate and the Holy Spirit fulfills a dynamic role in worship. Orthodox doctrine does not understand the laity to be passive observers, but full participants.

Orthodox seminaries include a strong emphasis on liturgies, and this includes musical as well as rubrical understanding. The liturgical year requires specific worship material for each feast and commemoration. Thus there are substantial worship resources such as liturgical guides, service books, and books of prayers and services, some of which are listed below.

Benjamin Williams

127 ✦ EVANGELICAL COVENANT CHURCHES

Worship in the Evangelical Covenant Church has been shaped by its Lutheran background in Sweden, by the Pietist movement of the seventeenth century, and by the evangelistic awakening of the nineteenth century. It has preserved the lectionary, the feast days, and a more frequent celebration of the Lord's Supper. Recent trends include the introduction of praise-and-worship music and the use of dramatic arts.

The Evangelical Covenant Church was organized in America in 1885. It was a church of immigrant Swedes who had experienced the spiritual renewal movements engendered by German Pietism, Moravianism, and Methodism. The Covenant Church in Sweden, organized in 1878, stemmed from the churchly tradition of the Lutheran state church and the conventicle tradition of Pietism.

Covenanters in Sweden. In the Lutheran church, worship was conducted according to the festivals of the church year, the assigned lectionary texts for reading and preaching, the given liturgical formulas used in worship, and the prescribed rites of the church. Lutheran chorales provided the hymnody.

Worship was also conducted in the conventicles held in homes, barns, and schools, which were at times illegal. The Bible was read, discussed, and applied to life. Social classes mattered little; all participants had an equal voice, which made the conventicles a political factor in the eventual democratization of Sweden. Seasons of free prayer occasioned a sense of closeness and intimacy with Jesus Christ and with each other, as lives were opened to faith, hope, and love. The music sung was that of Lina Sandell and Oscar Ahnfelt, an indigenous folk music preserving the relational character of the Christian life but not encouraging narcissistic subjectivism. The theme of Jesus' friendship was dominant and found expression in personal testimony as well as in song.

Churchly Influences. Both the churchly and conventicle traditions are in evidence in the development of Covenant worship in America. Covenanters preserved the lectionary and feast days; the lectionary currently used is the *Ecumenical Lectionary.* Infant baptism and confirmation were present from the beginning, although both infant baptism and the baptism of older persons are administered. The conventional term for baptism and the Holy Communion is *sacrament*, not ordinance.

Since 1900, five editions of pastoral handbooks or worship books have been issued; the sixth is to be published in 1995. The books published in 1900, 1960, and 1981 contain extensive treatments of the theology of worship, the meaning of symbolism, and to some extent, the explication of the Lord's Day service. Preaching remains the central act of the Sunday gatherings, though use of the lectionary is not as prevalent as in earlier times. One of the services provided for Holy Communion is the ancient classical form of the great thanksgiving in contemporary language but rich in biblical and eucharistic motifs.

Conventicle Influences. The conventicle tradition issues in a simpler service in which ritual and liturgical formulas are less prominent, though not totally absent. Space and time are frequently given for free prayer and testimony or, more formally, lay witness.

Pastoral prayers, sometimes composed beforehand and sometimes not, are in the pastor's own words and intercede for persons, world situations, and congregational concerns. Hymnody consists both of the chorale and conventicle songs, together with music of the wider church, and these varieties have been preserved for use in the six hymnals published by the Covenant Church. The seventh hymnal will be issued in 1995.

Revival Influences. Indigenous American influences stem particularly from revivalism. In the nineteenth and early twentieth centuries, the image of the pastor as an evangelist gained ascendancy. The service of worship itself held evangelistic potential. A major contributor to that end was the gospel song. Nearly three hundred of Ira Sankey's songs had been translated into Swedish by the late 1870s. More recently, praise music and Scripture songs, together with a variety of electronic instruments, find increasing use in Covenant churches. A hymnal supplement, published in 1990, provides a variety of resources in this area together with psalmody and other liturgical pieces. Newly planted churches in particular have used drama, puppetry, and other media to address the gospel to a culture that finds the language of Zion a foreign tongue.

Form and Freedom. Generally speaking, the service of morning worship corresponds to what classical liturgical literature calls the Service of the Word. Seasons of the church year, especially Advent, Christmas, Lent, Easter, Pentecost Sunday, and, not infrequently, All Saints Day are commemorated. Readings from both the Old Testament and New Testament are often used. The lectionary provides four readings per Sunday. The psalm for the day is often used as the call to worship. The use of the Gloria Patri finds its place as a response to the readings of Scripture. The Apostles' Creed is part of the Communion liturgy, baptismal liturgy, service of confirmation, and ordination.

One of the prayers appointed for uses of baptism closely resembles the narrative of Luther's "flood prayer," detailing the use God made of water in the history of redemption. Singing may include many types of music, including, on occasion, a period of sustained singing as a prelude to worship. Monthly celebration of Holy Communion is close to the norm. Congregations from Hispanic, African-American, Korean, and Southeast Asian backgrounds worship according to forms consistent with their cultures and with musical expressions that enable their praise and prayer and enrich the church at large. Pastors and congregations are not bound by canonical rites.

Worship is not standardized in Covenant churches. Wide divergence of forms exists. In the main, the hymnal and the book of worship are what congregations and pastors have in common. The classical and the contemporary, the churchly and the conventicle are kept in conversation, and the people who use these books are kept in touch with that which has given structure and spirit, form and freedom to the worship and service of the triune God. Covenant life and worship shows that the spontaneous need not be sacrificed to the standardized and intimacy to the institutional.

John Weborg

128 • EVANGELICAL FREE CHURCHES

The Evangelical Free Church does not dictate worship style to its congregations. For this reason, each community may respond to various trends. Some have been influenced by the liturgical renewal, but most are shaped by an evangelical gospel tradition or by the more recent praise-and-worship tradition.

The Evangelical Free Churches of America has no board or commission or committee that dictates or coordinates worship practices. In fact, protest against a policy-making board or commission in such matters is rooted in the denomination's tradition. The word _free_ in the title means that the churches are free from edicts and statements from headquarters that are intended to be adhered to by each and every church. This polity is both a unique strength and a peculiar weakness.

Autonomy and Diversity. Each church is autonomous in establishing methods and style of worship, choosing a pastor, and initiating evangelism programs. Consequently, any attempt to define worship renewal in the entire denomination will remind the reader of a place where the tides or currents of several confluent streams come together: there will be a swirling and a backwashing in the eddies that almost defy description of the movement and direction of the stream itself.

One may visit a church, perhaps in the eastern part of the United States, where there is a rather purposeful adherence to liturgical matters in the observance of the church year, the Eucharist, creedal statements, and various traditional ceremonies of long standing. But another Evangelical Free church may have, in marked contrast, a spontaneous, free-flowing style of corporate worship.

Musical Innovations. Most of the churches in the denomination are responding to some of the new methods, new sounds, and new materials for worship leadership. A survey published in the denomination's magazine, *The Evangelical Beacon,* in July of 1990 revealed that most of the responding churches are seeing increased use of rhythm instruments (drums, electric bass, guitars, synthesizers), as well as a growing use of choruses in equal proportion to hymns.

Furthermore, the two most popular hymnals in these churches are *Hymns for the Family of God* and the *Hymnal for Worship and Celebration.* This marks some movement away from traditional hymnal resources to more contemporary approaches to congregational music leadership. This would not be at all significant in some circles, but it is worthy of note for the Evangelical Free Church, with its Scandinavian and Midwestern roots.

Creative Planning. Innovation is also seen in the creative planning that is being given to corporate worship. The old picture of a pastor simply changing the page numbers of the hymns, responsive readings, and Scripture references is now being replaced by the conscious effort on the part of leadership to shape and mold the order of services in a variety of ways from week to week, so that there is flow, logic, sequence, and drama in the congregational experience.

Most of the ministers of music in the denomination realize the risk involved in such "tampering" with the order of service, but, as one music minister from Indiana put it, we "proceed with great caution and sensitivity to change, listening to what people say, making sure that our changes are *evolutionary, not revolutionary.*"

More and more of the churches appear to be developing greater consciousness of the mandate to be worshiping assemblies. More advance thought and self-examination is evident on the part of laity as well as clergy. Credence is given to the unifying themes and subjects of worship as church leadership is reading, discussing, attending conferences, and sharing experiences related to the challenge of worship.

Ways are being sought to encourage members of the congregation to be involved in worship, rather than be passive spectators. Some assemblies are allowing or encouraging the physical involvement of kneeling, raising hands, clapping, and standing. Others are incorporating elements of the liturgy in the use of creedal statements, doxologies, confessions, congregational readings of adoration, and symbols.

In a few instances there has been a conscious effort to build upon the church year with its consistent emphasis on the life of Christ and his ministry on earth. The Lord's Table has not taken on the formal, dramatic nature of the weekly Eucharist of mainline liturgical churches, but it remains as a monthly observance with slight variations in preparation and observance in most places.

In summary, the worship styles and form of most of the Evangelical Free churches are probably still focused on the sermon as the hub of the worship service. But time, thought, leadership, and attention is more and more being assigned to the equality of the worship events of adoration, praise, prayer, thanksgiving, confession, and forgiveness.

Howard Stevenson

129 • EVANGELICAL LUTHERAN CHURCH IN AMERICA

Lutheran worship renewal remains consistent with Lutheran directives to purify the Roman Mass and to refrain from legalism. Luther's concern for these goals is expressed in the simple and direct way in which the twentieth-century forms of renewal have been adopted and applied to Lutheran worship. Although change has been slow, the turn to ancient practices, charismatic worship, and inclusive elements is meeting with wider approval.

Lutheranism has been sometimes defined as a movement for reform of the Western Catholic church. Nowhere is this more evident than in worship practices. Martin Luther's principle, stated in his *Formula Missae,* was: "It is not now or ever has been our intention to abolish the liturgical service of God completely, but rather to purify the one that is now in use from the wretched accretions which corrupt it and to point out an evangelical use." Two programs were embedded in this statement: to prune the inherited rites of their many additions over the centuries so that their basic shape stands clear; and to promote a non-legalistic use. So concerned was Luther about not relapsing into the liturgical legalism of the Roman church that he wrote concerning his own _German Mass:_ "This or any other order shall be so used that whenever it becomes an abuse, it shall be straightway abolished and replaced by another." The important thing is that Scripture's gospel be proclaimed clearly in Word and sacrament.

Historic Church Orders

Lutheranism in the sixteenth century remained committed to the historic orders of the Mass, the daily prayer of the church (Matins and Vespers), and other occasional services. These might be sung in Latin or the local vernacular language (and often a combination of both), with preaching at every service, and opportunity for congregational song. Following Luther's lead, music and the arts of worship were also promoted. A rich musical life characterized the Lutheran churches of the Baroque period, culminating in the work of J. S. Bach.

There was a certain liturgical deterioration in the eighteenth and early nineteenth centuries as a result of the influence, first of Pietism, and then of rationalism, in which the subjective characteristics of worship were given primacy over the more objective characteristics. The recovery of Lutheran confessional theology in the mid-nineteenth century went hand-in-hand with liturgical recovery. But success has been difficult for both recoveries, especially in North America where eastern Lutherans were influenced by Pietistic revivals in their homelands.

The worship books used in English-speaking Lutheran congregations in North America during the twentieth century have reflected a commitment to the recovery of the historic sixteenth-century Lutheran church orders. The _Service Book and Hymnal_ (1958) and even more so the _Lutheran Book of Worship_ (1978) have also shown the influence of the ecumenical liturgical movement. The _LBW_ includes, among ecumenically inspired materials, its version of the three-year lectionary for Sundays and festivals, translations of canticles, creeds, and the Lord's Prayer by the International Consultation on English Texts, a psalter translation shared in common with _The Book of Common Prayer_ of the Episcopal Church in the USA, and a common core of ecumenical hymnody.

Common worship books have anticipated Lutheran organic unity in North America. The _Common Service Book_ (1917) preceded the formation of the United Lutheran Church in America (1918). The _Service Book and Hymnal_ preceded the formation of the American Lutheran Church (1960) and the Lutheran Church in America (1962). The _Lutheran Book of Worship_ preceded the formation of the Evangelical Lutheran Church in America (1988). The Lutheran Church–Missouri Synod participated in the Inter-Lutheran Commission on Worship that led to the _LBW,_ but withdrew its support at the last moment and produced its own book, _Lutheran Worship_ (1982).

Cultural Diversity

While the worship books provide a common resource, congregations have exercised their evangelical freedom in the use of the books. As a matter of principle, Lutheranism has been open to contextual cultural influences. Thus, some congregations, particularly in white suburbs, have embraced the worship practices of mainline Protestant or evangelical churches in the use of choral and instrumental music, congregational song, preaching styles, and expressions of fellowship—usually within a liturgical framework. Congregations in black or Hispanic communities have shown openness to worship expressions from these traditions, including gospel songs led by gospel choirs and worship in the Spanish language with guitar accompaniment. It seems that fewer congregations are committed to the continental European Lutheran heritage of chorales and exegetical sermons. Very few still provide worship in languages other than English. Lutheran publication houses increasingly provide musical settings and hymn collections to supplement the _LBW._

The Ecumenical Liturgical Movement

The commitment of Lutheranism generally to the received Catholic tradition has coincided with ecumenical efforts of the modern liturgical movement. This has provided Lutherans with an ecumenical repertoire of rites and symbols: a common shape of the liturgy (Entrance, Word, Table, Dismissal), a common use of the church-year calendar and lectionary, vestments and paraments in seasonal colors, customs of the church year such as Advent

The Trefoil and Triangle. This symbol of the Trinity, which combines the trefoil and the triangle, has been used frequently in stained glass, mural decoration, and church embroidery.

wreath and paschal candle, the use of litanies and bidding prayers, the enacted greeting of peace, body language such as the sign of the cross and praying with hands extended, and more frequent celebration of Holy Communion using a eucharistic prayer.

Congregations have moved, during the course of this century, from quarterly Communion, to monthly Communion, to bi-monthly Communion, to Communion every Sunday at one service, to the few that celebrate Communion every Sunday at every service. While the minister's edition of the *LBW* provides three great thanksgivings in addition to the one provided in the pew edition, most pastors still use the Words of Institution alone on both practical grounds (the great thanksgiving adds to the length of the service) and theological grounds (it confuses the "direction" of the sacrament from God to his people). It had been a historic Lutheran custom to sing hymns during the ministration of Holy Communion, and this custom is being recovered. While some Lutheran celebrations set up Communion stations, in most parish churches communicants still kneel at the altar rail to receive the sacrament. Sobriety and joy are held in tension in Lutheran Communion services.

Guidance to pastors and congregations is provided by denominational commissions or departments of worship. Most Lutheran seminaries have full-time professors of worship and also full- or part-time professors of church music. Worship conferences are sponsored by synods and regions of the ELCA. The annual Liturgical Institute of Valparaiso University has been held for nearly fifty years, and other church colleges are also beginning to provide worship and music conferences. The future worship practices in Lutheran churches promise to be as pluralistic as in the past. Meanwhile, present changes are being managed for the most part in pastorally sensitive and theologically responsible ways.

Frank C. Senn

130 • FRIENDS (QUAKERS)

Quaker worship has a tradition of silence. It eschews programmed worship, favoring instead meetings that are led by the prompting of the Spirit. Some Quaker groups have been influenced by American evangelicalism and have developed a somewhat more structured form of worship.

The silent meeting for worship is the most visible element of classical Quaker worship. Worshipers assemble without leader or program, stilling their minds and focusing their attention, waiting to sense the presence of the Spirit of God and then to respond as they are moved in their own spirits. The silent meeting for worship is but a means, however, for achieving the essential element of Quaker worship: the response of the soul to the felt presence and the moving of the Spirit of God. "Worship is the adoring response of the heart and mind to the influence of the Spirit of God," says the Richmond Declaration of Faith (1887). "It stands neither in forms nor in the formal disuse of forms; it may be without words as well as with them, but it must be in spirit and in truth."

Of the three broad types of worship—altar-centered, pulpit-centered, and congregation-centered—classical unprogrammed Quaker worship is the supreme example of the latter, which some call "waiting on the spirit." For three centuries Quakerism has adhered more closely to its early practices and ideals than any other Western tradition. But today its external distinctives are blurred, especially among evangelical Quakers whose structured or programmed worship shares much in common with pulpit-centered free church worship.

Classical Quaker Worship

The Quaker movement grew out of the experiences of George Fox who, as a troubled young man, searched for years for an answer to his personal turmoil. His search led ultimately to an experience of the Inner Light—a sense of the divine and direct working of Christ in the soul. This experience brought peace with God and himself as well as a strong dissatisfaction with the worship of the Puritan-dominated Established church. At the heart of the movement he began in 1646 lies the belief that the Inner Light he experienced is accessible to all and that the purpose of worship is a common waiting in silence for evidence of the presence and power of God.

The importance placed on the Inner Light led Quakers to reject formal ministry and all set forms of worship and to substitute spiritual communion and baptism for visible sacraments. Classical Quaker worship emphasizes, first, that true worship takes place only when the Spirit of God moves the hearts of those who are gathered for worship and that silence, not planning, is one of the surest means of guaranteeing the Spirit's freedom. "Ever since we were a people we have had a testimony against formal worship, being convinced . . . that the worship and prayers which God accepts are such only as are produced by the influence and assistance of his Holy Spirit" (_The Rules of Discipline of the Yearly Meeting, Held on Rhode Island for New England_, 1856). Secondly, the classical way emphasizes a first-hand encounter of the worshiper with God in the context of a strong corporate mysticism in which God speaks to the community through individuals to whom he has spoken.

The setting for classical Quaker worship is plain and simple. Traditional meetinghouses have rows of benches and often, facing them, a few raised benches for elders, "weighty Friends," and those who feel they may be led to speak—though the right to speak is extended to all who attend. Other meetinghouses often have benches or other, flexible seating arranged in hollow squares.

There is no pastoral leadership; the only prearranged responsibility is the selection of an elder to close the meeting by standing and turning to greet those near him. Elders are also responsible to ensure that the meeting stays within acceptable bounds.

As worshipers come together, they assemble in disciplined silence and "holy expectancy," waiting—without prearranged singing, Bible reading, prayers, or sermon—for the movement of God's Spirit. Each centers down in personal prayer and meditation and worship proceeds with mystical communion and with spoken ministry as individual worshipers are led by the Spirit to speak and pray. The meeting is said to be gathered—sometimes without a word having been spoken—when, in Thomas Kelley's words, the worshipers have become "wrapped in a sense of unity and of Presence such as quiets all words and enfolds (us) within an unspeakable calm and interknittedness within a vaster life" (_The Eternal Promise_ [1966]).

Contemporary Quaker Worship

Today Quaker worship is more diverse than at any other time in its history. Unprogrammed worship is still found, primarily on the East Coast of the United States and in England, among Quakers who tend to hold more liberal beliefs. Most Quaker worship in America—especially among evangelical Quakers—is either partially or fully programmed or structured.

Programmed worship began to be adopted, more for pragmatic than theological reasons, by many Quaker congregations during the nineteenth-century period of revival and renewal in American Protestantism. It differs little, externally at least, from pulpit-centered, congregational, free-church worship. These congregations employ pastors, and their worship includes prearranged music, Scripture readings, prayers, preaching, and occasional brief periods of silent worship. Their meetings for worship tend to involve two distinct movements: the first, often referred to as "worship," moves from the people toward God, consisting of singing and other music and, perhaps, Scripture reading and prayers. In the second, God speaks to the congregation through the sermon. Those congregations that practice partially programmed worship include a significant time of open or free worship based upon silent waiting, as in classical Quaker worship.

Change in contemporary Quaker worship is shaped to a degree from within as non-Quakers have become active in Quaker congregations. Such influence, understandably, has been quite diffuse.

In addition, there seems to have been two primary outside influences. The first was the free-church worship as found in the nineteenth-century period of revival and renewal that coincided largely with the opening of the American frontier. This influence brought to the Quakers a strengthened pastoral role and emphasis on biblical preaching, a reshaping of the form and content of worship, and a growing openness to the observance of Communion and baptism. Second, the recent praise-and-worship movement has given contemporary Quakers a vehicle—as silence once was—through which to sense and to respond to the Spirit of God in worship. Many churches now utilize extended periods of singing first to focus their attention and then to respond to the moving of the Spirit of God.

_____ **The Table** _____

Changing attitudes toward the sacraments represent the most visible and for some the most troublesome recent change in Quaker worship. In classical Quaker worship, all external elements—including words—are secondary to the real experience of the presence of Christ. The sacraments, therefore, are spiritualized and their inward reality emphasized. Visible sacraments are not necessary when one can experience Christ directly in community. For them, communion with the risen Lord does not come through eating and drinking perishable items but through spiritual communion with him through the Holy Spirit. And for them, the only baptism that counts is the inward baptism of the Spirit.

Today, a growing number of Quaker congregations are observing Communion. The practice began nearly one hundred years ago on the East Coast and is spreading today, especially among evangelical Quakers, at an increasing rate. There does not seem to be a distinct, guiding theology at this point, and observance tends to be inconspicuous and infrequent—once or twice a year, apart from regularly scheduled worship services. There is at least one distinctive aspect: While most other Protestant traditions would say that Communion and baptism are not necessary for salvation, they would insist that they are, as ordinances, matters of obedience, hence an aspect of discipleship. Quakers, however, hold them to be optional and therefore not necessary for discipleship. As a result, they may speak of the "elements," but tend to avoid reference to "sacraments" and "ordinances."

Warren Ediger

131 • INDEPENDENT EVANGELICAL & FUNDAMENTALIST CHURCHES

Traditional evangelical and fundamentalist worship is informal in style and emphasizes the sermon, singing, and prayer. Recent influences point to the need for more God-oriented worship and emotive music. Recently evangelicals have been borrowing from the liturgical and praise-and-worship traditions as well as utilizing the distinction between the seeker's service and believer's worship.

The formation of an independent evangelical congregation often springs out of a home Bible study group that has prospered. On other occasions a new congregation comes out of a church split, either from within a congregation or through the severing of ties with a denomination. The principal worship orientation is most often informal and folk-like in style. Since most new congregations begin with a constituency where everyone is known, there is a basic bias against any sort of formal structure for worship. Casualness and informality usually characterize the church's worship as well.

In the past, the format of the service was often an extension of the Bible study with time for singing, sharing, prayer, the study of Scripture, followed by refreshments. This format, combined with the revivalist meeting format that focused on the conversion of the lost, constituted the order of worship for most independent evangelical churches. Very often the order (liturgy) was announced as the service unfolded. In the broadest sense, all of this was considered worship. Congregations that own the title Fundamentalist are more likely to retain this style of worship.

_____ **Rethinking the Revival Format** _____

In the latter part of the 1980s modifications of this worship style became widespread. For many reasons there was an increasing awareness that the worship of God with a more vertical focus should have greater emphasis. Individual believers were no longer satisfied with the revivalist type of meeting where they generally sat, watched, and listened. An awareness of the spiritual nature of worship had grown from the abundance of books and articles on the topic that were published during the decade. A second large influence came from the charismatic service, particularly in its extensive use of emotive music. While many independent congregations did not fully embrace all that the charismatic experience included, they, nevertheless, took on a portion of its musical contribution both in style and in content.

Great variety remains in the worship patterns of independent evangelical churches. Some churches remain committed to the old revivalist tradition common twenty-five years ago. But many of the more forward looking churches have markedly altered their understanding and approach to worship. One of the most practical expressions of this change lies in the emergence of a staff position in the churches generally designated as minister of music and worship. This person is expected not only to plan and direct all musical activity but also to be knowledgeable and responsible for planning the worship services. This kind of position, relatively common in the 1990s, was very rare in the 1970s.

As a result of these changes much more thought is now given to the planning and execution of the worship service. Clergy and laity no longer assume that churchgoers know how to worship. Thus the teaching of worship is playing an increasingly important role in the development of the worship life of a congregation.

Despite the striking changes underway in independent evangelical churches, the sermon, "the feeding of the Word," is still considered by most pastors to be the primary purpose of gathering, as evidenced by the length of time allotted to it. For many, the sermon, not the Table, remains the focal point. Nevertheless, there is a greater openness to the fact that the service of worship contains more than the message from the pulpit.

New Formats

In the past, the order of the service had in it an enthusiastic welcome and "Good morning" response from the congregation, some inspirational singing, a prayer, a testimony, the offering, and the sermon. In many of the more energetic evangelical congregations this order has been altered greatly. The new format puts much greater emphasis on preparation of the individual worshiper, followed by a hymn or group of hymns that address God

rather than the human experience. Often these hymns are interwoven with praise music or Scripture songs.

Among other changes, confession of sin is assuming a more prominent role. Also, pastors are devoting more attention to the morning prayers. It is not uncommon to find a framework for the prayer sketched out or even to hear written prayers, rather than extemporaneous ones. Most often the offering still precedes the sermon, although occasionally it will follow the message in the Genevan tradition. Sometimes the bidding prayer is used in worship. The moment of greeting is in widespread use. Most probably, it is a kind of outgrowth of the kiss of peace taken in a very informal, casual manner.

Generally there are a few members in any congregation who regularly raise their hands at some point in the service. There is also more hand-clapping, though it is generally less an act of worship than an expression of appreciation for someone or some group that has just participated, especially if it is a children's choir. In some churches the congregation regularly stands for the reading of the Bible. On other occasions they may kneel for prayer. In fact, kneelers have been installed in many of the new sanctuaries built by evangelical congregations.

Drawing from Other Traditions

Thus, within the independent evangelical churches there is growing movement away from staid forms. There is greater freedom to draw from various traditions, and also an expectation that this should be done. A substantial number of the congregations in this kind of church have come from various denominations within Protestantism as well as from Western Catholicism and Eastern Orthodoxy. The parish as a whole has a broad background of experience. There are likewise many worshipers who have had no religious background at all. Consequently, it cannot be assumed that everyone understands the various practices and acts of worship. Teaching and explanation is important. Some of the practical expressions of borrowing from various traditions include:

Observance of Holy Week. It is common to find some form of services either in the evening or at noontime during this week. They are often simple and devotional in nature, patterned after the Office Hours.

Maundy Thursday Communion Service. In some congregations this has become one of the most moving, emotional services of the year. Borrowing from the Catholic tradition, there seems to be a greater willingness to look again at the death of Christ on the cross, in the context of the depth of his love for sinners. This is often a very creative worship service, especially when constructed as a Tenebrae service or Service of Darkness.

Communions that Frame the Church Year. Many independent evangelical churches celebrate Communion monthly, others quarterly. Some observe the Lord's Supper as a way of marking the first Sunday in Advent, the first Sunday in Lent, or Pentecost Sunday as part of the regular monthly observance. In general, worshipers manifest a growing desire for Communion to have greater spiritual significance; and there is less willingness simply to tack it on at the end of the service.

Advent. This season has taken on a higher priority with a different order of worship often being used during this time. It can be a special time to involve children in worship. There is also an increase in the use of Advent banners, candles, and wreaths as part of the celebration of this season.

Dedication of Children. Increased attention is being given to the dedication of children on the part of those who do not baptize them. The story of Hannah and Samuel is often related as a part of this service.

Other. Occasionally, during the High Holy Days, one will find an independent congregation that makes reference either in music or prayers to the Jewish background of the Christian faith. There may also be other services that use drama and dance as well. One major publishing house, Hope Publishing Company, has released a hymnal, *The Worshiping Church,* which contains an excellent breadth of traditions in historic hymnody, in newly composed serious hymns, in worship songs, and in a variety of liturgical material in the readings.

The independent evangelical churches that have the most effective worship will be those that teach the congregation how to worship and that borrow from a wide range of traditions. In borrowing and teaching they will be able to provide parishioners with not only a relevant sense of history, but introduce them to a deeper experience of the reality of worship.

Daniel Sharp

132 ✦ INTERNATIONAL CHURCH OF THE FOURSQUARE GOSPEL

The Foursquare Gospel Church, founded on the evangelistic and enthusiastic practices of Aimee Semple McPherson's Angelus Temple, has maintained the content of worship through various forms. In recent years it has benefited from the charismatic renewal movement.

Since its inception in 1923, the International Church of the Foursquare Gospel has understood worship as being a lifestyle of Spirit-produced, Christlike character, attitudes, and adherence to the biblical commands and principles, bringing glory to God and the gospel to others. It also includes a liturgy of corporate celebration that, when the local church comes together, offers praise to the Creator/Savior, celebrates redemption through grace, and communicates the daily mercies of the Lord. Though corporate in nature, the worship pattern of each congregation will be as diverse as its local setting, ethnicity, culture, language, taste in art form, and spiritual development of its members.

——————— **Angelus Temple** ———————

In the establishment of Angelus Temple, from which the Foursquare Church has now grown into over 24,000 congregations worldwide, founder Aimee Semple McPherson understood worship to be an expression of the believer, directed but not dictated, spontaneous yet using contemporary media and art forms. Angelus Temple was started in the center of the then-exploding Los Angeles, on the outskirts of Hollywood. Thus, according to Foursquare Church historian Nathaniel Van Cleave:

The doors of Angelus Temple opened with a convention enlivened by a Silver Band, a large choir, a golden harp, vocal and instrumental specials of great variety. Later, sacred operas and oratorios were composed and produced by Mrs. McPherson. . . . The music and the program appealed to rich and poor, black, brown and white, rural and urban, cultured and rustic, young and old. Hollywood stars would kneel alongside skid-row derelicts in quest of newness of life. (*The Vine and the Branches* [International Church of the Foursquare Gospel, 1992], 15)

Another major element in communicating the gospel in the vernacular was the illustrated and dramatized sermons that became the hallmark of Angelus Temple. Mrs. McPherson believed that by rendering visible her messages, the gospel would be more understandable and memorable. In the words of one newspaper writer, "Aimee Semple McPherson used the avenues of show business to instill the gospel's good news into the hearts of her multitudinous following" (Greg Rothwell, *Oxford Sentinel Review* [February 11, 1989]).

Above all, the goal of worship was to bring glory to God and people to Christ. On the pulpit of Angelus Temple was inscribed, "We would see Jesus," and in the first eighteenth months of the Temple's existence, there were more than 20,000 converts. In 1924, 3,000 were baptized in water; there were 3,000 new members, 3,600 reported healings and thousands experiencing the baptism with the Holy Spirit. It was her conviction that when worship was expressed from the heart, God's presence and power would be experienced in the life of the worshiper.

Historic Characteristics

Throughout its history, the Foursquare Gospel Church has embraced this heritage in its centricity of focus and in the flexibility of its forms. In almost every decade, members and leaders of the denomination have been used by God in the composing, arranging, and presenting of music, writing, and drama that have influenced the worship of the church worldwide. People such as Phil Kerr, Audrey Meier, Paul Mickelson, and Jack Hayford are just a few examples. In short, the Foursquare denomination has maintained strict adherence to the preeminence of Christocentric worship in the life of its congregations, but has allowed and even encouraged freedom of expression within biblically stipulated order.

During the decades of the 1950s and 1960s, the majority of Foursquare churches adopted a standardized worship form that included traditional hymns, Bible reading and special music, followed by the message of the day and benediction. Because of the church's Pentecostal tradition, there were the clapping and raising of hands by worshipers. Expressions of the vocal gifts, as delineated in 1 Corinthians 12, were allowed in public services. The sacraments of water baptism and Communion were observed regularly. Many churches practiced prayer for the sick and offered special programs for

children and adults on special days of the year, such as Easter and Christmas. Choirs and orchestras were used extensively in the worship setting. It must be noted, however, that uniformity seemed to exist as to when and how individual expressions of verbal praise would be permitted in the services. With few exceptions, as the decades progressed, the excitement of revivalism and spontaneity of experiential worship seemed to wane. According to one analysis, the decade of the 1960s was a time of reorientation and restudy of Pentecostal truth and worship (Van Cleave, 191).

Charismatic Influence and Openness

The beginning of the 1970s was accompanied by the charismatic movement among historic denominations. As people's spiritual hunger drew them to meetings where the power of the Holy Spirit appeared to be evident, the classical Pentecostal and historic denominations were challenged to encourage greater freedom of expression in their worship services. Though there were some unscriptural extremes, positive and lasting impact was made on the body of Christ.

Because of its inherent openness, as well as through the example of Foursquare pastors such as Jack Hayford in Van Nuys, California, Roy Hicks, Jr. in Eugene, Oregon, Jerry Cook in Gresham, Oregon, and Ralph Moore in Hermosa Beach, California, the Foursquare Church became involved with and received benefit from the charismatic renewal. Many Foursquare churches began to realize spiritual awakening and a renewal to a more informal, participant-centered, experiential form of worship. The result was remarkable growth, for the worship services made both charismatics and unbelievers feel at home.

Even among the churches mentioned above, the styles of worship patterns differed. From the highly organized, pulpit-centered worship form of Jack Hayford and The Church on the Way to the very decentralized style of Ralph Moore and Hope Chapel, which often met on the beach, diversity and adaptation to the local setting and mission of the congregation seemed to dictate the liturgy, stated or unstated. The common factor was the exaltation of Jesus Christ and a heart-response, corporately and individually, to him. And while, over the succeeding two decades, worship forms in most Foursquare churches have changed, there has been no disparagement of those congregations that have chosen to retain more traditional taste in music or manner of worship. Growth has been experienced in many of those churches as well.

At first, renewal of worship saw the congregations adopt the singing of Scripture and, later, experience-related choruses. Limited use of traditional hymns has now been reinstated, and in some cases, contemporary hymns are being composed. With certain exceptions, worship teams have replaced choirs and orchestras. The traditional expressions of hand-raising and clapping continue, but with little direction from the leader as to when such should occur. Times of extended praise (verbal or sung) are encouraged. Other body movement, such as moderate forms of dance, are used in some congregations. Prayer during worship services is often delegated to small-group sharing. Sacramental observance and the public use of spiritual gifts are included.

Whether it be in doctrine or in worship, the Foursquare Church has learned from its founder to maintain a middle-of-the-road balance. Thus, while allowing freedom, it is expected that any expression of praise be appropriate to all thinking, sober-minded believers. Any visible manifestations should be done in taste and in submission to the person leading the service.

─────── **Multicultural Challenges** ───────

In the 1990s, changing demographics are adding new dimensions and flavor to worship tastes in the Foursquare denomination. The immigration of millions to the cities of the United States from overseas is creating a new challenge. Already many Foursquare churches have been started, with others changing their previous focus in order to provide evangelism and worship opportunities to the new arrivals. The needs of various sub-cultures in the church as well as the advancements in media technology, call for greater creativity in contemporary worship and presentation of the gospel.

Thus, it could be said that the threefold content of worship in the International Church of the Foursquare Gospel has remained the same from its inception. However, that content is expressed in as many forms as there are congregations.

Ronald D. Williams

133 • LUTHERAN CHURCH–MISSOURI SYNOD

Worship in the Lutheran Church–Missouri Synod has retained the pattern set by Luther, with some modifications.

The liturgical, charismatic, and inclusive movements are making an impact here and there. But most churches practice traditional worship.

Changes in the Sunday worship of The Lutheran Church–Missouri Synod (LCMS) occur rather slowly. In its 150 year history there have been only three official English language hymnals (1912, 1941, 1982) and one German hymnal (1847). In recent decades individual congregations have experimented with texts, songs, and forms beyond these resources.

The pattern for worship set by Luther in his *Formual Missae* (a revision of the Latin Mass, 1523) and his *Deutsche Messe* (a German order of the Mass, 1525) continues to be an important influence. In these works he showed how to delete from the medieval mass that which contradicts the gospel and Scripture and to retain what is useful from tradition. He was anxious to provide excellent music and texts in the vernacular, and he led the way with his own hymn writing. In the German order he arranged chant melodies for the texts of the pastor's part, including the Gospel and Words of Institution, and provided hymnic versions of the people's liturgical texts.

Luther had little appreciation for those who abandoned useful traditions in order to restrict worship practice to that which is specifically mentioned in the New Testament. Doctrinally pure texts could combine with useful ceremony to help teach people the Christian faith. The services officially adopted by the LCMS follow Luther's reform, at least in spirit. As a condition of membership, the synod requires "exclusive use of doctrinally pure agenda, hymnbooks, and catechisms in church and school."

─────── **The Common Service** ───────

The form of the Sunday service with Holy Communion has remained essentially the same in the past eighty years. *The Lutheran Hymnal* (1941, hereafter *TLH*), employed the "Common Service" (1888) that was built from common elements in the services of European Lutherans in the sixteenth century as they developed their practice from Luther and the Lutheran confessional writings. The 1941 version of this service was essentially the same as the 1912 version, contained in the first official LCMS service book in English.

The *TLH* "Order of Holy Communion" is as follows: (1) Invocation of the Trinity, (2) Confession of Sins and Absolution, (3) Introit, (4) *Kyrie,* (5) *Gloria in Excelsis,* (6) Salutation and Collect [Service of the Word], (7) Epistle, (8) Gradual, (9) Gospel, (10) Nicene Creed, (11) Sermon, (12) Offertory, (13) General Prayer, (14) Preface and Proper Preface, (15) *Sanctus,* (16) Lord's Prayer, (17) Words of Institution, (18) *Pax Domini,* (19) *Agnus Dei,* (20) Distribution, (21) *Nunc Dimittis,* (22) Thanksgiving Versicle and Prayer, (23) Salutation and *Benedicamus,* (24) Benediction. Numbers two and twenty-four, and perhaps one, employ the sign of the cross. Approximately 40 percent of LCMS congregations, mostly the smaller ones, still use *TLH.*

Three Current Alternatives

Lutheran Worship (1982, hereafter *LW*) has three versions of the Holy Communion service. The first basically modernizes the English of the *TLH* service.

The second order, and most widely used, grew from the work of the Inter-Lutheran Commission on Worship (1966–1978), which had representatives from the LCMS and from congregations now belonging to the Evangelical Lutheran Church in America. The Common Service framework is somewhat altered in *LW.* The significant changes are as follows, with numbers given for comparison to the *TLH* order given above.

At the Introit (3) *LW* allows for a whole psalm or an entrance hymn to be sung. Instead of the threefold *Kyrie* (4), there is a dialogue prayer in which the people respond to each petition with "Lord, have mercy." A new scriptural canticle, "This is the Feast of Victory" (drawn from texts in Revelation), replaces the *Gloria in excelsis* (5) during the Easter season. A new three-year lectionary provides for three readings. A third Scripture reading, from the Old Testament, now precedes the epistle (7); the first reading is followed by a gradual (8) that may be replaced with a whole Psalm. Between the epistle and the gospel (9), where the former Gradual stood, there is now a verse. Its opening and closing alleluia, like the alleluia of the medieval Mass, is omitted from texts appointed for Lent. A hymn, related to the gospel, follows the gospel (9) and is called "the Hymn of the Day." The Nicene Creed (10) now follows the sermon (11). The prayer of the church (13) uses the pattern of a deacon's prayer with congregational responses after each petition (e.g., Leader: "Lord, in your mercy;" People: "Hear our prayer.") This prayer comes after the Creed and be-

fore the offering and offertory (12). New offertory texts are provided. After the preface and proper preface (14) and sanctus (15) a short prayer of thanksgiving is inserted—before the Lord's Prayer (16) and words of institution (17). The order allows for the kiss of peace just before the distribution (20) where the *Pax Domini* had always been but without the activity of greeting. An alternate canticle, "Thank the Lord" (based on Psalm 105), may replace the *Nunc Dimittis* (21) in appropriate seasons. There are two musical settings of this service.

A third order of Holy Communion employs hymns for the "ordinary" in the manner of Luther's *Deutsche Messe;* in fact, the hymns are translations of the sixteenth-century texts and use the sixteenth-century melodies.

Recent Developments

The most recent resources, a Hmong hymnal (1991) and a Spanish hymnal (1991), serve ethnic needs. An African-American hymnal is on the drawing board.

New cultural pressures, including language, ethnic heritage, or age group, cause congregations to seek alternatives in worship. Cross-cultural work demands adjustments to patterns of communication. New converts may seek songs and liturgical music that is easily accessible. Just as an unofficial set of Christian folk songs coexisted alongside the official hymnal in the 1960s and 1970s, so praise music and contemporary music now finds a similar path into the Sunday service. Practices of worship leadership and the dialogue nature of liturgy are frequently challenged by a desire for the appearance of informality. User-friendly formats for printed materials are in demand. Recorded music has raised expectations about performance quality within worship and for some instrumental sounds only possible in recorded formats.

Thus, some LCMS congregations, seeking to respond creatively to contemporary needs, are examining their worship for what they should keep and what they should change. Along with this process, proper catechesis (training in the scriptural essentials of Christian faith and life) is crucial as a preparation for worship. People are shaped by their worship. If worship is being shaped by those just entering the church, risks to its balance and fullness emerge. Other congregations use official books with enthusiasm and polish, finding their faith expressed and sustained by celebrating Christ's victory in traditional ways.

James L. Brauer

134 ◆ MENNONITE CHURCHES

The Mennonite tradition of worship has always placed emphasis on conversion and holy living. Since 1960 Mennonite worship has been affected by the modern liturgical movement, the charismatic movement, the praise-and-worship tradition, and the inclusion of other cultural forms of worship.

The traditional style of worship in Mennonite history has been simple, exhortatory, and penitential, focusing on conversion and holy living. Preaching has been the climax of the worship assembly.

In the 1960s various cultural influences and impatience with conventional patterns led to a continually widening liturgical diversity in the Mennonite mainstream. The more openly expressive worship of black congregations was, for the first time, noticed with approval by the larger church. Meanwhile, upwardly mobile, white, professional congregations turned to a more cerebral style in which the sermon became more or less a lecture followed by discussion. The charismatic movement led some congregations in a quite different direction. The marks of its influence were the singing of choruses repeatedly and intensely, encouragement of the extraordinary gifts of the Spirit like tongues, and attention to the immediate personal needs of worshipers through testimonies and prayers. A final influence was that of the liturgical movement, with its attention to aesthetics, the deliberate structuring of worship, the church year, and the lectionary.

The pursuit of Christian unity, whether with fellow-Mennonites beyond the North Atlantic world or with believers of other denominations next door, created a spirit of openness to change and diversity. The recent assemblies of the Mennonite World Conference have been showcases for diversity of form and spirit in worship.

Today in North America there are Mennonite congregations that worship much as they did a century ago. Others have defined themselves by one of the worship styles referred to above. Most, however, while fed by one or more of these newer sources, work at integrating innovations with existing patterns. Most of the worship resources published by most of the conferences occupy this middle

ground. This position also characterizes the new hymnal published in 1992 in cooperation with the Church of the Brethren.

——— The Sunday Service ———

Typical Sunday services might proceed in the following way. The congregational singing includes chorales, gospel songs, evangelical Scripture songs, and Roman Catholic contemporary hymns. The worship leader is a member of the local worship committee but is not a minister. After a few opening hymns, she welcomes the congregation and leads in an opening prayer taken from a contemporary volume of worship aids. One week a mixed adult choir might sing a nineteenth-century anthem; another week's service might include a guitar ensemble offering a Scripture song. One or more Bible passages are read, either the preacher's choice or selected according to the church calendar (use of which is usually limited to the weeks from Advent through Pentecost, often passing over Epiphany season and the early part of Lent). One of the passages might be rendered as readers' theater. A brief story or object lesson is presented to the children. The sermon, twenty to thirty minutes long, is occasionally expositional but more often a call for evangelism, peacemaking, or personal growth. Before the congregational prayer people are invited to share "joys and concerns." The intercessions follow, one week as a pastoral prayer, another as spontaneous offerings from the assembly, and yet another as a litany. A hymn and announcements follow after which the leader dismisses the people with a benediction.

The breaking of bread is not part of the weekly service, although it was in some settings at the time of the Reformation. Until recently most congregations celebrated Communion twice a year with a preparatory service and, in many congregations, footwashing. In evangelically influenced conferences and congregations a monthly Eucharist is common. Even where this influence is not predominant, the frequency with which the Supper is celebrated has increased to four to six times annually, most often on holy days like Good Friday and Pentecost. Sometimes the breaking of bread is followed by or incorporated into a fellowship meal.

——— Baptism and Other Practices ———

The baptism of believers occurs in public worship once or twice a year, usually a week after candidates have given a testimony of faith to the membership. This service is among the most solemn and festive gatherings of the year. It is usually concluded with Communion. In traditional congregations the holy kiss is given by the minister to baptismal candidates and mutually given at footwashing.

Some communities have begun to use the passing of the peace each Sunday or at the Lord's Table. Also, in these and in charismatic congregations, anointing with oil is observed for the sick. This is usually a private service.

Some striking, longstanding rituals are perpetuated in diverse Mennonite communities. In conservative Russian Mennonite churches, for example, care is taken to receive the Communion bread on a clean, white handkerchief. In some communities of Amish background the communicant bows halfway to the floor with the right knee after having partaken of the cup.

———— Form and Freedom ————

Most Mennonite congregations have become more conscious and deliberate in their commitment to both form and freedom. The widespread use of worship committees has led to long-range planning of worship that involves members and ministers and pays attention to diversity of themes and forms of expression. Books of prayers are commonly used and adapted by worship leaders. Friendliness and personalization are cultivated through, for example, individually welcoming guests and writing prayers or songs for particular occasions.

Since about 1980 one or more regional worship seminars has been held annually. The church press regularly features articles on worship, mostly of the "how to" variety. The 1992 hymnal has elevated the preparation of spoken worship resources to the same status as that of hymn tunes and texts. This new book of worship is set up according to the rhythm of praise rather than according to dogmatic categories. It begins with "gathering" and ends with "sending." For the first time in a congregational book there are separate services for the Lord's Supper and baptism.

The temperamental, spiritual, and liturgical diversity has immeasurably enlivened and deepened contemporary North American Mennonite worship life. Now that this expansion of the ways in which we come before each other and God is in place, care will need to be taken to nurture common memories, music, and gestures and to keep alive the simple

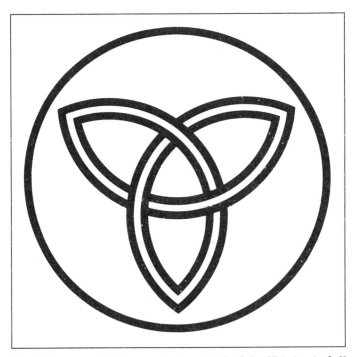

The Triquetra. This mystical symbol of the Trinity is full of meaning. The three equal arcs of the circle speak of the equality of the three Divine persons; the union of the three circles express the unity of divine essence; the continuous flow of the form symbolizes eternity; and the interwoven nature of the lines denotes the invisibility of the Blessed Trinity. The equilateral triangle in the center of the triqueta is the most ancient of the Trinity symbols, and each pair of arcs symbolizes God's glory.

reverence for which Mennonite worship has striven in the past.

John Rempel

135 • MESSIANIC SYNAGOGUE

Messianic Jews claim both Jewish identity and belief in Jesus as Messiah. The worship practices of the messianic synagogues are diverse and fluid, but most draw on the basic structure of Jewish worship while incorporating the New Testament in some way.

The contemporary Messianic Jewish movement locates its roots in the original Jewish community of believers in Jesus that flourished in the century following the Crucifixion. The movement seeks to reconstruct that indigenous messianic presence within the Jewish community today. The modern origins of Messianic Judaism lie both in the lives of believers who lived quietly within the Jewish community and in the ministries of evangelists and missionaries. The evangelistic efforts slowly bore fruit in the emergence of small mission congregations, several of which eventually became the early Messianic synagogues.

As an Aramaic-speaking Galilean, Jesus would probably have been called something like Yeshua bar-Yosef—Jesus, son of Joseph. The most universal characteristic of Messianic Judaism is the use of this or similar Jewish-based terminology (e.g., Yeshua *ha-Mashiᵃḥ,* Jesus the Messiah).

Also, Messianic Jews often draw on commonly used Jewish conventions for writing, such as C.E. (the Common Era) and B.C.E. (Before the Common Era) to replace the culturally pejorative usages A.D. (*anno domine,* "the year of our Lord") and B.C. (before Christ). Another often-used convention is "L-rd" or "G-d," derived from the custom of not pronouncing the tetragrammaton (YHWH).

The Messianic Movement Today

Messianic Judaism is a multifaceted renewal movement. It seeks both to rediscover a once-viable expression of Jewish faith and point towards the age-old goal of Christian renewal—to be like the New Testament church. Thus, it has the potential of incubating Christian renewal. It is also a renewal of what was once called Hebrew Christianity, a missionary outreach that less strongly identifies with the Jewish subculture than does Messianism.

Believer is the designation of choice for many Messianic Jews, due to cultural and historical baggage associated with the term *Christian.* For most Jews, "Christian" merely means someone who is not a Jew, whereas Messianic Jews claim to be simultaneously Jews and believers in Jesus.

Rapid growth followed the recovery of what one of the movement's pioneer spiritual leaders called "the Messianic distinctive," which contrasts it with the older Hebrew Christianity. In 1976 there were less than a dozen Messianic synagogues in only a few major cities. By 1982 there were thirty in twelve states and one province of Canada (plus some embryonic fellowships elsewhere). By early 1992 there were 146 congregations of varying sizes in thirty states and five Canadian provinces, plus others in Europe and Israel.

Generalizations about the specific worship practices of these congregations is difficult. According to Daniel C. Juster, former president of the Union of Messianic Congregations, approximately 5 to 10 percent of the messianic congregations adhere very strictly to the traditional Jewish liturgical prayers. On the other extreme 10 to 12 percent ignore liturgy altogether. By far the majority are divided into two schools of thought of approximately equal size. One of these is inclined to draw heavily on the Jewish liturgical tradition, with occasional efforts to rewrite prayers to draw out their messianic implications. The other draws on the prayers and rabbinic writings selectively, fitting the traditional materials into a worship service that may or may not conform to the parameters of traditional Jewish liturgy.

The Basic Structure of Jewish Worship

Traditionally, Jewish worship is Sabbath centered; although in Reform Judaism, early temples sometimes scheduled their worship services for Sunday morning. Similarly most Messianic synagogues hold their services on Friday evening or Saturday morning, or both. A few have Friday evening and Sunday morning services. Almost all observe *Shabbat* (the Sabbath), and only two have a Sunday worship service solely.

Although no single congregation necessarily utilizes every element of worship included in the following description, each of these elements is at least occasionally—in some places regularly—in use by some of the Messianic congregations. Traditionally, Jewish liturgical worship begins with prayers of praise, called *bᵉrakhot* (benedictions) or *piyyutim* (poems or hymns). Perhaps the most famous *erev Shabbat* (Friday evening) *piyyut* is "*Lacha Dodi,*" a later medieval hymn in praise of the Sabbath. It derives its name from the refrain, "*Lacha dodi, likrat kalah, p'nei Shabbat n'kab'la*" ("Come, my friend, the Bride to meet, The holy Sabbath let us greet"). Often, a *bᵉrakhah* is a quotation from Scripture (e.g., Exod. 31:16-17, Pss. 95–99). Saturday morning begins similarly, both services moving towards the *Barkhu,* the call to worship, followed by more praises, all of which focus the worshiper's attention on the next act of worship.

The *Shᵉma'* is the Jewish confession of faith: "Hear O Israel, the Lord is our God, the Lord is One." It is customarily chanted using the tune that is all but universal among Ashkenazic Jews (i.e., Jews of central or eastern European origin).

Following praise and confession, the Jewish service focuses on petition in the *Shᵉmoneh 'Esreh* (Eighteen Benedictions), often called the *Amidah* (the Standing Prayer). It is said quietly, but not silently, each worshiper standing as an individual before God. Everyone reads at his own pace and sits down when he has finished. Some or part of the prayer may then be chanted by the *ḥazzan* (Cantor).

On Sabbath morning, the Torah is read at this point in the service. Worship then concludes with a great thanksgiving prayer that points forward to the coming of the messianic kingdom—the *Alenu*—chanted to one of several variants of a commonly used synagogue tune.

The Torah Service

On Monday, Thursday, and Saturday mornings in Orthodox synagogues a portion of the Torah is read (Hayim Halevy Donin, *To Pray as a Jew* [New York, 1980], 233), following the *parshat* or *sidra,* the weekly lectionary. Although Messianic synagogues do not customarily have mid-week services, the lectionary is followed more in the breach than in regular observance. The custom of reading from the Torah at the Saturday service has been carefully maintained in many, probably a majority.

The Torah service begins with benedictions and with removing the Torah scroll from the *'Aron hakkodesh,* or "Ark," its cabinet. Many of the Messianic congregations own at least one scroll, and others have preparations under way to procure one. Arks are often of simple design in Messianic synagogues, in contrast to often ornate arks of older, more financially secure traditional congregations. However, great care is taken in the design and building of even the simplest Ark.

The Torah blessings that precede the reading of the Torah are of great antiquity. Much of this service was already in use during Jesus' lifetime, and thus constitutes a link with the Messiah and his times. Although abridgement often occurs, radical change is least likely in this section than, perhaps, any other segment of the liturgy. However, lack of adequate Hebrew education presents a challenge to the proper utilization of the Torah service. This problem is being addressed by curriculum development as well as by liturgical education in the service itself.

Reading from the Torah is an honor traditionally bestowed on a man but, following the example of Reform, increasingly bestowed on members with little regard to gender. The reader "ascends" to the *bemah*—the platform from which the worship leaders conduct the service—and says or chants at least the traditional benediction immediately preceding the reading, then reads from the Torah, usually an

English translation. After concluding with the traditional post-reading blessing, spoken or chanted, the reader returns to his or her place.

Following the reading of the Torah, a reader chants or reads the designated portion from the prophetic scriptures, followed by one or more of the four traditional post-*haftarah* blessings. The first recalls the veracity of God's Word, the second calls for the continued return of the Jewish people to Zion, the third recites the promise of the messianic coming (e.g., Yeshua's second coming) and the fourth is a thanksgiving for God's self-revelation in Scripture and in history. If a thirteen-year-old is having his or her *bar* or *bat mitzvah,* this segment is that child's moment to display skill in the liturgy and the tradition.

The unique feature of Messianic Jewish worship is the third reading, often called *B^erit haddashah*—the New Testament. As a congregation that believes the messiahship of Jesus, this reading is inevitable—and wholly without precedent in the synagogue liturgy. For this reason, there is no consensus about the liturgical setting, if any, surrounding this reading. Some congregations use the New Testament in education but have developed no liturgical setting for it. Others use it in worship with no liturgical surroundings. Still others use it in a liturgical setting as closely parallel that of the *Torah* or *Haftarah* as they can develop. Some of those using little liturgy use only one reading, often from the New Testament. Some of those using more liturgical tradition use it in addition to the *Torah* and *Haftarah* readings, while others use it instead of one or both of these. There simply has not been enough time for one or more "common usages" to emerge. Watching the Messianic movement may be instructive of the way in which the canon was handled in the first two centuries of church history.

Liturgical renewal within Messianic Judaism has been facilitated by the development of the *Machzor For High Holy Days* (Chicago: Congregation B'nai Maccabim, 1986) and *Messianic Services for Festival and Holy Day* (Palm Harbor, Florida: Menorah Ministries, 1992). As the Union of Messianic Congregations and individual Messianic congregations and rabbis continue to develop liturgical materials, worship patterns will likely become clearer, though diverse schools of thought will likely remain.

Kenneth Warren Rick

136 ✦ NATIONAL BAPTIST CONVENTION OF AMERICA

Worship in the constituency of the National Baptist Convention of America has been characterized by a free and emotionally powerful expression of faith in a God who promises liberation from oppressive circumstances. In recent years, worship has taken on greater structure without stifling freedom, and considerable resources have been devoted to enhancing the worship experience.

The divisions of the national black Baptist bodies do not represent distinctions in the types and modes of worship. The emergence of worship among all black Baptists can only be understood against the backdrop of the dehumanizing, servile status imposed upon them, which forced them to initiate the only form of worship they knew.

Their worship was unstructured because they could not reconcile themselves to the structure of their masters' worship nor their masters' God, who permitted freedom and servitude to obtain. The earliest worship of black Baptists consisted of spirituals calling upon God to give them strength to endure their servitude, hymns sung in long meter or no meter at all, long prayers uttered in the only language they knew, Scripture reading by those who could read, and a biblical exhortation by a respected leader. Worship occurred on their own time and its location was often at the end of a cotton row or a corn field.

Development of Black Baptist Worship

From its beginnings, worship in the black Baptist church centered in the sermon. The sermon was the crescendo in the worship experience. The content focused upon the hereafter and upon a God who gave his people hope in the midst of their despair and the mundane experiences of this life. Through the gift of his Son Jesus Christ, God would grant eternal liberation if they believed in him. The worship experience was very long, lasting sometimes for three hours and characterized by spontaneous expressions ("Amen," "Thank you, Lord"), crying, shouting, and seizurelike body movements representing release from everything that seemed to overpower the worshiper.

Remarkable changes affecting worship have occurred among the member churches of the National Baptist Convention of America, Incorporated. Among them are an improved educational status of both the pastors and the congregants, a shift from a "pie in the sky religion" to existential worship that recognizes the precarious nature of life's experiences and the necessity to apply the Christian message to daily living; greater emphasis upon the importance of the teaching ministry; and an abbreviated, more structured order of worship, with shorter sermons. The traditional "hellfire and brimstone" sermons of the first and second decades of the twentieth century have been gradually replaced by well-constructed, biblically based sermons focusing primarily upon redemption and hope and applicable to contemporary life.

Worship is now generally ordered around the following elements: call to worship, invocation, hymn of worship and praise, offering, intercessory prayer, hymn of preparation, responsive Scripture readings, choral music, pastoral prayer, invitation to Christian discipleship, and benediction.

Worship in the black Baptist tradition has always been free because freedom has always been a distinctive plank in the polity of the Baptist church. A more orderly format has not stymied the freedom of worshipers because they are provided opportunity for active participation. Moreover, black Baptists are spiritually motivated by the knowledge that God's Holy Spirit is always free and supersedes any prescribed forms or structures.

On the other hand, the Baptist insistence upon "freedom" in worship has often become a treadmill from which some Baptists have not been able to extricate themselves. Instead of being really free in worship, they have become trapped in restructured worship formats.

Since 1975, there has been a growing concern on the part of many black Baptist pastors and congregants to have meaningful worship experiences devoid of the stereotypes that characterized the earliest forms of black Baptist worship. Many black Baptist pastors are assimilating elements of worship from other traditions. Perhaps some of the most noticable changes since 1975 have been changes in musical styles.

The traditional and standard hymns, anthems, gospels, and inspirational renditions have been replaced by contemporary gospel songs and varied arrangements of anthems and standard Baptist hymns. Drums, other percussion instruments, woodwind instruments like the saxophone and the clarinet, and the trumpet, very seldom integral parts of the black Baptist worship experience seventy-five years ago, are now used in several churches.

While most member churches of the National Baptist Convention of America, Incorporated, have not made full use of the calendar year, many pastors and their parishioners are now using the Christian calendar in planning worship and as a teaching ministry aid.

Denominational Resources

Revisions in the _National Baptist Hymnal_ reflect the concern for future directions in black Baptist worship. Since 1977, black Baptists have produced six editions of the _National Baptist Hymnal_. The _New National Baptist Hymnal,_ 6th edition, was published in 1980 and represents a thorough examination of the theology and the biblical foundations of hymns for black Baptist worship. More importantly, the committee responsible for the publication represented a broad cross section of clergy and lay persons to upgrade the worship experience.

There are other hopeful signs of continued progress regarding worship. Pastors and lay persons are constantly being exposed to seminars, workshops, conferences, and a plethora of worship resources that have expanded the horizons for meaningful worship beyond the traditional sermon as the center of worship. Nonetheless, even with these new directions in worship, member churches of the National Baptist Convention of America, Incorporated, will continue to remain focused upon the mission of this particular aggregate of worshipers, which includes implementing the great commission at home and abroad, serving as an agency of Christian education, propagating Baptist doctrines of faith and practice, safeguarding full religious liberty and spiritual independence at home and on the foreign fields, and vouchsafing the principles of civil liberty, social justice, and equity of humankind as children of God.

Richard Rollins

137 ✦ NATIONAL BAPTIST CONVENTION OF THE USA, INCORPORATED

Worship in the churches of the National Baptist Convention of the USA, Inc., is a joyous expression of gratitude to God for deliverance, both social and spiritual. The traditional black Baptist style of fervent preaching and singing predominates, and recently a charismatic influence has been manifest in increased use of dance, raising of hands, and chanting.

Worship in the nearly 8 million-member National Baptist Convention, USA, Inc., centers on Christ and is African-American in cultural forms. The National Baptist Convention was formed in 1895 to meet the need for a strong national black Baptist organization independent of discriminatory white control (Leroy Fitts, _A History of Black Baptists_ [Nashville: Broadman Press, 1985], 78).

Worship as Gratitude

In the NBC-USA churches, worship is an exuberant expression of gratitude and joy to God for deliverance from physical and spiritual slavery. It functions as both an escape from and resistance to the societal reality of oppression. As H. H. Mitchell says, "The all-consuming, passionate abandon so characteristic of black culture worship has no doubt been an escape from brutal reality and a survival technique. But in a more positive sense this abandon, this freedom has been the evidence that spirit supersedes environment" (_Black Preaching_ [New York: Harper & Row, 1970], 34).

And while the content of worship is held in common by all churches (Fitts, 280), there is also extraordinary diversification in the liturgical form and emotional presentation. H. H. Mitchell writes, "The black congregation is very permissive. It accepts a considerable variety of behavior unrelated to the message, in order (consciously or unconsciously) to free preachers to be themselves" (Mitchell, 162–163). Each autonomous church may decide upon the order of worship service, as well as the style of worship—the length and fervor of the prayers; whether the church sings hymns or gospel music, high- or low-brow choral selections. The individual church also determines how the temporal business is conducted at Sunday services, or any other period (Thomas Elliott Huntley, _Huntley's Manual for Every Baptist_ [Elizabeth M. Huntley, 1963,1966], 48–49).

The liturgical form of Sunday morning service follows the pattern of the old Jewish order, as do most Protestant and Catholic worship services. The loose order is: call to worship, Scripture reading, invocational prayer, song, offertory, song, announcements of church events, altar call, pastor's remarks, sermon, invitation to discipleship, benedictory prayer.

Recent Trends

In recent years, there has been a growing movement with the NBC-USA churches toward more animated services that include dances, raising of both hands, chanting of praises, and in some churches, speaking in tongues. While the charismatic expression led to great deal of membership swapping with other Baptist churches, it doesn't appear to produce much new church membership.

Moreover, the great majority of churches have retained the more "traditional" method of singing songs with great emotion, encouraging spontaneous individual expression, and closing the service in the manner so well described by Mitchell: "We in African American tradition have cultural roots which demand that a sermon end in a celebration. For this we have a number of our own terms such as 'Coming on up' at the end, 'The Gravey,' the 'Rousement,' the 'Whoop,' or just the generic 'Climax.' . . . No sermon, in most quarters, dare end without one [an emotional climax]" (Henry H. Mitchell, *Celebrations and Experience in Preaching* ([1990], 12).

During the past ten years, there has been a decrease in the number of persons (usually women) who "shout" during regular Sunday morning worship. The "shout" is an expression of many emotions, such as joy and release from bondage or distress. Sometimes the shout represents a statement of determination to continue serving God in the face of great difficulty and/or personal loss, such as domestic turmoil, academic difficulty, financial problems, or professional frustrations (Mitchell, *Black Preaching,* 43–45).

Some issues related to worship practice are creating factions in the national body. Most prominent are questions concerning women preachers, the plenary inspiration of the Word of God, and the way in which the Holy Spirit is manifested in the body of believers.

Periodic Observances

Some special days and seasons of worship in the churches of the NBC-USA warrant mention. Communion for most Baptist churches is a memorial service to Christ. There are no times or dates established for when Communion should take place. However, most convention churches observe Com-

munion immediately following the morning sermon of the first Sunday. A large number of churches prefer to conduct an entire evening worship service, including choirs.

Generally, the baptismal observances are conducted at the same time as the Communion service. The candidates are dressed in white and immersed in water by the pastor (sometimes with the aid of a deacon), while the congregation sings hymns and prays for the candidates and the church. A reading of the church covenant usually precedes baptisms.

Special worship is held on major days of the church calendar such as Christmas, Easter, Good Friday, and Ash Wednesday. Individual congregations may also designate a variety of other days for special worship experiences. Typical examples include the church anniversary, choir day, men and women's day, youth day, young adult day, the pastor's anniversary, black history, Martin Luther King day, brotherhood week, and Thanksgiving day service.

Easter is the most highly reverenced day of the church year. Most convention churches participate in Easter morning services, and some have sunrise Easter services. In recent years, the emphasis has returned to more sincere worship of the risen Savior, rather than other activities not centered on the Resurrection. In addition, most churches participate in joint "Good Friday," commemorating the Crucifixion and seven last words of Jesus.

Lent and Ash Wednesday are highly visible in many convention churches. Ash Wednesday has not been observed as much as Palm Sunday, which also seems to be on the decline in recent years (Mitchell, *Black Preaching,* 43–45). In past generations, the observance of a forty-day and forty-night abstention for Lent was encouraged as part of the pre-Easter celebrations, but this is no longer prevalent.

Christmas is celebrated with enthusiasm. Most churches have special Christmas programs, which include plays, skits, and other depictions of the Christmas message and birth of Jesus. Frequently, special Christmas music expresses the birth of Jesus, the concept of the peace of God in human form, and the advent of messianic good will to humankind.

In the National Baptist Convention, USA, Inc., the worship experience has maintained a recognizable form which reflects the Christ-centered evangelical faith of the organizational founding fathers. It also has continued to reflect the heritage of the black

Baptist struggle to reverence Christ Jesus as Lord and Savior through the experience of slavery, segregation, and systematic repression.

Robert E. Davis

138 ✦ PRESBYTERIAN CHURCH IN AMERICA (PCA) AND OTHER PRESBYTERIAN CHURCHES

The Presbyterian Church in America practices a worship shaped by the updated Westminster Directory. However, because the directory is only a guide and not obligatory, there is no uniformity of worship in the PCA. Current trends in the church favor greater musical variety and increased congregational participation. Influences from the liturgical, charismatic, and inclusive movements are gaining in strength.

Several historic streams have shaped the worship of the relatively young Reformed denomination known as the Presbyterian Church in America (PCA). John Knox, father of Presbyterianism, came under the influence of John Calvin at Geneva and later wrote a liturgy known as "The Form of Prayer" (1556). Knox's spiritual descendants in the next century met at Westminster Abbey in London to produce the Westminster Confession and Catechisms, which form the theological basis for the PCA, as well as the Westminster _Directory for the Public Worship of God_ (1645). This directory included general rubrics and principles rather than a set liturgy. In 1661, however, Richard Baxter did produce a widely used liturgy known as the Savoy Liturgy. Out of these influences came the _Book of Common Worship_ (1906, 1932, 1946), which has set the stage for modern American Presbyterian worship.

———— Historic Characteristics ————

One general characteristic of Presbyterian worship has been adherence to the rubric provision method in contrast both to free liturgy and to a prescribed liturgy such as that of _The Book of Common Prayer._ This approach has provided some latitude for contemporary attempts at renewal. The _Westminster Directory_ is condensed and updated in the PCA's _Directory for the Worship of God,_ which claims to be "an approved guide and should be taken seriously as the mind of the Church agreeable to the Standards. However, it does not have the force of law and is not to be considered obligatory in all its parts." Consequently one finds great variety in

the worship of PCA churches within the accepted framework of Reformed covenantal theology.

A related characteristic has been adherence to the regulative principle of worship. This principle is found in chapter 21 of the Westminster Confession summarized in the Directory of Worship as follows: "Since the Holy Scriptures are the only infallible rule of faith and practice, the principles of public worship must be derived from the Bible, and from no other source. The Scriptures forbid the worshipping of God by images, or in any other way not appointed in his Word, and requires the receiving, observing, and keeping pure and entire all such religious worship and ordinances as God hath appointed in His Word (S.C. 51, 50)" (_Directory_ 47.1). Whereas church leaders can agree in principle that the elements of worship services must have biblical warrant, in practice there is difference of opinion as to how this principle should be implemented.

Thus in a few PCA churches one can find liturgical dance, whereas most would strongly reject such a practice. Some churches make abundant use of colorful, symbolic liturgical banners in the sanctuary, whereas other sanctuaries reflect more Puritan and Zwinglian visual simplicity. Nevertheless the regulative principle, though ignored and forgotten in some quarters, serves as a lodestar to guide attempts at liturgical renewal in the PCA.

Presbyterian worship traditionally has been characterized as emphasizing the verbal rather than the visual. Thus some have considered it very cerebral, appealing to literate congregations served by highly educated clergy. Some renewal efforts have attempted to recover more balance with activities designed to appeal to the emotional side of the worshipers.

Another characteristic has been a confessional element in the liturgy. This arises out of the Reformed theological emphasis on human depravity and unworthiness in the presence of a transcendent, holy God. Thus prayers of confession have formed an important part of traditional Presbyterian liturgy.

Perhaps the strongest characteristic of this Reformation denomination has been an emphasis on the preaching of the Word as central in the liturgy. This emphasis has been seen architecturally in the common use of a pulpit as the visual focal point at the center of the chancel. Historically these pulpits were large in size and elaborate in style. Prescribed lectionaries were replaced by the _lectio continua_ method of Calvin and Knox, in which consecutive passages of Scripture were read and preached from as the dominant component of the worship service. The PCA has emphasized a seminary educated clergy equipped to undertake preaching, which is an ordinance of God. "Preaching requires much study, meditation, and prayer, and ministers should prepare their sermons with care, and not indulge themselves in loose, extemporary harangues, nor serve God with that which costs them naught" (*Directory* 53.5).

Current Trends

Diversity increasingly marks worship in the more than one thousand churches constituting the PCA. Worship styles range from the more traditional televised services of the Coral Ridge Presbyterian Church, pastored by D. James Kennedy, to the more innovative services of several of the New Life Presbyterian churches and the New City Fellowship of Chattanooga. Nevertheless several general trends can be discerned.

Greater musical variety, in terms of style and range of instruments used, is evident across the country. The Reformed heritage, which once emphasized singing of Psalms exclusively, has broadened even beyond hymns and gospel songs to include contemporary choruses, praise songs, and Scripture songs. Some churches have introduced a time of praise singing for the first five or ten minutes of the service whereas others have incorporated such music into the service itself in deference to the changing preferences of the younger generations of parishioners. This has caused tensions in some congregations. Even the denomination's *Trinity Hymnal* (Philadelphia: Great Commission Publications; the Orthodox Presbyterian Church) in its 1990 edition includes numerous Scripture songs and contemporary praise choruses, some with guitar chords. The denomination's Christian Education and Publications department sponsors an annual national conference on "Music in Worship" to help raise church leaders' level of music competence.

Another trend is increased congregational participation in worship services. This includes open sharing and participatory prayer by worshipers, as well as increased use of lay people in leading services. Some PCA congregations use laity to assist the pastor as worship service planners.

The question of the participation of children in Communion has received considerable recent attention. Whereas the PCA is committed confessionally to baptism of the covenant children of believing parents, children have generally not partaken of Communion until they have come to understand the gospel and are admitted by the Session (elders) to the Lord's Supper, having made a public profession of their faith. Whereas this age can't be fixed it has traditionally been thought to be at least junior-high age. A study committee of the denomination explored this issue in recent years with a minority report arguing for pedo-Communion. The majority report concluded Communion should be open only to such as are of years and ability to examine themselves (1 Cor. 11:26-27).

Perhaps the most dominant trend in recent years in the PCA is increasing homogenization with evangelical Protestantism. The result is fewer denominational distinctives that distinguish a PCA worship service from that of any other evangelical church. Several factors may account for this. Rapid church growth, including a concerted effort to plant new churches, contributes to a blurring of distinctives. The PCA was organized in 1973 with 240 churches and by 1990 had over 1000 churches. For several years in the 1980s it was the fastest growing denomination in the United States. This growth, added to the mobility of parishioners, makes for increasing pluralism as people from many denominational backgrounds find their way into PCA churches with a few having had a Presbyterian background. This is accompanied by a lack of understanding of the historic distinctives of Presbyterianism on the part of the average worshiper.

More influential than historical precedents are cultural influences including religious radio and television. Worshipers from many denominations are exposed to the same contemporary Christian music and watch some of the same televangelists and religious programming. Parishioners bring these influences with them into their church worship services. On top of this one finds little emphasis on worship in the curricula of seminaries that train ministers for the PCA. Most of these seminaries offer only one liturgical course, and that often an elective.

All this contributes to the loss of denominational distinctives. It is a trend that is likely to continue into the next century as coming generations interact with cultural influences in seeking worship forms

Shield of the Holy Trinity. This is an example of the *Shield of the Blessed Trinity found in the stained glass of medieval churches. The figure is characterized by three curving sides, each exactly equal in length. At each angle is a small circle and in the center is a larger circle. Each of the outer circles that represent the Father (Pater), the Son (Filius), and the Holy Spirit (Spiritus Sanctus—abbreviated in the circle) is connected with the center circle, God (Deus). The* non est *of the outer band translates "is not" while the* est *of the inner band means "is." That is, the Father is not the Son, and the Son is not the Spirit, and the Spirit is not the Father, but the Father is God, and the Son is God, and the Spirit is God. Thus the unity and diversity of the Trinity is kept distinct.*

that enable parishioners to glorify God and enjoy him forever.

Paul E. Engle

139 • PRESBYTERIAN CHURCH (USA)

Presbyterian worship has felt the impact of the liturgical renewal movement. Members are expressing concern about remaining faithful to the Reformed tradition. The emphasis on preaching and singing remains strong, while renewed interest has emerged in the recovery Psalm singing, regular celebration of Communion, and the services of the Christian year. Some churches seek to incorporate charismatic and inclusive elements.

The theme of the Word of God incarnate in Christ and witnessed through the Bible is the focus of Presbyterian teaching on worship. The Psalms in metrical versions once were the exclusive fare for singing within the simple, even plain, Presbyterian orders of service. The Word was dominant.

In the American experience, Presbyterian worship has displayed almost all the fashions of evangelical church life, from revivalism through liturgical renewal. The PC (USA) still seeks to maintain a cohesive identity while living with a variety of notions about what makes Christian worship Presbyterian. Sermon-and-psalms no longer adequately describes this tradition.

The Renewal Impulse

Liturgical renewal in the PC (USA) stems from several factors, including the historical influence of both the Second Vatican Council and the continuing search for Reformed roots. An inner demand for renewal comes with membership decline and shifting demographic profiles. Presbyterians are reexamining their customs and practices with fresh eyes, concerned for the future of ministry and witness. They are more aware of ethnic traditions and customs in the church, and a secular American public to be reached. Justice, which affirms ethnic diversity and equality, and evangelism, which places priority on the needs of unchurched people, function as criteria for good worship, which increases the variety of what one finds on Sunday morning in congregations.

Seminary training is beginning to take liturgy seriously, and most Presbyterian seminaries have a worship position on the faculty, though few teachers hold earned Ph.D.s in the field of liturgy. The Theology and Worship Ministry Unit of the General Assembly includes staff in the areas of worship, arts, spirituality, and liturgical resources. The Unit coordinates worship conferences and events and publishes the quarterly journal *Reformed Liturgy & Music* (also the official publication of Presbyterian Association of Musicians).

Recent Developments

A new hymnal in 1990 (*The Presbyterian Hymnal: Hymns, Psalms, and Spiritual Songs*) selected music from several ethnic sources and represented a variety of styles of piety. This hymnal affirms the "centrality of the sacraments, ecumenical and mission dimensions, the perspectives of women, and the concerns of youth and age." The range is broad: classic and contemporary hymnody joins "praise-

and-worship" music, gospel songs, spirituals, ethnic contributions (Hispanic, Asian, Native American, and African-American). A section of psalms for singing in metrical and responsorial forms facilitates recovery of that practice. Some congregations keep one of the older denominational hymnals (1972, 1955, 1933) in use, while others use one of the commercial hymnals or music books. Supplemental collections for singing are often compiled and used locally.

Preaching continues to hold the most prominent place in worship, though there appear to be few true giants to emulate. The adoption of the Common Lectionary with the three-lesson plan of Sunday readings has had a major impact on preaching. Presbyterians first adapted the Roman Catholic lectionary of Vatican II in 1969. The older Presbyterian practice of reading and preaching through books of the Bible in course (called *lectio continua*) is still practiced by many preachers, with or without a view to the Common Lectionary.

The Unit on Theology and Worship has a staff position for the arts and worship, but program development lags in this area. Local churches and the seminaries experiment with dance and drama, but no strong precedent exists for a once-iconoclastic Presbyterianism to cultivate liturgical arts. Ecumenical and ethnic influences may be factors in new appreciations of movement, color, and texture that go beyond decoration to liturgical functions.

The liturgical calendar has proven very popular with the great majority of the PC (USA). Roughly one century after the first hesitant introduction of Christmas and Easter observances there is now widespread affirmation of the positive role of "seasons," with a growing number of holy days. The calendar is the post–Vatican II model increasingly common among North American churches. Efforts to reinforce the understanding of Sunday as Lord's Day and original feast day accompany the growing pedagogical interest in a calendar.

A new appreciation of the centrality of the sacraments is developing. The Lord's Supper, once observed at most four times in the year, is celebrated at least monthly in half the congregations. Change is not uniform, but a move toward greater frequency is widespread. Weekly celebration is the practice or a goal of a small but growing number of churches. The celebration of baptism increasingly involves the participation of the whole congregation and is less likely to be seen as strictly familial in significance.

In both sacraments the place and role of children is taken seriously, and their participation is encouraged.

The relationship between worship and other ministries cannot be generalized for all congregations of the PC (USA), but the ideal is clear—worship is the work of the Holy Spirit within the body of Christ, the source of the vitality of the people of God, and the offering of our failures and service to God in Christ. Presbyterians typically relate worship to education. Now, questions of justice within the worshiping community are being related increasingly to issues of justice in society. And, new church planting locates worship as the central activity of the church, and subjects worship practices to fresh demands for hospitality and relevance.

Resources for Renewal

The current *Directory for Worship* of the PC (USA) was adopted in 1989. It is the most ambitious directory ever adopted to govern and guide worship. It favors liturgical renewal, and assumes an educational rather than a strictly legislative role. A new "Brief Statement of Faith" was adopted in 1991 for liturgical use.

A book of services for the use of ministers is projected for 1993 and expected to be available in print and computer versions. Toward this end a series of *Supplemental Liturgical Resources* has been published (1984–1992) for trial use and review: *The Service for the Lord's Day* (No. 1, 1984); *Holy Baptism and Services for the Renewal of Baptism* (No. 2, 1985); *Christian Marriage* (No. 3, 1986); *The Funeral: A Service of Witness to the Resurrection* (No. 4, 1986); *Daily Prayer* (No. 5, 1987); *Service for Occasions of Pastoral Care* (No. 6, 1990); and *Liturgical Year* (No. 7, 1992). Spanish-language liturgical resources went into preparation in 1991. Service books are for voluntary use guided by the *Directory for Worship,* which is the constitutional provision for worship.

A complete *Psalter* is projected to appear in 1992–1993 for the use of cantors, choirs, and congregations. The style of the psalms is primarily responsorial. *The Common Lectionary for Sundays* gave the shape of the selection, but it will include biblical canticles to use in daily prayer along with psalms for Sunday.

Hughes Oliphant Old's studies in Presbyterian worship include *The Patristic Roots of Reformed Worship* (Neuchatel, 1974; Zurich: Theologischer

Verlag, 1975); _Praying with the Bible_ (Philadelphia: The Geneva Press, 1980); and _Worship That Is Reformed According to Scripture_ (Atlanta: John Knox Press, 1984), plus several articles on the daily prayer heritage of the Reformed tradition. Dr. Old's work, along with the writings of the prolific Methodist scholar James F. White, are used in seminary worship courses taught by Presbyterians.

Two major conferences are sponsored annually, at Montreat in North Carolina, and more recently, the Westminster Conference on Worship and Music (Presbyterian Association of Musicians), held in Pennsylvania. Workshops are held at the seminaries and by regional governing bodies of the denomination. Liturgical scholarship among Presbyterians is growing through academic programs, including the masters and Ph.D. programs of the University of Notre Dame, at Drew University, and other institutions. Presbyterian liturgists are now participating in greater numbers in international ecumenical bodies (e.g., North American Academy of Liturgy, and _Societas Liturgica_).

Response and Outlook

Liturgical renewal gained fresh interest among Presbyterians through new emphasis found in seminaries, through _Reformed Liturgy & Music_ and the impact of the Presbyterian Association of Musicians, and because of the latest generation of new resources (1984–1993). However, liturgical renewal has been unevenly understood and received. The claims to attention made by evangelism, social justice, and liturgical renewal are too often pursued in competition rather than developed into a faithful unity.

Monolithic visions for liturgical renewal will not prevail in the PC (USA) of the near future. Ethnic and other communities of loyalty and ministry will seek to preserve their own styles and spiritual genius. The success of renewal will be on the lines of a more pervasive care for teaching and doing liturgy.

The central gains of the post–Vatican II era continue to find stronger rootage: systematic hearing of Scripture, appreciation of the sacraments, and greater variety in music across lines of ethnic and theological diversity. Increased attention to spiritual gifts and the ministry of all the baptized integrates ecumenical insight with the continuing recovery of a Reformed heritage. Presbyterian worship has not ceased reforming and being reformed in the faithful service of the Word of God.

Stanley R. Hall

140 • PROGRESSIVE NATIONAL BAPTIST CONVENTION, INCORPORATED

Worship in the Progressive National Baptist Convention is rooted in a conviction of God's sovereignty and liberating character as revealed in the Exodus. The style of worship is participatory and uninhibited. Music, in a variety of styles, plays a vital role.

In his analysis of the distinctive character of African-American worship, Dearing E. King, editor of the _Progressive National Baptist Hymnal_, describes its most basic feature as "an unwavering faith in the absolute sovereignty of the supreme, infinite creator" ("Worship in the Black Church," in Emmanuel L. McCall, ed., _The Black Christian Experience_ [Nashville: Broadman Press, 1972], 34). He argues that this distinction enabled African-American worshipers "to affirm their personal identities in an authentic sharing of God's presence, grace, power, will and purpose for the betterment of their own lives and for others" (Ibid., 33).

In their worship experience, African-American Christians have long identified with the Hebrew slaves. The faith of the Hebrew slaves in the absolute sovereignty of God fortified them to deal with the oppression of Pharaoh. Identifying with Hebrew oppression continues even to this day to help African-American worshipers survive oppressive social structures. Faith in a gracious, liberating God enables them to make sense of the insanity of their disconnected, disturbed, and disorganized lives.

Freedom in Worship

Their response to God in worship is creative, spontaneous, and liberating. The language and liturgy are lyrical, poetic, majestic, and living. Although the worship has order and structure, there is no room for either inflexible religious routine or spiritual boredom. Traditional hymns and contemporary songs are sometimes rendered with the more personally meaningful through improvisation. Those who lead the services are not performing before _spectators_. The preaching, praying, and praising of God through musical expression are acts of _participation_ by the total community of worshipers. The aliveness of the worship experience is based on an awareness of God being in, with, and for the people in worship and in the totality of their lives.

African-American Christians make no sharp line of demarcation between their secular activities and their sacred responsibilities. Worship is the celebration of gratitude to the living God who never leaves the worshipers. So, in the worship services, they may sing and pray, "He woke me up this morning and started me on my way." This style of creativity and celebration is not limited to one socioeconomic class. Progressive National Baptist churches have members who have earned doctorates as well as members who have no degrees. The mixture of social classes contributes to the richness of diversity in the worship experience.

Although there is no single order of worship that is rigidly followed by all worshiping congregations in Progressive National Baptist tradition, there is an implicit commitment that worship is the grateful, creative, and celebrative response to the sovereignty of the liberating God, whom the worshipers have come to know in Jesus Christ. The worshipers recognize that this liberating God is absolute, supreme, infinite, and creative in maintaining a historical relationship of grace, mercy, and redemption with those who genuinely worship with an unwavering faith.

The expressions of worship are oral and uninhibited. There may be times of pensive silence, critical reflections, an oral utterance of "amen," hand-clapping, hand-raising, laughter, tears, or even ritualistic or spontaneous dance. All of this is accepted because the freedoms denied the worshipers in society are freedoms permitted as they worship God in the beauty of holiness. As Progressive National Baptist Scholar W. A. Jones would say, "There is a balance between sense and soul" (J. Alfred Smith, Sr., *Outstanding Black Sermons* [Valley Forge, Pa.: Judson Press, 1976], 7).

─────── **Musical Traditions** ───────

There was a time when all Progressive National churches had antiphonal singing or what is called "the lining of hymns." This method of singing has African roots. The words of the song sometimes were created spontaneously—as the leader was so inspired during the singing. The song leader would sing a line, and the audience would repeat the line as it had been sung. These songs have lasted through

the process of oral tradition. As the elders have moved on to the next world, successive generations have lost the art of antiphonal moaning and chanting of hymns. However, the Hampton University Ministers and Musicals Annual Conference, the L. K. Williams' Minister's Institute, and black church departments in well-known theological and divinity schools are helping to bring back antiphonal singing.

In many Progressive Baptist churches, two adult choirs lead the worship services. A gospel choir sings the gospel music made popular by the late Thomas A. Dorsey. This gospel tradition has been advanced and elaborated upon by musicians like Doris A. Akers, C. A. Tindley, Clara Ward, Lucy Campbell, Mahalia Jackson, Sallie and Roberta Martin, Aretha Franklin, J. Robert Bradley, Lucie Campbell, and the Reverend James Cleveland. Pastors like Cleophus Robinson, James Cleveland, Walter Hawkins, Clay Evans, Robert T. George, and M. T. Thompson are a few of the present-day pastors who keep the gospel tradition alive. The majority of pastors do a limited amount of singing to prepare the worshipers emotionally, psychologically, and spiritually to hear the preaching of the gospel.

The second adult choir is often called the sanctuary choir. This choir sings stately hymns, classical negro spirituals, anthems, and music often heard in Anglo-Protestant churches. On some Sundays this choir might be a children's choir, a youth choir, or a men's choir.

Music is a powerful carrier of "an unwavering faith in the absolute sovereignty of the supreme, infinite creator."

J. Alfred Smith, Sr.

141 • REFORMED CHURCH IN AMERICA

The Reformed Church in America has been influenced by the liturgical movement, the renaissance in the arts, and the praise-and-worship movement. While most churches observe a traditional approach to worship, a great variety of worship styles can be found in the RCA.

The Reformed Church in America is a semiliturgical church. Its liturgy is a part of its constitution (along with the creeds and the *Book of Church Order*). New liturgical forms join previously approved ones and together form the total corpus of the liturgy. Because liturgical forms are constitutional, they must be approved by the general synod and two-thirds of the district governing bodies (classes). The use of approved orders for the sacraments of baptism and the Lord's Supper is required.

Approach/Word/Response

The most significant event for RCA worship renewal in this century was the publication of _Liturgy and Psalms_ in 1968. These new orders, culminating work begun in 1950, constituted the first major liturgical change since 1906. _Liturgy and Psalms_ gave the church a basic three-part structure for worship: The Approach to God, The Word of God, and The Response to God. This pattern, which allows considerable freedom, brings flow and coherence to RCA worship. In the twenty-five years since this Approach/Word/Response form for Lord's Day worship was approved, it has gained wide acceptance throughout the church.

A directory for worship was approved in 1986 as an additional part of the constitution. The growing diversity of worship in the church prompted the Commission on Worship to develop principles that could assist churches in maintaining worship integrity within a variety of expression. Initially, there was a possibility that the RCA would become a "directory principle" church with the directory replacing the liturgy in the constitution. However, when the directory was incorporated into the constitution, the historic stance of the denomination was maintained. This directory is described as "equal in authority" to the liturgy. But the liturgy remains the dominant document, the directory being a commentary and instructional piece. The use of approved orders for sacrament and ordination/installation is still required. The directory principles guide both the development of official liturgy and provide sound guidance for those developing innovative liturgy in local congregations.

The principles guiding the Commission on Worship's liturgical development work since the late 1980s include (1) faithfulness to Reformed theology; (2) incorporation of vivid biblical imagery; (3) use of clear, concise language; (4) breadth in usage of imagery for God; (5) congregational participation; (6) historical sensitivity; (7) attention to the aural nature of language; and (8) sensitivity to emerging ecumenical liturgical convergence. These principles have affirmed within the RCA trends for worship renewal that are occurring in the broader ecumenical community.

Because RCA worship allows for great freedom within quite limited structure, there is enormous worship diversity. It is unlikely that any other communion has a greater variety of worship expression. The range of musical styles, congregational participation, degree of formality, and use of innovation in media, drama, or dance is almost limitless.

Liturgical Balance

RCA churches experiencing health and renewal in worship are moving from the historical dominance of the preached Word (and attendant worshiper passivity) to claim a healthy balance in worship. The integrity of worship as well as the experience of worshipers is enhanced when there is balance between liturgy, sermon, music, and sacrament. A number of trends are contributing to this renewal.

First, a more active role for congregations in responsive sentences, prayer, and music helps the service belong to the congregation, not just pastor and choir. Healthy congregations are moving away from our tradition's more passive worship style.

The Lord's Supper is being celebrated more frequently and with greater variety in mode of service. Historically, quarterly celebration has been required. Currently, at least 80 percent of churches celebrate more often than quarterly, 18 percent once a month or more. Most communicants are served in the pew, but more than 30 percent of congregations serve in a variety of ways. Increased frequency of the Supper shows recognition of the centrality of sacrament for the nurture of God's people and identifies the Word in sacrament as equal in importance to the Word in proclamation as a means of grace.

Increasingly the Common Lectionary serves as a foundation for worship. The lections have been printed on the denominational plan calendar since the early 1980s. Use of the Common Lectionary had grown to 29 percent by 1987. This use helps assure congregations of the breadth of the biblical message.

Observance of the church year has increased dramatically in the last two decades. The major seasons are kept by nearly all congregations with lesser festivals also observed by many. Reclaiming the richness of the liturgical year is a significant shift for a tradition that for centuries looked askance at many practices of historic Christianity. Embracing the church year gives helpful form and structure to worship while encouraging the use of the Common Lectionary.

The last decade has seen increased experimentation within worship. Liturgical drama, dance, and the use of various media has increased in many congregations. This has led to fresh expressions and less reliance on sermon for communication.

The role of music is changing. More congregations, whether using traditional hymnody praise music, Taizé chants, or some combination, are increasing congregational participation in the music of the service. The expanding role of music in the service is a more significant trend than the increasing variation in the type of music used.

All of these recent changes in the worship life of the RCA give worshipers a more active role. They help make worship the "work of the people."

Recent publications that reflect changes within the RCA include *Rejoice in the Lord,* 1985 (one of the first of the current crop of hymnal revisions, it incorporates inclusive language for people but doesn't reflect subsequent concern with God-language); *Worship the Lord,* 1987 (contains service orders approved between 1976 and 1986); *Understanding Worship in the RCA: The Lord's Day Service with the Directory for Worship,* 1988 (an illustrated educational resource); *Pray to the Lord,* 1988 (a treasury of prayers for corporate worship); *Liturgy and Confessions,* 1990 (a loose-leaf collection of all approved liturgy, confessions, and the Directory for Worship).

Worship in the Reformed Church in America covers a wide spectrum. It varies from formal to casual, carefully ordered to spontaneous, predictable to idiosyncratic. All its manifestations seek to follow the basic pattern of Approach/Word/Response in giving glory to God.

Carol Peterkin Myers

142 • REFORMED EPISCOPAL CHURCHES

The Reformed Episcopal Church continues to use the 1785 Book of Common Prayer but has added to its worship both the recovery of historic concerns, such as increased frequency of Communion, and the incorporation of contemporary forms, such as the use of praise songs. African-American congregations, which comprise about one-half of the denomination's membership, have incorporated African-American styles of worship as well.

Reformed Episcopal worship seeks to embody the evangelical tradition of Anglicanism. It was founded in 1873 by Bishop David Cummins, who wanted to preserve true catholicity around the principles of the ancient and Reformation churches. He wanted to maintain the final authority of Holy Scripture and the necessity of personal faith in Jesus Christ for salvation (emphases of the Reformation) in the context of traditional English prayer book worship and episcopal government (the ancient church). He did not wish to diminish either aspect of the Anglican tradition.

Bishop Cummins called the effort to uphold these combined elements, "a return to the old paths." He was deeply convinced that the catholicity of the church was in jeopardy. Given the tendency to draw lines around church polity at that time, he feared Christian witness would be eroded. He saw the historic Anglican emphases of catholicity centered on the Word of God and the sacraments as the correct basis for true unity. Because of his evangelism, he wanted all Christian churches to be able to commune together on the basis of their baptism in the name of the triune God and their common profession. In pursuing that goal he advanced a new denomination that reflected Anglican worship, strong preaching, and evangelism. These emphases have made for an important union of structure and evangelical expression in the worship of the Reformed Episcopal Church.

Flexible Use of the Prayer Book. The balance of form and freedom in worship has been worked out in the REC in a number of ways that provide greater opportunity for extemporaneous prayer as well as a flexible use of the prayer book. The services of *The Book of Common Prayer* are required on Sunday morning. Other services and forms worship can be used on Sunday evening and during the week.

Also, the REC has always permitted optional worship, such as praise services, before and/or after the regular Sunday morning services. The African-American congregations of the REC, for example, make use of this provision. These congregations diligently observe the order of the prayer book, but afterwards, traditional black preaching, singing, and giving occurs that makes for a lively evangelical service.

Renewal along Traditional Lines. The combination of the traditional and the extemporaneous have fed renewal in two directions. Along the more traditional lines, many Reformed Episcopal churches have revived ancient practices without relinquishing strong biblical and evangelical preaching. Some have instituted frequent Communion (weekly) and special services on high festival days (such as Ascension Day and the Feast of Pentecost) and biblical saints' days. They have also revived the musical practices of chanting and classical liturgical music. There is the wearing of vestments by presbyters and the historical episcopal robes (rochet and chamir) by the bishops. The sign of the cross is being used in the traditional sense of symbolizing the renewal of baptismal vows during the creed, before Communion, and at the benediction. Finally, other Anglican practices such as the imposition of ashes on Ash Wednesday are being restored.

Renewal along Contemporary Lines. Many different services are being developed along more contemporary lines. Some congregations are utilizing the Australian prayer book supplement to explore modern language services. Trial Communion liturgies with a more celebrative emphasis have been allowed during festive times of the church year such as Christmas, Easter, and Pentecost. One type of alternate eucharistic service simply combines the regular Morning Prayer service with Holy Communion. Praise music is being used during the Communion service, especially when Communion is actually being served. Also, services of ascent, which include contemporary music and active participation such as hand-clapping, are occurring before regular Sunday morning worship as well as at other times. Finally, some practices such as anointing for healing are taking place after Communion.

Thus, in no way does the traditional renewal inhibit significant contemporary developments in worship. At the same time as the REC is recovering its historic Anglican roots, contemporary language and practice is emerging. The basis for all of these developments can be found in the original desire to have a church that affirms the spirit of the invitation to Holy Communion, which says, "Our fellow Christians of other branches of Christ's Church [Ancient, reformational, and even modern] who love our Divine Lord and Savior Jesus Christ in sincerity are affectionately invited to the Lord's Table." The spirit of evangelical catholicity has opened the way for renewal of worship in a variety of forms. Moreover, to use a good Anglican phrase, this has

happened "decently and in order," and all in conjunction with the set forms of *The Book of Common Prayer.*

Ray R. Sutton

143 • ROMAN CATHOLIC CHURCHES

Renewal of Christian worship began in the nineteenth century and culminated in the reforms of the Second Vatican Council, which led to greater participation by the laity in the liturgy. Issues that must still be faced in ongoing discussions concern the theological and cultural appropriateness of the language of liturgical texts, the role of women, and the place of the laity in leadership.

The change in the worship experience of twentieth-century Roman Catholics may be appreciated by briefly looking at history. In the sixteenth century, Reformers had posed challenges to the lack of intelligibility of medieval Catholic worship experience to the laity. The Council of Trent (1545–1563) responded to the challenge by revising liturgical books, but the Latin language was retained and the textual uniformity remained. A Roman-centered Sacred Congregation of Rites insured a rubrical uniformity that often resulted in overemphasis on rubrics and underemphasis on people's prayer.

——— The Liturgical Movement ———

In the rapidly changing world of the seventeenth through nineteenth centuries, the minimal participation of the people in the liturgy and its lack of intelligibility became growing liabilities. The liturgical movement of the nineteenth and twentieth centuries would eventually address these liabilities with sound historical and biblical research. Dom Prosper Gueranger re-founded the Abbey of Solesme (1833) and dedicated it to scholarly study of sources of liturgy. This research, though medieval in emphasis, prompted other scholars to undertake varieties of studies that contributed to the flowering of twentieth-century liturgical renewal. Dom Lambert Beaudin, like others who joined him in the liturgical revival, emphasized the liturgy as the people's prayer. The essential unity of life and worship, of prayer and justice, was a constant thread of the liturgical movement.

Prior to Vatican II (1960–1965), Pope Pius XII gave official impetus to the liturgical renewal in *Mystici Corporis* (1943) and *Mediator Dei* (1947). The

Pontifical Commission for General Liturgical Restoration, which he established, effected restoration of the Easter Vigil (1951), reforms of Holy Week liturgies (1955), and greater participation of the people in the music and prayers of the liturgy (1958).

The successful impact of the liturgical movement can be seen in the early approval of "The Constitution on the Sacred Liturgy" (*Sacrosanctum Concilium*) at Vatican II in 1962. The document makes clear the centrality of the celebration of the paschal mystery for the life of the church: "The liturgy is the summit toward which the activity of the church is directed; at the same time it is the fount from which the church's power flows" (*S.C.,* 10). Liturgy is "the outstanding means whereby the faithful express in their lives and manifest to others the mystery of Christ and the real nature of the true Church" (*S.C.,* 2).

—— Implementing Liturgical Reform ——

The renewal and reform of Roman Catholic worship has taken many years, and is still ongoing. In 1964 Paul VI began the task of implementing the liturgical reforms called for by the "Constitution on the Sacred Liturgy." An international commission of experts (the Consilium) had the task of revising the liturgical books. In 1964 the International Commission for English in the Liturgy (ICEL) was established to accomplish the translation of prayer texts from Latin to English for all the English-speaking peoples.

In the United States, the national conference of bishops established the Bishop's Committee on the Liturgy (BCL) to monitor and mobilize ongoing liturgical reforms in the United States. In 1965, that committee started publishing a newsletter. Diocesan liturgical commissions were also established to implement the liturgical reforms in dioceses. The Federation of Diocesan Liturgical Commissions (FDLC) would supervise the various diocesan liturgical commissions.

The post–Vatican II liturgical reforms are still in process. The Liturgical Conference, established in 1950, continues to extend the liturgical apostolate in the United States and Canada. Its ecumenical liturgical publications and workshops have aided many pastoral ministers in varieties of Christian worship traditions. The National Association of Pastoral Musicians and the National Association of Liturgical Ministers continue to foster appreciation for and implementation of musical and liturgical renewal on local levels. The North American Academy of Liturgy, founded in 1973, and *Societas Liturgica* gathers liturgical scholars together for exchange of insights about many areas of liturgical renewal.

A series of revised liturgical books have been officially promulgated since 1970. A new Roman Missal, *Missale Romanum* (New York: Catholic Book Publishing Co.), with introductory theology and rubrical instructions, was promulgated in 1970 and revised in 1973 and 1975. This missal contains the variety of prayers for celebration of the Eucharist throughout the days and weeks of the liturgical year, including the lectionary readings for the daily and weekly eucharistic celebrations. A revised Lectionary is due in 1993.

The Liturgy of Hours was published in its four-volume English revision in 1975. Sacramental rituals of marriage, children's liturgies, initiation of children and adults, reconciliation, anointing, orders, and other ministries have been revised. *Rites I* (New York: Pueblo Publishing Co., 1976, 1983), *Rites IA* (New York: Pueblo, 1976, 1983, 1988), and *Rites II* (New York: Pueblo, 1980) contain these rituals. In an attempt to make ritual blessings more a part of family life, the Bishops' Committee on the Liturgy has published a book of blessings for various occasions.

The interest in liturgical music for the many occasions of sacramental worship can be seen in the variety of post–Vatican II hymnals using a wide variety of musical instruments and musical forms.

—— Progress and Remaining Challenges ——

There has been a great change in liturgical participation and appreciation since Vatican II. While some Roman Catholics still celebrate a "Latin mass" (Lord's Supper), the majority have embraced the renewed worship experience of sung and vocal prayers. A renewed interest in the Word of God has come through the hearing of more of the Scriptures in the Liturgy of the Word. Bodily movement and gestures, though still somewhat hindered by North American self-consciousness, have been encouraged in dance and other forms of expression.

At the same time, some of the texts and contexts for prayer are a matter of ongoing concern. Though some texts have been changed to reflect the inclusion of all in the mystery of the redemption, the exclusive nature of many liturgical readings, prayers, symbols, and metaphors requires ongoing critique and prayerful study. The multicultural population of Roman Catholicism requires respect for the cultural conditioning of the prayer experience and imaging of God. The Eurocentric male worldview that conditions prayer texts is too limited for a universal paschal mystery that touches everyone in some way.

A concern that requires further reflection is the increasing frequency of Sunday Communion services in absence of a priest. Due to the shortage of seminary-trained male clergy, Rome has decided that laity may lead the community in a service of the Word and also a Communion service. This denies the emphasis of Vatican II on the centrality of eucharistic liturgy as well as suggesting the Lord's Supper is the possession of ordained clergy.

The tradition of celebrating the oneness of the church calls for ongoing dialogue in which Christians look together at the meaning of belief in one Lord, one faith, and one baptism.

Shawn Madigan

144 • SALVATION ARMY

Salvation Army worship corresponds to its mission of saving sinners and meeting human need. It consists mainly of singing, testimonies, and calls to holy living.

The Salvation Army, founded in London in 1865 by William and Catherine Booth, is an international, evangelical part of the universal Christian church. Its mission is to preach the gospel of Jesus Christ and meet human need in his name without discrimination. Salvation Army officers (ordained leaders) and soldiers (lay members) operate corps community centers, schools, hospitals, shelters, feeding sites, and other programs in ninety-six countries around the world.

—————— Two-Front War ——————

From its beginning, the Salvation Army has been thoroughly evangelical. Its founder, William Booth, was a revivalist who served in the ministry of Wesleyan and New Connexion Methodism from 1849 to 1861, and conducted an independent ministry from 1861 to 1865. As an evangelist, Booth preached convincingly on the themes of personal conversion and sanctification. Using almost any means available—

The Three Fishes. The figure of the three fishes is a Trinitarian symbol found in many European churches. The fish is a very ancient symbol of the Savior since the Greek word for fish (ΙΧΘΥΣ, ICHTHUS) is composed of five letters that when used as an acronym means ''Jesus Christ, Son of God, Savior.'' The three fishes are based on John 3:16, which teaches that the three persons have part in our salvation.

open-air preaching, tambourines, brass instruments—to attract attention to his gospel message, Booth soon had a following of loyal supporters.

From the early open-air meetings, Salvation Army worship moved inside to disused pubs, dance halls, theatres, even a tent on a Quaker burial ground. The meetings were lively. Army musicians took secular tunes from pubs and dance halls and gave them unmistakably evangelistic words. For instance, ''Here's to good old whiskey, drink it down'' became ''Storm the forts of darkness, bring them down.'' Converts testified enthusiastically to the change wrought in their lives by salvation. Preaching by both men and women Salvationists was fiery and always aimed at the individual's need for salvation in Christ.

In an 1889 article, ''Salvation for Both Worlds,'' Booth expanded his message to include the social dimensions of salvation. Redemption meant not only individual, personal, and spiritual salvation, but corporate, social, and physical salvation as well. He and his followers believed that preaching had to be complemented by caring for the physical needs of the poor to whom they preached. Booth's book, *In Darkest England and the Way Out* (1890) became the textbook for an all-out, aggressive two-front war for the souls of people and for a rightly ordered society. Today, Salvationists are still fighting "The Great Salvation War" on those two fronts.

Worship and Theology

Salvation Army worship emphasizes spontaneity, personal experience, and congregational participation in worship. A typical worship service might include congregational singing with brass band accompaniment, spontaneous testimonies from members of the congregation, and an invitation for individuals to respond publicly to the biblical call to holy living.

In theology, The Salvation Army is Wesleyan. In philosophy it is practical. An Army slogan, "Heart to God, Hand to Man," explains the commitment of salvation soldiers around the world to preach, teach, counsel, shelter, feed, clothe, and befriend their brothers and sisters of all races, colors, creeds, and ages.

"We are a salvation people," William Booth wrote in 1879. "This is our specialty, getting saved, and then getting somebody else saved, and then getting saved ourselves more and more, until full salvation on earth makes the heaven within, which is finally perfected by the full salvation on the other side of the river." More than one hundred years later, the heart of all Salvation Army worship and work is still the preaching and personal experience of salvation for all people and sanctification from all sin.

Lesa Salyer

145 • SOUTHERN BAPTIST CONVENTION CHURCHES

The traditional hallmarks of Baptist worship have been the centrality of preaching, fervent singing, and extemporaneous prayer. Worship renewal in the Southern Baptist Convention is moving in divergent directions. Those influenced by the more formal British tradition seek renewal along the lines of the ecumenical consensus. Those more influenced by the revivalist tradition draw on the praise-and-worship style and the church growth movement.

Because of its congregational polity and the wide diversity in the social status of its membership, Southern Baptist worship today takes place in a wide variety of styles. As one Baptist pastor put it, "Some burn incense, others bay at the moon."

However most Baptist churches contain architectural clues that mark common characteristics in worship. The central pulpit predominates; Baptist worship has been characterized by the centrality of preaching. A prominent baptistry built into the wall behind the pulpit just above where the altar stands in many other communions is used in Baptists' most distinctive worship rite—believer's baptism by immersion. The placement of the Communion Table is in front of and below the pulpit. A prominent choir loft behind the pulpit and in front of the baptistry is a sign of the importance of music. The pews have no kneeling benches indicating that worship is more horizontal (*with* other believers) than vertical (a private worship *of* God). A scarcity, if not absence, of symbol in reaction against the heavy use of symbolism by Catholics and Anglicans is evidence that the ear is the most important organ in Baptist worship (the sanctuary is an *audi*torium).

Baptist worship began in the Puritan movement in England during the seventeenth century that sought to reform the Anglican *Book of Common Prayer* according to the "pure" Word of God. The earliest Baptist worship was held in homes and consisted of prayers, singing, and multiple sermons (by minister and lay people). There was no worship book. Worship was free, led by the Spirit. As Baptist worship developed its own standard form, these distinctives were maintained: the use of spontaneous and extemporaneous prayer (as opposed to set prayers), the centrality of preaching (as opposed to short homilies), and fervent hymn singing.

Charleston and Shady Creek

The Charleston and Shady Creek influences are the key influences shaping Southern Baptist worship. The Charleston tradition, closely tied to Baptists' British roots, had a set order of worship. The preachers, usually highly educated, sought to combine learning and piety. Services combined orderliness and stateliness with evangelical warmth. The primary thrust of worship was vertical—toward God.

The Sandy Creek tradition began in the revival fires of the eighteenth-century American frontier.

Informality, fiery preaching, spontaneous amens and shouts, gospel music, extemporaneous prayers, and personal testimonies marked revivalistic worship. It was more emotional than intellectual. Its thrust was more horizontal—toward a communal experience—than vertical. Its focus was more subjective than objective, stressing the faith and feeling of the worshiper more than God's nature and activity. The main goal of worship was the conversion and transformation of the worshiper.

Southern Baptist worship today bears the influence of both traditions. Charleston influence can be seen in the set order of worship, formality and dignity, hymns focusing on God, and sermons characterized by learning and piety, head and heart. Sandy Creek influence manifests itself in gospel hymns and songs focusing on the spiritual state of the worshiper, extemporaneous prayers, folksy informality, and fiery evangelistic sermons that leave ample room, even if carefully prepared, for spontaneous improvisation prompted by the Holy Spirit.

A typical (if there is such a thing) Southern Baptist worship service in the mid/late twentieth century would look like this:

Prelude
Call to Worship (choral or spoken)
Hymn of Praise
Invocation
Welcome and Announcements
Scripture
Pastoral Prayer
Offering
Anthem or Solo (instrumental or vocal)
Sermon
Hymn of Invitation
Presentation of "Decisions"
Benediction
Postlude

—— Contrasting Renewal Movements ——

The last ten years have seen two major developments in Southern Baptist worship. The first movement, found mostly in Charleston-tradition churches, has begun to draw upon the worship tradition of the larger ecumenical church. The congregations in this movement celebrate the major seasons of the Christian year (Advent, Lent, Easter, Pentecost). They make considerable use of symbols and other visual enhancements in worship such as banner art and sacred dance, celebrate Communion more often, and often include two Scripture readings. While the sermon is still central in these congregations, other features of worship take on an inherent importance rather than being simply "preliminaries" ancillary to the sermon.

The second movement is found mostly in conservative churches of the Sandy Creek tradition. It has been influenced by televised religion, the praise-and-worship movement, and the church growth movement. Worship is comprised of the song service, which includes the singing of many choruses and gospel songs as well as solo performances, and the preaching service, which includes the sermon and the invitation. Overhead projectors and other visual media are used to project song texts and sermon outlines. Hymn books are little used; set liturgy is nonexistent. The worship is performance and entertainment oriented, the solo and sermon being the main attractions. This movement seeks to make worship "user-friendly"—accessible and enjoyable to anyone who comes regardless of religious background. Denominational distinctiveness is minimized.

Both movements are considered "renewal" movements by their practitioners. Both are a response to a changing American religious culture where denominational lines are being blurred by social mobility. Both are trying to breathe new life into Baptist forms, some of which are becoming as ritualized as the Anglican worship that Baptists first sought to reform.

The ecumenically influenced movement responds by becoming ecumenical or multidenominational. It also entails a recovery of the historic roots of Christian worship in the New Testament and early church period. Its weakness is a tendency toward aestheticism and theological obscurantism.

The praise and evangelism movement responds by becoming post-, non-, or anti-denominational. It is fueled by intense desire to reach the unchurched and those disaffected by mainstream religion. Its adherents try to eliminate the "strangeness" of liturgy that becomes a barrier to the visitor and seeker. Its weaknesses are a proneness to reduce worship to entertainment and accommodate worship to the whims of American consumer culture. Worship then becomes a blend of Christianity, patriotism, self-help psychology, and self-help and feel-good religion.

Possibilities for furthering worship renewal in Southern Baptist congregations include the following:

- Increasing emphasis on the Table.
- Greater attention to baptism. As primary as believer's baptism by immersion is to Baptists, it is woefully neglected as a central dramatic act of worship. There are few baptism hymns and little baptismal theology.
- Greater use of Scripture; often one short reading connected to the sermon is all worshipers hear.
- Creative interaction with worship renewal going on in other denominations.
- A refocusing on God as the first audience of worship and worship as a dialogue with and offering to God.
- Continued exploration of the ever-important dialectic in worship between liturgy and liberty, order and ardor, set form and spiritual freedom.

H. Stephen Shoemaker

146 ✦ UNITED CHURCH OF CHRIST

The United Church of Christ is the union of four historic Congregational churches. It seeks to make Christ central in Word and sacrament, and is committed to a participatory worship, the use of inclusive language, and fostering a prophetic ministry. The 1986 Book of Worship *reflects a strong influence from the liturgical and inclusive movement. Some local churches have been influenced by charismatic worship as well.*

Worship in a "united and a uniting church" properly reflects the rich traditions of the four major denominational streams of the United Church of Christ (Congregational, Christian, Evangelical, and Reformed) and of the many ethnic communities within its membership. These traditions hold in common the Reformation understanding of the centrality of Jesus Christ in God's redemptive action in history. They also affirm the integral relationship between faithful congregational worship and prophetic ethical witness in society. Guided by the Holy Spirit, the entirety of the church's life and every individual Christian's life is worship offered to God.

Reformed and Always Reforming

In recent years, the United Church of Christ has sought to recover, in relation to congregational worship specifically, the Reformation conviction that "the only church truly reformed is the church always reforming." This has led the denomination to reexamine its rich worship history, and *not* to enshrine developments in the last century as more normative than roots that penetrate through the sixteenth-century Reformation to the patristic era and the primitive church of the New Testament.

This liturgical reformation is characterized by a willingness to encourage worship that is truly more participatory and socially prophetic. This includes increased congregational sharing in leadership, the recovery of the singing of the Psalms, a more full reading of the Scriptures (through the Common Lectionary), the use of the sign of peace, encouragement of movement, gestures, and the arts that show regard for our sensate nature, and the restoration of more frequent Holy Communion.

The reform of United Church worship is also shaped by a growing sensitivity to the power of language to hurt or heal. Consequently, great care is given to avoid words that exclude or judge others on the basis of gender, race, class, or some disability. For example, although it is acknowledged that in the past "man" was often used as a "generic" term inclusive of the human race, this usage is now seen as unjust. It leaves women, in their dignity as persons also made in the image of God, "out of sight and out of mind" in ways that contribute to their exploitation. In a similar way, the worship resources of the denomination seek to move beyond the exclusive use of male metaphors for God by recovering the biblical texts in which the feminine character of God is affirmed. In one instance this is expressed in a prayer of invocation by the phrase, "Gracious God, . . . you have brought us forth from the womb of your being and breathed into us the breath of life" (see Deut. 32:18, Hebrew text).

Word and Sacrament

Although no one order of service is mandated in the United Church of Christ, there is a growing appreciation of the historic pattern of Entrance, Word, Table, and Dismissal. The denomination is becoming more aware that in each of its historic streams the "ideal" set forth by the founding reformers was that full worship on the Lord's Day should include both Word and sacrament. There is also a growing consciousness that the Lord's Supper, in too many of our celebrations, was exclusively centered in Maundy Thursday and Good Friday, and had become a "death" meal cut off from the reality of Christ's resurrection.

The reclaiming of the Emmaus Road testimony to the sacrament has begun to transform the meal into a solemn but joyful feast that is as much an anticipation of the "coming again" of the Risen One as it is a proclamation of Christ's death. The orders for Holy Communion, with two full musical settings, seek to express this unitive wholeness of the salvation story. This has contributed to a shift from a quarterly celebration of Holy Communion to an almost universal minimum of monthly Holy Communion. In some local churches the weekly "ideal" is now a reality, at least in an early or alternate service.

The *Book of Worship*

The question of "forms" for use in worship has also been reexamined. The nineteenth-century aversion to most fixed forms in the Congregational and Christian parts of our heritage is well known. Current scholarship, however, shows conclusively the "*free* church does not translate simplistically into a church free *from* all forms. Rather, it denotes a church that includes within the parameters of its freedom the uninhibited liberty to use whatever forms prove to be consistent with its understanding and practice of the gospel" (*Book of Worship* [New York: United Church of Christ Office for Church Life and Leadership, 1986], 12).

This understanding of the balance between freedom and order is reflected in the action of the general synod to provide for a *Book of Worship* that is a resource and guide. Published in 1986, its only authority is its usefulness as local churches seek the continual reformation of their worship in response to the Scriptures and under the guidance of the Holy Spirit.

The production of the *Book of Worship* was the responsibility of the Office for Church Life and Leadership, which carries responsibility for most worship concerns. The process involved broad consultation with the entire denomination and with ecumenical partners, and disclosed a great interest in far more than orders for Sunday worship. Sections were added on the liturgical year, the use of the lectionary, services of anointing for healing, and

full orders for Holy Week, including footwashing, Tenebrae, and the Great Vigil of Easter. Orders for individual or corporate reconciliation, times of farewell when pastors or church members relocate, rites for celebrating the adoption of children, and a penitential order for the acknowledgement of the dissolution of a marriage were included in the final publication.

A unique mark of worship in the United Church of Christ is that each local church is a steward of its own liturgical life and cannot be compelled to conform to any one standard. At the same time, in this freedom, there is, in fact, not only rich diversity but a bond of unity expressed in forms common to all. This is apparent in the use of the *Book of Worship,* in the intense interest of the denomination in a new hymnal scheduled for publication by the United Church Board for Homeland Ministries in 1995, and in the increasing care given by their seven seminaries to liturgical theology and practice.

Thomas E. Dipko

147 • UNITED METHODIST CHURCHES

Worship in the United Methodist Church draws from both the Catholic and Protestant heritage. The denomination contains both strong liturgical and charismatic movements. Worship today is characterized by emphasis on the Christian year, frequent Communion, use of the arts, and commitment to inclusive language and women in liturgical leadership.

The United Methodist Church has a complex heritage that has predisposed it toward an eclectic style of worship and given it an openness to influences from many Christian traditions and contemporary worship renewal movements. The denomination was formed in 1968 by the union of the Methodist Church with the much smaller Evangelical United Brethren Church, the latter having been formed in 1946 by the union of the Evangelical Church and the United Brethren in Christ.

Formative Influences on Worship

The Methodist Church arose from a movement within the Church of England led by a priest named John Wesley (1703–1791). When this movement took root in America and organized itself as the Methodist Episcopal Church in 1784, Wesley sent an adaptation of the Anglican *Book of Common Prayer* that he entitled *Sunday Service of the Methodists in North America.* In a letter accompanying this service book he wrote, "I also advise the elders to administer the supper of the Lord on every Lord's day" (*John Wesley's Sunday Service of the Methodists in North America,* with intro. by James F. White [Nashville: United Methodist Publishing House and United Methodist Board of Higher Education, 1984], ii)—this at a time when quarterly Communion was the norm in Anglican parishes. On the other hand, Wesley frequently led informal services characterized by hymn singing and extemporaneous prayer and testimonies. In the letter with his *Sunday Service* he also wrote that the American Methodists "are now at full liberty, simply to follow the scriptures and the primitive church. And we judge it best that they should stand fast in that liberty, wherewith God has so strangely made them free" (Ibid., iii).

In 1792 the American Methodists, led by Francis Asbury (1745–1816), officially abandoned Wesley's *Sunday Service* as the norm for weekly worship, substituting a simple set of directions for a Service of the Word that reflected the Puritan and free-church worship style of the American frontier. The texts in the *Sunday Service* were, however, retained with adaptations for the Service of the Table, baptism, matrimony, the burial of the dead, and ordinations. The Lord's Supper became an occasional service, sometimes monthly and sometimes quarterly. This reduction in frequency was due to a severe shortage of ordained elders that caused most services to be conducted by lay preachers, the influence of Puritan worship patterns prevailing in America, and the uncongeniality of the printed text used for the Service of the Table to frontier worship.

At about the same time movements similar to Methodism were arising among German Americans. The Evangelical Church was formed under the leadership of a Lutheran lay preacher named Jacob Albright (1759–1808). The United Brethren in Christ organized under the leadership of a Reformed pastor named William Philip Otterbein (1726–1813) and a Mennonite preacher named Martin Boehm (1725–1812). These denominations adapted their inherited traditions to the Puritan and free-church worship styles of the American frontier.

The specific historical context of the traditions represented by the United Methodist Church is highly significant, for in it one can see the basis of the varied influences on worship in the denomination today. Each tradition arose as a reformation within Protestantism in the eighteenth century rather than as part of the sixteenth-century Protestant Reformation. They give United Methodists roots in all four major branches of the sixteenth-century Protestant Reformation—Anglican, Lutheran, Reformed, and Anabaptist/Mennonite. All were shaped in their formative years by Puritan and free-church traditions that had grown up between the sixteenth and eighteenth centuries, while at the same time inheriting Wesley's desire to follow the early church and broader catholic traditions.

In the early nineteenth century the churches that now form the United Methodist Church generally worshiped in a frontier style; but during the century that followed they increasingly worshiped in church buildings, with organs and choirs, and with orders of worship that included acts such as anthems, recitation of the Apostles' Creed, and responsive readings.

From the 1920s through the middle years of the twentieth century pulpit-centered auditoriums designed for preaching evangelism gave way to altar-centered nave-and-chancel "sanctuaries" designed for the worship of a God who was "high and lifted up"; and services increasingly became free adaptations of Episcopal Morning Prayer and Sermon—a relatively formal service of praise and prayer followed by announcements and offering and concluding with the sermon (framed by hymns).

Ecumenical Renewal

Since the union of 1968 the United Methodist Church has moved dramatically in the direction of the ecumenical worship renewal. Its Commission on Worship (after 1972 the Section on Worship of its General Board of Discipleship) conducted twenty years of study and development that led to the adoption of *The United Methodist Hymnal: Book of United Methodist Worship* in 1989. The Sunday services in the hymnal follow the ecumenical pattern of Entrance, Word, Table, and Dismissal. The full eucharistic pattern of Word and Table is treated as normative, but provision is made for the great majority of congregations that do not celebrate the Lord's Supper every Lord's Day. Within this pattern, there is a wide choice of old and new prayer texts and hymns, with encouragements given for extemporaneous and spontaneous praise and prayer. The new texts for the Lord's Supper are far more joyous than the old ones and celebrate all God's mighty acts in Christ rather than Christ's death alone. The services of daily prayer, baptism, marriage, death and resurrection likewise follow ecumenical worship patterns and understandings.

Whereas lectionaries were rarely used a generation ago, now the ecumenical Common Lectionary is officially endorsed and is used at least some of the time in the majority of congregations.

Also in the last generation there has been increasing affirmation of the diversity within the denomination. Patterns representing every period of the denomination's history survive and often flourish. A growing number of congregations celebrate the Lord's Supper weekly, though usually not at the main Sunday service. There is both a strong liturgical movement and a strong charismatic renewal movement. Such practices as spontaneous thanksgivings and intercessions, clapping, hand-raising, the exchange of the peace, chanting, drama, sacred dance, and use of visual arts are found in many congregations. African-American, Asian-American, Native American, and Hispanic worship traditions are encouraged. Sensitivity to women's concerns is growing under the leadership of an increasing number of female pastors. All this is affirmed and facilitated by the new hymnal and also by a supplemental book of worship for planners and leaders of worship published in 1992.

As the denomination looks to the future, there is widespread openness to the leading of the Spirit. An increasingly large proportion of pastors have studied and been trained in worship in seminary. Additional resources and training opportunities are offered each year. Joy increasingly pervades worship services, reflecting a firm trust in the living God through the risen Christ in the power of the Holy Spirit.

Hoyt L. Hickman

148 ✦ VINEYARD

The trademark of Vineyard worship is contemporary praise. Recently a great diversity of style is being embraced within the movement.

——— Theology of Worship ———

Vineyard worship is based on the belief and affirmation that God has commanded us to worship

The Cross and the Triangle. Church embroidery is characterized by certain combinations of the equilateral Triangle and the cross. This teaches that salvation is the work of the Son prompted by the Father's love, and applied by the Holy Spirit. Variations of this combination of cross and Triangle are found on embroidered altar frontals, pulpit and lectern hangings, and on book markers.

(Exod. 23:24, 25; Ps. 96:8-9; Matt. 4:8-10). What all of us struggle with is, How can we know the God we worship; why has God commanded worship; and what specifically is he commanding? We know from Scripture that God takes no delight in empty ritual, i.e., going through the motions of something with our heart detached (Isa. 29:13). We believe that just as we long for relationship with God, he longs for relationship with us. That relationship is meant to be honest, intimate, and full of life.

We believe this relationship is one of the main reasons God has commanded us to worship. As we acknowledge God in worship and realize who we are, it brings us to a place of recognizing our need of relationship with him. It fuels the desire for relationship because we all long for loving relationships, and through worship we come to know God's loving character.

Another reason God has commanded worship is because he is God. Period. Worship is not about us. Pure worship is a completely selfless act, focused on the one receiving the worship, not on the one giving it. Bowing down, kneeling, and humbling ourselves are very appropriate responses before God.

As we step through the door of selfless worship into the presence of God an amazing thing happens. God is love, so as we experience who God is, we encounter the pleasure of worship. In fact, worship becomes paradoxically the most "selfish" act because God is so satisfying. God created us as worshipers, with a capacity and a desire to worship. He knows he is the only one who can satisfy his worshipers, so it is the love of God for us that motivates his command for us to worship.

If worship is our destiny in eternity, we realize we will never fully exhaust its potential for relationship and knowing God, and we understand that a large part of worship will remain a mystery in this life.

What, then, is worship? There are a number of word pictures that can partly describe worship. Bowing, singing, kneeling, standing in awe, thanksgiving, music, silence, intimacy, reverence, service, and on and on. Yet even these word pictures cannot adequately express it, for our language cannot grasp it. We believe that worship can be found in all of these things. We believe that our worship is acceptable or in vain, based on how we live our entire life. Yet we recognize from Scripture (Exod. 20: 3-5; Matt. 2:11; Rev. 11:16-17) that worship is a specific, willing act of acknowledging who God is and submitting to him out of love.

——— The Shape of Vineyard Worship ———

The Vineyard usually gathers in a variety of public settings, including schools and community centers. The Langley Vineyard, on which the following description is based, gathers in a modified furniture warehouse. Inside, it is full of casually dressed people, lots of babies and young children (the primary age group is baby boomer and younger).

One of the things you notice as you come in is the low stage, filled with contemporary instruments, including a full drum set, synthesizers, electric piano, electric guitar, bass guitar, acoustic guitar, a number of vocal mikes, and some other percussion instruments.

The worship leader, dressed in a casual shirt and jeans, playing a guitar, welcomes everyone and begins the meeting with an upbeat song of praise. Newer people who have not yet learned songs are able to follow along by means of a songsheet (some Vineyards use overheads/slide projectors) that is up-dated every three months with new songs that have just been written. Many of the songs that they sing are written by the worship leader and others from the Vineyard. These new songs are continually being written out of what God is emphasizing to them through the teaching and their growth in areas of ministry, such as loving the poor, praying for the sick, and knowing the Father's love.

Usually, about forty minutes is given to gathered expression of worship, which is a flow of a number of songs with only a couple of minimal comments made by the leader. The length of the entire service is approximately two hours.

The musical style is contemporary, perhaps best described as pop rock or soft rock, but this varies slightly from Vineyard to Vineyard depending on the style of the worship leader and musicians. Vineyard worshipers believe strongly that music in the church should be comparable to the culture in which they live, in both quality and style. As a result, standards in both heart and skill are high and musicians work hard, rehearsing at least once a week. The worship pastor is often the second pastoral staff person hired.

The contents of songs are primarily honest, simple lyrics about the worshipers' relationship with God. Virtually all of them are directed to God. Occasionally they include a hymn as a way of joining with the historic church in expressing their worship, though the arrangement will be contemporary.

During the worship time people are free to sit, stand, kneel, and raise hands as they have desire and are moved by the Spirit to do so. Vineyards generally do not prescribe what people are to do, but leave them free to act out of their hearts. Some people will express their worship through dance, though only those who have been released by the leadership and are more mature in their gift may dance up front. Not all the dance is spontaneous; sometimes a number of dancers will prepare a choreographed dance for a specific song that will be included in the worship time.

As the worship time comes to a close, prayer both for the sick and for people who have responded to any words that have been given is offered. These words are like a "word of knowledge" (1 Cor. 12:8, KJV) that are given by either the teacher, home-group pastor, or lay leader, and often they describe a specific situation or physical condition to which God wants to bring healing.

While these people are being prayed for, the children are dismissed (they are present for the time of worship expression), and the people who are not involved in the prayer ministry are released to a fifteen-minute coffee break that encourages relationship and interaction. After the break there is fifty to sixty minutes of teaching time, which is not considered worship, although music and worship are employed to close the meeting or to help facilitate prayer ministry that is going on. Many times, healing will occur spontaneously without prayer ministry.

The overall style of a Vineyard meeting—an extended time of worship, teaching, and ministry—has not changed much since the inception. The worship expression has gone through some changes. The beginning of the movement was marked by intimate, slow, gentle songs of worship. Today that is still present, but there are more upbeat songs as well, plus some more complex songs. At this point, there is still little "special music" or performance music in the Vineyard; virtually all songs are participatory worship songs.

——————— Looking Ahead ———————

As the Vineyard looks ahead at more growth, most likely there will be more variety in musical expression of worship. At the same time, there is a sense of desiring the Vineyard's simple roots again, honest songs that help bring us face-to-face with God.

One other major trend in the Vineyard is an emphasis on evangelistic worship—taking the music outside of the church into the parks, streets, clubs, and other public places. Out of this movement, new songs and musicians are being released with a greater focus on evangelism. The Langley Vineyard is planting a country music church that will have an evangelism focus towards the "country music culture" that surrounds it.

One of the best ways to keep up to date with Vineyard worship is subscribing to the Worship Resource Center. Every three months, Vineyard Music produces a "live" worship tape/CD that consists of some of the new songs being written by the leaders and writers of the Vineyard. Along with the tape/CD and songbook comes a newsletter called _Worship Update_ with articles written by various Vineyard worship leaders among others. The Vineyard movement also hosts special worship seminars and events

in various locations that are an expression of where God is leading its members in worship.

Brian Doerksen

149 • WESLEYAN CHURCHES

Worship in the Wesleyan Church typifies that of the American holiness movement—relatively informal, centered on the sermon, and concerned with the holiness of the believer. One current renewal movement seeks to make worship a more praise-filled celebration, while another concentrates on recovering reverence through historic Christian liturgy.

True religion does not consist in any ritual observances, such as forms or ceremonies, even of the most excellent kind, be they ever so decent and significant, ever so expressive of inward things. The religion of Christ rises infinitely higher and lies infinitely deeper than all these. Let no man conceive that rites and ceremonies have an intrinsic worth, or that true worship cannot subsist without them. (_Discipline of the Wesleyan Church_ [Marion, Indiana: The Wesleyan Publishing House, 1968], 52)

This statement in the first _Discipline of the Wesleyan Church,_ adopted at its initial general conference in 1968, remains both a "special direction" of the denomination and a key to understanding its worship patterns.

——————— Plain Worship ———————

The Wesleyan Church was created by the merger of the Wesleyan Methodist Church and the Pilgrim Holiness Church, both of which were firmly rooted in the nineteenth-century holiness revival in America. As the denominational name indicates, the ties to John Wesley are strong.

The early shape of Wesleyan worship, then, was Methodist—not the traditional form Wesley himself preferred, but the modified variety, shaped by the American frontier. An early Wesleyan Methodist directive, "On Public Worship" (1849), speaks plainly about plain worship:

To establish uniformity among the churches in public worship on the Lord's Day, it is recommended that the following order be observed. Let the morning and afternoon service consist of, 1. Singing; 2. Prayer; 3. Reading the Scriptures; 4. Singing; 5. Preaching; 6. Singing; 7. Prayer; 8. Benediction. Let the evening service be the same, only omitting the reading of the Scriptures; or let there be a prayer meeting. Parts of this order may be omitted as particular times and circumstances may require.

We recommend the churches to dispense with the instrumental music. (*Discipline of the Wesleyan Church* [New York: The Wesleyan Methodist Connection, 1849], 65–66)

That basic order, or one similar to it, would be recognizable in a majority of Wesleyan churches a century and a half later—except that the afternoon service is now just a historical footnote and that instrumental music has long been universally accepted in the church.

Freedom Over Form

Wesleyan worship is still oriented more toward freedom than form, more toward simplicity than elaboration, more toward pulpit (or even pew) than Table. If James White is right in placing Methodism in the center of a worship continuum that stretches from order on one end to spontaneity on the other, the Wesleyan Church would join its holiness counterparts on the "free" side, though considerably short of Old-Style Quakers and Pentecostals (James White, *Protestant Worship: Traditions in Transition* [Louisville: Westminster/John Knox Press, 1989], 23).

Unlike some denominations, it is difficult to characterize the worship of a typical Wesleyan church. In most, a bulletin outlines an order of worship, but with few liturgical components. Gospel songs mix with Charles Wesley's hymns in the morning worship services, occasional "amens" punctuate the sermon (though less frequently than in the past), and evangelistic sermons lead to altar calls as seekers "pray through" at the front of the sanctuary. Communion is offered quarterly, baptism less often.

The Wesleyan version of the Christian year is simple, consisting of Christmas, Easter, and a collection of cultural holidays, like Mother's Day and Independence Day, that have been incorporated into the tradition. Revival meetings are scheduled for spring and fall, though the two-week meeting that was customary for the grandparents of today's worshipers was abbreviated to a ten-day meeting in their parents' generation and has since become a three- to five-day event in the modern church. Camp meeting is still a summer staple, but with fewer campers and more evening commuters. Often it is held in tandem with a church conference. Variations abound, but

this profile is generally accurate. In fact, it is a passable profile for the holiness movement as a whole.

Since in Scripture, from Isaiah 6 to the hymns of Revelation, the worship of God is inextricably linked to the holiness of God, it might be supposed that holiness churches would major on worship and set the pace for worship renewal in the Christian community. In reality, the emphasis in holiness circles has fallen more on the holiness God imparts to his people than on his own intrinsic holiness. "Be holy . . ." is stressed more than the rest of the verse, ". . . because I, the LORD your God, am holy" (Lev. 19:2; cf. 1 Pet. 1:16).

Simply put, worship in holiness churches has received less attention than the other marks of the church—evangelism, discipleship, fellowship, and service.

Celebration vs. Reverence

Like many sermon-focused traditions, Wesleyans have tended to regard the rest of the service as introductory and preparatory ("the preliminaries"). Since the 1970s, however, interest in the nature and purpose of worship has increased, judging from such indicators as worship-related articles in denominational publications, seminars at district and denominational gatherings, and worship attendance. Average attendance at Sunday morning worship surpassed Sunday school attendance for the first time in memory in 1980, a statistical trend that has continued. Perhaps the most significant renewal indicator, and certainly the most practical, is the frequency with which "worship leader" has begun appearing in pastoral staff job descriptions.

Renewal is apparent on two divergent fronts—one a trend toward praise and more freedom, the other an appreciation of liturgy and more form.

Praise-and-worship music is popular especially among younger congregations and newly planted churches, many of which are populated with first-generation Wesleyans. Overhead projectors are replacing hymnals for some, and clapping is increasingly accepted. Wesleyans do not practice glossolalia (tongues-speaking), but to many congregations worship renewal means a more charismatic style—lifted hands, contemporary choruses, an expanded role for music in the service, greater reliance on taped accompaniments. The emphasis is on *celebration*.

For others, worship renewal means a recovery of *reverence*. Wesleyans will never be "high church," but some congregations are adopting liturgical elements like the creed (two are printed at the front of the 1976 hymnal), choral responses, multiple Scripture lessons, and a greater participation in the Christian year. Lectionary use is not widespread, but some Wesleyan pastors follow it. Fixed prayers are still uncommon except for the sacraments, weddings, and the rituals of membership, ordination, and installation of leaders. Litanies appear on special occasions. It is a limited liturgy to be sure, but a journey of discovery for the participants.

The future degree and direction of change is difficult to predict, but the dialogue has begun. Wesleyans are thinking and talking about worship. Growth has brought a substantial number of new Wesleyans into the fold, and many bring with them worship patterns and preferences from previous denominations. The church is producing more seminarians than ever before, and at least one denominational college offers a course in Christian worship that focuses on liturgics and is required of all ministry candidates.

Both renewal movements will likely continue to act as catalysts for change. A denomination that has always defined itself doctrinally rather than liturgically will have room within its walls for contrasting—or complementary—worship styles.

Bob Black

150 • WISCONSIN EVANGELICAL LUTHERAN SYNOD

Throughout its history, the Wisconsin Evangelical Lutheran Synod has been slow to make changes in worship. Most of the church has resisted the liturgical, charismatic, and inclusive trends of the twentieth century. However, there is a new desire among some to be open to the new ways of worship.

The Wisconsin Evangelical Lutheran Synod (WELS), numbering some 400,000 members, has congregations in every state of the U.S. and several provinces of Canada. The church body conducts foreign mission work and supports its own worker-training system. Local congregations carry out parochial education on both the elementary and secondary level. The synod requires all its pastors to subscribe without reservation to the doctrines of the inspired Scriptures and to the Lutheran Confessions of the sixteenth century.

——— Pietistic and Confessional ———

Founded in 1850, the Wisconsin Synod has its roots in the pietistic mission societies of nineteenth-century Germany. During its first quarter century, however, the synod enthusiastically embraced the Lutheran orthodoxy championed in America by the Lutheran Church–Missouri Synod.

Although the Missouri Synod exerted a strong influence on its smaller sister in a variety of ways, WELS's attitudes toward worship continued to be influenced by the synod's pietistic roots for many years. Unlike Missouri, Wisconsin had no strong leader with the interest or desire to prepare and standardize a common liturgical rite. The synod did publish several German hymnals, but none contained an order of worship. Congregations continued to use the rites (in German or in translation) they had brought from their homeland. An English hymnal produced in 1920 included only a sampling of the Reformation chorales and a scant twenty pages of liturgical material.

While several synod leaders worked faithfully with Missouri's representatives in the production of *The Lutheran Hymnal* (1941), and while the book's confessional hymnody and the *Common Service* found quick acceptance in most congregations, there were voices still sounding in the 1950s against the new liturgy's "high church" forms. The increase in liturgical appreciation that might have accompanied the use of *The Lutheran Hymnal* was hindered as Wisconsin's pastors became convinced that the Missourians who were most interested in liturgical studies were also interested in fostering ecumenical discussions with Lutherans who were, from Wisconsin's point of view, decidedly nonconfessional.

Although the synod's colleges and preparatory schools placed a strong emphasis on church music of good quality, there was, even into the 1980s, little interest in liturgics, ecclesiastical art, or liturgical architecture. When the larger Lutheran church bodies produced new hymnals, the *Lutheran Book of Worship* (LBW) and *Lutheran Worship* (LW), neither WELS pastors nor congregations showed much enthusiasm.

——— Outreach and the New Hymnal ———

What did encourage an interest in worship renewal was a growing determination to attract and retain church members. Many argued that the Elizabethan language and the Germanic hymnody of *The*

Lutheran Hymnal diminished the church's appeal in contemporary society. The synod's 1983 delegate convention authorized the production of a new hymnal. By 1985 a project director, a music editor, and a twelve-member hymnal committee were in place and working. Final manuscripts for the new book were completed seven years later. The hymnal, published in 1993, appeared as *Christian Worship: A Lutheran Hymnal* (CW).

The synod's hymnal committee did not approach its task with the kind of pragmatism that initially had encouraged the project. *The Lutheran Hymnal*, in the committee's opinion, had been built on sound theological and liturgical presuppositions and deserved to set the standard for a new hymnal. While it was determined to contemporize language and incorporate new musical styles, the committee felt no desire to abandon the tradition of Lutheran liturgical worship. It hoped instead to build on the synod's experience with the "Common Service" and actually to encourage a stronger commitment to the liturgy, the church year, and the Supper. CW's liturgical section includes, besides a revision of the "Common Service," a new liturgical order, "Service of Word and Sacrament," a service of the Word, and new settings of Matins and Vespers. All were formed with a deep respect for the historic Christian forms.

With an eye toward encouraging more congregational participation, CW, in accordance Luther's teaching that "confession and absolution are nothing more than a reliving of one's baptism," CW attached the rite of Baptism to corporate confession in all the major services. The orders for Christian marriage and Christian funerals also involve the worshipers.

As the committee prepared the new book, it hoped to encourage a new understanding of the catholicity of the church's worship. Therefore, the book's hymn corpus includes a representation of hymns not only from sixteenth-century Germany and eighteenth- and nineteenth-century England, but also from the African-American heritage, the Southern harmony tradition, and the contemporary folk contributions. The translation of the Nicene Creed and of most of the liturgical canticles are those of the English Language Liturgical Consultation (ELLC). Settings of the canticles that appeared to be of enduring value were borrowed from other Lutheran worship books.

Given the liturgical history of the church body, the hymnal committee did not expect that the syn-od's willingness to accept new forms would be unlimited. A eucharistic prayer was considered but not included. The committee was impressed by the liturgical services of LBW and LW, but concluded that they were too sophisticated for the average WELS congregation. None of the hymnal's services encourage or even provide opportunities for the kiss of peace, lay readers, or processions.

Many of the synod's congregations received and used the new services and hymns with enthusiasm. The refrain/chant line settings of the Psalms (sixty psalms for worship appear in the book) became popular. A good number of pastors chose to chant the new Matins and Vesper services, both of which included the pastor's chant lines in the pew edition.

More than any other factor in recent history, *Christian Worship* is exerting a strong influence on the worship life of the Wisconsin Synod. However, the hymnal will have to overcome long-held fears of "Romanizing" and lingering suspicions that all changes in form signal changes in doctrine.

With its long history of confessionalism and its loyalty to the Scriptures, the WELS is not likely to move too far away from its present worship practices. However, more than a few of the synod's pastors, influenced by the times, contemplate worship from a pragmatic viewpoint. This is especially true of some who have become deeply committed to outreach. A feeling is spreading that the key to continued growth, both spiritual and numerical, is a renewed worship life that stands to be encouraged by the church's new hymnal.

James P. Tiefel

151 ✦ Women's Aglow Fellowship International

Aglow is an interdenominational ministry that touches over three-quarters of a million women each year in over 100 nations of the world. From the smaller monthly meetings (25 to 400 women) of the local fellowships to the larger annual conventions (2,000 to 10,000 women), praise and worship holds a prominent place in everything Aglow does.

Aglow believes in using all of the ways of praising and worshiping God that are set forth in both the Old and New Testaments: singing, shouting, prophesying, dancing, clapping, lifting hands, bowing, and kneeling.

Although Aglow has used the same general format

for worship in the last ten years, we have grown and matured as worshipers. From our formation twenty-five years ago to the present day, we still use psalms, hymns, spiritual songs, and songs of deliverance as part of our worship. In the last ten years we have also grown in our use of the arts such as mime, choreography, banners and flags, streamers, singing, and ballet. None of these are presented as a performance but rather as a means to stir and draw people closer to God in exaltation and as a celebration of worship.

Foremost and focal in the worship of Aglow is God's exhortation from Mark 12:32-33 to love the Lord our God with all our heart, all our mind, and all our strength. We believe this is best accomplished through "spirit to Spirit" worship of God, through an inner recognition of who God is and an outer overflow of ministry acts of service unto the God we worship.

We can also see a close parallel between the union of a bride and bridegroom and our spiritual and physical worship of God. In marriage bride and bridegroom bond and join both in the emotional as well as in the physical realm. The emotional bonding is at the core of the marriage relationship, this union stabilizing and strengthening the relationship. This emotional bonding also enhances the physical union.

So it is with worship; the more we bond and unite intimately in our soul and spirit, with our hearts touching God's heart, the more demonstrative we become in our physical response as our hearts rejoice, even to the point of singing and dancing before God as David did. Or we may find ourselves sitting quietly in his presence contemplating the wonder of our God in all of his majesty and glory!

There are times when the presence of God falls so strongly in Aglow worship that people find it hard to stand. Or we may just sit silently overwhelmed by God's love, listening to God's voice. Or as we come into God's presence we may experience fullness of joy, cleansing, healing, deliverance, release of burdens, anointing, intimacy, forgiveness, mercy, love for our neighbors, and unity in the body.

During our worship times, as we speak or sing words of adoration and affection to God, the love between us ignites a deep passion for more of his fullness. It is out of this type of heart-to-heart union with God that acts of service are then later offered to God, and these acts become the natural physical overflow of time spent in his presence.

We believe the moving of God's Spirit in Aglow's worship softens our hearts and draws us closer to Jesus—both to reveal him to us as well as helping us to truly know him (Heb. 3:6-14). The Holy Spirit reveals the triune God in a personal way rather than in a general or legalistic manner.

Oftentimes we use banners that display the different names and meanings of the names of Jesus (Lamb of God, Lion of Judah) as well as the facets of Christ's nature (the power of his might, his love for us, his provision, his healing power). Banners are often a special part of our biennial International Conferences, where over one hundred nations are represented. The attendees come from many different races, cultures, and denominations, and we have seen the Holy Spirit often break down the walls of division and prejudice by bringing us into unity through our fellowship around the common denominator of Jesus. Even though not everyone can understand English, we have found that worship is a language of the Spirit whereby our spirits touch God's Spirit and we are not limited by human language.

The song "Meet Me at the Cross" has been used widely throughout Aglow around the world to pull down strongholds of racism, prejudice, and division in the body of Christ. The words are:

> **Chorus**
> Meet me at the cross
>   where it all began.
> Let us gather there
>   sword to sword, hand in hand.
> Meet me where his blood
>   made us family, one race,
>   holy, through his grace.
>
> **Verses**
> Listen, hear the battle cry;
> The unseen war is raging on
>   beside us always.
> Listen, for the enemy is
>   whispering his lies
>   and has us fight each other.
>
> Listen, hear the trumpet call
>   the Spirit cries for nations
>   to rise up and follow.
> Let us put on holy armor
>   and gather where the
>   warrior King is waiting for us.

My brother, there is not much time
and the streets are filled with blood
where we have fought each other.
My sister, put your hand in mine
and let us fight together
for the Kingdom of the Father.

(From *The Warfare Musical,* copyright 1991, available through Ruth Collingridge, Sword-to-Sword Music, SpiritSong Celebration, 5114 Picnic Point Road, Edmonds, WA 98020).

Lorene Carlson and Ruth Collingridge

152 • ALTERNATIVE WORSHIP IN THE LITURGICAL TRADITIONS

St. Gregory Nyssen Episcopal Church draws from the rich worship tradition of the entire church, particularly the Eastern tradition and from various cultures around the world. In addition to Word and sacrament, this worship emphasizes community, space, movement, silence and meditation, and social concern.

Newcomers to St. Gregory Nyssen Episcopal Church in San Francisco, California (founded 1978), are often surprised to find diverse traditional sources supporting the worship of this contemporary American parish. The space seems exotically arranged with folk art from East and West; the congregation shares in much music, dance, and prayer from churches long divided. Yet this rich mixture feels authentic and joyous and welcomes each worshiper's progress in knowing and loving God. That progress was the passionate concern of Gregory Nyssen (Gregory of Nyssa), a fourth-century Greek bishop who wrote, "The one thing truly worthwhile is becoming God's friend." Without implementing Gregory's liturgical ideas (he wrote none down) or reconstructing the worship he knew (he discouraged historicist piety), worship at St. Gregory's Church follows him in affirming the whole human experience of God as a boundless progress in friendship, rich with gifts for Christ's people to share.

The 1979 *Book of Common Prayer* embraces creative diversity, and we intend our work to serve all who find it useful, as Christians from several denominations tell us they have done. Our liturgical choices mirror our choice of Gregory for our patron. People from many places receive and celebrate God's word. And like the bishop of Nyssa, our chief early models are Eastern models, which underlie the longest and sturdiest traditions of vernacular congregational worship. They have figured in most historical Christian revivals, particularly Anglican reforms. They serve today's interest in participatory liturgy and the ecumenical hunger for a loving fellowship spanning ages and cultures.

Architecture. Early Syrian Christian synagogues and Byzantine churches inspire our layout, a rectangle of two equal squares. The western square holds seats in rows facing each other across an aisle ("choir seating") and are used for the service of the Word. The aisle (*solea*) runs up to a platform (*bema*) at the end wall, holding a broad chair for the presiding presbyter (the chair is a handsome Thai elephant howdah), flanked by chairs for deacons and cantors, and bowl-shaped bells from Japan and Tibet. The bells produce a long ring that helps the whole congregation to fall into deep, reflective silence following each Scripture reading. They are already our most widely copied adaptation. At the aisle's other end, centering the building, a lectern rises with a standing censer before it, candelabra on either side, and a menorah behind it. A small forest of lacy brass Ethiopian processional crosses with their colorful cloth streamers at once close the square for the service of the Word and lead the eye eastward to the altar square. On the walls hang large Ethiopian, Russian, and American icons of Christ's birth, baptism, passion, and resurrection, and beloved saints whose lives exemplify his victory over sin and death.

The eastern square is mostly open space. At a sideboard by the north wall, arriving worshipers place canned goods for the poor and food for the eucharistic meal—an adaptation of a Jewish custom underlying diverse church practices. At the center, alone, stands the table where the congregation will give thanks, feast, and dance together. We cover the table in eye-catching cloth from African, Asian, or Native American folk weavers and dyers, following a calendar scheme of richness rather than color. Our Table is D-shaped, like dinner tables in Jesus' day. The shape invites people to gather around, and enables the clergy to reach vessels easily from the Table's flat western side, as ancient servants naturally needed to do. Thus the clergy preside among the people, rather than opposite them, and face always east, unifying both gatherings in a common movement, greeting Christ in his eucharistic banquet.

Music. We greet Christ with an ocean of song. Music is the most powerful element in worship, and the strongest agent for participation and renewal. Our musical fare includes plain and polyphonic chants, old and new, and metrical hymns from wide-ranging sources, including our own compositions and anonymous folk works.

We sing in parts (improvising these when appropriate), usually unaccompanied or supported by hand instruments scattered through the crowd. Our music director fills the church's most prominent lay office, and shares equally with the deacon in running our liturgy. The job demands skill in choral conducting and in inviting people to join in, no matter what their musical proficiency.

Entry. The opening sets any service's context, especially for newcomers. By adapting the popular entry from early Byzantine cathedral worship, we welcome and involve people from the start. The clergy and people gather in our open altar area, greet one another with the universal Christian shout, "Christ is risen!"/"He is risen indeed!" and rehearse music for the service. Then all pour into the seating area together, chanting a rhythmic Alleluia refrain and verses and lighting the menorah and lectern candles. This entry procession ends with a blessing that begins the liturgy of the Word, and the first censing. The deacon burns incense in the standing thurible as all sing a hymn—normally the early Christian morning hymn called _Gloria in Excelsis_. The president concludes the hymn with a morning collect—during most of the year, a classic prayer by Erasmus.

Scripture. Recalling Jewish worship as Jesus knew it, we open the Scriptures by singing the _Shᵉma_ and add two further readings from the Episcopal church's three-year Sunday lectionary, ending always with the Gospel. Lay people read all readings under the deacon's guidance, including the Gospel, which a soloist or chorus chants to one of several traditional melodies. Each lection leads to two full minutes' silence, begun and ended by deep bells (see above), followed by a song suiting the Scripture.

Because popular liturgy thrives on familiarity, we sing some texts constantly with a few varying musical settings, the changeable procession and dance hymns serve for two or three weeks at a time. "Sea-sonal" changes are scarce and simple. (Our people joke that there are two seasons at St. Gregory's: Easter and Easter's Coming.) From Easter to Pentecost we borrow the lively eastern Orthodox custom of singing the Easter _Troparion_ from Jerusalem repeatedly through the service, each time to a melody from a different ethnic heritage, sharing the musical gifts of every Christian people.

Sermon, Response, and Prayers. Following the Gospel and a second two-minute silence, the president preaches on the day's Scripture, sitting among the people as before, holding the Gospel book open for reference, and drawing always on personal experience.

Then a third silence, and the congregation share their own experience in response. This is no time for questions or argument, but rather for fulfilling the sermon by allowing the Spirit to speak from our church's own life. Visitors have likened this conversation to Quaker meetings, from whence in fact it comes. Soon the preacher thanks everyone and shoulders the Gospel book, carrying it around the church while a cantor chants psalm verses. The people sing Alleluia refrains, pressing forward to touch and kiss the Gospel as it passes by—a warm Jewish and Ethiopian Christian ceremony enabling all to express their love for the Christ who speaks to us in Scripture.

Announcements follow; then the people's prayers. We adapt the Lord's Prayer, likely used in New Testament times, for starting and guiding the congregation's prayer. All sing the Lord's Prayer (without doxology for now), and add their own spoken petitions and thanksgivings freely in a litany, as the congregation respond to each free petition. The deacon prompts these occasionally until prayer is offered for all the prayer book's recommended subjects. Then the president concludes with the prayer book's collect for the day; and all sing the Lord's Prayer doxology at the last. This method allows both fixed and free intercessions, and wraps each worshiper's prayer in the prayer of Christ. In conjunction with the prayers we may also welcome new members, or baptize using a portable font set on the _bema_ platform where all can see.

Dance and the Kiss of Peace. Congregational dance is a powerful primitive medium that European churches kept until modern times and that the Ethiopian church—the largest Eastern church—still keeps. Twice each Sunday, and for an hour on Easter, St. Gregory's people dance to hymns accompanied by Ethiopian *sistrum* rattles and African and native American drums. Our first dance follows the prayers, as the clergy lead the whole congregation to the table for the eucharistic banquet. Hands on each other's shoulders, we sing and march the simple *tripudium* step (three forward, one back—a fourth century step still used in Liechtenstein for this purpose). The procession circles the Table, censing it with belled Ethiopian thuribles, and then all exchange a moving kiss of peace.

Our children have followed their own service of study, play, and prayers in Sunday school. They join us during the hubbub. And while the peace continues, the deacon takes bread and wine from the sideboard, setting them out on the Table, at last calling everyone's attention for the preface and great thanksgiving prayer. Thus our "offertory" involves the whole congregation, in the earliest style, as the people move directly from prayers to peace to preface to feast, not stopping to watch clergy handle donations until after Communion.

Eucharist. The president blesses the congregation and summons their hearts heavenward. All stand round the table praying with hands raised high—the favorite early Christian prayer posture—while the president sings the entire great thanksgiving prayer (this normally follows an ancient Jewish Passover melody, now widely adapted). The people sing traditional response and acclamations. The president prays simply, without manual acts of any kind; the deacon attends to turn pages and shoo flies. Beside the prayers in *The Book of Common Prayer,* we often pray thanksgivings we have composed as the prayer book recommends. Following an early Syrian format, the thanksgivings recite salvation history in the light of the Scripture readings and end with the congregation singing the Sanctus and Benedictus hymns.

During the *Agnus Dei* (Lamb of God) hymn—another Syrian composition—the deacon brings extra vessels. The clergy divide the bread and wine for Communion, then raise these gifts, inviting all to eat and drink. Following Eastern custom, we give the Eucharist to each person by name, and all including the president receive from a fellow Christian's hand. The clergy give bread to each worshiper; the lay people administer chalices to each other, while lay ministers see to it the wine reaches everyone. As the remaining bread and wine return to the table, the president recites a prophecy from Baruch, promising salvation for all God's lost or oppressed people—a theme dear to Gregory of Nyssa. Then in thankful response to all God has given us, we gather money for the church's work and food for the hungry and lay these on the table with the remaining eucharistic gifts.

Our second dance, the carol, follows the collection. Singing a hymn again, the people join hands and spiral around the gift-laden table, dancing a repetitive Greek step that matches the hymn rhythm, and accompanied again by drums and sistrums. Greek steps supremely suit this moment, for they move gently sideways, affording dancers a sensous experience of the community moving together. Six easy Greek steps will fit nearly half the hymns in the Episcopal *Hymnal* of 1982. The oldest of these steps were certainly known to New Testament Christians. The carol ends in one last congregational songburst as the deacon leads us singing "God grant you many years!" to people celebrating birthdays and anniversaries, to new members, and to our occasional guest preacher. Coffee and cakes now join the other gifts on the table, and the feast continues until the congregation have consumed the bread, wine, coffee, treats, and each other's company to satiety. Thus the one eucharistic table centers and supports our whole community life.

Easter. We also offer other services in differing styles, including weekly Taizé meditation and the "Feast of Friends," an informal combined Eucharist and church supper following the second-century *Didache* text. But our chief variant, indeed the chief event of our congregation's life, is Easter. We keep this feast at night, as early Christians did, combining the ancient candlelight vigil of readings with a tumultuous Russian-style Easter party lasting until morning. After first experiencing the celebration, one member decided, "This is an Easter church; most churches are Christmas churches." A liturgy professor once told his students, "You have just had the closest possible experience to fourth-century Christian worship."

We do aim to share the early church's experience. But churches share one living, growing heritage

St. Patrick's Shamrock. The use of the shamrock as a sign of the Trinity originates from the legend of St. Patrick. It is reported that when the pagans demanded he prove the Trinity to them he plucked a shamrock leaf and asked, "Do I hold one leaf or three leaves? If one, why are there three lobes of equal size; if three, why only one stem?" His accusers were silenced for they could not explain. He then said, "If you cannot explain so simple a mystery as the shamrock, how can you hope to understand one so profound as the Holy Trinity?"

from those great missionary times, which we can use to bring our world into God's boundless friendship. That is always and everywhere the church's purpose: to build the one thing truly worthwhile.

Richard Fabian

153 ◆ Alternative Worship in the Free Church Tradition

At Grace Fellowship Church, worship dwells on the restoration of the world, which in turn creates the longing for worship. Worship draws from both the traditional and the contemporary and builds around a theme usually developed in acts of Entrance, Word, Table, and Dismissal. Both the influence of the liturgical movement and the praise-and-worship tradition is evident in this pattern of worship.

When our congregation was formed seven years ago, we wanted worship to be the first thing we did. For a while, it was the only thing we did. There were no programs to maintain, no agenda to fulfill;

the focus of our congregation was simply to be a worshiping people, open to the Spirit of God. What we've discovered is that the ministries and programs that have since sprung up have been born, not out of an isolated sense of what the church "ought" to do, but out of a growing commitment to worship.

Worship is the great integrator of our lives. If on Sunday we praise God for being the One who reigns, if we sing songs that speak of his majesty and dominion, then on Monday and throughout the week we must grieve with him over all the unfinished places in us and around us where the kingdom has not yet been received. In other words, being in worship feeds our longing to see ourselves and our world put back together, restored to wholeness. And being in the world feeds our longing to see God as rightful owner over all he has made, sovereign over sin, holy and lifted up in worship.

Tradition and Spirit in Tension

Because our worship reflects who we are as a congregation, it is always changing, always in process. We try to hold a continuity with the church's rich tradition and history in healthy tension with a sensitivity to the new work of the Spirit in us. The tradition keeps worship from becoming merely an excuse to enjoy ourselves, a "rootless" celebration, while the Spirit's ongoing influence keeps us from making "institutions" out of the living structure of worship.

Thus, we will affirm the ancient creeds (Apostles', Nicene) as well as the more modern ones (Barmen, Bread for the World). We will sing the _Kyrie_ during confession at Lent, employ ancient Christian symbols on our banners, and use the traditional greeting for passing the peace, but these actions are explained to our congregation in a way that encourages us to make them our own. We will sing hymns that give us a richer vocabulary in speaking of God, leading us to appreciate the mystery of who he is; and we'll sing choruses, which give us opportunities to express our love for him with great abandon. (We have often found Catholic choruses to be more "substantial" than others theologically and musically, while still allowing us to address God more freely.)

The freedom to enter into worship is not the result of techniques but of involvement. God draws us into intimate dialogue as we worship. Throughout the service, he speaks, we respond, and a relationship between God and his people is nurtured.

Thus, we do not have a song leader, whose job often seems like whipping up from nothing the congregation's enthusiasm. Rather, the task of "leading worship" belongs to the whole congregation. People who tend toward "expressive" worship have helped to open doors for others who just needed some company to expand their own way of worshiping. But there are no "musts" here, no need to prove our devotion, and this adds also to the freedom of the congregation.

Building a Theme

In planning the service, more time is spent on building the theme than on anything else. The theme comes most directly from the sermon, but everything before and everything after must reinforce that message. For instance, we recently worked on a service where the theme had to do with "selling ourselves" to the values of a world that has no room for God. The text was Hosea 2:2-13, which talks about both Gomer's and Israel's adulterous, idolatrous pursuits in the midst of their covenant relationships. We used as a Call to Worship the powerful text from Isaiah 44 that describes the absolute impotence of idols and the foolishness of those who trust in them, and contrasts this with the God who says to his beloved people, "O Israel, I will not forget you. . . . Return to me, for I have redeemed you." We chose hymns and songs throughout that praised God for his loyal pursuit of us and for his holiness that does not tolerate sin. In our prayer of confession, a litany written with the Hosea text in mind, we prayed for deliverance from the idols of success, comfort, and self. Those who had been sensitive to God's dialogue with us from the beginning of the service were better prepared to hear God speak into our lives (always an act of sheer grace) when the sermon came. The sermon was followed by the celebration of the Lord's Supper, where we rehearsed again the extent to which our Deliverer went in order to bring back a wandering, adulterous people. Building a theme in worship doesn't guarantee anything, but it does protect from a generic worship made of disconnected, interchangeable parts.

Eucharistic Transformation

The greatest change the congregation has experienced has to do with the celebration of the Eucharist. We began, seven years ago, coming to the Table quarterly, changed to monthly, and now we celebrate twice monthly. Most of us had come from a tradition of seeing the Lord's Table as a sacrament recalling the past rather than anticipating the future, more somber than joyous, more passive than active, more individual than corporate. There is now more of a sense of both the mystery of Christ's presence with us—he meets us in bread and cup—and the pure joy of receiving from him the grace to sustain our lives. Each of us comes to the front to receive the elements. We are addressed by name from those who serve us and told that the elements are indeed given to us by Christ, a very pastoral act. Often during this time, two of our elders sit with those who wish to be prayed for.

When Communion concludes, we pass the peace to one another. Passing the peace for us began as a somewhat awkward movement, where we could barely look each other in the eye. It is now becoming a time of much tenderness and healing as we affirm by look and word and touch the relationship we share in Christ.

This is what we've done in worship, but we hope this is not where we stop. Because God is a renewing God, who breathes life into dry bones, we pray that our worship of him might always reflect the renewing work he is doing in us.

Sharon Huey

154 • ALTERNATIVE WORSHIP IN THE PENTECOSTAL-CHARISMATIC TRADITION

The charismatic movement brought classical Pentecostalism into contact with other major traditions from which it had been estranged. Many younger Pentecostals are experiencing renewal in worship through this encounter, combining their Pentecostal heritage with evangelical and liturgical influences.

Classical Pentecostalism differs from the charismatic movement in many respects. A generation ago members of historic denominations that had experienced phenomena usually connected with Pentecostals, such as tongue-speaking, prophetic speech, and exorcism, were given the name "charismatic." The charismatics borrowed much from their Pentecostal friends, of course, but rejected much of their cultural mores.

The Pentecostal-Charismatic Encounter

The charismatic movement presented the classical Pentecostals with a real dilemma. They wanted to identify with the charismatics, but the conservative elements in Pentecostalism rejected the context in which the charismatics' experiences were happening. Early in its history Pentecostalism had divorced itself, and been divorced from, the rest of Christendom. As in most divorces, this one brought its share of hurt and bitterness. Pentecostals had learned to deal with the alienation by claiming to occupy at least a place of prominence in the Christian church, and sometimes even to have _replaced_ "backslidden" Christendom.

Now, after all these years, Pentecostals had to deal with the new tongues speakers. At first they put pressure on the charismatics to leave the historic denominations. The charismatics resisted this pressure for the most part, and in the cases where they did leave, they tended to form their own independent churches. Many of these new congregations became thriving megachurches, some of which began to exercise enormous influence on younger generations of Pentecostals. The younger people began to prefer the praise music and dance of the newer charismatics to the older traditions of spontaneous spiritual dance and frontier revivalistic hymns. All of this became the subject of many a conference and camp meeting.

The internal debates within classical Pentecostalism continue, but it is especially pronounced in the more isolated branches of the movement, such as the Church of God of Prophecy and the United Pentecostal Church. Larger bodies such as the Assemblies of God are not unaffected either, however. The struggle is nowhere more obvious than in style of worship.

The classical Pentecostals borrowed their worship from two main sources: the holiness Methodism of the frontier and the black churches. This background accounts for the mixture of high emotion together with what had been features of the more liturgical churches, such as anointing with oil and the laying on of hands. The Pentecostals retained the features of their own frontier background and rarely questioned whether the Pentecostal experience could ever emerge in any other cultural context.

Most of the independent charismatic megachurches tended to be Baptist in doctrine, church government, and preaching style. So as Pentecostals began to meet their charismatic counterparts, they first found themselves stretching to accommodate Baptist streams of thought. They had hardly caught their breath when they had to face as well the liturgical charismatics from Lutheran, Episcopalian, Roman Catholic, and Orthodox backgrounds. Their fathers had barely studied these people in Bible schools; this generation was meeting them face to face! The Pentecostals were like the Jewish friends of St. Peter at the house of Cornelius who came back to Jerusalem with the report, "we heard them speak with tongues as we did in the beginning." The younger Pentecostals began to experience an identity crisis. Who were they, and where were they going?

Pentecostal Diaspora

An understanding grew among them that the church of Jesus Christ, like her God, has a triune nature: sacramental, evangelical, and Pentecostal. Christians should reverence the majesty of God, proclaim the redemptive work of God, and announce the powerful kingdom of God. The church needs priestly pastors, rabbinical and scholarly teachers, and fiery prophets. The younger Pentecostals began to feel that it would take the whole church to reach the whole world. So while Pentecostalism was influencing the whole church, and the new generation of Pentecostals wanted to remain a part of that influence, they also believed it was time for the whole church to influence Pentecostalism. In other words, the younger Pentecostals no longer see renewal as something flowing in only one direction.

Some of the Pentecostal denominations are coping with this development better than others. In some groups the younger ministers have been routinely ostracized from the movement. Some of them, sadly, have been alienated even from their families. In response to this, several groups have sprung up that allow friends and colleagues to make their spiritual journey together. One of them, Global Christian Ministries, came into being in the early 1980s. By 1986 this group had developed a Confession of Faith based on the Apostles' Creed, and quickly become a network that brings together people from evangelical, Pentecostal, and liturgical backgrounds.

The churches and ministers involved in this Pentecostal diaspora are studying the church fathers, liturgies of churches Eastern and Western, and in general becoming connected with their Christian heritage, without, however, rejecting their own Pentecostal experience. As might be expected, this endeavor has had a great impact on the way they worship. Contemporary music, black gospel, charismatic praise choruses, and historic hymns blend in a strange but fulfilling collage of musical ecumenism. Written prayers mingle with highly charged extemporaneous intercession. Banners are carried in processionals into the sanctuary, accompanied by shouts of joy. The influence of the church year is growing, adding a new rhythm to the churches. Everywhere one sees copies of *The Book of Common Prayer.*

Some churches, such as the Church of the King in Valdosta, Georgia, have moved their affiliation from a Pentecostal denomination to that of a historical denomination (in their case, from the Assemblies of God to the Episcopal church). Most however, continue to move together in a loose network, studying, experimenting, interacting, and worshiping.

No one knows exactly what direction this movement will take, but it has already resulted in a deeper understanding of the sacraments, a pattern of worship closer to that of antiquity, and an experience of worship that combines celebration with adoration and solemnity.

Dan Scott

155 • THE SEEKERS' SERVICE/BELIEVERS' WORSHIP CHURCHES

Willow Creek Community Church in South Barrington, Illinois, the second largest church in the United States, has become well known for its pioneering efforts in the development of the seekers' service. This entry presents and explains this service, which is intended for the unchurched.

Willow Creek Community Church is unique because it avoids providing a worship service for believers on weekends. They must come instead to New Community on Wednesday or Thursday evenings at 7:30 P.M. to receive teaching from the Bible and to worship God with songs and prayers. Saturday night and Sunday morning services are devoted to seekers, who most probably are unchurched or unconverted but are curious about life-changing Christianity. In this sense, Willow Creek has started

its own tradition *sui generis* that is not derived directly from any denominational or sectarian source.

The essential twofold principle that guides those who "produce" either seeker or New Community services stresses both simplicity and depth. Willow Creek's patterns reflect some aspects of evangelical worship styles, but the leadership want even more to start something new. They represent a new generation of worship leaders that is challenging and encouraging a new generation of worshipers and seekers. They want every part of a service to concentrate on making a seeker service safe for inquirers or a New Community nourishing for believers.

Because Willow Creek has become one of the largest Christian churches in America, it has developed an extensive reservoir of talented volunteers who ensure that it services and ministries are well organized and run smoothly. They are fed into the specific area where they have a passion to serve by going through a series of seminars called "Network." Over a month, one night a week, men and women are taught from the Bible what God gave his church as spiritual gifts. Through prayer, low-key personality tests, and peer evaluation, they discover which ones they have been given and how they can use them at Willow Creek.

Many different ministries benefit from the influx of these volunteers, such as ushering, the band and orchestra, the vocal and drama teams, the actual stage crew, and others. For them, to serve is a form of worship. Supervised by the production team, they all contribute to achieving the overall service goals. This forms unique bonds of community within each group.

It must be stressed that the outcome of every service is not assured. Willow Creek has always made it a point to learn from mistakes and be open to new approaches. It is fortunate not to have denominational precedents to hinder such openness. Over the past seventeen years since the beginning, the church has been able to expand both its membership and its physical plant size. This growth brought more freedom to experiment and greater responsiveness to seekers and believers.

No liturgy is used at Willow Creek, though the sermon or message, following Protestant tradition, is still central to both kinds of services. A multiple teaching staff allows for flexibility and variety in speaking style and subject choice. They are chosen not primarily for their education or length of experience as much as for their communication skills, spiritual maturity, and commitment to Willow Creek's unique ministry vision. The preaching is largely topical, with current issues in American society providing much of the subject matter. When book studies are scheduled, the approach is expositional and meant to be more relevant to modern listeners than exhaustive in its scope.

Music plays a large part in Willow Creek's appeal to seekers and believers. Using volunteers, most of whom have some professional experience, the production team can put together a band, an orchestra, and several vocal teams with enough back-up members to ensure a powerful and well-conducted musical experience during the services. Much of the music used reflects more contemporary, even charismatic, sources than traditional ones. Material from several trademarks, such as Integrity or Maranatha! are widely draw upon and very popular. Many choruses are written by vocal team members themselves, another advantage of the broad talent base that Willow Creek enjoys.

Dramatic sketches are integral to both kinds of services, but primarily for the seekers' service. Written and performed by volunteers and supervised by a staff member, they prepare the way for the point of the message. They are meant to ask questions that the speaker will answer. The drama director works hard to make the sketches humorous or serious by turns, but always relevant. Occasionally, during the year, both music and drama teams will combine to do a "show" for a particular Christian holiday, such as Easter or Christmas. At other times a play will be performed simply as a special effort to reach inquirers and unbelievers. Such an outreach is seen by many as unconventional, but the leadership of Willow Creek is convinced by God's leading and the results that it is necessary in our present society.

New Community services at midweek represent the core of worship experience for believers at Willow Creek. A prayerful blending of music, message, and prayer can nourish and challenge the Christian who wants to meet God, even in the midst of thousands of other people. A large congregation can be intimidating, but because Willow Creek leadership places great emphasis on creating community among members and attenders, this is not a problem.

In fact, there are none of the usual distinguishing signs of traditional churches at Willow Creek at all, no crosses or other religious artwork. In a real sense, everything that is done is calculated for some effect. The reason is that the production team takes true worship of God most seriously of all.

The philosophy that underlies Willow Creek's approach to worship is fourfold. First, people must be personally involved because corporate worship arises from individual faithfulness to God's will in their lives. Second, careful planning allows the production team the freedom to make creative worship occur smoothly and orderly. Third, variety encourages and amplifies freshness of expression. Fourth, a worship service is centered on a single theme and each part promotes it, whether with drama, or music or by other means.

Future directions in worship at Willow Creek will include more congregational participation, responsive readers, and group seating by ministry involvement, among other additions. Willow Creek wants to draw its large congregation closer together by breaking up the whole into much smaller, more personally accountable parts. Like the neighborhood of long ago, people will be more in touch because they will see each other more often.

Steve Burdan

PART TWO

Introducing
Worship Renewal

✎ TWO ✎

What Is Worship Renewal?

═══════════════════════════════════════

What does it mean to renew our worship? Part 2 of this volume suggests how we can understand and recognize the renewal of worship. In chapter 2, several articles attempt to define worship renewal. More importantly, they describe pictures or signs of how renewed worship looks and sounds. Chapter 3 offers a typology of the range of styles to be found in renewing churches: liturgical, traditional Protestant, creative, charismatic, praise and worship, convergence, and seekers' service. Then follows a brief survey of major traditions with emphasis on signs of renewal in them.

During the twentieth century more study has been devoted to the subject of worship than in any other century of the Christian faith. This study has resulted in a rich variety of documents, resources, and experimentation, much of which has filtered down to the local church. A spiritual renewal has occurred in many churches, expressing itself in a vital faith and a participatory worship.

Worship renewal in the twentieth century has focused on two key issues: understanding what worship is and experiencing the power of worship. Both of these aspects of worship are addressed in the entries below.

═══════════════════════════════════════

156 • DEFINING WORSHIP

Because worship is multifaceted, no single definition completely captures it in full. The following attempts at definition express the richness and diversity of worship and show that a key to renewal is the awareness of worship as both a divine action and a human response.

That nothing else be done in [worship] than that our dear Lord Himself talk to us through His Holy Word and that we, in turn, talk to Him in prayer and songs of praise.

Martin Luther

Worship in all its grades and kinds is the response of the creature to the eternal.

Evelyn Underhill

[Worship] sums up and confirms ever afresh the process of saving history which has reached its culminating point in the intervention of Christ in hu-

man history, and through this summing up and ever-repeated confirmation Christ pursues His saving work by the operation of the Holy Spirit.

Jean-Jacques von Allmen

[Worship is] God acting to give His life to man and to bring men to partake of that life.

Paul W. Hoon

A Bible-centered approach to worship clearly reveals that worship is definitely not a God-built device to somehow get man to stroke a heavenly Ego. Neither is it a summons to a weekly reaffirmation of one's expertise in precision-cut declarations of doctrinaire posturing. Instead, the Scriptures consistently show God calling His creatures to worship in His presence that He might release, redeem, renew, and restore them.

Jack Hayford

[Worship is] the public act which sternly actualizes the nature of the church as the body of Christ, an act . . . which embraces, expresses, inspires and defines the whole church, her whole essential nature, her whole life.

Alexander Schmemann

[Worship is] an action wherein the testimony of God is heard and appropriated, the experience of the community is transformed, and the godly presence is disclosed.

Regis Duffy

Worship is an active response to God whereby we declare His worth.

Ronald Allen

The liturgy of the church is nothing other than that church's faith in motion.

Aidan Kavanagh

One basic principle to be learned from the Old Testament is that *worship implies the presence of God among his assembled people.* (This same principle can also be seen in the New Testament.) What does this principle imply for contemporary Christians? It means that when one enters a service of worship he is entering into the very presence of God. Just as God came to Israel and was present with them in a real way, so also is God present among Christians when they assemble together. *His name is upon them, his glory is manifested to them (in Jesus Christ) and he makes his face to shine upon them.*

Paul Engle

It is fitting and right to hymn you (to bless you, to praise you), to give you thanks, to worship you in all places of your dominion. For you are God, ineffa-

ble, inconceivable, invisible, incomprehensible, existing always and in the same way, you and your only-begotten Son and your Holy Spirit. You brought us out of not-being to being; and when we had fallen, you raised us up again; and did not cease to do everything until you had brought us up to heaven, and granted us the kingdom that is to come. For all these things we give thanks to you and to your only-begotten Son and to your Holy Spirit, for all that we know and do not know, your seen and unseen benefits that have come upon us. We give you thanks also for this ministry; vouchsafe to receive it from our hands, even though thousands of archangels and ten thousands of angels stand before you, cherubim and seraphim, with six wings and many eyes, flying on high singing the triumphal hymn proclaiming, crying, and saying: Holy, holy, holy, Lord of Sabbaoth; heaven and earth are full of your glory. Hosanna in the highest. Blessed is he who comes in the name of the Lord. Hosanna in the highest.

Preface to the Eucharistic Prayer,
The Divine Liturgy
of St. John Chrysostom

Worship is primarily a celebration of God's mighty deed of salvation accomplished through the living, dying, and rising again of Jesus Christ. Worship tells and enacts the story of God's victory over the powers of evil through Christ. And this worship, which is the work of the people, is done in the fellowship of the community of faith by the power of the Spirit as a response of praise and thanksgiving.

Robert E. Webber

When Christians gather in Christ's name, every first day of the week, our strongest impulse is to express the joyful praise which wells up in our lives. With readings and songs, sermons and prayers, gifts and sacred meals, we exult in the life God gives, adore the One who loves so fully, give thanks for Jesus our savior and friend, and renew our promises to serve God faithfully.

Keith Watkins

The Hand of God. The hand of God is a familiar and famous symbol of God the Father. The idea is based upon many Bible passages such as "his right hand and his holy arm have worked salvation for him" (Ps. 98:1).

157 • Signs of a Worship in Need of Renewal

The fourteen signs listed below are symptomatic of an apathetic worship and a passive congregation.

1. The congregation is passive and lacking in enthusiasm and a spirit of joy.
2. Visitors do not feel welcome or drawn into the community and its worship.
3. Worship is cerebral and oriented almost exclusively toward teaching.
4. Worship is evangelistic and oriented almost exclusively toward conversion.
5. Communication skills in preaching and leading worship are weak.
6. Sermons tend to be long, didactic, and lacking in application.
7. Communion is celebrated infrequently and when celebrated seems to be tacked on to the end of the service, often bearing the characteristics of a funeral.
8. People sit in a typical classroom formation with the back of another person's head as a major object of sight.
9. Singing lacks life, and the range of music is limited.
10. There is no sense in which the order of worship moves the congregation in a pattern that rehearses their faith and thus establishes, maintains, or repairs a relationship with God.
11. The Christian year is not practiced, or if it is practiced, it is not characterized by a sense of its gospel nature or used effectively as a means of ordering congregational spirituality.
12. The use of arts is shunned except on special occasions such as Christmas or Easter.
13. The people are not involved in responses, antiphons, prayer, ministry to each other, or the passing of the peace.
14. The senses are not adequately engaged in touch, smell, sight, or hearing.

Robert E. Webber

158 • Signs of a Renewing Worship

The objective and subjective characteristics of a renewed worship, as well as the results, are clearly discernible. The following list details these features.

A. Objective Characteristics
1. Restoration of a Christ-centered focus (worship celebrates the living, dying, and rising of Christ in which the powers of evil are overthrown, a sacrifice for sin is made, and an example for living is set forth)
2. Characterized by a good balance of order and freedom
3. Rediscovery of Christ's active presence in both Word and Table
4. Appropriation of the arts as servants of the text
5. Use of a wide range of music drawn from the history of the church and from various contemporary cultures
6. Heightened communication skills in both preaching and leading of worship
7. A space for worship that works for the participation of all the people

8. A worship that is intergenerational
9. A worship characterized by intimacy and pageantry
10. A warm and hospitable environment
11. Rediscovery of the evangelical nature of the church year

B. **Subjective Characteristics**
12. Aliveness of the people through active participation
13. An experience of joy, celebration, love, victory, and peace
14. A rehearsal of one's relationship to God
15. The engagement of the whole person—mind, heart, will, body, and senses
16. The experience of spontaneity
17. A feeling of personal involvement and corporate relatedness

C. **Results**
18. The ministry of people to one another in worship
19. A growing concern and commitment to evangelism and social outreach
20. A heightened spirituality, both personal and corporate
21. The experience of Christian community

Robert E. Webber

159 • Six Major Emphases of the Liturgical Movement

The impact of the liturgical movement is felt not only among liturgical churches, but among nonliturgical churches as well. The emphases presented below characterize worship reform not only in Catholic, Episcopal, and Lutheran circles, but also the renewal of worship among Presbyterians, Methodists, United Church of Christ, Disciples of Christ, and other denominations of the mainline Protestant churches.

A Return to the Scripture. A return to the Scripture has provided us with more readings and a revised lectionary. . . . There is now a more holistic sense to the liturgical readings. . . . The word is addressed to the whole person and not simply to the intellect. . . . The biblical understanding of memorial now predominates in the theology of the liturgy. . . . Liturgy is not primarily a looking to a past event. . . . Liturgy lives out of the future; it is an anticipation of what life is to be like when we live in union with God and through Christ.

Recovery of the Experience of the Early Church. This return to the sources has helped Roman Catholics realize that all sacramental activity is in response to the Word of God and that the Eucharist cannot bear the burden of all of one's worship life. It has meant for Anglicans and Protestants a renewed interest in the festive character of the Eucharist and the eucharistic prayer as praise and thanksgiving. This has resulted in more frequent eucharistic celebrations, as well as a less funeral character to the service of Holy Communion or the Lord's Supper.

A More Wholesome Ecclesiology. Ministry is no longer seen as the domain of the ordained, and the plurality of ministries is to find its reflection in the diversification of roles in the worshiping situation.

The Ecumenical Dimension of Worship. What is significant for liturgy is the convergence in the liturgical reforms of the various communions . . . probably more important than any specific liturgical agreement is the change in attitude wherein denominational differences no longer have the rigidity and intensity they once had.

Symbolism. To recover the fullness of the sign has always been a major point with those committed to liturgical reform. And much has been achieved here: a more generous anointing with oil, a greater experience of water in baptism, the extension of the cup to all. Today's liturgical students and facilitators are much more conscious of the studies of anthropologists, the work of modern artists, and the writers and philosophers of symbolism, as well as how symbols operate and grow, and the difference between a symbol, which sets up a situation of encounter, and a sign, which points away from itself to an absent reality.

Liturgy and Culture. This final plank of the liturgical movement's platform is the area where there is still the most to achieve. Up to the present, the liturgical reforms have been for a universal church and have been put together by experts known more for their sense of history, theology, and pastoral practice than for attention to national and ethnic differences.

James Empereur[1]

160 • WORSHIP AS CELEBRATION OF GOD'S SAVING DEEDS

The ultimate aim of worship is not to create a certain mood, nor is it the pragmatic goal of teaching or evangelism. Rather, the aim of worship is to joyfully respond to God's great deeds of salvation in Jesus Christ through praise and thanksgiving.

During the past two decades we have seen a renewal of interest in worship that has had both refreshing and disturbing features in the church.

On the positive side, we have seen a much needed emphasis upon worship as involving congregational praise to God. People have become involved in upward expression, as well as in listening. As the worship service has taken on an air of festivity and activity, many churches have been freed from a Bible-lecture mentality.

On the negative side, however, we have seen an unfortunate overemphasis upon "worship style." For example, we are told that a neocharismatic style of worship is definitely a proven attendance builder. Some years ago a worship-style clinician assured our congregation that if we could achieve a certain "sound" in chanted praise, it would "revolutionize" the life of the church. Mood was his aim.

Then the more flexible students tell us that any style that suits the tastes of the people in a given congregation is "the way to go." In other words, God works through many worship styles. Pragmatism is their secret, many pastors say.

In their absorption with "style," many churches have decided to seek dignity in worship. They have decided to borrow heavily from the traditional and liturgical churches, polishing up their previous information style with touches of tasteful order. Balance is their watchword.

There is probably some truth in all of the above. However, something vital is lost in this all-consuming concentration upon style in worship. It is simply this—that worship is not first of all a matter of style, but a matter of response to truth. Overemphasis upon the manner of worship has beclouded the purpose of praise.

Worship is our unified, celebrative response of thanksgiving to God for his creative and redemptive acts in Christ Jesus our Lord. This response involves our songs, prayers, offerings of thanks, ministry in the Word, mutual sharing of faith experience, and,

at regular intervals, the celebration of the Lord's Supper.

If the church is the foregleam of the future, then our worship has features that will culminate in the worship of the eternal world. This type of worship we find in chapter 5 of Revelation.

Here we see a great numberless throng breaking into utmost praise as it grasps the truth that Jesus Christ, the Lion and the Lamb, has become the conqueror. The heavenly hosts' worship is a response to truth about Christ.

Therefore, worship that becomes a quest for a certain style—whether neocharismatic or neodignified or a search for personal fulfillment and enjoyment, or a reaching out for a mood—misses the point. Although worship involves moods and experiences, it is not primarily a quest for these. It is

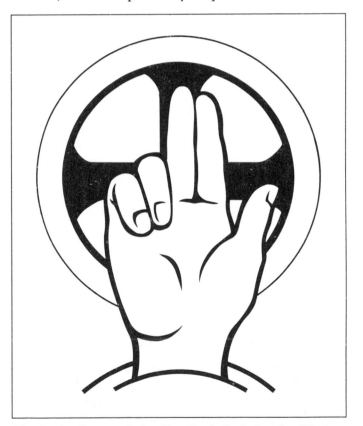

The Latin Form of the Hand of God. In the Western church the hand of God is frequently pictured with the thumb and the first two fingers extended and the third and fourth fingers closed. The three extended figures represent the Holy Trinity and the two closed fingers represent the twofold nature of the Son. The hand of God is appropriately surrounded with the circular nimbus with three rays. The nimbus is the sign of sanctity, and the three rays represent the triune nature of God. In the Roman church the benediction and blessings are always given with the hand in this position.

something we do in response to what God has already done in Christ.

Our total service then becomes worship. Certain portions of the service may bring us a more intense realization of the presence of God, but we do not apply the term *worship* to that experience in a special manner. We come as worshipers, participate as worshipers, and leave as worshipers.

In our congregation we like to say: We are not on a quest for long-delayed dignity, but on a quest for truth. Any intentional structuring of the service is for the sake of placing redemptive truth about Jesus Christ up front in song, word, and prayer. This helps us to avoid excessive talking about ourselves under the guise of "fellowship." The service must speak much about Jesus Christ.

When we discover that truth, not style, is the secret of New Testament worship—a response to truth inspired by the Holy Spirit—then that can be expressed under various styles. It is then no longer the simplistic idea that "any style works," but the biblical principle that the central saving truth about Jesus Christ will inspire worship in any culture.

We also need to remind ourselves that worship is not primarily a period devoted to refueling church workers, nor a pep rally for church growth—although activity and growth should be natural results of our life together. The church is first of all a community of working *worshipers,* not a community of worshiping *workers.* In worship we present ourselves to God first in a response of thanksgiving and praise, centered around the truth in Christ—then in a response of service.

Henry Jauhiainen

161 ✦ Worship Open to Change

Worship renewal depends on a congregation open to change. Rather than changing for change's sake, the renewed church draws on biblical and historical worship traditions and is receptive to the leading of the Spirit.

It wasn't long ago that Reformed churches in this country approached public worship in a rather uniform way. We all basically agreed what elements were appropriate in worship and what form our Sunday morning services should take. But during the past ten to twenty years that predictability has begun to disappear. Many congregations are involving other voices than the pastor's in worship.

Stringed instruments, drums, tambourines, and other instruments are used alongside the more traditional piano and organ. People raise their hands in praise and prayer to God and give public testimonies to God's grace. Some congregations have introduced ecclesiastical dance into their services. Joy and celebration seem to be the keynote of these newer celebrations as churches in our tradition move toward a more liturgical worship style.

Change is always unsettling and generally raises a host of questions. What *is* Reformed worship? How does the Bible regulate worship? How do these new practices stand up in the light of scriptural teachings?

——— The Regulative Principle ———

Our worship—as all of life—must be regulated by the Scriptures. Historically, at least for Presbyterians, the "regulative principle" has always provided the foundational direction for worship, guiding our churches to include only those elements directly commanded by Scripture or those (such as infant baptism) arrived at by good and necessary inference.

In this century the regulative principle recently has received a sharp challenge from Ralph J. Gore, Jr., in his doctoral thesis *The Pursuit of Plainness: Rethinking the Puritan Principle of Worship,* submitted to Westminster Seminary in 1911. One of Gore's strongest arguments is that Jesus did not follow the regulative principle. He regularly worshiped in the synagogue, which has no biblical warrant for existence. And he was involved in at least one feast, the Feast of Dedication (John 10:22ff), which also has no biblical warrant. If Jesus did not follow the regulative principle of worship, claims Gore, then neither should we.

Gore's thesis may provoke some rethinking of principles of worship in years to come. But whether or not it is right to include elements of worship that fall beyond the commands of Scripture, we should *surely* include elements that are commanded expressly by God. Many of the newer practices fall into that category.

Exuberant Praise. Many people are unsettled when they attend services in which hand-clapping and praise-shouting are a regular part of worship. If that is your reaction, you should use a concordance to check out God's directives for worship. Here are some samples: "Clap your hands, all you nations;

shout to God with cries of joy" (Ps. 47:1); "Come, let us sing for joy to the LORD; let us shout aloud to the Rock of our salvation" (Ps. 95:1); "Shout for joy to the LORD, all the earth, burst into jubilant song with music; make music to the LORD with the harp, with the harp and the sound of singing, with trumpets and the blast of the ram's horn—shout for joy before the LORD, the King" (Ps. 98:4-6).

Who can doubt that we are urged to shout in the context of worship? Who can believe that only the preacher has that privilege? What seems strange and unsettling to many of us is actually a response to clear biblical directives.

What about the introduction of new instruments, even percussion instruments, into worship? They can help us catch the sense of awe-filled joy found in Psalm 150, which begins "Praise God in his sanctuary" and continues "Praise him with the sounding of the trumpet, praise him with the harp and lyre, praise him with tambourine and dancing, praise him with the strings and flute, praise him with the clash of cymbals, praise him with resounding cymbals"(vv. 1, 3-5). The principle seems to be to use everything we have to bring praise to God—and that certainly includes musical solos, choirs, and accordions.

Notice that dancing, too, was a part of Old Testament worship. There have been times during worship that I was so full of the joy of the Lord that I felt like dancing. I was held back by natural inhibitions, a total lack of rhythm, and ignorance of what kind of dancing would be appropriate for worship. I've never witnessed dancing in worship, but I'm convinced that those congregations who include it in their services may be responding to biblical directives.

Raised Hands. When I first attended an Orthodox Presbyterian church where many people raised their hands in prayer, I was startled and uncomfortable. _What's going on here?_ I wondered. _Only Pentecostals do this sort of thing._

That got me searching the Bible, and I found 1 Timothy 2:8: "I want men everywhere to lift up holy hands in prayer." It was also eye-opening to find that the solidly Reformed John Calvin said in his commentary on this passage: "This attitude has been generally used in worship during all ages. . . . Let us learn that the attitude is in accordance with true godliness."

Widespread Congregational Participation. I grew up being told that we don't include testimonies in worship because we want to focus on God rather than on people. I also heard numerous lurid accounts of congregations who abused this practice.

So, as the pastor of a rather traditional church, I tended to avoid the testimony—except at Thanksgiving. On that holiday I gave people a chance to publicly express their thanks to God for blessings during the past year. Many people told me it was the best service of the year. Slowly it began to dawn on us that if testimonies were good once a year they could be a blessing at other times. After all, the Scriptures do indicate the importance of bringing personal expressions of thanksgiving and intercession to God (Phil. 4:6; 1 Tim. 2).

We've discovered that when others (besides the minister) participate in worship by speaking out their praise to God and leading other parts of worship, the life of the church as the body of Christ is more evident. Such wider participation was apparently also part of worship in the early church (1 Cor. 14). Paul seems to assume that a number of people will speak, pray, and testify in worship and gives at least tacit approval to multiple worship leaders.

My congregation and I have also discovered that it is important to be open to change and that it's healthy to have a variety of approaches to worship—as long as the regulative principle is followed. Certainly we shouldn't accept new ideas just to be different or because they seem entertaining. We should look carefully at new practices that could divert us from true worship. At the same time, we should carefully consider changes when they have biblical warrant.

B. J. Stonehouse[2]

162 • BIBLIOGRAPHY ON RENEWAL WORSHIP

Abba, Raymond. _Principles of Christian Worship: With Special Reference to the Free Churches._ New York: Oxford University Press, 1957. Congregational. An early free church look at worship renewal.

Allen, Ronald and Gordon Borrow. _Worship: Rediscovering the Missing Jewel._ Portland, Oreg.: Multnomah Press, 1982. Protestant. Collaboration of an evangelical theologian and musician. Deals with popular issues: Defining, planning, moods of worship, reading, singing, environment.

Alternative Futures for Worship. Collegeville, Minn.: Liturgical Press, 1987. Catholic. A seven-volume collaboration by a number of contemporary scholars. Examines social sciences, directed toward pastors. The seven volumes are:

Duffy, Regis, O.F.M., ed. *General Introduction.* Vol. 1. Examines the role of ritual and symbol, drawing on sociological and psychological studies.

Searle, Mark, ed. *Baptism and Confirmation.* Vol. 2. Examines baptism and confirmation as aspects of conversion process. Emphasis is on process and development. Draws on the social sciences.

Bernard, J. Lee, ed. *The Eucharist.* Vol. 3. Examines the Eucharist in relation to the human sciences—especially as the Eucharist pertains to church as intentional community. Sample liturgies.

Fink, Peter E., ed. *Reconciliation.* Vol. 4. Examines the act of reconciliation in light of psychology and applies reconciliation to groups as well as individuals. Contains excellent history of the rite. Sample liturgies.

Cooke, Bernard, ed. *Christian Marriage.* Vol. 5. Examines marriage in relation to socio-behavioral insights. Also contains excellent chapters on the history of marriage and the theology of marriage. Sample liturgies.

Cowan, Michael A., ed. *Leadership Ministry in Community.* Vol. 6. Examines various ministries in the church from the perspective of the social sciences. Excellent material on images of community, leadership, stewardship, empowerment, and theological assumptions and ministerial style. Sample liturgies.

Fink, Peter E., ed. *Anointing of the Sick.* Vol. 7. Examines the process of healing in light of the human sciences. Chapters on pastoral theology and anointing healing in the church. Sample liturgies.

Beachy, Alvin J. *Worship as Celebration of Covenant and Incarnation.* Newton, Kans.: Faith and Life Press, 1968. The material of this book represent the collective thought of Anabaptist worship theologians and leaders. The theme of covenant represents the worship of the Old Testament while the theme of Incarnation represents the worship of the New Testament. The argument is that the exterior form of worship represented in the Old Testament is translated into an interior meaning in the New.

Burkhart, John E. *Worship.* Philadelphia: Westminster Press, 1982. Protestant. Presbyterian professor draws from scholarly sources. Readable material on why we worship, the meaning of assembly, the meaning of Word and Table, and the relation of worship to social action and evangelism.

Clark, Neville. *Call to Worship.* London: SCM Press, 1960. A British Baptist perspective.

Coleman, Michael and Ed Lindquist. *Come and Worship: Tap into God's Power through Praise and Worship.* Tarrytown, N.Y.: Fleming Revell, 1989. A popular and very helpful book describing how to achieve and experience charismatic worship.

Collins, Mary. *Worship: Renewal to Practice.* Washington, D.C.: Pastoral Press, 1987. Catholic. Based on scholarship. Addresses the renewal of worship, spirituality. The study of worship (rituals), the words of worship (inclusive language), and the practice of worship (obstacles to liturgical creativity).

Cornwall, Judson. *Let Us Worship: The Believer's Response to God.* South Plainfield, N.J.: Bridge Publishing, 1983. A charismatic presentation of worship that deals with a number of issues such as the call to worship, holiness and worship, praise and worship, and many other issues.

Daniels, Harold M. *What to Do with Sunday Morning.* Philadelphia: Westminster Press, 1979. Protestant. Presbyterian scholar addresses the matter of change in worship. Guidelines for the development of new forms, the centrality of the Lord's Supper, the use of art forms, and creative possibilities for worship.

Dayton, Donald, ed. *"The Higher Christian Life": Sources for the Study of the Holiness, Pentecostal, and Keswick Movement.* New York: Garland, 1985. A bibliographic overview of all the Holiness and Pentecostal movements, their theology and worship.

Dix, Gregory. *The Shape of the Liturgy.* New York: Harper & Row, 1945. Ecumenical. A classic scholarly work. Emphasis is on the development of worship in the early church, particularly the first three centuries.

Dunstan, Alan. *Interpreting Worship.* Waco, Tex.:

Word Books, 1985. Protestant. Popular. Anglican leader addresses why worship, recovering mystery, presenting the Bible in worship, the authority of preaching, prayer, the sacraments, psalms, hymns, songs, and service in the world.

Empereur, James. _Worship: Exploring the Sacred_. Washington, D.C.: Pastoral Press, 1987. Catholic. Based on good scholarship. Addresses worship as the Experience process (the search for meaning in worship), the Reflection (models of worship), the Process (planning), and the Challenges (creativity).

Engle, Paul E. _Discovering the Fullness of Worship_. Philadelphia: Great Commission Publications, 1978. Popular. Protestant. Presbyterian leader explores worship under the old covenant, worship under the new covenant, and the history of Christian worship. Strong on biblical material.

Erickson, Craig Douglas. _Participating in Worship_. Louisville: Westminster/John Knox Press, 1989. Protestant. Based on good scholarship. Emphasis on participation. Deals with priesthood of the church, perspectives on participation, utterances of the Spirit, silence, prayer, preaching, lay-led worship, communication, participation in the mystery of Christ.

Fink, Peter C. and James M. Schellman, eds. _Shaping English Liturgy_. Washington, D.C. : Pastoral Press, 1991. This work, written in honor of Archbishop Dennis Hurley, contains articles on ritual reform, language and liturgy, culture and liturgy, justice and liturgy, lectionary and scripture.

Gusmer, Charles. _Wholesome Worship_. Washington, D.C. : Pastoral Press, 1989. Catholic. Based on good scholarship. Deals with the many dimensions of ritual, services of Sunday and week days, reconciliation and healing, and seasons of the year.

Harakas, Stanley S. _Living the Liturgy_. Minneapolis: Life and Light Press, 1974. Orthodox. Popular. Deals with both the objective and subjective side of the St. John Chrysostom liturgy. Argues for worship as a lived experience and shows how to make the liturgy live.

Hardy, Daniel W. and David F. Ford, _Praising and Knowing God_. Philadelphia: Westminster Press, 1985. Protestant. Deals with the issue of praise, biblical praise, praise in the historical tradition, basic Christian existence as praise, evil, suffering and death, knowing God, Jesus in our praise, praise and prophecy, with an appendix on the systematics of praise.

Hayford, Jack W. _Worship His Majesty_. Philadelphia: Westminster Press, 1987. Protestant. Popular. Charismatic preacher and song writer (author of "Majesty") deals with themes of renewing worship. In fourteen chapters touches on all the themes of morning worship—Word, Table, song, structure, and practical "how to" matters of planning and leading.

Hickman, Hoyt L. _A Primer for Church Worship_. Nashville: Abingdon Press, 1984. Protestant. Popular but based on good scholarship. This United Methodist minister explores the structure of worship, helping readers understand what is behind worship, the what and why of worship in Entrance, Word, Table, and Christian year.

Jones, Cheslyn, Geoffrey Wainwright, and Edward Yarnold, eds. _The Study of Liturgy_. New York: Oxford University Press, 1978. Ecumenical. Scholarly. A standard text book in liturgy dealing with the impact of twentieth-century scholarship in the origins and developments of worship. Covers general matters, initiation, Eucharist, ordination, the divine office, the calendar, and the setting of worship.

Kelsey, Morton. _Tongues Speaking: The History and Meaning of Charismatic Experience_. New York: Crossroad, 1981. A brief history from the day of Pentecost to the contemporary time with an approach to the meaning of tongues.

Kavanagh, Aidan. _On Liturgical Theology_. New York: Pueblo, 1984. Catholic. Popular but based on good scholarship. Lectures given in seminary settings. Addresses discoursing about the church and the world, and liturgy and theology.

Kendrick, Graham. _Learning to Worship as a Way of Life_. Minneapolis: Bethany House Publications, 1984. Protestant. Popular. Leader of the charismatic movement in England and popular songwriter addresses practical matters such as dethroning the powers of evil and worshiping in the Spirit. Also includes a helpful section on how to lead worship.

Kilmartin, Edward J. _Christian Liturgy_. London: Sheed & Ward, 1988. Catholic. Scholarly. Addresses the theology of the sacraments with a concern for the recovery of mystery in worship.

Kreider, Eleanor. *Enter His Gates.* Scottdale, Pa.: Herald Press, 1990. An excellent introduction to convergence worship from an Anabaptist perspective. Addresses the design of worship with chapters on form and freedom, planning worship and songs ancient and brand-new. Also includes a number of worship models.

Last, Carl, ed. *Remembering the Future: Vatican II and Tomorrow's Liturgical Agenda.* New York: Paulist Press, 1983.

Lebon, Jean. *How to Understand the Liturgy.* New York: Crossroad, 1988. Catholic. Popular but based on contemporary scholarship. Deals with the act of celebrating (worship as action), with matters of liturgy (signs, postures, communicating), and the liturgy itself (assembling, Word, Table, dismissal).

Liesch, Barry. *People in the Presence of God.* Grand Rapids: Zondervan, 1988. Popular. Evangelical explores biblical worship with strong emphasis on creativity and the arts: Principles, family, small group and large group worship.

Marshall, Michael. *Renewal in Worship.* Wilton, Conn.: Morehouse-Barlow, 1985. Protestant. Popular but based on contemporary scholarship. Anglican writer discusses general subjects such as the nature of worship, flexibility, music, signs, symbols, ceremonies, the Word, and service to the world.

Martimort, A.-G., ed. *The Church at Prayer.* 4 vols. Collegeville, Minn.: Liturgical Press, 1986–1988. An excellent scholarly set of books addressing major issues of worship: Vol. 1: *Principles of the Liturgy;* Vol. 2: *The Eucharist;* Vol. 3: *The Sacraments;* Vol. 4: *Liturgy of Time.*

Martin, Ralph P. *The Worship of God.* Grand Rapids: Eerdmans, 1982. Protestant. Based on contemporary scholarship. A study of worship in the New Testament touching on matters of praise, praying, singing, the offering, confession, the sermon, baptism, Table, Holy Spirit in worship, and the unity and diversity of New Testament worship.

Micks, Marianne H. *The Future Present.* New York: Seabury Press, 1970. Protestant. Based on scholarly sources. In two parts, summoning the future and shaping the present, the author faces a variety of issues in the changing patterns of worship: motion and emotion, speaking and hearing, silence, hope, touch and feel, architectural space, taste and see, worship and action.

McMinn, Don. *Entering His Presence: Experiencing the Joy of True Worship.* South Plainfield, N.J.: Bridge Publishing, 1986. A popular Protestant inspirational book on worship themes.

Myers, Warren and Ruth. *Praise: A Door to God's Presence.* Colorado Springs: NavPress, 1987. This work probes the relationship between worship and praise, and teaches how to praise God in all of life.

Newman, David R. *Worship as Praise and Empowerment.* New York: Pilgrim Press, 1988. Examines the origin of worship and argues for new discoveries of worship in the face of the loss of transcendence. Concludes with a protection of what can happen in a renewed worship.

Ostdiek, Gilbert. *Catechesis for Liturgy.* Washington, D.C.: Pastoral Press, 1986. This work invites congregations to work toward a participatory worship through an integrated program of pastoral care for the liturgy consisting of catechesis, preparation, and evaluation. Through this process, applied to space, action, time, and speech, a congregation may develop a dynamic process of involving all the people as participants in worship.

Peterson, Randy. *Giving to the Giver: Worship That Pleases God.* Wheaton, Ill.: Tyndale House, 1990. A popular Protestant examination of various themes of worship.

Powers, David. *Unsearchable Riches.* New York: Pueblo Publishing Co., 1984. Catholic. Scholarly. Explores the importance of symbol in worship. Asks, "Does symbol capture peoples' experience and express it meaningfully?"

Ramshaw, Gail. *Worship: Searching for Language.* Washington, D.C.: Pastoral Press, 1988. Examines how words reveal both God and the self. Writes about words we choose to explore the mystery of God, express motherhood and fatherhood of God, verbalize our belief in the Trinity and other matters.

Rayburn, Robert G. *O Come, Let Us Worship.* Grand Rapids: Baker, 1980. A Reformed perspective on worship including a very strong and helpful section on Isaac Watts.

Robeck, Cecil M., Jr., ed. *Charismatic Experiences in History.* Peabody, Mass.: Hendricksen Publishers, 1985. This book is a collection of essays on the charismatic experience. While touching on particular historical periods, it is not a history or development of the charismatic experience throughout history. Articles deal with the charismatic experience in the New Testament on historical figures such as Origen and on movements such as the Pentecostal revival of 1906.

Schaper, Robert N. _In His Presence._ Westminster, Md.: Newman Press, 1984. Protestant. Popular evangelical Anglican touches on biblical, historical, developments in worship as well as contemporary concerns for symbols, congregational participation.

Schmemann, Alexander. _For the Life of the World._ Crestwood, N.Y.: St. Vladimir's Seminary Press, 1973. Orthodox. Popular but based on scholarly research. Addresses how worship is by definition and act a reality with cosmic, historical, and eschatological dimensions of Christian truth. Worship is not mere piety but an expression of worldview.

Schmemann, Alexander. _Introduction to Liturgical Theology._ Crestwood, N.Y.: St. Vladimir's Seminary Press, 1966. Orthodox. Scholarly. Addresses problems in Eastern worship. Deals with the task and method of liturgical theology, the origin and development of orthodox worship, and the Byzantine synthesis.

Segler, Franklin M. _Christian Worship._ Nashville: Broadman Press, 1967. Protestant. Popular. A Southern Baptist deals with basic issues such as the meaning of worship, a means of expressing worship, and planning and conducting worship.

Shephard, Lancelot, ed. _The People Worship: A History of the Liturgical Movement._ New York: Hawthorn Books, 1967. Explores the history of the liturgical movement; investigates the fundamental ideas of the liturgical revival, the advances made by the liturgical movement, and the documents of liturgical renewal.

Skoglund, John E. _Worship in the Free Churches._ Valley Forge, Pa.: Judson Press, 1965. This out-of-print book is a major source for the study of free worship. Arguing that free church worship is in trouble, the author points toward a future of worship that draws from the past yet retains the freedom of the church's tradition.

Talley, Thomas J. _Worship: Reforming Tradition._ Washington, D.C.: Pastoral Press, 1990. Ecumenical. Scholarly. Examines major issues affecting worship renewal such as priesthood in baptism and ordination, healing, reconciliation, the primitive Pascha, origin of Lent, the Feast of All Saints, sources and structure of the eucharistic prayer, and the liturgical year.

Taylor, Michael J., ed. _Liturgical Renewal in the Christian Churches._ Baltimore: Helicon Press, 1967.

Thompson, Bard. _A Bibliography of Christian Worship._ Metuchen, N.J.: Scarecrow Press, 1989. Ecumenical. Comprehensive if not exhaustive bibliography on worship through 1981. Almost 800 pages of extremely valuable references.

Underhill, Evelyn. _Worship._ New York: Continuum Books, 1989. Ecumenical. Popular but based on good scholarship. A classic. Anglican author deals with the nature of worship; ritual and symbol; sacrament and sacrifice; characters of Christian worship; principles of corporate worship; liturgical elements; Eucharist; personal worship; Jewish worship; origins of Christian worship, Catholic worship, Reformed worship, free church worship, Anglican.

Vasileios, Archimandrite. _Hymn of Entry._ Crestwood, N.Y.: St. Vladimir's Seminary Press, 1984. Orthodox. Popular but based on scholarship. Relates worship and theology through a study of the structure of the St. John Chrysostom liturgy.

Wardle, Terry Howard. _Exalt Him._ 2d ed. Camp Hill, Pa.: Christian Publication, 1992. Protestant. Popular Christian Missionary Alliance pastor writes to an evangelical audience, providing stimulus to make worship glorify God, be Christ-centered, edify believers, and appeal to visitors. The new edition contains a section on spiritual warfare.

Webber, Robert. _Signs of Wonder._ Nashville: Abbott Martyn Press, 1992. Protestant. Popular but based on scholarship. Develops the six areas of current worship renewal: (1) pre-conditions for worship renewal; (2) renewal of Sunday worship and preaching; (3) the place of music and the arts in worship; (4) the services of the Christian year; (5) sacraments, ordinances, and sacred actions of the church; (6) worship and related areas: evangelism, social action, education, spirituality.

_____. _Worship Is a Verb._ Nashville: Abbott Martyn Press, 1992. Protestant. Popular but based on scholarship. Develops four principles of worship and their implication for renewal: (1) worship celebrates Christ; (2) in worship God speaks and acts; (3) in worship we respond to God and to each other; (4) all creation joins in worship.

————. *Worship Old and New.* Grand Rapids: Zondervan, 1982. Protestant. Based on contemporary scholarship. An introduction to the biblical roots of worship, its historical development, an understanding of its theology, and a grasp of the relationship of worship to space, time, sound, and the world.

————. *Worship Workshop.* Grand Rapids: Zondervan, 1990. Designed as a week-by-week study of worship in the heart, in the home, in the church, and in the world.

$\textcircled{\tiny ▶}$ THREE $\textcircled{\tiny ◀}$

Descriptions of Worship Renewal

This chapter surveys styles of worship and the ways in which renewal is restoring or modifying those styles. The seven styles include liturgical, traditional Protestant, creative, charismatic, praise and worship, convergence, and seekers'/believers' worship. The survey suggests that in many traditions renewal means not only discovering new ways to worship, but also rediscovering the roots of the worshipers' particular heritage. Much renewal in worship blends two or more of these styles into a new hybrid.

163 • SEVEN STYLES OF MORNING WORSHIP

Broadly speaking, the contemporary renewal of worship in the Western world can be classified as follows: (1) liturgical; (2) traditional Protestant; (3) creative; (4) charismatic; (5) praise-and-worship tradition; (6) convergence; (7) the seekers' service/believers' worship pattern.

Liturgical Worship. This model of worship is found among the oldest churches—Orthodox, Catholic, Anglican, and Lutheran. A strong emphasis is placed on the Eucharist.

Traditional Protestant Worship. This model of worship is found among groups of Christians that are able to trace their historic roots either to the Reformation era or to reforming movements among Protestant Christians prior to 1950. This includes mainline denominations, evangelical denominations, holiness denominations, Anabaptist denominations, and the independent churches related to movements prior to 1950. A strong emphasis is placed on the Word. However, most of these groups are being affected by the liturgical renewal and are returning to a model of worship shaped by the early church and twentieth-century concerns. This model, often called the ecumenical model, is characterized by a fourfold shape—Acts of Entrance, Service of the Word, Service of the Table, Acts of Dismissal.

Creative Worship. The creative model of worship is perhaps better considered a modification of any of the other models than an independent model. Cre-

ativity has always had a part in shaping any given worship experience, but its current manifestation is more far-reaching than ever before and can be found among both small and large churches, mostly of independent origins. These churches seek to contextualize worship to the masses, draw heavily on the arts, and have strong appeal to the post-Enlightenment generation, especially the baby boomers. More traditional churches exercise creativity within the bounds defined by the tradition, but that often leaves much room for creative expression. Creative worship also often involves a church rooted in one model borrowing elements from another model. The extreme of this kind of blending merges into the convergence model.

Charismatic Worship. The charismatic tradition of worship, which has emerged since the middle of the 1960s, is a phenomena that attempts to recapture the worship of the New Testament church, particularly that of the Corinthian church (see 1 Cor. 12–14). It emphasizes the Spirit and the role of the gifts in worship. While there are particular charismatic groups, the movement itself has affected the worship of nearly every denomination.

The Praise-and-Worship Tradition. The praise-and-worship tradition of worship is a phenomenon influenced by the charismatic movement of the sixties. It places a strong emphasis on music, involvement of the whole person, and healing. It enjoys a strong following among post-Enlightenment-oriented people, especially those who desire a free-form participation in worship.

The Convergence Model of Worship. The convergence model of worship is an approach to worship that draws on all the traditions. It seeks to achieve a balance of Word and Table, draws on liturgical resources, and incorporates the arts and music from the praise-and-worship tradition. It is an emerging worship found in nearly every denomination.

Seekers' Service/Believers' Worship. In this style of worship a distinction is made between a service of outreach (evangelism) and the worship of the community of faith. The seekers' service replaces the typical Sunday morning worship, whereas the believers' worship is conducted during the week.

These seven styles of worship are discussed more thoroughly in the entries below.

Robert E. Webber

164 • LITURGICAL WORSHIP

Liturgical worship is found mainly among the churches of ancient origin—Catholic, Orthodox, and some Protestant churches such as Lutheran and Anglican. More recently, many mainline Protestant churches are drawing from the liturgical traditions and are modeling their worship according to the early Christian church. The article below looks at worship as an act.

We are all beginners in the liturgy, really. All of us—from the first-time visitor who finds himself or herself paging helplessly through the prayer book wondering what is happening, to the aged priest who has known it all by heart for half a century—are only on the lower slopes of worship. If the great seraphim themselves cover their faces in the presence of the Divine Majesty, who of us will claim to be experts at the act of approaching the throne with offerings of adoration and praise?

For that is what worship is: an act. It is not primarily an "experience," although we often hear people talking about having "a beautiful worship experience." This is a fine sentiment but partly misses the point. God commands us to worship him, and you cannot command an experience. Like love (which is also commanded), worship may be *attended* by exalted feelings; but the thing itself is the *act* of bringing laud and honor to the Most High.

The word *liturgy* catches this. It means "the work

of the people," if we translate literally the two Greek words which make up the word *liturgy.* And this work of the people—the people of God—is to offer themselves and their substance and their praises as an oblation (offering) to God, made acceptable by virtue of the One Offering, namely the sacrifice of our Lord Jesus Christ.

Three questions seem to present themselves when we come to this matter of liturgy.

Why Do We Have Ritual and Ceremony?

It is an odd but significant thing about us human beings that when we come to the highest and deepest experiences of life (birth, love, and death) we reach for ceremony. All tribes, cultures, and civilizations testify to this. Obstetrics can tell us a great deal about birth, for example, but it is not enough: there must be candles and cake and pink and blue and frills. Obstetrics cannot approach the mystery at work in birth. Biology and genetics can tell us what happens when a man and woman come together, but it is not enough: there must be music and hush and slow processions. Medical science cannot approach the mystery at work in death.

Worship is the act in which we approach the highest mystery of all, namely, God. Hebrews and Christians have from the beginning given this act a structure, not leaving it to the whim of the moment, nor to the rather thin resources furnished by spontaneity—although spontaneous bursts of praise are a lovely thing in their place: it is just that the *corporate* worship of Hebrews and Christians was never, until the modern age, done in an off-the-cuff way. Once in a while you hear someone wondering whether "the liberty of the Spirit" is not somehow hampered by structured worship, and whether that liberty is not synonymous with spontaneity. The most helpful thing to point out here is the fact that the Spirit of God, which, like the wind, bloweth where it listeth, has always been the architect of order. We need only look at Creation, or the moral law, or the early church, to see examples of this. Nothing is left to chance.

Ritual, strictly speaking, refers to the *words* in the liturgy. All of us are familiar with the Christian use of hymns and psalms in worship, and in these we have ritual, that is, fixed, "secondhand" words furnishing us with the very capacity our own imaginations lack to say what we would like to say. All hymns are ritualistic in this sense: the words, which somebody else has written, and which are "imposed" on us, turn out, lo and behold, to set us free. They help us to say what we wish we could say but cannot, left to our own spontaneous devices. Old and New Testament worship operated on this principle. The ritual you find in the Christian liturgy is a matter of words that have been ripened by wise and widespread usage in the church.

Ceremony, strictly speaking, refers to the _actions_ in the liturgy. Every movement—kneeling, standing, processing, the priest's gestures at the altar—is significant. We are all, of course, accustomed to this business of gestures and movements carrying a weight of significance: a kiss, a handshake, a wave, a victory march—these are all examples of this sort of thing. You _do_ something: merely talking about things does not always suffice. The Christian liturgy is a glorious unfurling of ceremony (significant movement) being brought to the highest service of all, namely, the worship of God. The liturgy is an _enactment,_ in which the church proclaims the whole gospel drama. Every celebration of the liturgy unfolds the entire drama of salvation. It is well for us to remember that actions as well as words are means of communicating significance. Many Christian churches in Renaissance Europe, and then America, decided to limit themselves in their worship to verbal methods of expression, as though words alone are true vehicles of meaning. No human being ever lives on this principle in any other realm of experience, and it would seem to be something of a pity to huddle worship into this sort of limitation.

─────────── **What Is Sacrament?** ───────────

Sacrament is the Latin word for "mystery." In the sacraments (e.g., the bread and wine at Communion, or the water of baptism) we encounter something that runs through the whole story of redemption, namely, that physical things may be the point at which the eternal touches time. The unseen touches the seen. There are religions that tell us that matter has nothing to do with God and that true sanctity is a matter of our fleeing from the visible realm of flesh and blood into a world of vision and contemplation and "inner reality" alone. Christianity rejects and abhors this, since it celebrates Creation (God made all this and saw that it was good), and redemption (he salvaged it all from ruin: apparently, it was worth salvaging). The whole drama of redemption was played out in very physical terms:

lambs, blood, altars, gold, and—supremely—the Incarnation, with God himself taking our flesh and carrying out the great work of redemption, incarnation, passion, resurrection, ascension, Pentecost: look at those great events. Every one of them involves our flesh-and-blood humanity. The sacraments are, of course, of one cloth with all this. They make present to us humans the whole mystery of God taking our world and our flesh into his purposes of redemption. There are some Christian churches that have ruled out all mystery here: for them the sacraments are simply reminders of long-ago events. That is a somewhat modern idea (a product of the Protestant Reformation), and no Hebrew or early Christian would have quite understood it. The sacraments are not magic, of course, but neither are they reasonable. They are, precisely, mysteries. Magic tries to dodge around one side of mysteries, and reason tries to dodge around the other. Neither will work. When our Lord said at the Last Supper, "This is my body," he did not mean less than what he said: but we cannot unravel the mystery here with either magic or reason. We receive it with faith, which is the only faculty we have by which we may receive any of the gospel at all. We are neither required nor able to _understand_ it. Worship begins when we reach the point when we must say with St. Paul, "Oh, the depths!"

─────────── **What Is the Eucharist?** ───────────

Eucharist is a Greek word meaning "thanksgiving," and it refers to the Lord's Table, or the Holy Communion, or the Mass, or the Divine Liturgy, or whatever the various Christian traditions have called this rite. It is a useful word since it is very ancient and crosses all sectarian lines. It strikes the note that something got lost in the late Middle Ages and the Reformation, of this meal being a time of great joy and gladness. Many traditional settings for the Eucharist strike a note mainly of fear or mere penitentiality. These are attitudes always appropriate to us mortals as we approach the Most High, of course, but the attitude that marked the early Christians' gathering for this feast was overridingly one of great joy. "Christ our Passover is sacrificed for us." "Therefore let us keep the feast!" they exclaimed.

Two further roles may be appropriate here. First, the initial thing that we usually find occurring when we come to church to worship is the playing of organ music. This is not technically part of the liturgy proper, and hence it is not provided for in the prayer book. This music is sometimes thought of as a sort of fence or buffer between the clutter of the week and the hush of Sunday morning worship, furnishing us with a few moments to collect our wits. This is not really the main idea in having organ music here, however. From the beginning of human history, and indeed from long before that, music has been offered to God in praise. It does not have to be music with "religious" words attached to it. In the Old Testament, trumpets and cymbals and harps were used all the time in worship. The church has carried on this tradition. There are, again, ways of offering worship that are not verbal.

Second, in liturgical churches, as in many others, we often find that the choir and servers and clergy enter the church in procession during the singing of a hymn. Once more the liturgy itself has not yet strictly speaking begun, although in the Orthodox church the view is somewhat different here. But the church, that is, the people of God, is gathered now, and we begin to enact here, in this building with this congregation, what is true on an infinitely more vast scale, namely, that the church here on earth, together with the church in heaven, moves in its worship up to the place of God's dwelling. The train of choir, acolytes (servers), readers, and clergy follows the cross (a vivid picture of what is true) into the "sacred space" of the church proper and up to the altar. Everything, even space, is sanctified by the gospel, and the church building is a sign of that. All is set apart for God—this building as a sign of all buildings which, in the Christian view, *ought* to be made for no other purpose than the glory of God, whether they are pigsties, gas stations, or cottages. All of us in the congregation, and all of the people of God everywhere, are "in" the procession as it moves toward the altar, singing with angels and the saints of all ages. The whole thing is a visible *enactment* of what all Christians believe to be true. Again, there are ways other than words on a printed page of proclaiming what is true. Enactment is one of these ways—ancient and thoroughly biblical.

Thomas Howard[3]

165 • TRADITIONAL PROTESTANT WORSHIP

Traditional Protestant worship has benefited from the findings of modern scholarship regarding early Christian practices. Like those involved in liturgical renewal, these Protestants recognize that worship is a celebration of God's saving deeds,

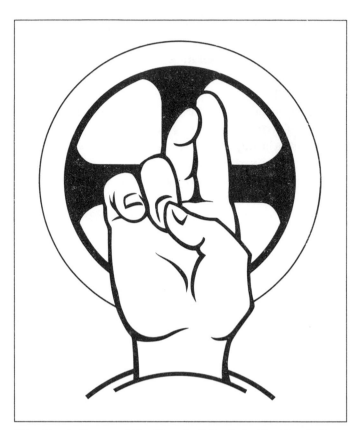

The Greek Form of the Hand of God. In the Greek form of the hand of God that is used in benedictions and blessings, the first finger is extended, the second finger is curved, the thumb and the third finger are crossed, and the fourth finger is curved. This configuration forms the Greek letters IXΘΥΣ, *which is the ancient Greek symbol for the Name, the Lord Jesus Christ. The message of the symbol is that God the Father has blessed the world through his Son.*

a celebration that makes the benefit and power of God's healing action available to the worshiping community.

During recent years many churches have experimented, separately and together, in the effort to be faithful to their own life and to find renewal. It is now possible to identify six convictions or principles that are emerging from this period of liturgical reform, principles that may help us think afresh the purpose, pattern, and practice of Christian worship.

Retelling the Biblical Story. *Authentic worship is rooted in the church's experience of the gospel, especially as it is expressed in the Bible and in the church's living experience through history.* Churches are rediscovering the significance of "recital," the importance of retelling in worship the wonderful deeds of God. From the Exodus and Easter to contemporary examples of new birth, from

Abraham to Mother Teresa and Desmond Tutu, these stories show how our own lives may be shaped by God. The touchstone for comprehending God's action in our lives is most certainly Scripture; but Scripture itself is a product of the early Christian community and is necessarily reinterpreted in each succeeding generation if it is to be a living witness to the love and power of God.

Scripture and "tradition" thus form an inseparable basis for our worship (something disciples have not always appreciated). Together they testify that the disclosure of God-in-Christ to which the Bible witnesses is a living, present reality. To say that worship is rooted in Scripture, therefore, is not simply a call for solemn recollection of what God once did, but an acknowledgment that worship is encounter with the divine here and now.

Theological Worship. *Worship is deeply and inevitably theological.* Worship expresses ideas about God, God's relationship to the world, and the world's response to God. Other aspects of theology are also implied in worship, including ideas about Jesus Christ and the Holy Spirit, the church, salvation, and the meaning of life. This theological quality is present in the service not only as a whole but also in its parts—from the order of its parts to the wording of all that is spoken or sung, to the manner in which the service is conducted. Thus the key question for the service as a whole and all its parts is this: Does this act of worship speak the truth? Decisions about worship are sometimes made on the basis of practicality: "Will it work?" This criterion, though useful, is incomplete. Prior to every other criterion for worship is that of faithfulness to the will of God.

Diversity. *The church encompasses significant diversity in the theological positions on which its worship is based.* Principles two and three must be held together, for the church contains not *one* but *several* theologies, all of which are intended to witness to the one true and living God.

For example, how should we answer this question: Is worship primarily a matter of God's gift (grace) or of our human response to that gift (faith)? Most churches are now able to answer, "Both." Christ's presence at the Lord's Supper, for example, does not depend upon our faith, for that would limit the freedom of God; but we now agree that the faith needed to discern it is also the worshipful celebration of a believing community.

To take another example, is worship primarily a remembrance of God's saving acts or an anticipation of God's sovereign reign which is to come? Do we emphasize the great tradition of Christian witness or the dynamic presence of the Spirit that opens us to the possibility of genuine newness? Again, the churches in ecumenical discussion are able to resist either/or answers, insisting that authentic anticipation is rooted in the memory of what God has done for our salvation.

Disciples have long espoused a commitment to theological diversity. What this has often meant, however, is simply a lack of attention to theological issues, leaving the patterns of our worship to be determined by functional considerations. An authentic appreciation of diversity should lead us to take theology more seriously, not less so. While we happily acknowledge that there is no one correct way to offer thankful praise, it remains true that "as we worship, so shall we believe." Every tradition thus needs to give close attention to the theology expressed in its worship.

Worship and Mission. *Worship is intimately connected with the church's mission, including its struggles for peace and justice in the world.* This connection goes back to Christianity's Jewish heritage in which sacrifice, meditation on the law, and a life of obedience to God are intertwined. Christians, however, have often forgotten, or preferred to ignore, this relationship between worship and mission. Worship, they argue, is something that happens between individuals and God at certain specified times and places and should not be confused with social concerns.

The churches involved in the new consensus on worship have strongly rejected this line of thinking. The experience of God's presence in worship should lead, they argue, to responsible care for God's creation, and especially for those creatures who bear God's image. Thankful praise is rendered not just by what we say and think, but by what we do. God is glorified through the lives of Christians in the world, even as those lives are renewed and sustained by coming together and sharing food in worship.

The very language of worship can reflect a commitment to justice. Many Christians now believe that their worship will be renewed only when its language moves beyond the traditional masculine bias with its unjust exclusion of women. We affirm this belief and strive for language that is inclusive of both genders and thereby reflective of the whole people of God.

Universal and Local. *While worship involves ideas that are timeless and universal, it should be expressed through the culture of the local worshiping community.* This principle may seem obvious, but it masks difficulties and dangers. On the one hand, the unity of the church demands that Christian worship in each place be recognizable as such to Christians from other contexts. We share the same Lord, the same faith, the same baptism, the same Scripture across all differences of language and culture. Surely our worship should reflect this universal inheritance.

On the other hand, people must hear the gospel and pray to God in speech that is their own, using art and ritual borrowed from their distinctive contexts. The modern consensus regarding worship recognizes that such contextualization inevitably takes place. The task is to encourage this process, while at the same time, insisting that the indigenous elements be carriers of the gospel that transcends all particular ideas and experiences.

Creative and Traditional. *Worship should be both open to creative transformation and conformed to enduring standards in its meaning and patterns.* The churches have been divided into two groups: those that require the use of officially prescribed books and services and those that expect ministers and congregations to order worship locally. Today, the two groups are moving much closer together. Although they still use officially required service books, Catholics, Lutherans, and Episcopalians have increased the choices that may be made by leaders of worship, and the mood of these prayers and services is very much like the mood that has characterized free church worship. The new publications of churches in the Methodist and Presbyterian families are examples of movement in the other direction. While continuing to value freedom of choice in the congregations, these churches are giving much more attention than before to sacramental worship and to form and order in their services.

Keith Watkins[4]

166 ✦ CREATIVE WORSHIP

Liturgical creativity is the process by which succeeding generations make traditions of Christian worship their own, through exercise of the gifts of the Spirit in the church.

Creativity in worship means calling forth the gifts of the leaders and all participants. Among these gifts are the ability to write and speak prayers that express the faith and praise of the community; the ability to use space, the visual arts, and movement for fitting praise of God; and musical gifts. Litugical creativity is not the same as liturgical innovation—for the goal is not to entertain through the novel, but to call forth authentic contemporary praise of God, whether in local, denominational, or ecumenical settings. Learning what is done in other worshiping communities can feed liturgical creativity, but creativity is not imitation, since it depends on specific gifts and abilities in each worshiping community.

The process of evoking creative gifts for worship is not uniform, since it involves the working of the Spirit. However, some stategies can assist the process. First, leaders of denominations and congregations must find ways to honor and nurture gifts which can contribute to worship. Second, the work of planning and leading worship must be surrounded by prayer. Third, liturgical creativity requires a commitment of time as worship leaders and committees seek ways to speak to and from the heights and depths of Christian experience rather than seizing upon the first suggestion or resource that comes their way.

A particular challenge which calls on the creativity of planners and leaders of worship is to work with past traditions so that they continue to be intelligible and consistent with a community's theological understandings. For example, the early church drew on Jewish worship traditions while expressing distinctive Christian insights; thus the Passover *seder* became the paschal liturgy. Sometimes the transition is linguistic, for example the movement from Latin to the vernacular or from King James to contemporary English. Sometimes the transition is theological, for example, the revision of baptismal rites in the last three decades in accordance with a renewed theology of baptism and Christian mission. At times, transition involves a radical change, when church leaders seek to bring out basic meanings and actions in rites which have lost their focus over time. In all cases, liturgical creativity calls for awareness of the piety and sensitivities of worshiping communities. It is important to understand what worship traditions mean to a community before revising or eliminating them.

In recent years, the Roman lectionary and other

lectionaries based upon it have become a major source of liturgical creativity, as many Christian churches seek to give Scripture a more central place in their worship. Hymns, anthems, and prayers composed in response to lectionary text can enrich and unify Christian worship.

Ruth C. Duck[5]

167 • CHARISMATIC WORSHIP

Charismatic worship is in itself a renewal movement that has had an impact on almost every denomination. It might be called worship that focuses on the sovereignty of the Holy Spirit. Its hallmarks are free expression, both verbal and somatic, within the bounds established by the tradition; participation by all members; the encouragement and exercise of the gifts of the Spirit; and the expectation that the Holy Spirit will minister to each member of the congregation.

It is late Sunday afternoon. A group of ten has gathered for prayer in the chapel of the Second Presbyterian Church. These persons, believing that they have special spiritual gifts for planning and leading worship, have committed themselves to provide an opportunity for free-flowing worship for the members of their congregation who find this worship style meaningful. Weekly they meet as a growth group to study worship, to rehearse the music and liturgies that will be used at Sunday vespers, and to plan ahead. Now they have gathered for an hour of prayer as they enter into that spirit of worship and adoration into which the congregation will come.

About half an hour before the announced time of the service, the musicians—two guitarists, a pianist, and a drummer—begin to play the music of charismatic worship, folklike settings of Scripture passages intermixed with "praise songs" that use scriptural motifs but that also weave in exclamations of personal devotion and wonder. As the people gather, they may greet one another with smiles and embraces, or they may quietly seek a seat and enter into prayer, meditation, or the singing which has informally begun. Because the goal of each worshiper is to sense as fully as possible the presence of God, the mode of participation will vary from person to person. One may remain bowed with eyes closed, others may lift hands toward heaven in the familiar "charismatic" gesture of praise. Some will pray softly under their breaths in "tongues," the ecstatic prayer language which has been the most controversial element in Pentecostal worship. Still others may enter into soft conversations, talks that move unself-consciously into prayers for one another's particular burdens.

The Order of Worship

A scriptural call to worship begins the time of adoration and praise, in which singing, prayer, and witness to God's powerful actions in individual lives are vital elements. Though the jubilant singing seems spontaneous, much of it has been planned by the worship group to flow from theme to theme. For example, the first songs may cluster around the praise of the Creator and Provider, the next around the name of Jesus, and the third, the person and work of the Holy Spirit. Between these song clusters come spontaneous or planned sharings from Scripture, personal testimonies of praise, or offerings of song or prayer from individual members.

Times of confession follow. Sometimes these grow out of biblical readings about the grace of God in Christ. There may be a period of silence followed by confessions voiced by a worship leader, or they may simply be spoken by individual worshipers. Assurance of pardon is followed by prayers, songs, and hymns of thanksgiving. A sermon or teaching leads to a time of self-offering and of commitment through the Lord's Supper.

This congregation has come to think of the Lord's Supper as one of the most important means of grace, and now celebrates it every Sunday night. Because the number of persons who attend the Sunday Vesper service is small, a spirit of intimacy surrounds the Supper. People are invited forward to partake as they kneel in prayer around the Table. If there are special needs, people are urged to make these known to the serving elder and receive prayer, with the laying on of hands and perhaps anointing with oil (James 5:14). A time of prayer for healing naturally grows out of the sharing in Christ's broken body and the elders pray individually with those seeking health as the congregation joins in supportive prayer by breaking into groups of two, three, and four for ministry. Hymns and songs of commitment or of reconciliation close the service.

It is probably not strictly accurate to say that this service is typical of worship in those congregations which have experienced charismatic renewal, for variations from congregation to congregation, and even from service to service within a congregation, are innumerable. Yet almost anyone visiting from such a congregation will feel at home here, comfortable that these folk seek to respond to the creating initiative of the Spirit, always spontaneous and always orderly.

The purpose of such worship is not to produce spiritual fireworks, but "to be drawn to God through Jesus Christ, acknowledging the sovereignty of the Spirit," observes Calvin H. Chambers in his study of charismatic worship in Reformed tradition, *In Spirit and In Truth: Charismatic Worship and the Reformed Tradition* ([Ardmore, Pa: Dorrance, 1980], 5–6). Worship in the charismatic community, like that of all believers, seeks to offer a worthy response under the guidance of the Holy Spirit to God's initiative (*Book of Order,* Presbyterian Church, USA, S-2.0100).

It is distinctive in four major emphases. First, it is *guided by the free church tradition of resisting imposed forms yet seeking to re-create the worship described in the Word of God.* Spontaneity is a criterion for meaningful worship in this mode. Though much planning, even rehearsal, goes into a celebration of worship, the order of worship is fluid, moving from adoration to confession to thanksgiving, from teaching to intercession to self-giving. While there are set worship leaders, any worshiper may at any time move into leadership by beginning a song, uttering a prayer of prophecy, moving to embrace someone. Such spontaneous leadership seeks to submit itself to Paul's criterion for decency and order in 1 Corinthians 14.

The principle of spontaneity does not preclude the use of prepared liturgies. Many congregations use a sophisticated liturgy while cultivating the freedom to adapt, enhance, or depart from its use when the needs of worshipers or the movement of the Spirit seem to provide fresh new direction.

A second distinguishing principle is the degree to which every worshiper unself-consciously participates in leadership. The Reformers' doctrine of *the priesthood of all believers is more completely realized in this kind of worship than in many mainline services.* Because the Spirit is believed to anoint at will people from every walk of life, participation of every worshiper is a desideratum. Each person feels free to bring a hymn or prayer, to pass the elements of the Lord's Supper with words of blessing, to respond to the sermon or the teaching in a worship that is "corporate, communal, and congregational" (Stephen Winward, *The Reformation of Our Worship* [Richmond, Va.: John Knox Press, 1964], 96).

Thus, in the charismatic tradition, worship is the "work of the people" and truly inclusive. The result is a sense of community and oneness reflecting the biblical metaphor of the body of Christ, with each member interacting harmoniously with all the others in a diapason of praise.

Paul uses this metaphor in 1 Corinthians 12–14 in discussing *the role of spiritual gifts.* The use of these gifts in worship as well as in service is a third major characteristic of congregations experiencing charismatic renewal. Preaching and teaching, encouragement and exhortation are used in charismatic worship just as they are in any gathering of God's people. During periods of intercessory prayer, gifts of wisdom, discernment, knowledge, and mercy may all be brought into ministry. Supernatural gifts like healing or praying in the spirit (tongues) may also be a part of intercessory prayer. Also, sacraments and ordinances may be marked by a prophetic blessing upon a baptisand, a couple being married, or new members received.

The conviction that the Holy Spirit will minister directly to members of the congregation is a part of the *expectancy* that is the fourth characteristic peculiar to charismatic worship. All worship, of course, has an experiential dimension, but gathered charismatics await with a kind of communal mysticism the revelation of God's presence among them. They expect that their own lives will be touched and changed as God speaks to and through them, heals, delivers, and transforms.

Such an eagerness to experience the presence of God results in the great emphasis on prayer and praise, since "God inhabits the praises of the people." People want to respond holistically to the holy presence, loving the Lord with "heart, soul, strength, and mind." Thus, they enact prayer and praise as well as giving them verbal expression. They stand, kneel, clap, lift hands and faces, dance, embrace each other. There is also much silence as people call upon heart and mind to join body and soul in experiencing the presence of God.

Prayer

Prayer is at the heart of charismatic worship. Although the going forth of the Word is still central in the rather free-flowing order of worship, so much worship time is devoted to prayers—silent, sung, spoken, and enacted—that the proclamation/teaching event is itself one aspect of the listening which is integral to prayer.

Often a third of the worship time is spent in prayers of _adoration and praise:_

- singing the Psalms and other Scripture;
- uttering brief ascriptions of adoration;
- reading or reciting passages of Scripture that exalt the triune God, sometimes with brief comments of personal praise:
- praying "set" prayers from a prepared liturgy or led by appointed lay persons or pastors;
- dancing, spontaneous or carefully choreographed and prepared as an offering of praise;
- enacting prayer in other ways—bowing, kneeling, standing with raised hands, clasping hands.

Prayers of _confession_ follow—silent, sung, spoken spontaneously as various members acknowledge sin, read together, or lead in a bidding prayer. Often these prayers are enacted. People may write confessions, which are collected in a brazier and burnt, may bow silently and light candles as they complete private confessions, or turn to one another with exclamations of praise: "Our sins are forgiven in Christ!"

Prayers of _thanksgiving_ are usually brief sentence prayers spoken by the grateful. They may be offerings of Scripture read or sung, material gifts, or gifts of talents. They may take the form of "sharing," which in charismatic circles has the particular meaning of rehearsing the mighty acts of God in one's own recent spiritual journey.

Prayers of _intercession and of supplication_ may take another third of the time allotted for worship. Often there are spoken requests or petitions from members, with a kind of collect following. Other congregations may provide a healing service with a heavily liturgical form derived from Anglican and Episcopal healing rites. (See Robert G. Bayley, _The Healing Ministry of the Local Church_ [Oklahoma City: Presbyterian and Reformed Renewal Ministries]). One approach particularly in favor in congregations of Reformed tradition derives from that developed by John Wimber and taught in the "Signs and Wonders" course at one time taught at Fuller Seminary (See John Wimber, _Power Evangelism_ [San Francisco: Harper and Row, 1985]).

These intercessions involve:

- quiet listening to the Spirit to hear what God is doing rather than making assumptions;
- questioning and listening to persons who request prayer for themselves or others, in an effort truly to hear the person's needs and concerns;
- verbal prayers of intercession and where appropriate of confession, forgiveness, "release," and reconciliation;
- praying "in the spirit," particularly when one does not know how to pray in particular instances, so that "through the Spirit we are now able to speak . . . but we are not speaking; God is speaking for us" (Hans-Joachim Kraus, _The Threat and the Power_ [Richmond, Va: John Knox Press, 1966], 97).
- praying in small groups, so that each person can receive prayer as needed.

The climax of an evening of prayer and praise is likely to be the offering of prayers of _commitment_ to discipleship in services of commissioning for special acts of ministry. Many of the churches which have been touched by charismatic renewal are also deeply committed to social witness. The charismata which equip for ministry within the particular fellowship are intended, they believe, for the service of God in the world and in the larger church. In one church, the past several months have been commissionings for youth to build churches and a library in Haiti; an elder to serve as a commissioner to the PC (USA) General Assembly; an engaged couple to serve one another in the discipleship of marriage; a college man to tutor children in an inner-city community; a woman to ask forgiveness of a neglected parent; and a pastor to lead Bible studies for fraternal workers overseas. Such prayers are enacted by the laying on of hands on the part of the whole congregation whom the commissioned will represent in the task for which they are set aside. The prayers may be varied by spontaneous Scripture readings, pledges of support, intercessions, prophesies, and encouragement.

Music

Much of the prayer so central to charismatic worship is expressed in song. Spontaneous music is apt to burst forth at any point in the service as an expression of praise, joy and thanksgiving, or need.

Most mainline Protestant charismatics love the worship hymns of the ages: "A Mighty Fortress,"

"Holy, Holy, Holy," "O Worship the King," Oswald Chambers comments that "as a congregation is renewed in the Spirit, a strong desire for . . . a magnifying God for his redemptive work in Jesus Christ [is felt]. . . . People . . . request hymns centered upon the praise of God rather than those which express human desires."

The music most associated with charismatic worship is the Scripture song, born of the 1960s and in the idiom of Dylan and Baez. Roman Catholics have contributed overtones of plainsong and the Gregorian chant, while Messianic Judaism has brought in the rhythms and scales of Israeli dances, especially in settings for the Psalms.

The singing of Scripture paraphrases is a vital characteristic of charismatic worship. Because of the spontaneity of enacted prayer that accompanies the singing, Calvin's Geneva might not recognize their kingship. Eric Routley describes the reaction of Saul's daughter to David's sacred dance as expressing "the essential shockableness of conventional religion" and suggests that responsible musicians might join David in calling such stodginess "superstition." Believing that the whole person is called to worship, and that the Pauline principle of order gives forms to the principle of freedom rather than enforcing a conventional passivity, "Spirit-led" worshipers clap, snap fingers, join hands, and sway as they sing, kneel in the aisles or at their places, dance to celebrate the mighty power of God.

One misunderstood aspect of the singing of Scripture songs is the continued repetition of a single verse, three, four, or half a dozen times. This is an intentional moving from a logical-intellectual mode of perception to one of meditation and spiritual understanding. The call "Let all that is within me bless God's holy name" is extended to harmonize left and right brain!

The Lord's Supper

Sacraments take on a new importance when congregations share a new vitality of faith. In their sense of personal renewal, many members ask for a second baptism in order to bear public witness to their new life in Christ. Understanding the sacrament of baptism, we must offer frequent opportunities for public reaffirmation of promises made at baptism. The Lord's Supper gives such opportunity on a recurrent basis. Moreover people filled with a new dimension of love for Christ yearn for frequent cele-

brations of the Supper. And one of the effects of the Spirit's work in any congregation is to create a sense of family that is fulfilled as we gather around the Table of the Lord. Thus many renewing churches have returned to Calvin's original design, the weekly celebration of the Lord's Supper.

The manner of receiving reflects the concept of lay ministry. Many charismatics prefer to rise and go forward to receive from a single loaf and chalice, or to pass cup and bread to one another as they assure each other, "This is the body . . . this is the blood." Spontaneous songs, prayers, exclamations of thanksgiving may enliven the time of receiving, or the sacrament may be received in the absolute silence of meditation; but most often ministry within the body may be a part of the celebration.

Because charismatics believe in divine healing, the healing dimension of the Lord's Supper has been restored to the prominence it has had in the Roman, the Orthodox, and the Anglican churches. Congregations experiencing charismatic renewal therefore offer opportunities for special prayers for healing—physical, emotional, spiritual—in conjunction with the Supper. For the healing of relationships, opportunities for confession and reconciliation between those present may precede the Supper; and passing the peace, with embraces and expressions of reconciliation, follows.

Balance and Harmony

One of the beauties of the charismatic renewal in the Presbyterian and Reformed families of faith is the balance between the tough logic and rigorous devotion to doctrinal truth inherent in Calvinism with the freedom and mysticism once available only in other cultures or traditions. Surely the God who created day/night, sea/land, and female/male rejoices in the happy syzygy of praise offered by Calvinist/charismatic voices!

Melicent Huneycutt Vergeer[6]

168 • PRAISE AND WORSHIP

The praise-and-worship tradition is found mainly among charismatic churches and those churches influenced by recent innovations in both liturgical and nonliturgical bodies. The article below makes a distinction between praise, which is directed to God for God's acts, and worship, which is directed to God for God's person.

Some ten years ago, when I wrote the book _Let Us Praise,_ I consistently interchanged the words _praise_ and _worship_ for, at that level of my walk with God, I accepted them as synonymous terms. During the intervening years I have observed that the Scriptures do not interchange these words but rather teach that praise prepares us for worship, or that praise is a prelude to worship. Psalm 95 is a good example of this principle. It begins:

> O come, let us sing unto the LORD: let us make a joyful noise to the rock of our salvation. Let us come before his presence with thanksgiving, and make a joyful noise unto him with psalms. (vv. 1-2, KJV)

That this is praise none would dispute. It is joyful, melodious, demonstrated, and declared praise directed to God. But it is only after this praise has been fully expressed unto God that the psalmist invites us:

> O come, let us worship and bow down: let us kneel before the LORD our maker. (v. 6)

The order is praise first, worship second. The same pattern is found in Psalm 96, where we are reminded:

> For the Lord is great, and greatly to be praised: he is to be feared above all gods. Give unto the Lord, O ye kindreds of the people, give unto the Lord . . . the glory due unto his name: bring an offering, and come into his courts. (vv. 4, 7-8)

It is only after clearly orchestrating the form of praise that was to be offered unto God that the inspired writer added, "O worship the Lord in the beauty of holiness: fear before Him, all the earth" (v. 9). So while worship may be dependent upon praise, praise is not a substitute for worship; it is, however, a blessed supplement to it.

The frontal attack of praise is a positive response Godward, based far more upon his deeds than on his person. Repeatedly the psalmist urges us to praise the Lord for the _things_ he has _done._ Moses wrote the song of praise extolling God's dramatic rescue of Israel through the Red Sea; Hannah sang praises to God for giving Samuel to her after a long period of childlessness; and Psalm 107 three times exhorts us, "Oh that men would praise the Lord for his goodness, and for his wonderful works to the children of men!" (verses 8, 21, 31, KJV).

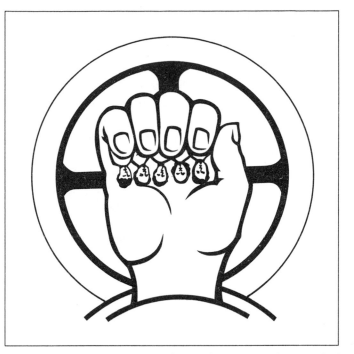

The Hand of God Holding the Righteous. _In this symbol of the Father, the hand of God extends from a bright cloud, and within the hand are five tiny human figures who represent the souls of all the righteous. The idea is based on Psalm 139:10 (KJV), "Thy right hand shall hold me," and on the book of Wisdom "the souls of the righteous are in the hand of God" (3:1)._

This thrust of praise is prescribed, proper, and very profitable, and it is certainly a step beyond thanksgiving; but it is admittedly concerned far more with what God has done for us than with who God actually is. Praise tends to be more concerned with God's _presents_ than with God's _presence._

A diversity between praise and worship might be the method of expression used. Each must be expressed through the channel of our bodies, so quite obviously, there will be many similarities between them, but a trained observer will also see great dissimilarities.

For instance, praise is very vocal, while worship is often void of much speaking. Some declare that praise is the vocal end of worship, and while there is some truth in that statement, it bypasses the very real possibility and common reality of praising without ever worshiping. Two lovers on a walk have much to talk about, but when they are locked in an embrace, words seem superfluous. So it is, often, in worship.

Praise is often physically demonstrative with great action, while deep worship is far more likely to be physically submissive than physically active. We might say that praise tends to be emotional while worship is devotional, and that praise is often loudly exuberant while worship is more apt to be quietly exultant.

Would we better understand this contrast if we said that praise puts love into words and action while worship puts love into touch and relationship? Each is important, but worship is higher and the more intimate.

We cannot bypass praise or negate it, for it is the route into worship. The musical channel for the release of praise is perhaps the most gentle route into worship that God has given us. But we do not desire to remain in praise when God's presence makes worship a distinct possibility.

Judson Cornwall[7]

169 ✦ CONVERGENCE WORSHIP

Convergence worship is the coming together of historic and contemporary worship. This approach to worship follows the fourfold approach to worship, draws on an ancient hymnody, and incorporates contemporary music and other arts.

There seems to be a considerable amount of evidence suggesting that the future of Christian worship is at an uncertain crossroads. One of the major reasons for this uncertainty is the breakdown of distinct denominational worshiping styles. What is emerging from this breakdown is an interdenominational approach to worship. This may be called the convergence of worship old and new.

The day of remaining in the same worshiping community from birth to death is increasingly a phenomena of the past. I speak and worship in a number of different denominational and ecumenical settings. In many churches the denominational mix of people is rather impressive.

For this reason, there seems to be a great deal of anxiety among pastors and other worship leaders. What kind of worship could possibly meet the needs and expectations of such a variety of people?

There are three responses to this question. First, there are the traditionalists, who want worship to be as it was. These are the people who resist change or are so deeply committed to a particular historical model of worship that talk of incorporating new styles of worship is intolerable. Second, there are those who wish to jettison traditional worship as irrelevant and go in search of a worship that is con-

temporary. Contemporary worship is difficult to pinpoint since there are so many forms of creative contemporary worship, ranging from the guitar Mass to entertainment models of worship.

Convergence worship is a third approach to worship. It is both old and new, a worship that respects the tradition, yet seeks to incorporate worship styles formed by contemporary culture.

General Principles of Convergence Worship

Convergence worship is first of all characterized by a willingness to reopen all the questions about worship. For convergence worshipers the reformational theme of *semper reformanda* is taken seriously. Even though ecumenical worship has recently asked what is worship, and why do we worship, convergence worshipers believe these basic questions need to be continually addressed from the biblical, historical, and social science perspectives.

Second, convergence worship is characterized by a willingness to learn from the entire worshiping community. Consequently convergence worshipers look sympathetically at both liturgical worship and the worship of evangelicals, blacks, Anabaptists, Pentecostals and charismatics. They continually ask what can be learned from traditions quite different from our own.

Third, convergence worship is characterized by a healthy respect for the past. Because convergence worshipers are not isolationist in their attitude toward other forms of worship throughout history, they seek to be aware of the way worship has remained faithful to its Jewish and early Christian roots and how it has been adapted in various historical time periods and among diversified cultures.

Finally, convergence worship is characterized by an absolute commitment to contemporary relevance. Those who espouse convergence worship are mindful that worship is an act of communication between God and God's people. Consequently these worship leaders feel worship must touch the lives of people, stimulate personal and spiritual formation, and result in the healing of the inner person and of relationships.

Specific Characteristics of Convergence Worship

First, convergence worship is committed to the ecumenical consensus of the fourfold approach to worship: Acts of Entrance, the Service of the Word, the Service of the Table, and the Acts of Dismissal. Leaders of convergence worship recognize how these four acts are characterized by a narrative quality: they both tell and act out the story of God's saving deeds. These acts also draw the worshiper into the experience of rehearsing a relationship to God through a joyful entrance that brings the worshiping community into God's presence; the reading and preaching of Scripture that speaks to felt needs; a eucharistic response that celebrates Christ's healing presence at the Table; and a mission-oriented dismissal that sends them forth into the world to love and serve the Lord.

Next, convergence worship is committed to the festal character of worship. Festivity goes beyond a mere rote ritual or a cerebral pedagogical approach to worship. It is a celebration of both creation and recreation and is more Davidic (celebrative) in style than Mosaic (somber). For this reason both the Acts of Entrance and the Service of the Table are characterized by text and music that are expressive, enthusiastic, and exuberant.

The festal character of worship leads into the third characteristic of convergence worship: a broad range of musical content and style. For example, the gathering may be characterized by friendly folk songs or contemporary choruses, while the Entrance hymn may be an ancient processional hymn of great joy accompanied by stringed instruments, brass, and a joyful procession of people led by a dancer, banners, and flags that express the festive nature of coming before God; the responsorial psalm may be led by a cantor with the people responding with a compelling refrain; and the Communion songs may be mixture of Taizé music and appropriate contemporary choruses.

A final characteristic of convergence worship is the recovery of the arts. In worship renewal today, there is an increased attention to the arts and to the use of artistic gifts. There is a new sense of the power of visual symbol, a new attention to congregational movement and physical participation, to an appropriate use of drama, to the recovery of the senses, and to the engagement of the whole person in worship.

A Brief Description of Convergence Worship

The description of convergence worship that follows is only one of several possible models. It represents a service that can be adapted to the local customs of worship in a particular congregation. A brief explanation of its four parts shows that it is a celebration of God's saving deeds. It is also the context in which God acts in the midst of the community and calls for a response of praise and thanksgiving.

As a preliminary matter, note the architectural setting. The church gathers around the symbols of storytelling and feasting (pulpit and table), possibly in a semicircular form so people can see, hear, taste, feel, and fully participate in the celebration of the body of Christ.

The first act of worship is simply that of gathering, coming together into the presence of the Lord. The procession at the opening hymn symbolizes coming before the Lord. Then, like Isaiah who saw the Lord seated on the throne, high and lifted up, the church praises God through song. The church sings God's worth and celebrates with great joy its access to the God of gods, the King of kings.

Next, God speaks to the church as it recites the story of God's love shown through revelation. In keeping with the consensus of centuries, the church hears God speak from the Hebrew Scriptures, then through an Epistle, and finally through the words of a Gospel reading. To these "voices of God" the church responds with a Psalm and an Alleluia. Then God's Word is interpreted and applied through a sermon. After that, the church responds to God's voice through the affirmation of faith, by the lifting of hearts in intercessory prayer, and by sharing with the sign of reconciliation to God and to each other through the Kiss of Peace. In these acts the church has told and acted out the story of faith, the story that gives meaning to the story of life.

But then, because God has not only spoken through revelation but has become one of us in the Incarnation, the church enters into intimate relationship with God in the meal of bread and wine, that symbol of Christ's victory, that sign of our own healing. This part of the service is ordered around the fourfold action of Christ at the Last Supper—he took, blessed, broke, and gave. Drawing from the oldest known prayers of thanksgiving (dating back to the second century but updated into modern language) the church celebrates his victory over sin and makes Eucharist (thanks). As Christ in his death and resurrection said yes to the church, so the church eats and drinks with him at his Table, saying yes to him and to his victory _for us_ over evil. The prayers at the Table recite the history of our salvation, call us to remembrance, and plead for the Holy Spirit to be with us. The songs sung during the reception of the bread and wine are songs of celebration and victory, songs of triumph and of the exaltation of Jesus. And because the Holy Spirit is always present to apply the benefits of Christ's saving work to personal needs, the ministry of healing broken and wounded lives and spirits occurs simultaneously with the meal and singing. The meal part of the service then concludes with a burst of doxological praise.

Finally, God sends the church forth to serve God in the world, to live in the power of God's name, and to witness to God's mighty deeds. A special blessing grounded in God's powerful name is proclaimed over the people of God. And then the recessional hymn symbolizes the church going forth into the world to serve.

Conclusion

In brief, convergence worship is an alternative worship that is concerned for order *and freedom,* the historical *and the contemporary,* the verbal *and the symbolic.*

This kind of alternative worship should be seen as a challenge and not a threat. It builds on the best of the biblical, historical, and traditional elements of worship. It is concerned that worship be authentic and real, characterized by a sense of fullness, the feeling of deep joy, and the experience of comfort and healing.

It is, in a word, a post-Enlightenment worship that is in tune with the dynamic faith of biblical Christianity and the changing cultural patterns of modern life. This is the kind of worship that will attract and hold people in the church and give direction to their confused lives.

Convergence worship stands as a signpost at the uncertain crossroad of future worship. It says, "Here is a way to preserve the best of the past and to walk with confidence into the future." Because of this it can be seen as one example of *semper reformanda* (the church must always be reforming itself).

Robert E. Webber

170 • SEEKERS' SERVICE/BELIEVERS' WORSHIP

The seekers' service is a form of evangelism more than a form of actual worship. The model has been developed at Willow Creek Church in South Barrington, Illinois, and has spread across the United States, particularly among newer churches.

Normally, Sunday morning is reserved for a nonthreatening presentation of the gospel through Christian entertainment, a public witness of faith, and a sermon on a real-life issue that reflects a Christian point of view. Believers bring their unchurched friends to this service as a way of introducing them to the Christian faith and community.

Believers' worship is conducted during the week. This service consists mainly of singing (praise-and-worship style) plus instruction and a monthly celebration of the Lord's Supper. Believers are organized into small groups for prayer, Bible study, fellowship, ministry, and service and usually meet in these groups weekly.

Service for Seekers: An Analysis

Leaders involved in the ministry at Willow Creek Community Church believe that it is not possible to evangelize, edify, and worship within the confines of one service and minister effectively to those who have needs in each of these areas. Seekers, the recipients of the evangelistic message, have needs that differ vastly from those of believers. It is difficult for a seeker to relate to the terminology, customs, and routines that are often part of a service that incorporates worship and teaching designed to minister to the believer. Willow Creek Community Church strives to reach these individuals by providing a service that is designed specifically to meet their needs.

Market Research and Analysis. The service for seekers was developed from the results of a community survey taken by leaders of the church prior to the establishment of the church in 1975. Members of the community were asked one question: "Do you actively attend a local church?" If the response was yes, those conducting the survey thanked them for their time and left. If the answer was no, they asked them why. The survey results strongly indicated that individuals with no interest in church attendance had five basic reasons for their indifference.

1. Churches are always asking for money (yet nothing significant seems to be happening through the use of the money).
2. Church services are boring and lifeless.
3. Church services are predictable and repetitive.
4. Sermons are irrelevant to daily life as it is lived in the real world.

5. The pastor makes people feel guilty and ignorant, so they leave church feeling worse than when they entered the doors.

If a church for unchurched individuals was to be developed, it was important that the obstacles hindering their attendance be identified and removed. For this reason the church leaders took the results of the survey seriously when they began designing a church service for those who had given up on the church ever holding any significance in their life.

These leaders also believed that it was important to identify a target audience. Knowing who they wanted to reach allowed them to focus their efforts and energies. It was not enough just to state that the target audience was the unchurched individual, but rather to become more specific and narrow down the target audience.

Professional men between the ages of twenty-five and fifty are the target audience for the Willow Creek Community Church service for seekers. The community surrounding the church encompasses many individuals who are employed in professional positions. All age groups are represented at Willow Creek Community Church, but the service is targeted for those between the ages of twenty-five and fifty. Since men are more difficult to reach with the gospel message and are forceful in their demands upon the church, the services are designed to speak and appeal to men. Women tend to be more open, forgiving, and easier to please in church matters. Therefore, if the service for seekers reaches men, it will reach women as well. Additionally, men are traditionally the role model within the family. If the man in the household is not involved in the spiritual life of the family, the spiritual growth of the family is curtailed.

Philosophical Principles. Foundational values and principles must be identified before embarking on any major endeavor. In order to know what would and would not be done in a service for seekers, it was important to discover the basic philosophical beliefs that would guide the formation of a service and the attitude toward the seeker. Willow Creek Community Church is founded on the following philosophical principles:

1. All people matter to God; therefore, they must matter to us.

2. Lost people need to be sought out and found.
3. Evangelism and edification cannot effectively be done in the same service since the needs of the churched and nonchurched individual differ greatly.
4. Respect for the spiritual journey of the seeker must be communicated, allowed for, and legitimized.
5. Seekers do not want to be embarrassed, singled out, pressured, or identified.
6. Excellence reflects the glory of God and has a positive effect on people.

Strategy

Identifying the obstacles and the philosophical principles allows Willow Creek Community Church to develop aggressively and thoughtfully a strategy for a service for seekers. Every aspect of the unchurched individual's experience is filtered through these principles and obstacles to determine how best to reach him or her with the message.

The ingredients of a service for seekers:

1. A belief in the biblical mandate to evangelize the world, beginning with our own community.
2. The desire to never bore anyone out of the kingdom of God; therefore a commitment to being contemporary and creative.
3. A deep respect for the anonymity of the seeker.
4. An understanding of the seeker's need for time in making a decision; therefore, an emphasis on the process, not the event.
5. The recognition of the need for excellence in everything we do, especially with those things that communicate the very character and nature of God.
6. An understanding that people will desire to support the cause with their time, talents, and treasures since the cause is handled with excellence, integrity, and honesty, and leads to results.
7. Commitment to providing a relevant connection between Christianity and the seeker's daily life.

Seekers who come to Willow Creek Community Church are aware of every component of the church that they encounter. Looking for anything that will discredit what they are about to experience, the unbeliever scrutinizes all aspects of the church, including the facility, the grounds, and the actual service. For this reason, staff members and volunteers at Willow Creek Community Church are dedicated to excellence. This dedication permeates all areas of ministry, from building and grounds maintenance through every aspect of the actual service. The experience that a seeker will encounter upon visiting Willow Creek Community Church is described below.

The first impression of the church is given as soon as a seeker enters the grounds. Initially he will encounter policemen at the entrance to the grounds who are there to facilitate traffic control. The grounds are immaculate, the lawns are mowed, trees and flowers have been planted, and the overall appearance is pleasing to the eye. Entering the grounds, he is assisted in parking by members of the traffic control team who are easily identifiable by their bright orange uniforms. As he approaches the church he is once again assisted by a member of the traffic control team who monitors the crosswalks, stopping traffic to allow people access to the church building. Once inside the building, the seeker will find individuals who are happy to answer any questions he may have but who are careful not to overwhelm him with friendliness.

Upon entering the auditorium, the seeker is handed a bulletin that contains information on activities that he as a seeker might find relevant. As he sits down in the auditorium he will find himself listening to taped music that is designed to allow him to feel comfortable since silence is unsettling for most people. Examining the auditorium he finds nothing that is offensive or even questionable. There are no crosses or other religious symbols that may distract him. The entire experience is designed to put him at ease and allow him to be receptive to the message.

The seeker is surrounded by creativity and variety in every aspect of his everyday life. To capture the attention of the seeker it is imperative that all aspects of the service be interesting and contemporary. It is important to inform the seeker through music, drama, and media that leadership at Willow Creek Community Church is in touch with reality and that they know what is going on in the secular world.

Components that make up the programming session of the service are described as follows:

Music: The music performed is upbeat and contemporary. The seeker is invited to participate in one chorus during the service. The remaining musical selections, designed to minister to the unbeliever, are relevant to the message that will be given during the service. Musical selections may be performed by members of the vocal team, orchestra, or band.

Drama: The majority of weekend services include a sketch performed by Suitcase, the Willow Creek Community Church drama team. Drama does not attempt to preach or answer questions; rather, it is used to provoke questions, provide identification with the issue, and prepare the thought process for the message. These sketches deal humorously or dramatically as well as sensitively with current issues and concerns and are relevant to the message that will be given during the service.

Scripture Reading: A member of the ministry staff is responsible for the Scripture reading each week. Generally a personal story or current event corresponding with the Scripture is related, illustrating the fact that Scripture is relevant in today's culture. The Scripture reading is always relevant to the message that will be given during the service.

Announcements: Announcements are given by a member of the ministry staff and are informative for the seeker as well as the regular attender. This portion of the program is not designed to give details of an upcoming church picnic or to ask for volunteers to teach Sunday school; this time is designated to welcome everyone who is in attendance and to inform those who would like additional information about the church how to obtain this information. Registration details regarding upcoming classes that may be of interest to seekers are also relayed. The announcements provide a smooth transition into the offering portion of the service. General announcements, service opportunities, and employment opportunities are given in the New Community Update, which is distributed at the midweek service.

Offering: This portion of the service for seekers is presented in a very low-key style. A disclaimer is given at the beginning of the offering by the staff member who has made the announcements. The seeker is told that he is a guest and that as a guest he is not expected to participate in this portion of the service. This is designed to put the seeker at ease, and to reinforce the fact that he is welcome at Willow Creek Community Church for himself and not for his financial contribution.

Message: The message or sermon is the final component in the service for seekers. The pastor giving the message strives to ensure that the message is relevant to the audience that has been targeted. Using contemporary examples to illustrate biblical principles, the message deals with current issues and problems and emphasizes the relevancy of Jesus Christ in the lives of seekers and believers today.

Anonymity: An underlying belief that permeates every aspect of the service for seekers is that seekers desire anonymity. Participation for the seeker during the service is limited to singing one short chorus and greeting those sitting around him. Every other aspect of the service requires only the attention of the seeker, and it is the responsibility of the programming department to capture his attention. An altar call is not given during a seeker service because it is the belief of the key leaders within Willow Creek Community Church that seekers need time to assimilate the information that they have received prior to making a life-changing decision.

Choosing not to be event-oriented, but rather process-oriented, leaders at Willow Creek Community Church recognize that it will take a seeker a period of time to come to a rational understanding of a need for Christ. It has been determined through the testimonies of those who participate in baptism that it takes an average of six to eight months for a seeker, once he has set foot in the doors of the church, to make that decision. During that process, the nonchurched person is encouraged to consider the claims of Christ, talk about them with the friend who brought him, and become involved in other activities and classes designed to assist in his search. When he is ready to acknowledge his desire to enter into a personal relationship with Jesus Christ, members of the church body are available to guide him as he embarks on his spiritual journey.

Although the weekend services at Willow Creek Community Church have been designated as seeker services, the truth of the Word is such that it will help all who attend. It is recognized, however, that the believer needs an opportunity not only to receive more "meaty" teaching, but also to join in corporate worship of the God who has called each person to himself. Therefore believers are encouraged to attend the New Community service, which is held midweek. The New Community service is designed specifically to meet the edification and worship needs of the believer.

Willow Creek Community Church Leaders

Models of Renewing Worship

This chapter presents models of renewing worship from the major traditions of the Christian church. These models are intended to be studied and used, adapted and implemented. A congregation may follow these examples and make changes appropriate to its own worship.

The introduction to each of the worship models provides the reader with a brief understanding of the setting from which the worship derives; the main text invites the reader and student to study the flow of worship in the tradition represented; and the commentary summarizes the distinctive features of that worship pattern.

In all of the following models that include text as well as outline, bold indicates congregational parts; normal type, the pastoral parts; and italics, directions.

171 ◆ ADVENTIST WORSHIP

Seventh-day Adventist worship follows in the tradition of free church worship, featuring much hymn singing, expository sermons, and informal atmosphere. Some churches use the Common Lectionary, and the Communion Service is becoming more prominent. A representative order of worship is organized around four areas: God's presence, God's gifts, God's Word, and God's grace. In outline, a renewed pattern of Adventist worship is as follows:

———— Preparation for Worship ————

Sabbath Focus. The entire congregation gathers in a time of intergenerational activity. A special feature may be presented by the children; slides of an overseas mission or community service/action project may be shown; or some inspirational story, poem, or minidrama of interest to all ages may be presented. The "Focus" is specifically planned to bring together and involve everyone present as the church body. Prior planning is essential to effective intergenerational programming. Individual creativity on the part of the coordinator is also a key to success.

Songs of Praise. The intergenerational emphasis is continued. Often a group of children will come to the platform to sing a cradle roll, primary, or junior song. The adults will be invited to join in the singing and act out any motions illustrating the song. Most songs are piano accompanied, but often a guitar is used. On rare occasions a flute and a viola are added; other instruments could be added with availability. Praise choruses and Scripture songs are sung on occasion, using an overhead projector. Generally the *Seventh-day Adventist Hymnal* is used for the "adult" songs. Gospel songs with a praise emphasis predominate. The leaders regularly plan a thematic sequence and almost always make sure the singing time is upbeat. "Songs of Praise" serve to further meld individual worshipers into a worshiping congregation. This active, informal expression of praise gives way to greater formality later in the service and prepares the worshipers to better meet God in Word and prayer.

Celebration and News. Events in the lives of congregants that call for gratitude, concerns that call for action and/or prayer, announcements about church life activities, and explanation or instructions relating to the day's worship are presented here in the context of the community of faith.

Lambs' Offering. All the young children walk among the worshipers collecting an offering for Christian education. The value of this activity to our worship time seems to rest primarily in the great pleasure it gives to a large majority of worshipers. In addition, the children feel included in the service, and physical activity here also helps the children to sit more quietly later, since at present there is no nursery service. At times a children's lesson (or story) relating to the worship theme is presented before or after the Lambs' Offering.

We Celebrate God's Presence

Up to this point in our worship the atmosphere and attitude has been decidedly informal. It has been intentionally planned to meet the fellowship/family needs of congregants in a worship setting and is essentially preparation of the community for worship.

Following this point the character of our service is designed to be considerably more formal, enabling the congregation to experience the depth and breadth and at least a token of the richness that comes from using some of the forms of historical Christian worship. (In a process of education and renewal we add features from time to time or on special occasions.) Our order of worship is organized under four areas of celebration: God's presence, God's gifts, God's Word, and God's grace.

While the local pastor is the worship leader, "local elders" lead portions of the service. Moreover, worship is specifically planned to include congregational participation as much as possible.

Lakeside is currently one of the few Seventh-day Adventist churches that uses the Common Lectionary as the scriptural basis for planning weekly worship. Worship is, of course, on Saturday; when I refer to a lection, it is the one prescribed for the Sunday immediately following. The order of worship may have a title such as Advent I or First Week in Advent, or there may be a note in the bulletin announcements regarding the day or season of the Christian year.

The worship environment includes a fresh floral bouquet as a symbol of creation and the beauty of the Creator, a table with a hand-carved cross and often other symbols or artifacts (these often are not verbally explained) to illustrate the worship theme and/or sermon, and seasonal banners (often left hanging until the next season). In the worship used as a model for this article, Triumphal Entry and Easter banners were displayed and the usual line drawing of the church building on the service bulletin was replaced with one illustrating the Ascension.

Ganged chairs form a modified semicircle around the platform, but are rearranged on occasion to facilitate greater participation. An electronic organ is the primary musical instrument for worship, but it is regularly and frequently joined by the piano. A pipe organ is included in the long-range plans of the church. Occasionally a guest musician offers a solo on some other instrument such as flute, cello, saxophone, or trumpet.

Organ Prelude. This time of meditation and absence of vocal sound follows the informal, more physically active time. Silent prayer is encouraged. The local elders come forward to the platform pews, joining the pastor. On the relatively infrequent occasions when candles are used, acolytes light them during the prelude. If symbolism is better served because of a specific reference in the call to worship or the hymn of praise, the candles are lit at that point. During Advent there is a lighting ceremony at the Advent wreath each week.

Call to Worship. Though in various ways worship has already been happening, the call to worship formally opens worship, signaling clearly the direction of thought and action. Most often it is responsive, thus vocally involving the people in what they are about to do. Most of the time ministers will adapt the lectionary psalm for the day so that it becomes specifically a call to worship, including elements of the human cry, assurance, and praise. Very occasionally they use a prepared call from some worship resource material. Less often they use a more traditional liturgical form. While it is not listed in the order, some leaders follow the call to worship with an invocation that invites God's presence in words related to the call to worship and the worship theme of the day.

Hymn of Praise. This hymn is specifically chosen to direct thought toward God and express adoration of him, magnifying who he is and what he does more than voicing our experience. If such a hymn can also relate to or introduce the day's theme, so much the better. It may do so by contrast, enhancement, or as in this model service, fill out another part of the biblical story that is related to the theme.

We Celebrate God's Gifts

Tithes and Offerings. The tithes and offerings provide the monetary means for conducting the work of God on earth, which is an aspect of worship. Importantly, they also symbolize the gift of oneself to God. Additionally, the act of giving funds is praise to God for his love and blessings. The musical offertory during this time enhances the auditory and aesthetic beauty of worship. At Lakeside a prayer begins the offertory actions and continues with the offertory in music and placing a gift in the plate. At one church in Virginia a doxology that changes every two to three months is sung prior to the prayer that concludes this section of worship.

Our Prayers. This prayer voices the praise, supplication, and confession of the congregation. It is offered by a lay leader, who on occasion asks the congregation for specific needs for prayer. The congregation kneels for prayer and participates by singing a prayer invocation (changed every few months or for special seasons, e.g., the refrain of "O Come, All Ye Faithful" during Advent) and a prayer response.

———— We Celebrate God's Word ————

Old Testament. When used, the Old Testament lesson may be the one listed in the lectionary, particularly if it relates to the worship theme. On occasion it is chosen apart from the lectionary to fit the worship theme. Other times, again particularly if it fits the theme, I use the Psalm, as in this model service.

Hymn. The hymn in this position is often meditational in nature, may reflect on the Scripture before or after it, and usually is related to the sermon in some way. If there is a vocal or instrumental solo or an ensemble, it occurs at this spot in the order. Lakeside does not have a choir; if it did, an anthem would be sung here.

New Testament. This may be the second reading (Epistle) of the Lectionary, or it may be the Gospel lection. In this model service it is a responsive reading from the hymnal that tells the story of the day's worship emphasis (Ascension). We do not necessarily have both Old Testament and New Testament and/or Gospel lections every week. Sometimes there is just one Scripture lesson, which usually is one of the lections of the day, but which is sometimes chosen to complement or enhance the worship theme in a way the designated lections cannot. One of the lessons will often be the sermon passage.

The vast majority of the time the Scripture lessons for the service will be arranged to involve congregational participation. Most commonly it will be an ordinary responsive reading, but regularly it will be antiphonal, or use men and women, or various sections of the congregation, or it will be formatted and presented as a readers' theater, etc. At times

special illustrative effects will be added, as in the Old Testament lesson in the model service.

Hymn. This hymn has, in general, the same characteristics as the one between the lessons, enhancing the worship theme and/or preparing for the sermon. Most of the time only one hymn rather than two (as in this model) will be used in these positions.

Sermon. The expository sermon is based on a biblical passage, most often one of the lections for the day. I preach a topical sermon very rarely. The worship theme comes into clear focus in the sermon and ties all the elements of the service together. Those elements in turn enhance and enlarge the worship theme and the message of the sermon.

———— We Celebrate God's Grace ————

Hymn of Response. This hymn serves to summarize the sermon, to make an appeal relating to the message, to complete the worship theme, and to provide a powerful verbal vehicle enabling the congregation to respond to the entire worship. The ideal hymn for this spot will do all four. At times I write my own hymn (using a familiar tune) if I cannot find what I need in the hymnal.

Benediction. The service is usually concluded by a lay leader, frequently using a scriptural benediction, but occasionally taking the form of a closing prayer.

Dismissal. The spoken dismissal includes an invitation to fellowship and refreshments. The dismissal line in the bulletin generally includes the phrase, "as we are dismissed to fellowship and service beyond."

——————— Holy Communion ——————— [optional]

The Service of the Table is not included in the model of full worship because historically the Seventh-day Adventist Church has celebrated Holy Communion only quarterly (four times per year). The Service of the Table nevertheless deserves important comment in the context of this article on renewing worship in the Seventh-day Adventist Church.

Our present pattern at Lakeside is to have Candlelight Communions on the Friday evening just before Christmas and on Good Friday evening, plus two Communions during the year at a regular Sabbath morning worship, usually in June and September. My personal goal at the present time is to encourage the church to celebrate Communion at least bi-monthly or preferably monthly.

I believe that the Service of the Table is the culmination, the high point of worship. However, many Adventists tend to shy away from Communion. Therefore, for both reasons, I devote very significant time and effort to planning Communions that are unusually beautiful, rich in meaning, full of the joy and mystery of salvation (as opposed to the feelings of unworthiness that keep worshipers away), and have some different feature each time—for example, having the congregation come to the Table to take a six-ounce cup instead of being served the ordinary tiny Communion cup; again, using a six-ounce cup filled with sparkling red grape juice rather than the usual purple Welch's; baking a loaf of bread in the form of a cross and having the members of the congregation break off their own piece instead of being served the small wafer; interspersing readings; and using a brilliant hymn of praise for salvation at the end in place of a traditional near-dirge.

The Service of Feetwashing is included with the Service of the Table for Communion in the Seventh-day Adventist Church. I try also to give it fresh meaning by changing the room environment, suggesting prayers for partners, adding perfume or bath oil to the water, and so forth.

Merle J. Whitney

172 ✦ AFRICAN-AMERICAN WORSHIP

African-American worship has been a renewal movement from the beginning, when African-American slaves gathered to affirm God and in turn were affirmed, renewed, and transformed by the presence and power of God. The African-American tradition in worship encourages free and creative response to all that happens in worship, from gestures to song to the spoken and preached Word. Music is fundamentally communal and varies widely, particularly in instrumentation. African-American churches are not concerned so much with ecumenical worship trends as with "Discovery and Recovery" of African and early African-American worship.

Renewal in worship is not a new concept for some African-American worshipers. This fact becomes evident when one participates with understanding in services of worship where there is some apparent continuity between the unique early African-American worship history and current practices.

From an African heritage, worshipers understood that God alone was the source of restoration and renewal when the ontological balance between the divine and human had been tilted. In many African traditions there were occasions and rites for making and renewing contact between divinity and humanity.

The African-American slave community at worship gathered as a clandestine body and sought renewal, restoration, and reaffirmation of the control of Almighty God in their disrupted and confused lives. Worship provided opportunities for the revival of the soul and the regaining of spiritual and physical vigor necessary for holistic survival in a strange and alien land. In worship, through the enabling power of the Holy Spirit, the impetus to live was "made new again" (renewed) and worshipers were freed "to walk a new walk, and talk a new talk." Renewal in this context means a celebration of the mysteries of Christ by a particular group of believers with the needs and concerns of the community especially highlighted.

This understanding of renewal is predicated on forced existential conditions that negated the humanity of African Americans, causing them to be ostracized and marginalized. Separate times and places for worship allowed direct and personal contact with the Word of God, and freedom to respond

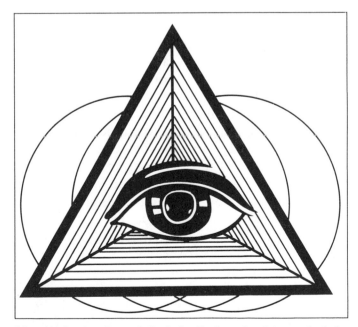

The All-Seeing Eye of God the Father. _In this symbol the eye of God is placed within an equilateral triangle. This symbol is found in many restored English churches, particularly those with the triple-decker pulpits._

in joyful celebration of the gospel. The Good News, which affirms that the presence and power of God, is available for all of God's people and is equally renewing, transforming, and empowering, *in* and *beyond* the worshiping environment. The gathered community at worship could shape and reshape its own liturgy from common symbols of worship as a means of communication *and* as a means of survival. The unity established and maintained between African Americans in the *koinonia* and the *diakonia* initially transcended doctrinal matters. Renewal in worship made it possible to live and work in an oppressive, racist society without muting the memory of suffering and ultimate victory in Christ.

Where there has been continuity from Africa through the period of slavery in America to the present age, it is conceivable that some form of continuing renewal takes place whenever African Americans worship. Amidst community-defined order, and under the power of the Holy Spirit, worshipers respond freely and creatively to the acts of God in history. In services of worship where congregations follow a basic order established by the denomination, one finds a variety of liturgical styles reflective of particular needs and cultural variances.

Verbal expressions such as Scripture readings, preaching, prayers, community concerns, and liturgical directions also vary according to the leadership style of the clergy and congregational needs. The unity of the whole church throughout the world is noted in prayers, sermons, and in the increasing use of songs from other traditions and cultures. There is also a growing tendency to use inclusive language in spoken and preached words.

The improvisatory gifts of worshipers are demonstrated especially in the interaction of African-American liturgical music (forms and styles), with musical performances outside of the worshiping environment. Both traditional spirituals and the form identified as black Gospel music reflect the shaping as well as vocal and instrumental improvisations of the church and concert stage. This is indicative of the traditional blending of "sacred and secular" in offering praise to God. Music holds in constant tension an emphasis on present situations in "this world" and life in the Spirit, which also transcends the moment. As music ministers to the whole person, it connects the liberating message of the gospel with concerns for social justice throughout the world. Music repertoires also include hymns by African Americans, stylized "metered hymns" (or "Dr. Watts"), hymns by Euro-Americans, and more recently, hymns from other cultural traditions. Performance practices may vary, however, from one congregation to another. "Renewal music for worship," including the contemporary praise and Scripture songs from other traditions, is freely transformed (or reshaped) and incorporated to meet the needs of local congregations.

Music in African-American worship is first and foremost *communal* music and therefore lends itself to the renewal of individuals and communities of faith. Regardless of personal depths of faith or levels of suffering, individuals find meaning and renewal through music as they identify with others whose existential journeys are similar.

The piano and electronic organ are the most frequently used musical instruments for worship. Pipe organs and guitars are also used in some services, and more recently, percussive instruments—drum sets of varying sizes—have become acceptable liturgical instruments. It is not unusual for the organist or pianist to accompany prayers and the sermon. A gifted sermon accompanist is able to help the preacher establish, maintain, or modulate the pitch of his or her voice and enhance special points in the sermon. Some pastors prefer to have keyboard accompaniment during the entire service.

The current liturgical renewal movement among Euro-American denominations that emerged following Vatican II may not be the source of renewal for African Americans. The concept most apparent among African-American congregations is "Discovery and Recovery," with reference to African and early African-American modes of worship. This concept is predicated on events surrounding the civil rights movement, which called attention to the fact that the church universal was not yet practicing what it had attempted to teach about ecumenical unity. Forms of renewal are not limited to acts of worship but to more direct action and involvement in mission and ministry, local and worldwide.

While there are specific times in the orders of worship where particular responses are elicited, there is an inherent rhythmic "call-and-response" pattern in African-American services of worship that occurs throughout the service and peaks during the sermon. The renewing Word of God is expressed, not only in the preached message, but also in the faith of the preacher. The intent of the preacher is to be used by God, so that the faith, life, and total being of the hearer may be transformed into a new person—the person that God would have them become. The preacher and hearer thus are holistically involved in the preaching event.

The model which follows is based on an order of worship that draws on traditional African-American worship and current liturgical trends. A written document alone cannot do justice to the service itself, since the real "work of the people" varies from one congregation to another.

The Basic Pattern

A Time of Gathering. As the people gather they may greet each other warmly and then prepare for worship in quiet meditation, or there may be a period of corporate devotion. The devotional period could be led by officers, youth groups (if officers do not include youth), or other organizations in the church. Care should be taken to allow spontaneous response within a basic structure, carrying forth themes of the liturgical year so that integrity is not lost. The sacred space should be conducive to a variety of styles of worship.

Prelude/Instrumental Voluntary. Music appropriate to the season of the Christian year or to the theme of the day is offered as the gathered community continues in preparation.

Call to Worship. Sentences of Scripture or words which appropriately proclaim that God, in Jesus the Christ, has taken the initiative to call God's people to worship may be spoken by a leader (liturgist) or read responsively by the leader and congregation. The call could be a responsorial setting of the Psalm for the day. This may be preceded or followed by a choral call to worship (introit) by the choir or choir and congregation.

Praise, Adoration, and Thanksgiving

Hymn or Song of Praise and Adoration. The people respond to the call and promises of the grace of God in song.

Prayer of Adoration and Thanksgiving. In continuing response, an opening prayer is offered that includes elements of adoration, praise, and thanksgiving to Almighty God who, in Jesus Christ, continues to make worship opportunities possible.

Choral Response. An appropriate choral response to the prayer is offered, or the people may chant the Lord's Prayer.

Anthem, Spiritual, or Gospel Song of Praise. The choir offers a continuation of praise in song on behalf of the people gathered.

Testimonies (optional). In some gatherings, the people are given an opportunity to express personal instances of divine intervention and renewal during the week, which can be claimed by the entire community as reasons for praise and thanksgiving and as witness to what God can and will do. This might also occur during "community concerns."

Call to Confession and Confession of Sin. Fully aware of the awesome power of God, who is praised, adored, and offered thanksgiving, the people are called to recognize their nakedness in the presence of the majesty and holiness of the Almighty, and the human propensity to sin against God and each other. A prayer of confession is offered by the leader or is prayed in unison by the people. A period of silent confession may precede or follow the prayer.

Assurance of Pardon. The leader declares God's forgiving grace, mercy, and empowering love to all who truly and earnestly repent of their sins.

Gloria Patri **or Doxology.** A Trinitarian ascription of praise sung by the whole congregation is appropriate at this time. To use a traditional ascription is a reminder that God's promise of forgiveness is an everlasting gift to sinners saved by grace.

Affirmation of Faith or Credal Statement (optional). The people may affirm their faith in God with the whole church at this point or following the sermon.

Welcome to Visitors. Visitors are acknowledged, welcomed, and encouraged to feel that they are part of the worshiping community.

Community Concerns. Announcements and parish notices that need to be highlighted and concerns of the congregation and community are shared.

Altar Call/Prayers for Healing/Intercessory Prayers (optional). Some congregations may opt to include intercessory prayers at this point in the service. People are invited to come forward and kneel at the kneeling rails or stand around the symbolic sacred space—pulpit, Table, and font. Concerns of the people, personal prayer needs, and prayers for healing may be combined with prayers for the world.

The Renewing Word of God

Old Testament Lesson. A prayer for illumination, which invokes the blessing of the Holy Spirit upon the readers and hearers of the Word, may be prayed prior to the reading of the first Scripture. Although the primacy of Scripture has always been a given in African-American worship, there has not always been an intentional inclusion of readings from both Testaments and the Psalms. The use of a lectionary would facilitate the choice of Scriptures, allow for consistency in following the Christian year, provide an orderly or systematic use of Scriptures, and allow the community of faith to hear more of the fullness of the Bible over a period of years.

Anthem, Spiritual, or Gospel Songs. The choir may sing words that either provide commentary on the Old Testament Scripture or prepare the people for the New Testament lessons; or a setting of the Psalm for the day may be sung.

New Testament Lesson(s). It is appropriate to use two Scriptures, one from the New Testament other than the Gospels and a reading from one of the four Gospels.

Congregational Song. The music offered here further helps to prepare and free the preacher and the people to "hear the Word" that they might be willing "doers" of the Word. In some settings, this song is eliminated so that the preacher moves directly from the Scripture to the sermon.

Sermon. One or more of the Scripture readings are interpreted. Faithful preaching confronts us with the liberating, renewing Word, and witnesses to God's continuing activity among the people and in the life of the world.

Response to the Word of God

Invitation to Discipleship. The call to discipleship is a continuation of the call to make or renew personal commitment to God in Jesus Christ given in Scriptures, song, and sermon. It may also symbolize the "opening of the doors of the church" to receive new members into the universal church.

Hymn or Song of Affirmation or Commitment. The song chosen should continue the call to renewal, commitment, and an affirmation of faith. This might

also be the place for an "Altar Call" as people are called through the Word of God in song and sermon to respond to the Word of God. This period may be followed by an affirmation of faith or an ecumenical credal statement that further reminds the local congregation of its connection with the whole body of Christ.

Offertory. The offertory, placed at this point, symbolizes a continuation of the response to the Word of God. It is a symbolic offering of ourselves and all that we have to God, not merely monetary gifts. Nevertheless, the offertory may occur earlier in the service.

Baptism and the Lord's Supper

The Lord's Supper (when scheduled). Baptism and the Lord's Supper are appropriate acts of worship to follow in response to the preached Word since both historically symbolize the Word enacted. Through the waters of baptism, the people of God are born (and borne) into the body of Christ. The Lord's Supper renews all that baptism signified and sealed. When either is to be celebrated, it should follow the preaching of the Word.

Since African Americans are members of a variety of denominations with different doctrines, polities, and practices, one could expect to find these acts of worship located at other places in services of worship. There are also differences in whether baptism is required before one can partake of the Lord's Supper.

Sending and Going Forth in God's Name

Hymn or Song. "When they had sung a hymn, they went out" (Matt. 26:30; Mark 14:26). In keeping with the Scripture, the people have fed upon the Word and now sing a song as they prepare to leave.

Charge and Benediction. Using words that capture the essence of the sermon, the minister charges the congregation to go forth into the world to continue the mission and ministry as set forth in the gospel. The blessing of God is then given as the pastor and people look at each other.

Recessional. The choir and worship leaders may sing a song as they recess, symbolizing the going forth into the world.

Melva Wilson Costen

173 ◆ ANABAPTIST WORSHIP

Churches in the Anabaptist traditions are characterized by great variety in worship. Some have adopted habits from mainstream Protestant churches, while others have maintained a long-held communal ethos and some distinctive worship practices. Among the challenges to the churches that are eager to find life in the Anabaptist tradition are these questions: Does public worship shape the character of individuals and the community by Jesus' way—by the marks of mercy, love, humility, and peace? Do worship and ethics reflect each other? Does worship build up a loving, disciplined, participatory, accountable congregation? Does worship engage us in God's mission of reconciliation and justice in the world? If so, the churches will realize the best in the Anabaptist tradition.

Hymn singing traditionally sung in parts without accompaniment serves the congregation on several levels. Besides conveying the texts (praise, dogma, confession, commitment), the hymns are a focus of realizing unity in the community, as well as an expression of an aesthetic dimension which is often undervalued in worship. People sometimes say worship was "good" or "not so good" on the basis of how moved they were by the congregational singing. _The Hymnal: A Worship Book_ (1992) includes music and resources from a wide variety of Christian traditions, notably including subcultures within North America.

Liturgically distinctive is the (at least annual) three-part Love Feast—feetwashing, an agape meal, and the bread and cup Communion. Preparation for the Love Feast underscores reconciliation among the members as an integral part of reconciliation with God. Feetwashing symbolizes themes of humility, forgiveness, and service. The agape meal is a foretaste of the banquet of the kingdom. Celebrated in the cup and bread Communion are unity with Christ, with members of the faith community, and with the church universal. True unity means commitment to "full obedience" in a life of "following after" Jesus.

Most Mennonites and Brethren observe the Lord's Supper quarterly. A period of preparation, including making peace with all, self examination, and prayer is traditional. Feetwashing services, which dramatize a commitment to follow Jesus in humble service, are not universal.

Water baptism on confession of a person's faith is foundational. Baptism is always public and involves commitment to membership and service in a particular congregation.

Below is the basic pattern of Mennonite worship with a commentary.

The Basic Pattern

Call to Worship. Transition from anteroom chatter to worship in the meeting room is sometimes bridged by pre-service singing of hymns or quiet instrumental music. The worship leader may introduce the service by saying, "It is our custom to begin worship with a short period of silence." A one-sentence welcome and greeting in Jesus' name are sufficient before the Scripture sentences or psalm portions with prayer that combine with several hymns and songs of praise to form the opening section. The song leader and the worship leader may stand side by side to lead a smoothly integrated period of singing, prayer, and Scripture reading. They will direct attention toward God in this section.

Hymns and Songs

Children's Time. Skillful storytellers can invite children forward for a short period specifically directed to them. Object lessons or brief interviews with visitors can be effective. But problems lie with adults who laugh at children's reactions, with the wide range of ages among the children, and with necessity for continuous novelty in ideas. More helpful is a visual or dramatic presentation of the service's theme which addresses "the child within" adults as well as the children. This requires simple language, visual aids, or an interactive story. In this section it is important to avoid moralizing and to leave the lesson open to further reflection.

Offering. Although often a fairly perfunctory item, the offering can be surrounded with joy and thanksgiving. A proper biblical reticence in not letting the left hand see what the right hand gives can be balanced by conscious enjoyment of communal projects that include personal time and innovative gifts, as well as money and material goods. An accent on offerings is especially appropriate in Communion services.

Bible Reading. Bible reading is strangely neglected in this self-confessed "biblical tradition." Besides the passage associated with the sermon, other readings can be chosen by use of a lectionary, woven into opening and closing sections of the service, presented dramatically, or read serially from one week to the next (especially Old Testament narratives). Bible portions told by memory are especially direct and moving. It can be useful to find the gifted readers and train them, valuing them as much as the musicians and preachers.

Sermon. Traditionally the focus and longest section, the sermon is under scrutiny these days. Polished rhetorical delivery is valued less than clear, simple biblical explanation with practical application. Preachers are working with interactive, dramatic, and narrative approaches. Most congregations encourage the preaching gifts of several members besides the minister. The traditional "giving liberty" (on-the-spot invitation to preach) to visiting preachers can remind us to expect the Holy Spirit to inspire a timely message from an unexpected quarter.

Sharing of Concerns. A recent liturgical innovation, the period of sharing news and concerns has the strength of its rootedness in everyday experience, its earthy quality, and its emphasis on relationships. If poorly led, however, it may ramble or be inaudible or trivial. It may actually exclude newcomers and visitors with in-language and references to unknown programs or to people by first names only. The best hope for the "sharing time" is to incorporate its concerns into prayers, to have some prepared announcements along with opportunities for informal comments, and to exercise loving discipline upon it.

Pastoral or Morning Prayer. Usually led by a minister, the main prayer often focuses primarily on pastoral concerns for the local church. This is the part of worship that needs the greatest enrichment and must be allowed plenty of time. An outline structure can help to ensure that the prayers are wide-ranging. Confession, both for individuals and for the congregation, can be followed by intercessions for global concerns, for government, for the earth, for all who work for peace and justice, as well as for immediate local needs. Prayers and anointing with oil for for-

giveness, healing, and ministry are well known in the tradition, and can also be incorporated into the morning prayers. Two or three people can jointly lead such a series of integrated prayers. All prayers are best framed with thanksgivings to God and can be concluded with the congregation praying together the Lord's Prayer.

Benediction. There is untapped potential in the closing benediction. It links the story we celebrate in worship—God's love for the world and commitment to its healing—to our daily lives. Every week the members can commission each other to love God anew and to learn more about loving the neighbor. They can pledge to help each other to follow Jesus' way and to breathe deeply of the Spirit. Worship leaders may write special blessings or use biblical or poetic benedictions. The congregation may regularly use a memorized benediction.

Eleanor Kreider

174 • BAPTIST WORSHIP

Baptists do not "own" a liturgy; rather, they share broadly with other denominations. The order of worship in most Baptist churches normally will not differ significantly from free church congregations. Those Baptists following a more formal order often borrow from Episcopal or Lutheran resources—or from the recently published resources developed by the United Methodists and Presbyterians PC (USA).

The service outlined here is the result of post–Vatican II scholarship and practice. Within the *structure* described, unlimitable possibilities are present. Nearly any worship *style* found in modern Western Christianity can be accommodated within this structure. Our test for validity of structure and style is twofold: whether the *story*—the gospel of Christ—is faithfully proclaimed, and whether the body of Christ, the church, is nurtured by the liturgy we follow as we offer worship to God. The service outlined here is both responsive to the ancient practice of the church (of Justin and Hippolytus) and as fresh as tomorrow. Whether it is acceptable and worthy to offer to God is not simply the result of the outline or the words and acts we choose, but is ever and always wholly dependent upon the intent of the hearts of those who gather to worship God.

Unfortunately, a "worship script," as read off the

page of the Sunday bulletin (or out of a prayerbook), bears little resemblance to the drama that is enacted from its "stage directions." Different congregations—and even the same congregation at different times—will read and enact the "script" differently. For this outline of liturgy, as for any liturgy, the final "director" is the Holy Spirit, who may, at any time, invite us to depart from the "script" and worship _ad lib_. We find it much easier to _ad lib_ in response to the "inbreaking" of the Spirit when we are _not ad libbing_ on our own all the time. In fact, it is _then_ that these occasions truly "blow fresh" through our assembly, when we all—pastors and congregation—are surprised by God.

The Lord's Supper may be ordered according to any of the several traditions known among the churches and may involve any of the various methods of the distribution and partaking of the elements. We most often observe "traditional Baptist" practices of "Communion in the pews," though we vary this for seasonal use.

On Ash Wednesday we may come to the table, kneel, and feed each other by twos. Maundy Thursday we may sit at the banquet table (Southern Presbyterian style) ten to twenty at a time, serving each other "family style" around the table. Easter dawn we come forward to the Table and are fed standing. Christmas Eve we may form a circle around the room, pass the elements round the circle, then, afterward, pass the candles for lighting.

On occasion we may use any of the forms for the Communion service presently in use among the churches. Often the form is simple and relatively unornamented. At other times we may use a more formal style, which may include sung response. When we use our more formal outline, it may follow a format similar to Basic Pattern that follows. (Items in bold indicate congregational participation, and stars indicate the points in the service where the congregation is to stand.)

——————— The Basic Pattern ———————

The Worship of God
Month NN, 1992
Nth Sunday after (_Feast Name_)

Date, time, day of the church year are indicated to help worshipers center (orient) themselves as they arrive.

Prepare to Worship

(Text of quote for use as meditative reading)
  Author's Name

Personal Reading before Worship (Psalm NN). Persons are encouraged to arrive early so that upon entering the place for worship they have time to quietly greet others and then to gather (center) themselves into a spirit of receptivity to God. A brief quotation and a suggested Scripture passage (usually the Psalm for the day) that focus on the theme for the day are provided to facilitate meditation.

Announcements for the Week, Welcome, and Attendance Registration. When the choir, clergy, and other worship leaders have entered, the liturgist (a layperson) makes any necessary announcements and invites the congregation to greet each other and to record their presence in the attendance registers located in the pews. Before the formal opening of worship, the congregation is invited to "draw near to the throne of grace, lay down our burdens, and encourage each other with our joys." As an act of mutual love and care, this act also allows the congregation to free themselves of any pressing concerns as a preparation for the worship to follow. Once unburdened and encouraged, worshipers become better able to approach God in the praise to follow.

———— Concerns & Celebrations ————

Organ Meditation/Intercessory Prayer & Lord's Prayer ("debts" translation). We pray for the requested intercessions and for "those concerns which still lie unspoken on our hearts." In the Lord's Prayer, we pray for ourselves and our own strengthening. (It is most appropriate that the liturgist lead the concerns & celebrations and the prayers.)

Response No. 585 "Hear Our Prayer, O Lord." _(Response numbers are the numbers in the church hymnal.)_ The congregation sings the Response as closure and for transition. Though Baptists are traditionally indifferent to posture, local custom usually provides attention to airing certain acts and postures (though it is exceptionally difficult to get many—if not most—Baptists on their knees).

———— Gather in God's Name ————

Prelude (and chimes)/Greeting/Introit/Singspiration. The people gathered turn their thoughts and hearts to worship. A greeting appropriate to the day and season, given by the president or the musicians, formally begins the service. The greeting may be a few verses of Scripture, a call to worship, a sung introit, a congregational hymn-sing, or some other introductory act which proclaims, "We are gathered before God; let us worship God."

*Praise/Processional Hymn. The congregation responds (or continues) with a hymn of praise, followed by an act of affirmation, which may be a litany, unison or responsive reading, recitation of a statement of faith, an act of confession and absolution, reading and renewing the church covenant (especially on the Sunday after Epiphany, at the Easter dawn service, and any time there is a dedication or baptism), or a collect (prayer) of the day.

*Affirmation of Faith No. NN. The number is given only if the affirmation text is in the hymnal; otherwise, it is printed in the bulletin or on an insert.

During Advent, the affirmation includes lighting the Advent candles; Christmas through Epiphany, the (re)lighting of the Christ candle; in Lent, a penitential act; and, in Eastertide, acts of joy and celebration.

*Response No. 575 *"Gloria Patri."* The *Gloria Patri* is sung as a joyous response to the affirmation.

Proclaim God's Word. God's Word is read and expounded. Interspersed among the readings may be choral anthems or congregational singing of psalm verses and/or other music.

Hebrew Scripture/Apostolic Writing/Choir Anthem/Moment with the Children. The "children's moment," though theologically and kerygmatically suspect, is a popular custom in many churches today. We use it to let our children know that they are valued and that their participation in worship is important.

Gospel/*Response No. 587 "Let the Words of My Mouth." Sung by all, the response (Ps. 19:14) expresses the desire that the sermon will be rightly spoken and heard, in keeping with the lessons just read. The *Common Lectionary* (revised beginning Advent 1992) is used (on a three-year cycle) to help the preachers work through most of Scripture and to not fall prey to their own "pet" topics, though there are occasions when other lessons are chosen, based on local need and the Spirit's leading. Three lessons are usually read: one from the Old Testament, one from apostolic writings (Acts—Revelation), and one from the Gospels. The first two

lessons are usually read by a lay reader; the Gospel, by the preacher.

Sermon. A prayer for illumination (a collect) may be prayed before the Sermon. The end of the sermon may include an "invitation to discipleship," for any who wish to be received during the next hymn or another time in the service.

Giving Thanks to God/*Discipleship Hymn/*Affirmation of Faith (optional). The congregation responds to hearing the Word by acknowledging the source of salvation and by acts of thanksgiving and charity. (The affirmation shown here may be used instead of or in addition to the affirmation shown above, with a different focus than the first.) If not done before the prelude, the announcements, concerns, prayers, and response are included here.

(If not done above:)

Concerns and Celebrations ___ (Announcements)

Intercessory Prayer/Lord's Prayer (Debts)/*Response No. 585, "Hear Our Prayer, O Lord"/Offertory Invitation/Offertory (music during collection). Alms are solicited and collected, and presented with thanksgiving; the presentation prayer includes a re-dedication of our whole hearts and being.

*Doxology No. 572 and Prayer of Dedication. This is the usual place where new members are welcomed and received into fellowship, usually on a Communion Sunday. If children are to be dedicated, they are brought forward at the Doxology and are dedicated after the alms and tithes are presented. If there is to be baptism, candidates come forward at the Doxology, take their baptismal vows, then go to prepare for the baptism. Sample orders for dedication and baptism are available. Baptism and dedication are normally scheduled on the Sunday before a Communion Sunday, and are done at the place marked here for the Lord's Supper.

The Lord's Supper (or Dedication or Baptism). As often as agreed (weekly, if possible), our Lord's Supper (Eucharist or Holy Communion) is included in its rightful place as the climax of the service.

The Great Thanksgiving
(One = President or Designated Leader)
Dialogue *(standing)*

One: God be with you.
All: **And also with you.**

One: Lift up your hearts.
All: **We lift them up to God.**
One: Let us give thanks to the Lord our God.
All: **It is right to give God our thanks and praise.**

Recital of the Acts of God *(standing)*. Here the president alone, or responsively with the congregation, recounts some of the mighty acts of God which have particular relevance to this service, as appropriate to this season, day, or occasion. The end of this part usually includes the following dialogue, with the first response being sung:

One: Therefore we praise you, joining our voices with Angels and Archangels and with all the company of heaven, who forever sing this hymn to proclaim the glory of your Name:
All: **Holy, holy, holy! Lord God Almighty! All thy works shall praise thy name; In earth and sky and sea; Holy, holy, holy! Merciful and Mighty! God in three persons, Blessed Trinity! Amen**

This is the fourth stanza of the familiar hymn, "Holy, Holy, Holy" (the first stanza is sometimes used in morning services), used as an alternative where the congregation does not know a more traditional "Sanctus" setting and text. Baptists will sing this even when they resist singing another "Sanctus."

One: Blessed is the One who comes in the name of the Lord.
All: **Hosanna in the highest.**

Remembrance of Christ *(seated)*. Here the "Institution Narrative" is recited, either by the president alone or in a **responsive dialogue** with the congregation. We usually use whole loaves of fresh bread (Challah, Portuguese sweet bread, round Italian, Boule, English toasting bread, etc., at the discretion of the deacon providing it for that service), which are broken at the words "given for you." At the word "poured," the chalice is emptied into two or three (empty) individual glasses in the top tray of each stack of trays. (We prefer to use red grape juice or nonalcoholic wine, again dependent on the choice of the deacon providing it for that service.) Also, we usually recite traditional Jewish blessings for the cup and bread as part of this remembrance.

At the end of this part, the following dialogue or one similar to it is said or sung:

One: Therefore we proclaim the mystery of faith:
All: **Christ has died. Christ is risen. Christ will come again.**

Invocation of the Holy Spirit *(seated or kneeling). Here we complete the Trinitarian structure of the Great Thanksgiving by offering the "oblation" to God and by calling the Holy Spirit "down" onto us and our assembly. This part ends with the following dialogue (with the response, "By Christ . . ." sung or said:)*

One: All this we ask through our Lord Jesus Christ, in whose name we gather.
All: **By Christ, with Christ, in Christ, in the unity of the Holy Spirit, all honor and glory are yours, Almighty God, now and forever. Amen.**

Conclusion *(seated or standing)*.

One: Christ is made our Passover:
All: **Therefore let us keep the feast. Alleluia.**

Sharing Loaf and Cup *(seated, standing, or kneeling, as appropriate for this service)*. Elements are taken to the congregation in the pews, or the people move as requested to the place(s) where they may partake. Any directions not part of a "typical" service are usually given both in writing in the bulletin and verbally by the president or a deacon. Depending on the type of service, we may either partake simultaneously or individually, as is appropriate.

Thanks after the Meal *(standing). (This optional part is included at the most formal occasions:)*

One: You have given yourself to us, Lord.
All: **Now we give ourselves to others.**
One: Your love makes us a new people;
All: **As people of love we serve you with joy.**
One: Your glory fills our hearts;
All: **Help us glorify you in all things.**

Go Forth in God's Name
*Closing/Recessional Hymn
*Blessing
*Congregational Response
Postlude
*Greet Each Other/Share the Peace of God

Blessing
Blessing of Oil
*Calling Forward

Laying on of Hands and Anointing
Dismissal with Blessing

Brief Order for Anointing and Healing. Another option in services is the Order of Anointing and Healing, which would usually come after communion or just before dismissal.

Ronal and Inga Freyer Nicholas

175 ◆ CHARISMATIC WORSHIP

All the trappings of historic and well-ordered worship do nothing for the worshiper who is not consumed with the desire to enter into the presence of the Lord "in Spirit and in truth." A people who have seen a vision of the glory of the living Lord, whose lives have been touched by his covenant love and faithfulness, and whose spirits have been caught up in a heartfelt response to the movement of his Spirit—such a people will worship with a worship at once individual and corporate, timeless and contemporary, ordered and free.

The theme of the covenant is a basic theme of worship and is present in the service below in several ways: in the proclamation of the covenant commandments; in the celebration of the new covenant at the Lord's Table, with its emphasis on personal renewal in his presence; and in the sermon, which brings out the covenant bond of the body of Christ as worshipers seek to "admonish one another."

——— An Order of Worship ———

This entry describes a worship service that took place on a Communion Sunday in an independent charismatic church in a Chicago suburb. There is great diversity in the way charismatic pastors conduct worship, and this service is typical in some respects and atypical in others. In a general way, it conforms to the pattern: Entrance, Service of the Word, Service of the Lord's Table, and Dismissal.

Praise and Worship in Song (30–40 minutes in free-flowing contemporary style). The service is conducted by a worship leader for approximately the first half hour. There is no formal opening of worship; instead, the organ and piano are playing familiar choruses as the people gather in the place of worship. At the time for worship to begin, the leader steps to the pulpit and begins the first chorus; the people stand and will remain standing through the first half hour or so.

Choruses are selected for both theme and key relationship, so that one may follow another with-out pause for announcement. The projector operator simply puts the next chorus on the screen when the leader begins it. The congregation is familiar with several hundred choruses, so the projected words are mainly for newcomers. Many of the choruses used are adapted directly from Scripture.

The choruses begin with a note of celebrative praise. The leader then offers a prayer of invocation, based on a traditional collect from the Anglican tradition: "Almighty God, to You all hearts are open, all desires known, and from You no secrets are hid; cleanse the thoughts of our hearts by the inspiration of Your Holy Spirit, that we may more perfectly love You, and more worthily magnify Your holy name, through Christ our Lord." Amen. After this the choruses continue.

The singing of choruses is accompanied, where appropriate, by rhythmic clapping, and worshipers may raise their hands in the scriptural posture of praise and prayer. Although the choruses follow one another without a break, the sequence of choruses may be punctuated with the "song of the Lord." That is, the congregation breaks into spontaneous praise, sung around one chord in both English and the worshipers' personal "tongues." Spontaneous applause may also break out in praise to the Lord. On some occasions one or more words of prophecy may arise out of the congregation at an appropriate moment.

Scripture Reading. On this Sunday the leader has chosen this moment to read from the Old Testament. He begins with Psalm 50:1-7. This is followed by the reading of the Ten Commandments from Exodus 20, and concluded by Leviticus 19:2 (NKJV): "You shall be holy, for I the LORD your God am holy." This serves as an appropriate introduction to the signing of the traditional hymn, "Holy, Holy, Holy, Lord God Almighty!" All four stanzas are sung, leading directly into a worshipful slower chorus based on Isaiah 6:3.

After the subsiding of spontaneous praise following this chorus, the leader reads the Gospel from Luke 24:13-15. This passage is the narrative of how Christ made himself known to the disciples at Emmaus after his resurrection in the breaking of the bread. It has been selected because this is both the first Sunday after Easter and a Communion Sunday. Slower, more contemplative choruses follow.

Announcements/Offering (with Vocal Duet). The order of service then shifts to a less intense mood, with announcements and offering. During the offering, the music director and a student sing a vocal duet, "He's More than Wonderful," to a taped accompaniment.

Prayer for Special Needs. Prayer requests have been turned in with the offering, and the pastor responds to these in a time of prayer before the sermon.

Sermon. The sermon is part of a series on the "each other" verses of the Bible, and the theme of the day is "Admonish One Another," which relates well with the Old Testament Scriptures on the law of God which have been read earlier. A brief time of prayer concludes the service.

The Lord's Supper. At this point the pastors step to the Communion Table and officiate in a simple administration of the Lord's Supper. According to the usual custom, the unleavened bread is first distributed to the people by the deacons, and all worshipers partake together. The cup is received in the same fashion.

Concluding Chorus. Communion is concluded with the singing of the simple chorus, "Alleluia!" which serves as a dismissal.

While not following a traditional order of worship, the service described above incorporates a number of traditional elements of the Holy Communion service in the Anglo-American liturgical tradition: the collect for purity of heart, the proclamation of the commandments, the "Holy, Holy, Holy Lord" or _Sanctus._ Yet these elements are woven into a more free-flowing charismatic structure emphasizing praise and worship in the presence of the Lord.

Richard C. Leonard

176 ✦ CHRISTIAN CHURCH (DISCIPLES OF CHRIST) WORSHIP

The service of worship in the Christian Church follows the ecumenical consensus of the fourfold order. However, it breaks the Service of the Word into two parts, having one section for the proclamation of the Word and another for the response to the Word. Because the Christian Church stands in the free church tradition (a worship tradition that does not use a text or prayer book), the form of worship (which follows the same pattern of the text tradition) is set forth in an outline rather than a complete text.

Elements considered essential to the Sunday service are indicated in **bold** type. While the basic pattern of this service is strongly recommended, the details are flexible. The first hymn, for example, could easily precede the greeting or follow the opening prayer.

The headings to the five sections of the service deliberately emphasize the corporate character of worship. It is possible, however, to shorten them as follows:

Coming Together to Serve God in Worship
Proclaiming the Word of God
Responding to the Word
Coming Together around the Lord's Table
Going Forth in Mission

—————— The Basic Pattern ——————

**The Community Comes Together
to Serve God in Worship**
Gathering of the Community
Opening Music
Greeting
Hymn

Music, especially communal singing, is vital to Christian worship. There is no particular point,

The Creator's Star. The six-pointed star, which speaks of God's Act of Creation, is made from two equilateral triangles (the symbol of the Trinity) superimposed upon each other. This symbol is quite common in Christian art.

however, at which the singing of hymns is fixed. The hymn usually included in the time of "coming together" is normally a hymn of praise. Other hymns (this order suggests three) should reflect the distinctive character of the moments in the service when they occur.

Opening Prayer(s)
The Community Proclaims the Word of God
First Reading from the Bible

The reading from the Bible is essential to Christian worship. While three scriptural readings are recommended in this commentary, the number is not an absolute requirement. The first reading is ordinarily from the Old Testament, and the third reading ordinarily comes from one of the four Gospels. The second reading comes from another part of the Apostolic Writings.

Psalm or Other Response
Second Reading from the Bible
Anthem or Other Response
Reading from the Gospel
Sermon

A children's sermon, if used, may come at this point in the service.

The Community Responds to the Word of God
Call to Discipleship
Hymn
Affirmation of Faith
Prayers of the People

**The Community Comes Together
  around the Lord's Table**
Invitation to the Lord's Table
Offering

The offering is a part of the service in which the congregation brings gifts of money and the communion elements, and with these set the table. A musical response, prayer of dedication, and communion hymn may be included.

Prayers at the Table

The text includes several models for prayer at the Table. Each includes the major themes of this climactic act of worship: thankful praise, remembrance of Jesus, prayer for the Holy Spirit, and renewal of the covenant with God. The words of institution are always included as warrant, as part of the "prayers" preceding the "offering."

Words of Institution and Breaking of the Bread
Lord's Prayer
Peace

The peace also may come at other points in the service—for example, following a prayer of confession before the readings from Scripture.

Communion
Prayer after Communion
The Community Goes Forth to Serve God in Mission
Hymn
Closing Words

The closing words often precede the final hymn.

Closing Music

Keith Watkins[8]

177 • EASTERN ORTHODOX WORSHIP

The rule of prayer is the rule of faith. We pray what we believe and we believe what we pray. Christ handed down to his apostles not only the rule of faith (the doctrine of the apostles) but also the rule of prayer (the worship of the apostles).

Perhaps the most provocative questions asked by pastors, ministers of music, and students today are these: Can we know what the worship of the ancient church was like? And can that worship be adapted to our current situation? The answer to both is yes.

The Divine Liturgy of St. John Chrysostom has preserved the ancient practices of the church handed down to us through the apostolic tradition, and it is being used today not only by churches united to the ancient patriarchates in the East (Antioch, Jerusalem, Alexandria, and Constantinople), but also by churches here in North America made up largely of former evangelical, Protestant, and charismatic Christians who have been united to those ancient sees.

At first glance the Liturgy of St. John Chrysostom may seem foreign, flowery, and long. But a careful examination of the prayers and hymns reveals that the orthodox faith, once for all handed down to us, is imprinted in the worship itself.

Certain guidelines in adapting this Liturgy to the contemporary scene should be followed:

1. The Liturgy needs a leader (celebrant), an assistant (deacon), and a congregation. It is also very beneficial to have a choir to help and inspire the participation of the congregation.

2. The liturgy is best rendered as a sung liturgy (i.e., the various sections of the liturgy are chanted rather than read). This technique can be learned and incorporated into the Liturgy on a gradual basis.

3. The music of the responses ("Amen"; "Lord, have mercy"; "To You, O Lord"; and others) as well as the music of the antiphons and hymns should be set very simply in order to encourage full congregational participation.

4. In adapting the texts of the hymns of the church, great care must be exercised to preserve their theological meaning.

5. The prayers of the celebrant should be prayed aloud for the edification of the people.

6. Certain portions of the Liturgy may be omitted for the sake of time, but the order of the service should not be changed.

The Basic Pattern

THE DIVINE LITURGY OF ST. JOHN CHRYSOSTOM

St. John Chrysostom was a fourth-century saint from Antioch. He was called Chrysostom, or "Golden Mouth," because of his incredible gift of preaching. St. John eventually became bishop of Constantinople in 398 and died in A.D. 404.

The word *liturgy* means the work of the people. The worship of the church is the corporate work of the royal priesthood (1 Pet. 2:9). The Liturgy is an action in which a group of people corporately become something that they had not been as a mere collection of individuals. Christ stands at the head of the congregation as the Great High Priest—a minister (or liturgist) of the sanctuary and of the true tabernacle which the Lord, not humans, erected.

Opening Benediction

Celebrant: Blessed is the kingdom of the Father and of the Son and of the Holy Spirit, now and ever and unto ages of ages.

People: Amen.

The Liturgy is a joyous gathering of those who are to meet the risen Lord and to enter with him into the bridal chamber. It is a journey of the church into the dimension of the kingdom of God. Christ said, "My kingdom is not of this world" (John 18:36).

The congregation responds "Amen," and in so doing, accepts the journey to the kingdom of God as their ultimate goal.

Great Litany

Deacon: In peace, let us pray to the Lord.

People: Lord, have mercy.

Deacon: For the peace from above and for the salvation of our souls, for the peace of the whole world, for the stability of the holy churches of God, and for the union of all, let us pray to the Lord.

People: Lord, have mercy.

Deacon: For this holy house and for all who enter with faith, reverence, and the fear of God, for our Metropolitan *Name,* for the honorable priests and deacons in Christ, and for all the clergy and the people, let us pray to the Lord.

People: Lord, have mercy.

Deacon: For this country and for every authority and power within it, for this city, for every city and for the faithful living in them, let us pray to the Lord.

People: Lord, have mercy.

Deacon: For seasonable weather, for an abundance of the fruits of the earth, and for peaceful times, for those who travel by land, air, and sea, the sick and suffering, those under persecution and for their deliverance, let us pray to the Lord.

People: Lord, have mercy.

Deacon: For our deliverance from all affliction, anger, danger, and need, help us, save us, have mercy on us and keep us, O God, by Your grace.

People: Lord, have mercy.

Deacon: Remembering our most holy, most pure, most blessed and glorious Lady, the Mother of God, and Ever-virgin Mary, with all the saints, let us commit ourselves and each other and all our life unto Christ our God.

People: To You, O Lord.

Celebrant: O Lord, our God, Whose power is unimaginable and Whose glory is inconceivable, Whose mercy is immeasurable and Whose love for mankind is beyond all words, in Your compassion, O Lord, look down on us and on this holy house, and grant us and those who are praying with us the riches of Your mercy and compassion. For to You are due all glory, honor, and worship, to the Father and to the Son and to the Holy Spirit, now and ever and unto ages of ages.

People: Amen.

Great Litany to Prayer of the Entrance. The petitions of the Great Litany refer to all the needs of the church, the world, the praying community, and each individual. In its petitions we find the true order of prayer and discover truly Christian priorities and values.

This prayer is not simply the prayer of a man or a group of people, but the prayer of Christ himself to his Father, which has been granted to us. This prayer is made possible only by Christ himself, who is our peace (Eph. 2:14). Therefore, we pray in him, with confidence that because of him, our prayer is being accepted by God. By responding "Lord, have mercy," we commit the outcome of each petition to the will of God.

First Antiphon

Deacon: Let us pray to the Lord.
People: Lord, have mercy.
Celebrant: O Lord our God, save Your people and bless Your inheritance. Guard the fullness of Your Church, sanctify those who love the beauty of Your House, glorify them by Your divine power, and do not forsake us who hope in You. For Yours is the dominion and the Kingdom and the power and the glory of the Father and of the Son and of the Holy Spirit, now and ever and unto ages of ages.
People: Amen.

Second Antiphon Hymn (Only-Begotten Son)

People: **Only-begotten Son and Word of God, although You are immortal, yet for our salvation You condescended to be made flesh by the holy Mother of God and Ever-virgin Mary. Without undergoing change You became Man and were crucified, trampling down death by death. O Christ our**

God, Who are One of the Holy Trinity and are glorified with the Father and the Holy Spirit, save us!
Deacon: Let us pray to the Lord.
People: Lord, have mercy.
Celebrant: O Lord, Who have given us the grace to pray together in peace and harmony, and Who promise to grant the requests of two or three who agree in Your Name, fulfill even now the petitions of Your servants as is best for us, giving us in this age the knowledge of Your truth, and in the age to come, eternal life. For You are good, O our God, and You love mankind, and we send up glory to You, to the Father and to the Son and to the Holy Spirit, now and ever and unto ages of ages.
People: Amen.

Third Antiphon/Processional Hymn
Prayer of the Entrance

Deacon: Let us pray to the Lord.
People: Lord, have mercy.
Celebrant: O Sovereign Lord, our God, Who appointed in heaven the orders and armies of angels and archangels for the service of Your glory, grant that the holy angels may enter with us, to serve and glorify Your goodness with us. For You are due all glory, honor, and worship, to the Father and to the Son and to the Holy Spirit, now and ever and unto ages of ages.
People: Amen.
Deacon: Father, bless the entrance.
Celebrant: Blessed is the entrance of Your saints, always, now and ever and unto ages of ages.
People: Amen.
Deacon: Wisdom! Let us attend!

Entrance with the Gospels to Feast-Day Hymn/ Prayer before the Trisagion Hymn. The Eucharist is a procession of the church following the ascension of Christ (Heb. 9:11–12:29). This entire passage from the book of Hebrews is best understood as a progressive discourse about a heavenly place to which we can spiritually ascend in worship and in prayer. We experience this heavenly dimension fundamentally in the Divine Liturgy, and this ascent is revealed when the celebrant enters into the altar with the Book of the Gospels.

We can ascend to the place where we are surrounded by "so great a cloud of witnesses" (Heb. 12:1, KJV). This is not a physical place (v. 18) but a spiritual realm, Mt. Zion, the city of the living God, the heavenly Jerusalem (v. 22), inhabited by God, the angels, and "the spirits of just men made perfect" (v. 23). In Hebrews 9:11-12 we see that Christ came to the greater and more perfect tabernacle, obtaining eternal redemption for us. Since we believe this tabernacle is the same spiritual place mentioned in Hebrews 12:22, we can enter that holy place with Christ by virtue of our union with him (10:19-20). We enter into this heavenly and invisible place fundamentally in corporate worship (12:28-29). The content of this worship includes remembering the righteous (11:4-40); (cf. Prov. 10:7 and Ps. 112:1-6). We join the timeless worship of the angels that is already taking place around the throne of God; we are standing in heaven and we sing their hymn (Isa. 6).

| Deacon/Choir: | O come, let us worship and bow down before Christ. |
| People: | **O Son of God, Who rose from the dead, save us who sing to You, alleluia.** |

Feast-Day Hymn
Hymn to the Patron Saint
Feast-Day Hymn
Prayer before the Trisagion Hymn

Deacon:	Let us pray to the Lord.
People:	**Lord, have mercy.**
Celebrant:	O Holy God, Who rest in the saints, Who with the Trisagion Hymn are praised by the Seraphim, glorified by the Cherubim and worshiped by all the heavenly powers, Who out of nothing brought all things into being, Who created man in Your image and likeness and adorned him with every gift of Your grace, Who give wisdom and understanding to anyone asking for them, and Who do not disregard the sinner, but have appointed repentance for salvation, Who have made us Your humble and unworthy servants, even at this hour, to stand before the glory of Your

holy altar, and to offer You the worship and praise due to You: accept, O Lord, from the mouths of us sinners the Trisagion Hymn and visit us in Your goodness. Forgive us every transgression, whether voluntary or involuntary. Sanctify our souls and bodies, grant that we may worship You in holiness all the days of our life, through the intercessions of the holy Mother of God and of all the saints who have pleased You from the beginning. For You are holy, O our God, and we send up glory to You, to the Father and to the Son and to the Holy Spirit, now and ever . . .

| Deacon: | . . . and unto ages of ages. |
| People: | **Amen.** |

The Trisagion Hymn. According to the tradition of the church, this hymn was divinely inspired. When Proculus was archbishop, the people of Constantinople were praying in public to avert some threat of divine wrath. At that time, a child was taken up out of the crowd and was taught the Trisagion (Thrice-Holy) Hymn by some angelic choirmasters in the following manner: "Holy God, Holy Mighty, Holy Immortal, have mercy on us." When the child came back again and told what he had been taught, the whole crowd sang the hymn, and the threat was averted. The Trisagion Hymn was also sung in this manner at the Fourth Ecumenical Council held in Chalcedon in A.D. 451.

| People: | **Holy God, Holy Mighty, Holy Immortal, have mercy on us. (3 times) Glory to the Father and to the Son and to the Holy Spirit, now and ever and unto ages of ages. Amen. Holy Immortal, have mercy on us. Holy God, Holy Mighty, Holy Immortal, have mercy on us.** |
| Deacon: | Let us attend! |

The Liturgy of the Word (Opening Greeting to Sermon). The Liturgy is a manifestation of the Word of God. The Lord will speak to us through the readings from Scripture. We cannot understand our worship without knowing the Scriptures. The Bible is the key to the understanding of the Liturgy. Yet the opposite is also true since the meaning of the Scriptures is disclosed in worship, supplying us with a key to the interpretation. In other words, the Liturgy is a living explanation of the Bible. Furthermore, the whole structure and spirit of Orthodox worship is intimately linked with the Scriptures and is deeply rooted in them.

Opening Greeting

Celebrant:	Peace be to all!
People:	**And to your spirit!**
Deacon:	Wisdom!

Gradual Psalm

Deacon:	Wisdom!
Reader:	**The Reading from the Epistle of the holy Apostle N. to the N.**
Deacon:	Let us attend!

Epistle Lesson
Alleluia Psalm

Deacon:	Let us pray to the Lord.
People:	**Lord, have mercy.**
Celebrant:	O Sovereign Lord and lover of mankind, enlighten our hearts with the pure light of Your divine knowledge and open the eyes of our minds to understand Your evangelical proclamations. Instill in us also the fear of Your blessed commandments, so that trampling down all sinful desires, we may live a spiritual life, both thinking and doing everything pleasing to You. For You are the enlightenment of our souls and bodies, O Christ our God, and we send up glory to You, together with Your Father, Who is without beginning, and Your all-holy, good and life-giving Spirit, now and ever and unto ages of ages.
People:	**Amen.**
Deacon:	Wisdom! Let us listen to the holy Gospel.
Celebrant:	Peace be to all.
People:	**And to your spirit.**
Reader:	The reading from the holy Gospel according to St. (*N.*).
People:	**Glory to You, O Lord, glory to You.**
Deacon:	Let us attend!

Gospel Lesson

People:	**Glory to You, O Lord, glory to You.**

Sermon/Litany of Fervent Supplication. As we continue our ascent to the heavenly Holy of Holies, we pray for the actual and immediate needs of the congregation. Here the church prays for individuals and particular needs by name. We intercede as a royal priesthood before the Lord.

Deacon:	Let us say with all our soul and with all our mind, let us say,
People:	**Lord, have mercy.**
Deacon:	O Lord Almighty, the God of our fathers, hear us we pray and have mercy.
People:	**Lord, have mercy.**
Deacon:	Have mercy on us, O God, in Your great mercy, hear us we pray and have mercy.
People:	**Lord, have mercy. Lord, have mercy. Lord, have mercy.**
Deacon:	Again we pray for the godly and Orthodox Christians; for our Metropolitan *N.;* for the priests, deacons, and all other clergy; and for all our brethren in Christ.
People:	**Lord, have mercy. Lord, have mercy. Lord, have mercy.**
Deacon:	Again we pray for the blessed and ever-memorable founders of this holy Church; and for all our fathers and brethren, the Orthodox Christians departed this life before us, especially (*N.N.*), who here and in all the world lie asleep in the Lord.
People:	**Lord, have mercy. Lord, have mercy. Lord, have mercy.**
Deacon:	Again we pray for mercy, life, peace, health, salvation, and visitation, for the servants of God (*N.N.*), and for pardon and remission of their sins.
People:	**Lord, have mercy. Lord, have mercy. Lord, have mercy.**
Deacon:	Again we pray for those who bring tithes and offerings and do good works in Your holy Church; for those who serve and those who sing; and for all the people here present, who desire Your great and bountiful mercies.
People:	**Lord, have mercy. Lord, have mercy. Lord, have mercy.**

Celebrant: For You are a merciful God and love mankind, and we send up glory to You, to the Father and to the Son and to the Holy Spirit, now and ever and unto ages of ages.

People: Amen.

The Liturgy of the Faithful. The Eucharist is a mystery; the mystery of the church, the mystery of the heavenly kingdom and the fullness and manifestation of the church as the age to come.

Deacon: Let us, the faithful, pray to the Lord.

People: **Lord, have mercy.**

Celebrant: Often and again we fall down before You and implore You, O gracious Lord and Lover of mankind, to regard our prayer and to purify our souls and bodies from all defilement of flesh and spirit. And grant that we may stand before Your holy altar without guilt or condemnation. And grant us, O God, and those praying with us, progress in life, faith, and spiritual understanding. Grant that they may always worship You and partake of Your holy Mysteries with fear and love and without guilt or condemnation, and that they may be made worthy of Your heavenly Kingdom.

Deacon: Help us, save us, have mercy on us, and keep us, O God, by Your grace.

People: **Lord, have mercy.**

Deacon: Wisdom!

Celebrant: That always being protected by Your power, we may send up glory to You, to the Father and to the Son and to the Holy Spirit, now and ever and unto ages of ages.

People: Amen.

Cherubic Hymn. The Eucharist is the mystery of universal remembrance. Remembrance is an act of love in which God remembers us. His remembrance—his love—is the foundation of the world. In Christ, we remember, also, the church in its separation from "this world" on its journey to heaven remembers the world, remembers all men, remembers the whole creation, and takes it in love to God. We remember his life, his death, his resurrection: one movement of sacrifice, love, and dedication

to his Father and to men—this is the inexhaustible content of our remembrance.

Choir: Let us who mystically represent the Cherubim, and who sing the Trisagion Hymn to the Life-creating Trinity, lay aside all earthly cares . . .

Deacon: All of you, may the Lord our God remember in His kingdom, always, now and ever and unto ages of ages.

People: Amen.

Entrance with the Holy Gifts. The Eucharist is an entrance of the church into the joy of the Lord. It is an entrance into the risen life of Christ—the very movement of the church as passage from the old into the new, from "this world" into the "world to come." God is holy. We cannot enter his heavenly Holy of Holies without the proper offering. That offering is the once-for-all sacrifice of our Lord and Savior Jesus Christ. We join now with him in the continual presentation of his body and blood before the Father.

The Eucharist is a movement: a movement of adoration and praise in which all joy and suffering, all beauty and all frustration, all hunger and all satisfaction are referred to their ultimate end and finally become meaningful. It is a movement of love toward God, the only movement in which the meaning and the value of all that exists can be revealed and fulfilled.

Choir: . . . that we may receive the King of all, invisibly attended by the Angelic Hosts. Alleluia! Alleluia! Alleluia!

Litany of the Offertory to the Creed. As Christians we live and worship in a unity of love and faith. Our love is expressed in the kiss of peace and our faith in the Nicene Creed.

Deacon: Let us complete our prayer to the Lord.

People: **Lord, have mercy.**

Deacon: For the precious Gifts that have been offered, let us pray to the Lord.

People: **Lord, have mercy.**

Deacon: For this holy house and for all who enter with faith, reverence, and the fear of God, let us pray to the Lord.

People: **Lord, have mercy.**

Deacon: For our deliverance from all affliction, anger, danger, and need, let us pray to the Lord.

People: **Lord, have mercy.**

Deacon: Help us, save us, have mercy on us, and keep us, O God, by Your grace.

People: **Lord, have mercy.**

Deacon: That this whole day may be perfect, holy, peaceful, and sinless, let us ask of the Lord.

People: **Grant this, O Lord.**

Deacon: For an angel of peace, a faithful guide and guardian of our souls and bodies, let us ask of the Lord.

People: **Grant this, O Lord.**

Deacon: For pardon and remission of our sins and transgressions, let us ask of the Lord.

People: **Grant this, O Lord,**

Deacon: For all that is good and profitable for our souls and for peace in the world, let us ask of the Lord.

People: **Grant this, O Lord.**

Deacon: That we may spend the remainder of our life in peace and repentance, let us ask of the Lord.

People: **Grant this, O Lord.**

Deacon: For a Christian end to our life, painless, blameless, and peaceful, and for a good defense before the dread judgment seat of Christ, let us ask of the Lord.

People: **Grant this, O Lord.**

Deacon: Remembering our most holy, most pure, most blessed and glorious Lady, the Mother of God, and Ever-virgin Mary, with all the saints, let us commit ourselves and each other and all our life unto Christ, our God.

People: **To You, O Lord.**

Celebrant: O Lord God, Ruler of all, Who alone are holy, Who accept a sacrifice a praise from those who call upon You with all their heart, receive also the prayer of us sinners, and bring us to Your holy altar. And make us worthy to offer You gifts and spiritual sacrifices for our sins and for the errors of Your people. And grant us to find grace in Your eyes, so that our sacrifice may be acceptable to You, and that the good Spirit of Your grace may rest on us and on all Your people and on these Gifts set before You:

through the mercies of Your Only-begotten Son, with Whom You are blessed, together with Your all-holy good and Life-giving Spirit, now and ever and unto ages of ages.

People: **Amen.**

Celebrant: Peace be to all.

People: **And to your spirit.**

Deacon: Let us love one another that with one accord we may confess:

People: **Father, Son and Holy Spirit, the Trinity, one in essence and undivided.**

Kiss of Peace. The kiss of peace is an act of love in which the members of the church acknowledge their reconciliation with God, with all people, and with the whole creation. We are a reconciled people. God the Father has reconciled us to himself through Jesus Christ our Lord. We are also reconciled to each other as we walk in the light together. As we exchange the kiss of peace, we say, "Christ is in our midst. He is and shall be."

Celebrant: Christ is in our midst.

Deacon: He is and shall be.

Deacon: The doors! The doors! In wisdom, let us attend!

The exclamation "The doors! The doors!" is probably a reference to the practice of reserving the eucharistic liturgy for the intiated alone.

The Creed

People: I believe in one God, the Father Almighty, Maker of heaven and earth, and of all things visible and invisible; And in one Lord Jesus Christ, the Son of God, the Only-begotten, Begotten of the Father before all worlds. Light of Light, Very God of Very God, Begotten, not made; of one essence with the Father, by Whom all things were made: Who for us men and for our salvation came down from heaven, was incarnate of the Holy Spirit and the Virgin Mary, and was made man; And was crucified also for us under Pontius Pilate, and suffered and was buried; And the third day He rose again, according to the Scriptures; And ascended into heaven, and sits at the right hand of the Father; And He shall come again with glory to judge the living and the dead, Whose Kingdom shall have no end. And I believe in the Holy Spirit, the Lord, and Giver of Life, Who proceeds from the Father, Who with the Father and the Son together is worshiped and glorified, Who spoke by the Prophets; And I believe in One Holy Catholic and Apostolic Church. I acknowledge one Baptism for the remission of sins. I look for the Resurrection of the dead, and the Life of the world to come. Amen.

The Nicene Creed was formulated at the Ecumenical Council of Nicaea in A.D. 325 and affirmed at Constantinople in A.D. 381. Arius, a heretic from Alexandria, had said that there was a time when the Son of God was not, i.e., a time when he did not exist. St. Athanasius, one of the heroes of the Council, upheld the universal understanding of the church that the Son of God was begotten from the Father before all time and was equal with the Father. He said, "There never was a time when He was not."

The Thanksgiving. The Eucharist is the "lifting up" of our offering and of ourselves. It is our offering to him of ourselves, of our lives, and of the whole world—as a Russian poet once said, "To take in our hands the whole world as if it were an apple!"

The Eucharist is the ascension of the church to heaven. We have entered the eschaton (the age to come, the kingdom of God) and are now standing beyond time and space. It is because all this has first happened to us that something will happen to bread and wine. It is our ascension to Christ.

The Eucharist is the state of human perfection. When man or woman stands before the throne of God, when he or she has fulfilled all that God has given the person to fulfill, when all sins are forgiven, all joy restored, then there is nothing else to do but to give thanks. When a person stands before God face to face, accepted into this presence, when sins are forgiven and when he or she has recovered a pristine beauty, the Eucharist—thanksgiving, adoration, worship—is truly the ultimate and the total expression of his or her whole being. It is the divine element, the image of God in us. It is the life of paradise, the only full and real response of human beings to God's creation, redemption, and gift of heaven. It is a new style of life and the ultimate expression of the only true relationship between God and the world.

The Eucharist is Christ himself: "It is He who offers and it is He who is offered." Christ is the perfect human being who stands before God. Christ alone is the perfect eucharistic being. In and through this Eucharist the whole creation becomes what it always was meant to be and yet failed to be.

Humans are sacrificial beings because they find their life in love, and love is sacrificial: it puts the value, the very meaning of life in the other and gives life to the other, and in this giving, in this sacrifice, finds the meaning and joy of life. It is indeed a sacrifice offered "for everyone and for everything."

The Eucharist is the "breakthrough" that brings us to the table in the kingdom, raises us to heaven, and makes us partakers of the divine food. The Eucharist is the end of the movement. We are at the paschal table of the kingdom—the end of the journey and the end of time. We have arrived at a vantage point from which we can see more deeply into the reality of the world.

The Eucharist is communion with the whole church. It is the supreme revelation of the "communion of the saints"—the unity and interdependence of all the members of the body of Christ. But it is judgment and condemnation to people who do not see Christ in the church, but rather see human pride and arrogance, selfishness and the spirit of "this world."

Deacon:	Let us stand well! Let us stand with fear! Let us attend that we may offer the holy offering in peace.
People:	**An offering of peace! A sacrifice of praise!**
Celebrant:	The grace of our Lord Jesus Christ, the love of God the Father, and the communion of the Holy Spirit be with you all.
People:	**And with your spirit.**
Celebrant:	Let us lift up your hearts.
People:	**We lift them up unto the Lord.**
Celebrant:	Let us give thanks unto the Lord.
People:	**It is fitting and right.**
Celebrant:	It is fitting and right to sing to You, to bless You, to praise You, to give thanks to You, to worship You in every place of Your dominion. For You are God, beyond description, beyond understanding, invisible, in-

comprehensible, always existing, always the same; You and Your Only-begotten Son and Your Holy Spirit. Out of nothing You brought us into being and when we had fallen, raised us up again, and You have not ceased doing everything until You brought us to heaven and graciously gave us Your future Kingdom. For all these things, we thank You and Your Only-begotten Son and Your Holy Spirit; for all that we know and do not know, for the open and hidden benefits bestowed upon us. We thank You also for this Liturgy which You are pleased to accept from our hands, though there stand before You thousands of archangels and myriads of angels, Cherubim and Seraphim, six-winged, many-eyed, soaring high on their wings; singing, proclaiming, shouting the Hymn of Victory.

People: **Holy! holy! holy! Lord of Hosts!
Heaven and earth are filled with Your glory.
Hosanna in the highest!
Blessed is He Who comes in the Name of the Lord!
Hosanna in the highest!**

Celebrant: With these blessed powers, O Lord Who loves mankind, we also cry aloud and say: You are holy, most holy, You and Your Only-begotten Son and Your Holy Spirit. You are holy, most holy, and magnificent is Your glory. You have so loved the world that You gave Your Only-begotten Son, that whoever believes in Him should not perish but have everlasting life. And after He had come and accomplished all that was appointed, on the night in which He was given up, or rather gave Himself up for the life of the world, took bread in His holy, most pure, and blameless hands, and when He had given thanks and blessed and sanctified and broken it, He gave it to His holy disciples and apostles, saying: "Take! Eat! This is My Body which is broken for you for the remission of sins!"

People: **Amen.**

Celebrant: And likewise, after supper, He took the cup, saying: "Drink from it, all of you! This is My Blood of the New Testament which is shed for you and for many for the remission of sins!"

People: **Amen.**

Celebrant: Remembering this saving commandment and all that has been done for us, the cross, the tomb, the resurrection on the third day, the ascension into heaven, the sitting at the right hand, and the second and glorious coming, we offer You Your own, from what is Your own, for everyone and for everything.

People: **We praise You, We bless You,
We give thanks to You, O Lord,
And we pray unto You our God.**

Celebrant: Furthermore, we offer You this spiritual and unbloody worship and implore You and pray and supplicate You; send down Your Holy Spirit upon us and upon these Gifts set before You. And make this bread the precious Body of Your Christ.

People: **Amen.**

Celebrant: And what is in this cup the precious Blood of Your Christ.

People: **Amen.**

Celebrant: Changing them by Your Holy Spirit.

People: **Amen. Amen. Amen.**

Celebrant: That to those who partake of these Gifts, they may be for the cleansing of soul, for remission of sins, for communion with Your Holy Spirit, for the fullness of the Kingdom of Heaven, for freedom in prayer toward You and not for judgment or for condemnation. Furthermore we offer to You this spiritual worship for those who in faith have gone on before us to their rest: forefathers, fathers, patriarchs, prophets, apostles, preachers, evangelists, martyrs, confessors, ascetics and every righteous spirit made perfect in faith, especially for our most holy, most pure, most blessed and glorious Lady, the Mother of God and Ever-virgin Mary.

Hymn to the Mother of God to the Lord's Prayer. We recite the Lord's Prayer together, not only on our own behalf, but for all Christendom.

Celebrant: We also offer this spiritual worship for the holy Prophet and Forerunner, John the Baptist, for the holy, glorious, and all-honorable apostles, for St. *(N.)*, whose memory we commemorate today, and for all Your saints, through whose intercessions watch over us, O God. And remember all who have fallen asleep in hope of the resurrection to eternal life, especially *(N.N.)* and give them rest where the light of Your countenance watches over them.

Furthermore, we implore You: remember, O Lord, every Orthodox bishop who rightly teaches the word of Your truth, and all the priests and deacons in Christ, and every order of the clergy. We also offer You this reasonable and spiritual worship for the whole world, for the holy, catholic, and apostolic Church, for those who live a pure and holy life, for all civil authorities and armed forces. Grant them, O Lord, peaceful times so that we may live a quiet and peaceful life in all godliness and holiness.

Among the first, remember, O Lord, our Metropolitan *(N.)*, and grant him to Your holy Church for many years in peace, safety, honor, health, and in rightly teaching the word of Your truth.

Deacon: And remember also those men and women whom each of us has in mind.

Celebrant: Remember also, O Lord, this city in which we live, and every city and country, and all the faithful living in them. Remember, O Lord, those who travel by land, air, and sea, the sick and suffering, those under persecution, and for their deliverance. Remember, O Lord, those who remember the poor, and pour out Your

mercies on us all. And grant that with one mouth and one heart we may glorify Your all-honorable and majestic Name, of the Father and of the Son and of the Holy Spirit, now and ever and unto ages of ages.

People: **Amen.**

The Communion of our Lord's Body and Blood

Celebrant: And may the mercies of our Great God and Savior Jesus Christ be with you all.

People: **And with your spirit.**

Celebrant: And make us worthy, O Lord, that with boldness and without condemnation we may dare to call upon You, the heavenly God and Father and say:

The Lord's Prayer

People: **Our Father, Who art in heaven, hallowed be Thy Name. Thy Kingdom come, Thy will be done on earth as it is in heaven. Give us this day our daily bread, and forgive us our trespasses, as we forgive those who trespass against us; and lead us not into temptation, but deliver us from evil.**

Celebrant: For Thine is the Kingdom and the power and the glory of the Father and of the Son and of the Holy Spirit, now and ever and unto ages of ages.

People: **Amen.**

Celebrant: Peace be to all.

People: **And to your spirit.**

Deacon: Let us bow our heads to the Lord.

People: **To You, O Lord.**

Celebrant: We give thanks to You, O Invisible King, Who by measureless power and in the greatness of Your mercy, brought all things from non-existence into being, look down from heaven, O Master, upon those who have bowed their heads to You; for they have not bowed to flesh and blood, but to You, the awesome God. Therefore, O Master, distribute these gifts offered to all of us for our own good according to the individual need of each person; through the grace and compassion and love for mankind of Your Only-begotten Son, with Whom You are blessed, together with Your all-holy, good, and life-giving Spirit, now and ever and unto ages of ages.

People: Amen.

Celebrant: Hear us, O Lord Jesus Christ our God, from Your holy dwelling place and from the glorious throne of Your kingdom, and come to sanctify us, You Who sit on high with the Father and are here invisibly present with us. And make us worthy by Your mighty hand to be given Your most pure Body and precious Blood and through us to all Your people.

The Elevation to the Breaking of the Bread. The Eucharist is the breaking of the bread, the one source of life that redeems the unity of all humanity under one head, that is, Christ. It is the mystery of forgiveness, the mystery of reconciliation achieved by Christ and eternally granted to those who believe in him. It is the essential food of the Christian, strengthening his or her spiritual life, healing diseases, affirming faith, creating the possibility of leading a truly Christian life in this world. It is the gift of eternal life, an anticipation of the joy, peace, and fullness of the kingdom, a foretaste of its light. It is both partaking of Christ's suffering (the expression of our readiness to accept his "way of life") and sharing in his victory and triumph—a sacrificial meal and a joyful banquet. In this meal, his body is broken and his blood is shed, and, partaking of them, we accept the Cross. Yet by the Cross joy has entered the world, and this joy is ours when we are at the Lord's Table.

Deacon: Let us attend!

Celebrant: The holy Gifts for holy people!

People: One is holy. One is the Lord Jesus Christ,
To the glory of God the Father. Amen.

The Breaking of the Bread

Celebrant: Broken and distributed is the Lamb of God, broken, but not divided; forever eaten and never consumed, but sanctifying those who partake.

People: Amen.

Celebrant: The fullness of the cup, of the Faith, of the Holy Spirit.

People: Amen.

The Blessing of the Water to Prayer before Communion. As the body of the Lord is broken for us and his blood is poured out for us, we proclaim his death until he comes. We eat the holy sacrifice in the presence of the Lord and we partake of the power of Christ. The Eucharist is also given to me personally in order to transform me into a "member of Christ," to unite me with all those who receive him, and to reveal the church as a fellowship of love.

Celebrant: Blessed is the warmth of Your saints, always, now and ever and unto ages of ages.

People: Amen.

Deacon: The warmth of faith full of the Holy Spirit.

People: Amen.

Prayer before Communion

People: I believe, O Lord, and I confess that You are truly the Christ, the Son of the Living God, Who came into the world to save sinners, of whom I am chief. I also believe that this itself is Your most pure Body and this itself Your precious Blood. Therefore I implore You, have mercy on me and forgive me my transgressions, whether voluntary or involuntary, whether in word or in deed, whether in knowledge or in ignorance. And make me worthy to partake of Your most pure Mysteries without condemnation, for the remission of sins, and for eternal life.

At Your Mystical Supper, O Son of God, receive me today as a communicant; for I will not speak of the Mystery to Your enemies, nor will I give You a kiss like Judas, but like the thief I will confess You: remember me, O Lord, when You come in Your Kingdom. Amen.

Not for judgment nor for condemnation be my partaking of Your Holy Mysteries, O Lord, but for healing of soul and body.

Communion Hymn to Hymn after Communion. The Eucharist is our joy and certitude, our source of inspiration and growth, the victory that overcomes evil, the presence that makes our whole life—in sum, our life in Christ.

Deacon: With the fear of God, with faith and love, draw near.

People: **Blessed is He Who comes in the Name of the Lord, God is the Lord and has revealed Himself to us.**

Other Communion hymns may be sung at this time.

Celebrant: O God, save Your people and bless Your inheritance.

Hymn after Communion. _On most days we sing the following hymn:_

People: **We have seen the true Light, we have received the heavenly Spirit, we have found the true Faith worshiping the undivided Trinity, Who has saved us.**

Priest: Blessed is our God, always, now and ever and unto ages of ages.

People: **Amen.**
Let our mouths be filled with Your praise, O Lord, that we may sing of Your glory; for You have made us worthy to partake of Your holy, divine, immortal, and life-giving Mysteries. Keep us in Your holiness, that all day long we may meditate on Your righteousness. Alleluia! Alleluia! Alleluia!

Deacon: Let us attend! Having received the holy, most pure, immortal, heavenly, life-giving, and awesome Mysteries of Christ, let us worthily give thanks to the Lord.

Prayer of Thanksgiving. We have been doing several important things in the Eucharist. Most important is our worship of the Blessed Trinity. The second is our partaking of the body and blood of the Lord Jesus Christ. Third, we have presented ourselves afresh as a living sacrifice to God. Now we offer our thanksgiving to God and enjoy fellowship together.

We have been nourished and fortified by the Lord's body and blood. We have partaken of the benefits of his death and the power of his resurrection. We go forth from this holy place as a believing people, equipped and able to face life in this world. The Eucharist has been transformed into a new beginning, and things that were impossible to us are revealed again as possible. The time of the world has become the time of the church, the time of salvation and redemption.

Celebrant: We thank You, O Sovereign Lord and Lover of mankind, Benefactor of our souls and bodies, that You have made us worthy today of Your heavenly and immortal Mysteries. Direct our way, strengthen all of us in Your fear, guard our life, guide our steps, through the prayers and intercessions of the glorious Mother of God and Ever-virgin Mary, and of all Your saints, for You are our sanctification and we give glory to You, to the Father and to the Son and to the Holy Spirit, now and ever and unto ages of ages.

People: **Amen.**

Celebrant: Let us go forth in peace.

People: **In the Name of the Lord.**

People: **Blessed be the Name of the Lord, from this time forth and forevermore. (3 times)**

Celebrant: The blessing of the Lord and His mercy come upon you through His grace and love towards mankind, always, now and ever and unto ages of ages.

People: **Amen.**

Celebrant: Glory to You, O Christ our God and our Hope, glory to You.

People: **Glory to the Father and to the Son and to the Holy Spirit, now and ever and unto ages of ages. Amen.**
Lord, have mercy. Lord, have mercy. Lord, have mercy.
Father, bless.

Celebrant: May Christ our true God (Who has risen from the dead) through the intercessions of His most pure and holy Mother, the holy, glorious, and all-honorable apostles, (_The Patron Saint of the church_), St. (_N._), whose memory we commemorate today, and of all the saints, have mercy on us and save us, for He is good and loves mankind.

Through the prayers of our holy fathers, O Lord Jesus Christ our God, have mercy on us and save us.

People: Amen.

John David Finley

178 • EPISCOPAL WORSHIP

The eucharistic liturgy, refined by twenty centuries of usage, has two distinct parts which form a unity. The first consists of gathering, listening, and responding to God's written Word. The second is making Eucharist or thanksgiving. This involves receiving bread and wine, praying over these gifts, thanking the Father for the work of Jesus, and receiving back the consecrated elements of bread and wine.

Participation by the community of the baptized at the eucharistic celebration is essential. In fact, liturgy, a word derived from Greek, means "the work of the people." On the Lord's Day, the "work" of the covenant community is to listen afresh to God's mighty and saving work and to give him thanks. The eucharistic assembly is more than an aggregate of individuals. It is to be understood as a representative gathering of the body of Christ, the church universal.

There is an orderly flow to eucharistic liturgy which is both spiritually and psychologically satisfying:

Gathering in the Lord's name
Proclaiming and responding to God's Holy Word
Praying for the created order and for the church
Exchanging Christ's peace
Preparing the Table
Making eucharistic prayer
Breaking the bread
Sharing the bread of heaven and the cup of salvation
Sending into the world

The following is the text of Rite II in the American *Book of Common Prayer* (1979). Throughout, the general rule for the people is to stand for prayer, sit for hearing, and kneel for confessing.

——————— **The Basic Pattern** ———————

The Word of God/The Service of the Word. The Gathering of the Community: People must be gathered and united to do liturgical "work." Before the liturgy there may be praise music, a prelude, or congregational rehearsal of a new musical item in the worship service. A welcome should be given here, especially if visitors are present, in order to set a tone of community and welcome. The ceremonies of gathering will vary but often include being welcomed by an usher and being seated in silence. The quiet space supports the purpose of preparing to worship the living God.

A hymn, psalm, or anthem may be sung.

[In high churches this may accompany the procession.]

The first act of the gathered community is a song of praise which is accompanied by a formal or informal procession of the ministers of the worship. This may be a well-known, traditional English or German hymn or chorale—usually a praise theme or hymn addressed to Jesus. Banners, incense, cross, and candles can be used in the procession. A full procession would consist of a thurifer (incense bearer), crucifer (cross bearer), acolytes bearing candles, choir, and ministers.

The people stand.

Celebrant: Blessed be God: Father, Son and Holy Spirit.

People: **And blessed be his kingdom, now and for ever.**
            Amen.

In place of the above, from Easter Day through the Day of Pentecost,

Celebrant: Alleluia. Christ is risen.

People: **The Lord is risen indeed. Alleluia.**

In Lent and on other penitential occasions,

Celebrant: Bless the Lord who forgives all our sins;

People: **His mercy endures for ever.**

When the procession has ended and priests, deacons, acolytes, and choir have taken their places, the priest and people bless the Trinity and the kingdom of God. This act of blessing sets the tone of active participation for the whole liturgy. In Lent or Advent the service may begin with a penitential order which includes the decalogue or summary of the law and the general confession.

The Celebrant may say,

Almighty God, to you all hearts are open, all desires known, and from you no secrets are hid: Cleanse the thoughts of our hearts by the inspiration of your Holy Spirit, that we may perfectly love you, and worthily magnify your holy Name; through Christ our Lord. _Amen._

Then follows one of the treasures of the English liturgy, Thomas Cranmer's collect for purity.

When appointed, the following hymn or some other song of praise is sung or said, all standing:

> Glory to God in the highest,
> and peace to his people on earth.
> Lord God, heavenly King,
> almighty God and Father,
> we worship you, we give you thanks,
> we praise you for your glory.
> Lord Jesus Christ, only Son of the Father,
> Lord God, Lamb of God,
> you take away the sin of the world:
> have mercy on us;
> you are seated at the right hand of the
> Father:
> receive our prayer.
> For you alone are the Holy One,
> you are alone are the Lord,
> you alone are the Most High,
> Jesus Christ,
> with the Holy Spirit,
> in the glory of God the Father. Amen.

On other occasions the following is used:

> Lord, have mercy   Kyrie eleison.
> Christ, have mercy   or   Christe eleison.
> Lord, have mercy.   Kryie eleison.

or this

> Holy God,
> Holy and Mighty,
> Holy Immortal One,
> Have mercy upon us.

This is followed by an act of praise such as the _Gloria in Excelsis Deo_ or a canticle. In Lent and Advent either the _Kyrie_ ("Lord Have Mercy") or the ancient Greek _Trisagion_ ("Holy God") is sung; during Christmas and Epiphany—the song of the angels, _Gloria in Excelsis,_ is used; Eastertide brings The "Te Deum" or "Christ Our Passover" or a festive hymn, such as Carl Schalk's "This Is the Feast" (p. 417 in the _Hymnal, 1982_). During the Pentecost (Ordinary Time) season any act of praise is appropriate—the Doxology or "Father, We Adore You"

could be used. On Marian feasts the Magnificat can be employed.

The Collect of the Day

Celebrant: The Lord be with you.
People: _And also with you._
Celebrant: Let us pray.

The Celebrant says the Collect.

People: **Amen.**

The opening acts are concluded by the prayer of the day (as set by the liturgical calendar).

The Lessons

The people sit. One or two Lessons, as appointed, are read, the Reader first saying

> A Reading (Lesson) from _____

A citation giving chapter and verse may be added.
After each Reading, the Reader may say,

> The Word of the Lord.

People: **Thanks be to God.**

or the Reader may say,

> Here ends the Reading (Epistle).

Silence may follow.

Proclaiming and Responding to God's Holy Word. It is important to recognize that in liturgical eucharistic worship Word and sacrament stand in a dynamic relationship with each other. The Scripture readings, the sermon, the prayers of the people, and confession of sin combine into a cohesive whole. The reading from the Holy Gospel forms the axle upon which the other Bible readings and the prayers turn. How the Gospel Book is handled by the deacon suggests its dignity; so also does the ceremony surrounding the reading of the Gospel. For example, the assembly stands to hear the Gospel, and the Gospel Book, carried in procession with candle-bearing acolytes to a place in the midst of the people, may be elevated, censed, and/or kissed by the deacon who reads it. All of the readings proceed from a three-year cycle lectionary ("an orderly arrangement of Scripture according to the Church Year") and are frequently addressed by the homily or sermon. Silence may follow the readings in order to permit reflection.

Psalm/Hymn/Anthem. A psalm, hymn, or anthem may follow each reading.

The psalm after the Old Testament reading is sung, following the historical and biblical use of the Psalms as a song book; most churches use the Responsorial Refrains or Anglican chant or Plainsong. After the New Testament reading the alleluia verse may be sung. Most churches follow the "Eight-Fold Alleluia" or a simple plainsong tone repeated after a cantor. In Lent "Alleluia" is not used but is replaced by a verse of Scripture set to music (such as "Create in me a clean heart, O God"). A very short choir motet or anthem could work here as long as it maintains the theme set in the Scripture.

Then, all standing, the Deacon or a Priest reads the Gospel, first saying,

> The Holy Gospel of our Lord Jesus Christ according to _____.

People: **Glory to you, Lord Christ.**

After the Gospel, the Reader says,

> The Gospel of the Lord.

People: **Praise to you, Lord Christ.**

The Gospel may be read, chanted, acted out in story form, or told as a children's story.

The Sermon. The sermon, in the best tradition, is based on one or more of the lectionary texts.

On Sundays and other Major Feasts there follows, all standing,

The Nicene Creed. The entire assembly affirms the Nicene Creed, either spoken in unison, sung in a hymnal setting, or chanted monotone with instrumental accompaniment that modulates in keeping with the sense of the phrases. This act is seen as a weekly renewal of the baptismal covenant.

The Prayers of the People (Form VI). *The Leader and People pray responsively.*

> In peace, we pray to you, Lord God.

Silence

L: For all people in their daily life and work;
P: **For our families, friends, and neighbors, and for those who are alone.**
L: For this community, the nation, and the world;
P: **For all who work for justice, freedom, and peace.**
L: For the just and proper use of your creation;
P: **For the victims of hunger, fear, injustice, and oppression.**

L: For all who are in danger, sorrow, or any kind of trouble;
P: **For those who minister to the sick, the friendless, and the needy.**
L: For the peace and unity of the Church of God;
P: **For all who proclaim the Gospel, and all who seek the Truth.**
L: For [*N.* our Presiding Bishop, and *N.* (*N.*) our Bishop(s); and for] all bishops and other ministers;
P: **For all who serve God in his Church.**
L: For the special needs and concerns of this congregation.

Silence
The People may add their own petitions.

L: Hear us Lord;
P: **For your mercy is great.**
L: We thank you, Lord, for all the blessings of this life.

Silence
The People may add their own thanksgivings.

L: We will exalt you, O God our King;
P: **And praise your Name for ever and ever.**
L: We pray for all who have died, that they may have a place in your eternal kingdom.

Silence
The People may add their own petitions.

L: Lord, let your loving-kindness be upon them;
P: Who put their trust in you.

Silence may be kept.

Praying for the created order and the church. We respond to the Word by praying for the world and for the church. The Word of the Lord has given us the boldness to believe that our prayer is heard.

Leader and People
> Have mercy upon us, most merciful Father;
> in your compassion forgive us our sins, known and unknown,
> things done and left undone;
> and so uphold us by your Spirit
> that we may live and serve you in newness of life,
> to the honor and glory of your Name;
> through Jesus Christ our Lord. Amen.

The Celebrant concludes with an absolution or a suitable Collect.

If the service did not begin with the penitential order and general confession, it may be included here. The text shown here is the most recent revision of the general confession. A form of the classic Anglican general confession may be found in the text of Rite I (the prayer beginning, "Almighty God, Father of our Lord Jesus Christ, maker of all things, judge of all men: We acknowledge and bewail our manifold sins and wickedness, which we from time to time have most grievously have committed, by thought, word, and deed, against thy divine Majesty . . .").

The Peace. _All stand. The Celebrant says to the people,_

> The peace of the Lord be always with you.
>
> People: **And also with you.**

Then the Ministers and People may greet one another in the name of the Lord.

Exchanging Christ's Peace. A mood shift takes place in the assembly at this point in the liturgy. Having heard the Word and having responded to it by prayer and confession of sin we instinctively share the Lord's peace with others. It is a liturgical acting out of I John 4:20. We do this in word by saying: "The peace of the Lord be always with you" and in action by a handshake or hug. A song may be sung such as the Taizé "Ubi caritas."

The Holy Communion. _The Celebrant may begin the Offertory with one of the sentences on page 376 (The Book of Common Prayer, 1979), or with some other sentence of Scripture._

During the Offertory a hymn, psalm, or anthem may be sung.

Representatives of the congregation bring the people's offerings of bread and wine, money, or other gifts to the deacon or celebrant. The people stand while the offerings are presented and placed on the Altar.

The Service of the Table

Preparing the Table. Offerings of bread, wine, and money are received. Many parishes have members of the congregation carry these elements to the altar Table. This is iconographic of the fact that they are the people's gifts. Up to this point the prayer desk, ambo (pulpit), and pews have been the center of activity. The altar/table now forms the center of focus for the baptized community. The money, bread, and wine represent our life and labor.

The Great Thanksgiving: Eucharistic Prayer A

Making Eucharistic Prayer. This prayer is modeled on Jewish table prayer and bears the theme of the Jewish Passover. The eucharistic prayer celebrates Christ as our Passover. The prayer comprises four elements: (1) praise and thanksgiving proceeding from (2) the remembrance (_anamnesis_) of Christ's saving work; (3) Jesus' words at the Last Supper; (4) the offering of ourselves to the Lord and his service, and (4) the calling down of the Holy Spirit upon the bread, wine, and congregation. The congregation may stand or kneel for these prayers.

Prayer A is an adaptation of one of Cranmer's eucharistic prayers in the _BCP._ In addition, the Prayer Book includes Prayer B, a shortened form, Prayer C, a contemprary prayer with responses by the people and featuring some contemporary concerns such as the environment; Prayer D, a prayer derived from Syrian and Eastern Orthodox liturgies; and "An Order for Celebrating the Holy Eucharist," a more free outline with short forms for the Great Thanksgiving.

The people remain standing. The celebrant, whether bishop or priest, faces them and sings or says,

> The Lord be with you.
>
> People: **And also with you.**
>
> Celebrant: Lift up your hearts.
>
> People: **We lift them to the Lord.**
>
> Celebrant: Let us give thanks to the Lord our God.
>
> People: **It is right to give him thanks and praise.**

The Great Thanksgiving begins with the ancient dialogue found in Hippolytus and many other liturgies. These lines, then, are the classic greeting in Christianity. The second exchange is called the _Sursum corda_—"lift up your hearts" not only suggests high-heartedness but is an act of union with the praise of heaven, a reference to the heavenly banquet in which the communion to come participates.

Then, facing the Holy Table, the Celebrant proceeds,

> It is right, and a good and joyful thing, always and everywhere to give thanks to

you, Father Almighty, Creator of heaven and earth.

Here a Proper Preface is sung or said on all Sundays, and on other occasions as appointed.

Therefore we praise you, joining our voices with Angels and Archangels and with all the company of heaven, who forever sing this hymn to proclaim the glory of your Name:

Giving thanks is a joyful obligation—an obligation because it is "right," an appropriate response to God. The proper preface is a variable prayer that is thematically related to the season or feast being celebrated. In liturgical terminology, "proper" means elements proper to the particular celebration, whereas "ordinary" refers to the invariable parts of the liturgy, those parts always present in any celebration of the Eucharist.

Celebrant and People:
Holy, holy, holy Lord, God of power and might, heaven and earth are full of your glory.
Hosanna in the highest.
Blessed is he who comes in the name of the Lord.
Hosanna in the highest.

The *Sanctus* (Holy, holy, holy . . .), based on Isaiah's vision of the worship of heaven, is followed by the *Benedictus,* which echoes the praise offered to Jesus at his Triumphal Entry into Jerusalem.
The people stand or kneel.
Then the Celebrant continues,

Holy and gracious Father: In your infinite love you made us for yourself; and, when we had fallen into sin and become subject to evil and death, you, in your mercy, sent Jesus Christ, your only and eternal Son, to share our human nature, to live and die as one of us, to reconcile us to you, the God and Father of all.

He stretched out his arms upon the cross, and offered himself, in obedience to your will, a perfect sacrifice for the whole world.

The eucharistic prayer proper begins here.
At the following words concerning the bread, the Celebrant is to hold it, or lay a hand upon it; and at the words concerning the cup, to hold or place a hand upon the cup and any other vessel containing wine to be consecrated.

On the night he was handed over to suffering and death, our Lord Jesus Christ took bread; and when he had given thanks to you, he broke it, and gave it to his disciples, and said, "Take, eat: This is my Body, which is given for you. Do this for the remembrance of me." After supper he took the cup of wine; and when he had given thanks, he gave it to them, and said, "Drink this, all of you: This is my Blood of the new Covenant, which is shed for you and for many for the forgiveness of sins. Whenever you drink it, do this for the remembrance of me."

The text of this section is called the Institution Narrative, taken from Paul's account of the Last Supper in 1 Corinthians 11:23-25.

Therefore we proclaim the mystery of faith:

Celebrant and People:
Christ has died.
Christ is risen.
Christ will come again.

The acclamation in which the people express the substance of their praise—the reason why the celebration is happening.
The Celebrant continues:

We celebrate the memorial of our redemption, O Father, in this sacrifice of praise and thanksgiving. Recalling his death, resurrection, and ascension, we offer you these gifts.

The "memorial" is more than just a memory. The Greek word for it, *anamnesis,* suggests the present reality in this celebration of the historic work of Christ. In this the church followed the Hebrew notion of memorial participation in previous events.

Sanctify them by your Holy Spirit to be for your people the Body and Blood of your Son, the holy food and drink of new and unending life in him. Sanctify us also that we may faithfully receive this holy Sacrament, and serve you in unity, constancy, and peace; and at the last day bring us with all your saints into the joy of your eternal kingdom.

The *epiclesis* calls upon the Holy Spirit to sanctify the gifts of bread and wine and to sanctify the people who partake of them. Note the phrase "for your people," which attempts to steer clear of a radical view of transsubstantiation.

> All this we ask through your Son Jesus Christ. By him, and with him, and in him, in the unity of the Holy Spirit all honor and glory is yours, Almighty Father, now and for ever. **Amen.**

The conclusion of the prayer is the Great Doxology, and the Amen is the Great Amen.

> And now, as our Savior
> Christ has taught us,
> we are bold to say,

People and Celebrant:
> Our Father, who art in heaven,
> hallowed be thy Name
> thy kingdom come,
> thy will be done,
> on earth as it is in heaven.
> Give us this day our daily bread.
> And forgive us our trespasses,
> as we forgive those
> who trespass against us.
> And lead us not into temptation,
> but deliver us from evil.
> For thine is the kingdom,
> and the power, and the glory,
> for ever and ever. Amen.

The Our Father has always been a staple of the liturgy. In the old Roman liturgy and the eastern rights, this summation of petitions followed another group of petition that had the character of the prayers of the people.

The Breaking of the Bread. *The Celebrant breaks the consecrated Bread.*
> *A period of silence is kept.*
> *Then may be sung or said*

Celebrant: [Alleluia.] Christ our Passover is sacrificed for us;
People: Therefore let us keep the feast. [Alleluia.]

In Lent Alleluia is omitted and may be omitted at other times except during Easter Season.
> *In place of, or in addition to, the preceding, some other suitable anthem may be used.*

Breaking the Bread. The celebrant, priest, or bishop holds the bread high and breaks it. Since the body of Christ was broken on the cross, it is broken for

the people of God so that each person has a portion in the eucharistic feast. The breaking of the bread is usually climaxed by a congregational "Alleluia!"

Facing the people, the Celebrant says the following Invitation:
> The Gifts of God for the People of God.

and may add
> Take them in remembrance that Christ died for you,
> and feed on him in your hearts by faith, with thanksgiving.

The ministers receive the Sacrament in both kinds, and then immediately deliver it to the people.
> *The bread and the Cup are given to the communicants with these words:*
> The Body (Blood) of our Lord Jesus Christ keep you in everlasting life. **Amen.**

or with these words:
> The Body of Christ, the bread of heaven. **Amen.**
> The Blood of Christ, the cup of salvation. **Amen.**

Sharing the Bread of Heaven and the Cup of Salvation. The priest invites the people to communion by lifting the gifts. The additional words ("Take them in remembrance . . .") were added to the invitation by Cranmer as a Protestant explanation of the manner in which the body and blood of Christ are received. The bread and wine are given to the baptized in either a standing or kneeling posture. The walk to the front of the worship space is an important aspect of the reception. In this respect, liturgical churches have a weekly "altar call." This is the part of the liturgy that is rightly called Holy Communion.

During the ministration of Communion, hymns, psalms, or anthems may be sung.
> *When necessary, the celebrant consecrates additional bread and wine, using the form on page 408* (The Book of Common Prayer, *1979).*
> *After Communion, the Celebrant says,*
> Let us pray.

During the administration of the Holy Communion there may be silence or suitable music such as hymns, Taizé songs, Scripture songs, or appropriate choruses. After Communion persons who so wish may receive the anointing of oil and then return to their seats, ready to do the work of the kingdom.

Celebrant and People:

> Eternal God, heavenly Father,
> you have graciously accepted us as living
> members of your Son our Savior Jesus
> Christ, and you have fed us with spiritual
> food in the Sacrament of his Body and
> Blood.
> Send us now into the world in peace,
> and grant us strength and courage
> to love and serve you with gladness and
> singleness of heart; through Christ our
> Lord. Amen.

or the following:

> Almighty and ever living God,
> we thank you for feeding us with the spiri-
> tual food
> of the most precious Body and Blood
> of your Son our Savior Jesus Christ;
> and for assuring us in these holy mysteries
> that we are living members of the Body of
> your Son,
> and heirs of your eternal kingdom.
> And now, Father, send us out
> to do the work you have given us to do,
> to love and serve you
> as faithful witnesses of Christ our Lord.
> To him, to you, and to the Holy Spirit,
> be honor and glory, now and for ever.
> Amen.

The Thanksgiving after Communion. Some churches invite spontaneous thanksgivings from the people, spoken or silent, which then are gathered up in this prayer.

The Bishop, when present, or the Priest, may bless the people.

A concluding blessing is almost always given. Frequently it consists of a series of three blessings with a seasonal theme.

The Deacon, or the Celebrant, dismisses them with these words:

> Let us go forth in the name of Christ.
>
> People: Thanks be to God.

or this:

> Deacon: Go in peace to love and serve the
>   Lord.
> People: Thanks be to God.

or this:

> Deacon: Let us go forth into the world, rejoic-
>   ing in the power of the Spirit.
> People: Thanks be to God.

or this:

> Deacon: Let us bless the Lord.
> People: Thanks be to God.

From the Easter Vigil through the Day of Pentecost, "Alleluia, alleluia" may be added to any of the dismissals.

> *The People respond*
>
> Thanks be to God. Alleluia, alleluia.

(*The Book of Common Prayer* [New York: Church Hymnal Corp., 1977], pp 353–366, 392–393.)

Dismissal. The deacon then dismisses the assembly. For that congregation the liturgy has ended, but the Eucharist has not. Christians are called to be eucharistic people, a people of thanksgiving in all circumstances. Alleluia! Christ our Passover is sacrificed for us. Therefore let us keep the Feast. Alleluia!

Richard Lobs and Larry Nyberg

179 ◆ EVANGELICAL WORSHIP

Evangelical churches may be defined as those that have stressed historically the authority of Scripture, personal commitment to serve Jesus Christ, and an evangelistic outreach to their community and world. Models of worship renewal in evangelical churches may be as numerous as the number of churches involved in such renewal. These churches usually function independently in the ordering of their church life, even where they cooperate with fellowships of like mind and tradition in matters of witness to the greater community.

At the same time, a survey of worship renewal in evangelical circles discloses some common trends. The underlying purpose of renewal is usually articulated as reaching people for Jesus Christ and involving them more effectively in Christian growth and the corporate life of the local church. It is unlikely that an evangelical church would pursue the worship renewal if it did not appear that these goals were being addressed.

Evangelical churches have moved into renewal as a recognition that older styles of church services have increasingly lost points of contact with people living in contemporary North American culture. *Relevance,* therefore, is the key word. As Doug Thiessen, music minister of First Evangelical Free

Church in Rockford, Illinois, puts it, "When people discover that God speaks through a contemporary idiom, they find they can respond to him that way." The target group in worship renewal tends to be those whom Thiessen calls "raw recruits"—those with minimal Christian background—although others who had a church background in the past, but have dropped out, also discover new meaning in renewed forms of worship that emphasize a life-changing encounter with the mystery of God rather than a rationalist, word-oriented type of corporate gathering.

Frequently an evangelical church will retain a more traditional service for those who prefer it, while adding a service in contemporary style. Others have been able to mix the two, introducing elements of renewal into a "standard" format. Some churches periodically schedule special occasions for renewed worship at times other than Sunday morning.

Several influences are at work to shape the renewal of worship in evangelical congregations. The "praise-and-worship" style has been popularized through recordings, Christian broadcasting, and exposure of church members to the worship of other churches in the community. Evangelical worship leaders have been able to introduce this less formal style to their congregations partly because it has always been present to a degree in their church life, in the worship of specialized groups such as children's ministries or youth camps and conferences. Although evangelical churches tend towards a more "laid-back" approach to celebrative worship than what might be encountered in some charismatic churches, one may often observe features formerly associated only with Pentecostals and charismatics, such as clapping or lifting of the hands. In a few evangelical congregations made up largely of people who have come from Catholic or liturgical Protestant backgrounds, contemporary worship resources from those traditions may be incorporated into renewed celebration, especially for Holy Communion.

The use of a worship team of lead singers and instrumentalists, in place of the traditional choir, is another practice adapted from the "praise-and-worship" movement. The worship team not only provides musical support but also functions to encourage worshipers to become more involved in the act of Christian celebration. The technology of the "praise-and-worship" movement also makes its appearance in overhead projectors and enhanced sound systems.

Renewed worship may also incorporate a time for open prayer and testimony from members of the congregation, a practice influenced not only by liturgical renewal in the Catholic community and by charismatic worship, but also by the format of the traditional midweek prayer meeting of many evangelical churches.

Worship, formerly a neglected area in many evangelical churches, is being rediscovered as (in A. W. Tozer's words) "the missing jewel of the evangelical church." More and more, the exaltation of God and the direct expression of love to him, as well as instruction in his Word, is being viewed as a priority in congregational life. Some churches have created the staff position of *minister of worship* (not just "minister of music") or have assigned greater responsibility to their worship committees. Carl Stam, of Chapel Hill Bible Church in North Carolina, writes:

> Exalting Christ as Lord means to thoughtfully worship him—to come with adoration, exultation, and thanksgiving, acknowledging him as Lord. The congregation and the elders feel it's worth having someone trained to do these things. I'm the one they look to to develop a philosophy and a means of worship so that the congregation can be more thoughtful in what they do. ("Worship That Integrates Faith and Music," *Worship Leader* [February/March 1993]: 20)

The Basic Pattern

The following representative orders of worship come from the First Evangelical Free Church of Rockford, Illinois, and from South Park Church, an independent evangelical church in Park Ridge, Illinois, in January 1993.

First Evangelical Free Church

The salient features of the contemporary worship service at First Free Church, Rockford, are *theme* and *flexibility;* the order of worship varies from week to week depending on the theme of the service, though it always moves through the three stages of adoration, exhortation, and dedication. The sermon and its worship context are an integrated whole.

Adoration

Choruses (may include Scripture readings)
Prayer
Offering

The evangelical tendency to turn worship into instruction is countered, however, by the fact that the opening segment always focuses on praise offered directly to God. The service begins with up-tempo, hand-clapping choruses that phase into those in a more intimate mode of personal adoration. The music may proceed without interruption, or the theme of the day may be introduced during the opening segment through drama or Scripture readings. The music itself may introduce the theme; for example, the motif of stewardship may be expressed through the chorus "Jehovah Jireh, My Provider," or that of thanksgiving through "It is Good to Give Thanks to the Lord." Solos as well as congregational singing may be included in this segment, but often the music is familiar to worshipers through Christian media, and they may join in singing a refrain. The transition into the exhortation phase occurs with the offering.

Exhortation

Drama (may appear earlier)

In a culture steeped in entertainment media, drama is an effective means of focusing on issues of Christian faith and life in the worship setting. Larger churches (First Free is the largest congregation of its denomination) especially have the resources for this kind of ministry. The model for worship drama is ultimately a biblical one; the worship of Israel was essentially a representation of the historic saving deeds of the Lord, and the Lord's Supper is a dramatic visualization of Christ's action.

Scripture Reading
Sermon
Prayer

The Scripture reading and sermon bring the theme for the day to a clear focus and may lead the worshiper to a point of decision. The sermon concludes with a prayer summing up its theme, leading into the dedication phase of the service.

Dedication

Chorus in Response to the Word
Benediction
Invitation to Fellowship

The final chorus is a response to the theme; for example, if stewardship is the motif the chorus might be "We Are an Offering." The benediction is taken from one of the scriptural blessings, and the service ends informally with the pastor's invitation for worshipers to greet one another.

South Park Church

The order of service from South Park Church shows some similarities to First Free's, and some variations. South Park's service is *flexible* but stresses *participation* more than theme.

Praise and Worship in song

(may include Scripture)
Welcome and Announcements
Morning Prayer
Offering (with special music ministry)
Scripture Option:
  Scripture Reading
  Responsive Reading
  Dramatic Reading

The service opens with a period of praise in song, led by a worship team. Following the pastor's welcome, announcements are made from both platform and congregation as appropriate; the pastor then offers general prayer for church concerns. A solo or other act of music ministry accompanies the offering, after which the Scripture lesson is read. The Scripture may also take the form of a responsive or dramatic reading.

Sharing Options:

  Servant's Word
  Sharing Time
  Witness of Faith
  Baby Dedication

The next segment, a time of congregational participation, may follow several optional formats. Someone involved in a ministry opportunity may share it with the congregation in the "servant's word." A general "sharing time" may provide for open expression of prayer concerns, a Scripture passage a worshiper has found especially meaningful, or a testimony to God's working in the life of a believer. When new members join the church, they are given the opportunity to tell how they have come to Christ in the "witness of faith." In a congregation including many younger families, infant dedication occurs regularly during this segment.

Hymn or Song

Message (may incorporate drama)

Response in Song
Benediction

A hymn or song of praise and worship, during which children are dismissed to their own special groups, precedes the message. The issues to be addressed by the pastor's message may be presented beforehand in a short drama or skit. Following the sermon, the congregation responds in song and is dismissed with a benediction.

For Alan Koetz, minister of music and worship at South Park Church, what makes worship contemporary is not the style of music, drama, or the like which it uses, but the ability to be flexible in responding to the needs of the congregation. He stresses the difference between entertainment and enjoyment. When worship _entertains,_ the focus has shifted away from the Lord and onto the worshiper. However, God and his worship are always to be _enjoyed._ Koetz's view is another way of summing up the motivation behind worship renewal in evangelical churches.

God, the Almighty. When various Hebrew names of God are used in Christian art as above (El Shaddai), they are surrounded with rays of light. This symbol speaks of the inexpressible nature of God, who dwells in glorious light.

Conclusion

The pulpit-centered approach of these churches still places limitations on the extent of worship renewal; most congregations have stopped short of restoring the Lord's Table to its historic position as the basic act and climax of Christian worship. Within this self-imposed restraint, however, evangelical churches are showing increased creativity in their approach to the weekly corporate gathering.

Richard C. Leonard

180 ♦ Holiness Worship

The Holiness movement is Wesleyan in origin. It emphasizes the sanctification of life and conduct. Sanctification is normally seen as a second work of grace subsequent to personal regeneration. Holiness churches also believe in divine healing, a rite some congregations are beginning to recover.

Most of the Holiness churches began in the late nineteenth century. Worship was strongly emotional and often employed the use of the "mourners bench" (as in Nazarene worship), where people came to confess their sins and get right with God. This movement was a forebear of the Pentecostal movement.

Worship among the churches of the holiness tradition—Wesleyan, Nazarene, and Christian and Missionary Alliance churches—may vary from place to place. Those holiness churches that seek to draw on historical worship patterns

while retaining their own distinctive practices have created orders similar to the one described in this article. The service that follows is from a Church of the Nazarene.

The Basic Pattern

Acts of Entrance/Prelude. As the congregation gathers for worship, an organ prelude featuring celebratory and Christocentric but familiar hymn tunes is offered with authority. While some congregants use this time to greet each other, others quietly read Scripture, peruse the worship folder, or join the pastoral staff and worship leaders at the altar for prayer.

Procession. As the service time draws near, the robed ministers of music (choir) gather at the back of the sanctuary and the worship team advances to the platform. When the organist concludes the prelude, the service begins while the ministers of music are still in the foyer, singing a choral call to worship a capella.

Call to Worship/Hymn. When the call is given, the pastor stands and moves toward the pulpit, inviting the congregation to stand as well. The first spoken words are from Scripture. "Now, therefore, you are no longer strangers and foreigners, but fellow citizens with the saints and members of the household of God." (Eph. 2:19, NKJV). "As fellow citizens of his kingdom, let us stand and offer our praise unto God by singing Hymn 73, "Praise Ye the Lord, the Almighty." As the congregation sings all verses of the hymn, the ministers of music process from the back of the sanctuary, led by the children's choir.

Prayer of Blessing/*Gloria Patri*. While the congregation remains standing, the pastor offers the prayer of blessing. Here the pastor asks God's help so that the congregation may confess what they must and confess what they can so that all may offer worship "in spirit and in truth." The prayer may include the Lord's Prayer, prayed in unison, followed by the singing of the Gloria Patri.

Act of Praise/Ministry of Music. Having confessed and sought blessing, the ministers of music sing a selection, inviting the congregation to unite in praise. The number is always done with a sense of thanksgiving, adoration, and triumph. As a footnote to the camp-meeting tradition in which the Nazarene church was shaped, the congregation regularly responds to the choir selections by spontaneous shouts of "amen," "praise the Lord," or "glory."

Apostles' Creed. While individuals may respond in those ways, the pastor invites the entire congregation to stand and confess resurrection truth. About once a month, the confession will be followed with the Apostles' Creed.

Children's Choir. After this the children's choir sings. Generally their selections have a resurrection motif and often include unison recitation of Scripture. The children are used every week in this fashion for two reasons. (1) They actually and quite naturally lead the congregation in the spirit of celebratory worship, and (2) their regular involvement diminishes any sense in which they are a "cute" addition to the service. They are a consistent and meaningful part of congregational life.

Christian Greetings. The greeting is the first time the pastor actually talks with the congregation. "Greetings to you in Christ's name." "May the peace of the Lord be with you!" "We extend welcome and grace to those who worship with us for the first time and to those who worship with us week by week." "We have been called by the Christ who graces us with his presence." "As the children go to

the service prepared for them, stand and extend the peace of Christ to each other."

Announcements are not mentioned. Instead, the pastor may refer to the insert in the worship folder concerning various aspects of congregational life. Persons for whom the congregation is asked to pray are listed as are other needs, both local and global. The greeting may last no more than a minute or two.

The Service of the Word/First Lesson, Psalm, Second Lesson. When the congregation is seated, a lay reader introduces the first lesson, which is taken from the standard lectionary. The reader gives a brief introduction of the context of the passage before reading. Between the first and second lesson, the choir sings a psalm selection or other appropriate number. While a few respond to the reading of the Word by saying, "Thanks be to God," or simply "Amen," the majority are silent but reflective, a response called for after the reading of the second lesson.

Hymn. A hymn prior to the prayers of the people is introduced by a phrase of Scripture. "Be anxious for nothing, but in everything by prayer and supplication, with thanksgiving, let your requests be made known to God" (Phil. 4:6, NKJV). "Let us stand and sing unto God, Hymn 94."

Prayers of the People/Song of Response. Except for the word of written invitation, nothing is said about the congregation joining the pastor at the altar. Routinely, as the last verse of the hymn is sung, the pastor moves to the altar for prayer while persons from every part of the sanctuary join in kneeling at the altar, with Communion table and the cross in view.

The prayers of the people are largely intercessory, asking God's blessing on the healthy and ill, the employed and unemployed, those present and those absent, those in leadership and those under authority, those at peace and those at war. If the Lord's Prayer has not been used earlier, it may be sung as the conclusion of the people's prayer. When it is not used in that way, the congregation joins in singing a contemporary response.

Offering. The offering is introduced by an invitation to read the printed Scripture in unison, after which the pastor offers an extemporaneous prayer. As the ushers receive the offering, a vocal selection is sung to live accompaniment. The church attempts to use the spiritual gifts of those present in lieu of taped accompaniment, discouraging any semblance to entertainment.

Gospel Lesson/Sermon. The gospel lesson, which frequently is the text for the sermon, is read by the pastor. The congregation stands in reverence to the reading of the Gospel, and after it is read, the pastor says, "The Gospel of Christ." The congregation responds by singing the Doxology, after which the Word is preached.

The Service of Response/Invitation or Lord's Supper. The vast majority of Nazarene churches use the mourners bench (altar) as a response to the preached Word. A hymn of invitation or gospel song that corresponds with the sermon may be sung as seekers are invited to pray at the altar. On occasions when Communion is served, appropriate Scripture is read and the sacraments are blessed and served in lieu of the song of invitation and closing prayer.

Acts of Dismissal/Hymn and/or Closing Prayer or Words of Dismissal. The service concludes with a biblical benediction followed by words of exhortation. "Go in peace to love and serve the Lord." The postlude sounds the final note of triumph, as the pastor and choir recess, reminding worshipers that "we are more than conquerors through Him who loved us" (Rom. 8:37, NKJV).

Randall Davies

181 ◆ LUTHERAN WORSHIP

Imagine a welcoming narthex that opens onto the room of assembly where there is a great baptismal pool, full of clear and flowing water and situated just at the place where the narthex opens onto a nave. The assembly room itself is furnished with a central reading desk, a gracious and significant table, visible chairs for a few leaders, and worthy chairs for all the people who gather. Here are visible invitations to baptism, the Word, the meal, and the leadership, as well as a good space for the participating community.

As people arrive, doorkeepers hand out the liturgy books. Candles flicker at each of the central places, marking especially the reading desk and the table. A great white linen cloth covers the table, and both reading desk and table may also be marked with cloth in the color of the season or the day. Near the entrance, at a place that can be seen, stands a table holding the loaf of bread that someone has brought, and a glass flagon of amber or white wine. Music, light though intense, fills the room—a solo flute, a small ensemble, _an organ—but, in any case, music which points to the hymns that soon will be sung. All these things—the water in the pool, the open but centered space, candles and cloth and colors, doorkeepers, the waiting bread and wine, music—are meant to welcome the arriving persons into the mystery which will be celebrated here: Christ present in the assembled community, in baptism remembered, in Word read and preached, in the Holy Supper celebrated. Such is the setting of Lutheran worship._

Lutheran worship follows this pattern: four acts of Entrance, Word, Table, and Dismissal. The service often begins with a penitential act, the Brief Order for Confession and Forgiveness (see below). The Lutheran Book of Worship contains three settings for worship and a choral service of Holy Communion. The service below is Setting One. (Variable prayers offered in Setting One are not included.)

—————— The Basic Pattern ——————

Brief Order for Confession and Forgiveness/Entrance. If the assembly is small enough and if not too many of its members have difficulty in standing or walking, all those who arrive gather in a growing circle around the pool. They wait there, greeting each other and quietly talking. If this will not work, they take their places in the assembly room now, but they prepare to stand and face the pool. As the music draws to a close, a small procession joins those who stand at the font: a cross-bearer, a person carrying the assembly's large Bible, two candlebearers with lit torches, the choir, at least one _lay_ assisting minister and a presiding minister who is the congregation's pastor. Each of these persons is clothed in an alb, the white garment of baptism. They wear this robe because it is the garment that belongs to all who have "put on Christ," and these leaders are fulfilling tasks for the sake of an assembly of those who are so "clothed." The presiding minister also wears a stole and an amply cut, gracious, but very simple chasuble in the color of the season or the day, marking him or her as both the community's leader and primary representative of the tradition and of the other churches to which this community is linked.

Then, as a proclamation of the new baptism from which this community lives—as a return to the word of grace that lives in baptism and as a way to go "through the water" into this meeting again—a simple order for confession and forgiveness is enacted by the pool.

(Stand)

1. The minister leads the congregation in the invocation. The sign of the cross may be made by all in remembrance of their baptism.

Presiding Minister: In the name of the Father, and of the Son, and of the Holy Spirit.

Congregation: **Amen.**

Presiding Minister: Almighty God, to whom all hearts are open, all desires known, and from whom no secrets are hid: Cleanse the thoughts of our hearts by the inspiration of your Holy Spirit, that we may perfectly love you and worthily magnify your holy name, through Jesus Christ our Lord.

Congregation: **Amen.**

Presiding Minister: If we say we have no sin, we deceive ourselves, and the truth is not in us. But if we confess our sins, God who is faithful and just will forgive our sins and cleanse us from all unrighteousness.

(Kneel/Stand)

2. Silence for reflection and self-examination.

Presiding Minister: Most merciful God,

Congregation: **we confess that we are in bondage to sin and cannot free ourselves. We have sinned against you in thought, word, and deed, by what we have done and by what we have left undone. We have not loved you with our whole heart; we have not loved our neighbors as ourselves. For the sake of your Son, Jesus Christ, have mercy on us. Forgive us, renew us, and lead us, so that we may delight in your will and walk in your ways, to the glory of your holy name. Amen.**

3. The minister stands and addresses the congregation.

Presiding Minister: Almighty God, in his mercy, has given his Son to die for us and, for his sake, forgives us all our sins. As a called and ordained minister of the church of Christ, and by his authority, I therefore declare to you the entire forgiveness of all your sins, in the name of the Father, and of the Son, and of the Holy Spirit.

Holy Communion

Setting One

1. The Brief Order for Confession and Forgiveness may be used before this service.

2. The minister may announce the day and its significance before the Entrance Hymn, before the lessons, or at another appropriate time.

3. When there is no Communion, the service is concluded after the Creed as indicated.

(Stand)

4. The ENTRANCE HYMN or Psalm is sung.

The musicians then introduce the Entrance hymn. The entire community—or the small procession, representing the community—enters the assembly room, singing this hymn. The principal assisting minister and the presiding minister take their places at the chairs of leadership. The choir has a place from which they can be heard, a place that also makes clear that they are part of the assembly. If they have just come from the font, the other members of the assembly find their places as well. With everyone still standing, the presider makes an open gesture of welcome and speaks the apostolic greeting (2 Cor. 13:13), a greeting meant to proclaim the triune life of God in which this assembly gathers. The congregation's response intends to make sure that the presider is also included in this proclamation.

5. The minister greets the congregation.

Presiding Minister: The grace of our Lord Jesus Christ, the love of God, and the communion of the Holy Spirit be with you all.

Congregation: **And also with you.**

6. The KYRIE may follow:

Now the principal assisting minister intones the bids of the *Kyrie*, the whole assembly responding as if, on the way to the heart of the meeting, we mean to remember where we are and how great is our need of God. The same assisting minister continues by intoning the ancient Gloria in Excelsis, that poetic trope on the song of the angels at the Incarnation, as if the word we are about to hear is the very presence of that Incarnate One. The whole congregation takes up the song, making the angels' chorus audible in this world. These chants and all the subsequent classical liturgical texts are sung according to one of the three musical settings of the liturgy provided in the book or according to one of the many alternate settings in circulation. Finally, the presider, still standing at the chair, raises his or her hands in the old posture of prayer which will be used throughout this service and speaks the prayer of the day that sums up all this gathering, singing, and moving—all this activity of entrance.

Assisting Minister:	In peace, let us pray to the Lord.
Congregation:	**Lord, have mercy.**
Assisting Minister:	For the peace from above, and for our salvation, let us pray to the Lord.
Congregation:	**Lord, have mercy.**
Assisting Minister:	For the peace of the whole world, for the well-being of the Church of God and for the unity of all, let us pray to the Lord.
Congregation:	**Lord, have mercy.**
Assisting Minister:	For this holy house, and for all who offer here their worship and praise, let us pray to the Lord.
Congregation:	**Lord, have mercy.**
Assisting Minister:	Help, save, comfort, and defend us, gracious Lord.
Congregation:	**Amen.**

7. The HYMN OF PRAISE or another appropriate hymn may be sung.

Assisting Minister:	Glory to God in the highest, and peace to his people on earth.

Congregation:
Lord God, heavenly king, almighty God and Father:
We worship you, we give you thanks,
we praise you for your glory.
Lord Jesus Christ, only Son of the Father,

Lord God, Lamb of God:
You take away the sin of the world;
have mercy on us.
You are seated at the right hand of the Father; receive our prayer.
For you alone are the Holy One,
You alone are the Lord,
you alone are the Most High, Jesus Christ with the Holy Spirit,
in the glory of God the Father. Amen.

or

Song: "This is the feast of victory for our God"

8. The PRAYER OF THE DAY is said; the salutation may precede it.

Presiding Minister:	The Lord be with you.
Congregation:	**And also with you.**
Presiding Minister:	Let us pray. . . .
Congregation:	**Amen.**

(Sit)

9. The FIRST LESSON is announced and read.

Assisting Minister:	The First Lesson is from the _____ chapter of _____.

Word. Then we all sit down and proceed with the heart of the meeting. A lector rises from the congregation and comes to the reading desk, where the great Bible has been placed. The first lesson, a reading from the Hebrew Scriptures appointed in the lectionary, is read.

10. After the lesson the reader may say: "Here ends the reading."

11. The appointed PSALM is sung or said.

A voice from the choir then begins the psalm and soon the entire assembly joins in antiphonal song with the choir, singing through this response to the first reading.

12. The SECOND LESSON is announced and read.

The lector then reads the second lesson, a reading from the Epistles of the New Testament.

Assisting Minister:	The Second Lesson is from the _____ chapter of _____.

13. After the lesson the reader may say: "Here ends the reading."

14. The appointed VERSE is sung by the choir, or the congregation may sing the appropriate Verse below:

Everybody then stands to welcome the Gospel reading as a sign of the presence of the risen Christ amidst all these biblical words. While the choir sings an ''Alleluia'' verse, verbally expressing that welcome, the Bible is carried into the midst of the assembly, flanked by candlebearers. The presider comes to the book to do the reading. The congregation sings acclamations to the risen one before and after the reading itself.

(Stand)

| Congregation: | Alleluia. Lord, to whom shall we go? You have the words of eternal life. Alleluia. Alleluia. |

(LENT)

| Congregation: | Return to the Lord, your God, for he is gracious and merciful, slow to anger, and abounding in steadfast love. |

15. *The GOSPEL is announced.*

| Presiding Minister: | The Holy Gospel according to St. _____, the _____ chapter. |
| Congregation: | Glory to you, O Lord. |

16. *After the reading the minister may say: ''The Gospel of the Lord.''*

| Congregation: | Praise to you, O Christ. |

17. *The Hymn of the Day may be sung before the Sermon.*

(Sit)

18. *The SERMON. Silence for reflection may follow.*

Then the presider returns to the reading desk where he or she preaches, opening the texts which have just been read so that they clearly speak to us today the law of God and the gospel of God's mercy in Christ.

(Stand)

19. *The HYMN OF THE DAY is sung.*

Four actions follow and receive this central reading and preaching of Scripture. First, there is a long and deep silence. Second, the hymn of the day is sung: a great, classic hymn which brings to expression, in words that the congregation takes up, any of the themes of the readings. This hymn is frequently sung in alternation with the choir or between two parts of the congregation.

20. *The CREED may be said. The Nicene Creed is said on all festivals and on Sundays in the seasons of Advent, Christmas, Lent, and Easter. The Apostles' Creed is said at other times. The Creed is omitted here if the service of Holy Baptism or another rite with a creed is used.*

Third, one of the classic creeds is confessed.

NICENE CREED

21. *When there is no Communion, the service continues on page 171.*

22. *THE PRAYERS are said.*

And finally, the assisting minister, standing before his or her chair, speaks out the bids of the prayers. These prayers are always for others, for the deep needs of world and church, as well as for the sick and dying of the parish. It is as if the grace of God, which has been proclaimed to us in the Word, is sought also for the needs of the world beyond this present circle.

| Assisting Minister: | Let us pray for the whole people of God in Christ Jesus, and for all people according to their needs. |

Prayers are included for the whole church, the nations, those in need, the parish, special concerns.

The congregation may be invited to offer petitions and thanksgivings.

Prayers of confession may be included if the Brief Order for Confession and Forgiveness has not been used earlier.

The minister gives thanks for the faithful departed, especially for those who recently have died.

After each portion of the prayers:

| Assisting Minister: | Lord, in your mercy, |
| Congregation: | hear our prayer. |

The prayers conclude:

| Presiding Minister: | Into your hands, O Lord, we commend all for whom we pray, trusting in your mercy; through your Son Jesus Christ or Lord. |
| Congregation: | Amen. |

23. *The PEACE is shared at this time or after the Lord's Prayer, prior to the distribution.*

Table. As a ''seal'' on these prayers (cf. Mark 11:24-25) and as a preparation to gather the gifts we have brought (Matt. 5:23-24), the congregation shares a sign of peace with each other—a handshake, an embrace, a gesture, but always the words of greeting. This shared sign thus becomes the bridge to the second central action of this meeting, the Lord's Supper.

Presiding Minister: The peace of the Lord be with you always.

Congregation: **And also with you.**

The ministers and congregation may greet one another in the name of the Lord.

Peace be with you. Peace be with you.

(Sit)

24. _The OFFERING is received as the Lord's Table is prepared._

A collection is received, intended both for the poor and for the support of the church's mission. While these gifts are being gathered, the assisting minister spreads another linen cloth on the table and sets a large chalice on that cloth. Then, as the collection is brought forward, together with the bread and wine, which had been set out at the entrance and which also are gifts drawn from our common life, the assembly stands and the choir interprets this action with an offertory verse, praising God as the giver of all things and proclaiming that all we can finally give is our utter need of God. The assisting minister sums up this entire action—collection, table-setting, and song—with a simple prayer.

25. _The appointed OFFERTORY may be sung by the choir as the gifts are presented, or the congregation may sing one of the following offertories or an appropriate hymn or psalm._

(Stand)

Congregation: What shall I render to the Lord for all his benefits to me? I will offer the sacrifice of thanksgiving and will call on the name of the Lord. I will take the cup of salvation and will call on the name of the Lord. I will pay my vows to the Lord now in the presence of all his people, in the courts of the Lord's house, in the midst of you, O Jerusalem.

26. _After the gifts have been presented, one of these prayers is said._

Assisting Minister: Let us pray.
Assisting Minister: Merciful Father,
Congregation: **we offer with joy and thanksgiving what you have first given us—our selves, our time, and our possessions, signs of your gracious love. Receive them for the sake of him who offered himself for us, Jesus Christ our Lord. Amen.**

or

Assisting Minister: Blessed are you,
Congregation: **O Lord our God, Maker of all things. Through your goodness you have blessed us with these gifts. With them we offer ourselves to your service and dedicate our lives to the care and redemption of all that you have made, for the sake of him who gave himself for us, Jesus Christ our Lord. Amen.**

27. _The ministers make ready the bread and wine._

28. _The GREAT THANKSGIVING is begun by the minister standing at the altar._

If the Gospel reading and the sermon together constituted the first center of the service, we are now at the second: thanksgiving and eating and drinking. The presider joins the assisting minister at the table. The chalice is poured from the flagon and the loaf is uncovered. The dialogue is chanted, drawing all the assembly into the thanksgiving which follows. The proper beginning of the prayer (the proper or proclamatory preface) is sung, and the great prayer is spoken.

Presiding Minister: The Lord be with you.
Congregation: **And also with you.**
Presiding Minister: Lift up your hearts.
Congregation: **We lift them to the Lord.**
Presiding Minister: Let us give thanks to the Lord our God.
Congregation: **It is right to give him thanks and praise.**

29. _The preface appropriate to the day or season is sung or said._

The flow of the prayer is joined by the congregation as it speaks acclamations and sings yet another angelic song (a pastiche of Isa. 6 and Ps. 118), the mystery present in this meal being at the very heart of the angelic worship.

> Presiding Minister: It is indeed right and salutary . . . we praise your name and join their unending hymn:
>
> Congregation: **Holy, holy, holy Lord, God of pow'r and might:**
> **Heaven and earth are full of your glory.**
> **Hosanna, Hosanna, Hosanna in the highest.**
> **Blessed is he who comes in the name of the Lord.**
> **Hosanna in the highest.**

30. The minister continues [one of two eucharistic prayers may be said), using one of the sections below:

31. The minister may say:

But our prayers are never enough to proclaim the greatness of the promise of God, so we sum up this thanksgiving with a simple recitation of the Lord's Prayer, trusting that this meal of Christ's body and blood, given to us on, in, and under the food we set out, will be "our daily bread," a sufficient foretaste of the feast to come.

> Presiding Minister: Holy God, mighty Lord, gracious Father:
> Endless is your mercy and eternal your reign.
> You have filled all creation with light and life;
> heaven and earth are full of your glory.
> Through Abraham you promised to bless all nations.
> You rescued Israel, your chosen people.

Through the prophets you renewed your promise; and, at this end of all the ages, you sent your Son, who in words and deeds proclaimed your kingdom and was obedient to your will, even to giving his life.

In the night in which he was betrayed, our Lord Jesus took bread, and gave thanks; broke it, and gave it to his disciples, saying: Take and eat; this is my body, given for you. Do this for the remembrance of me.

Again, after supper, he took the cup, gave thanks, and gave it for all to drink, saying: This cup is the new covenant in my blood, shed for you and for all people for the forgiveness of sin. Do this for the remembrance of me.

For as often as we eat of this bread and drink from this cup we proclaim the Lord's death, until he comes.

> Congregation: **Christ has died. Christ is risen. Christ will come again.**
>
> Presiding Minister: Therefore, gracious Father, with this bread and cup we remember the life our Lord offered for us. And, believing the witness of his resurrection, we await his coming in power to share with us the great and promised feast.
>
> Congregation: **Amen. Come, Lord Jesus.**
>
> Presiding Minister: Send now, we pray, your Holy Spirit, the spirit of our Lord and of his resurrection, that we who receive the Lord's body and blood may live to the praise of your glory and receive our inheritance with all your saints in light.
>
> Congregation: **Amen. Come, Holy Spirit.**
>
> Presiding Minister: Join our prayers with those of your servants of every time and every place, and unite them with the ceaseless petitions of our great high priest until he comes as victorious Lord of all.
>
> Congregation: **Through him, with him, in him, in the unity of the Holy Spirit, all honor and glory is yours, almighty Father, now and forever. Amen.**
>
> Congregation: **Our Father in heaven, hallowed be your name, your kingdom come, your will be done, on earth as in heaven. Give us today our daily bread. Forgive us our sins as we forgive those who sin against us. Save us from the time of trial and deliver us from evil. For the kingdom,**

the power, and the glory are yours, now and forever. Amen.

(Sit)

32. The COMMUNION follows. The bread may be broken for distribution.

As the loaf is peacefully broken into smaller pieces, sufficient to feed the congregation, and as the wine is poured out into another chalice or two, if the size of the community warrants, the Agnus Dei is sung. Then people begin to come forward in turn, to stand near the table, receive the bread from the presider and the chalice from an assisting minister, and return to their places. All baptized Christians are welcome. During the Communion, a solo instrument may play, the choir may sing, silence may reign, hymns may be sung, or the assembly may take up a repeated _ostinato_ refrain, any of these choices being intended to interpret the encounter with God's grace.

33. The Presiding Minister and the Assisting Ministers receive the bread and wine and then give them to those who come to receive. As the ministers give the bread and wine, they say these words to each communicant:

> The body of Christ, given for you.
> The blood of Christ, shed for you.

34. The communicant may say: "Amen."

35. Hymns and other music may be used during the ministration of Communion.

(Stand)

38. After all have returned to their places, the minister may say these or similar words.

Presiding Minister:	The body and the blood of our Lord Jesus Christ strengthen you and keep you in his grace.
Congregation:	Amen.

39. The POST-COMMUNION canticle or an appropriate hymn is sung as the table is cleared.

Dismissal. When the meal is finished, the service comes quickly to an end. The congregation stands to sing the _Nunc dimittis_ (Luke 2:20-32), as if each one who has communed were old Simeon, bodily receiving Christ and so seeing the very salvation of God present in the world.

Congregation:	Lord, now you let your servant go in peace; your word

has been fulfilled. My own eyes have seen the salvation which you have prepared in the sight of every people: A light to reveal you to the nations and the glory of your people Israel. Glory to the Father, and to the Son, and to the Holy Spirit, as it was in the beginning, is now, and will be forever. Amen.

40. One of these prayers is said (there are three options):

Assisting Minister:	Let us pray.

The assisting minister prays, simply thanking God for the gifts of this meal.

Assisting Minister:	We give you thanks, almighty God, that you have refreshed us through the healing power of this gift of life; and we pray that in your mercy you would strengthen us, through this gift, in faith toward you and in fervent love toward one another; for the sake of Jesus Christ our Lord.
Congregation:	Amen.

41. Silence for reflection.

42. The minister blesses the congregation.

Both Word and Table are summed up in the words of the Aaronic benediction (Num. 6:24-26), which the presider dares to "put on" the people. And the assisting minister dismisses the people. There is no "recessional," though the musicians may play strong and celebrative music as the worshipers make their way into the world of mission.

Imagine it is Sunday and this congregation comes away, having seen, at the pool and in the word and at the table, an entirely new and gracious way to understand the world.

Presiding Minister:	Almighty God, Father, Son, and Holy Spirit, bless you now . . . and forever.

or

Presiding Minister:	The Lord bless you and keep you.
	The Lord make his face shine on you and be gracious to you.

The Lord look upon you with favor and give you peace.

Congregation: Amen.

43. The minister may dismiss the congregation.

Assistant Minister: Go in peace. Serve the Lord.
Congregation: **Thanks be to God.**

(*Lutheran Book of Worship* [Minneapolis, Minn.: Augsburg Publishing House, 1978], 56–74)

Gordon Lathrop

182 • METHODIST WORSHIP

The Methodist movement, led by John and Charles Wesley, began in the Church of England in the eighteenth century and spread beyond England and the Church of England into America. Born in the revival fires of Wesley, Methodist worship remained respectful of its Anglican roots and expressed the warmth of the presence of the Holy Spirit, which infused its worship with enthusiasm and joy. This warmth found expression in gospel song and evangelistic worship which gave shape not only to Methodist worship but also worship in numerous independent evangelical associations and local churches. The United Methodist Church has been impacted by the liturgical renewal, and now in its publications and new hymnal urges congregations to adopt the fourfold model of worship.

—————— The Basic Pattern ——————

The United Methodist Hymnal, 1989
A SERVICE OF WORD AND TABLE I
A congregation may use this text for the entire service.
Parts of the service marked in brackets [ ] are optional.

Entrance/Gathering. In the United Methodist tradition we see our gathering for worship as a statement of the grace of God at work in us and in our world. The church gathers in answer to the prior action of God's grace.

Worship is social, and as we prepare for it we are particularly aware of our community. We see our friends and greet them. We take a moment to catch up on the latest news. Children seek out the friends they hope to sit with during worship. More often than not the organ music serves as background music for the hive of activity as the community prepares for the hour ahead.

Some churchgoers find this raucous form of gathering to be inappropriate, even irreverent. But we appreciate this time to bring our relationships, our social identity, before the altar of God. Wherever the Spirit comes there is a stir.

Greeting. Worship is ordered by the very presence of God, and so the pastor greets the congregation in the name of the Lord. This can be formal or informal, but it is important to set the context for worship: we are human beings who have come before the presence of the living Christ. The holy God is in our midst. And our response to God is praise and thanksgiving and supplication. And so we worship.

This greeting time is an important place to interpret worship to the congregation. Once worship has begun, we should avoid the temptation to talk continually about what we are doing. But it can be very helpful, at this point, to be reminded that our time of worship is ordered by God's presence. Any announcements and prayer requests can be made at this time.

The grace of the Lord Jesus Christ be with you.
And also with you.
The risen Christ is with us.
Praise the Lord!

The following (or a prayer of the day) is offered:

Opening Prayers and Praise. The opening of worship is always in a major key. Here we confidently proclaim the goodness of our God: we look to the Father's faithfulness, Christ's majesty, the Holy Spirit's nearness.

Opening prayers and responses may often speak of the human needs that our God addresses, but the primary focus at this point in the service is on God's being. Opening hymns should be brisk and objective (rather than subjective).

Other ways of representing God's glory are appropriate at this time, including processional banners, crosses, and candles. As helpful as liturgical art can be, however, it should never be so overwhelming or intrusive that it becomes an end in itself; God must always be the focus of our wonder and praise. Good liturgical art grabs our attention and directs it at God. It should be straightforward and thoroughly integrated into the pattern of worship itself.

Almighty God,
to you all hearts are open, all desires known,
and from you no secrets are hidden.
Cleanse the thoughts of our hearts
by the inspiration of your Holy Spirit,

that we may perfectly love you,
and worthily magnify your holy name,
through Christ our Lord.
Amen.

Act of Praise/Proclamation and Response/Scripture.
The Word of God orders our worship. The Word
isn't a matter of proposition only, but of presence:
the Book is always in the hands of the Master even
as we hold it in our hands. We proclaim the Word
through readings from the Old and New Testaments.
Readings may be few or many, long or short. They
should be read with clarity and understanding and
with a sense of reverence.

In striving to make worship "comfortable" we are
sometimes tempted to paraphrase or "retell" passages of Scripture. This practice patronizingly assumes that the rough edges of Scripture are too
offensive for the congregation; it deprives worship
of its "objective" focus in God's activity and
plunges it into a muddle of subjectivism. Scripture
should be discussed in the sermon.

Scripture may be used creatively at other points
in the service, for example, as prayers and response.
The Word addresses us through Scripture, but these
words also direct our address of God.

Prayer for Illumination

Lord, open our hears and minds
by the power of your Holy Spirit,
that, as the Scriptures are read
and your Word proclaimed,
we may hear with joy what you say to us today.
Amen.
Scripture Lesson
[Psalm] *May be sung or spoken.*

**Scripture Lesson/Hymn or Song/Gospel Lesson/Ser-
mon.** The Word must always be proclaimed. The
proclaimed Word is appropriate to the field and
streets, but always in the church. And it is the task
of the preacher to make Christ known to the congregation. Preaching is integral to the sacramental presence; it is a means by which God draws us into his
presence.

Sermons should be engaging communication, but
they are not essentially entertainment. The job of
the preacher is to bring God's Word to the doorsteps
of our lives. The job of the listener is not to critique
the sermon, but to listen for God's Word to herself
or himself.

Response to the Word. Our response to God's Word
will be both ritualized and spontaneous, personal
and social. The order of worship moves us to review
our lives as framed by the Word: as individuals (How
is God's redeeming work being carried on in my
life?), our life as a church (How are we as people
being sanctified and bringing God's holiness into
the word?), and as members of the human race
(What are the needs set before us in God's love?).
Having drawn near to God, we find ourselves better
able to love the world that Christ so loves.

Response to the Word may include a creed
(though this may also be used as a summary of Scripture), concerns and prayers, confession, pardon,
and the peace. In addition to personal confession
we confess our sins as a church. The congregation
offers pardon to the pastor even as the pastor offers
Christ's pardon to the people.

Silent prayer is particularly effective at this time
in that it gives people an opportunity for spontaneous and deeply personal response.

*Response may include one or more of the follow-
ing acts:*

- *Invitation to Christian discipleship, followed
  by a hymn of invitation or of response, or a
  baptism or confirmation hymn*
- *Baptism, confirmation, reaffirmation of faith,
  or other reception of members*
- *The following or another creed:*

I believe in God, the Father Almighty,
creator of heaven and earth.
I believe in Jesus Christ, his only Son, our Lord,
who was conceived by the Holy Spirit,
born of the Virgin Mary,
suffered under Pontius Pilate,
was crucified, died, and was buried;
he descended to the dead.
On the third day he rose again;
he ascended into heaven,
is seated at the right hand of the Father,
and will come again to judge the living and the
    dead.
I believe in the Holy Spirit,
the holy catholic church,
the communion of saints,
the forgiveness of sins,
the resurrection of the body,
and the life everlasting. Amen.

Concerns and Prayers. *Brief intercessions, petitions, and thanksgivings may be prayed by the leader, or spontaneously by members of the congregation. To each of these, all may make a common response, such as: "Lord, hear our prayer." Or, a litany of intercession and petition may be prayed.*

Or, a pastoral prayer may be prayed.

Invitation

Christ our Lord invites to his table all who love
   him,
who earnestly repent of their sin
and seek to live in peace with one another.
   Therefore, let us confess our sin before God and
   one another.

Confession and Pardon

         Merciful God,
we confess that we have not loved you with our
   whole heart.
We have failed to be an obedient church.
We have not done your will,
we have broken your law,
we have rebelled against your love,
we have not loved our neighbors,
and we have not heard the cry of the needy.
Forgive us, we pray.
Free us for joyful obedience,
through Jesus Christ our Lord.

All pray in silence.

Leader to People:
Hear the good news:
   Christ died for us while we were yet sinners;
   that proves God's love toward us.
In the name of Jesus Christ, you are forgiven!

People to leader:
   In the name of Jesus Christ, you are forgiven!

Leader and People:
   Glory to God. Amen.

The Peace. Let us offer one another signs of reconciliation and love.
All exchange signs and words of God's peace.

Offering. As we make our offering to God, we offer our lives as well as our tithes. And so we move toward the Lord's Table, where our offerings to God meet God's offering to us in Jesus Christ. At the Table of the Lord we offer our gifts to God and receive them back again transformed by God's holiness. Wesley emphasized this connection between our worship and our daily work when he said "make all you can, save all you can, give all you can."

As forgiven and reconciled people,
   let us offer ourselves and our gifts to God.

A hymn, psalm, or anthem may be sung as the offering is received. The bread and wine are brought by representatives of the people to the Lord's Table with the other gifts, or uncovered if already in place. A hymn, doxology, or other response may be sung as the gifts are presented.

If a Great Thanksgiving other than that which follows here is to be used, the service proceeds with "A Service of Word and Table III." Otherwise, the service continues as follows:

Thanksgiving and Communion. Communion has often been a somber affair focused primarily on our unworthiness (this we inherited in part through the influences of Cranmer's liturgy and Pietism). As it becomes a more regular element in our Sunday worship, it reflects the range of tones appropriate to the seasons of the church year: it can be somber; it can be festive; it can be appreciative; it can emphasize Christ's sacrifice or Christ's resurrection; it can emphasize our need for God or our union with God.

Taking the Bread and Cup. *The pastor takes the bread and cup, and the bread and wine are prepared for the meal.*

Great Thanksgiving. The prayer of thanksgiving can be varied according to the liturgical season, but its substance remains the same: we address the Father with gratitude for the mighty works of salvation; we remember the Son and his great sacrifice of love for us and pray its work upon us and in us. We call upon the sanctifying work of the Holy Spirit.

United Methodists have been particularly sensitive to issues of gender and language about God. But the formal liturgy of the church retains the formative ancient economy of prayer: to the Father, through the Son, and in the Holy Spirit. Alternative forms of address (such as Creator, Redeemer, and Sustainer) that do not clearly articulate the relationship of persons in the triune God are not recommended in the formal liturgy.

This prayer is not only read, it is dramatized in the gestures of the pastor. The pastor stretches out her hands in gratitude; she holds up the bread and the cup as the prayer continues and offers them across the table to the hungry congregation; she holds out her hands over the elements and the gathered community as the Spirit is called upon.

The prayer alternates between the recitation of God's great works and our response as God's people to them. Congregational responses, including the Sanctus, the Acclamation, and the Amen, may be sung as a way of highlighting their responsive character.

The musical settings on pages 17–25 (The United Methodist Hymnal, 1989) *may be used if desired.*

The Lord be with you.
And also with you.
Lift up your hearts.
We lift them up to the Lord.
Let us give thanks to the Lord our God.

It is right to give our thanks and praise.
It is right, and a good and joyful thing,
always and everywhere to give thanks to you,
Father Almighty, creator of heaven and earth.
You formed us in your image
and breathed into us the breath of life.
When we turned away, and our love failed,
your love remained steadfast.
You delivered us from captivity,
made covenant to be our sovereign God,
and spoke to us through your prophets.
And so,
with your people on earth
and all the company of heaven
we praise your name and join their unending
   hymn:
Holy, holy, holy Lord, God of power and might,
heaven and earth are full of your glory.
Hosanna in the highest.
Blessed is he who comes in the name of the Lord.
Hosanna in the highest.
Holy are you, and blessed is your Son Jesus
   Christ.
Your Spirit anointed him
to preach good news to the poor,
to proclaim release to the captives
and recovering of sight to the blind,
to set at liberty those who are oppressed,
and to announce that the time had come
when you would save your people.
He healed the sick, fed the hungry, and ate with
   sinners.

By the baptism of his suffering, death, and
   resurrection
you gave birth to your church,
delivered us from slavery to sin and death,
and made with us a new covenant
by water and the Spirit.
When the Lord Jesus ascended,
he promised to be with us always,
in the power of your Word and Holy Spirit.
On the night in which he gave himself up for us,
he took bread, gave thanks to you, broke the
   bread,
gave it to his disciples, and said:
"Take, eat; this is my body which is given for
   you.
Do this in remembrance of me."
When the supper was over, he took the cup,
gave thanks to you, gave it to his disciples, and
   said:
"Drink from this, all of you;
this is my blood of the new covenant,
poured out for you and for many
for the forgiveness of sins.
Do this, as often as you drink it,
in remembrance of me."
And so,
in remembrance of these your mighty acts in
   Jesus Christ,
we offer ourselves in praise and thanksgiving
as a holy and living sacrifice,
in union with Christ's offering for us,
as we proclaim the mystery of faith.
Christ has died; Christ is risen; Christ will come
   again.
Pour out your Holy Spirit on us gathered here,
and on these gifts of bread and wine.
Make them be for us the body and blood of
   Christ,
that we may be for the world the body of Christ,
redeemed by his blood.
By your Spirit make us one with Christ,
one with each other,
and one in ministry to all the world,
until Christ comes in final victory
and we feast at his heavenly banquet.
Through your Son Jesus Christ,
with the Holy Spirit in your holy church,

all honor and glory is yours, almighty Father,
now and for ever.
Amen.

Lord's Prayer. The Lord's Prayer is never a private prayer. The prayer directs us to "our" Father. And as we come before "our Father," we are made aware of the needs of the kingdom. Even before Communion we are not allowed to think only about ourselves.

The pastor says:

And now, with the confidence of children of God, let us pray:

Our Father in heaven,
hallowed be your name,
your kingdom come,
your will be done,
on earth as in heaven.
Give us today our daily bread.
Forgive us our sins
as we forgive those who sin against us.
Save us from the time of trial,
and deliver us from evil.
For the kingdom, the power, and the glory are
  yours
now and for ever. Amen.

Breaking of the Bread and Giving the Bread and the Cup. United Methodists (in the tradition of the Wesleys) are prodigal in their invitation: children are invited to the Lord's Supper; sincere seekers (baptized or unbaptized) are encouraged to come. Let them all come and meet the Lord their God.

The congregation comes forward to receive the Communion meal at Christ's invitation. In doing so we present ourselves to Christ. This is the altar call of the early church, and our movement from pew to altar and back again is a crucial means of confirming our commitment to God with gratitude and loving humility. It is one way we open our lives to Christ's continuing work of sanctifying love.

We receive by kneeling or standing (this depends, in part, on the mood and focus of the service) but the physical act of coming forward is crucial to our understanding of this meal.

The pastor breaks the bread in silence, or while saying:

Because there is one loaf,
we, who are many, are one body, for we all
  partake of the one loaf.

The bread which we break is a sharing in the
  body of Christ.

The pastor lifts the cup in silence, or while saying:

The cup over which we give thanks is a sharing in
  the blood of Christ.

Giving the Bread and Cup

The bread and wine are given to the people, with these or other words being exchanged:

The body of Christ, given for you. Amen.
The blood of Christ, given for you. Amen.

The congregation sings hymns while the bread and cup are given.

When all have received, the Lord's Table is put in order.

The following prayer is then offered by the pastor or by all:

Eternal God, we give you thanks for this holy
  mystery
      in which you have given yourself to us.
Grant that we may go into the world
      in the strength of your Spirit,
      to give ourselves for others,
in the name of Jesus Christ our Lord,
Amen.

Sending Forth/Dismissal. The dismissal is full of expectation. We go forth as Christ's people to a world which he is already redeeming and sanctifying; a world in which much remains to be done. It is never enough to be sent out with a blessing; we are sent *as* a blessing to the world.

Hymn or Song
Dismissal with Blessing

Go forth in peace.
The grace of the Lord Jesus Christ,
and the love of God,
and the communion of the Holy Spirit
be with you all.
Amen.

Mark Horst

183 • PENTECOSTAL WORSHIP

The structure of Pentecostal worship has been and generally continues to be comprised of three basic units:
  Preliminaries
  Sermon
  Invitation/Altar Service

Within this tripartite structure, spontaneity and informality are the key operatives that flesh out the basic form.

The inclusion, order, and length of preliminaries such as congregational singing, testimonies, manifestations of the Spirit, special music, and prayer (to name a few possibilities) are generally different from church to church and service to service. Pentecostals shy away from codifying and writing down an invariable liturgy because of their belief that Spirit-led worship means flexibility in following the changing promptings of the Spirit.

Nevertheless, in actual practice each Pentecostal church and pastor generally settles on an order of service that tends to be fairly constant. Though the congregation seldom has the written order, worship leaders often have copies. This alleviates the need for a "master of ceremonies" having to announce each part of the service as it progresses.

In keeping with the Pentecostal predilection for spontaneity and extemporaneity, yet in recognition of the practice of using a somewhat similar order of service from week to week, it would seem useful to develop an outline for a Pentecostal morning worship service that centers around the gospel and takes into account the Pentecostal historic heritage. This is only a suggested order, of course. Changes due to time constraints and other considerations as the Spirit directs may be made.

The Basic Pattern

Preparation for Worship. One means of preparation is a Saturday intercessory prayer meeting for the following day's service. This may take any number of forms:

- A general prayer meeting at church for the entire congregation.
- Specific organizations within the church (choir, board, teachers, Women's Missionary Council) providing prayer support (may meet at church or in various homes).
- All members of the assembly praying individually in their homes for the Lord's anointing on Sunday's services.
- Fasting, confession, and penitential emphases on an individual basis. The time immediately before the service should be spent in repentance, reflection, and contemplation. Prayer may be silent or aloud (Pentecostals often pray aloud all at once). Visiting, talking, and other distractions should be avoided.

Opening Acclamation. This is an opportunity to affirm the sacred nature and purpose of the meeting. The acclamation may take various forms:

- A brief scriptural statement such as Psalm 41:13 or 72:18-19.
- A call to worship such as Psalm 95:1, Psalm 99:5, or Psalm 100:4.
- A song by the congregation and/or choir such as "All Hail King Jesus" (Dave Moody); "Brethren [People, Christians] We Have Met to Worship" (William Moore), stanzas 1 and 4; "All Hail the Power of Jesus' Name" (Oliver Holden), stanza 1.

Invocation. This is a gathering prayer, which sets the stage for what is to take place. It invites the Almighty to visit his people and reminds the congregation that God is worshiped through Jesus Christ in the power of the Holy Spirit.

Songs of Praise. The emphasis should be on hymns rich in biblical and theological content. They should focus on God rather than on the individual. Avoid musical expressions that are trite or overly emotional. Congregational music ministry should reflect much prayer and creativity. Plan well, and plan long-term. The spiritual impact of congregational music is a direct result of the seriousness with which the church's leaders view this aspect of church worship and are willing to make it all that it can be in any given situation. (See _Discipling Music Ministry: Twenty-first Century Directions_ [Peabody, Mass.: Hendrickson Publishers], 112–42). Avoid stereotyping the direction of the song service. Do not always end with slow worship songs or begin with fast, peppy ones. Above all, use music whose composition is compatible with the integrity of Scripture. Do not use music as entertainment or emotional manipulation.

Prayers of the Assembly. Leaders should vary: pastor, elders or others leaders, choir, or members of the congregation. The idea is to pray together as a community with fervor and with intensity on a wide range of topics. The people should be given a chance to voice their own petitions.

Pastoral Greeting. A time of informal welcome to all, especially newcomers.

Congregational Witness. Shared praises, admonitions, and words of edification and encouragement by members of the assembly give a sense of family community. General ground rules should apply: brevity (two minutes), emphasis on the positive, the focal point of each witness to bring glory to God. Persons may be asked in advance or invited to share extemporaneously.

Giving of Tithes and Offerings. The manner of collection and its accompanying activity may be varied:

- The congregation may process to the altar and place their tithes in the offering plate on the Table. This symbolism of placing the work of one's hands on the altar for God is very powerful.
- Ushers may take the offering.

It is best to accompany the taking of the offering with some important activity so that its meaning be heightened. To think of this as dead time and to treat it accordingly with background music is to strip the act of its symbolism.

- A choir anthem may be sung.
- Well-prepared vocal or instrumental music may be sung or played.
- Congregational singing of an appropriate song is possible.

Choir Anthem. If the choir has not sung an anthem at the offertory, it may do so at this point.

The Reading of Scripture. The public reading of Scripture harks back to the practice of the synagogue and the New testament church. It is good if the sermon is based on the readings, but if that is not always possible, the value of reading Scripture in worship is not diminished. God's Word, read under the anointing of the Holy Spirit, stands on its own merit. Having a common link or theme between passages from the Old Testament, Psalms, and New Testament is highly recommended. There are numerous lectionaries from which common readings may be drawn. The Old Testament passage is read by a lay member of the assembly. The psalm should be *sung* (it was written to be sung and

was always done that way in Old and New Testament times—see *Discipling Music Ministry: Twenty-first Century Directions,* 119–23, for further explanation and instruction). The congregation may remain seated. The New Testament text is read by another member of the laity. It is suggested that reading may be assigned well in advance for the sake of practice. At this point a short chorus with words on an alleluia theme, or on the theme of the importance of God's Word may be sung. The pastor may move to the pulpit and the people may stand as a sign of respect for the words of Jesus about to be read. The Gospel reading is done by the pastor. If three readings and a psalm are not feasible, at minimum something from the Old Testament and New Testament should be read. The importance of publicly reading God's Holy Word cannot be overestimated.

Sermon. The sermon may or may not be taken from the previous Scripture readings.

Congregational Song. This hymn or series of choruses may be linked to the sermon, invitation, or the celebration of the Lord's Supper.

Commmunion: Pastoral Instruction and Admonition. The service of the Lord's Table is so filled with significance that the congregation would profit from a short, succint reminder about the nature and meaning of Communion.

Blessing over the Bread and Cup. The blessing may be done by the pastor or one of the elders.

Distribution and Partaking of the Bread and Cup. The people may come to the altar to receive the bread and cup, or the ushers may distribute them at the appropriate time. Silence is best during the distribution and partaking of the Lord's Supper. However, if the time is lengthy, music based on the themes of Christ's death and resurrection may be played or sung. (Refrain from always using sad and doleful music).

Song(s) of Thanksgiving. It would be fitting to sing a cappella one or more meditative songs or choruses of thanksgiving for the gift of God's Son.

Invitation/Altar Service. A general invitation or a more specific one—for salvation, anointing with oil, or recommitment—may be given.

Closing Song. The subject matter of this song will depend on circumstances. It might be one of invitation, praise, or benediction.

Benediction. These words of closure may be given from the rear of the church so that the pastor will be in position to greet the people.

——— Body Ministry and Acoustics ———

The Pentecostal tradition encourages body ministry—individuals in the congregation ministering to one another. This often takes the form of a member of the congregation addressing the entire assembly with a tongue, interpretation, prophecy, word of knowledge, admonition, scriptural quotation, or word of edification quite extemporaneously from one's location in the pews. It is not practical to have microphones readily available to everyone. Yet unless everyone can hear, the ministering word is of little use.

The answer to the widespread problem of being unable to hear well is a worship space which is acoustically "live." (A lengthy reverberation time with a proper decay curve will enhance the spoken word so that it may be understood at any point in the room without electric amplification.) Body ministry is maximized when such conditions exist. The fine acoustics necessary for this particular Pentecostal emphasis is the result of architectural foresight and planning, especially when the building seats over two hundred people.

Calvin Johansson

184 ◆ PRESBYTERIAN WORSHIP PC (USA)

In the Presbyterian Church (USA), formal congregational worship is planned and conducted by the pastor and others. The order of service involves the congregation in praying and singing; listening and speaking; receiving and giving; and using the Bible, hymnals, and service books, all of which are guided by a directory for worship. The influential model for such directories has been A Directory for the Public Worship of God _(1644), first published in England by the Westminster Assembly of Divines._

Presbyterians have occasionally revised their directories. Recently they have developed new service books that are modelled on those used in Geneva and in Scotland. Originally approved for "voluntary" use, these books have become more widely used by pastors. Among these are The Book of Common Worship _(1946) and_ The Worshipbook _(1970)._

Recently, as part of the ongoing project of creating a new service book, Presbyterians have issued a series of supplemental liturgical resources (1984–1992), including The Service for the Lord's Day _(1984). That book and_ The Presbyterian Hymnal _(1990) now seek to define the basic structure of Prebyterian worship._

Such worship, while retaining something of its Puritan roots, has also been enriched by a recovery of the liturgical contributions of sixteenth-century reformers such as Martin Bucer, John Calvin, and John Knox—who had their own ecumenical and restorative interests in the patristic period.

——— The Basic Pattern ———

Assemble in God's Name
Gathering of People
Call to Worship
Hymn of Praise, Psalm, or Spiritual
Confession and Pardon
Act of Praise
The Peace

Assembly. Worship begins as the people gather, becoming "church" as they are "called together." Words from Scripture, usually spoken by the pastor, define the gathering as worship. Pastor and people join in singing praises to God. The people pray together, confessing their sins. The pastor assures them of God's pardon. The people say or sing their praise for God's forgiveness. They greet one another, speaking, shaking hands, or embracing to express joy in the peace of God.

Proclaim God's Word
Prayer for Illumination
First Lesson
Psalm
Second Lesson
Hymn, Spiritual, or Anthem
Gospel Lesson
Sermon
Hymn or Spiritual
Creed or Affirmation of Faith
(Baptism or an Ordinance of the Church)
Prayers of Intercession
Offering

Proclamation. This part of the service is the Liturgy of the Word. The focus is upon the hearing of Scripture. Since it is the Holy Spirit who gives understanding, the readings are prefaced with a request for illumination. Since the sixteenth century, Presbyterians have customarily included a reading from the Old Testament. If the reading is a psalm, it may be read, sung, or recited. Many Presbyterians now use the common lectionary with readings from Old Testament, Epistle, and Gospel. The music may be selected in relation to the theme in the lessons and/or sermon. The sequence of the readings may be changed so that the Scripture from which the sermon flows is in this section.

The sermon is understood in itself as a word from God. Through music the people begin their response to the message of the sermon and continue by reciting the Apostles' Creed. Baptism, prayers on behalf of the people, and an offering may occur during this segment of worship.

Give Thanks to God
Preparation of the Table
Great Prayer of Thanksgiving, concluding with the Lord's Prayer
Breaking of the Bread
Communion of the People

Thanksgiving. The celebration of the Lord's Supper has become more frequent among Presbyterians, and many now share Calvin's desire for weekly observance. When the Supper is not celebrated, this is still the appropriate place for prayers of thanksgiving. If the bread and wine have been covered, their coverings are reverently removed. While the service includes the "words of institution," the heart of the liturgy of the Table is giving thanks to God. The "one presiding is to take the bread and break it in the view of the people." Bread and cup are distributed according to local customs. Since Jesus is the host, all his people, including baptized children, are welcome to receive the bread and cup.

Go in God's Name
Hymn, Spiritual, or Psalm
Charge and Blessing
Going Forth

Sending. Those who have been called together are now sent forth as ambassadors of the Gospel. The people hear, usually from their pastor, words of encouragement that God goes with them into the world where their "service" continues. To this charge and blessing they respond with the "Amen" of voices and lives.

John E. Burkhart

The Good Shepherd. A dominant symbol of Jesus Christ in the early church is the Good Shepherd. This symbol, based on the words of of Jesus, "I am the good shepherd" (John 10:11), shows Jesus as the strong shepherd who is able to carry and defend his lambs against the attack of wild beasts.

185 ◆ REFORMED WORSHIP

Rooted in Calvinism and in a strong confessionalism, Reformed churches are being shaped significantly by liturgical and charismatic trends. Although these influences are creating tension and upheaval, the RCA is attempting to deal constructively with change.

The Basic Pattern

The Approach to God. The congregation approaches God through the following:

Votum. While the word *votum* is peculiar to the liturgy of the Reformed church in America, its content is Psalm 124:8. The votum begins worship by announcing who God is and who we are: "Our help is in the name of the LORD, the Maker of heaven and earth." A Latin word, *votum* means "desire," in this context meaning the desire of the congregation that its whole life is to be lived in the acknowledgment of God's help. The people affirm this to be true with a vocal Amen.

Sentences. The sentences continue the approach with scriptural words setting the tone of the service. When used responsively, they enable the congregation to be immediately participant.

Salutation. The salutation is given by the minister on behalf of Christ, reminding us that he is in our midst, bringing grace, mercy, and peace. The colloquial "good morning" or "hello" are tawdry substitutes for the biblical salutations bearing the fruits of our redemption in Christ's precious blood and as such are both inadequate and inappropriate. The salutation is to be delivered in joy and love.

Hymn. The hymn is the congregation's outburst of praise in light of Christ's grace, mercy, and peace.

Prayer of Confession. In the medieval church people went to confession before going to church—at least when they partook of the sacrament. In many Reformation churches the service began with confession. While entering the gates of the Lord with praise, we are quick to acknowledge who we are, sinners in need of forgiveness, and thus we together confess our sin. The Reformation renewed the awareness of the corporate nature of sin. Thus it is highly appropriate that we make corporate confession. Some congregations also allow a time for silent, personal confession.

Kyrie. The *Kyrie Eleison* (Lord Have Mercy), while usually sung as a reiteration of confession, in its original sense was a declaration of the power of the Lord to grant mercy. Its prevalence throughout the church is such that it retains its Greek title.

Assurance of Pardon. The assurance of pardon is made by the minister in his office as Christ's representative. It is made in the words of Scripture, emphasizing the fact that it is not by human power, but by the power and promises of God that sin is forgiven.

The Law of God. The Law of God in this position in the liturgy is one of the contributions of the Reformed to the church. Calvin emphasized that the third use of the law was as a guide to Christian living. And in the Heidelberg Catechism the law is explained in the section on gratitude. We manifest our gratitude to God by living according to his law—thus it is read *after* the forgiveness of sin, not before.

Psalter and *Gloria Patri*. The Psalter and *Gloria Patri* are a fitting response to this encapsulation of the Christian life in confession, pardon, and law. A hymn of praise by the choir can also take place at this time, although it is better when the whole congregation participates.

Word of God in Proclamation and Sacrament. The heart of the service is the Word of God in proclamation and sacrament. God's living Word, Christ Jesus, comes to us in both proclamation and sacrament. While in practice most RCA churches do not celebrate the sacrament each Lord's Day, frequency is increasing. For the first time in the history of the RCA, the Lord's Supper is printed in the liturgy as normative for the Sunday service.

Prayer for Illumination. The prayer for illumination recognizes that it is through Word and Spirit that proclamation will be effective.

Hymn. Because of the desire to tie together the reading of Scripture and the sermon, it is suggested that the hymn precede the reading of Scripture, although its ancient position in praise for the Scripture is also recognized.

Lessons. There is presently a shift from reading a single portion of Scripture to reading the lectionary passages from Old Testament, Epistle, and Gospel, with appropriate responses of praise by the congregation.

Sermon. Hopefully the sermon will find its source in one or more of the lections for the day. *Lectio continua,* preaching consecutively through a book of the Bible, still has some advocates, and it is to be hoped that preaching from the church year is supplanting topical preaching.

Prayer for Blessing. Prayer for blessing on the proclamation.

Confession of Faith. Most frequently this is the Apostles' Creed, although the Nicene Creed is growing in favor. The general synod of the RCA has voted to put the filioque clause of the Nicene Creed ("who proceeds from the Father [*and the Son*]") in brackets to indicate its later insertion into the Creed by the Latin church.

At times a question and answer from the Heidelberg Catechism or a portion of "Our Song of Hope" (*Worship the Lord*, 80–85), a contemporary confession of the RCA, will be used.

Peace. The peace is given at this time to indicate that we live in peace and forgiveness with one another, even as we have been forgiven. Unfortunately, there are still too many congregations that have a secularized version of the peace in the form of a welcome, greeting, or handshake of friendship. Where the peace is used, the words "The peace of Christ be with you" are accompanied with a smile, handshake, hug, or kiss, as is appropriate and comfortable within the congregation.

Offering/Doxology. The offering in most congregations is the receiving of monetary gifts, although a few are restoring the ancient practice of also bringing the bread and wine for the Lord's Supper at this time. Often the choir will also do its anthem during or after the offering is received. As the offering is brought forward, the people stand and sing the Doxology.

Meaning of the Sacrament/Communion. The meaning of the sacrament is then read by the minister, explaining the Lord's Supper as a feast of the remembrance of Christ's passion and our reconciliation; our communion with the risen Christ who is with us always; and our hope in his coming again of which this Communion is a foretaste.

Invitation. An invitation is given to all who have confessed their faith in Christ and are members of a Christian church to come to the Lord's Table.

Communion Prayer. The Communion prayer precedes the fraction and delivery, wherein thanks are given for the gifts of Creation and redemption, and the congregation responds with the words of the Trisagion of Isaiah, the heavenly hosts of Revelation, and the crowds at the Triumphal Entry. There follows the prayer for the presence and power of the Holy Spirit that the bread and wine may indeed become for us the communion of the body and blood of Christ.

Communion. The Communion includes the biblical words of institution at the fracture. Delivery is most frequently done by taking bread already broken (cubed) and little cups of grape juice to the people in their pews. In some churches people are invited to come forward to stand or sit about the table to receive the elements. In such churches a loaf and common cup with wine are frequently used.

The Response to God
Thanksgiving after Communion
Intercessions and Lord's Prayer
Hymn
Benediction

Response to God. Having completed that portion of the service where we have received the word of God in proclamation and sacrament, it is concluded by our response to God, in which there is first a thanksgiving, frequently Psalm 103 with additions. Then follow prayers of intercession for the congregation, church, and world, concluding with the Lord's Prayer, after which a hymn of thanksgiving is sung. The minister on behalf of Christ gives to the congregation a biblical benediction.

─────── **Baptism** ───────

When the sacrament of baptism is celebrated, it is always done as a part of a service of worship with the entire congregation present. Sprinkling, pouring, or immersion are all used, albeit sprinkling is by far the most common gesture. The liturgical action of baptism has not yet begun to catch up with our theology of baptism, which is probably why baptism is so undervalued among the laity.

While as recently as 1968 the recommended place in the service for baptism was after the offering and doxology as a response to the Word proclaimed and in positional parallel with the Lord's Supper, more recently a place in the service of approach has been advocated as symbolic of our entry into the church. The liturgy for baptism is then used instead of the confession, pardon, and law sequence, equivalents of which are a part of the liturgy for baptism.

Liturgical renewal continues within the Reformed Church in America with the goal of preserving that which was best in the Reformation while recovering those elements of practice which have nurtured the church catholic, and which Calvin sought in and described as "The Form of Church Prayers . . . According to the Custom of the Ancient Church."

Donald J. Bruggink

186 • ROMAN CATHOLIC WORSHIP

The Roman Catholic Sunday liturgy, the Mass, or more properly, the Eucharist, is composed of two primary parts: the Liturgy of the Word, which is concerned primarily with the reading of Scripture, and the Liturgy of the Eucharist, which is centered on the prayer of thanksgiving and Communion. In addition to these two primary parts, there are several introductory rites, a dismissal rite, and transitional rites between the two primary sections. In outline, the Mass includes:

Introductory Rites
    Entrance Song
    Greeting
    Penitential Rite
    Gloria
    Opening Prayer
Liturgy of the Word
    First Reading
    Responsorial Psalm
    Second Reading
    Alleluia or Gospel Acclamation
    Gospel
    Homily
    Profession of Faith
    General Intercessions
Liturgy of the Eucharist
    Preparation of the Altar and the Gifts
    Prayer over the Gifts
    Preface
    Holy, Holy, Holy
    Eucharistic Prayer with Acclamation
    Communion Rite
    Lord's Prayer
    Doxology
    Sign of Peace
    Breaking of the Bread
    Communion
    Prayer after Communion
Concluding Rite
    Greeting
    Blessing
    Dismissal

The Basic Pattern

Introductory Rites. The _General Instruction of the Roman Missal_ (_GIRM_) states that the individual rites that make up this first part of the liturgy enable "the faithful coming together to take on the form of a community and prepare themselves to listen to God's word and celebrate the eucharist" (_GIRM,_ 24).

Entrance Song. _After the people have assembled, the priest and the ministers go to the altar while the Entrance Song is being sung. When the priest comes to the altar, he makes the customary reverence with the ministers, kisses the altar, and (if incense is used) censes it. Then, with the ministers, he goes to the chair._

The Entrance song gathers the community, focuses their attention on the season or feast, and accompanies the procession of liturgical ministers (_GIRM,_ 25). Since the 1975 edition of the _GIRM,_ however, the lived experience of the song has led to its more common title, the gathering song, which reflects its unifying purpose. The procession, while still common, is no longer the deciding factor in choosing the music, and may even be omitted during certain times of the year (such as Lent). The procession, especially on feast days, usually begins with incense (either in a thurible or danced in with bowls); followed by a processional cross or the paschal candle in Easter; the reader with the lectionary or deacon with the Gospel book; acolytes; and the presiding minister ("presider" from presbyter, the official title of what is usually known as priest). The procession ends with the presider moving to the chair after reverencing the altar (most properly a bow), and kissing the altar.

Greeting. The Trinitarian greeting with the gesture of tracing the cross on oneself is a reminder of baptism: the words are those of the baptismal formula, the tracing of the cross a remembrance of being claimed in baptism with the "brand" or sign of Christ. The greeting continues with one of three dialogical options in which the presider extends the peace of Christ given at baptism to all those present, and they return the greeting.

After the Entrance song, the priest and the faithful remain standing and make the sign of the cross, as the priest says:

In the name of the Father, and of the Son, and of the Holy Spirit.

The people answer:

Amen.

Then the priest, facing the people, extends his hands and greets all present with one of the following greetings:

The grace of our Lord Jesus Christ and the love of God and the fellowship of the Holy Spirit be with you all.

The people answer:

And also with you.

The priest, deacon, or other suitable minister may very briefly introduce the Mass of the day.

A. The rite of blessing and sprinkling holy water may be celebrated in all churches and chapels at all Sunday Masses celebrated on Sunday or on Saturday evening.

or

B. The penitential rite follows.

or

C. If the Mass is preceded by some part of the liturgy of the hours, the penitential rite is omitted, and the Kyrie may be omitted. (See General Instruction on the Liturgy of the Hours, nos. 94–96).

Penitential Rite. Following this ritual greeting the liturgy continues with two options, the most common being the misnamed penitential rite. After an introduction that should ideally echo the readings and prayers of the day, one of three options can be chosen, the third being most faithful to the spirit of the acclamation of praise, "Lord, have mercy," (or the original Greek, *Kyrie eleison*). The series of three prayers, addressed to Christ alone, praise him for different facets of salvation and can be chosen to reflect seasons of the year. This litany, designed to be sung, is an inheritance of the original procession to the church in the centuries of urban stational liturgies, and its presence on an every-Sunday basis is now being debated.

The option to the penitential rite is the *Blessing and Sprinkling of Holy Water,* commonly used during the Easter season as a reminder of baptism.

After the introduction to the day's Mass, the priest invites the people to recall their sins and to repent of them in silence. He may use these or similar words:

Coming together as God's family, with confidence let us ask the Father's forgiveness, for he is full of gentleness and compassion.

A pause for silent reflection follows. After the silence, one of the following three forms is chosen:

Gloria. The hymn of praise which follows is most frequently sung alternating between cantor and congregation (the form in which many new compositions are written). Like the penitential rite, its use on an every-Sunday basis is strongly disputed, and it is increasingly omitted in many parishes wishing to streamline the introductory rites. Its perceived duplication of the gathering song, its origins in morning prayer and not the eucharistic liturgy, and its identification with the themes of the Christmas season suggest that it should be used only at particular times of the year.

This hymn is said or sung on Sundays outside Advent and Lent, on solemnities and feasts, and in solemn local celebrations.

Glory to God in the highest,
and peace to his people on earth.
Lord God, heavenly King,
almighty God and Father,
we worship you, we give you thanks,
we praise you for your glory.

Lord Jesus Christ, only Son of the Father,
Lord God, Lamb of God,
you take away the sin of the world:
have mercy on us;
you are seated on the right hand of the Father:
receive our prayer.

For you alone are the Holy One,
you alone are the Lord,
you alone are the Most High,
Jesus Christ,
with the Holy Spirit,
in the glory of God the Father. Amen.

Opening Prayer. The original beginning of the liturgy still carries the title of *Opening Prayer* in its English translation. The text of this prayer is proper to each Sunday (the example here is for the Tenth Sunday in Ordinary Time), with each Sunday having two choices. The form of the prayer is the collect (pronounced with the accent on the first syllable): the presider invites everyone to pray, all pray in silence, and then the presider collects the prayers of the congregation in the concluding section. This prayer is one of the presidential prayers—in other words, one of those prayers in which the presider prays in the name of all gathered together, signified by the ancient posture of prayer, the *orans* (standing, with arms raised).

Afterwards, the priest, with hands joined, sings or says:

Let us pray.

Priest and people pray silently for a while.

Then the priest extends his hands and sings or says the opening prayer, at the end of which the people respond: **Amen.**

Priest: Let us pray [for the guidance of the Holy Spirit]

Pause for silent prayer.

God of wisdom and love,
source of all good,
send your Spirit to teach us your truth
and guide our actions in your way of
  peace.
We ask this through our Lord Jesus Christ,
  your Son,
who lives and reigns with you and the
  Holy Spirit,
one God, for ever and ever.

Liturgy of the Word. The proclamation of the Word of God, in which "God is speaking to his people, opening up to them the mystery of redemption and salvation" (*GIRM*, 33) centers on the three Scripture readings, two chants, and the homily. The first reading is assigned for each Sunday from the three-year lectionary, in which the Old Testament reading was chosen for its relationship to the Gospel reading. During the season of Easter, the first reading is taken from the Acts of the Apostles. The second reading, taken from the New Testament, follows its own semicontinuous cycle. Both of these readings have liturgical beginnings ("A reading from . . .") and endings. (The examples are from the Tenth Sunday in Ordinary Time, Cycle A.)

First Reading. *The reader goes to the lectern for the first reading. All sit and listen. To indicate the end, the reader adds:* This is the Word of the Lord.

All respond: **Thanks be to God.**

Responsorial Psalm. The psalm, which comes between the first two readings, is sung by the cantor and the assembly, the cantor singing the verses and the assembly alternating with the short refrain (hence its title, responsorial). Like the readings, there is a proper psalm assigned for each Sunday, which can be replaced by a common psalm of the season.

The cantor sings or recites the Psalm, and the people respond.

Second Reading. *When there is a second reading, it is read at the lectern as before. To indicate the end, the reader adds:* This is the Word of the Lord.

All respond: **Thanks be to God.**

Alleluia or Gospel Acclamation. This acclamation, usually an Alleluia except during Lent, is sung to acclaim and announce the Gospel. The congregation stands, the Gospel book (increasingly a separate ritual book from the lectionary) is carried in procession from the stand or altar to the ambo or middle of the church, from where it will be proclaimed. Frequently it is accompanied by candles and incense, signs of honor for the presence of Christ in the Gospel. On feast days (such as Easter and Christmas), it is preferable that the Gospel be sung, either by a single voice or by several, for which settings are now readily available.

The Alleluia or other chant follows. It is to be omitted if not sung.

Gospel. *Meanwhile, if incense is used, the priests puts some in the censer. Then the deacon who is to proclaim the Gospel bows to the priest and in a low voice asks his blessing:*

Father, give me your blessing.

The priest says in a low voice:

The Lord be in your heart and on your lips that you may worthily proclaim his gospel. In the name of the Father, and of the Son, and of the Holy Spirit.

The deacon answers:

Amen.

Then the deacon (or the priest) goes to the lectern. He may be accompanied by ministers with incense and candles. He sings or says:

The Lord be with you.

The people answer:

And also with you.

The deacon (or priest) sings or says:

A reading from the holy Gospel according to *N.*

He makes the sign of the cross on the book, and then on his forehead, lips and breast.

The people respond:

Glory to you, Lord.

Then, if incense is used, the deacon (or priest) incenses the book, and proclaims the Gospel.

At the end of the Gospel, the deacon (or priest) adds:

This is the Gospel of the Lord.

All respond:

Praise to you, Lord Jesus Christ.

Then he kisses the book, saying inaudibly:

May the words of the Gospel wipe away our sins.

Homily. *A homily shall be given on all Sundays and holy days of obligation; it is recommended for other days.*

The proclamation of the homily (or sermon) follows the Gospel and links the reading of Scripture with the action of the Eucharist to follow. The homily's purpose is not to teach about the Scripture, rather it is preached *from* the Scriptures "to interpret people's lives in such a way that they will be able to celebrate Eucharist" (*Fulfilled in Your Hearing,* 52).

Profession of Faith. Since the Middle Ages the baptismal creed has been added to the eucharistic liturgy, usually in the form of the Nicene Creed. While it is still officially part of every Sunday's liturgy, its interruption of the prayer of the people in response to the homily and its redundancy in a liturgy that is essentially a profession of faith in itself are considered by many to be valid reasons for its omission.

After the homily, the profession of faith is said on Sundays and solemnities; it may also be said in solemn local celebrations.

We believe in one God,
the Father, the Almighty
maker of heaven and earth,
of all that is seen and unseen.

> We believe in one Lord, Jesus Christ
> the only Son of God,
> eternally begotten of the Father,
> God from God, Light from Light,
> true God from true God,
> begotten, not made, one in Being with the
> Father.
> Through him all things were made.

For us men and for our salvation
he came down from heaven:

All bow during these two lines:

> by the power of the Holy Spirit
> he was born of the Virgin Mary, and became
> man.

For our sake he was crucified under Pontius
Pilate;
he suffered, died, and was buried.
On the third day he rose again
in fulfillment of the Scriptures;
he ascended into heaven
and is seated at the right hand of the Father.
He will come again in glory to judge the living
and the dead,
> and his kingdom will have no end.

We believe in the Holy Spirit, the Lord, the giver
of life,
> who proceeds from the Father and the
> Son.
> With the Father and the Son he is
> worshiped and glorified.

He has spoken through the Prophets.
We believe in one holy catholic and apostolic
Church.
We acknowledge one baptism for the forgiveness
of sins.
We look for the resurrection of the dead, and the
life of the world to come. Amen.

General Intercessions. *Then follow the general intercessions (prayer of the faithful). The priest presides at the prayer. With a brief introduction, he invites the people to pray; after the intentions he says the concluding prayer. It is desirable that the intentions be announced by the deacon, cantor, or other person.*

The restored prayer of the faithful is a series of prayers for the world, the church, the community, and individuals. Because it exercises the ministry of baptized Christians, praying with the efficacy of the Spirit, it was the first "ministry" done by the newly baptized; this is also the reason for the dismissal of the catechumens (those preparing for baptism) before this prayer. In the restored catechumenate, that dismissal again takes place here in preparation for the Liturgy of the Eucharist, which is only for fully initiated Christians.

The intercessions can be spoken or sung, although they are usually spoken because the prayers themselves are voiced by lectors.

Liturgy of the Eucharist. The Eucharist, literally "thanksgiving," centers on the eucharistic prayer, recalling the wonderful works of God and especially the gift of Jesus himself, the breaking of the "one bread of unity," and Communion, in which the faithful "receive the Lord's body and blood in the same way the apostles received them from Christ's own hands" (_GIRM_, 48).

Preparation of the Altar and the Gifts. In the transitional rites between the Liturgy of the Word and the Liturgy of the Eucharist, the gifts of bread and wine are brought in procession to the altar by parishioners. During the accompanying music, the collection may also be taken up and brought in procession, but the money is never placed on the altar. Once the bread and wine are brought to the altar, they are prepared either by the parishioners themselves or, more likely, the acolytes assisting in the liturgy.

The presider then says a blessing over the bread and wine, a form derived from Jewish table blessings, and washes his hands, originally a necessity after incensing the altar, gifts, and people. If incensing is included at this point in the liturgy, it would always include an incensation of all present as a sign of honor for all the baptized. A brief dialogue symbolizing the role of the congregation in the offering and a variable prayer (proper to each Sunday) precede the eucharistic prayer.

After the Liturgy of the Word, the offertory song is begun. Meanwhile the ministers place the corporal, the purificator, the chalice, and the missal on the altar.

Sufficient hosts (and wine) for the Communion of the faithful are to be prepared. It is most important that the faithful should receive the body of the Lord in hosts consecrated at the same Mass and should share the cup when it is permitted. Communion is thus a clearer sign of sharing in the sacrifice which is actually taking place.

It is desirable that the participation of the faithful be expressed by members of the congregation bringing up the bread and wine for the celebration of the Eucharist or other gifts for the needs of the Church and the poor.

The priest, standing at the altar, takes the paten with the bread and, holding it slightly raised above the altar, says inaudibly:

> Blessed are you, Lord, God of all creation.
> Through your goodness we have this
>   bread to offer,
> which earth has given and human hands
>   have made.
> It will become for us the bread of life.

Then he places the paten with the bread on the corporal.

If no offertory song is sung, the priest may say the preceding words in an audible voice; then the people may respond.

> **Blessed be God for ever.**

The deacon (or the priest) pours wine and a little water into the chalice.

Then the priest takes the chalice, and, holding it slightly raised above the altar, says inaudibly:

> Blessed are you, Lord, God of all creation.
> Through your goodness we have this
>   wine to offer,
> fruit of the vine and work of human
>   hands.
> It will become our spiritual drink.

Then he places the chalice on the corporal.

If no offertory song is sung, the priest may say the preceding words in an audible voice; then the people may respond:

> **Blessed be God for ever.**

Standing at the center of the altar, facing the people, he extends and then joins his hands saying:

> Pray, brethren, that our sacrifice
> may be acceptable to God, the almighty
>   Father.

The people respond:

> **May the Lord accept the sacrifice at your
>   hands
> for the praise and glory of his name,
> for our good, and the good of all his
>   Church.**

Prayer over the Gifts

> Pray, brethren . . .
> Lord, look with love on our service.
> Accept the gifts we bring
> and help us grow in Christian love.
> Grant this through Christ our Lord.

With hands extended, the priest sings or says the prayer over the gifts, at the end of which the people respond:

Amen.

**[Sundays in Ordinary Time VI
The Pledge of an Eternal Easter]**

Preface. *This preface is said on Sundays in ordinary time.*

The prayer begins with the ancient dialogue of Jewish origins, exchanging peace and focusing on heavenly things. The preface that follows is variable according to feast and season. During ordinary time (our sample liturgy uses the prayers of the Tenth Sunday in Ordinary Time) there are eight Sunday prefaces from which to choose, left to the discretion of the person preparing the liturgy.

The preface leads into the first of three eucharistic acclamations, the *Holy, Holy, Holy* (often referred to by its Latin title, the *Sanctus*). This is sung by all present; the text remains constant, the music can be chosen from many different settings, but in order to reflect the unity of the whole prayer it is desirable that all three acclamations be from the same musical setting.

Priest: The Lord be with you.
People: **And also with you.**
Priest: Lift up your hearts.
People: **We lift them up to the Lord.**
Priest: Let us give thanks to the Lord or God.
People: **It is right to give him thanks and praise.**
Priest: Father, all-powerful and ever-living God,
we do well always and everywhere to give you thanks.
In you we live and move and have our being.
Each day you show us a Father's love;
your Holy Spirit, dwelling within us,
gives us on earth the hope of unending joy.
Your gift of the Spirit,
who raised Jesus from the dead,
is the foretaste and promise
of the paschal feast of heaven.
With thankful praise,

in company with the angels,
we glorify the wonders of your power:

Holy, Holy, Holy

A. Holy, holy, holy Lord, God of power and might,
heaven and earth are fully of your glory.
Hosanna in the highest.
Blessed is he who comes in the name of the Lord.
Hosanna in the highest.

B. Lord Jesus, you came to gather the nations
into the peace of God's kingdom:
Lord, have mercy.

The people answer.

Lord, have mercy.
Priest: You come in word and sacrament to strengthen us in holiness:
Christ have mercy.
People: **Christ, have mercy.**
Priest: Lord, have mercy.

The priest says the absolution:

May almighty God have mercy on us,
forgive us our sins,
and bring us to everlasting life.

The people answer:

Amen.

**Eucharistic Prayer with Acclamation
[Eucharistic Prayer III]**

Eucharistic Prayer. The invariable part of the great prayer of thanksgiving follows, the example chosen is Prayer III, one of nine official eucharistic prayers in the current sacramentary. The entire eucharistic prayer can be sung (the original intention behind the sung acclamations of the assembly) or just the parts noted in the text.

The priest, with hands extended, says:

Father, you are holy indeed,
and all creation rightly gives your praise.
All life, all holiness comes from you
through your Son, Jesus Christ our Lord,
by the working of the Holy Spirit.
From age to age you gather a people to yourself,
so that from east to west

a perfect offering may be made
to the glory of your name.

He joins his hands and, holding them outstretched over the offerings, says:

And so, Father, we bring you these gifts.
We ask you to make them holy by the
power of your Spirit,

He joins his hands and, making the sign of the cross once over both bread and chalice, says:

that they may become the body and
blood
of your Son, our Lord Jesus Christ,
at whose command we celebrate this
Eucharist.

The *epiclesis,* the ancient prayer invoking the Holy Spirit's blessing on the bread and wine, follows, accompanied by a gesture symbolic of the Holy Spirit and the sign of the cross of the gifts. This portion of the eucharistic prayer has been maintained in the Eastern Christian tradition but was neglected in the West. The revised Roman sacramentary restores it in this prayer.

He joins his hands.

The words of the Lord in the following formulas should be spoken clearly and distinctly, as their meaning demands.

On the night he was betrayed

He takes the bread and, raising it a little above the altar, continues:

he took bread and gave you thanks and
praise,
He broke the bread, gave it to his
disciples, and said:

He bows slightly.

Take this, all of you, and eat it:
this is my body which will be given up
for you.

He shows the consecrated host to the people, places it on the paten, and genuflects in adoration.

Then he continues:

When supper was ended, he took the cup.

He takes the chalice and, raising it a little above the altar, continues:

Again he gave you thanks and praise,
gave the cup to his disciples, and said:

He bows slightly.

Take this, all of you, and drink from it:
this is the cup of my blood,
the blood of the new and everlasting
covenant.
It will be shed for you and for all
so that sins may be forgiven.
Do this in memory of me.

He shows the chalice to the people, places it on the corporal, and genuflects in adoration.

This section contains the words of institution, the words of Christ at the Last Supper as reported by the apostle Paul. They have always been regarded as essential to eucharistic consecration. Again, the gestures indicate in the text are an essential part of the prayer.

Then he sings or says:

Let us proclaim the mystery of faith:

A.   *People with celebrant and concelebrants:*
**Christ has died,
Christ is risen,
Christ will come again.**

B.   **Dying you destroyed our death,
rising you restored our life.
Lord Jesus, come in glory.**

C.   **When we eat this bread and drink this
cup,
we proclaim your death, Lord Jesus,
until you come in glory.**

D.   **Lord, by your cross and resurrection
you have set us free.
You are the Savior of the world.**

The second sung acclamation of the people follows, using one of the four texts printed.

With hands extended, the priest says:

Father, calling to mind the death your Son
endured for our salvation, his glorious resurrection and ascension into heaven, and
ready to greet him when he comes again,
we offer you in thanksgiving this holy and
living sacrifice.

The *anamnesis.* This means "memorial" or "remembrance," but in the strong sense of remembering in such a way as to make present the historical reality. It suggests the joining of the offering of this liturgy to the offering of Christ given in his death. But it also includes the reality of the Resurrection and Ascension and looks forward to Christ's return.

Look with favor on your Church's offering, and
see the Victim whose death has reconciled us
to yourself.

Grant that we, who are nourished by his body
and blood, may be filled with his Holy Spirit,
and become one body one spirit in Christ. May
he make us an everlasting gift to you and enable
us to share in the inheritance of your saints, with
Mary, the virgin Mother of God; with the
apostles, the martyrs (*saying N.* [*the saint of the
day or the patron saint*]) and all your saints, on
whose constant intercession we rely for help.

Lord, may this sacrifice, which has made our
peace with you,
advance the peace and salvation of all the world.
Strengthen in faith and love your pilgrim Church
on earth;
your servant, Pope *N.*, our bishop *N.*, and all
bishops,
with the clergy and the entire people your Son
has gained for you.
Father, hear the prayers of the family you have
gathered here before you.
In mercy and love unite all your children
wherever they may be.
We hope to enjoy for ever the vision of the glory,
through Christ our Lord, from whom all good
things come.

The intercessions bring the whole concerns of the
church and its people and saints (in all times and
places) into the action of the liturgy.

*He takes the chalice and the paten with the host
and, lifting them up, sings or says:*

Through him, with him, in him, in the unity of
the Holy Spirit,
all glory and honor is yours, almighty Father, for
ever and ever. Amen.

The people respond. **Amen.**

The eucharistic prayer concludes with the Doxology and the final acclamation of the people, the
Great Amen.

Communion Rite/Lord's Prayer. The Lord's Prayer is
then sung or said by all present; at eucharistic liturgies the embolism is added prior to the doxological
ending.

*The priest sets down the chalice and paten and
with hands joined sings or says the following:*

Let us pray with confidence to the Father in the
words our Savior gave us.

Our Father, who art in heaven, hallowed be thy
name; thy kingdom come; thy will be done on
earth as it is in heaven. Give us this day our
daily bread; and forgive us our trespasses as
we forgive those who trespass against us; and
lead us not into temptation, but deliver us
from evil.

With hands extended, the priest continues alone:

Deliver us, Lord, from every evil, and grant us
peace in our day.
In your mercy keep us free from sin and protect
us from all anxiety as we wait in joyful hope
for the coming of our Savior, Jesus Christ.

He joins his hands.

Doxology. *The people end the prayer with the acclamation:*

For the kingdom, the power and the glory are
yours, now and for ever.

Sign of Peace. Originally this gesture preceded the
eucharistic liturgy (concluding the general intercessions) and its location in the liturgy is currently a
topic of discussion. The ritual includes the prayer of
the presider (addressed to Jesus), the dialogue, and
the exchange of peace between all present, which
usually takes the form of a hug or handshake in
American churches.

Then the priest, with hands extended, says aloud:

Lord, you said to your apostles:
I leave you peace, my peace I give you.
Look not on our sins, but on the faith of
your Church,
and grant us the peace and unity of your
kingdom,

He joins his hands.

where you live for ever and ever.

The people answer:

Amen.

The priest, extending and joining his hands, adds:

The peace of the Lord be with you always.

The people answer:

And also with you.

Then the deacon (or the priest) may add:

Let us offer each other the sign of peace.

*All make an appropriate sign of peace, according
to local custom.*

The priest gives the sign of peace to the deacon or minister.

Breaking of the Bread. The breaking of the bread and pouring of wine is accompanied by the *Lamb of God,* a ritual music composition that continues as long as the action of breaking and pouring takes place. The breaking of bread (one of four fundamental actions of eucharistic liturgy: taking, blessing, breaking, giving) is both practical, in preparation for the distribution of Communion, and symbolic of the one loaf of unity now broken like the body of Christ.

Then the following is sung or said:

Lamb of God, you take away the sins of the
    world:
have mercy on us.
Lamb of God, you take away the sins of the
    world:
have mercy on us.
Lamb of God, you take away the sins of the
    world:
grant us peace.

This may be repeated until the breaking of the bread is finished, but the last phrase is always "grant us peace."

Communion. The invitation to Communion (in the form of a dialogue between presider and congregation), the distribution of Communion, and the post-Communion prayer make up this rite. Communion is ordinarily (and preferably) received under both species, bread and wine. Most American parishes have parishioners who fulfill the ministry of eucharistic minister, both distributing the Eucharist to the congregation and bringing Communion to the sick or shut-ins of the parish. After processing to the front of the church and receiving a piece of bread and drinking from the common cup, the congregation returns to their seats, either remaining standing as a sign of solidarity with all, or kneeling in private prayer. During the distribution of Communion there is usually singing, either by the congregation, cantor, choir, or a combination of these.

The priest genuflects. Taking the host, he raises it slightly over the paten and, facing the people, says aloud:

This is the Lamb of God
who takes away the sins of the world.

Happy are those who are called to his
    supper.

He adds, once only, with the people:

Lord, I am not worthy to receive you,
but only say the word and I shall be
    healed.

Facing the altar, the priest says inaudibly:

May the body of Christ bring me to ever-
    lasting life.

He reverently consumes the body of Christ. Then he takes the chalice and says inaudibly:

May the blood of Christ bring me to ever-
    lasting life.

He reverently drinks the blood of Christ.

After this he takes the paten or other vessel and goes to the communicants. He takes a host for each one, raises it a little, and shows it, saying:

The body of Christ.

The communicant answers:

Amen.

and receives Communion.

When a deacon gives Communion, he does the same.

The sign of comunion is more complete when given under both kinds, since the sign of the eucharistic meal appears more clearly. The intention of Christ that the new and eternal covenant be ratified in his blood is better expressed, as is the relation of the eucharistic banquet to the heavenly banquet.

If any are receiving in both kinds, the rite described elsewhere is followed. When he presents the chalice, the priest or deacon says:

The blood of Christ.

The communicant answers:

Amen.

and drinks it.

The deacon and other ministers may receive communion from the chalice.

A period of silence may be observed after Communion, or a psalm or song of praise may be sung.

Prayer after Communion

Let us pray.

Pause for silent prayer, if this has not preceded.

Lord,
may your healing love
turn us from sin

and keep us on the way that leads to you.
We ask this in the name of Jesus the Lord.

Following a brief silence, the post-Communion prayer, another presidential prayer proper to Sunday, is prayed.

Concluding Rite. The Sunday liturgy ends far more briefly than it began in the introductory rites. If there are any announcements regarding the life of the parish, they are done at this time, and then the liturgy concludes with the blessing.

The blessing begins with a dialogue symbolic of the presence of the Spirit in each one present, and then follows one of three forms, the simplest being given here. The dismissal, technically a diaconal task dating from the centuries when the deacon announced the location of the next week's liturgy, follows.

The recessional is optional; the presider kisses the altar, and with the other ministers reverences the altar. All recess out if there is a recessional song. The music may take the form of a sung piece or an instrumental selection.

If there are any brief announcements, they are made at this time.

Greeting
The rite of dismissal takes place.

Facing the people, the priest extends his hands and sings or says:

> The Lord be with you.

The people answer:

> **And also with you.**

Blessing
Simple form
> *The priest blesses the people with these words:*

> > May almighty God bless you,
> > the Father, and the Son, and the Holy
> > Spirit.

The people answer:

> **Amen.**

Dismissal. *The dismissal sends each member of the congregation to do good works, praising and blessing the Lord.*

The deacon (or the priest), with hands joined, sings or says:

> Go in peace to love and serve the Lord.

The people answer:

> Thanks be to God.

The priest kisses the altar as at the beginning. Then he makes the customary reverence with the ministers and leaves.

If any liturgical service follows immediately, the rite of dismissal is omitted.

Lizette Larson-Miller

187 • United Church of Christ Worship

Worship life in the United Church of Christ (UCC) exhibits both continuity and variety. A journey on any given Sunday to congregations across the country would reveal substantial similarities. The Sunday service is fundamentally a preaching service; only the Lord's Supper and baptism are celebrated as sacraments; the Lord's Supper is celebrated occasionally, at high points of the church year or, in some congregations, monthly. Yet it is the structure of these services that defines the UCC worship tradition most clearly. In the past worship services used to climax with the sermon, but over the past thirty years a more balanced tripartite structure of gathering, Word, and offering has evolved.

The Basic Pattern

Gathering. The gathering serves to orient the congregation toward God. Beginning with a prelude and opening prayers or call to worship, this section may also include an act of adoration, a corporate confession, a pastoral prayer, an anthem, and a hymn. When celebrated, baptism most often falls in this section.

Word. The reading of Scriptures and the preaching of a sermon lend this section its defining character. One might find here a children's sermon, an affirmation of faith, an anthem, and a hymn. If baptism is celebrated at this point in the service, it is understood to be a response to the Word.

Offering. The offering celebrated is twofold: what God has offered us and what we have to offer to God. This twofold understanding has always been present in the ritual which surrounds the giving of money for church and mission. Through the use of the Doxology, the money is interpreted as a symbol of those many blessings that flow from God; the prayer of dedication takes the giving of this money to be an indication of our willingness to commit our lives to God. The Lord's Supper, which invariably falls in this section, celebrates the full Christological import of this mutual offering. Aspects of it also can be conveyed through a pastoral prayer, announcements, and a dismissal or commissioning. This section may include an anthem and a hymn; it always concludes with a benediction and a postlude.

———————— **Commentary** ————————

Theologically speaking, UCC worship is structured as a dialogue between God and the world. After gathering from the world and turning toward God, worshipers are moved through God's Word to offer themselves to the world.

While this basic pattern remains constant, its execution is varied. Although UCC worship typically contains an act of adoration, that act may be expressed as a psalm, a hymn, a dance, a prayer, or an anthem. Communion may be celebrated using a common cup, instinction, or individual Communion glasses; it may be received standing or sitting or kneeling. The eucharistic prayer may be a full one, complete with sung parts, or a lean one comprised of barely more than the Words of Institution. A person may be baptized by sprinkling, pouring, or immersion, according to the traditional Trinitarian formula or "in the name of Jesus." This diversity of worship is guaranteed by the polity of the UCC, based as it is on the autonomy of the local congregation.

The particular UCC character of this worship is created by the pushes and pulls felt between three dichotomies: (1) order and freedom, (2) tradition and practice, (3) culture and community.

The contrast of _order and freedom_ in the worship of the UCC has its roots in the denominations that merged to form it. The Congregational Christian churches (CC) valued freedom in worship. Both the Puritan and revivalistic sects of the Congregationalists held fixed prayer and ritual in suspicion, valuing instead free prayer and simple ceremony. Whenever a book of worship was published by an agency of the CC, it was _de rigueur_ for the authors to acknowledge its optional status.

In contrast to the CC, the Evangelical and Reformed (E & R) brought a significant liturgical tradition into the merger. Through the influence of the Mercersburg Liturgical movement and under the leadership of its national synod, this denomination had moved beyond the particular liturgical traditions of the German Reformation. Specifically, it developed an appreciation for liturgical forms from the Catholic tradition: the church year, a lectionary, and the prayers and symbols of the church. This was an act of evangelical freedom, an attempt to balance Protestant subjectivity with Catholic objectivity, to breathe a Protestant spirit into Catholic forms.

While striving to create its own liturgical tradition, the UCC has continued to honor the tradition of the denominations that merged to form it. These liturgical strains still can be discerned as one moves from one congregation to another.

Worship in the UCC also lives in the tension between _tradition and practice._ Along with other American denominations, both mainline Protestant and Roman Catholic, the UCC participated in the ecumenical liturgical convergence that took place in the latter half of the twentieth century. Aspects of this ecumenical liturgical tradition include an acknowledgment of the service of Word and sacrament as the norm for worship, an understanding of baptism as a sacrament of the church, the use of the liturgical year, the adoption of a lectionary, and a greater sensitivity to the rituals and symbols of the church. In the UCC this commitment to an ecumenical liturgical tradition stands in some tension with the local liturgical practice of individual congregations. Former E & R congregations found it more amenable than former CCs. Yet throughout the denomination the encounter with this tradition has given rise to an appreciation for the presence of God in symbols as well as words. This accounts for the introduction of banners for sanctuary decoration, the celebration of the liturgical year, the use of the New Revised Common Lectionary, and an attentiveness to sacramental symbols and ritual life. On Pentecost Sunday, for example, some congregations offer an assortment of breads used for communion in order to symbolize the oneness of all peoples in Christ: pita bread from the Middle East, matzo from Israel, croissants from France, black bread from Russia, and hard rolls from Germany.

Lastly, UCC worship unfolds in the tension between _culture and community._ The UCC was formed just as a number of social developments challenged the ascendancy of WASP culture: the civil rights movement, the rise of black power, the controversies over the Vietnam conflict. These developments called into question the traditional WASP belief in the compatibility between American cultural values and the Christian faith. Whereas before 1960 it was understood that a faithful Christian could affirm traditional values, after that time a strong element in the UCC held that Christian faith demanded a critical reappraisal of these values. For this group, God was present not in the mainstream of culture but in that community called by its faith to witness against problematic cultural values such as racism, sexism, ageism, and militarism. In recent years this sectarian vision has been forcefully articulated by the women's movement.

The tension between culture and community has impacted worship in a variety of ways. Most significantly, it has influenced the way many members of the UCC talk about God. Those critical of older cultural norms seek to find a God language that is neither gender-biased nor hierarchical. In the UCC *Book of Worship* God is referred to as "Father" in only two instances: The Lord's Prayer and the Trinitarian baptismal formula. Those who see a compatibility between faith and traditional American culture hold to the traditional language. Those affirming this view would dress the altar with the American and Christian flags; those critical of traditionalism are offended to find American flags in places of worship. Adherents of cultural change prefer a relational worship which seeks God in the world, while those of a more conservative bent embrace a clergy-centered worship whose God orders the world for good.

A concept large enough to embrace all three of these dichotomies is to be found in the writings of the UCC theologian H. Richard Niebuhr. He suggests that a full understanding of the church must contain within it two principles, the Catholic and the Protestant. With these terms Niebuhr was not referring to the two Western traditions of the faith known to history, but rather to those inner principles necessary for all Christian communions. The Catholic principle is the principle of incarnation by which the faith must become enfleshed in historical forms, be they the church or saints or symbols. By the Protestant principle he meant an attitude of protest which warms at every turn against the danger of confusing the penultimate with the Ultimate, the finite with the Infinite, the symbol with the

Holy. Within the dichotomies of order and freedom, tradition and practice, culture and community, the UCC seeks a worship life which can hold these principles in a balanced tension.

Fritz West

188 ✦ Creative Worship: Taizé

Taizé is a small village in eastern France where young adults from all over the world have gathered together since the early 1950s. They come to pray, to worship, and to seek the meaning of life in communion with Christ and sisters and brothers of many races and cultures. The founder and mentor of this ecumenical community is Brother Roger, a "bearer of trust, reconciliation, and peace." Today there are almost one hundred brothers in the Taizé community from over twenty different countries. They share their material goods, talents, and faith together in a celibate life, and lead Bible study groups, prayer services, and worship for the thousands of young adults who make a pilgrimage to their community. Common prayer is at the center of their life together, whether they are at Taizé or travel to share the life of the poor in India, Africa, or Central America.

Taizé worship takes place three times a day and includes meditative and sung prayer, Scripture reading, and silence. The singing, often in four-part harmony or in a round, is offered in many languages. Sometimes instruments play an obligato part as voices sing a short, chantlike number. Solo verses might be added by one of the brothers or a child who serves as cantor. The simple yet magnificent music that is repeated over and over again continues on in the heart long after worship has ended.

The Worship Environment

To create a Taizé worship environment, the sanctuary needs to be dark. On window sills and the worship table/altar, place many small votive or tea candles at different heights, on differing sizes and shapes of wood or bricks. At several positions in the room place icons, pictures of Christ, and a cross. Worshipers sit in rows facing the chancel area, for, as Brother Roger says, the focus is to be on Christ, not each other. People may sit in pews or on cushions on the floor. Scripture readers, cantors, and leaders of intercessory prayer (representing the brothers and sisters in the Taizé community) are seated on chairs or cushions in rows in the middle aisle, with the other worshipers on either side. A choir and instrumentalists may sit together near the front of the congregation to begin the songs. No one sits in the chancel area. Worship leadership rises from the congregation, with the "brothers" (and "sisters") who sit in the middle aisle providing direction.

A Worship Service in the Style of Taizé

Opening Songs. All the music used in this service is found in *Hymnal: A Worship Book,* published in 1992 by Brethren Press (Elgin, Ill.); Faith and Life Press (Newton, Kans.); and Mennonite Publishing House (Scottsdale, Pa.). Solo and instrumental parts are found in the *Accompaniment Book* to *Hymnal: A Worship Book,* published in 1993. Page numbers of the music are included in the order of worship. Several other recently published denominational hymnals contain Taizé music.

> *Gloria,* No. 204
> *Veni sancte spiritus,* No. 298

Reading of Psalm 63. The congregation sings the "Alleluia," and one or two persons read the verses of the psalm.

Alleluia, No. 101. In the Taizé service, songs are sung several times, possibly even for several minutes, for it is prayer itself. Worshipers sing their prayers in a meditative, and thus repetitious way. "Alleluia" is sung before the reading of the psalm and between verses as noted. *"Kyrie eleison"* is sung before the prayers of petition and intercession begin and after each prayer. The prayers are spoken by one of the "leaders." Other prayers that express the needs of the congregation may be written or spoken spontaneously by the worshipers. It is very effective to have prayers spoken in languages other than English.

> O God, you are my God, I seek you
> my soul thirsts for you;
> My flesh faints for you,
> as in a dry and weary land
> where there is no water.
> Alleluia
> So I have looked upon you in
> the sanctuary,
> beholding your power and glory,
> Because your steadfast love is
> better than life,

my lips will praise you.
So I will bless you as long as I live;
I will lift up my hands and call
upon your name.
Alleluia
My soul is satisfied as with a
rich feast,
and my mouth praises you with
joyful lips
when I think of you on my bed,
and meditate on you in the
watches of the night;
Alleluia

Gospel Reading: John 4:1-15
> Song: *Ubi caritas et amor,* No. 452
> Epistle Reading: Philippians 4:4-7
> Song: *Nada te turbe,* No. 562

Silence. The time of silence should be five to ten minutes long. If silence is new to the congregation, a statement might be said after *"Nada te turbe"* such as: "We will continue in prayer with a few moments of silence."

Prayers of Petition and Intercession. The congregation sings *Kyrie eleison* ("Lord, have mercy") before the prayers begin, and after each prayer.

> *Kyrie eleison,* No. 152
> *Kyrie eleison*
> O Christ, you suffered for our sakes;
> make us willing to suffer for others.
> *Kyrie eleison*
> Jesus, son of God, you gave water to the
>   thirsty,
> and to the hungry you gave food;
> may we give sustenance to those who
> cry for help.
> *Kyrie eleison*
> O Christ, when our hearts are troubled,
> give to us your peace.
> *Kyrie eleison*
> Christ of compassion, remember those
>   who are
> victims of violence and injustice.
> *Kyrie eleison*
> Loving God, you break down the walls of
> separation between people and nations.
> Reconcile us as families, friends,
>   countries.

Kyrie eleison
Spirit of the living God, fall afresh on
your people and renew your church.

(other prayers from the congregation)

The Lord's Prayer/Concluding Prayer. The concluding prayer included in this service is one of many by
Brother Roger. The Taizé service usually ends with
one of his prayers. This prayer and others by
Brother Roger are found in *Songs and Prayers from
Taizé* (London: Geoffrey Chapman/Mowbray,
1991). This book is an excellent resource for Taizé
services, including songs, prayers, and Scripture
readings. There are other books and videos on the
Taizé community and its worship available at local
and religious bookstores.

> O Christ,
> you take upon yourself all our burdens
> so that freed of all that weighs us down,
> we can constantly begin anew to walk
> with lightened step,
> from worry towards trusting,
> from the shadows towards the clear
> flowing water,
> from our own will towards the vision of
> the coming
> Kingdom.
> And, then we know,
> though we had hardly dared hope it,
> that you offer to make every human being
> a reflection of your face. Amen.

(Prayer by Brother Roger, from *Songs and Prayers
from Taizé,* 33)

Song: *Jubilate Deo omnis terra,* No. 103. At the end
of each Taizé service, one or more songs are sung
over and over again as each person prays privately,
and, when ready, moves out into the world. "*Jubilate Deo omnis terra*" is sung in at least a two-part
canon, often accompanied by several different instruments taking turns playing an obligato part, and
then joining together in a restatement of the joyful
melody. People often continue singing as they move
out from the sanctuary, so that the "sung prayer"
lives on in their hearts.

Prayers around the Cross and the resurrection of
Christ are celebrated each week on Friday and Saturday evenings in the Taizé community. Descriptions

of these celebrations with appropriate music are
found in *Songs and Prayers from Taizé.*

Nancy Rosenberger Faus

189 ✦ CONVERGENCE WORSHIP

*The convergence model, which draws from a variety of tradi-
tions, exists in nearly every denomination. Liturgical churches
that incorporate praise music can be regarded as convergence
models. So too can praise-and-worship churches that incorporate liturgical resources. All traditions contribute in some
way to convergence worship. Liturgical resources, as well as
traditional Protestant resources, provide order and depth;
creative resources heighten communication; the praise-and-
worship resources, especially the music and the rites of healing, create a sense of the immediacy of the Spirit. This
growing tradition has made a break with the cerebral, didactic
style that has characterized worship since the Enlightenment.
Instead, convergence strives to engage the whole person in
worship: mind, body, and senses.*

─── The Basic Pattern ───

Acts of Entrance are those elements of worship that
bring us into the presence of the Lord. Entering into

*The Fish. The fish is a very early symbol based on the
Greek word* ΙΧΘΥΣ *(ICHTHUS), which is translated
"fish." The early Christians saw in the letters of* ΙΧΘΥΣ
*an acronym composed of the first letters of the words in
the sentence:* "Ἰησουσ Χριστοσ Θεου Ὑιοσ Σωτερ" *(Iesous
Christos Theou (H)uios Soter), meaning "Jesus Christ
God's Son our Savior."*

God's presence involves a slow but deliberate shift in focus from those events and people around us to the Lord himself.

Welcome

Invitation to Center Down. The people are encouraged to put away the cares and events of the morning and concentrate on spiritual things. This is accomplished through a brief exhortation to "center down"—an old Quaker phrase for focusing on the Lord. This is followed by a time of silent meditation.

Welcome and Announcements. A simple greeting and welcome is followed by a brief time of pertinent announcements. By placing the announcements at the beginning, we can take care of all housekeeping without interrupting the flow of the service.

Invocation for Gifts and Ministries. Our convergence style worship incorporates body ministry. We invite the Holy Spirit to come and release his giftings through the body assembled and use them to edify the church as we worship.

Processional. The processional usually involves the singing of a hymn or chorus, during which time a cross and several banners are carried in on long poles, followed by liturgical dancers. The ministers sometimes enter with this processional. This element is seen not only as an *entering in* but as an *ascension up* into the worship of heaven.

Opening Sentences/Opening Prayer. Usually taken from *The Book of Common Prayer,* opening sentences invite the people to worship. A verse such as: "The Lord is in his holy temple" or an antiphonal response: "Blessed be God: Father, Son, and Holy Spirit." ["And blessed be His Kingdom, now and for ever, Amen"] are used.

Ministry of Praise and Worship

Music and Acts of Praise and Worship/Operation of Gifts. We "enter his gates with thanksgiving and his courts with praise" during thirty minutes of worship through hymns and contemporary choruses. Directed by a worship leader (with worship team of musicians and singers), keyboards, guitars, drums, and solo instruments are used. Additionally, we involve pageantry with banners, expressive movement, liturgical dance, singing, mime, and drama. Opportunity is given during this time for the ministry of the Holy Spirit through prophecy, spontane-

ous praise acclamations, Scripture readings, words of knowledge and wisdom, gifts of healing, and other acts. Anything to be offered to the body publicly must first be approved by one of the elders present. Joy, healings on various levels, repentance, and renewal can all take place during our entrance into God's presence.

Worship through Readings and Responses

Ministry of the Word. The acts of entrance bring us to a place of hearing and responding to God's Word. All readings follow the lectionary in *The Book of Common Prayer,* 1979.

Collect for the Day. This section begins with a collect—a special prayer with three distinct parts: an address to God, a specific petition that usually focuses on a theme, and a meditation. Our collects are usually taken from *The Book of Common Prayer* and set the theme and tone for the readings that follow.

First Reading. This reading usually comes from the Old Testament and is offered by a member of the congregation who comes forward to share the Word. He or she begins by saying, "A reading from _____." The reading is followed by the words and response, "The Word of the Lord *[Thanks be to God].*" After the reading opportunity is given for further exhortation or prophetic expression.

Psalm. Optionally, a psalm or canticle from *The Book of Common Prayer* is said or sung between the readings.

Second Reading. The second reading, from the New Testament Acts or Epistles, is handled the same as the first reading.

Gradual. The gradual—a hymn or chorus—is the processional to the reading of the Gospel. The people stand to honor the Lord of the Gospel.

Gospel Reading. Where the first two readings were instructional, the Gospel is the expression of Christ, the Word. It is read by one of the presiding ministers. He begins by saying, "The Holy Gospel of our Lord Jesus Christ according to _____" and ends with the response, "Glory to you, Lord Christ." After the reading he says, "The Gospel of the Lord" followed by the response, "Praise to You, Lord Christ."

Ministry of the Word

Message. The hearing of God's Word leads us to a time of expounding the Word through teaching, preaching, or other forms of proclamation such as drama, dramatic vignettes, and audio-visual media. The message, either taken from the lectionary readings or a completely different passage, is Word-centered and usually expositional in approach. We see the message as the culmination of our pilgrimage. Having come into the presence of God, he speaks to us from his timeless Word. The remainder of the service is a response to what we have heard.

Responses and Ministry. The message is followed by a time of application. The congregation personally and corporately is invited to respond to the truth presented. Many times an invitation is given for people to receive Jesus Christ as Savior and Lord.

Creed. We then share together in a corporate declaration of faith through the saying or singing of a creed, usually either the Apostles' or Nicene Creed. From time to time other creeds taken from Scripture are used to focus on a specific theme or event.

Prayers of the People

Intercession. Intercession follows the creed and is led by a member of the congregation. Prayers are offered in a number of ways: spontaneous, written, and "directed prayer," in which a topic is presented to the congregation, who then pray privately. As each topic is prayed for, the leader says, "Lord, in your mercy," to which the congregation responds, "Hear our prayer."

Confession of Sin. An exhortation is then given to examine our lives and repent of any and all sin. Quiet personal confession is followed by a public corporate confession.

Ministry of Hospitality. The end of the ministry of the Word comes with the "passing of peace," where we, as cleansed and forgiven people, greet one another with love, joy, and the peace of Christ. As people take their seats, a special welcome for visitors is offered along with any additional announcements.

Offertory. People are invited to continue their worship through the giving of tithes and offerings. Special music is usually sung by a soloist or group. Sometimes dance, sign, or mime is also used. As the gifts are being offered, the bread and wine are brought forward and prepared for the time of the Holy Communion. In its convergence worship, our local congregation has begun using various vestments as signs and symbols. During the offertory the ministers exit the sanctuary and return in albs and stoles for the celebration of the Eucharist.

Holy Communion

Great Thanksgiving. While earlier parts of our worship have been taken from *The Book of Common Prayer,* we are using a different book of liturgies for eucharistic prayers and consecration of the elements as an act of respect for the custodians of the BCP (since we are not in the Anglican Communion). Some parts, such as the Sanctus, are usually sung.

Administration of the Elements. The people come forward, as worship choruses are sung, to receive the bread and common cup (which is preferred to signify our oneness in Christ). While they are free to drink from the cup, most prefer instinction—the dipping of bread into the cup—as the servers administer the elements.

Ministry of Healing. During Holy Communion prayer teams are assembled on the platform to minister physical, emotional, and spiritual healing to those who so present themselves after receiving the elements. The Lord's presence has powerfully met many during these times, bringing renewal, healing, restoration of relationships, and encouragement.

Dismissal

Final Words of Exhortation. After the post-Communion prayer, the presiding minister shares words of comfort or encouragement, and any last-minute announcements.

Blessing/Benediction. A blessing and/or scriptural benediction is then given by the chief celebrant.

Hymn or Song of Sending. The service is ended with a commissioning hymn or "song of sending." Usually up-tempo, the song focuses on the ministry we have in the Word, etc. People are joyfully released as they sing. We have signs over the door leading out of the sanctuary that say, _You Are Now Entering the Mission Field._

Randolph Sly

190 ❖ PRAISE AND WORSHIP

Below is a praise service celebrated by the Zion Christian Reformed Church of Oshawa, Ontario, Canada, in a worship conference dealing with the liturgical year from Advent through Pentecost. This particular service celebrated the theme of Epiphany. Since it is a creative form of worship, the praise-and-worship style will vary from community to community.

The Basic Pattern

Praise and Adoration in Songs. The service began with a piano prelude of praise songs. On the platform there were a group of fifteen singers, two trumpeters, a drummer, two guitars, and a synthesizer, plus the regular organ and piano. Three dancers were also part of the singing group. The joy expressed by the praise group was contagious as they led the time of praise.

Welcome and Call to Worship. The praise songs were followed by an extemporaneous welcome that ended with a call to worship: "Come, let us join hearts, hands, and voices and praise of God."

Entrance Hymn. The praise songs were immediately followed with "Praise to the Lord, the Almighty" with organ, piano, and trumpets.

Acts of Praise and Adoration. The acts of praise and adoration were a medley of praise songs with piano synthesizer, guitar, and drums, including "Sing unto the Lord a New Song," "I Will Exalt," and "Jesus Put This Song into Our Hearts." Praise songs were followed by the reading of Psalm 33:1-4 and a praise group medley of adoration including "I Will Bless the Lord," "Give Thanks with a Grateful Heart," "I Love You, Lord," and "Father, I Adore You." A member of the praise group then read Psalm 33:18-22. This section closed with the hymn of conviction "Jesus Shall Reign."

The Sharing of Joy, Blessings, and Answers to Prayer. Members of the congregation were invited to stand up and share. This was concluded by a prayer led by a member of the praise group. The prayer was followed by the congregational singing of "Bless the Lord, O My Soul."

The Sharing of Needs and Concerns. Members of the congregation were invited to stand and state their needs for prayer. Again, this was concluded by a prayer of intercession led by a person from the praise group. The prayer ended with congregational singing of "Peace I Give to You."

Growth in Grace/Responsive Reading. A collection of Scripture presenting the Epiphany theme was proclaimed responsively by various members of the praise team (a readers' theater).

Hymn of Response. The hymn of response was "Arise, Shine, for Your Light Has Come." Verses were sung by soloists, and all joined in on the refrain (including dancers, accompanied with piano, guitars, synthesizer, trumpets, and drums.)

Scripture Reading. The Scripture reading for this particular Sunday was Luke 4:14-21, a passage that points to Jesus' calling to preach and proclaim the good news of the kingdom to a suffering humanity.

Message. The title of the sermon was "His Mandate and Ours."

God's People Respond

Benediction/Closing Hymn. The closing hymn was "Alleluia, He Is Coming." Dancers led the audience in simple, expressive motions. This song transitioned the congregation into a few moments of silent meditation, which was ended by the pianist quietly beginning a postlude of praise songs.

Henry Wildeboer

191a ❖ SEEKERS' SERVICE

The seeker services, on Saturday evenings at 5 and 7 and on Sunday mornings at 9 and 11:15, are meant to provide a safe place for unchurched visitors to hear the gospel in ways relevant to their lives. This is not primarily a worship service for Christians. A free-will offering, directed to members and believers, is taken at some point in the service, usually before the message.

The program for a weekend service is more detailed than that for "New Community" because seekers and visitors are more interested in seeing the order unfold. The following is an example of a service that took place at Willow Creek Community Church in South Barrington, Illinois.

The Basic Pattern

Prelude. The band plays some light jazz as people enter to talk and take their seats.

Welcome. A vocal team member welcomes and greets everyone. He or she leads the congregation in singing a short chorus that is printed in the bulletin for convenience.

Vocal Duet. A duet and small ensemble perform music ("Good for Me") that focuses attention on the coming message about modern marriages. They are accompanied by the band.

Drama. Four drama team members perform a sketch about an older married couple who want to inject a bit of balanced perspective into a soon-to-be married younger couple. The accent is on humor.

Scripture. A woman reads a portion of Scripture that deals with the marriage relationship and adds her own contextual comments.

Song. Another song ("That's What Love Is All About") is performed, accompanied by the band.

Announcements. In the announcements segment, the programming director of the church highlights important events and ministries at Willow Creek that would be of interest to seekers.

Offering. An offering is then taken, but seekers and visitors are told that they need not contribute. This service is for them.

Message. For his message, Bill Hybels begins a series that discusses and explores modern American marriages and the difference that God through Christ can make in them. He closes the service with a short prayer. (The message lasts approximately thirty minutes. The whole service is scheduled for one hour.)

Discussion and Fellowship. Post-service discussion and fellowship in the auditorium and the new atrium is encouraged. While the gospel is not always overtly presented to seekers in this service, an evangelical approach to issues and programming, songs and drama, is fundamental.

191b • Believers' Worship

Midweek services, called New Community, meet on Wednesday and Thursday evenings at 7:30. These gatherings are meant for believers, who may or may not be members of Willow Creek Church. The primary purpose of each service is to teach them deeper truths and lessons from the Bible and to worship God through various hymns and choruses. The model for a midweek service is very simple and yet highly effective. The example below is from Willow Creek Church.

The Basic Pattern

Prelude. Before the service begins, a musical prelude by the orchestra or band plays behind a closed curtain and an empty stage as people file in to talk and take their seats. At the appointed time either an elder, teacher, or music leader begins the service with an introductory greeting.

Exaltation. A vocal team member leads the congregation in a series of choruses and hymns, chosen to create a worshipful atmosphere and to prepare for the message. He is accompanied by the church band and punctuates the songs with his own spiritual insights. (This part takes approximately twenty minutes.)

Family Concerns. The pastor, Bill Hybels, highlights various announcements in the New Community Update, the service bulletin. The tithe offering is taken, with a musical interlude.

Message. "Spiritual Warfare—Part II, Ephesians 6:10-24." Associate pastor and teacher, Don Cousins, continues his series and follows an outline printed on the update. (The sermon lasts approximately forty-five minutes.)

Exaltation. More praise-and-worship songs emphasize both the power and help that believers have in God. A closing prayer concludes the service.

Conclusion

While there is no set order each week, the worship components remain the same. Occasionally, a short drama piece or video is used in conjunction with the point of the message. Humorous bits are used also to stress a particular project or concern of Willow Creek. The programming team prayerfully concentrates on organizing the service around the point of the message, whether topical, expositional, or part of a longer series.

Steve Burdan

PART THREE

Resources for Sunday Worship

❧ FIVE ❧

Styles of Worship

═══

A glance at the orders of worship of various churches gives evidence of both commonalities and distinctives. Part 3 attempts to provide specific directions and textual resources for the range of possible service parts included in the Entrance rites, the Service of the Word, the celebration of the Lord's Supper (service of the sacrament), and the acts of Dismissal. These are introduced by a general descriptive and theological approach to the nature of the worshiping assembly itself and to the various styles of worship employed in those assemblies.

The two foremost styles of renewing worship in our time are the fourfold pattern of worship and the contemporary praise-and-worship movement. The fourfold pattern of worship is rooted in the biblical and historical research of the twentieth century and represents a return to the order of worship in the early church. The praise-and-worship order is an offshoot of the charismatic movement, the Jesus movement of the 1970s, and the influence of the new praise songs. This chapter also looks at a convergence worship, which seeks to bring together the traditional and the contemporary in the fourfold pattern of worship.

═══

192 ◆ ASSEMBLING THE PEOPLE

In both early Israel and the church, the assembly of the people is essential to worship. The act of assembling constitutes the ekklesia, *the people of God, who come together in response to the Lord's call and celebrate communally Word and sacrament. This act of assembly begins by gathering together the people of God.*

The worship assembly is the gathering of baptized Christians who, in response to God's call, come together at periodic but regular intervals to celebrate the liturgy of the church. The assembly of a local church is the subject of the liturgy; what the assembly does is the corporate action of worship. Worship assemblies are also events in the life of the church: they are Christian communities called to assembly. These events are not only regular meetings of the church for the central celebrations of Word and Eucharist but also for other liturgical occasions in the life of specific Christian communities. Worship assemblies can be understood as gatherings to celebrate the official liturgies of those churches that have authorized books of worship, but they can also refer to gatherings for worship that is not so

clearly designated as the "official prayer of the church." In either case, gathering in assembly for worship at regular intervals constitutes an essential dimension of Christian life. There is no Christian church without assembly.

The renewed interest in recent years in the worship assembly and the emphasis on the central role of assembling for worship in Christian identity and life is the fruit of the biblical and liturgical renewal movements of the earlier part of this century. During the 1950s, Roman Catholic scholars in particular explored the meaning and practice of assembling in an effort to overcome what they saw as the clericalizing tendencies within Roman Catholic worship and the lack of full participation of all members of the gathered church. Their research included a study of a biblical theology of the assembly (both Old and New Testament), early church theology and practice of assembling, and the fate of the assembly from the early church to the present time. Their judgment at mid-century was that a retrieval of a theology of the liturgical assembly was central to a renewal of Christian life in general and a renewal of the liturgy in particular. The impact of their research on Roman Catholic liturgical reforms cannot be underestimated, but it would be a mistake to suggest that their influence was limited to Roman Catholic practice alone. However, a systematic treatment of the liturgical assembly in the practice and theology across all the Christian denominations remains to be done.

Biblical Theology

In an effort to enlarge their understanding of the mystery of the church, biblical scholars and theologians of the first half of the twentieth century traced Christian images, structures, vocabulary, and liturgical practices to their Jewish antecedents. The examination of the New Testament term *ekklesia* led to studies of the Septuagint's use of *ekklesia* and *synagoge* and the Hebrew equivalents of *qahal* and *edah*. For those interested in the worship assembly, the Hebrew term *qahal* and the theology which developed around *qahal* were of primary interest.

Thierry Maertens argues that the Hebrew Scriptures testify to a practice and a theology of the assembly that developed over a period of four centuries (seventh to third centuries BCE), starting with the Deuteronomic reforms. During this time, both practice and theology were shaped by the religious, cultural, political, and historical factors influencing Israel's life. Maertens suggests that a distinctive character of Israel's solemn assemblies and a basic structure of the assembly event were sustained into the New Testament period. In his judgment, an emerging theology of assembly also helped Israel interpret its identity and God's intention for its people. This theology included past events, present experience, and future promise.

The assembly of Israel was a divine convocation: God took the initiative and called together a disparate crowd, making them one. God was the great assembler (Jer. 23:3; 29:14), although various personages throughout Israel's history called the assembly together in God's name (Num. 16:3, 8-11). The people thus created were the assembly of God, the *qahal YHWH*.

There was an intimate connection between the act of assembling and the identity of the people. In their solemn assemblies Israel could take cognizance of itself as a people called by God: the *qahal YHWH*. In this sense, the assembly could be understood as the gathering of the people themselves. It was in their physically coming together that their identity as God's assembly was instilled and strengthened. Their identity was tied to God and

God's intention for them; God's holiness was communicated to them in the assembly (Lev. 24:16; Num. 19:20). Formative events in the life of Israel, such as the Sinai covenant, evidenced a theology of the assembly. The whole Sinai event could be seen as the "Day of Assembly" (Deut. 4:10; 9:10; 10:4; 18:16).

God gathered the people together by means of a word (Deut. 4:10) in order to proclaim a word to them (Deut. 9:10). The Scriptures not only testified to God's action in history; they constituted the divine presence in the local assembly. The dynamic of the assembly was call and response; it was an event of encounter. God initiated the assembly and the community responded by gathering, by listening, and by making a response in the form of a profession of faith, a sacrifice, or prayers of blessing and thanksgiving. Covenant relationships were renewed through solemn liturgical assemblies.

The assembly as event in the life of the people had a clear structure and organization. The Scriptures were central, as was instruction in the Scriptures in the later postexilic assemblies. After the response of the assembly to the Scriptures, dismissals constituted a final structural element of the assembly. Dismissals had a dual purpose. They marked the boundary between the solemn assembly and the rest of the life of the people. Second, they sent the people back to their daily tasks imbued with a moral imperative to carry out the exigencies of the covenant or to rejoice in the knowledge of what God had done (1 Kings 8:66; Josh. 24:28; 2 Chron. 7:10; 31:1).

The issue of who was allowed to participate in the solemn assemblies was a matter of considerable importance. Especially in the Deuteronomic period, the call to assembly was notably inclusive; the assembly was ecumenical in nature: God's call was ultimately universal. Experiences of exile and growing nationalistic tendencies modified practices and theology of inclusion and exclusion (cf. Lev. 21:18; 2 Sam. 5:8; Neh. 10:31). Particularly under priestly influence, notions of distinction, separation, holiness, and uncleanness were brought to bear.

Once again stressing God's universal call, the prophetic literature reintroduced the inclusive nature of the liturgical assembly (Jer. 23:3; 29:14). The prophets portrayed God as shepherd, gathering the peoples and leading them to good pasture (Mic. 2:12; 4:6; Ezek. 11:17; 34:13). The prophets also added an eschatological emphasis to their theology of assembly. Solemn liturgical assemblies were understood as signs of the definitive assembly that is yet to take place. In the final section of Isaiah, to be part of the assembly even then was to be a part in sign and in action of God's intention to gather all peoples.

Research into the New Testament reveals that Jesus redefined and reinterpreted the theology of the assembly, as did the early Christian community. Jesus now became the "great assembler"; he is the true shepherd calling all, particularly the lost, to good pasture. His ministry was especially to those who were excluded from assemblies and/or places of assembly or given secondary status in them—those with physical ailments, sinners, and whole classes of people such as women, children, and pagans. It was to these that Jesus reached out often for their inclusion in the assemblies. The blind and lame were healed, frequently in the temple surroundings; the banquet parables repeatedly stressed the inclusion of all; women and children were noticeably included in the gatherings around Jesus.

Jesus' own person became the new focus of the assembly, replacing the temple and other cultic places as the gathering place of the assembly (Matt. 23:37-39). While the revelation of God in the assembly was always a central element of the assembly, within the Christian dispensation Jesus the Christ was God's new word of disclosure. In the Christian assembly God's presence is communicated in both Word and in sign, most fully in the eucharistic sign of eating and drinking.

———— Christian Assemblies ————

Apostolic and postapostolic accounts suggest that the early church understood itself as the continuation of Israel in general and of the _qahal YHWH_ in particular. A typological reading of the Hebrew scriptures allowed the apostolic church to see itself as the new "people of God," "a chosen race," "a holy nation," "a people set apart." The Greek equivalent of the Hebrew _qahal YHWH, ekklesia tou Theou,_ with its rich heritage described above, was applied to the whole Christian people and its assembly, while the term _epi to auto_ (gathering together in one place) also became a technical term for Christian assemblies of prayer. Gregory Dix suggests that until the third century the word _ekklesia_ (church) was used to refer not to the building for worship but to the "solemn assembly for the liturgy, and by extension those who have a right to take part in this"

(_The Shape of the Liturgy_ [Westminster: Dacre Press, 1945], 19).

The apostolic church also took over the eschatological meaning of the assembly. Just as the final assembly gathers all peoples from all nations and overcomes all divisions, so too must the Christian assembly show forth these characteristics, even if imperfectly. The most obvious difference of Christian assemblies was, of course, the centrality of Christ. Their prayer was in and through Christ, and their liturgies were in memorial of the saving action of Jesus' life, death, and resurrection. At the earliest stage of church life, the leadership of the assemblies was tied to witness to the risen Christ.

In the post-apostolic period, numerous church orders, accounts of the martyrs, and patristic writings indicate that gathering in assembly stood at the heart of ecclesial life. To be a Christian was to be one who assembled, and this assembly had a profoundly social character. The body of Christ was built up by each one's presence and diminished by each one's absence. Individual faith was nourished and strengthened in these gatherings, and the prayer of the whole body gathered into one voice had an efficacy beyond that of individual prayer. All had a responsibility to attend and to encourage other members to do so as well.

The Sunday assembly took on greater prominence in the post-apostolic period, and its meaning was developed. The preeminence of Sunday rested on the resurrection of Christ on the first day of the week. Sunday became the "Lord's Day" and the "Day of the Resurrection." It was also the first and eighth day, the day of the new creation inaugurated in Christ and the eschatological sign of the world to come.

———— Characteristics of the Assembly ————

As well as retrieving the biblical and early church foundations for a theology of the worshiping assembly, liturgical scholars of this century also outlined abiding characteristics of the assembly and its relationship with ecclesial life. An important methodological move was to consider the assembly in light of its relationship to the church. The conclusion of the worshiping scholars studying this issue at mid-century was that the assembly, like the church, can be considered in the realm of mystery. In other words, it is a theological reality rooted in God's call and sustained by God's grace. While the church precedes and supersedes the liturgical assembly, the assembly is a sign and manifestation of the church. Through the actual gathering in assembly for worship, the church actualizes itself in its essential nature. Although the life of the church encompasses more than its gathering for worship, the action of gathering into assembly for worship is so tied to ecclesial identity that A.-G. Martimort can say that there is no church without assembly ("Dimanche, assemblée et paroisse." *La Maison Dieu* 57 [1959]: 58). Assembling for worship is constitutive of the church's being; it is the church in action, becoming itself and expressing the fullness of its being.

If the worship assembly is a sign and manifestation of the church, then what characterizes the church in its apostolic ministry characterizes the assembly as well. The assembly, like the church, is a sign of salvation. The assembly nourishes and builds the faith of the baptized, but it also is a sign to those outside the baptized community of the unity and charity of all in God. Like the assembly of Israel, to participate in the assembly is to participate in God's mission, now seen through the life and mission of Christ Jesus, of gathering all into one.

At another level, to claim that the assembly manifests the church means that the particular structure and organization of the church will be manifest in the assembly. It is the consensus of liturgical scholarship that the worship assembly is a united but differentiated body. Not all members do the same thing, but all members have an essential role to play in the celebration of the liturgy. While this general statement can be made across all Christian communions, the actual assignment of roles and responsibilities within the assembly will be related to the actual ordering of a particular church and to its theology of ministry.

While recognizing the many differences on ministry and order that still remain among the Christian churches, it is fair to say that the scholarship on the worship assembly helped to focus contemporary efforts in liturgical renewal on a new role for liturgical ministers and more enhanced participation of the entire assembly. Particularly for the churches that had succumbed to a clericalization of the liturgy, this scholarship pointed to the need for worship ministers to focus their attention on the assembly as well as on the unfolding of the rites. A.-G. Martimort was particularly responsible for reclaiming the ordained minister's role as "president" or "presider" of the assembly. By situating the ordained celebrant as leader, facilitator, or mediator

within a community of active participants, both the communal nature of the assembly and the communal nature of the liturgy are maintained. The revival of ancient ministries of lector or reader and the creation of new ministries (such as that of lay eucharistic ministers) has broken the presiding celebrant's hold on liturgical ministries and has opened those ministries to many more of the Christian faithful, both women and men. Investigation of individual church practices would reveal distinct legislation on the participation of the laity in these ministries as well as a possible distinction between women and men in some ministries.

Some scholars have suggested that entrance into the assembly and departure from it makes stringent demands on the participants. Because the assembly is a sign of the eschatological gathering of all into unity and charity, actual Christian assemblies need to reflect that unity in concrete ways. Accordingly, participants are challenged to set aside the prejudices and biases that mark daily life and allow the promised grace to transform their behavior and attitudes. More recent scholarship has addressed this issue in terms of justice. Our liturgical gatherings must be manifestations of just relationships or we risk losing the authenticity of our worship. On the other hand, the vision and patterns of justice expressed in assembly must be carried beyond the confines of the assembly into every aspect of life.

Function of Liturgical Assemblies

It is clear from what has been said above that recent liturgical scholarship places great emphasis on the necessity for worship assemblies for the very existence of the church. However it is possible to explore more deliberately the function of such assemblies in the life of the Christian people. Liturgical assemblies are events where the Christian community responds to God's call, expresses its faith, and celebrates its salvation in Christ Jesus and the power of the Spirit. Thus it can be said that Christians have a right to assembly for worship and a right to the eucharistic assembly as the preeminent assembly to which all others are ordered. This challenges all churches to overcome any obstacles that would inhibit the gathering of the community or the celebration of its central mystery.

Worship assemblies are also events that continually shape the faith of the baptized and form the faith of those seeking to join the community. This implies that individual Christians can expect both presence and active participation in the liturgical assemblies. The communal nature of the assembly and the liturgy demands them; the faith of the participants is nourished or impoverished by them. This challenges the churches to address the quality of their assemblies and to consider the role of assembling in the formation of new members.

Finally, by insisting on the relationship between participation in the worship assembly and Christian identity, churches must consider whether the actual practice of the church supports such extravagant claims. If not, they must consider what changes at the level of liturgical praxis and catechesis would enable such a conviction to take root once again.

Conclusions

While the impetus for the research into the liturgical assembly arose from a specific pastoral concern of the Roman Catholic church, the fruit of this research has much to offer all Christian churches in their current efforts at liturgical renewal. There is need, however, for each denomination to review its own history and explore the fate of the assembly within its own specific context. More constructive work on the theology of the assembly also needs to be done. As in all cases, there are no liturgical concerns that are not ecclesial concerns. A theology of the liturgical assembly and its actual organization, structure, and practice will be conditioned by the particular ecclesiology of the church gathering. At the same time, the actual practice of liturgical assembling will shape the faith and identity of the church.

Catherine Vincie

The liturgy of the Eucharist is best understood as a journey or procession. It is the journey of the church into the dimension of the kingdom. . . . Our _entrance_ into the presence of Christ is an entrance into a fourth dimension that allows us to see the ultimate reality of life. It is not an escape from the world, rather it is the arrival at a vantage point from which we can see more deeply into the reality of the world.

The journey begins when Christians leave their homes and beds. They leave, indeed, their life in this present and concrete world, and whether they have to drive fifteen minutes or walk a few blocks, a sacramental act is already taking place, an act that is the very condition of everything else that is to hap-

pen. For they are now on their way to _constitute the church,_ or to be more exact, to be transformed into the church of God. They have been individuals, some white, some black, some poor, some rich, they have been the "natural" world and a natural community. And now they have been called to "come together in one place," to bring their lives, their very "world" with them and to be more than they were: a _new_ community with a new life. We are already far beyond the categories of common worship and prayer. The purpose of this "coming together" is not simply to add a religious dimension to the natural community, to make it "better"— more responsible, more Christian. The purpose is to _fulfill the church,_ and that means to make present the One in whom all things are at their _end,_ and all things are at their _beginning._

Alexander Schmemann[9]

193 • A CASE FOR THE PLURALITY OF WORSHIP STYLES

Christian worship from the beginning has been characterized by a variety of styles. Contemporary scholarship suggests that there was no single original style of worship, but rather that worship patterns varied from place to place in the early church. Knowing this fact, we can see the current range of worship practices as a positive characteristic that enriches the church.

When the serious scientific study of liturgy began to be pursued in the nineteenth century, it was primarily as a historical discipline: scholars wanted to know how we had reached the forms of worship practiced in the present, how liturgy had changed and developed throughout the history of the church. Although more recently the scope of liturgical studies has expanded to include other methods of analysis, the historical approach still tends to occupy the position of primary importance in scholarship. More importantly still, those engaged in liturgical revision and renewal in many Christian churches in the present have as their aim the recovery and restoration of ancient forms of worship. There is a tendency to view the early church as the "golden age" of Christianity and its forms of worship as embodying better than all later liturgies the true meaning and spirit of the Christian faith. So, for example, the common shape that is emerging in many eucharistic rites today is modeled upon what is thought—however mistakenly—to have been the pattern of eucharistic worship in the early church, and the structure of initiation rites (baptism and confirmation) is in large measure an archaeological enterprise, reconstructing the practice of the fourth century. However, I believe that there are three serious defects in this approach.

First, we do not know anywhere near as much about the details of the worship of the early church as we once thought we did, and so our attempts at the reconstruction of the past are more often a romantic idealizing than an accurate reflection of what really happened. Moreover, what we do know suggests less the existence of a single, standardized liturgical practice and more a pluriform and variegated style of worship within different communities that only very slowly and belatedly accepted some measure of conformity under the pressures caused by the need to define orthodoxy over heresy in the fourth century. If we really wanted to model ourselves on the worship of the early church, therefore, the liturgies of our various traditions would actually look much less like one another than they tend to.

Second, even if we were in a position to be able to produce an exact replica of early Christian worship in our churches, there would still remain the question of whether we ought in fact to do so. In other words, is the past normative for the present and the future? Previous generations of scholars thought that it was, but that assumption can be challenged. The liturgical customs and theology of primitive Christianity do offer us insights into the nature of Christian worship that we would be unable to get in any other way, but so for that matter do the practices of later centuries and of our own day. Authentic Christian worship does not have to reproduce precisely the pattern of third-century worship. Though we may claim to possess the faith once delivered to the saints, no Christian today holds exactly the same beliefs and doctrine as a Christian of the ante-Nicene period, and no Christian today lives in a cultural context identical to that of the early church, however striking the parallels may be in some situations. Why then must we force contemporary believers to wear nothing but the liturgical dress of the former ages?

Third, underlying both of the previous points there is a more fundamental question: Can or should any single liturgical form at all be considered as universally normative for Christians, regardless of whether that form originated in the third century, the sixteenth century, or the twentieth century? To posit universal norms for worship, to speak of the liturgy rather than of liturgies, implies that there exists in heaven some Platonic ideal of the perfect act of worship that we must constantly struggle to replicate here on earth. It is a static rather than a dynamic view of liturgy that suggests that God does not delight in the infinite variety and richness of creation but wants to be worshiped only in one predetermined manner. Should we not rather expect acts of worship to reflect both the diversity of the beliefs of particular groups of Christians and the variegated cultures in which they are set?

This critique is not meant to imply that there are no norms at all for Christian worship, that anything goes and people should be free to do whatever they like by way of liturgical practice. What it is trying to say is that the rightness or quality of an act of worship cannot be measured against some universal yardstick. We need instead to ask such questions as: Does the rite enable the people engaging in it effectively to express their own particular piety, or does it try to impose a false piety upon them? Is it an authentic expression of the beliefs of that specific community or tradition? Does it "work"; does it succeed in doing for the group whatever it is meant to do, or does it hinder that process? For in the end liturgies can only be judged good of their kind and in their context, and not in an absolute sense.

Paul F. Bradshaw

194 ✦ STORY, STRUCTURE, STYLE

Story, structure, and style are three elements of a paradigm first formulated by family therapist Salvador Minuchin. To the person interested in finding a useful way to think about the act of divine worship, this paradigm may be helpful.

Many of us, when we think of worship, think of it as "the way we do it in our church"; that is, as a complex system of words, actions, events, history, and emotions, all tied up in God. When one attempts to say something useful about worship, one therefore needs a way to discuss it in less complicated and less "loaded" terms. Thus, we offer this paradigm as a way to identify and clarify what we know, think, feel, believe, and understand about Christian worship, given the breadth and depth in which worship is discussed in these volumes.

Christians are storytellers. We have a gospel that tells the story of our Lord Jesus Christ, who himself used stories to proclaim his message. Though the first generation of Christians had only the Hebrew Bible as Scripture, once the stories of Jesus were committed to writing, together with the Epistles and other texts, and once these texts—and no others—were received as authoritative ("canonical") by the church of Christ, they became the defining standard of what Christians are and do.

Scripture, then, becomes the text, the rule, the standard form of the STORY, by which Christians identify themselves and recognize each other. As far as the Christian is concerned, the story is wholly objective, not subject to opinion, addition, or omission; it is constant. When we think of the Christian story, we may ask several useful questions:

- Whose story is being told? Who "owns" it?
- What kind of story is it? A story of rules and laws? of relationships? of crime and punishment? of love and mercy? of history?
- As an individual Christian, how does my personal story interweave with the Christian story, the story of Christ and the church? Do I make the story conform to my experience and understanding or do I grow to become part of the story?
- How does the story of my particular congregation, or my denomination, or my social or ethnic group interweave with the Christian story?
- How does the liturgy—the corporate worship—in my church contribute to the undistorted telling of the Christian story?
- If I consider how another congregation or denomination tells the Christian story in its life and worship, how does it differ from mine? Is it the same story? Does moving from one building or denomination or ethnic group to another actually change the content—the central message—of the Christian story as I understand it?

Once we consider these questions, we may then be prepared to face the ultimate question of whether or not we "heard" the Christian story "straight" when it was told to us and whether or not we are "telling" the story "straight" to those we are teaching to be disciples of Christ.

Thus, story is the "bottom line" of everything that happens in Christian liturgy. The story of the gospel of Jesus Christ is the unchanging center of the life, work, and worship of the church. It is the thing that defines us, tests us, and judges us, as we seek to be faithful communicators of this gospel we serve. Therefore, if the story changes when we communicate it in worship, then we are obligated—in fact, commanded—by our Lord to adjust our message in our worship until it faithfully communicates his message.

Structure, the second point of the paradigm, deals with how the Christian story is "managed" in the telling. Structure is the context in which the story is told. Structures are mostly objective and relatively permanent, though they may be changed for good cause. When we think of structure, we may ask such questions as:

- What forms and forces direct or try to direct how we tell the story? Am I aware of how I have been shaped (educated, indoctrinated) as a Christian? Am I conscious of the assumptions, the "givens," the "relative absolutes" of my life which have conditioned the way I receive and transmit the story?
- How do power structures (such as denominational affiliations, political and socioeconomic status, and organizational structures) exert their influence on how I and my congregation communicate the story?
- Which forms and forces are relatively rigid, and which are somewhat flexible? How do time, space, tradition, and denominational doctrine condition the context in which we tell the story? Would the story change if we changed the furniture, the meeting time, the order for worship, the selection of music, or how the worship leaders dress and comb their hair?
- How might present structures be examined, evaluated, and changed, if necessary, to make certain that the undistorted story is being communicated to the next generation of Christians we are teaching right now?

Most of us worship in buildings, use songbooks, use Bible translations, and organize our congregations according to what prior generations of Christians thought were appropriate and correct. If we could design and construct our own forms and structures, what shape might they take? If I designed the worship space, how would it look? What would I see, hear, feel, taste, experience, and do in that space? When would I want to be there? With whom? All these considerations are the structure, the framework, the context that we use—and that more often uses us—to communicate the story.

Finally, style is the "stuff" we bring to the discussion. Style is concerned with how we communicate, or "express," the story within our structures. Style and structure interact strongly with each other and changes in one often necessitate changes in the other, but that is as it should be—only the story remains constant. Ask yourself, *Would Justin Martyr or Paul or Hippolytus "fit in" in your church this Sunday? Would they understand the language? know the songs? figure out the bulletin?* Of course, in the abstract sense, they ought to be able to recognize a Christian service with its praise, prayer, preaching, confession, communion, and care; but the specific elements of your service, most likely not.

Unlike story and structure, style is mostly subjective; that is, style is subject to trends, fads, fancies, personal tastes, and conventional wisdom. Style most often becomes the battleground of worship, because it is the most subjective, and is most easily subject to congregational power struggles. Even in 1880, Henry Martyn Dexter understood this crucial difference and so was able to write to his congregational, free-church contemporaries:

> Any Congregational church, whose taste and sense of expediency may so incline it, is at perfect liberty to order its worship by the liturgy of the Church of England, or the Protestant or Reformed Episcopal Church of the United States, or by a liturgy of its own. So long as it does nothing which shall give reasonable ground of offense to the other churches with which it is in fellowship, it may order its prayers, its praise, and all the methods of its worship, to its own entire content; and its pastor, remaining true to our fundamentals of doctrine and polity, though enrobed and endowed . . . with "chausuble, albe, amice, stole, maniple and zone, with two blessed towels, and all their appendages," would remain, in good faith and entirely, a Congregational minister still.

It is not unreasonable to infer that Dexter understood that, to a point, even choosing structures is a matter of style. Questions of style that might be useful include:

- What style does our congregation use—in our worship space, at the times we gather—to communicate the story?

- Is our style so rigid, predictable, and unyielding that it is more like a structure?
- Does our congregation understand and accept that styles and structures are not integral parts of the story itself?
- Do we know that styles and structures may change without violating the essential message of the gospel? Do we understand that styles and structures are humans' contributions to the Christian story and not God's?

Considering the whole paradigm, we must ask if our congregation has an effective means of keeping the three elements of the paradigm separate. Are we clear on which things we have added and which things are essential and unchangeable? We must be ever careful to distinguish the message (the story) from the medium (the structure and style) by which it is transmitted.

At present, there is much discussion on what kinds of worship are "best" or "most attractive." Some people strongly advocate something called "contemporary" or "charismatic" or "traditional," and so on. Some use terms like "doxological," "pedagogical," "evangelical," "liturgical," "spontaneous," or "planned." As the following chapters will show, all of these terms relate to style and structure, and none of them is part of the story itself. Most of the divisions congregations and denominations experience relate to opinions about structure and style.

When the veneers of denominational doctrines are finally peeled away, each Christian must consider: Where, when, and how is the undistorted Christian story being communicated? How do I know it is undistorted? Am I doing it? Why or why not? And am I sure that God is pleased with my effort and the effort of my congregation when we appear before God in worship?

Inga and Ronal Freyer Nicholas

195 ◆ THE TRADITIONAL FOURFOLD PATTERN OF WORSHIP

The order below represents the traditional worship of the Western church. With some variation, it is found today mostly among liturgical and mainline churches.

The Entrance

The Gathering of God's People
The Entrance Song

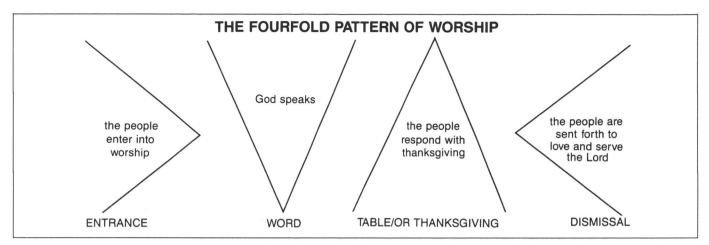

THE FOURFOLD PATTERN OF WORSHIP

God speaks

the people enter into worship

the people respond with thanksgiving

the people are sent forth to love and serve the Lord

ENTRANCE   WORD   TABLE/OR THANKSGIVING   DISMISSAL

The Fourfold Pattern of Worship. The lines provide a sense of the movement of worship. Worship is not a program but a movement of God's people who ENTER to hear the WORD, respond in THANKSGIVING, and GO FORTH to love and serve the Lord. On those Sundays when the TABLE of the Lord is not being celebrated, the response of thanksgiving may consist of songs or prayers of thanksgiving.

The Greeting(s)
The Penitential Rite
Acts of Praise
The Prayer of the Day

The Acts of Entrance bring the people before God, form them into the body of Christ, and ready them to hear the Word of the Lord.

The Service of the Word

Hearing God Speak
The Old Testament Lesson
The Psalm (responsive)
The Epistle Lesson
The Alleluia (or other response)
The Gospel Lesson
The Sermon

Emphasis is placed on the full range of God's revelation. Readings are chosen from a three-year lectionary. Some shorten the readings to two. Readings may be dramatized or told as story.

Responding to God
The Creed (or some other response)
The Prayers of the People
The Kiss of Peace

The response to God comes after God has spoken. A great deal of variation of forms may be used to accomplish the response.

The Service of the Table

The Offertory (bringing of bread and wine, taking of offering, anthem or hymn)

Invitation to the Lord's Table
Salutation
Sursum Corda (Lift up your hearts)
Prayer of Proclamation
Sanctus (Holy, Holy, Holy)
The Words of Institution
The Epiclesis (prayer for coming of the Holy Spirit)
The Prayer of Intercession (Lord's Prayer)
The Fraction (Breaking of Bread)
The Distribution
Communion Songs and Hymns
The Closing Prayer

There is a fourfold action at the Table following the action of our Lord—he took, blessed, broke, and gave (see Matt. 26:26). Approaches to the Table vary from very simple and compressed forms to the more elaborate. Listed here are the major parts of the service that can be done simply or expanded into a more elaborately sung Eucharist. Anointing with oil may accompany the eucharistic action. Communion songs with an upbeat resurrection motif have been restored in many churches.

The Dismissal

Announcements
Benediction (Blessing)
Hymn of Dismissal
Words of Dismissal

Because the people are being sent forth in mission, announcements are frequently given before the words of dismissal. Various acts of worship then bring closure to worship and send the people forth.

196 • THE STYLE OF CONTEMPORARY WORSHIP

Sustained sections of praise are now being used successfully in worship by young congregations. Instead of organizing their services into a series of discrete events—a single hymn followed by a prayer, another hymn, the choir, the offering, a solo, a Scripture reading, and then the sermon—they make time for sustained, unbroken, flowing praise that often lasts anywhere from ten to fifty minutes. After a time of teaching, people are invited to come forward for salvation, healing, and deliverance. In churches with a more charismatic flavor, the extended time of worship includes opportunities for healing, words of knowledge, exhortations from the congregation, prophetic utterances, and dance both from those in the congregation and from trained dance teams.

Another pattern followed by many contemporary worship leaders is the fourfold pattern based on the tabernacle. In this pattern the worship leaders lead the worshipers through the gates, into the outer court, into the inner court, and finally into the Holy of Holies. There is a narrative quality to the movement as the worshipers travel through distinct moods and stages of spiritual intensity through the use of music.

The Five-Phase Worship Pattern

John Wimber and Eddie Espinosa have developed a five-phase pattern for guiding their long worship song service, or as they term it, "worship set." Evangelical churches may find aspects of it useful for their Sunday morning or evening services, as well as weekday small-group meetings.

Wimber and Espinosa have used this pattern for several years in leading both groups of a thousand people and small home praise groups. The idea for this pattern evolved from their experience, practice, and Bible reading. They became aware that there are different types of choruses and that these can be categorized in a sequence. The five phases are *invitation, engagement, exaltation, adoration,* and *intimacy* (plus a closing).

The *invitation phase* is like a call to worship. The lyrics used in this phase should address the people and draw their attention to worship, as in the choruses "I Just Came to Praise the Lord" or "Don't You Know It's Time to Praise the Lord." They may be accompanied with hand-clapping where appropriate. For a vigorous call to worship with hand

clapping, the Hebrew chorus "The Celebration Song" (Chambers) is excellent. A mellower opener could be "Let's Forget about Ourselves and Magnify the Lord and Worship Him." More traditional churches might wish to have a mix of speaking, reading, and singing. They might include Scripture readings in the call and substitute hymns for choruses.

The key is that the lyrics of the song can now do the inviting and focusing without the song leader having to resort to verbal exhortation. The leader can continue with hymns and choruses until he or she has made contact with the people and they with him or her and everyone is focused.

In the *engagement phase* the people begin to draw near to God, and the lyrics should reflect that. They are now singing to God, not encouraging one another. Espinosa likens it to the engagement period before marriage (e.g., "Praise Song").

In the *exaltation phase* the people sing out with power in response to key words in these choruses like *great, majestic, worthy, reigns, Lord, mountains,* and so on (e.g., "Our God Reigns"). The pitch spans of the melodies are generally greater than in the other phases.

In the *adoration phase* the dynamics may gradually subside and melody may have a smaller range. The key words may be *you* or *Jesus* (e.g., "Father, I Adore You").

The last phase before the close, the *intimacy phase,* is the quietest and most personal. It's like addressing God as *Abba* or "Daddy" (e.g., "In Moments like These" or "O Lord, You're Beautiful"). This is the "kiss." One meaning of the Greek word for worship, *proskuneo,* is "to turn toward to kiss," as in kissing the feet, the hands, or the lips. Closeness is required for kissing; this closeness can happen in worship only if it is properly prepared for in the phases that precede it.

It all ends with a closing chorus or hymn that leads out of intimacy and helps the people to adjust to the next event in the service.

Using the Five-Phase Style

The five-phase progression has a beautifully balanced and graduated arch shape with the high point in the middle. Use it as handy frame to guide your own worship practice, but *feel free to be flexible with it.*

You can be flexible about time; the same progres-

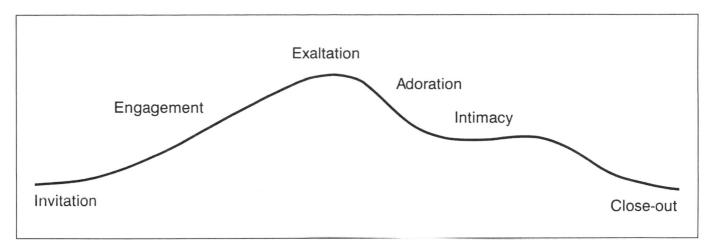

Exaltation

Adoration

Engagement

Intimacy

Invitation

Close-out

The Five-Phase Pattern of Worship. *This pattern of Entrance is used by many Vineyard churches and narrates their movement toward the Service of the Word. Source: Barry Liesch, People in the Presence of God* (Grand Rapids, Mich.: Zondervan, 1988), 92.

sion can be used in either long or short worship sets. You can also be flexible about content; use all choruses, all hymns, or a mixture of hymns and choruses (or even humming and prayers).

You can even rearrange the phases. For example, you can give a single phase like adoration more weight than the others, or limit a set to one or two of the phases. I've experimented successfully with short sets (ten to fifteen minutes) toward the middle of the morning service that focus on adoration pieces exclusively. It works especially well when the set emerges out of a time of prayer. I've also tried moving from exaltation to adoration and vice versa—or even from exaltation to adoration and back to exaltation.

One benefit of the order is that it encourages us not to jump around between categories in a worship set when we select choruses and hymns. This jerking about tends to be confusing and results in a lack of direction. It's like a home decorated with uncoordinated colors, furniture, and paintings.

Another advantage of the progression is that if a group is leading the song service, group members don't need to know the exact sequencing of the individual tunes. They can identify the phase they are in from the lyrics and the progression of songs over time and know how they should be functioning musically to achieve an ensemble effect.

Here is one more thought on linking choruses. Try to find key words and similar thoughts. Many choruses have only one key thought. Two choruses back-to-back that reiterate the key word *love,* for example, will promote a sense of continuity rather

than patchiness. *You* or *Jesus* are other examples of key words.

Barry Liesch[10]

The Four-Phase Tabernacle Style

During the first phase of coming through the gates the congregation may sing a chorus such as "I Will Enter His Gates with Thanksgiving in My Heart." This song may be accompanied by loud shouts of joy and dancing. Once in the inner court, the congregation may continue to sing songs about coming to worship such as "Come Let Us Worship and Bow Down" as well as songs of confession and repentance such as "Change My Heart, Oh God." Next, when the congregation passes into the inner court, songs are sung about God such as "My God How Wonderful Thou Art" and "Turn Your Eyes upon Jesus." Finally when the congregation is brought into the Holy of Holies songs are sung to God such as "I Love You, Lord," "Father, I Adore You," and "Jesus, What a Wonder You Are."

Charismatic churches include the operation of various spiritual gifts throughout all the phases of worship. Many churches are now requiring that any participation from people in the congregation is first approved by a designated elder or staff member who assists the worship leader in releasing these gifts at the proper time in the service.

In charismatic and some contemporary churches, the use of "open worship" such as the "singing the new song," prophetic songs, or singing in the Spirit often precedes or follows some choruses during the

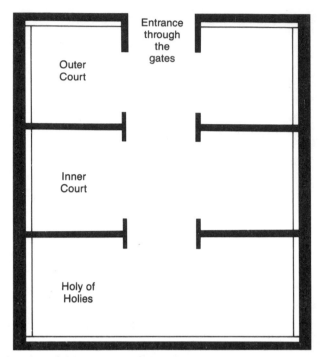

The Fourfold Pattern of the Entrance. Many charismatics and praise and worship communities follow the above pattern of worship, fulfilling the narrative of being brought to the Word. Singing interlaced with Scripture admonitions may take twenty to thirty minutes.

exaltation and adoration phases. Building on one or a few chords, the congregation is encouraged to lift their own personal songs to the Lord with the rest of the congregation. Sometimes a person may even have a prophetic song for the congregation, where he or she sings a melodic message of insight or encouragement. This must be accomplished only by the most trusted worshipers.

Churches involved in long periods of praise, worship, and the operation of spiritual gifts must be cautioned against seeing this section of the service as the total expression of worship. Recently, many churches have become aware of richness brought to worship by bringing back certain traditional dynamics of liturgy and structure.

197 • A PATTERN FOR THE CONVERGENCE OF TRADITIONAL AND CONTEMPORARY WORSHIP

Worship that draws on liturgical and historical resources as well as charismatic and contemporary sources will vary from church to church. Churches that are liturgical will likely continue to follow traditional styles but may incorporate contemporary elements at appropriate places. Likewise, char-

ismatic or contemporary churches may find certain liturgical practices helpful and will incorporate them in their worship. Below is a basic pattern of convergence worship. Each church will have to experiment with this pattern to find a style and content most suitable to its character.

Acts of Entrance

The Gathering. The gathering happens as God's people come together to worship. It may begin ten or fifteen minutes before the starting time of worship and contain one or more of the following acts:

    Informal singing of praise choruses
    Formal organ prelude
    Instrumental music
    Informal greetings
    Announcements
    Words of welcome
    Rehearsal of congregational music
    Quiet meditation

Opening Acts of Worship. The opening acts of worship are characterized by a joyful spirit and a narrative quality. They gleefully fulfill the task of bringing the congregation into the presence of God and readying them to hear the Word of God. Because the opening acts are a joyful journey to the Word, instructive elements of worship are inappropriate. The opening acts of worship may include one or more of the following:

Entrance Hymn or Song. Because the entrance into worship is an act of joy, the hymn or song may be accompanied by many musical instruments such as organ, piano, synthesizer, band, trumpets, and flutes, and with a procession of the choir(s) with banners and dance.

Greeting. The greeting is a simple word of welcome or biblical greeting such as "The grace of our Lord Jesus Christ be with you." More charismatic churches may engage in the holy shout to the Lord.

Invocation or Gathering Prayer. The invocation is a prayer calling upon God to be present in the worship of the people.

Confession and Acts of Pardon. Some churches place the confession and pardon in the Entrance, others in the Service of the Word after the prayers. Confessions and acts of pardon may range from written prayers to informal prayer or silent meditation. In some churches the confession and pardon may be incorporated into the praise choruses.

Acts of Praise. In the acts of praise a great variety of songs of praise may occur, ranging from ancient acts of praise such as _Gloria in Excelsis Deo_ or canticles such as the _Te Deum_ to anthems, psalms, or praise choruses that lead the congregation from the outer court through the inner court to the Holy of Holies. These acts of praise may conclude with a time of singing in the Spirit or singing individual words of praise together.

Opening Prayer (Collect of the Day). The opening prayer brings closure to the Acts of Entrance and is a transition to the Service of the Word. The theme is usually expressed in the opening prayer. In some churches the opening prayer may be the singing in the Spirit, as above.

Service of the Word

The Service of the Word is the central act of worship. The Acts of Entrance have brought the people to the Word where they will dwell. The character of the acts of worship in the Service of the Word is instructional. The basic structure of the Service of the Word is proclamation and response. God speaks and the people respond. The mood of the Service of the Word shifts from the mood of the Entrance to a more meditative mood.

The Service of the Word includes the following:

Scripture Readings. The focal point of the Service of the Word is the reading and proclamation of Scripture. Two or three Scripture readings may be read (Old Testament, Epistle, Gospel) interspersed with psalms, canticles, or choruses. Scripture content may be communicated through reader's theater, drama, or storytelling. For example:

Formal Style

Old Testament Reading
Responsorial Psalm
Epistle
Canticle or Anthem
Gospel

or

Informal Style

First Reading
Chorus(es) Response
Second Reading

Sermon. A text or the theme of the text is interpreted.

Response to the Word. The structure of the Service of the Word is proclamation and response. The people now respond to the Word using a variety of possible responses such as:

- Nicene Creed or some other appropriate affirmation of faith drawn from Scripture.
- Discussion and application of the sermon in small groups of four to six people seated near each other.
- Hymn of response.
- Invitation to receive Jesus, to rededicate one's life to the Lord, or to come for baptism or church membership.

Sometimes opportunity is given for other members of the ministry team of the church to give additional insights, clarification, or specific application to the message preached. Often called "Prophetic Responses," these are usually three-to-five minute exhortations based on the insights and impressions from the Spirit received during the message.

Many contemporary churches are now viewing the time of response as more than a traditional altar call; it has become a "laboratory of the Holy Spirit." Often time is given for the Lord to direct in offering specific ministries to people who are experiencing physical, emotional, or spiritual problems.

Prayer of the People. The congregation, having responded to the Word of God, is now ready to present its prayers to God. In some congregations people with special needs or prayer requests will come forward to a kneeling bench. Prayers may be offered in a number of ways such as:

- Group Prayer: The people may stand and turn to form small groups of four to six people.
- Bidding Prayers: The prayer leader says: "I bid you to pray for . . . ," and the people offer prayers aloud.
- Litany Prayers: A prayer is said and the people respond with a written response or with "Lord, hear our prayer" or other appropriate words.
- Pastoral Prayer (sometimes called "The Long Prayer").

- Intervention Prayers: The leader invites people to name specific burdens for intercession or personal needs aloud, followed by prayer from another individual about the situation.
- Directed Prayer: After the leader names a specific theme or topic to be prayed for, the people pray quietly to themselves. The leader then introduces another topic. Often this type of prayer is accompanied by specific prayer ministry in the front of the church offered quietly by a prayer team. The prayer may end with a prayer of confession and forgiveness (unless done in the Acts of Entrance).

Passing of the Peace. The people offer the peace of the Lord to each other as they shake hands or embrace saying, "The Peace of the Lord be with you."

Offering/Offertory. Having been reconciled with God and each other, the people now bring gifts of thanksgiving. As the collection of money is taken, the choir may sing an anthem or the congregation may sing a hymn. If the Table of the Lord is to follow, the bread and wine may be brought at this time. In some free churches the individual cups are prepared in advance, but a loaf (and a symbolic chalice) may be brought forward at the offering.

——— The Service of Thanksgiving ———

The Service of the Table and/or Thanksgiving is by nature a response to the Service of the Word, the central act of worship. In the early church, it was normative to celebrate the Eucharist weekly. (The word *Eucharist* means "thanksgiving," and in the early church it was called the great thanksgiving.) Renewing churches are moving toward the practice of weekly Eucharist as advocated by the Reformers. Where it is not yet the custom to celebrate the Eucharist weekly, contemporary worshiping communities sing songs of praise and thanksgiving followed by the Lord's Prayer. The mood of thanksgiving is celebrative, not sober. The acts at the Service of the Table include one or more of the following:

Thanks at the Table of the Lord. Preparation of the bread and the cup. The pastor invites the people to lift their hearts in praise to God. In many churches the ancient invitation to thanksgiving has been restored. It is:

The Lord be with you (or, God be with you).
And also with you.
Lift up your hearts.
We lift them up to the Lord (or, to God).
Let us give thanks unto our Lord God (or, unto the Lord our God).
It is right to give him (God) thanks and praise.

Preface Prayer. The pastor prays a brief prayer indicating that the earthly community has joined the heavenly community around the throne of God with all the angels and archangels.

Sanctus (Holy, Holy, Holy). The congregation now joins the heavenly choir in singing the new song. Formal congregations may sing the ancient *Sanctus*. More informal congregations may sing contemporary versions of the "Holy, Holy, Holy."

Thanksgiving. The pastor prays a prayer of thanksgiving for the bread and the wine.

Institution Narrative. The pastor says the Words of Institution over the bread and the wine, lifting the bread and cup for all to see.

Memorial. The pastor says Words of Remembrance such as "This do in remembrance of me" and/or words that recall the passion, the tomb, and the Resurrection.

Acclamation. The people may respond with the words of the mystery of faith:

> **Christ has died,**
> **Christ is risen,**
> **Christ will come again.**

Invocation of the Holy Spirit. The pastor may pray for the Holy Spirit to come down upon the people to gather them into one and to confirm them in the faith.

The Communion. The pastor invites the people to receive the bread and the cup. The people may come forward to receive at the Table or remain in their seats. The people sing songs of praise and thanksgiving. Hymns or praise choruses expressing the joy of the resurrection and exaltation of Christ may be sung.

Special Prayer. Elders and other ministers of the church may administer prayer with the anointing of oil and the laying on of hands. The people may come forward to stations of prayer or, after receiving the bread and the wine, they may remain at the altar rail or step aside to the station of prayer.

Closing Prayer. The pastor leads in a closing prayer of thanksgiving.

Thanks without the Table of the Lord. On those Sundays when the Table of the Lord is not celebrated, the people may give thanks through a prayer of thanksgiving or through hymns or choruses of praise and thanksgiving. This time of thanks may be concluded with the Lord's Prayer if it has not been prayed previously.

The Acts of Dismissal

The Acts of Dismissal bring closure to public worship. The pastor should send the people forth in joyful recognition of their responsible service to the world. The mood is one of joy and the sense is that of going forth. The Acts of Dismissal include one or more of the following:

Announcements. If announcements have not been given in the gathering, they may be given here. As the people go forth they are reminded of the activities of the people of God during the week.

Benediction (or Blessing). The people are blessed with a word from God that empowers them for life in the world.

Dismissal Hymn or Song. The hymn signals going forth. If the Entrance Hymn was accompanied by a procession with music, banners, dance, etc., the Dismissal Hymns should do the same.

Words of Dismissal. These words close the worship and send the people forth. For example:

Go forth into the world to love and serve the Lord.
Thanks be to God! Alleluia! Alleluia!

In some congregations the service ends with clapping to the Lord.

Robert E. Webber[11]

SIX

Resources for the Acts of Entrance

By using the following resources, a congregation may fulfill the very purpose of the Entrance: coming into the presence of God and preparing themselves to hear the Word of the Lord. Nevertheless, it must be remembered that such resources alone do not fulfill the purposes of the Entrance. They are the forms through which the Spirit becomes present. Consequently they are to be offered in the same way a prayer is offered—in a spirit full of joy and enthusiasm at being in the presence of God.

The resources of this section are primarily for churches that follow a traditional pattern of worship. Contemporary worship generally fulfills the Acts of Entrance with songs and choruses that often are displayed with overhead or slide projectors. Contemporary worship leaders, however, may wish to study traditional acts of worship as a guide to selecting songs that bring worshipers into God's presence.

The following four chapters include a few words about seasonal variations in worship. For further models of seasonal elements presented in greater detail, see Volume 5: The Services of the Christian Year.

198 • WHAT DOES AN ENTRANCE DO?

The acts of worship in the Entrance assemble the people and prepare them to hear the Word of God.

In the Entrance the people are gathered together through acts of worship that represent both the beginning of worship and the formation of the people of God into a worshiping community. The commonly accepted parts of the Entrance in worship renewal today, in liturgical and most traditional Protestant communities, include: the gathering, the Entrance song, a greeting, call to worship, a confession of sin (optional), an act of praise, and opening prayer of the day. Because the spirit of Entrance is doxological (joyful) and not instructive, care should be taken to preserve the joyful spirit of the Entrance through acts of worship that emphasize the act of coming together. Even in Lent, when the Entrance may be silent, the spirit of joy can remain as an inward flame of expectation and longing.

The order and content of these acts of opening may vary from church to church and the content will change slightly from one season of the Christian year to another. The purpose of these Entrance acts must always be kept in mind. Their function is narrative. They order the experience and story that brings the people into the presence of God and forms them into a joyful people ready to hear the Word of God. For this reason the Entrance is usually brief and moves quickly, with the people standing for the entire time (except possibly for the gathering).

To understand the variety of Entrance styles, see the models of renewing worship in chapter 4 of this volume.

199 • THE PRELUDE

The word prelude *derives from the Latin* praelludium *and means "to play beforehand." It is a key musical piece in the Entrance.*

In Protestant worship the prelude refers to the music played before the formal worship begins.

This music is often a classical piece or an arrangement of a hymn, anthem, chorale, or other church music, usually performed on the organ. In many contemporary approaches to worship the prelude has been replaced by gathering songs. However, it is possible to sing gathering songs, then have a prelude before the Entrance hymn.

200 • THE GATHERING

The gathering allows the people to take their seats and ready themselves for worship.

Gathering is used to signal the congregation that their attention should begin moving from each other to the worship leaders.

Establish a normative pattern of gathering that can become a familiar signal to the congregation. In some churches where no processional is held, the pastors enter the sanctuary and kneel to pray, indicating that worship has begun. In other places, the worship team begins by playing and singing some "pre-worship" music that helps the congregation focus toward worship.

The gathering may include such things as greetings to friends and acquaintances, announcements, practice of portions of worship, the act of being seated in quiet reverence, prayerful preparation before the service begins, and an organ prelude or community song. While there are no resources as such to deal with the gathering, there are several principles that may be helpful.

- Regard the entire act of gathering as part of worship. Place the word _gathering_ in the bulletin. Encourage the people to see the time of coming together as a vital element of the worship experience.
- Establish a tradition that signals the end of the gathering. In some churches the gathering is followed by a brief explanation of the service and/or a time to practice an antiphon or some other unfamiliar aspect of the service.
- Observe a brief time of silence before the Entrance song. This is an appropriate time to use the traditional introit, prelude, or sung or instrumental music to bring the congregation to quietness and a state of preparedness.

201 • GATHERING SONG(S)

Gathering songs are songs which are sung as people take their places in the worship space.

In a contemporary worship style the gathering song(s) replace the traditional prelude. As people are coming into the worship space, a song leader may be leading the congregation in singing. This singing is most often that of praise songs or folk songs, but can also include hymns. The music is usually upbeat and spirited to express the joy of coming into the presence of God. Examples of the gathering songs are:

Hymns
"Brethren, We Have Met to Worship"
"Come We That Love the Lord"
"Praise the Lord! O Heavens Adore Him"
"I Will Sing of the Mercies"
"The Gathering"

Choruses
"We Bring a Sacrifice of Praise"
"It Is Good to Give Thanks"
"All Hail King Jesus"
"Praise the Name of Jesus"
"We Want to Bless You"
"Come and Worship"
"Glorify Your Name"
"Clap Your Hands"

202 • THE ENTRANCE SONG

The Entrance song or hymn often signals the beginning of the formal acts of worship, particularly the procession and the entrance of the leaders of worship.

The purpose of the Entrance song is to focus the mind, heart, and spirit of the worshiping community on the praise of God. The Entrance song also accompanies the action of the ministers, choir, and others who process into their places. Consequently, it is best to sing familiar music to convey the sense of coming before the Lord.

The Entrance song(s) and the entrance of ministers, readers, and choir is a very important part of worship because it signals the community coming before God. The entrance of clergy and choir—whether formal, from the back of the sanctuary, or casual, from side doors—should symbolize more than minister and choir taking their seats. In many worship renewal churches the procession is being revived because of the vital symbolic significance it expresses of coming before the Lord.

During Lent, in many traditional churches the Entrance song is omitted in favor of a silent procession, or is preceded by a penitential rite directed from the rear of the congregation.

Examples of the Entrance song are as follows:

Hymns
"Praise to the Lord, the Almighty"
"Immortal, Invisible, God Only Wise"
"Alleluia! Sing to Jesus"
"Holy, Holy, Holy, Lord God Almighty"
"A Mighty Fortress"
"O God Our Help in Ages Past"
"When Morning Gilds the Skies"
"The God of Abraham Praise"
"O Christ, the Word Incarnate"
"Crown Him with Many Crowns"
"All Creatures of Our God and King"
"All Hail the Power of Jesus' Name"
"O for a Thousand Tongues to Sing"
"Praise My Soul the King of Heaven"

Choruses
"All Hail King Jesus"
"Be Exalted, O God"
"Enter into His Gates"
"Hail to the King"
"I Extol You"
"Let There Be Glory, Honor, and Praises"
"To Thee We Ascribe Glory"
"We Bring a Sacrifice of Praise"
"Good Morning, Jesus"
"Praise Ye the Lord"
"The Lord Is Present"
"Hymn of Glory"
"This, This Is the Day"

203 ✦ Guidelines for the Procession

A procession is an act of movement in worship by a group of people for the sake of all. In the Entrance, the procession symbolizes the entire congregation coming before the Lord.

General norms for the conduct of the procession are as follows:

a. The people who are to process into the sanctuary line up in order of entrance at the back of the church or some other convenient and inconspicuous place.

b. The order of personnel in the Entrance should be:
   • the cross bearer (if a cross is used)
   • acolytes or candle bearers (if used)
   • the banner carriers (if banners are used)
   • the Scripture readers (who may carry a Bible or Gospel book or lectionary)
   • the choir
   • the ministers; in liturgical churches deacons first (carrying Gospel book) then priest(s) or pastor(s).

c. As the Entrance song is sung the procession enters.

d. The people processing will best signify the meaning of the entrance as they:
   • sing heartily, offering leadership to the worshiping community.
   • assume a demeanor of prayerful reverence.
   • do not look around or cast greetings. This is not a show in which persons in the procession are on display.

The procession, when done in the right spirit, provides strong leadership to the beginning of worship and calls forth hearty singing from the people. This profound and joyous sense of coming before the Lord establishes a spirit of joyful anticipation that give life to worship.

During the seasons of the Christian year, it is important to use music, banners, and colors that express the theme of the season (see Volume 5: *The Services of the Christian Year*).

204 ✦ The Greeting

The greeting in worship is a Christian exchange between the worship leader and the people.

After the Entrance song is completed and the minister, choir, readers, and others are in their places, worship continues with the simple and straightforward act of greeting extended to the people. It is best to keep this section simple and short.

In terms of spatial communication, worship leaders have found that it is best not to do the greeting standing in front of the pulpit, if possible. This is true of other parts of the Entrance as well. The constant movement from chair to pulpit by the person or persons leading the Entrance does not adequately communicate the sense that worship is an

The Procession. *The procession establishes the meaning of worship as entering into the Lord's presence. The order of procession personnel generally includes (a) cross-bearer, (b) acolytes or candle-bearers, (c) banner carriers, (d) Scripture readers with Bible, (e) choir, (f) clergy (in liturgical churches, deacons first, carrying in Gospel Book, followed by priest(s) or pastor(s).*

action going on between God and the entire worshiping community (including the leader). When the action takes place between the pulpit and the congregation, it symbolizes communication between leader and congregation. Therefore, churches have found it is best to lead from a chair set sideways on the bema (platform). Standing, the leader may turn at the conclusion of the Entrance song, face the congregation, and say in a loud, clear, and cheerful voice, "Good morning," to which the people respond, "Good morning." Or, "The Lord be with you," to which the people respond, "And also with you." In this way the bodily position of the leader works together with the words to communicate what is being said. Symbolic action and verbal communication work in concert to establish the meaning of the greeting. Examples of the greeting are below:

Traditional Forms of the Greeting

> The LORD be with you.
> **And also with you.** (Ruth 2:4)

or

The grace of our Lord Jesus Christ
be with you all.
And also with you. (2 Thess. 3:18)

or

Grace and peace to you
from God our Father
and from the Lord Jesus Christ.
And also with you. (Rom. 1:17)

or

Other passages of Scripture that can be used as a greeting to the congregation:

2 Corinthians 13:14	2 Peter 1:2
2 Timothy 1:2	Revelation 1:4-5

Contemporary Forms of the Greeting

A greeting can often be prepared from the Scripture texts of the day. The greeting works best when it is short. Take a phrase out of one of the Scripture readings and put it into a form of greeting similar to the examples below.

Leader: Brothers and sisters in Christ,
Today I greet you with the words of St. Paul taken from today's Epistle reading, Ephesians 1:9: God has "made known to us the mystery of His will."

People: **Thanks be to God.**

or

May God be gracious to us and bless us.
Amen.
May his face be illuminated for us
Amen.
May his salvation come upon us in Jesus, his Son, our Lord.
Amen.

(Adapted from Lucien Deiss, *Reflections on His Word, Cycle A* [Schiller Park, Ill.: World Library Publications, 1980], 158.)

In the name of the Father
who loves us from all eternity
(Eph. 2:4)
and who calls us;
In the name of the Son
who knocks down the wall of hostility
(Eph. 2:14-15)
and gathers us all into a single new man (creature);

In the name of the Holy Spirit
who makes the peace and the joy of
    heaven
flourish on our earth:
May the grace and the joy of God be
    always with us.
Brothers and sisters,
let us praise the Lord Jesus!
He is our Good Shepherd (Ps. 23).
He gathers us together today for the
    feast of his Word;
he sets for us the table of his
    Eucharist.
May his grace and goodness
    accompany us
all the days of our lives
and open for us the door of the
    eternal feast!

(Adapted from Lucien Deiss, *Reflections on His Word: Sunday Prayers, Cycle B* [Schiller Park, Ill.: World Library Publications, 1981], 171.)

205 ✦ THE CALL TO WORSHIP

A call to worship is directed to the people by God through the worship leader. It is an act that brings the worshiping community into being.

The call to worship is directed toward the people. It is a call to focus mind, heart, and intention on the worship of God. Therefore, it is brief and emotive, not lengthy and intellectual. It has the character of an acclamation, not a teaching. One exception to this rule may occur during Lent when the character of the preparation changes significantly to convey the mood of sobriety and identification with Christ through the use of penitential litany.

The call to worship is not a time for responsive readings. Responsive readings are kept for the Service of the Word when content and instruction constitute the goal of the worshiping community. In the Entrance the goal is to come before the Lord. Consequently the acts of worship such as a call to worship are characterized by simplicity and brevity.

Below are two examples. One, an antiphonal reading, is an example of *what not to do*. It is too long, tends to be instructive, and requires reading. This instructive form is more appropriate for the Service of the Word. The second, a short proclamatory statement, is more appropriate for the call to worship, fitting the nature of the call which is doxological, not instructive.

Avoid This Kind of Call to Worship

Leader: Lord, we have gathered together today to worship you.

People: **We come from many walks and conditions of life. Some of us are discouraged, some of us battle illness, some of us have experienced financial loss.**

Leader: But we come O God to worship you.

People: **We bring our joys and hurts, our struggles and victories, our losses and gains to you, O Lord.**

Leader: Be present to us, O Lord, and receive the worship we offer you in Christ's name.

Strive for This Kind of Call to Worship

Leader: Blessed be God, Father, Son, and Holy Spirit.

People: **And blessed be God's kingdom forever and ever.**

Traditional Examples of the Call to Worship

Blessed be God; Father, Son, and Holy
    Spirit
**And blessed be his kingdom, now and
    forever. Amen.**

or

This is the day the LORD has made.
Let us be glad and rejoice in it.
    (Ps. 118:24)

or

Glorify the LORD with me;
Let us exalt his name together. (Ps. 34:3)

or

Give thanks to the LORD,
for he is good;
His love endures forever. (Ps. 106:1)

or

The earth is the LORD's, and everything in
    it,
the world and all who live in it. (Ps. 24:1)

or

Clap your hands, all you nations!
Shout to God with cries of joy. (Ps. 47:1)

or

O LORD, open ours lips
and our mouths will declare your praise.
(Ps. 51:15)

or

The LORD is in his holy temple.
Let all the earth be silent before him.
(Hab. 2:20)

Contemporary Examples of the Call to Worship

The call to worship may be written from contemporary sources such as a familiar song or from the Scriptures of the day, particularly the psalm. When preparing your own call to worship, keep in mind the following guidelines:

- Structure the call to worship.
- Keep it brief so it functions as an acclamation, not an instruction.

Here is an example of a call to worship that adapts material from the Vesper service of the Orthodox church. In this example the Proclamation is made in the leader's first line. All the remaining parts are response.

Leader:	Blessed is our God always; now and ever, and unto ages of ages.
People:	**O come, let us worship and fall down before God our King.**
Leader:	O come let us worship and fall down before Christ our King and our God.
All:	**Amen.**

or

God created us;
Praise God.
The Son recreates us;
Glory to the Son.
The Spirit creates new life in us;
Honor to the Spirit.
Praise, glory, and honor
To the triune God,
The cause of our worship,
The source of our joy.
We will ever praise the triune God!

(E. Lee Phillips, *Breaking Silence before the Lord* [Grand Rapids: Baker Book House, 1986], 23)

or

O sing to the Lord a new song; tell of
God's salvation from day today.
For great is the Lord, and greatly to be
praised; God is to be feared above
all gods.
Worship the Lord in holy array;
tremble before God, all the earth!
Honor and majesty are before God;
strength and beauty are in God's
sanctuary.

(James G. Kirk, *When We Gather: Year A* [Philadelphia: Geneva Press, 1983], 26)

Examples for Seasons of the Christian Year

Advent:

Repent, for the kingdom of heaven is near.
Everything God says we will do. (Matt. 3:2)
Prepare the way for the LORD;
Make straight in the wilderness a highway for
our God. (Isa. 40:3)

Christmas:

I bring you good news of great joy that will be for all the people. Today in the town of David a savior has been born to you; he is Christ the Lord. (Luke 2:10-11)
Thanks be to God.

Epiphany:

"My name will be great among the nations, from the rising to the setting of the sun. In every place incense and pure offerings will be brought to my name, because my name will be great among the nations," says the LORD Almighty. (Mal. 1:11)
We worship and adore you, King of the Universe.

Lent:

Bless the Lord who forgives all our sins.
His mercy endures forever.

or

Rend your heart
and not your garments.

Return to the LORD your God,
for he is gracious and compassionate,
slow to anger and abounding in love. (Joel 2:13)
Everything God asks us we will do.

or

The sacrifices of God are a broken spirit;
A broken and contrite heart,
O God, you will not despise. (Ps. 51:17)
Receive our repentance, O Lord.

or

I will set out and go back to my father and say to
him
**Father, I have sinned against heaven and against
you.**
I am no longer worthy to be called your son.
(Luke 15:18-19)

Good Friday:

Is it nothing to you, all you who pass by?
Look around and see.
Is there any suffering like my suffering
that was inflicted on me . . .
in the day of his fierce anger? (Lam. 1:12)

Easter:

[Alleluia.] Christ is risen.
The Lord is risen indeed. [Alleluia.] (Mark 16:6;
Luke 24:34)

or

[Alleluia.] He is risen.
He is risen indeed! [Alleluia.]

or

[Alleluia.] Christ is risen.
Christ is risen indeed! [Alleluia.]

Ascension:

Since we have a great high priest who has gone
through the heavens . . .
Let us then approach the throne of grace with
confidence
So that we may receive mercy and find grace to
help us in our time of need. (Heb. 4:14-16)
Thanks be to God.

Pentecost Sunday:

You will receive power when the Holy Spirit
comes on you; and you will be my witnesses in
Jerusalem, and in all Judea and Samaria, and to
the ends of the earth. (Acts 1:8)
Thanks be to God.

Thanksgiving Day:

Honor the LORD with your wealth,
With the firstfruits of all your crops;
Then your barns will be filled to overflowing,
And your vats will brim over with new wine.
(Prov. 3:9-10)

206 ✦ THE INVOCATION (OR GATHERING PRAYER)

*The invocation calls upon God to be present to the worshiping
community.*

The word *invocation* is derived from the Latin
invocatio and means the act or process of petition-
ing for help or support. In worship there are three
times when a prayer of invocation is appropriate:
(1) in the Entrance, when we ask God to be present
in our worship; (2) in the Service of the Word, when
we ask God to be present through preaching (sometimes called the prayer of illumination); (3) in the
prayers of the Table, when we ask God to send the
Holy Spirit upon the people and gifts of bread and
wine for the confirmation of faith in truth (called
the *epiclesis*).

The Entrance invocation calls on God to be present to the worshiping community and usually follows the call to worship. It is very brief and is often
preceded by the traditional *salutation* to prayer:

The Lord be with you.
And also with you.
Let us pray.

The salutation engages the people in prayer and
expresses the dialogic nature of worship. It is spoken quickly and firmly, and the people respond
strongly. The use of this short response, when approached in the right spirit, helps to build a sense of
unity and expectancy in the congregation. After the
words "Let us pray" it is best to keep silence for a
moment, then pray. The time of silence allows for a
measure of stillness to fall on the congregation before prayer.

Spatially, the invocation, like the greeting, is said
while standing sideways to the congregation. This is
prayer addressed to God, not to the congregation.
Consequently, the bodily position corresponds to
the purpose of the prayer.

Traditional Examples of the Invocation

> Almighty God,
> to whom all hearts are open,
> all desires known,
> and from whom no secrets are hid:
> cleanse the thoughts of our hearts
> by the inspiration of your Holy Spirit,
> that we may perfectly love you
> and worthily magnify your holy name;
> through Christ our Lord.
> **Amen.**

(*The Gregorian Sacramentary,* seventh century; as adapted in *The Book of Common Prayer*)

or

> O God,
> who makest us glad with the weekly
>   remembrance
> of the glorious resurrection of thy Son our Lord:
> Grant us this day such blessing through our
>   worship of thee,
> that the days to come may be spent in thy favor;
> through the same Jesus Christ our Lord. Amen.

(The Book of Common Prayer)

Contemporary Examples of the Invocation

> Father in heaven,
> from the days of Abraham and Moses
> until this gathering of your church in prayer,
> you have formed a people in the image of your
>   Son.
> Bless this people with the gift of your kingdom.
> May we serve you with our every desire
> and show love for one another
> even as you have loved us.
> Grant this through Christ our Lord.

or

> Father in heaven,
> form in us the likeness of your Son
> and deepen his life within us.
> Send us as witnesses of gospel joy
> Into a world of fragile peace and broken
>   promises.
> Touch the hearts of all men with your love
> that they in turn may love one another.
> We ask this through Christ our Lord.

or

> In faith and love we ask you, Father,
> to watch over your family gathered here.
> In your mercy and loving kindness
> no thought of ours is left unguarded,
> no tear unheeded, no joy unnoticed.
> Through the prayer of Jesus
> may the blessings promised to the poor in spirit
> lead us to the treasures of your heavenly
>   kingdom.
> We ask this in the name of Jesus the Lord.

(*Christian Prayer* [New York: Catholic Book Publishing Co., 1976])

Directions for Preparing an Invocation ("Collect"). For those who wish to prepare an invocation, there are four steps to keep in mind. They are:

Direction	Example
1. Begin with a salutation to God.	Almighty God,
2. Continue with a description of God in which some aspect of God's character or action is extolled.	To whom all hearts are open, all desires known, and from whom no secrets are hid:
3. Next comes the petition, the heart of the invocation. The petition is often followed by a statement of the end or purpose of the petition.	Cleanse the thoughts of our hearts by the inspiration of your Holy Spirit, that we may perfectly love you and worthily magnify your holy Name;
4. Conclude with an ascription of praise.	Through Christ our Lord.

Invocations may often be prepared out of the Scripture texts for the day.

Invocation for Seasons of the Christian Year

Advent:

> Father in heaven,
> our hearts desire the warmth of your love
> and our minds are searching for the light of your
>   Word.
> Increase our longing for Christ our Savior
> and give us the strength to grow in love,
> that the dawn of his coming
> may find us rejoicing in his presence
> and welcoming the light of his truth.
> We ask this in the name of Jesus the Lord.

Christmas Eve:

Come, Lord Jesus,
do not delay;
give new courage to your people who trust in
your love.
By your coming, raise us to the joy of your
kingdom,
where you live and reign with the Father and the
Holy Spirit,
one God, forever and ever.

Christmas:

Almighty God and Father of light,
a child is born for us and a son is given to us.
Your eternal Word leaped down from heaven
in the silent watches of the night,
and now your church is filled with wonder
at the nearness of her God.
Open our hearts to receive his life
and increase our vision with the rising of dawn,
that our lives may be filled with his glory and his
peace,
who lives and reigns forever and ever.

Epiphany:

Father of light, unchanging God,
today you reveal to men [people] of faith
the resplendent fact of the Word made flesh.
Your light is strong,
your love is near;
draw us beyond the limits that this world
imposes,
to the life where your Spirit makes all life
complete.
We ask this through Christ our Lord.

Ash Wednesday:

Lord,
protect us in our struggle against evil.
As we begin the discipline of Lent,
make this day holy by our self-denial.
Grant this through our Lord Jesus Christ, your
Son,
who lives and reigns with you and the Holy
Spirit,
one God forever and ever.

Lent:

Father,
through our observance of Lent,
help us to understand the meaning

of your Son's death and resurrection,
and teach us to reflect it in our lives.
Grant this through our Lord Jesus Christ, your
Son,
who lives and reigns with you and the Holy
Spirit,
one God, forever and ever.

Palm Sunday:

Almighty, ever-living God,
you have given the human race Jesus Christ our
Savior
as a model of humility.
He fulfilled your will
by becoming mortal and giving his life on the
cross.
Help us to bear witness to you
by following his example of suffering
and make us worthy to share in his resurrection.
We ask this through our Lord Jesus Christ, your
Son,
who lives and reigns with you and the Holy
Spirit,
one God, forever and ever.

Maundy Thursday:

Father,
for your glory and our salvation
you appointed Jesus Christ eternal High Priest.
May the people he gained for you by his blood
come to share in the power of his cross and
resurrection
by celebrating his memorial in this Eucharist,
for he lives and reigns with you and the Holy
Spirit,
one God, forever and ever.

Good Friday:

Father,
look with love upon your faithful people,
the love which our Lord Jesus Christ showed us
when he delivered himself to evil people
and suffered the agony of the cross,
for he lives and reigns with you and the Holy
Spirit,
one God, forever and ever.

Holy Saturday:

All-powerful and ever-living God,
your only Son went down among the dead
and rose again in glory.
In your goodness

raise up your faithful people,
buried with him in baptism,
to be one with him
in the eternal life of heaven,
where he lives and reigns with you and the Holy
    Spirit,
one God, forever and ever.

Easter:

God our Father, Creator of all,
today is the day of Easter joy.
This is the morning on which the Lord appeared
    to men
[those] who had begun to lose hope
and opened their eyes to what the Scriptures
    foretold:
that first he must die, and then he would rise
and ascend into his Father's glorious presence.
May the risen Lord
breathe on our minds and open our eyes
that we may know him in the breaking of bread,
and follow him in his risen life.
Grant this through Christ our Lord.

Pentecost:

Father in heaven,
fifty days have celebrated the fullness
of the mystery of your revealed love.
See your people gathered in prayer,
open to receive the Spirit's flame.
May it come to rest in our hearts
and disperse the divisions of word and tongue.
With one voice and one song
may we praise your name in joy and
    thanksgiving.
Grant this through Christ our Lord.

(*Christian Prayer* [New York: Catholic Book Publishing Co., 1976])

207 • THE ACT OF PRAISE

*The act of praise recognizes God's transcendence and char-
acter.*

After the confession of sin and words of forgiveness, the people are ready to offer an act of praise.
Traditionally the act of praise has been either the
Gloria in Excelsis Deo or the *Gloria Patri.* The act
of praise may also be an appropriate hymn, canticle,
psalm, or Scripture praise song.

In the Western churches, the Gloria is generally
dropped during penitential seasons such as Advent
and Lent. The loss of this gladsome hymn of praise
is a reminder of the need to repent and prepare for
the coming of Christ (Advent) and for his death
(Lent). (Bold type indicates the people's response.)

Traditional Examples
of the Act of Praise

The *Gloria in Excelsis Deo.* The *Gloria in Excelsis
Deo,* which is also known as the Greater Doxology,
dates back to the fourth-century church and,
through the centuries, has been established as the
most appropriate ascription of praise to the triune
God used in the Entrance. In much of contemporary worship renewal this Gloria has been restored
to its original place and is rapidly gaining universal
use in all the churches. It may be said or sung. Most
recent hymn books contain one or more tunes.

This Greater Doxology expresses the meaning of
coming before God as in Isaiah 6:1-7 and seeing
God in all splendor and glory. While it is highly
recommended that the Greater Doxology be used
in the Entrance, it can be substituted by a suitable
hymn or canticle that expresses God's glory. A substitute for the Greater Doxology may be used on
occasion; however, only those substitutes that truly
worship God in his majesty should be used.

Traditional Language Version:

Glory be to God on high,
and on earth peace, good will toward men.
We praise thee, we bless thee,
we worship thee,
we glorify thee,
we give thanks to thee for thy great glory,
O Lord God, heavenly King, God the Father
    Almighty.
O Lord, the only-begotten Son, Jesus Christ;
O Lord God, Lamb of God, Son of the Father,
that takest away the sins of the world,
have mercy upon us.
Thou that takest away the sins of the world,
receive our prayer,
Thou that sittest at the right hand of God the
    Father,
have mercy upon us.
For thou only art holy;
thou only art the Lord;
thou only, O Christ,
with the Holy Ghost,

art most high in the glory of God the Father.
Amen.

Contemporary Language Version:

> Glory to God in the highest,
>   and peace to his people on earth.
> Lord God, heavenly King,
> almighty God and Father,
>   we worship you, we give you thanks,
>   we praise you for your glory.
> Lord Jesus Christ, only Son of the Father,
> Lord God, Lamb of God,
> you take away the sin of the world:
>   have mercy on us;
> you are seated at the right hand of the Father:
>   receive our prayer.
> For you alone are the Holy One,
> you alone are the Lord,
> you alone are the Most High,
>   Jesus Christ,
>   with the Holy Spirit,
>   in the glory of God the Father. Amen.

Current tunes are found in many of the new hymnals. For example, see *The Hymnal 1982* (New York: Church Hymnal Corporation, 1982), S201, S202, S203, S204.

The *Gloria Patri*. The *Gloria Patri,* known as the Lesser Doxology, was added as an ascription of praise offered to the Trinity at the end of the psalms and canticles. However, many Protestant churches have given this shorter form of the Gloria an independent place in worship. Its purpose, like that of the Greater Doxology, is to praise the triune God. In the spiritual rhythm of the Entrance it normally comes after the confession of sin and before the collect or opening prayer of the day. When the Gloria in Excelsis Deo is not used, the more simple form is an appropriate replacement.

> Glory be to the Father
> and to the Son,
> and to the Holy Ghost;
> As it was in the beginning,
> is now, and ever shall be
> world without end. Amen.

Contemporary Examples of the Act of Praise

One or more of the following choruses expresses the acts of praise intended by the more traditional Glorias. (New choruses that may fit are being written constantly. Check current song books and resources for up-to-date songs that may be used as acts of praise.)

> "Be Exalted, O God"
> "Blessing, Glory, and Honor"
> "Glorify Thy Name"
> "I Exalt Thee"
> "I Extol Thee"
> "To Thee We Ascribe Glory"

Canticles Used as an Act of Praise (said or sung)

A Song of Praise *(Benedictus es, Domine)*
Song of the Three Young Men, 29–34

> Blessed art Thou, O Lord God of our Fathers;
> **praised and exalted above all forever.**
> Blessed art Thou for the name of thy majesty;
> **praised and exalted above all forever.**
> Blessed art Thou in the temple of thy holiness;
> **praised and exalted above all forever.**
> Blessed art Thou that beholdest no depths.
> and dwellest between the cherubim;
> **praised and exalted above all forever.**
> Blessed art Thou in the glorious throne of thy
>   kingdom;
> **praised and exalted above all forever.**
> Blessed art Thou in the firmament of heaven;
> **praised and exalted above all forever.**
> Blessed art Thou, O Father, Son and Holy Spirit;
> **praised and exalted above all forever.**

or

A Song of Praise *(Benedictus es, Domine)*
Song of the Three Young Men, 29–34

> Glory to you, Lord God of our fathers;
> **you are worthy of praise; glory to you.**
> Glory to you for the radiance of your holy Name;
> **we will praise you and highly exalt you**
>   **forever.**
> Glory to you in the splendor of your temple
> **on the throne of your majesty, glory to you.**
> Glory to you, seated between the cherubim;
> **we will praise you and highly exalt you**
>   **forever.**
> Glory to you, beholding the depths;
> **in the high vault of heaven, glory to you.**
> Glory to you, Father, Son, and Holy Spirit;
> **we will praise you and highly exalt you forever.**

or

Venite

Psalm 95:1-7

Come, let us sing to the Lord
**let us shout for joy to the Rock of our
salvation.**
Let us come before his presence with
thanksgiving
and raise a loud shout to him with psalms.
For the Lord is a great God,
and a great King above all gods.
In his hand are the caverns of the earth,
and the heights of the hills are his also.
The sea is his, for he made it,
and his hands have molded the dry land.
Come, let us bow down, and bend the knee,
and kneel before the Lord our Maker.
For he is our God,
and we are the people of his pasture and the
sheep of his hand.
**Oh, that today you would hearken to his
voice!**

(from _The Book of Common Prayer,_ 1979)

Jubilate

Psalm 100

Be joyful in the Lord, all you lands;
**serve the Lord with gladness
and come before his presence with a song.**
Know this: The Lord himself is God;
**he himself has made us, and we are his;
we are his people and the sheep of his pasture.**
Enter his gates with thanksgiving;
go into his courts with praise;
give thanks to him and call upon his Name.
For the Lord is good;
**his mercy is everlasting;
and his faithfulness endures from age to age.**

(from _The Book of Common Prayer_)

or

A Song to the Lamb _(Dignus es)_

based on Revelation 4:11; 5:9-10, 13

Splendor and honor and kingly power
are yours by right, O Lord our God,
From every family, language, people, and nation,
a kingdom of priests to serve our God.
And so, to him who sits upon the throne,
and to Christ the Lamb,

Be worship and praise, dominion and splendor,
forever and for evermore.

or

The Song of the Redeemed _(Magna et mirabilia)_

based on Revelation 15:3-4

O ruler of the universe, Lord God,
**great deeds are they that you have done,
surpassing human understanding.**
Your ways are ways of righteousness and truth,
O King of all the ages.
Who can fail to do you homage, Lord,
and sing the praise of your Name?
for you only are the holy One.
All nations will draw near and fall down before
you,
**because your just and holy works have been
revealed.**
Glory to the Father, and to the Son, and to the
Holy Spirit:
**as it was in the beginning is now, and will be
forever. Amen.**

or

You Are God _(Te Deum laudamus)_

You are God:
We praise you;
You are the Lord:
We acclaim you;
You are the eternal Father:
All creation worships you.
To you all angels, all the powers of heaven,
cherubim and seraphim, sing in endless praise:
**Holy, holy, holy Lord, God of power and
might,**
heaven and earth are full of your glory.
The glorious company of apostles praise you.
**The noble fellowship of prophets praise you.
The white-robed army of martyrs praise you.
Throughout the world the holy church acclaims
you;**
Father, of majesty unbounded,
your true and only Son, worthy of all worship,
and the Holy Spirit, advocate and guide.
You, Christ, are the king of glory,
the eternal Son of the Father.
When you became man to set us free
you did not shun the Virgin's womb.
You overcame the sting of death

and opened the kingdom of heaven to all
  believers.
You are seated at God's right hand in glory.
We believe that you will come and be our judge.
  Come then, Lord, and help your people,
bought with the price of your own blood,
and bring us with your saints
to glory everlasting.

208 • THE CONFESSION OF SIN

A confession of sin is an act of repentance, motivated by faith and characterized by the expectation of forgiveness.

Protestant traditions have rooted the confession of sin in the experience of Isaiah. When Isaiah saw the Lord seated on the throne (Isa. 6:1-7), his response was "Woe to me! I am ruined!" In the presence of God we see ourselves as sinners, confess our sin, and hear the Word of forgiveness. Thus the purpose of the confession is to rehearse our relationship to God.

When the confession of sin fits best in worship is a matter of dispute. Some churches place it in the Entrance, arguing that the best time to confess sin is when we initially come into the presence of God. Others argue that the joyful note of the Entrance should not be marred by a confession. They prefer to place the confession of sin either after the Prayers of the People or in the beginning of the acts of worship at the Table of the Lord. Others argue that because worship is a celebration of the Resurrection there is no need for a confession of sin.

During Advent and Lent the confession is often placed in the Entrance because these seasons are penitential in nature.

Biblical Examples of the Confession of Sin

A Form for Biblical Confession of Sin

Leader: *Quote the Scripture and end with words such as:* "Let us confess our sins in silence" *(see below).*
People: *Silence.*
Leader: *Speak the words of forgiveness (see below).*

Scripture Sentences for the Confession of Sin

Jesus said: "Love the Lord your God with all your heart and with all your soul and with all your mind and with all your strength" and "Love your neighbor as yourself." (Mark 12:29-31)

or

St. John says: "If we claim to be without sin, we deceive ourselves and the truth is not in us. If we confess our sins, he is faithful and just and will forgive us our sins and purify us from all unrighteousness." (1 John 1:8-9)

or

The writer of Hebrews says: "Since we have a great high priest who has gone through the heavens, Jesus the Son of God, let us then approach the throne of grace with confidence, so that we may receive mercy and find grace to help us in our time of need."

Traditional Examples of the Confession of Sin

Traditional Language Version:

Let us humbly confess our sins unto Almighty God.

Silence may be kept.

  Minister and People:
  Almighty and most merciful Father,
  we have erred and strayed from thy ways like
    lost sheep,
  we have followed too much the devices and
    desires of our own hearts,
  we have offended against thy holy laws,
  we have left undone those things which we
    ought to have done,
  and we have done those things which we
    ought not to have done.
  But thou, O Lord, have mercy upon us,
  spare thou those who confess their faults,
  restore thou those who are penitent,
  according to thy promises declared unto
    mankind
  in Jesus Christ our Lord;
  and grant, O most merciful Father, for his sake,
  that we may hereafter live a godly, righteous,
    and sober life,
  to the glory of thy holy Name. Amen.

(*The Book of Common Prayer*)

or

Contemporary Language Version:

Let us confess our sins against God and our neighbor.

Silence may be kept.

Minister and People:
Most merciful God,
we confess that we have sinned against you
in thought, word, and deed,
by what we have done,
and by what we have left undone.
We have not loved you with our whole heart;
we have not loved our neighbors as ourselves,
We are truly sorry and we humbly repent,
For the sake of your Son Jesus Christ,
have mercy on us and forgive us;
that we may delight in your will,
and walk in your ways,
to the glory of your Name. Amen.

(The Book of Common Prayer)

or

Lord, have mercy.
Christ, have mercy.
Lord, have mercy.

or

Kyrie eleison.
Christie eleison.
Kyrie eleison.

(The *Kyrie*)

or

Holy God
Holy and Mighty
Holy Immortal One,
Have mercy upon us.

(The Ancient *Trisagion*)

or

Hear the commandments of God to his
people:
I am the Lord your God who brought you out
of bondage.
You shall have no other gods but me.
Amen. Lord have mercy.
You shall not make for yourself any idol.
Amen. Lord have mercy.
Remember the Sabbath Day and keep it holy.
Amen. Lord have mercy.

Honor your father and your mother.
Amen. Lord have mercy.
You shall not commit murder.
Amen. Lord have mercy.
You shall not steal.
Amen. Lord have mercy.
You shall not be a false witness.
Amen. Lord have mercy.
You shall not covet anything that belongs to
your neighbor.
Amen. Lord have mercy.

(The Book of Common Prayer)

Contemporary Examples of a Confession of Sin

There is therefore now no condemnation for
those
who are in Christ Jesus.
**I do not understand my own actions. For I do
not do
what I want, but I do the very thing I hate.**
There is therefore now no condemnation for
those
who are in Christ Jesus.
**So then it is no longer I that do it, but sin
which
dwells within me.**
There is therefore now no condemnation for
those
who are in Christ Jesus.
I can will what is right, but I cannot do it.
There is therefore now no condemnation for
those
who are in Christ Jesus.
**Miserable creature that I am! Who is there to
deliver me from this body of death?**
God alone, through Jesus Christ our Lord!
Thanks be to God!

(James G. Kirk, *When We Gather* [Philadelphia: Geneva Press, 1983], 96–97)

or

Have mercy on us, O God,
Father God Almighty,
God most high,
God of hosts,
Lord of the world,
God invisible,
God incorruptible,

God immortal,
God all-merciful,
God all-perfect,
have mercy on us.
God of the earth,
God of the fire,
God of the fresh waters,
God of the great winds,
God of the shining stars,
God who made the world,
God of the many tongues,
God of the nations,
God of golden goodness,
Heavenly Father [Parent]
have mercy on us.

(Padraig O' Fiannachta, *Saltair: Prayers from The Irish Tradition* [Blackrock, Ireland: Columba Press, 1988], 62)

or

Righteous Father [God],
We who own more than we use,
    Proclaim more than we experience,
    And request more than we need,
    Come asking Thy forgiveness.
We seek Thy salvation—then act like we save
    ourselves.
We beg Thy forgiveness—then repeat our
    errors.
We experience Thy grace—then act defeated.
We rely on Thy power—but only in hard
    times.
We have become confused and misguided.
Forgive our every defection.
Bring us to an unbroken commitment and a
    steady trust,
Through Him
who is the *way* of hope,
the *truth* of God, and
the *life* of love.
Now and always.
Amen.

(E. Lee Phillips, *Breaking Silence Before the Lord* [Grand Rapids: Baker Book House, 1986], 68)

or

Sin chains us;
grace frees us.
Let us recognize that we are sinners

and let us implore our freedom.
Lord Jesus,
you break the chains of the old slavery
    (Gal. 5:1)
and you want us to walk in the freedom of the
    Spirit (Gal. 5:16).
Free us from sin and have mercy on us.
Lord Jesus,
you break the bonds of falsehood
and you deliver us through your truth
    (John 8:32).
Free us from sin and have mercy on us.
Heavy are the chains that we carry.
Show us mercy, Almighty God.
Break the chains of our old slavery
and lead us to eternal life. (Gal. 5:1)

(Lucien Deiss, *Reflections on His Word: Sunday Prayers, Cycle C* [Schiller Park, Ill.: World Library Publications, 1982], 172)

209 • THE WORDS OF FORGIVENESS (ABSOLUTION)

In God's place, the minister or worship leader speaks words of forgiveness and healing to those who repent in true faith.

Traditionally the act of confession is followed by the words of forgiveness spoken by the minister. These are words of assurance to the effect that those who have truly repented of their sin may know with certainty that God has heard their confession and extends a gracious pardon to their request. The words of forgiveness should be short and to the point. This act is essential and should not be omitted.

Biblical Examples of the Word of Forgiveness

Hear the words of St. John:

If we confess our sins
he is faithful and just
and will forgive us our sins
and purify us from all unrighteousness
    (1 John 1:9).

or

Hear the words of Jesus:

Where are those who accuse you?
Is there no one to condemn you?

Neither do I.
Go! and sin no more! (based on John 8:10-11)

or

Since we have been justified through faith,
We have peace with God
Through our Lord Jesus Christ. (Rom. 5:1)

Traditional Examples of the Words of Forgiveness

Almighty God, our heavenly Father, who of his great mercy hath promised forgiveness of sins to all who with hearty repentance and true faith turn unto him, have mercy upon you, pardon and deliver you from all your sins, confirm and strengthen you in all goodness, and bring you to everlasting life; through Jesus Christ our Lord. Amen.

(The Book of Common Prayer)

or

Almighty God have mercy on you, forgive you all your sins through our Lord Jesus Christ, strengthen you in all goodness, and by the power of the Holy Spirit keep you in eternal life. Amen.

(The Book of Common Prayer)

or

The mercy of the Lord
is from everlasting to everlasting.
I declare to you, in the name of Jesus Christ,
you are forgiven.

May the God of mercy,
who forgives you all your sins,
strengthen you in all goodness,
and by the power of the Holy Spirit
keep you in eternal life.
Amen.

The Service for the Lord's Day [Louisville: Westminster/John Knox Press, 1984], 87)

Preparing the Proclamation of the Words of Forgiveness

The following pattern of proclamation may be used by those who desire to prepare the words of forgiveness.

Direction	Example
1. A salutation addressed to God	Almighty God
2. An application regarding God's character of mercy or forgiveness	Have mercy on you [us],
3. A description of God's favorable disposition toward the repentant	forgive you [us] all your [our] sins through our Lord Jesus Christ, strengthen you in all goodness, and by the power of the Holy Spirit keep you [us] in eternal life.
4. A concluding ascription or prayer closure	Amen.

210 • OPENING PRAYER OF THE DAY (COLLECT)

A collect is a prayer that "collects" the prayers of the people in summary fashion, places them in a context appropriate to the seasonal or thematic focus of the day, and offers them to God.

The function of the collect (pronounced with emphasis on the first syllable) is to bring together the prayers of the people, to bring to a close the Entrance to worship, and to proclaim the theme of the day. The worship leader may face the people with outstretched arms, bid them to pray, wait until their prayers surface or allow a time for silent prayer, then pray, bringing the congregation and their prayers before God. The congregation assents with an Amen.

Traditional Examples of the Opening Prayer

General Prayers

O holy God
You who rest in the holy place,
You who are hymned by the seraphim,
You who are glorified by the cherubim
and worshiped by all the heavenly powers;
You brought all things into being out of nothing.
You created us out of your image and likeness
and adorned us with many gifts;
You give to those who ask wisdom and understanding;
You do not despise the sinner,

but call them to repentance;
You have given to us, your humble and
    unworthy servants,
To stand before you and offer you the praise
    and worship
due your name;
Accept our praise O God and give us your
    goodness,
Forgive us our sins known and unknown,
Sanctify our souls and bodies, and
Grant us the power to serve you in holiness
All the days of our life.
For you only are Holy, O Lord
And unto you alone do we ascribe glory:
To the Father, to the Son, and to the Holy
    Spirit,
Now and forever, and unto ages of ages. Amen.

(Adapted from the Prayer of the Trisagion, *St. John
Chrysostom Liturgy)*

or

O Lord
You who are bountiful and compassionate,
You who are longsuffering and plenteous in
    mercy,
Open your ears to our prayer and
listen to our pleading voice;
Work within us your good work and
Lead us in your way so that
We may walk in your truth.
Make our hearts glad
That we may fear your holy name.
For O Lord you are great and you do great
    things
You save all who trust in your Holy Name.
For unto you is due all glory, honor and
    worship:
To the Father, to the Son, and to the Holy
    Spirit,
Now and forever until ages of ages. Amen.

(Adapted from Vespers,
Prayer of the Eastern Orthodox Church)

or

O Lord
Do not rebuke us in your displeasure
Nor chasten us in your wrath:
but deal with us according to your mercy,
O physician and healer of our souls.
Guide us into the haven of your will.
Open the eyes of our hearts

to the knowledge of your truth,
keep us from sin and give us peace
throughout our life.
For yours is the majesty
and yours is the kingdom and the power and
    the glory:
of the Father, and of the Son, and of the Holy
    Spirit:
Now and forever and to the ages of ages.
    Amen.

(Adapted from Vespers, Prayer 2 of the Eastern Orthodox Church)

or

O Lord our God
Remember us sinners and servants
When we call upon your name
And do not disappoint us
in the expectation of your mercy:
But give us, O Lord, all our petitions
Which lead to salvation and
cause us to love and fear you
with all our hearts and
To do your will in all things.
For you are a good God and
you love all people and unto you
We ascribe all glory:
To the Father, and to the Son,
And to the Holy Spirit:
Now and forever and
unto ages of ages. Amen.

(Adapted from Vespers, Prayer 3 of the Eastern Orthodox Church)

or

O Lord God
You are hymned by the holy powers
With never-ceasing hymns and songs of praise
Grant us a participation in the inheritance
of all those who fear you and keep your
    commandments
For to you is all glory, honor and worship:
To the Father, to the Son, and to the Holy
    Spirit,
Now and ever and to ages of ages. Amen.

(Adapted from Vespers, Prayer 4 of the Eastern Orthodox Church)

or

O Lord our God
You uphold all things in the hollow of your
　　pure hand;
You show longsuffering to all people and
sorrow over the calamities we endure:
Remember the fullness of your mercy.
Visit us with your lovingkindness:
And grant us this day
to avoid the snares of evil;
Through the grace of your Holy Spirit.
We ask this through the mercy and love of
　　your Son
With whom you are blessed, together with
　　your
all holy, and good, and life-giving Spirit:
Now and forever, and to the ages of ages.
　　Amen.

(Adapted from Vespers, Prayer 5 of the Eastern Orthodox Church)

or

O God you are great and wonderful
With your own inscrutable wisdom and
With the great riches of providence you order
　　all things
and give us the good things of earth;
You have given us a pledge of the coming
　　kingdom
through the good things you have already
　　given us,
And you make us shun evil:
Grant us the power to live this day and
　　throughout our lives
Without reproach before you, and
Cause us to hymn and glorify you,
The only good one, our God, who loves all
　　people;
For you are our God and
Unto you we ascribe all glory:
To the Father and to the Son and to the Holy
　　Spirit:
Now and forever, and to the ages of ages.
　　Amen.

(Adapted from Vespers, Prayer 6 of the Eastern Orthodox Church)

or

O great and most high God
You alone are eternal and
you alone dwell in unapproachable light;
You made all creation out of your wisdom;

You divided the light from the darkness,
You appointed the sun to rule the day,
The moon and stars to rule the night;
You also cause us sinners to come before your
　　presence
with confession and to offer you sacrifices of
　　praise:
O Lord, you who love all people,
direct our worship to come before you
and accept it as sweet incense;
Empower us with your light,
Move us to remember your Holy Name,
cause us to be filled with joy and
to glorify your goodness.
For you are a good God and you love all
　　people;
We ascribe glory to your Holy Name:
To the Father and to the Son and to the Holy
　　Spirit:
Now and forever and to the ages of ages.
　　Amen.

(Adapted from Vespers, Prayer 7 of the Eastern Orthodox Church)

or

You are holy,
O Lord, our Creator and Father,
giving us mercies beyond number.
You are holy,
O Savior Jesus Christ,
loving and setting us free.
You are holy,
O Spirit of truth and peace,
leading us in ways that are right.
O holy, eternal Trinity,
we praise you forever and ever.
Amen.

(_The Service for the Lord's Day_ [Louisville: West-
minster/John Knox Press, 1984], 57)

or

You do hear the prayers of your people, O God,
and give heed to their supplications. Your faithfulness spans generations and nations, as a
cloak of protection sewn with benevolent care.
You promise your presence as your Spirit
abides in our midst. We bow down before you,
as our mothers and fathers have done before
us, in praise and adoration of your gracious
name.

(James G. Kirk, *When We Gather: Year A* [Philadelphia: Geneva Press, 1983], 104)

Opening Prayers for the Seasons of the Christian Year

(For opening prayers appropriate to the seasons, Sundays, and feast days of the Christian year, see Volume 5: *The Services of the Christian Year; The Book of Common Prayer;* The Roman Missal; or other liturgical books.)

Preparing an Opening Prayer. For those who prepare a creative Opening Prayer the following form may be used as a guide:

Direction	Example
1. An address to God	O God,
2. A reference to some divine attribute or act as the ground of prayer	you have prepared for those who love you such good things as surpass our understanding:
3. (a) A petition related to the day's theme or the position in the church's year, (b) often with a clause describing the end or purpose of the petition	Pour into our hearts such love towards you, that we, loving you in all things and above all things, may obtain your promises, which exceed all that we can desire;
4. A concluding doxology	through Jesus Christ our Lord, who lives and reigns with you and the Holy Spirit, one God, forever and ever. *Amen.*

This format is a generalization, and not every classic or modern collect fits it. Many variations exist, and a look at them will reveal the appropriate bounds of the form. For example, the collect for the First Sunday of Advent does not have a section devoted to an attribute of God, but rather implies attributes in the petition itself:

[1] Almighty God

[3a] give us grace to cast away the works of darkness and put on the armour of light, now in the time of this mortal life in which your Son Jesus Christ came to visit us in great humility;

[3b] that in the last day, when he shall come again in his glorious majesty to judge both the living and the dead, we may rise to the life immortal;

[4] through him who lives and reigns with you and the Holy Spirit, one God, now and forever. Amen.

The petition here not only asks for something; it tells part of the story of salvation with its characteristic Advent references to the Incarnation and to the return of Christ, and in so doing reveals the character of God in sending his Son.

Another example, from the Third Sunday of Advent (often called the "Stirrup Prayer" because of its opening words), begins with the petition immediately, which also suggests an attribute of God and then interjects the address to God. The prayer then proceeds to a second, closely related petition:

[3, 2 implicit] Stir up your power,

[1] O Lord,

[3] and with great might come among us;

[3] and, because we are sorely hindered by our sins, let your bountiful grace and mercy speedily help and deliver us;

[4] through Jesus Christ our Lord, to whom, with you and the Holy Spirit, be honor and glory, now and forever. Amen.

Robert E. Webber
with Larry J. Nyberg
Randolph Sly
Ronal Freyer Nicholas

SEVEN

Resources for the Service of the Word

The Service of the Word has always held a central place in worship. In the beginning of Christian worship, the Service of the Word was a dialogue that involved the entire congregation. Today's worship renewal seeks to return the Word to the congregation so that the truth spoken remains in the heart and finds expression in the lifestyle.

211 • WHAT DOES THE SERVICE OF THE WORD DO?

The service of the word rehearses the story of God's redeeming actions and calls us to see God at work in our own histories.

In the Service of the Word the mood shifts from the joyful and *doxological* note of the Entrance to an *instructive* mood. By its very nature the Service of the Word is more cognitive than the Entrance. The emphasis is on reading, hearing, listening, and responding to the story of God's action in history.

The origin of the Service of the Word and its instructive orientation lies in the synagogue. The early Christians who were Jews probably adapted what they did in the synagogue to the context of Christian worship.

After the Scripture readings, punctuated by psalms (as in the synagogue), early Christian worship contained a sermon followed by several responses to the Word such as discussion of the sermon, prayers of the people, and the Kiss of Peace. Later, another response was added, the Creed. Placed after the sermon, it replaced the discussion of the smaller communities.

The emphasis on Scripture in the Service of the Word is captured in these words of Justin Martyr: "The memoirs of the Apostles or the writings of the prophets are read as long as time permits." These Scriptures were not simply read but probably discussed as they were in the synagogue.

Today many renewing churches have restored the ancient tradition of Scripture readings punctuated by psalms and the response to God's Word which includes responses such as occasional discussion, the saying of the creed, the prayers of intercession, and the passing of the peace. There are, of course, a variety of ways of doing these acts of worship, ranging from traditional models to contemporary models. In all of these acts—the historical recitation of the Scriptures, the singing of the psalms, the hearing of the sermon—God is speaking and the people are responding.

Liturgical traditions have been prone to regard the Service of the Word as an optional preamble to the "real" worship in the eucharistic liturgy. The Reformers called the church back to the Word, but that call is being sounded again in many liturgical churches as more attention is given to the Word and its indispensability for complete worship is recognized.

Free churches historically have been tempted to emphasize the Service of the Word to excess, making Sunday worship "Sunday school for adults." Many free churches, however, are now emphasizing exhortation and encouragement somewhat more than instruction in the sermon, to keep the sermon from descending into a lecture.

Without being trite, trivial, or shallow, many free churches are now using the *kerygma* (the church's basic proclamation) in worship and offer the "rest of the story," the in-depth *didache* (teaching), in a separate instructional session.

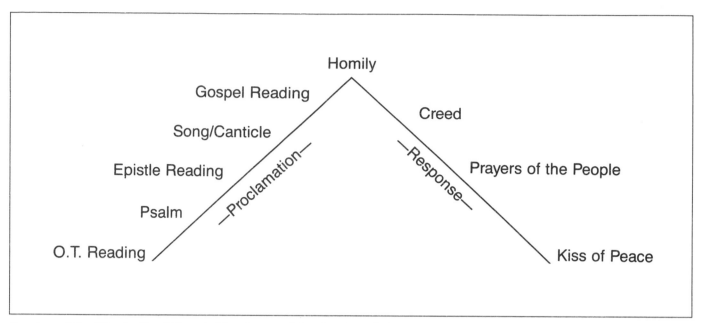

Service of the Word—Traditional. The shape of the Service of the Word in liturgical churches.

212 ✦ THE SHAPE OF THE SERVICE OF THE WORD

Broadly speaking, the form of the Service of the Word is similar in both traditional and contemporary churches: Scripture reading, sermon, and response to the Word.

Scripture. Two or three Scriptures are usually read, often from the lectionary texts. When lectionary texts are not used, careful attention is given to the choice of texts throughout the year so that the people may hear a broad range of biblical material.

Scripture readings are generally interspersed with psalms (sung or spoken); a special acclamation such as a sung Alleluia or an appropriate chorus often precedes the reading of the gospel.

Sermon. The sermon interprets and applies one or more of the Scripture readings. A prayer for illumination is often said before the sermon.

Response to the Word. Responses such as invitations to follow Christ, hymns, creeds, anthems, prayers, and offering, as well as baptisms, dedications, and reception into membership of the church, generally come *after* the sermon, not before. Thus the structure of proclamation/response is maintained.

Passing of the Peace. The ancient custom of expressing the peace of Christ has been restored in many Protestant churches as a fitting conclusion to the Service of the Word and an appropriate transition into the Service of the Table.

213 ✦ GUIDELINES TO ENLIVENING THE SERVICE OF THE WORD

As this article indicates, the liveliness of the Service of the Word depends on the full and conscious participation of every person in the dialogue of worship.

Because the nature of the Service of the Word is instructive, it, more than any other part of worship, is subject to cerebral overkill. The following guidelines will help a congregation break through the impasse of a passive, noninvolved approach to the Service of the Word.

1. As the Service of the Word is planned, recognize that its pattern is proclamation and response.
2. Introduce the reading of Scripture in such a way that people will be encouraged to listen attentively.
3. Establish a form of response to the Scripture reading.
4. Find new ways to communicate Scripture (drama, readers' theater, storytelling).
5. Increase the use of the psalms, said or sung.
6. Include acclamations at appropriate places (e.g., "Thanks be to God").
7. Develop a conscious response to the sermon (talk-back sermon).
8. Develop a form of prayer that returns prayer to the people (e.g., bidding prayers).

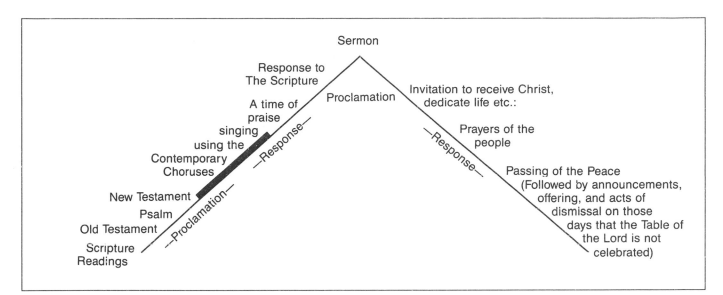

Service of the Word—Praise and Worship. _A model of the Service of the Word for contemporary praise-and-worship churches._

9. Find ways to enhance the text through the arts.
10. Encourage the Passing of Peace as a joyous occasion.

Each local church may have its own way of eliciting response. By following the above guidelines and employing a form of response familiar to the people, the Service of the Word will fulfill the pattern of God speaking and the people responding.

214 ◆ THE USE OF THE ARTS IN THE SERVICE OF THE WORD

The arts are intended to enhance the text, not dominate the worship. Their function is to highlight, festoon, illustrate, or express the Word.

Because modern worship renewalists recognize the Service of the Word as an act of communication, a new interest has emerged in the use of the communication arts. The reading of the Scripture may be done through reader's theater, dialogic readings, drama, and storytelling. The sermon or message may also be communicated through a storytelling approach and may include a time for feedback and application. Dance also has an appropriate place in the Service of the Word as a means of festooning the reading of the gospel or as a response to the sermon.

Great care should be taken in the use of the arts to prevent them from taking on the character of a "performance." The arts are servants of the text; they interpret the text and assist in the communication of the text and are never an end in themselves. It is well to recognize that the use of arts in expressing a reading is always an interpretation. It may illuminate the text in a new way, but it may also limit the meaning or stand in the way of God's speaking to the church through his Word. Drama and reading teams should be instructed in these matters, perhaps as a part of some preliminary spiritual exercises for the group. It is best to limit the use of the Arts to one act of worship and no more in the Service of the Word.

For more information on the arts in worship, see Vol. 4: _Music and the Arts in Christian Worship._

215 ◆ THE PLACE OF SCRIPTURE IN THE SERVICE OF THE WORD

The reading and preaching of God's Word in worship is the central act of divine action.

Centrality of Scripture. Scripture holds the place of centrality in worship. Thus in the Entrance the people come into the presence of God and prepare to hear the Word of God. At the Table the people respond to the Word in what the early church called the great thanksgiving (Eucharist). Thus the Word is to be seen as the central act of proclamation and the Eucharist is the great response of thanksgiving for the Word. Consequently the celebration of the Eucharist is never a diminishing of the Word, but the most appropriate response of thanks the congregation can give to the Word. When this relationship between Word and Table is properly understood, both Word and Table are most likely to receive their true place in worship. The reading and hearing of Scripture in Christian worship is *not* optional; it is one of the defining "marks" that distinguishes Christian worship.

Scripture as Worship. The Bible is not so much a message-book as it is a voice-book. Yes, it speaks not only about worship but also speaks as worship. It gives voice to the presence of the living God. We are at worship as we meditate on its words—from Genesis to Revelation.

LeRoy E. Kennell[12]

216 • THE PUBLIC READING OF THE SCRIPTURE

Because Scripture is the living Word, it should be read with feeling, inflection, and conviction. Many renewing churches have established a lay readers group—people who have as their specific calling and ministry the reading of the Word in worship. This group will meet to rehearse and practice the reading of the Word so that its reading becomes an "event" in worship.

Scripture Reading in the Early Church

The earliest source of our liturgy of the Word is the Jewish synagogue service, in which any adult male Jew could be invited to proclaim from the Jewish Scripture and to give a commentary. Jesus himself was a forerunner of the Christian lector. In the Nazareth synagogue, he unrolled the scroll of Isaiah, proclaimed a passage from the lectionary, and announced that he was the Spirit-filled servant described by Isaiah (Luke 4:16-22).

Another source of Christian proclamation was the activity of first-century missionaries, such as Paul and Barnabas. Because the entire Christian community assumed responsibility for proclamation we would be in error if we described the urgent task of first-century evangelization and proclamation as the exclusive activity of ordained bishops and presbyters. Commissioned and sent by their community, itinerant ministers of the Word announced the good news of salvation in the risen Lord. They invited their listeners to conversion, which meant rejection

of sin and acceptance of God's saving activity in Jesus.

Liturgical ministries in this period were diversified and shared. Christ's command, "do this in memory of me," was accepted as a commissioning of the entire community to celebrate Eucharist. Who led the celebration? Usually the local bishop. Who proclaimed Paul's letters and the Old Testament Scriptures? Designated baptized (lay) members of the community.

Jerry and Gail DuCharme[13]

Learning How to Read Effectively

I find that the most helpful approach for lectors comes from the discipline of oral interpretation. It is not that this discipline is going to solve all the problems, but it does provide a good starting point to examine our relationship to the Word that we proclaim. First, what is "oral interpretation"? I like Charlotte Lee's definition: "Oral interpretation is the art of communicating to an audience a work of literary art in its intellectual, emotional, and aesthetic entirety." Let us look at this definition more closely.

The art of communicating to an audience . . . "We are involved here with a skill that can rise to become an art—a skill of communicating to an audience or a congregation. The focus is outgoing, toward the listeners, becoming one of them, for that is the purpose of any communication. Readers and listeners are brought into communion through *"a work of literary art . . ."* If such communion is possible through a work of Shakespeare or Dickens or Faulkner, how much more so in the case of the living Word of God, who desires that, in his Son, there be no division or separation. But for this to happen, the Word must be communicated *"in its intellectual, emotional, and aesthetic entirety."* First the lector must understand what he or she is communicating, the development of thought in the passage, whether it is the words of Jeremiah or Paul or a retelling of one of the stories of the Old Testament or the Acts of the Apostles. The lector must intellectually grasp what is being said. This will demand close study of the passage. Then the lector must communicate the emotional tone of the piece; so if it is the anger of Paul in his letter to the Galatians or the joyful anticipation of the prophet Isaiah envisioning when the wolf will be a guest of the lamb, this feeling must be felt and communicated.

Scripture Reading. Central to worship is the proclamation of the Word of God.

Finally, there is the aesthetic dimension of any piece, all those qualities that make the passage a work of beauty. It could include the rhythm in which a psalm has been translated, with its three or four stresses per line. Or it might be the way a story builds up to a conclusion—for instance the story of the death of David's son Absalom, which ends with David's grief-filled words: "O my son Absalom! My son, my son Absalom! If only I had died instead of you—O Absalom, my son, my son!" (2 Sam. 18:33). Or it could mean highlighting the words of a passage from the book of Wisdom, allowing for the silence before moving on to the next thought. The aesthetic concern is a concern for how all the parts fit together so that the listener has a total experience of the passage.

James Wallace[14]

Group Readings

What Is Group Reading? Group reading is a stimulating, refreshing means of communication. Two or more oral readers share with an audience a piece of literature. By means of oral and physical cues, all the scenes, characters, and action exist in the imagination of the hearers rather than on platform. Attention focuses on the reading rather than on the reader.

You may have encountered group reading in several forms—concert reading, multiple reading, readers' theater, or staged readings.

Where Did Group Reading Originate? The recently revived art is said to have originated in Greece in the fifth century. Since then it has experienced revival at various times in various forms. The present resurgence holds a challenge for us as Christians.

Why Use Group Reading? Little or no staging, costuming, or memorization are required in group reading. Consider the saving here in time and funds. This is not to say, however, that group reading can be done effectively without taking time for thorough individual and group practice.

Young people of all ages are given an opportunity to share the Christian message with others through group readings. The reading from Jonah, for instance, has been presented successfully by young missionaries and in a modified form by children in a Christian day school.

The variety of voices and faces in group reading makes it possible to present longer readings than one person could attempt without risking loss of attention.

Finally, group reading "brings alive" the printed page in a remarkable way. This is invariably the first comment heard after the readings are presented.

Charlotte E. Arnold[15]

217 • FORMS FOR THE READING OF SCRIPTURE

Traditional and contemporary ways of reading the Scriptures for public worship are explained in the following article.

Traditional Forms

The Old Testament reader, rising out of the congregation or from the seats where the leaders of worship sit, may walk to the pulpit or some other place and say "A reading from the book of _____." The reader then reads the appointed lesson in a clear and forceful voice, ending with the words "This is the Word of the Lord." When this action is done with conviction, the people can respond with an equally strong statement— "Thanks be to God"—as a way of showing their acceptance of the Word.

After a responsorial psalm, the Epistle reader rises out of the congregation or from the seats where the leaders of worship sit, walks to the pulpit or some other place and says, "A reading from the [First/Second/Third] Epistle [Letter] of [Paul to the] _____." The reader then reads in a clear and forceful voice, ending the reading with the words, "This is the Word of the Lord." The congregation again responds, "Thanks be to God."

After the gospel acclamation, the gospel is read. The action of reading the gospel is of utmost importance. It ought not to be stiff and formal, communicating a sober, distant, and cold God. Nor should it be casual and hip, communicating a carefree "hail fellow well met" God. Since the action of walking among the people with the gospel communicates the incarnate Christ, the goal is to express a reverence for the gospel shown not only through the processional movement but through the raising of the gospel book over the head, the signing of the cross over the pages to be read, the introductory words, the proclamatory spirit in which the gospel is read, and the kissing of the gospel by the reader before the procession returns to its seats. When the gospel is read, it is often read by the minister from the center of the congregation. The minister, together with servers such as the one who will hold the gospel book as it is read, and candle bearers who walk with the gospel reader, walk halfway down the center aisle (in less formal churches the gospel reader will read from in front of the congregation or walk down the center aisle alone), where the gospel reading is preceded by the words "The Holy Gospel of our Lord Jesus Christ according to _____." The people then respond "Glory to you, Lord [Christ]." After the reading the reader may say "The Gospel of the Lord" and the people may respond "Praise to you, Lord [Jesus] Christ."

The general norm today is to read three lessons interspersed with psalms and acclamations. The lessons are usually from the Old Testament, an epistle, and the gospel. These texts are listed in the lectionary. Sometimes lessons from Acts and Revelation replace Old Testament lections (e.g., at Eastertide and the feast of Christ the King).

Contemporary Forms for the Reading of Scripture

Those congregations that do not choose to use the traditional form for the introduction of Scripture readings may choose one of the following ways to introduce Scripture:

Before the Reading

A paragraph or two explaining the text is either read or said extemporaneously.

or

The hearer is asked to attend to the reading of Scripture with the sense of smell, touch, sight, and/or hearing.

or

The hearer is asked to see a picture rather than to hear words.

or

The hearer is asked to listen with the feeling side of the being, to get into touch with the noncognitive part of the person that may be affected by the Scripture lesson.

After the Reading. A comment may be made such as:

May the Lord add his blessing to the reading of the Word.

or

May God cause his Word to take up residence in our lives.

The people may respond with:

A chorus such as "Thy Word is a lamp to my feet,"

or

Words such as "All the Lord asks we will do."

218 • THE RESPONSORIAL PSALM

The responsorial psalm is sung as a response to the reading of the Old Testament lesson. The lesson is proclamation; the psalm, response.

The tradition of interspersing Scripture readings with psalms and acclamations goes back to the early church and has been maintained formally in liturgical churches. This tradition has been revived today among many other churches as well.

When the psalm is said, it may be said responsively, in an antiphonal manner, in unison, or in any other agreed-upon way. When sung, any appropriate tune may be chosen (when the psalm tune is new or difficult it may be practiced in the beginning of the service during the gathering).

The responsorial psalm is very important because it is the people's response to Scripture. The people should be encouraged to respond with fervor. A strong response expresses a willingness to hear the Word of God and creates an atmosphere of a lively communal worship. When the responses are weak, instruct the congregation concerning the importance of the response and practice the way the responses should be done at the beginning of the service (during the gathering).

There are five different types of psalm singing: _chant,_ which is most appropriate in a liturgical church; _plainsong,_ which works well in traditional Protestant and contemporary creative worship; _metrical,_ which can be used effectively in all types of worship; _antiphonal,_ which can be used in all traditions, and _psalms_ prepared in contemporary chorus style which is used predominantly in charismatic/praise tradition worship.

219 • THE GOSPEL ACCLAMATION

In liturgical worship an acclamation is sung after the Epistle reading and before the gospel reading.

—— A Liturgical Gospel Acclamation ——

Explanation of the Liturgical Gospel Acclamation. After the Epistle reading and before the gospel, the congregation stands to sing the gospel acclamation. The gospel acclamation is normally an alleluia (which means "praise Yahweh"). If the gospel reading is to be read from the center aisle of the sanctuary, the reader (and assistants) may process to the place of reading during the alleluia.

As the gospel acclamation begins, the people stand. The gospel acclamation is then sung in the following way:

1. The alleluia is sung first by a cantor.
2. The alleluia is then repeated by the congregation and choir.
3. The verse is sung by the cantor.
4. The alleluia is repeated by the congregation and choir.

Example of the Liturgical Gospel Acclamation
Cantor:
  Alleluia, Alleluia, Alleluia.
Congregation:
  [Repeats the Alleluia.]
Cantor:
  [Sings verse or verses of the psalm.]
Cantor and Congregation:
  [Sing the Alleluia together.]

(This sequence is repeated until the psalm is completed.)

—— A Contemporary Gospel Acclamation ——

In the nonliturgical churches the ancient gospel acclamation may be replaced by a more contemporary song such as a psalm, a canticle, or a praise tradition song. The purpose of the song is to adorn the reading of the gospel and thus serve the gospel.

Before the gospel is read, the people stand and the worship minister or choir leads them in the singing of a song that adorns the reading of the gospel and prepares the hearts of the people to hear the Word of the Lord.

Examples of Songs That May Adorn the Reading of the Gospel

  "Alleluia"
  "Change My Heart, O God"
  "Give Praise to Jesus"
  "Great Are You Lord"
  "Here in Your Presence"
  "Thy Word"

220 • PRAYER BEFORE THE SERMON

In many traditions a brief prayer is said before the sermon. Generally, if the people have been standing for the gospel, the prayer is said with the people standing. After the prayer they are seated. This is sometimes called the "prayer of illumination."

A Biblical Example of the Prayer Before the Sermon

Let the words of my mouth and the meditations of our hearts be acceptable in your sight, O Lord our strength and our redeemer. Amen.

or

In the name of the Father, the Son, and the Holy Spirit. Amen.

Traditional Examples of the Prayer Before the Sermon

O Master,
Illumine our hearts with the pure light of divine knowledge;
Open the eyes of our mind to understand your gospel;
implant in us the fear of your blessed commandments;
and trample down all our worldly desires:
That we may live in the Spirit,
Thanking you and doing the things that please you
For you are the illumination of our life.
And unto you we ascribe all glory,
For you live forever with the Father
Who is everlasting and with the Holy Spirit
Who is all-holy and the giver of life.
Now and forever and unto ages of ages. Amen.

(Adapted from the *Liturgy of St. John Chrysostom*)

or

Blessed Lord, who caused all holy Scriptures to be written for our learning: Grant us so to hear them, read, mark, learn, and inwardly digest them, that we may embrace and ever hold fast the blessed hope of everlasting life, which you have given us in our Saviour Jesus Christ; who lives and reigns with you and the Holy Spirit, one God, forever and ever. Amen.

(The Book of Common Prayer)

Guidelines for Preparing a Prayer of Illumination

Direction	Example
1. An ascription to God	Blessed Lord,
2. A description of God's work with reference to Scripture	who caused all holy Scripture to be written for our learning:
3. The petition	Grant us . . . that we may . . .
4. A closing doxology	who lives and reigns . . .

221 • Creeds in Worship (Traditional)

A creed is a summary of God's mighty acts of salvation. Saying or singing the creed in worship is a way of rehearsing the salvation story.

After the sermon, the people respond with an affirmation of faith. The affirmation of faith serves as a way for the congregation to express faith in God through a response to the Scripture readings and the sermon. Formal affirmations of faith include the Nicene Creed and the Apostles' Creed. The Nicene Creed, which originated in A.D. 325 and was set in its final form in 381, has always been looked on as the most appropriate creed for morning worship. The Apostles' Creed, which originated as a baptismal statement of faith, is always used when a baptism occurs.

A problem in the recitation of creeds is that the people tend to say the creed in an intellectual way. Originally the creed was doxological witness, a cry of faith from the heart, not a mere belief system to be recited from the head. Congregations should be taught to express the creed in an effective way. This can be accomplished by singing the creed or by saying it in a proclamatory way. Congregations must be instructed and taught how to do this. Use the time in the gathering to practice a heartfelt way of expressing faith through the creed.

Some churches prefer to prepare an affirmation of faith from Scripture texts instead of the traditional Nicene Creed or Apostles' Creed. These creeds may be said in unison, in an antiphonal manner, or in some other suitable way.

Other churches (especially charismatic), prefer to have brief spontaneous Statements of faith said or sung by members of the congregation. People may respond with acclamations of faith such as "God has been real to me in my suffering," "I know God loves me," or with statements that refer to characteristics of God such as, "Blessed be God who is filled with compassion and love," "Praise God who is sovereign over the affairs of people and nations."

When this approach to an affirmation of faith is used, care must be given to its introduction, to involvement of all the people, and to its conclusion. An affirmation of faith can also be achieved through a talk-back time to the Sermon. This form of response is particularly effective in the small or informal church. Simply ask: "What did you hear God saying to you?" and allow a specific amount of time for response.

Some churches are also asking for response to the sermon through brief groups discussions or talk-back sermons.

Biblical Creeds

Some churches do not use the traditional creeds of the church, preferring creeds that are strictly biblical. Below are several biblical creeds.

We stand in the good news
that Christ died for our sins according to the
    Scriptures,
that he was buried,
that he was raised on the third day,
and that he appeared to Peter,
then to the Twelve
and to many faithful witnesses.
We proclaim him to be the Christ,
the Son of the living God;
We confess that he is the first and the last,
the beginning and end;
And we commit our lives to him as our Lord and
    our God. Amen.

(Adapted from St. Paul)

or

We are convinced
there is no condemnation
for those who are in Christ Jesus,
and we have experienced
that in everything God works good
for those who love him
and are called according to his purpose.
We are also sure
that neither death,
nor life, nor angels,
nor principalities,
nor things present,
nor things to come,
nor powers,
nor height,
nor depth,
nor anything else
visible or invisible
will be able to separate us
from the love of God
in Christ Jesus our Lord. Amen.

(Adapted from St. Paul)

Examples of Traditional Creeds

The Nicene Creed is traditionally used in Sunday worship while the Apostles' Creed is used at baptism. Many churches, however, use the Apostles' Creed in morning worship as well.

The Nicene Creed

We believe in one God,
the Father, the Almighty,
Maker of heaven and earth,
of all that is, seen and unseen.
We believe in one Lord, Jesus Christ,
the only Son of God,
eternally begotten of the Father,
God from God, Light from Light,
true God from true God,
begotten, not made,
of one being with the Father.
Through him all things were made.
For us and for our salvation
he came down from heaven:
by the power of the Holy Spirit
he became incarnate from the Virgin Mary,
and was made man.
For our sake he was crucified under Pontius
    Pilate;
he suffered death and was buried.
On the third day he rose again
in accordance with the Scriptures;
he ascended into heaven
and is seated at the right hand of the Father.
He will come again in glory to judge the living
    and the dead,
and his kingdom will have no end.
We believe in the Holy Spirit, the Lord, the giver
    of life,
who proceeds from the Father [and the Son].
With the Father and the Son he is worshiped and
    glorified.
He has spoken through the Prophets.
We believe in one holy catholic and apostolic
    church.
We acknowledge one baptism for the forgiveness
    of sins.
We look for the resurrection of the dead,
and the life of the world to come. Amen.

(The Book of Common Prayer)

The Apostle's Creed

> I believe in God, the Father almighty,
> Creator of heaven and earth.
> I believe in Jesus Christ, his only Son, our Lord.
> He was conceived by the power of the Holy
> Spirit
> and born of the Virgin Mary.
> He suffered under Pontius Pilate,
> was crucified, died, and was buried.
> He descended to the dead.
> On the third day he rose again.
> He ascended into heaven,
> and is seated at the right hand of the Father.
> He will come again to judge the living and the
> dead.
> I believe in the Holy Spirit,
> the holy catholic church,
> the communion of saints,
> the forgiveness of sins,
> the resurrection of the body,
> and the life everlasting. Amen.

(The Book of Common Prayer)

Apostles Creed (Contemporary Version). Many renewing churches have kept the basic doctrines and teaching of the historic creeds while placing them in a more contemporary framework. In recent years Graham Kendrick wrote a musical version of the Apostles' Creed called "We Believe."

Barry Liesch, in his book *People in the Presence,* also provides us with a poetic version of the creed designed to be sung to the tune of "Glorious Things of Thee Are Spoken."

> I believe in God the Father Maker of the heaven
> and earth,
> And in Jesus Christ, our Savior, God's own Son of
> matchless worth;
> By the Holy Ghost conceived, Virgin Mary bore
> God's Son,
> He, in whom I have believed, God Almighty,
> Three in One.
> Suffered under Pontius Pilate, crucified for me
> He died.
> Laid within the grave so silent, gates of Hell He
> opened wide,
> And the stone-sealed tomb was empty, on the
> third day He arose,
> Into heaven made His entry, Mighty Conqueror
> of His foes.

> At God's right hand He is seated, till His coming,
> as He said,
> Final judgment will be meted to the living and
> the dead,
> I confess the Holy Spirit has been sent through
> Christ the Son,
> To apply salvation's merit, God the Spirit—Three
> in One.
> I believe that all believers form one body as a
> whole,
> We are one throughout the ages, with the saints I
> lift my soul.
> I believe sins are forgiven, that our bodies will be
> raised,
> Everlasting life in heaven, Amen, let His name be
> praised!

(Barry Liesch, *People in the Presence of God* [Grand Rapids: Zondervan, 1988], 108)

222 • CREEDS IN WORSHIP (CONTEMPORARY)

In contemporary and in praise-and-worship traditions, the response of faith is becoming a common practice. Some churches are using historical or contemporary creeds, while others are encouraging people to sing or say their own acclamations of faith or to engage in a talk-back sermon as a way of responding in faith to the Scripture readings and the proclamation of the gospel.

Form for Congregational Responses of Faith. The minister invites these responses of faith and people will say or sing such acclamations as "You are God," "I love you Lord," "You are faithful," "I bless you for your mercy and forgiveness." A form to be used for a spontaneous response of faith is below:

Minister:	In response to the Scripture readings and sermon, I invite you to offer brief acclamations of faith.
People:	[*Spontaneous responses of faith are made.*]
Minister:	The Lord's name be praised.
People:	**Amen.**

Resource: A number of excellent affirmations of faith are found in various prayer books.

A Form for Small Group Response of Faith

Minister:	Please stand. Please turn and group yourselves with four to six people and respond to the sermon by saying, "I heard God speak to me in . . ."

Minister: *Bring the response to a close with a song.*

A Form for a Talk-Back Sermon. After completing the sermon the minister may sit in a chair in a place where he/she can be seen by all. The minister may then say, "What did God say to you through the Scripture and sermon today? Please stand and speak clearly so that all may hear." The people may then respond with brief statements. These personal responses should not be sermons directed *at* people, but a witness to what has been heard in Scripture or Sermon and how that may be applied to this spiritual pilgrimage.

223 • THE PRAYERS OF THE PEOPLE

In contemporary worship renewal, the prayers of the people are said after the confession of faith. These prayers are known as the litany (Latin, "to entreat"). In many churches, this practice is replacing the more traditional pastoral prayer.

A litany is a prayer form in which a deacon, priest, cantor, or other worship minister says or sings a petition followed by a congregational response. Litanies were prepared in the early church, spreading from Antioch to Constantinople and throughout the Christian world. The litany form was developed particularly by the church at Constantinople and are found to this day in the liturgies of the East, particularly the St. John Chrysostom Liturgy. In the West the litany form fell into disuse after the sixth century but has been recovered since Vatican II. Consequently many new litany prayers have been developed for both Catholic and Protestant worshiping communities.

In addition to the forms for the prayers of the people found in the major worship books of various traditions, there are a number of very good contemporary collections. See the section on prayers in the bibliography at the end of chapter 9 of this volume.

——— Examples of the Litany Prayer ———

An Early Church Litany

We beg you, Lord, to help and defend us.
Deliver the oppressed. **Amen.**
Pity the insignificant. **Amen.**
Raise the fallen. **Amen.**
Show yourself to the needy. **Amen.**

Heal the sick. **Amen.**
Bring back those of your people who have gone
  astray. **Amen.**
Feed the hungry. **Amen.**
Lift up the weak. **Amen.**
Take off the prisoner's chains. **Amen.**
May every nation come to know
that you alone are God,
that Jesus Christ is your Child,
that we are your people, the sheep that you
  pasture. **Amen.**

(Clement of Rome, first century)

Contemporary Litanies

Father, we pray for your holy catholic church;
That we all may be one.

Grant that every member of the church may
  truly and humbly serve you;
That your Name may be glorified by all people.

We pray for all bishops, priests, and deacons;
**That they may be faithful ministers of your Word
  and Sacraments.**

We pray for all who govern and hold authority in
  the nations of the world;
That there may be justice and peace on earth.

Give us grace to do your will in all that we
  undertake;
That our works may find favor in your sight.

Have compassion on those who suffer from any
  grief or trouble;
That they may be delivered from their distress.

Give to the departed eternal rest;
Let light perpetual shine upon them.

We praise you for your saints who have entered
  into you;
**May we also come to share in your heavenly
  kingdom.**

Let us pray for our own needs and those of
  others.

Silence.
The People may add their own petitions.
The minister proceeds to the confession of sin when Communion is celebrated, unless a confession has been made in the Preparation. Otherwise conclude with the following prayer:

Lord, hear the prayers of your people; and what
we have asked faithfully, grant that we may obtain

effectually, to the glory of your name; through Jesus Christ our Lord. **Amen.**

(The Book of Common Prayer)

or

On behalf of all and for all, in peace, let us pray to the Lord . . .

Saying, "Lord, hear our prayer."

1. For peace from on high, for the salvation of our souls, and for the fulfillment of creation, let us pray to the Lord . . .
2. For good weather, for an abundance of the fruits of the earth, for the protection of our homes, the safety of our neighborhoods, and for a clean and healthy environment, let us pray to the Lord . . . .
3. For our civil authorities, the mayor of this city, the president of the United States, for _____, and for all world leaders, let us pray to the Lord . . .
4. For the pope, John Paul; our bishop, _____; our priest, _____; and for all the holy servants of God, let us pray to the Lord . . .
5. For those who have done good for us; for our parents, relatives, and friends, especially: _____; and for all who celebrate birthdays and anniversaries this week, especially: _____, let us pray to the Lord . . .
6. For those who are visiting with us for the first time: _____ and for all those who are recorded in (your parish's) Book of Life, let us pray to the Lord . . .
7. For _____ let us pray to the Lord . . . .
8. For the poor, the hungry, the homeless and imprisoned; for exiles and refugees; for the aged, the lonely and the bereaved; especially: _____ and for all those who are in need, let us pray to the Lord . . . .
9. For the sick, especially: _____ and for all those who are in need, let us pray to the Lord . . . .
10. For those who have departed from this life, especially: _____ and for all who lie asleep in the Lord, let us pray to the Lord . . . .
11. For all the people of this parish, both living and dead, especially those who were baptized or married here, and those who were

buried from this holy church, and for all present here this day, let us pray to the Lord . . . .
12. Remembering the Holy Mother of God, Saints (of day and coming week) _____ _____ and all the saints, we offer to you, O Lord, our whole lives, on behalf of all, and for all, let us pray to the Lord . . . (final response is "To you, O Lord!")

(*Modern Liturgy,* 12, 9 [1985]:9)

Preparing Litany Prayers

1. Develop a prayer or prayers for each of the four traditional areas of intercessory concern.
   • the church
   • the world and nation
   • the poor, the oppressed, and the sick
   • the work and needs of the local church
2. Prepare responses that are specific to the intercession.
3. Responses should be short.

The Bidding Prayer

Many renewing congregations are using the ancient bidding prayers for the congregational intercessions. In the bidding prayer the prayer leader introduces an area of prayer concern and the congregation then prays the concerns of that particular area. This form of prayer has the advantage of eliciting congregational participation in prayer and has been used very successfully in congregations that have been taught to pray.

In smaller congregations or cell-based worshiping communities, the intervention prayer model is being used as a modification of bidding prayers. The leader would begin the prayer time with instruction, stating that after an opening prayer, those in the congregation are free to offer publicly those concerns that are on their hearts. After the concern is voiced, either the one who shares the request or another leads in a short prayer focused on that need. If the persons are present, laying on of hands by the ministers or members of the body during the prayer time is recommended.

Directed Prayer. Another variation of the bidding prayer is the directed prayer model. It is usually practiced in larger churches or in churches that also practice a ministry time at the platform during Prayers of the People. In Directed Prayer, the minister leads the people in an opening prayer and then begins to mention various areas of prayer focus. After mentioning the need, time is given for the congregation to pray silently or quietly about that specific need. The minister can then list another need or end the prayer by simply saying, "Lord, hear our prayer." This more quiet version of bidding prayer offers time for counsel and ministry to take place in the front of the church during the prayer time, where people can be anointed for healing or prayed for by prayer team members who have gathered to support them.

A Form for a Extemporaneous Bidding Prayer

Leader: Please stand together for the Prayers of the People. I will announce topics of prayer and ask you to respond with short sentence prayers. After each prayer, please end the prayer with the word "Lord" so that the congregation may respond "Hear our prayer."

Leader: Let us pray for the church universal, for all its people and especially for those who work and minister in the church.

People: (Prayers are offered.)

Leader: Let us pray for the needs of the world, for those who lead the nations and for this nation.

People: *(Prayers are offered.)*

Leader: Let us pray for the poor, the needy, and the sick.

People: *(Prayers are offered.)*

Leader: Let us pray for the needs and the work of this local church.

People: *(Prayers are offered.)*

Leader: *(May close with a prayer, a confession of sin, or the Lord's Prayer.)*

or

The following form may be used to supplement the preceding prayers or the entire prayers of intercession may be developed in a fashion similar to this prayer and placed as an insert in the bulletin for congregational prayer. The constant supplication for people that this prayer presents emphasizes a growing sense of community.

Leader: Let us pray for the needs of . . .
(Michelle, Diane, Pat, Elizabeth, Michael, Zachary, Rachel, Laurie, the McKain family, all prisoners and hostages . . . any others)

People: **Lord in your mercy . . . hear our prayer.**

Leader: Let us remember those who are shut in, especially . . .
(Virginia, Frances, Bob . . . any others)

People: **Lord in your mercy . . . hear our prayer.**

Leader: Let us remember those needing prayers for health and healing . . .
(Frances, Cynthia, Agnes, Margaret, Hazel, Gertrude, Norah, Dick, Madoka, Dana, Stan, Sandy, Helen, Pauline, Sarah, Bunny, Pat, Erin, Frank, Christopher, Mary Ann, John . . . any others)

People: **Lord in your mercy . . . hear our prayer.**

Leader: Let us pray for those who celebrate their birthday this week . . .
(Steward Ruch
Robert Frederick
Michael Horn
Marjorie Benolken)

People: **Thanks be to God.**

Leader: Let us give thanks for the life and witness of those who have died and pray for the strengthening of their families . . . .
(Jean Huff Kirstein
Shina Kadoyama
George Watanabe
Frank Kastner)

People: **Lord in your mercy . . . hear our prayer.**

Leader: Let us give thanks for God's blessings in our lives . . .
(Spontaneous prayer)

Leader: *(Closing prayer.)*

(From Church of the Resurrection, West Chicago, Illinois)

224 • CONFESSION OF SIN

When a confession of sin is not used in the Entrance and will not be used as an examination of conscience (before the Table prayers), a confession may be used at the end of the prayers of the people.

A Liturgical Example
— of the Confession at the End —
of the Prayers of the People

We pray to you also for the forgiveness of our
   sins.

Silence may be kept.

Leader and People:
> Have mercy on us, most merciful Father;
> in your compassion forgive us our sins,
> known and unknown,
> things done and left undone;
> and so uphold us by your Spirit
> that we may live and serve you in
>   newness of life,
> to the honor and glory of your Name;
> through Jesus Christ our Lord. Amen.

*The Celebrant concludes with an absolution or a
suitable Collect.*

A Nonliturgical Approach to the
—— Confession of Sin at the End of ——
the Prayers of the People

The minister may say,

Let us confess our sin to Almighty God.

*Silence may be kept or the minister may make Con-
fession for all by proclaiming a list of sins personal,
institutional, and national.*

*The minister may conclude with an extempora-
neous prayer and proclamation of God's forgiveness.*

225 ✦ THE PASSING OF THE PEACE

*The kiss of peace concludes the response to the Word. The
kiss of peace, a handshake, or a hug extended to other people*
*in the congregation expresses the reconciliation Christ has
made not only with God, but also on the horizontal level
between people. This has become a joyful time, a time to
greet each other with a Christian greeting and to express a
feeling of love through a physical gesture. Encourage great
freedom and hospitality in this action as a way of expressing
and experiencing the warmth and love of the community of
faith.*

Form for Passing the Kiss of Peace

The Peace of the Lord be always with you.

or

The Peace of Christ be with you.
And also with you.

or

As our Lord said to his disciples,
"Peace be with you."
And also with you.

These words are said first by the minister or worship
leader. Then, as the people exchange the peace they
say these words to each other. The meaning of the
words and the sequence is that this is not a simple
greeting among friends, but it is a gift of God's own
peace passed from one to another. It is worth taking
time occasionally to reinforce this meaning of the
peace. However, in most warm and friendly congregations the time of passing the peace tends to get
happily chaotic and is indeed a special time of community bonding. The exchange of the peace occurs
with a handshake, a hug, or a kiss.

Robert E. Webber with
Randolph Sly
Ronal Freyer Nicholas

EIGHT

Resources for the Service of the Table

In the early church, worship consisted of both Word and Table. The Word proclaimed the saving deed of God in Jesus Christ, and the Table was the response of thanksgiving (Eucharist is the Greek word for thanks). During medieval times, the Roman Catholic church did not maintain the ancient balance of Word and Table, allowing the reading and preaching of the Word to go into decline. The Protestant Reformation restored the Word to its rightful place in worship and sought to maintain the ancient balance of Word and Table. Unfortunately the Reformers' wishes in this regard were left largely unfulfilled, and among Protestants, the Table of the Lord has been celebrated infrequently and without adequate understanding. However, as worship renewal seeks to recover the worship of the early church, both Word and Table are receiving new attention from Catholics and Protestants.

Contemporary worship renewal has recognized the need to recover the experience of resurrection joy at the table while not abandoning the focus on Christ's death and passion. This has been accomplished through the use of (1) various contemporary and traditional forms of the ancient Prayer of Thanksgiving, (2) Communion songs, which can bring a mood of celebration or meditation (or both) to the Table, and (3) the Rite of Anointing, which emphasizes the healing virtues of Christ's resurrection power. All three actions restore the joy and communicate the presence of Christ's saving grace among the people.

The theology and individual elements of the eucharistic prayers are discussed in more detail in Volume 6: The Sacred Actions of Christian Worship, Part 4: History, Theology, and Practice of the Lord's Table.

226 • WHAT DOES THE SERVICE OF THE TABLE DO?

The acts of worship at the Table of the Lord enact the story of how God in Jesus Christ, who gave himself as a sacrifice for sin, overthrew the powers of evil and left an example of life lived by love. Contemporary worship accents the joy of God's salvation and healing available at the Table.

Originally the church met in houses for the breaking of the bread (Acts 2:42-47). These celebrations, known as the Agape feast (Love feast), were full meals and were occasions of great joy because of the presence of the resurrection of Christ.

Later, due to the misuse of the Agape feast, the apostle Paul instructed people to eat their meals at home and to remember the death of Christ when they gather for the Lord's Supper (1 Cor. 11:23-26).

In the history of Table worship there has always been tension between the sobriety of the Corinthian model, which emphasizes the death of Christ and the more primitive model in Acts, which emphasizes the joyous experience of his Resurrection. The Western church, both Catholic and Protestant, has had a long history of emphasizing the death of Christ without an adequate experience of the Resurrection. Consequently Table worship has been sober, meditative, and penitential (and, too often, dreary).

Contemporary worship renewal recognizes the

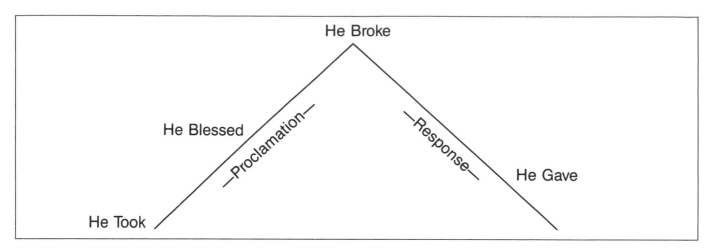

The Shape of Table Worship. *The basic shape of Table worship is patterned on the actions of Jesus (Matt. 26:26).*

need to recover the experience of resurrection joy at the Table. This has been accomplished through the recovery of (1) the ancient Prayer of Thanksgiving, (2) the use of Communion songs, and (3) the Rite of Anointing. All three of these actions restore the experience of resurrection joy and communicate the presence of Christ's saving action among the people.

227 • BIBLICAL TERMS FOR THE SERVICE OF THE TABLE

The New Testament uses four terms to describe worship at the Table: Breaking of the Bread, the Lord's Supper, Communion, and Eucharist.

1. **Breaking of the Bread** (Acts 2:42). The emphasis is on the presence of the resurrected Christ in the feast. The term *breaking of bread* is reminiscent of the appearance of Jesus to the disciples, in the breaking of bread (Luke 24:31, 35).

2. **The Lord's Supper** (1 Cor. 11:17-34). The emphasis is on the death of Christ. The experience recalls the sobriety of the Last Supper and Jesus' impending death.

3. **Communion** (1 Cor. 10:16). The emphasis is on a participation in the broken body and shed blood. The word *communion* means participation, and refers to the thanksgiving God's people give for the death and resurrection of Christ.

4. **Eucharist** (John 6:11; 1 Cor. 11:24). The word *Eucharist* means "giving thanks." The prayers at the Table are called the great Thanksgiving.

228 • THE SHAPE OF TABLE WORSHIP

From the very beginnings of Table worship, its various parts have been discernible.

The service of the Table originated at the Last Supper (see Matt. 26:29) and consisted of seven parts, in which Jesus:

1. took bread,
2. blessed the bread,
3. broke the bread,
4. gave bread to his disciples,
5. took a cup,
6. gave thanks,
7. gave the cup to his disciples.

In the process of time, these seven actions were condensed into four. For example, Luke may have been aware of these four actions of the Table when he wrote "he *took* bread, gave thanks, *broke* it and began to give it to them" (Luke 24:30, italics added). Thus in the ancient church, the universal action at the Table compresses the four rites over the bread and three rites over the wine into four parts that incorporate the blessing and giving of bread and wine into single actions:

1. the taking
2. the blessing (over both bread and wine)
3. the breaking
4. the distribution (of both bread and wine)

As worship developed, each of these four parts of Table worship were expanded with prayers, response, and symbolic actions. In the medieval era these sub-parts of the service became excessively elaborate with all sorts of ceremonial actions. The Reformers sought to return the worship of the Table to its more primitive simplicity, but in the process lost certain parts of Table worship grounded in the ancient tradition. Today the Reformation concern for simplicity is retained, but a greater emphasis is placed on recovering the substance of Table worship developed in the first five centuries of the church.

The renewal of Table worship today is not merely the recovery of ancient forms for the sake of antiquity. Rather, because these forms of worship are unique in their biblical imagery, they contain a greater power to deliver the meaning of what is happening at the Table. Consequently, the revised forms of the ancient eucharistic prayers used in renewal worship today are significant because of their faithfulness to the biblical and historical tradition of eucharistic worship. As such, they deliver a keener sense of the presence of Christ and call the worshiper into a deeper response to the benefits of Christ's work made available at the Table.

229 ✦ THE STRUCTURE OF TABLE WORSHIP IN THE EARLY CHURCH

The oldest prayer of Thanksgiving is found in Hippolytus, The Apostolic Tradition, dated about A.D. 215. Because Hippolytus remembered this prayer from his youth, it is generally thought the prayer reaches back to 150. Through this prayer we can see the developed parts of the ancient eucharistic prayer. Consequently, this prayer has served as a model for the contemporary restructuring of the prayers said at the Table.

The Text of Hippolytus is shown in its entirety on the following page.

230 ✦ GUIDELINES FOR A CONTEMPORARY MODEL OF THE LORD'S SUPPER

The following is an example of the Lord's Supper as it might be conducted in a contemporary church such as a creative or a praise-and-worship assembly. It presupposes careful preparation on the part of the minister and people. A bulletin insert may provide the order of service, the responses, and Communion hymns. The service is a single whole and is to be celebrated without announcement and in the spirit of celebration and joy.

General Guidelines

Below are six guidelines for those who lead Table worship without the use of a book of prayer and/or a set form.

1. Examples of the eucharistic prayer should be received in the same spirit in which Hippolytus set forth the first known eucharistic prayer. He exhorted his readers to view the eucharistic canon as a model but not one to be slavishly followed.

2. Each pastor and local congregation of the non-liturgical traditions should study the content of the Table prayers and freely develop a form most suitable to their own local customs and tastes, seeking to retain the historic substance, meaning, and spirit of the prayers and responses.

3. Because the underlying structure of the prayer, like other parts of worship, is proclamation and response, serious attention should be given to the incorporation of the response in the eucharistic prayer. Note especially the _Sursum Corda,_ the _Sanctus,_ the _Memorial Acclamation,_ the _Lord's Prayer,_ and the _Agnus Dei,_ or response in the breaking of the bread. Either these responses or appropriate substitutes should be used to maintain the structure of proclamation and response and to involve the congregation in a participatory way in the _Prayer of Thanksgiving._

4. Because an important aspect of receiving the Communion is the personal "yes" said to the death and resurrection of Christ (for me), careful consideration should be given to the manner of reception. Symbols that strengthen the personal element of faith response include:
   • Coming forward to receive the bread and wine
   • Giving the bread and wine to each person by name
   • Touching the hand of the receiver as the bread is placed in the palm of the hand
   • Instructing the receiver to say "Amen" to the words of giving both the bread and the wine

5. Because the overriding mood of Table worship is the joy of the Resurrection, special attention should be paid to the Communion song and its power to help the congregation achieve a spirit of praise.

The Text of Hippolytus

ORDER	TEXT	COMMENTARY
Dominus vobiscum	The Lord be with you *And all shall say:* And with your spirit.	
Sursum Corda (Lift up your hearts)	Lift up your hearts. We have them with the Lord. Let us give thanks to the Lord. It is fitting and right.	Worship ascends into heaven around the throne of God.
Preface Prayer	We render thanks to you O God, through your beloved child Jesus Christ, whom in the last times you sent to us as savior and redeemer and angel of your will; . . .	The preface to the prayer of thanksgiving is a proclamation.
Sanctus	(Not found in Hippolytus)	In the Sanctus, the church joins with the angels and archangels in the heavenly song.
Prayer of Thanksgiving	. . . who is your inseparable Word, through whom you made all things, and in whom you are well pleased. You sent Him from heaven into the Virgin's womb; and, conceived in the womb, he was made flesh and was manifested as your Son, being born of the Holy Spirit and the Virgin. Fulfilling your will and gaining for you a holy people, he stretched out his hands when he should suffer, that he might release from suffering those who have believed in you. And when he was betrayed to voluntary suffering that he might destroy death, and break the bonds of the devil, and tread down hell, and shine upon the righteous, and fix the limit, and manifest the resurrection, . . .	The prayer of thanksgiving is a recall of God's mighty acts in history, particularly God's act of salvation in Jesus Christ. Note the creedal nature of the prayer as it recounts creation, incarnation, death, resurrection, overthrow of evil, and establishment of the church.
Words of Institution	. . . he took bread and gave thanks to you, saying, "Take, eat, this is my body which shall be broken for you." Likewise also the cup saying, "This is my blood, which is shed for you; when you do this you make my remembrance."	The repetition of the words of Jesus lie at the heart of the Table action.
Anamnesis (Remembrance)	Remembering therefore his death and resurrection, we offer to you the bread and the cup, giving you thanks because you have held us worthy to stand before you and minister to you.	The word "anamnesis" means recall and refers not to a mental memory, but a divine action in which Christ, the head of the church, is remembered with the body.
Offering		The offering is the offering of the church's praise, which ministers to God.
Epiclesis	And we ask that you send your Holy Spirit upon the offering of your holy church; that, gathering them into one, you would grant to all who partake of the holy things (to partake) for the fullness of the Holy Spirit for the confirmation of faith in truth; . . .	The Holy Spirit is invoked so that those who partake may be confirmed in truth by the work of the Spirit.
Closing Doxology	. . . that we may praise and glorify you through your child Jesus Christ, through whom be glory and honor to you, to the Father and the Son with the Holy Spirit, in your holy Church, both now and to the ages of ages. (Amen.)	The prayer ends with a trinitarian doxology.

(R. C. D. Jasper and G. J. Cuming, eds., Prayers of the Eucharist: Early and Reformed, *2d ed. [New York: Oxford University Press, 1980], 22–23)*

6. Because Table worship is a special encounter with the risen Christ, who heals our infirmities, special attention should be paid to the rite of healing in connection with the reception of the elements.

Specific Guidelines for Table Prayers and Leadership

Invitation to the Table and Confession of Sin. The leader may make a few comments inviting all who have faith in Christ to come to his Table. These comments may be followed by an invitation to examine conscience through singing a chorus such as "Create in Me a Clean Heart," followed by "We Bring the Sacrifice of Praise" or some other such song.

The Prayer of Thanksgiving/The Preface Prayer. The minister may pray, giving thanks to God for who he is, for his act of creation, and for his activity in history with the patriarchs, the prophets, and with the people of this congregation.

Sanctus. The people may then sing choruses praising God for his person, such as "Thou Art Worthy," "Blessed be the Lord God Almighty," "Glorify Thy Name," "Holy, Holy, Holy Is the Lord of Hosts."

Thanksgiving. The minister then gives thanks to God for the birth, life, death, resurrection, ascension, and coming again of Christ.

Words of Institution. The minister then says the words of institution.

The Acclamation. The people sing again, acclaiming the wonder of Christ and the gospel in songs such as "All Hail King Jesus," "Jesus, Name Above All Names," "Worthy Is the Lamb."

The Remembrance. The minister continues in prayer, remembering the Cross, the tomb, the Resurrection, and the overthrow of the powers of evil.

The Invocation of the Spirit. The people then sing a prayer invoking the presence of the Holy Spirit in their midst such as "Come, Holy Spirit," "Holy Spirit," "Spirit of the God," "Spirit Song."

The Lord's Prayer. The people continue by singing the Lord's Prayer.

The Breaking of the Bread. The minister lifts the bread and breaks it and lifts the cup for all to see. Words of acclamation, such as "The Body of Christ Broken For Us" and "The Blood of Christ Shed for Us," may accompany the action.

Communion. The people are invited to receive the bread and wine. They either walk forward and receive it at the Table, or bread and wine is served in the pew. During the reception, choruses move the people through the death and into the Resurrection. Choruses such as "O the Blood," "You Are the Vine," "Seek Ye First," "Praise the Name of Jesus," "Emmanuel," "His Name Is Wonderful," "The Lord Liveth," or "God Reigns," are sung.

Laying on of Hands. After the people have communed, a prayer line may be formed for the laying on of hands and the rite of healing. The people continue to sing until all have received and been prayed for.

Doxology. A closing prayer may be said by the minister, or the people may sing a closing doxology such as "Lord Be Glorified" or "All Thy Works Shall Praise Thee."

231 ✦ THE MEANING OF TABLE WORSHIP

At the Table of the Lord, the church recalls God's saving acts in Christ and experiences the benefit of healing.

For some, the complicated set of prayers that belong to the Table through biblical precedent and historical tradition may seem tedious and unnecessary. However, let it be remembered that, at the Table, God's people celebrated the entire history of salvation from creation through God's calling of Israel to the Incarnation, death, Resurrection, ascension, and coming in glory of Christ together with the church's response of faith. The Table is a drama of the meaning and mystery of human existence revealed in Christ. Consequently, Table worship should not be done haphazardly or in haste as something tacked on to the end of worship. Indeed, what is done at the Table is the supreme act of Christian worship, the act that makes Christian worship uniquely different from Hebrew worship and that of other religions of the world.

232 ✦ THE PLACE OF THE ARTS AT TABLE WORSHIP

The arts are vehicles of communication. They are not used for their own sake, but rather a means through which an encounter with the risen Christ is enhanced.

There are two places where the arts serve the action of the Table.

1. Dance may accompany the song sung during the bringing of the gifts and wine to the Table.
2. Communion songs may be sung during the reception of bread and wine as a way of expressing the mystery of the death and Resurrection.

233 ◆ THE PRESENTATION OF BREAD AND WINE (HE TOOK)

The taking consists of bringing the bread and wine to the Table, where the elements are prepared by the presider. The taking, which is primarily a symbolic action, conveys many powerful ideas. Because the primary symbol is that of an offering made to God, a number of offerings may occur simultaneously. For example, as the bread and wine are brought to the Table, an anthem may be sung and an offering of money taken. What is important in this action is the sense that the whole congregation is making an offering of praise and thanksgiving to almighty God. When the people are able to make connection with the symbolic action, their own offering of praise becomes more intense and moving.

The Presentation in Liturgical Churches

In liturgical churches, the Table remains bare through the Service of the Word. After the kiss of peace, an ascription of praise is made and then, as the choir sings an anthem, two persons (or a family) will carry the bread and wine down the center aisle and hand them to the minister, who places them on the Table and prepares for the Eucharist with various prayers and actions. The ushers follow behind the bread and wine bearers and receive the offering as the choir sings (or a congregational song may be sung), and the bread and wine bearers return to their seats. The order of the taking in liturgical churches is as follows:

- After the kiss of peace, announcements may be made.
- Then, facing the congregation with outstretched hands, the minister may say the ascription of praise, such as "O Taste and See That the Lord is Good."

- Next, the choir may sing an anthem or a congregational hymn may be sung.
- Then, as the above action is taking place, the bearers of bread and wine and the ushers process to the Table.
- The minister receives the bread and wine, the bearers of bread and wine turn and return to their seats and the ushers receive the offering.
- As these actions are taking place, the minister prepares the Table with one or more of the following actions:
  Silent prayers over bread and wine
  Mingling of water and wine in the chalice
  Incensation
  Washing of the hands
- The hymn or anthem ended, the ushers bring the offering forward as the congregation sings, "Praise God From Whom All Blessings Flow." The minister prays, thanking God for the offering. The ushers return. The minister now begins the prayer of thanksgiving.

The Presentation in Contemporary Churches

An order of presentation of the gifts of bread and wine for churches not following a set liturgical tradition is as follows:

- The Table may be prepared beforehand, in which case the taking does not occur in public.
- The deacons or others who serve may walk forward during a hymn and take their places by the minister at the Table.
- At the conclusion of the hymn, the minister may call the congregation to the examination of conscience through a Scripture reading or through a prayer.

Many nonliturgical churches are now setting the Table during worship and adapt the order of the liturgical style of the taking to their own situation.

234 ◆ THE ASCRIPTION OF PRAISE

The ascription of praise is a statement made by the minister that signals the beginning of the service of the Table. It is said just after the kiss of peace or after the announcements (if the announcements are between the Service of the Word and the Service of the Table). One of the following or some other appropriate sentence of Scripture may be used in both liturgical and contemporary worship.

> Sacrifice thank offerings to God, fulfill your vows to the Most High. (Ps. 50:14)

> Ascribe to the LORD the glory due his name; bring an offering and come into his courts. (Ps. 96:8)

> If you are offering your gift at the altar and there remember that your brother has something against you leave your gift there in front of the altar. First go and be reconciled to your brother; then come and offer your gift. (Matt. 5:23-24)

> Therefore, I urge you, brothers, in view of God's mercy, to offer your bodies as living sacrifices, holy and pleasing to God—this is your spiritual act of worship. (Rom. 12:1)

> Live a life of love, just as Christ loved us and gave himself up for us as a fragrant offering and sacrifice to God. (Eph. 5:2)

235 • THE OFFERTORY HYMN

The offertory hymn expresses the action of bringing bread and wine and of coming to the Table of the Lord.

Examples of Traditional Offertory Hymns

"Come Down, O Love Divine"
"I Bind unto Myself"
"I Come with Joy to Meet My Lord"
"All My Hope on God Is Founded"
"Christ Is Made the Sure Foundation"
"At the Name of Jesus Every Knee Shall Bow"
"Let All Mortal Flesh Keep Silence" (used regularly in the fourth century)
"A Banquet Is Prepared"
"Come to Me, All Who Are Weary"

Examples of Offertory Praise Music

"Eat This Bread"
"Let Us Break Bread Together"
"One Bread, One Body"
"You Are Our Living Bread"
"Come into the Holy of Holies"
"To Thee We Ascribe Glory"

236 • THE PREPARATION OF THE TABLE

The following instructions are especially suited for liturgical churches. However, contemporary churches may adapt these traditions to local usage and custom.

Preparation of the Table in Liturgical Churches

Bread and Wine. While the wine or grape juice is purchased at a store or through liturgical supply vendors, many churches have appointed persons to bake the bread at home. Homemade bread adds a personal quality to the service and engages the gifts of the breadmaker in worship. Several brands of nonalcoholic wine (such as St. Regis) are now available for those who want wine but avoid alcohol.

Table Setting. The Table is bare except for candles. The deacon or server sets the Table by placing on it the corporal (tablecloth), the purificator (napkin), the chalice (drinking cup), the paten (plate for the bread), and the missal (the book of prayers).

Prayers Over the Bread and Wine. The celebrant takes the paten with the bread and lifts it slightly for the people to see, saying a brief prayer (said audibly or inaudibly), praising God for the gifts of creation (a Jewish tradition, not a prayer over bread, but a prayer blessing God). The Jewish prayer said with the bread is:

> Blessed be God, King of the Universe, who brings forth bread from the earth.

The same may be done with the cup. The Jewish prayer with the cup is:

> Blessed art thou, O Lord God, King eternal, who createst the fruit of the vine.

Mingling of Water and Wine. A server brings a vial of water to the celebrant. Water is poured into the wine. This symbolizes the water and blood flowing from the side of Jesus. Some suggest, however, that it symbolizes the two natures in the person of Christ or the union between Christ and his people.

Prayer of the Celebrant. The celebrant then prays a brief audible or inaudible prayer professing his or her own need of pardon. In some traditions this prayer takes the form of a congregational prayer known as the prayer of humble access (see the traditional rite in _The Book of Common Prayer_).

Incensation. The Table, bread, and wine, are incensed as a sign of prayer going up to God.

Washing of the Hands. The celebrant washes his or her hands as a symbol of cleansing, while reciting audibly or inaudibly Psalm 51:4 "Against you, you only, have I sinned and done what is evil in your sight."

Preparation of the Table in Contemporary Churches

When the Table is prepared before the service, the work should be done in the spirit of prayer. While one is preparing bread and wine and setting the Table, the Lord's Prayer may be repeated, Scripture may be quoted, or a song may be sung. When the Table is prepared in worship, an adaptation of the liturgical approach is made according to local usage and custom.

237 • THE EXAMINATION OF CONSCIENCE

The examination of conscience before the Table is used when there has been no confession of sin in either the acts of Entrance or after the prayers of the people.

The examination of conscience may occur as follows:

The minister may say:

Hear the words of the apostle Paul "Examine yourselves, and only then eat of the bread and drink of the cup" (1 Cor. 11:28, NRSV).

Here follows silence, an extemporaneous prayer, or one of the following prayers said by minister and people together.

> Father,
> Lord of Heaven and earth,
> I confess to you all hidden and open sins
> of my heart and mind,
> which I have committed until this day.
> Wherefore I beg of you,
> The merciful and righteous judge,
> Forgiveness and grace to sin no more. Amen.

(Eastern Orthodox)

or

> O Lord our God,
> Our Creator and our Judge;

> Proved every day, yet strong and patient;
> Forgive we beseech you,
> Our rebellion against your will.

or

> Our forgetfulness of your law,
> Our complacency, apathy,
> Our culpable ignorance,
> Our tolerance of intolerable wrongs.
> Have mercy upon us, O Lord,
> And turn our hearts,
> Through Jesus Christ, our blessed Lord and
>   Savior.
> Amen.

(Unknown)

When writing or preparing an examination of conscience, observe the following structural guidelines:

Definition	Example
An ascription to God	Father
A description of an attribute of God	Lord of heaven and earth
The confession	I confess to you, etc.
God's property of mercy	The merciful and righteous Judge
The application of God's property	Forgiveness and grace to sin no more

238 • THE PRAYER OF THANKSGIVING (HE BLESSED)

The blessing, which is also known as the eucharistic prayer or prayer of thanksgiving, originated from the Jewish Bᵉrakah (blessing). It passed through various stages of development, reaching a fixed content in the fourth and fifth century. In the medieval era it became excessively elaborate. The Reformers simplified the prayer, and today the forms of the ancient church are being restored to common use in the church.

Some scholars believe the prayer of thanksgiving is a modification of the Jewish Bᵉrakah (blessing). The Bᵉrakah said on both private and public occasions reflects the prayer most likely said at the Last Supper. It contains three parts:

1. Praise
2. Commemoration
3. Petition

During the early centuries of Christianity, the prayers of thanksgiving may have been an adaptation of this form. By the end of the fourth century the development of this prayer was complete, resulting in the prayer known as the _eucharistic prayer_ in the West (_anaphora_ in the East). The prayer appears to have three parts, corresponding with the three parts of the _B^erekah_ prayer along with subparts that express the theme. Here is the basic outline of the prayer:

1. Praise
   The Opening Dialogue
   The Preface
   The _Sanctus_
2. Commemoration
   Thanksgiving for Salvation History
   The Institution Narrative
   The Prayer of Offering and Remembrance
3. Petition
   Invocation of the Holy Spirit
   Intercessions
   Doxology
   Amen

This prayer, which is known as the great thanksgiving, is a powerful representation of Christ's work, the work that delivers us from the power of the evil one. The content is therefore characterized by historical commemoration and eschatological anticipation. It tells the story of the death and Resurrection of Jesus in both word and action. The story of the prayer recites everything from Creation to consummation, emphasizing the restoration of all things in Christ. Great care must be given to tell and

Praise. With hands lifted the minister bids the congregation to lift up their hearts in praise.

act out this story with a mixture of both solemnity and joy in order to adequately express both the death and the resurrection. The people may be carried through the death and Resurrection as a rehearsal of their own faith not only through the words and symbols of the service, but also through the music, which serves as a powerful vehicle for the communication of God's saving presence at the Table of the Lord.

239 • THE STRUCTURE OF THE PRAYER OF THANKSGIVING

The following examples are intended to provide the reader with a sense both of the structure and of the content of the prayer of thanksgiving. For more examples, see chapter 4 in this volume.

See pages 260–261 for structure and commentary.

240 • GUIDELINES FOR AN EXTEMPORANEOUS PRAYER OF THANKSGIVING

Traditions that do not use fixed prayers may follow the suggestions below:

- Begin with thanks for the goodness of God made available to us in Creation.
- Recall the people of faith such as Abraham, Moses, David, prophets, Miriam, Deborah, Ruth, Hulda, Elizabeth, Dorcas, Priscilla, or others through whom the continued witness of God's activity in the world has been made.
- Make thanks for God's salvific action in Jesus Christ, in his incarnation, death, and resurrection.
- Repeat Christ's words at the institution of the Lord's Supper.
- Pray a prayer to the effect that participation in Communion is an offering of praise and an offering of one's life to God.
- Briefly proclaim the death, Resurrection, and the coming again of Christ at the end of history.
- Invoke the Holy Spirit to come upon people and gifts to confirm their faith in truth.
- Lead the people in the Lord's Prayer.

The Prayer of Thanksgiving

The Lord be with you
And also with you.
Lift up your hearts
We lift them to the Lord.
Let us give thanks to the Lord our God
It is right to give Him thanks and praise.

Minister:
It is right, and a good and joyful thing, always and everywhere to give thanks to you, Father Almighty, Creator of heaven and earth.

Here the minister continues with a Preface Prayer suited to the particular occasion of worship. This prayer ends with words such as: And so, with your people on earth, and all the company of heaven, we praise your name, and join their unending hymn:

Minister and People Say or Sing:

Holy, holy, holy Lord,
God of power and might, heaven and earth are full of your glory.
Hosanna in the highest.
Blessed is He who comes in the name of the Lord.
Hosanna in the highest.

The people stand or kneel as the minister continues with the prayer:

Holy and gracious Father: In your infinite love you made us for yourself; and, when we had fallen into sin and become subject to evil and death, you in your mercy sent Jesus Christ, your only and eternal Son, to share our human nature, to live and die as one of us, to reconcile us to you, the God and Father of all. He stretched out his arms upon the cross, and offered himself, in obedience to your will, a perfect sacrifice for the whole world.

At the following words concerning the bread, the minister may hold it or lay a hand upon it; and at the words concerning the cup, to hold or place a hand upon the cup and any other vessel containing wine to be consecrated.

On the night he was handed over to suffering and death, our Lord Jesus Christ took bread; and when he had given thanks to you, he broke it, and gave it to his disciples, and said, "Take, eat: This is my body, which is given for you. Do this for the remembrance of me."

After supper he took the cup of wine; and when he had given thanks, he gave it to them, and said, "Drink this, all of you. This is my blood of the New Covenant, which is shed for you and for many for the forgiveness of sins. Whenever you drink it, do this for the remembrance of me."

Therefore we proclaim the mystery of faith:

Minister and People respond:
Christ has died
Christ is risen
Christ will come again

The Minister continues:
We celebrate the memorial of our redemption, O Father, in this sacrifice of praise and thanksgiving. Recalling his death, resurrection and ascension, we offer you these gifts.

Structure and Commentary

Sursum Corda

This ancient opening dialogue is now used universally.

The Preface Prayer

The content of the preface prayer is related to the Sunday in the church year or to the theme of the celebration.

Sanctus

The *Sanctus* has been set to many different tunes available in denominational hymn books. Contemporary, creative, praise tradition, and charismatic may replace the traditional *Sanctus* with a contemporary Holy, Holy, Holy (or a stanza from a familiar hymn)

Commemoration

Here, saving events in Jesus Christ are recalled.

Words of Institution

It is universally taught that a proper Communion cannot take place without the words of institution.

Memorial Acclamation
The Memorial acclamation provides an opportunity for the people to respond to the Prayer of Thanksgiving.

Anamnesis and Oblation
A prayer containing the remembrance and an offering of the gifts, as well as an offering of sacrifice and praise.

THE PRAYER OF THANKSGIVING (cont.)

Sanctify them by your Holy Spirit to be for your people the body and blood of your Son, the holy food and drink of new and unending life in him. Sanctify us also that we may faithfully receive this Holy Sacrament, and serve you in unity, constancy, and peace; and at the last day bring us with all good saints into the joy of your eternal kingdom. All this we ask through your Son Jesus Christ.

Minister and People:
By him, and with him, in the unity of the Holy Spirit all honor and glory is yours,
Almighty Father, now and forever.
Amen.

And now, our Savior Christ has taught us, we are bold to say.

Here minister and people say or sing the Lord's Prayer.

STRUCTURE AND COMMENTARY

Epiclesis

A prayer invoking the Holy Spirit to be present with the people, confirming faith and bringing healing to mind, body, and soul.

The Lord's Prayer

In the ancient church, prayers of intercession were often said at the end of the Eucharistic prayer. Today the Lord's Prayer serves that place in Western worship.

The text of the prayer is from The Book of Common Prayer.

241 ✦ THE BREAKING OF THE BREAD (HE BROKE)

Not only is Christ the broken bread: the church also is to become the bread broken for others.

In the early church a prominent position was given to the third part of the Table, the breaking of the bread. Breaking bread was so central that the entire service of the Table in the primitive community was named the breaking of the bread (Acts 2:42). Paul interpreted the bread as a sign of Christ, the Bread of Life, in whom the many people of the church are made one body (1 Cor. 10:17). The *Didache,* a document dating around the turn of the first century, preserves an early Christian prayer over the bread, a prayer that shows the significance of the unity of the body of Christ expressed in the loaf "as this piece [of bread] was scattered over the hills and then was brought together and made one, so let your church be brought together from the ends of the earth into your kingdom. For yours is the glory and the power through Jesus, your child forever."

Accordingly, the entire tradition of the church affirms that the bread should be made of wheat (current practice is returning to the use of a full loaf of bread made of wheat and water). The broken bread is the symbol of Christ broken for his people, the church, the body united with him in his death and resurrection.

After the breaking of the bread, an antiphonal anthem may be sung by the choir and the people. Then the celebrant or minister invites the people to come and receive the bread and wine.

242 ✦ THE FORMS FOR THE BREAKING OF THE BREAD

In liturgical churches, the breaking of the bread is accompanied by a litany of response between the celebrant and leader. This litany is often sung.

——————— **Liturgical Form** ———————

The Celebrant breaks the consecrated Bread. A period of silence is kept. Then may be sung or said:

[Alleluia] Christ our Passover is sacrificed for us;
Therefore let us keep the feast. [Alleluia]

In Lent, Alleluia is omitted, and may be omitted at other times except during Easter Season.

In place of, or in addition to, the preceding, the following or some other suitable anthem may be sung or said here.

O Lamb of God, that takest away the sins of the world,
    have mercy upon us.

O Lamb of God, that takest away the sins of the
world,
  have mercy upon us.
O Lamb of God, that takest away the sins of the
world,
  grant us thy peace.

The following prayer may be said. In the Anglican tradition it is called the Prayer of Humble Access. The People may join in saying this prayer:

We do not presume to come to this thy Table, O merciful Lord, trusting in our own righteousness, but in thy manifold and great mercies. We are not worthy so much as to gather up the crumbs under thy Table. But thou art the same Lord whose property is always to have mercy. Grant us therefore gracious Lord, so as to eat the flesh of thy dear Son Jesus Christ, and to drink his blood, that we may evermore dwell in him, and he in us. Amen.

(*The Book of Common Prayer*)

─────── **A Contemporary Form** ───────

The minister silently lifts the bread for all to see
The minister then breaks or tears the bread as a sign of Christ's body broken for salvation. As the bread is torn, the minister may say, "The body of Christ broken for you."
The minister may then pour wine into the cup

Breaking of the Bread. *The bread is broken to proclaim the body of Christ broken for us.*

and, raising it for all to see, say, "The blood of Christ shed for you."

The cantor, the choir, the congregation, or all together may sing a song such as the Agnus Dei (Lamb of God) *or a chorus such as* "O the Blood of Jesus" *as an appropriate response to the symbolic action of Christ's broken body.*

The minister may say, "Alleluia Christ our Passover is sacrificed for us."

The congregation may respond, "Therefore, let us keep the feast. Alleluia."

243 • THE INVITATION TO RECEIVE COMMUNION

Before the distribution of the bread and wine, the celebrant, holding up or indicating the gifts, invites the people to Communion. This moment, of course, is most effective when the people come up from their seats to receive.

The celebrant says a private prayer of preparation before receiving the Communion, as the members of the congregation also pray silently. In liturgical worship the celebrant genuflects, then, taking the bread and cup and holding it for the people to see, says,

This is the Lamb of God who takes away the sins of the world. Happy are those who are called to his supper.

He adds, once only, with the people:

Lord, I am not worthy to receive you, but only say the word and I shall be healed.

(Catholic tradition, *The Roman Missal*)

or

The gifts of God for the people of God.

The celebrant may add:

Take them in remembrance that Christ died for you, and feed on him in your hearts by faith, with thanksgiving.

(*The Book of Common Prayer*)

The servers and choir are served first, then the people come forward as ushers lead them from the pew toward the Table.

The Invitation to Receive Communion in Contemporary Worship. In churches where the bread and wine will be carried to the people in the pew, the minister may say one of the following words before the bread and wine is passed:

Traditional

The gifts of God for the people of God. Take them in remembrance that Christ died for you, and feed on him in your hearts by faith, with thanksgiving.

(The Book of Common Prayer)

Contemporary (Biblical)

O taste and see that the Lord is good.

Contemporary

Come to the feast and celebrate with Christ at his Table.

244 ✦ THE RECEPTION OF BREAD AND WINE (HE GAVE)

The giving of the bread and wine is the action of Christ communicated through human hands and speech.

The Common Actions of the Giving of Bread and Wine

The various parts of the giving include the following:

Invitation. The minister lifts the bread and wine for all to see and invites the people to come and receive the bread of heaven and the cup of salvation.

- Walking forward to receive (or receiving in the pew)
- Receiving the bread with appropriate words
- Receiving the wine with appropriate words
- Singing hymns, choruses, spiritual songs of celebration
- A closing doxology (similar to the doxology of the _B^erakah_)

The Giving in Liturgical Churches. In liturgical communities the people stand and walk forward to receive the bread and wine, kneel, or stand at a Communion rail, or stand at designated stations in the worship space. Walking forward requires the involvement of the body in worship, which corresponds to inward coming forward to receive Christ. This action occurs as the entire congregation sings songs of resurrection and praise.

The Giving in Contemporary Churches. In most nonliturgical churches, the elements are taken to the person seated in the pew, and after being received, the entire congregation eats and drinks at the same time. The action of taking bread and wine together expresses the unity of the congregation. Many nonliturgical churches are now asking the people to come forward to receive the bread and wine and accompany this action with the Communion song.

245 ✦ THE WORDS OF RECEPTION

The words of reception are those words of faith said by both minister and people at the giving and receiving of the bread and wine.

The Words of Reception in Liturgical Churches

As people are kneeling at the rail or standing before the Table to receive the bread and wine, the server and the people say one of the following phrases:

Traditional

The body of our Lord Jesus Christ, which was given for thee, preserve thy body and soul unto everlasting life. Take and eat this in remembrance that Christ died for thee, and feed on him in thy heart by faith, with thanksgiving.

The blood of our Lord Jesus Christ, which was shed for thee, preserve thy body and soul unto everlasting life. Drink this in remembrance that Christ's blood was shed for thee, and be thankful.

or

The body (blood) of our Lord Jesus Christ keep you in everlasting life. Amen.

or

The body of Christ, the bread of heaven. Amen.
The blood of Christ, the cup of salvation. Amen.

or

The body of Christ given for you. Amen.
The blood of Christ shed for you. Amen.

or

The Bread of heaven.
The cup of salvation.

(*The Book of Common Prayer*)

The Words of Reception in Nonliturgical Churches. When the bread and wine are delivered to the people in the pew, the minister may say:

Reception. The people receive the bread and wine, the symbols of forgiveness, healing, and new life in Christ.

Over the Bread: Take eat; this is my body which is broken for you; do this in remembrance of me (1 Cor. 11:24).

Over the Wine: This cup is the new covenant in my blood. This do, as often as you drink it, in remembrance of me (1 Cor. 11:25).

When the congregation walks forward to receive the bread and wine, one or more of the options in the section above (The Words of Reception in Liturgical Churches) are used.

246 • THE COMMUNION SONG

The Communion song is sung by the congregation during the reception of bread and wine.

One of the most important features of worship renewal today is the recovery of the Communion song. In Communion song the congregation sing songs of resurrection, victory, and the reign of Christ. These songs shift Communion from a preoccupation with the death of Christ toward a celebration of the Resurrection, and from private introspection to communal celebration. Consequently, the importance of the Communion song sung by the entire congregation during the administration of bread and wine cannot be overemphasized.

The purpose of the Communion song is threefold. First, it expresses the unity of the church as all the people sing together. This is not a time for instrumental music or choir anthems or song. Second, the Communion song organizes the spiritual experience of the congregation by ordering their memory of both the death and the resurrection of Christ. The first song or two may dwell on the death of Christ. However, the majority of songs sung here should express the joy of the Resurrection and the immediacy of the Spirit. Third, the Communion song prevents a mere verbalization of the death and Resurrection and creates a sense of the mystery of faith. Song is a more powerful way to approach mystery than are words alone.

Some churches that have begun celebrating Communion more regularly and have a strong emphasis on music in worship have opted to hold their extended times of praise after Communion. This emphasizes the joyous freedom and victory of the Christian due to Christ's victorious death and resurrection that works in us today. Dancers can also become a significant part of this type of praise time. From the Table, the congregation is moved into worship musically, ending either with a sending hymn or a recessional. Here are some examples of Communion song:

Traditional Hymns

"Just As I Am"
"Breathe on Me Breath of God"
"Now My Tongue the Mystery Telling"
"Let All Mortal Flesh Keep Silence"
"Be Thou My Vision"
"You Lord We Praise in Songs of Celebration"

Praise Tradition

"O the Blood of Jesus"
"I Exalt Thee"
"More Precious than Silver"
"Jesus Remember Me"
"Gloria, Gloria, Gloria"
"We Bring the Sacrifice of Praise"
"Abba, Father"
"Worthy Is the Lamb"
"Jesus Is Lord, Alleluia"
"Broken for Me"

247 • THE RITE OF HEALING

The church has always practiced anointing with oil for healing. Renewing worship connects the rite of healing with Table worship. Here at the Table, the bread and wine, as well as the oil with the laying on of hands, communicates an encounter with the healing power of the risen Lord. Renewing churches are increasingly using the time immediately after a person has received Communion for the laying on of hands with a prayer for healing.

A Form for Prayer of Healing. _A person with the gift for the ministry of healing may stand at an appropriate place near the Table. After receiving the bread and wine, the one desiring prayer may present him- or herself to the minister. There is no need for the exchange of words. The minister may lay hands on the one being prayed for and say:_

I anoint you in the name of the Father, Son, and Holy Spirit (_making the sign of the cross with oil on the forehead_).

Then, clasping hands around the head, the minister may say:

May the Holy Spirit bring healing into your whole person, mind, body, soul, and Spirit, and may you be filled with the presence of Christ.

(The peace may be exchanged.)

Most charismatic and renewal churches are more comfortable practicing a thorough ministry of healing, which includes interview, anointing, prayer for guidance, and healing prayers. Teams that have been raised up in such churches can be stationed near the Communion rail to offer such a healing ministry. As they leave the Table, persons can receive in-depth help while others communicate. This ministry can continue even after Communion and into the time of dismissal and sending, if necessary.

Some churches employ prayer teams or eucharistic healing teams during Communion. After receiving the elements, the people are invited to move to a specific place in the front of the sanctuary for the ministry of healing. This allows more time for prayer and anointing, while allowing others to receive Communion.

248 • THE CLOSING COMMUNION DOXOLOGY

The concluding prayer of the Eucharist is a laudatory statement of praise. Following the primitive model of the Jewish meal prayer, the prayer gives glory to God for his provision; the people respond with the Amen. In this way the worship at the Table ends on a strong note of praise. Here are several examples:

Traditional

Through him, glory to thee, and honor, to the Father and to the Son, with the Holy Spirit, in the holy church, now and forever. Amen.

(Hippolytus, _The Apostolic Tradition_)

Contemporary

Eternal God, heavenly Father, you have graciously accepted us as living members of your Son our Savior Jesus Christ in the Sacrament of his Body and Blood. Send us now into the world in peace, and grant us strength and courage to love and serve you with gladness and singleness of heart; through Christ our Lord. Amen.

(The Book of Common Prayer)

or

Almighty and ever-living God, we thank you for feeding us with the spiritual food of the most precious Body and Blood and for assuring us in these holy mysteries that we are living members of the Body of your Son, and heirs of your eternal kingdom. And now, Father send us out to do the work you have given us to do, to love and serve you as faithful witnesses of Christ our Lord. To him, to you, and to the Holy Spirit, be honor and glory, now and forever. Amen.

(*The Book of Common Prayer*)

Instructions for Preparing the Closing Doxology

Direction	Example
Begin with an ascription of praise.	Eternal God, heavenly Father,
Continue with a proclamation of what God has done for the congregation in the Communion.	You have graciously accepted us as living members of your Son, our Savior Jesus Christ, and you have fed us with spiritual food in the sacrament of his Body and Blood.
Continue with a request for God's continued presence in life and work.	Send us now into the world in peace, and grant us strength and courage to love and serve you with gladness and singleness of heart;
End with an appropriate ascription.	Through Christ our Lord.

Robert E. Webber with
Randolph Sly
Ronal Freyer Nicholas

❧ NINE ❧

Resources for the Acts of Dismissal

The Dismissal is an integral part of worship because it brings closure to the public act of worship and sends God's people forth into the world, where their private worship is expressed in relationships, in leisure, and in work. For this reason, worship renewalists are paying attention to the content and style of the Dismissal.

---

249 • WHAT DOES A DISMISSAL DO?

The Dismissal consists of those acts of worship that send out people from the assembly to love and serve God and their neighbors in the world.

The fourth part of worship, the Dismissal, retains the celebrative mood of the Eucharist and adds to it the sense of being sent forth. Like any meeting, whether formal or informal, the Dismissal contains acts of departure or going forth. So naturally, public worship, which has a beginning, must also have an ending. Consequently, the acts of worship in the Dismissal simply send the people forth. For this reason the announcements are put by many worshiping communities after the Table worship at the beginning of the Dismissal. Because the announcements represent the ongoing activity of the worshiping community, their inclusion in the Dismissal is entirely appropriate. Naturally, announcements should be brief and to the point.

Next, the blessing is said over the people. The blessing, or benediction, which is Jewish in origin, is an authoritative declaration of God's favor on the people. Like the Aaronic blessing of the Hebrew form (Num. 6:24-26), the Christian blessing proclaims God's continued presence with the people of God's name, "And the peace of God, which transcends all understanding, will guard your hearts and your minds in Christ Jesus" (Phil. 4:7).

After the blessing, it is normal to sing a recessional hymn. This hymn is more than a concluding song.

It is an expression of continuing worship. The praise not only of our lips but our lives. Consequently, it should be chosen with care and sung enthusiastically with joyful praise.

Finally the service of worship is concluded with the words of Dismissal, which sends the people into the world to do what they have experienced in worship—works of love in the context of prayer and praise.

250 • A MODEL FOR THE DISMISSAL

The Dismissal is standard in all Christian traditions and generally follows the order below.

Announcements (optional)
Benediction (blessing)
Recessional or closing hymn or song
Words of Dismissal

251 • THE PLACE OF THE ARTS IN THE DISMISSAL

The arts serve the text and accompany the action of worship. They are never performances within worship.

In liturgical and some contemporary gatherings, the recessional hymn may be accompanied by a recession of the choir, worship leaders, and minister and may be led by a liturgical dance, which by its movement symbolizes the going forth of the congregation.

252 • THE BLESSING (BENEDICTION)

The benediction sends people forth with the blessing of God's power over their lives.

Explanation of the Benediction

Although announcements are part of the Dismissal, the first liturgical act of the Dismissal is the blessing or benediction. In the liturgical tradition, the pastor stretches forth his or her right hand and, forming a gesture symbolizing the cross, speaks the words of Dismissal. The people, watching, do the sign of the cross and respond with the Amen. In contemporary worship, the minister will raise his or her hands and arms (one or both) above the head, a gesture that symbolizes the laying on of hands, and say the benediction over the people as they stand with heads bowed. The response is "Amen."

In worship renewal today a significant emphasis is placed on the importance of recapturing the true nature of the benediction in both word and meaning. Consequently, the preparation of statements that truly bless the people and send them forth with their lives, their homes, their work and leisure, and their service to neighbor and the world truly blessed is being recaptured.

Benediction. The tradition gesture of benediction is the right arm with open palm extended toward the congregation.

Examples of the Traditional Blessing (Benediction)

May the grace of the Lord Jesus Christ
and the love of God,
and the fellowship of the Holy Spirit be with you all.
Amen.

(2 Cor. 13:14)

or

The LORD bless you and keep you;
the LORD make his face shine upon you and be gracious to you;
the LORD turn his face toward you and give you peace.

(Num. 6:24-26)

or

The Lord bless you and keep you. [**Amen.**]
The Lord make his face to shine upon you and be gracious to you. [**Amen.**]
The Lord lift up his countenance upon you and give you peace. [**Amen.**]

or

The peace of God, which passes all understanding,
keep your hearts and minds
in the knowledge and love of God,
and of God's Son Jesus Christ our Lord;
and the blessing of God almighty,
the Father, the Son, and the Holy Spirit,
remain with you always.
Amen.

(see Phil. 4:7)

or

May the God of peace
make you holy in every way
and keep your whole being—
spirit, soul, and body—
free from every fault
at the coming of our Lord Jesus Christ.
Amen.

(1 Thess. 5:23, TEV)

or

May the God of hope
fill you with all joy and peace in believing
so that by the power of the Holy Spirit

you may abound in hope.
Amen.

(Rom. 15:13, RSV)

or

Now may the God of peace
who brought back from the dead our Lord Jesus,
the great shepherd of the sheep,
by the blood of the eternal covenant,
make you complete in everything good
so that you may do God's will,
working among you
that which is pleasing in God's sight,
through Jesus Christ,
to whom be glory forever and ever.

(Adapted from Heb. 13:20-21)

— Examples of Contemporary Blessings —

The minister asks the people to lift the right hand to shoulder height and make a circle, connecting the thumb and the small finger. The other three fingers are raised. The minister explains that the circle represents eternity and the three fingers the Trinity. The minister now proceeds with the blessing.

Direction: Place your right hand on your fore-
head.
Blessing: May God the Father bless you.
Direction: Put your hand on your heart.
Blessing: May God the Son heal you.
Direction: Cross your arms over your heart.
Blessing: May God the Holy Spirit heal you.

As arms remain across the chest, the minister says:

And now may the love of God fill you and make you a loving person; may the grace of the Lord Jesus Christ reside within you and make you a gracious person; and may the fellowship of the Holy Spirit touch all your relationships. In the name of the Father, and of the Son and of the Holy Spirit. And all the people said:

Amen.

or

May our God and Father,
the fountain of life and the source
of all mercy,
bring you to himself throughout
this week.

May you bring to him
a true faith and sincere repentance,
and in this way
prepare your heart for Jesus Christ,
the heavenly King,
to whom belong all honor and praise
forever and ever.
Amen.

Chuck Smith, Jr.

or

Now may the Mighty God,
Ruler of heaven and earth,
watch over your life
and give you protection through this
new week.
May his Spirit fill you with the hope
of knowing that his Son,
our Lord Jesus Christ,
is soon to appear.
And may that hope
help you become a better person,
who knows God and
performs his will,
and gives him praise,
both now and always,
Amen.

253 • THE DISMISSAL HYMN

The Dismissal hymn sends the people forth into the world with a sense of mission and Christian purpose.

Just as an Entrance hymn symbolizes coming into the presence of God, so a Dismissal hymn symbolizes going forth into the world to serve God. Therefore it is most appropriate to sing a sending forth hymn that touches on service, mission, or the Christian life.

During the hymn, leaders of worship recess to the back of the sanctuary. In the liturgical tradition, the order of recessing is the same as the order of the procession.

- the cross bearer (if a cross is used)
- the banner carriers (if banners are used)
- the Scripture readers
- the choir
- the ministers

The ministers of the Dismissal gather at the back of the sanctuary, where they lead the singing of the final hymn. During a festal season the choir may offer a special number at the end of the service as a way of accenting the meaning of the season's worship.

Examples of the Dismissal Hymn and Songs

Hymns
"A Charge to Keep I Have"
"Be Thou My Vision"
"Christ Be My Leader"
"Forth In Your Name Lord I Go"
"Go, Tell It on the Mountain"
"God Be With You"
"I Have Decided to Follow Jesus"
"Lead On, O King Eternal"
"Living for Jesus a Life That Is True"

Choruses
"Go Forth"
"Heal Our Land"
"Raise Up an Army"
"Revival in the Land"

254 ◈ THE WORDS OF DISMISSAL

The words of Dismissal are words of closure and of sending forth.

The minister, from the back of the congregation, ends public worship with a proclamation that begins the Christian service in the world. An example may be: "Go in peace to love and serve the Lord" to which the people respond, "Thanks be to God."

— Examples of the Words of Dismissal —

Go out into the world in peace;
have courage;
hold on to what is good;
return no one evil for evil;
strengthen the fainthearted;
support the weak, and help the suffering;
honor everyone;
love and serve the Lord,
rejoicing in the power of the Holy Spirit.

(1 Cor. 16:13; 2 Tim. 2:1; Eph. 6:10; 1 Thess. 5:13-22; 1 Peter 2:17)

or

Be watchful;
stand firm in your faith;
be courageous and strong.
Let all that you do be done in love.

(1 Cor. 16:13-14, RSV)

or

Whatever you do, in word or deed,
do everything in the name of the Lord Jesus,
giving thanks to God the Father through him.

(Col. 3:17)

or

Go out into the world in peace.
Love the Lord your God
    with all your heart,
    with all your soul,
    with all your mind.
This is the greatest commandment;
    it comes first.
The second is like it;
Love your neighbor as yourself.
Everything in the law and the prophets
hangs on these two commandments.

(based on Matt. 22:37-40)

or

Go in peace to love and serve the Lord.
Thanks be to God. [Alleluia, alleluia]

or

Go in peace to serve the Lord, in the name of
    Christ.
Thanks be to God. [Alleluia, alleluia]

or

Let us go forth into the world,
rejoicing in the power of the Holy Spirit.
Thanks be to God. [Alleluia, alleluia]

255 ◈ VARIATION IN THE DISMISSAL

There is very little that can be done or even should be done in the Dismissal by way of variation. The Dismissal is best kept brief and to the point, serving the function of sending the people forth. Nevertheless, here are several suggestions to enhance the Dismissal.

Dance. Use a dance during the Dismissal hymn. In the Dismissal procession, God transcends the congregation and is experienced as the One who goes before the church, leading his people into the world to serve. When the Dismissal hymn is choreographed for dance and led by a dancer, the movement itself can be a powerful spiritual experience of going into the world with the God who goes before us.

Special Music. Have the choir sing a special number after the recession from the back of the church. This approach is very effective during the festive season. For example, the Dismissal on the last Sunday after Epiphany may be characterized by a "Goodbye to the Alleluias," since the Alleluias will not be sung again until Easter. The "Goodbye to the Alleluias" serves the Paschal event in an eschatological way by creating a memory during Lent that creates a longing for the Resurrection symbolized in the return of the Alleluia.

Clapping. In charismatic and other churches the congregation may end worship with several celebration choruses followed by clapping. The clap is for God and expresses the joy of having been in the presence of God.

Robert E. Webber with
Randolph Sly
Ronal Freyer Nicholas

256 ◆ BIBLIOGRAPHY OF RESOURCES FOR THE RITES OF WORSHIP

Service Books and Supplementary Resources

Allen, Ronald J., et. al. *Thankful Praise*. St. Louis: CPB Press, 1987. Created to "strengthen Christian public worship and especially the celebration of the Lord's Supper," this volume corresponds to the *Common Lectionary* and contains prayers, calls to worship, and other resources that may be incorporated in Sunday worship. Christian Church (Disciples of Christ).

Cox, James W., ed. *The Minister's Manual*. New York: Harper and Row, 1989. Complete minister's manual published yearly with 130 new sermons, 156 outlines keyed to lectionary readings, 52 stories and sermons for children, worship aids and service orders, sermon illustrations, ministry ideas for churches, and indices for all material.

Duck, Ruth C., ed. *Bread for the Journey*. New York: Pilgrim, 1981. Similar to companion volume *Flames of the Spirit* and introduces material from many sources and traditions. Scripturally based and theologically sound.

_____. *Flames of the Spirit*. New York: Pilgrim, 1985. Resources based on the ecumenical lectionary and liturgical year. Calls to worship, prayers, litanies, doxologies, faith affirmation, confessions, creeds, and etc. grouped under special occasion services titles and resources appropriate to all seasons. Also elements for pastoral prayer, special services (groundbreaking for new facilities, ordination, etc.), sacraments, and rites.

Ecumenical Services of Prayer. New York: Paulist Press, 1983. The Consultation on Common Texts, a constituent body of ten church denominations (Catholic and Protestant), has produced this volume for times when Christians of varying traditions get together for public prayer or for those who have covenanted to pray privately as individuals about matters of common concern. Ecumenical.

Esther, James R., and Donald J. Bruggink, eds. *Worship the Lord*. Grand Rapids: Eerdmans, 1987. This volume offers liturgical forms for public worship in congregations and classes of the Reformed Church in America, and contains orders of worship for the Lord's Supper, baptism, marriage, healing, burial, reception into communicant membership, and ordination and installation of elders, deacons, ministers, and missionaries. Text for "Our Song of Hope" is also present.

Gray, Henry David. *Congregational Worshipbook*. Arcadia, Calif.: Michillinda Press, 1990. Complete worship source for Congregational churches. Topics: Sunday worship, sacraments, holy rites, Christian year, orders of worship for festive days, compendium of commoration (funerals), prayers for all seasons, church celebrations, music in congregational worship, congregational usage (about the denomination and all matters pertaining to the local community), and catechism.

Hickman, Hoyt L. *Holy Communion*. Nashville: Abingdon Press, 1987. This is essentially a service book for ministers/presiders at Communion to be used in conducting services. The Order of Holy Communion is prepared for United Methodists.

Johnson, Lawrence. *The Word and Eucharist Handbook*. San Jose, Calif.: Resource Publications, 1986. Consideration of the Eucharist/Communion in its historical, theological, and liturgical aspects. Volume takes the reader/planner through the liturgy from preparation and introduction to concluding rites. Comprehensive and easy to read and follow. Bibliography.

Keller, Wayne H. *Lectionary Worship Workbook*. Lima, Ohio: C.S.S. Publishing, 1988. One of the most complete volumes on the subject offers a "parade" of creative alternatives for liturgy, music, preaching, and prayer for every Sunday of Cycle C in the lectionary calendar. A helpful worship planner page which includes suggestions regarding banners and the like accompanies each service. Ecumenical/Presbyterian.

Kemper, Frederick W. *Variety for Worship*. St. Louis: Concordia, 1977. Resources for approximately thirteen festival worship liturgies which include all seasons. Each complete service includes introductory notes and primer thoughts. Some alternative services given provide variety. Lutheran.

Mitman, F. Russell. *Worship Vessels*. San Francisco: Harper and Row, 1987. This book contains over 300 worship resources for seasons and festivals, worship acts incorporating familiar and new hymns, guides for structuring traditional and alternative services, orders for baptism, marriage, and burial. Also, practical helps for creating meaningful bulletins. Resources for renewal in the United Church of Christ.

Presbyterian Church (USA). *The Service for the Lord's Day*. Philadelphia: Westminster Press, 1984. A liturgical resource divided into three parts: Order of Service for the Lord's Day, Liturgical Texts (prayers, words of greeting, creeds, etc.), and Commentary on the Order of Service for the Lord's Day. Bibliography. Presbyterian.

The Sacramentary. New York: Catholic Book Publishing, 1985. The Roman missal, liturgical resource for the Roman Catholic church. Contains all material related to the church year and for the conduct of the Mass. Appendices and indices.

United Methodist Church. *The Book of Services*. Nashville: Abingdon Press, 1984. A collection of services of Word and Table that emphasizes flexibility and contains longer forms, brief and minimum texts for special circumstances. Baptism, membership, marriage, confirmation, and burial services are included as well as other special services. United Methodist.

Prayers

Prayer transcends the boundaries of tradition. In each entry, the tradition is noted for reference of the reader. It would be good for the reader to go beyond the spirituality of his or her tradition and sample the prayers of another.

Adam, David. *The Edge of Glory*. Wilton, Conn.: Morehouse-Barlow, 1985. Prayers in the Celtic tradition which the author discovered as distinctive in their ability to discern and express the attributes and activity (divine glory) of God in everyday life (ordinariness). A unique volume for both private and public worship. Anglican.

Albrecht, Earl. *Altar Prayer Workbook*. 3 vols. Lima, Ohio: C.S.S. Publishing, 1984–1986. Altar prayers for every Sunday of the church year with cross-cultural sensitivity. Volumes are designed to lie flat for use during liturgy. Series A, B, and C for use with Common (Consensus) and Lutheran and Roman Catholic lectionaries. Ecumenical.

Appleton, George, ed. *The Oxford Book of Prayer*. New York: Oxford University Press, 1985. An ecumenical effort that includes divisions: Prayers of Adoration, from the Scriptures, of Christians (personal and occasional), of the Church, as Listening, from Other Traditions (Jewish, Indian, Buddhist, Chinese, Zoroastrian, etc.), and Prayers toward the Unity of Humanity. Text and general resource. Ecumenical.

Arnold, Duane W. *Prayers of the Martyrs*. Grand Rapids: Zondervan, 1991. A powerfully unique volume of the intimate prayers of those martyred for their profession of faith. Endnotes provide personal profiles and sketches of the context of each prayer. Valuable for public and private worship and for historical investigation. Ecumenical.

Blackwood, Andrew. *Prayers for All Occasions*. 4th edition. Grand Rapids: Baker Book House, 1988. The book is a compilation of prayers from sixty-six pastors, educators, and church leaders arranged alphabetically for seasons, the church year, special occasions (baptism, funerals, marriage, etc.), and United States holidays. Evangelical/Protestant.

Bornhoeft, Theodore. *Prayers Responsively*. St. Louis: Concordia, 1984. A collection of responsive prayers for the three-year lectionary which are written to encourage congregational involvement and include major and minor festivals and special occasions. An opportunity for personal intercession is offered with each prayer. May be photocopied without permission. Ecumenical.

Bowyer, O. Richard, Betty Hart, and Charlotte Meade. *Prayer in the Black Tradition*. Nashville: Upper Room, 1986. The volume offers access to both black heritage and rich spirituality as expressed in prayer for public worship and special occasions, personal devotions, black literature, and song. It is replete with printed examples of prayers compiled through taping and transcription. Bowyer introduces the book with an overview. Ecumenical/United Methodist.

Brooke, Avery. _Plain Prayers for a Complicated World._ New York: Reader's Digest, 1975. Short prayers in this volume are written by the author for the everyday concerns that are encountered by everyone. Primarily intended for personal use, these prayers may be creatively used in the public forum. Format is by topic, with a thematically grouped index at the end. Ecumenical.

Carlozzi, Carl G. ed. _Prayers for Pastor and People._ New York: Church Hymnal Corp., 1984. A compendium that is thematically arranged; drawn from prayer books, private collections, and priest's and pastor's manuals; and accounts for prayer of: Community, Nation and World, Personal and Corporate Concerns, Family and Home, Thanksgivings, Church and Ministry, Sick, Departed and Bereaved, Dedications, Blessings and Absolutions, Saints and Seasons, Litanies, General Intercessions, and Bidding Prayers. Reference. Ecumenical/Episcopal.

Cassidy, Sheila. _Prayer for Pilgrims._ New York: Crossroad, 1982. Cassidy has written a book on prayer that attempts to expand the experience of a "life of prayer" by achieving balance in one's relationships—vertical to God and horizontal to humanity—in the context of one's "coming and going" with God in the world. Prayers evidence deep spirituality and everyday concerns. Ecumenical/Roman Catholic.

Coggan, Donald. _The Prayers of the New Testament._ New York: Harper and Row, 1967. Coggan delivers a commentary on all of the prayers in the New Testament. It is a "direction and exposition" of prayers he hopes will become models for biblical study and devotion. Ecumenical/Anglican.

Colquhoun, Frank, ed. _Prayers for Every Occasion._ Wilton, Conn.: Morehouse-Barlow, 1974. A collection of over 1,800 prayers. Each prayer is numbered and found under appropriate headings and titles. This is perhaps one of the more inclusive and complete prayerbooks available. It also contains indices for biblical and subject reference. Though Anglican in style, it is valuable to all. Ecumenical/Episcopal.

Cunningham, Agnes. _Prayer: Personal and Liturgical._ Wilmington, Del.: Michael Glazier, 1986. The

message of the Fathers to the church regarding prayer is the author's focus. It is a study of Patristic prayer that includes introductory notes on the doctrine and forms of prayer and contains a good number of examples. The period of scholarship ranges from the primitive church to 636 CE in the West and 749 CE in the East. Ecumenical.

Davies, Horton, and Morris D. Silfer. _Prayers and Other Resources for Public Worship._ New York: Abingdon Press, 1976. The volume is an anthology of public prayers and other resources to be used in the context of public worship. The book's chapters are arranged in the order prayers might occur in the liturgy, and is a helpful volume from opening sentences to Dismissal and blessing. Ecumenical/United Church of Christ.

Deiss, Lucien. _Reflections of His Word._ Chicago: World Library Publications, 1982. "Biblicality" is the contribution of this prayerbook, which elaborates primarily on scriptural sources. Prayers are presented in the order in which they would occur in the liturgy and offer options within some of the sections depending on imagery preferred in the service or on "voices" (accusatory vs. acclamatory, etc.) intended. The book may be used in a variety of contexts. Ecumenical/Episcopal.

Dunlop, Laurence. _Patterns of Prayer in the Psalms._ New York: Seabury Press, 1982. Dunlop's contribution regards the heartfelt prayer experience of the "real people" in the Psalms. Examples of psalmic prayer are enhanced by exegetical and explanatory notes. Prayers are interspersed throughout the text of the book, which is divided thematically and according to subject. Ecumenical.

Forristal, Desmond, ed. _Saltair._ Dublin: Columba, 1988. Desmond Forristal's collection of Celtic prayers is unique for its cultural insights and bilingual approach. Text of prayers is printed in both Irish and English on facing pages for easy reference and includes ancient and modern simple, common prayers as well as those of theologians. Prayers in the Irish tradition. Catholic.

Garrotto, Alfred. _Christians and Prayer._ Minneapolis: Winston Press, 1980. The volume is a unique prayer study with text, daily Scripture reflection, theological "notes," interesting weekly assignments, and thought-provoking worksheets as a part of the book. It focuses on adult continuing education in prayer, and may be used in a variety of contexts. Ecumenical/Roman Catholic. ❧

Godshall, C. David. *Prayers in Dialogue.* 3 vols. Lima, Ohio: C.S.S. Publishing, 1984–1986. The volumes blend the voices of minister(s), worship assistant(s), and the people in prayer as a creative substitute for long, pastoral prayers. May be photocopied. Series A, B, and C for use with Common (Consensus) and Lutheran lectionaries. Lutheran/Common.

Grenz, Stanley J. *The Cry for the Kingdom.* Peabody, Mass.: Hendrickson, 1988. A challenge to the modern individual and church to discover the prayer ministry of the early church in order to experience renewal. Text lends itself to personal or corporate study, and could be used as preparation for clergy, worship committees/assistants, and the overall church. Answers questions on the nature, person, persistence, and influence of prayer. Baptist/Ecumenical.

Hard, Larry, Dick Pope, and Dwight Bowers. *Contemporary Altar Prayers.* Lima, Ohio: C.S.S. Publishing, 1988. Honest, forthright, contemporary prayers for all of the seasons and special occasions from three parish ministers. Text lies flat for altar use and contains fifty prayers. United Methodist.

Hoffman, Lawrence A. *The Art of Public Prayer.* Washington, D.C.: Pastoral Press, 1988. Hoffman asserts that worship in North American churches and synagogues is banal and failing, a system in trouble with its structuring of time, lost symbols, worship systems, and communications. He proposes that corrections include new understandings of worship, worship as art, redesigned sacred space, prayer-scripts both spoken and sung, and general "system intervention." Not for clergy only. Ecumenical/Jewish.

Hollings, Michael, and Etta Gullick. *Into Your Hands.* Mystic, Conn.: Twenty-Third Publications, 1989. Prayers for times of depression in a poetic form along with notes introducing each section. The authors have included prayers for both chronic and situational depression, including prayers anticipating depression. A unique work of empathy and inspiration. Ecumenical.

Hostetter, B. David. *Psalms and Prayers for Congregational Participation.* 3 vols. Lima, Ohio: C.S.S. Publishing, 1983–1985. Each order of service includes a psalm that has been distilled and compressed by the author for use as responsive prayer. Series A, B, and C for use with Common (Consensus) Lectionary. Language is contemporary and meaningful. Ecumenical/Presbyterian.

House, Garth. *Litanies for All Occasions.* Valley Forge, Penn: Judson Press, 1989. The author's thoughtful original litanies include church year and holiday celebrations. There are also special compositions for facing challenges in the "passages" of life. Baptist.

Huffman, Walter C. *The Prayer of the Faithful.* Minneapolis: Augsburg Publishing House, 1986. Huffman focuses on prayer as "praise-making," formative, the articulation of faithfulness, and as intercession. He contends that liturgists have paid more attention to eucharistic prayers than to other forms, and advocates increased attention to these. He also includes a section on guidelines concerning the practice of public prayer. Ecumenical/Lutheran.

Hurley, Dermot. *Our Daily Prayer.* London: Collins, 1986. This small book is a primer on personal prayer that is full of information on and examples of the subject. It exhibits simplicity, variety, and contemporary comprehensiveness. There is a particularly helpful guide to New Testament passages suitable for prayer. Roman Catholic.

Jesus Christ—The Life of the World. Geneva: World Council of Churches, 1976. This is the Sixth Assembly Worshipbook for the World Council of Churches, Vancouver 1983. It is a collection of Biblical affirmations, Scripture Passages, Responsive Readings, and Litanies and Prayers (in English, French, German, and Spanish) that may be used for services with the stated theme. Ecumenical.

Kirk, James G. *When We Gather.* 3 vols. Philadelphia: Geneva Press, 1983–1985. The author has composed original prayers for use in the liturgy that are intended to ensure the same breadth in prayer that the lectionary attempts to achieve in Scripture readings. Prayers have been edited especially for rhythm, making them easier to read aloud. Language is modern and gender-inclusive. Series A, B, and C for use with Common (Consensus) Lectionary. Ecumenical.

McDonnell, Rea. *Prayer Pilgrimage through Scripture.* New York: Paulist Press, 1984. The author uses Scripture to teach prayer which seeks to produce "biblical spirituality" and deepen one's knowledge of God. There is commentary on all major types of biblical literature and its individual authors, along with "guided prayers" and exercises that reflect the unique concerns of the writers of Scripture and their particular concerns. Ecumenical/Roman Catholic.

Paradis, Jean-Guy. _Lord, Teach Me to Pray._ Mystic, Conn.: Twenty-Third Publications, 1987. A collection of texts from the Bible and liturgy that is "simple, free, unconventional . . . and inspired by the Bible," and was compiled in the context of the author's ministry to university and college students. The format is participatory, beginning with a Scripture reading by the leader, moment of silent reflection, spontaneous prayer, and corporate prayer. Ecumenical.

Phillips, E. Lee. _Breaking Silence before the Lord._ Grand Rapids: Baker, 1986. Prayer is "breaking silence" before the Lord, the result being a public testimony of private thoughts shaped by reflective, productive meditation of the Holy. Prayers contained in the volume are thoughtful, poetic, dignified, and contemporary. They reflect all of the great prayer traditions and include all types of prayer found in liturgy for regular and special occasion use. Useful bibliography of "classic" works on prayer. Ecumenical.

Phillips, E. Lee. _Prayers for Worship._ Grand Rapids: Baker, 1979. Advocating the vital importance of public prayer, Phillips authors an excellent small volume on the subject that commences with insights on prayer preparation that are relational and invaluable. "Prayer is us!" he affirms, and produces excellent original compositions for every liturgical use. Book and interview bibliography. Ecumenical.

Prayers of Blessing and Praise for All Occasions. Mystic, Conn.: Twenty-Third Publications, 1987. The volume may be termed "prayer for everyday and everyone," as its approach is topical and relevant to human life situations. Prayers may be used in private and public contexts and are especially suited to interfaith opportunities in prayer. Roman Catholic.

Prayers of the Faithful. New York: Pueblo, 1977. The volume is a catalog of general intercessory prayers for use in the Sunday eucharistic liturgy and for solemnities for the three-year cycle. It is a valuable consultative resource for all. Source: Roman Catholic.

Prayers, Thanksgivings, and Litanies. New York: Church Hymnal Corp., 1973. Prayers offered are in contemporary language and thought forms, arranged under headings and titles, and keyed to _The Book of Common Prayer._ The volume also includes a history of intercessory prayer, appendices, and indices. Ecumenical/Episcopal.

Quoist, Michel. _Prayers._ Kansas City, Mo.: Sheed and Ward, 1963. Quoist's unique volume is a collection of unusual prayers in "stinging" everyday speech. Subjects range from the drunken man in the middle of the street to the telephone that has just been returned to its receiver. It is simple, profound, contemporaneous, and urban, and even includes what Quoist thinks God might say in answer to our prayers. Not to be missed. Ecumenical.

Rahner, Karl. _Prayers for a Lifetime._ New York: Crossroad, 1989. "Before God," "With Christ," and "In the Holy Spirit," Rahner's collected and grouped prayers reveal a man of deep spirituality. It is an insightful volume for students of the eminent theologian and a didactic resource for those who would be seduced by the temptation to pursue theological endeavors devoid of private piety. Ecumenical/Roman Catholic.

Ramshaw, Gail, ed. _Intercessions for the Christian People._ New York: Pueblo, 1988. A collection of prayers (intercessory) of the people edited by Ramshaw from over fifty sources, based on the three-year cycle used by Roman Catholic, Episcopal, and Lutheran traditions, and intended for use with the Lectionary.

Rogahn, Kenneth W. _Begin with Prayer._ St. Louis: Concordia, 1985. The volume is especially designed to provide opening forms for just about any type of church or group meeting. Scripture readings, songs, and a prayer are given for each of 121 appropriately short openings. Ecumenical.

Rowthorn, Jeffery. _The Wideness of God's Mercy._ 2 vols. Minneapolis: Winston Press, 1985. Both volumes are collections of intercessory prayers in the form of litanies for all occasions with the intent to "enlarge" prayer both in quality and in numbers of participants. The author advocates a return to prayer that is broad in scope, highly regarded, regular, and participatory in order to recover what is considered to be an early church objective lost through years of clerical praying. Ecumenical.

Rupp, Anne Neufeld. _Prayer in Corporate Worship._ Newton, Kans.: Faith and Life, 1981. The pamphlet is a prayer primer, with a concise introduction of prayer and its public ministry, the language of prayer, an excellent short list of types of prayer, and a section on pastoral prayers with congregational involvement. Good for private use and as introductory material for a worship committee. Bibliography. Ecumenical/Mennonite.

Senger, Basil. *Living Prayers.* New York: Catholic Book Publishing, 1984. The volume is divided into thematic prayers especially suited to the life situations of adolescents, teens, and younger adults. There are morning and evening prayers, prayers for forgiveness and gratitude, of praise and commitment, for family and friends and all people. Prayers for young Catholics. Illustrated.

Ulanov, Barry. *Prayers of St. Augustine.* Minneapolis: Seabury Press, 1983. Ulanov has collected the prayers of the ancient theologians as "a geography of [the] interior space" of Augustine and ourselves under five themes: Splendor, Signs, Insistent Desire, Trust, and Inner Knowledge. The book gives insight concerning the complex individual and commanding rhetorician but is valuable for its remarkable ability to demonstrate the contemporary spirit of this Christian ancestor's life and prayers.

Wade, David L. *Lord, Forgive Me.* Lima, Ohio: C.S.S. Publishing, 1987. A fresh and creative collection of prayers of confession in the first person that reflects the author's wish for prayers that are "calls to honesty." Each prayer is related to a Scripture text and follows the three-year church cycle for Lutheran, Episcopal, and Roman communions. Ecumenical.

Weil, Louis. *Gathered to Pray.* Cambridge, Mass.: Cowley, 1986. Weil's book is particularly appropriate for parish worship committees or those studying the nature of prayer in the public forum. The type of liturgical prayer considered here is the "collect," a form of intercessory prayer, and the author considers its construction along with specific technical, linguistic, and pastoral guidelines. Episcopal.

PART FOUR

Resources for Preaching in Worship

TEN

A Brief History of Preaching

Preaching has always been a significant moment in the church's worship. During the Middle Ages, preaching became almost completely irrelevant to the people as the consecration of the eucharistic elements became the sole focus of the liturgy. Fewer and fewer people could understand the Latin of the service. The mendicant preachers of the late Middle Ages began to restore preaching to the people, but the Reformation brought a new focus on preaching, often to the exclusion of the Eucharist. The current consensus views preaching as an essential part of the Service of the Word, which is balanced and completed by the Service of the Table.

The following entries seek to provide resources for preaching while making no presumption of being exhaustive. In chapter 10, a brief overview of the history of preaching explores the development of the essential methods of preaching (textual, expository, and evangelistic) that were in place by the time of John Wesley. The sections on styles and approaches in preaching delineate the essential methods of preaching while attempting to offer a glimpse into other more recent and creative trends in preaching.

The history of preaching follows the natural divisions of Old Testament, New Testament, early church, fourth and fifth centuries, Middle Ages, Reformation, and modern era. First, the roots of biblical preaching are described in its Jewish background and later development by Jesus and Paul. The next three centuries of preaching are represented by Melito of Sardis, Origen, John Chrysostom, and Augustine, each with distinct methods and results. This history resumes, after a medieval lull, with the monastic Bernard of Clairvaux, the scholastic Thomas Aquinas, and the mystic John Tauler. Next we look at the preaching styles of the Reformers Martin Luther and John Calvin and conclude with the revivalistic style of John Wesley and George Whitefield.

---

257 • THE JEWISH ROOTS OF THE CHRISTIAN SERMON

The sermon has its unique roots in Jewish tradition and was carried on and explored in the Christian tradition, as this entry demonstrates.

The Beginnings of Preaching

The First Sermon. It can be said that the sermon and spoken word is at the very source and origin of the Jewish experience. Even God began his intervention in the universe with the spoken word. When God said: "Let there be light," it can be said that we have the first sermon with instant results.

To be sure, historians of the Jewish sermon, qua sermon, situate the earliest sermon in the Tannaitic period, with at least one complete sermon, as such, so recorded. It is a sermon by Rabbi Eleazar ben Azaraiah, found in Hagigah 3a in the Babylonian Talmud.

Abraham as Preacher. However, it is possible to suggest that Abraham, the first Jew, began his career with the spoken word. To be sure, the inference comes from an exegetical interpretation of the text, in a way that some scholars would never accept. It is my feeling that the rabbinic interpreters of Scripture had such a feel for what really went on that their comments have a dependability on which we can count. For the most part they had the right "feel" for the context, and very often it is very useful to turn to them.

Nevertheless, when we are informed that after

accepting God's command to leave his home and his native land, and to go to a land that God would show him, the text records that Abraham [then Abram] took with him his wife Sarah [then Sarai], his flocks, and "the souls that they had gotten in Haran" (Gen. 12:5, KJV).

That last phrase cries out for interpretation. What could it possibly mean? The sages interpreted it to mean the converts he had made to the One God he had newly discovered. And how did he convert them? By talking to them, of course! By preaching to them! Hence Abraham must have been the first *darshan!*

Moses as Preacher. So the sages see Abraham as the first preacher. Then how about Moses? What is the Torah that Moses receives at Sinai if not one great "Sermon on the Mount"? What is it if not a roaring, fiery sermon that sets the Jewish people on its course of destiny? Moses, in this sense is the *darshan* par excellence. This is apparent at the beginning of his career at Mount Sinai. It is apparent throughout his career. It is especially apparent at the end of his career in those two masterful sermons in the book of Deuteronomy, written in such limpid prose and soaring poetry. I refer of course to his great sermon that encompasses the whole book, and that sermon-poem *Ha'azinu* at the conclusion, where he calls heaven and earth to witness as he outlines, for the last time to his people, their story, their destiny, and their covenant obligation.

Of this poem, an early *midrash* [Sifrei, to Deut. 32] says:

> Great is song
> for it contains the present, the past and the
>   future
> things of this world and things of the world
>   to come.

This is prophetic speech. Its inspiration comes directly from God, and the prophet speaks the word to the people. It is direct speech. It is not text centered and text oriented. The prophet does not prepare his text. He is the human vessel, divinely chosen to project God's message to the people. It is the Mount Sinai syndrome, continued throughout the period of the first commonwealth.

As we speak of prophecy in relation to the development of preaching and of the sermon, it is wise to remember the root meaning of the Hebrew word for prophet. The root meaning of the word *navi'* is

"spokesman." Moses, as we know, was a stammerer, and when he raised this objection with God with respect to his role, his brother Aaron was assigned to be his spokesman; and the term used is *navi'*. When we come to the meturgeman, the first actual preacher, a little later, we will see its first echo in Aaron.

That, indeed, is how Rashi and Ibn Ezra describe him. The *midrash* to this Exodus passage tells us that Moses and Aaron would go among the people in Egypt, teaching, instructing, and inspiring them. In fact, we are told that "they had scrolls from which they entertained the people, in order to persuade them that God would redeem them" (Exodus Rabbah 80:5).

The Power of the Spoken Word in the Bible

The power of the spoken word in this sense emerges clearly throughout the Bible. A few examples will suffice. When Samuel, the seer-prophet, comes upon the scene to lead the people, it is because "the word of God was rare in those days." It had dried up and disappeared, and now it was restored.

King David could also be seen as preacher, communicating with the harp through his psalms. I can just see the modern folk singer with the guitar, speaking to the soul of the people through folk songs, speaking of their hopes, fears, and aspirations. All the ingredients for the sermon-derasha-folk communication are there

When Solomon, the wisest man of his time, expounded his wisdom, and it was finally brought together in a book, that book was called *Qohelet*. *Qohelet* means "preacher." It comes from the word *qahal*, which means "community." *Qohelet* really means "community-communicator." Let us take a glance at a pertinent passage from the *Midrash Qohelet:*

> All the people would gather together in the presence of Solomon to listen to words of wisdom which God had placed in his heart. That is why he was called *Qohelet* because his words were spoken before the community [*qahal*]. [*Midrash,* Yalkut Shim'oni II, par. 965]

Prophetic Speech. We return, however to the prophet and prophetic speech, for that is the central factor in the process of development. Prophetic speech provided the core and kernel, which the various forms of *derashah* presented. For the words of the prophets were words of insight. They were words of warning, of denunciation, of consolation. By and large the prophet is at odds with the people because he tells them what they do not wish to hear.

Who can forget Isaiah's denunciation of the selfishness and insensitivity of the people who followed their pleasures and forgot God's directions? Who can forget the intensity and power of Jeremiah's temple sermon, which ends with the traumatic prediction of the destruction of the temple where he was speaking?

Who can forget the fight for social justice of Amos and his cry?

> Assuredly, because you impose a tax on the poor and exact from him a levy of grain, you have built houses of hewn stone, but you shall not live in them; you have planted delightful vineyards, but you shall not drink their wine. (Amos 5:11, author's translation)

Who can forget Micah's prescription for decent conduct, his "do justly, love mercy, and walk humbly with thy God"? Who can forget Deutero-Isaiah's words of consolation, when, after the destruction and his pain, he could bind the wounds with his "*Nahamu, nahamu 'ammi* [comfort ye, comfort ye, my people]"?

And who can forget those last words of Malachi, that Malachi who, as we have already noted, may be one with Ezra, bridge from prophet to rabbinic/pharisaic/sage?

> Remember ye the law of Moses my servant, which I commanded unto him in Horeb for all Israel, with the statutes and judgments. (Mal. 4:4, KJV)

Prophecy ceases, but God can henceforth speak to the people through Torah. The task of finding what God's message is and communicating it to the people becomes the task of the sages. They train other sages by teaching them how to exegete and communicate love of Torah, and what it teaches, and how one must react when it is tested; their purpose is to teach all the people through the derashah and sermon.

The End of Prophecy. These words of Malachi mark a shift in the nature of the communication of God's way to the people. Up to now it had been through the prophets, directly inspired by God. The prophets did not speak out of texts. They communicated what God commanded them to say. From Jeremiah we learn how painful this could be:

> When your words were offered, I devoured them; your word brought me delight and joy. . . . Why must my pain be endless, my wound incurable? (Jer. 15:16, 18, author's translation)

But painful or not, that is the way it was. With the destruction of the first commonwealth, the sacking of the temple, and the exile of the people, something changed and changed drastically.

For this catastrophe marked the end of many things. But most of all, it marked the end of prophecy. This reality is preserved in the Talmudic dictum: "When the Temple was destroyed prophecy ceased" (Sanhedrin 11a). The children of Israel had heard from God directly at Sinai, and for the next six hundred years the word of God comes to them from the prophets. But now, with the destruction and the end of prophecy, they were another step removed. Henceforth the divine will would be mediated through the sacred texts, brought together and prepared for them by the sages, and mediated by the sages through the process of *midrash*.

Since ultimately the Jewish people were to be God's witness to the world and the bearers of the covenant promise and heritage, the people needed to know; the people needed to be taught.

Reading of the Torah

It was Ezra—and if we are to believe the Targum comment Malachi-become-Ezra, or prophet transformed into scribe/sage/pharisee—who makes the crucial change. The Torah, hitherto in possession of the priests and read infrequently to the people, is now to become part of their regular discipline. It is to be read to them regularly and interpreted to them. It is to be introduced into the liturgy.

The Babylonian Talmud records ten innovations credited to Ezra, and the first two, clearly in their eyes the most important, have to do with this. Thus we read in Baba Kama, folio 82a:

> The following ten enactment's were ordained by Ezra: that the Torah be read publicly in the Minha [afternoon] service on Sabbath; that the Torah be read [publicly] on Mondays and Thursdays; that Courts be held on Mondays and Thursdays. . . .

Every Sabbath a portion from the Pentateuch is to be read, and the same portion is to be read on Mondays and Thursdays at morning prayers. Why Mondays and Thursdays? Because that was when people came into the market, so before they gathered to earn their daily bread, the Torah was read and interpreted, and the courts were to be in session.

Listen to the account of this innovation, as we read it in the book of Nehemiah (8:4, 7-8, KJV):

> And Ezra the scribe stood upon a pulpit of wood, which they had made for the purpose; and beside him stood Mattithiah and Shema, and Anaiah, and Urijah, and Hilkiah, and Maaseiah, on his right hand; and on his left hand, Pedaiah, and Mishael, and Malchiah, and Hashum, and Hashbadana, Zechariah, and Meshullam. . . . And the Levites caused the people to understand the law: and the people stood in their place. *So they read in the book in the law of God distinctly, and gave the sense, and caused them to understand the reading* [emphasis added].

Here, with the reference to those who "read in the book in the law of God distinctly and gave the sense, and caused them to understand the reading," we have the first clue to the origins of the *darshan.*

—— The Emergence of Meturgeman ——

Some time thereafter we become aware of the structure of the meturgeman. *Meturgeman* is an Aramaic word that means "one who translates," but the "one who translates" became also the "one who interprets."

The fact that the earliest term for this craft is Aramaic and not Hebrew is very significant. Recall the destruction of the first temple and the letter of Jeremiah to the exiles. Recall that the Babylonian community persisted and grew, always out of reach of the Roman expansion. Recall how after the destruction of the second commonwealth, it was rabbinic Judaism of the long-range messianic type that moved first to Jabneh, then to the Galilee, and finally back to the Parthian empire, out of the reach of Rome.

The Judaism that developed thus developed among Jews whose language was no longer Hebrew. Their language was Aramaic, the *lingua franca* of the Middle East. By the second century, even Galilee had become Aramaicized. It was Jews from Babylonia who returned with Ezra and Nehemiah to build

the second temple. It is doubtful that most of them by this time knew Hebrew well.

The changeover probably began with the Assyrian destruction of the northern kingdom, Israel, and the siege of Jerusalem, which was miraculously terminated because of a plague in the Assyrian forces. However, at the height of the siege, and a bitter siege it was, the Assyrian general, Rab-shakeh, called for surrender as he parlayed with the leaders:

> Then said Eliakim the son of Hilkiah, and Shebna, and Joah, unto Rab-shakeh: Speak, I pray thee, to thy servants in the [Aramean] language; for we understand it: and talk not with us in the Jews' language in the ears of the people that are on the wall. [Despite this plea] Rab-shakeh stood and cried with a loud voice in the Jews' language, and spake, saying . . . (2 Kings 18:26, 28, KJV)

Language process changes do not occur overnight. Within a space of perhaps three centuries from the Assyrian invasion to the years following the confrontation with Babylonia and the destruction of Jerusalem, the change takes place, and Aramaic becomes the language of a majority of the people. And according to tradition, Rab-shakeh, who spoke for the Assyrians, was a convert from Judaism.

Evidence of this Aramaicization is to be found in the books of Ezra and Nehemiah, as well as in the book of Daniel, where significant portions are in Aramaic. The Kaddish prayer itself, used at the conclusion of the period of study, and in the Hebrew liturgy to act as a division between the sections of the service, and to serve as a prayer for the dead, was in Aramaic.

So it becomes clear that the public reading of the Torah meant translation into Aramaic by the meturgeman. This was his principal role, as it developed in Babylonia. The Torah would first be read in Hebrew, and then translated into Aramaic. These Aramaic translations have persisted, as Targum, and to this day are printed side by side in the Rabbinic texts of the Bible. In fact, the custom persisted, long after Aramaic ceased to be the current language of Jews, to read the weekly portion of the Torah at home once in Hebrew and twice in Aramaic.

The Targumim as Expansions and Amplifications. Although there are no collections of early sermons of this period, a careful reading of the Targumim illustrates that these were not simply direct translations of the texts. They were expansions and amplifications, such as a later preacher or *darshan* would do. It is indeed an early echo of the preaching process.

In the second version of the Creation story, in Genesis 2:7, we read:

> And the Lord formed man of the dust of the ground, and breathed into his nostrils the breath of life; and Adam became a living creature. (author's translation)

The Targum to the last phrase is more than just a translation. It reads: "and it became in Adam the spirit of uttering speech." The meturgeman is not simply translating *nefesh hayyah,* he is exegeting it. He is suggesting that the power of speech was the unique quality of Adam, as, by implication, the power of speech through *derashah* was a unique quality for the Jewish people in the spread of Torah.

Then we come to the story of the Garden of Eden and the expulsion of Adam and Eve because of the temptation of the serpent. Adam is told that because of this sin he will henceforth earn his bread by the sweat of his brow. Eve is informed that she will bear children in pain. And to the serpent God says:

> And I will put enmity between thee and the woman, and between thy seed and her seed; it shall bruise thy head, and thou shalt bruise his heel. (Gen. 3:15, KJV)

The Targum to the last phrase is not simply a translation of "it shall bruise thy head, and thou shalt bruise his heel," but an elaboration, which again has the germ of a homily, if not given in full, then at least clearly suggested: "He [humankind] will remind you of what you did to him in the past, and you will preserve your hatred for him into the future." From the beginning the serpent/human relationship had a deep and enduring psychological impact.

When Adam and Eve sinned, God had a twinge of regret for having created them. After all, he had, according to one *midrash,* been warned against this by a group of his angels, but he had ignored the advice. In any event we read: "And God repented that he had made man on earth, and it grieved him at his heart" (Gen. 6:6, author's translation). The translation to this comes out as: "He determined upon breaking their power according to his will." Quite a change, is it not? Not man's downfall, but his defeat by God through man's loss of power is

central. We almost hear an echo of the Prometheus myth!

Another instance deals with the moment at Mount Sinai after the people have heard the Ten Commandments proclaimed and have cried out with one voice, "All that the LORD hath said, we will do, and be obedient" (Exod. 24:7, KJV). Afterward Moses, Aaron, Nadab, and Abihu go up to the mountain for a revelation of the divine, and the heavens are opened in all their radiant glory for the people to see. The people are included in this experience:

> And upon the nobles of the children of Israel he laid not his hand: also they saw God, and did eat and drink. (Exod. 24:11, KJV)

This passage troubled the meturgeman. The image of feasting at such a moment, an act of total self-indulgence, was not to his liking. Hence his translation reads:

> They beheld God's glory and gladly offered sacrifices which were received with favor *as though they had eaten and drunk.* [emphasis added]

Targumim Linked to Talmudic Tradition. Furthermore, we find on some occasions that the variants of translation in the Targum are clearly linked to a Talmudic tradition, which had by this time developed. For example, in the legal code that follows the proclamation of the Ten Commandments in Exodus, where the damages for injury are recorded, we read:

> If he then gets up and walks outdoors upon his staff, the assailant shall go unpunished, except that he must pay for his idleness and for his cure. (Exod. 21:19, author's translation)

The Targum reads: "He shall pay him for the hire of a physician," which is exactly the formula we find in the Talmud. Similarly, in Deuteronomy, where we are told that the "Levites shall have equal portions to eat except for that which is sold according to their patrimony" (Deut. 18:8, author's translation), Targum reads: "They shall have equal portions to eat except for that which is sold accrues to them from their tour of duty, for thus their fathers have decreed." What is vague in the Torah text comes out clearly as their daily wage, and it is thus specified in the Talmud (Sukkah 56a).

Here then are glimpses of how the meturgeman

functioned, and what he did by way of not only interpreting but expounding the Torah. We have to dig for the evidence and ferret it out, but when it is put together, the portrait begins to emerge.

We watch this role of meturgeman grow and expand, as the process of rabbinic exegesis develops and the Talmud emerges. There was a two-level process of communication. The sage taught his students in smaller groups, but as these grew in size, and the sages were not always good speakers, they required someone who could do this for them.

Such a role was known as meturgeman or amora. The commentator Rashi, who in the eleventh century in the Rhineland wrote the classic commentary of the Talmud, making its study possible in the West, found it necessary to describe the role as follows:

> Amora—the translator who stands at the side of the preaching sage while the latter quietly whispers to him in Hebrew what he wishes to say, while the former translates it into the language the people understand. (Rashi to Yoma 20b and Ketubot 106a)

In another source we learn that Rav Huna had thirteen meturgemanim, so large were his classes. They were scattered throughout the audience, and they listened to what he said and repeated it to the assembly on either side, and from the front and rear of the audience, positioning themselves in every section of the crowd (Ketubot 106a).

How would a lecture be stopped? If it was deemed improper it was stopped with the command: "Remove the meturgeman." In our own time they would say: "Turn off the public-address system!" For example, it was related that one time when Rabban Gamliel was publicly insulting Rabbi Joshua ben Hananiah, the sages put an end to it by ordering Huzpit the meturgeman to halt!

The Prevalence of the *Darshan*/Meturgeman Role. We find here and there in the Talmud the listing by name of the meturgeman to a given scholar. Judah the Prince, the man who finally edited the Mishnah (c. 200), had a meturgeman whose name was Abba Yudan (Jerusalem Talmud, Berakhot 1:1). Rav, his son-in-law, who with Samuel moved the academies to Babylonia, was the meturgeman for his uncle Hiyya and for the great sage Shila (Yoma 20b). We are informed that he had a special talent as a popular *darshan,* that he had a very attractive voice, and often acted as cantor (Teshuvat ha Geonim, Sha'arei Teshuva 178). Judah ben Nahmani was meturgeman

for Simeon ben Lakish (Hagiga 15a). Bar Yehuda was meturgeman for Abbahu (Megillah 14:7) and Rabbi Pedat was meturgeman for Yissa. The mere citation of these names and references shows the wide prevalence of the *darshan*/meturgeman role.

One need only look into the Code of Maimonides, in which the whole corpus of Talmudic exegesis and development is fixed and codified as Judaism develops in the Middle Ages to the modern era, to see how this role emerges as a fixed institution in the process of teaching and continuing Judaism. In the section dealing with the laws surrounding the study of Torah, the entire gamut of this process that is at the heart of Judaism is explored in direct and pithy statements as to what is required.

Dealing with how a teacher must teach, how the teacher must relate to his students, and the students to their master: Does one sit or does one stand when a class is in session? Does the teacher stand and the class sit, or vice versa? Who respects whom and how? What are the grounds for excommunicating a teacher and a student? When must a busy person study? In the midst of this, we suddenly encounter the following:

> If he [the Sage] was teaching through a meturgeman, the [meturgeman] between him and his students, the Sage speaks to the meturgeman and the meturgeman speaks to all the students. When they [the students] ask a question of the meturgeman, he asks the Sage and the Sage gives the answer to the meturgeman, and the meturgeman gives the answer to the students. . . .

What Maimonides was here describing was clearly something institutionalized and part of the learning process. What is more, there was a whole series of mutual obligations and a whole ethic of relationship. See how he continues:

> The sage may not speak louder than the meturgeman, nor shall the meturgeman speak louder than the sage when he asks a question of the sage. The meturgeman may neither subtract from nor add to what the Sage has said, nor may he change anything unless he happens to be the Sage's father or teacher.

What we see is a carefully balanced and orchestrated relationship designed to respect the status of each. One perceptive commentator raised the question, and rightly so, that if the class were large, the meturgeman would have to speak louder than he spoke to the sage. And the answer comes through in the affirmative. But the mutual respect is what is really important.

God as Meturgeman

The commentator invokes God to make his point, and God, in this connection, is given the role of meturgeman! How does the commentator make the deduction? By describing the moment at Sinai when God and Moses spoke to each other. He quotes the account from Exodus: "And when the voice of the trumpet sounded long, and waxed louder and louder, Moses spake, and God answered him by a voice" (Exod. 19:19, KJV). The question is: With what kind of voice? Being God's, was it louder and more powerful, as clearly it had to be? No, came the answer. God responded to Moses in exactly the same level of voice with which Moses spoke, just as any good meturgeman was required to do (Num. Rabbah XIV:3).

Preaching in rabbinic Judaism and early Christianity came out of the same source, developed in the creative years of the second commonwealth. They emerged as reactions to the cataclysmic end of that commonwealth. They shared and developed a common basis in sacred text, spread its word, each according to its own light, through the spoken word.

Hayim Goren Perelmuter[16]

258 • THE SERMON IN SYNAGOGUE WORSHIP

The sermon in synagogue worship was always in the context of prayers, benedictions, psalms, hymns, and the reading of Scripture. When Hebrew was no longer the spoken language for many Jews, the Scripture was first read in Hebrew, then translated into the spoken language. This translation from one language to another necessitated an interpretation. The interpretation, which at first may have been offhand comments, gradually grew into a more formal presentation.

Preaching in the Synagogue

Preaching in the synagogue took place within the established Jewish liturgy. The service in the synagogue would begin with the recitation of the *sh*e*ma*? This was a confession of God's greatness and was taken from Deuteronomy 6:4-9; 11:13-21; and Numbers 15:37-41. There would then be a time of prayer that would usually be one of a cycle of eighteen prayers called "The Prayer." Following the prayers

The Lion of the Tribe of Judah. This symbol, based on Revelation 5:5, is one of the best-known symbols of Jesus Christ. The ancients believed the lion obliterated his tracks by his tail. So the Lord concealed his glory from his enemies and accomplished the will of his Father despite evil plottings. Also, because lion cubs were born with their eyes closed, it was believed that they were born dead but were brought to life on the third day. In the same manner Jesus was brought to life in the third day.

came the reading of Scripture, which would first be a text from the Law, followed by a text from the prophets. An interpreter would then translate the Hebrew into Aramaic so the people could understand it. The text from the Law was one of one hundred fifty that were to be read, so that over a three-year period the whole Law would be covered. The texts from the prophets would differ depending on the reader. The preaching of the sermon would follow, which was an exposition on the previously read texts.

The reading of Scripture and exposition of it can be dated back to Ezra. "They read from the Book of the Law of God, making it clear [translating it] and giving the meaning so that the people could understand what was being read"(Neh. 8:8). The practice of public reading of Scripture followed by exposition was a part of the Jewish worship centuries before Christianity.

The synagogue required that ten men (male over the age of thirteen) be present for the Scripture to be read. It could be read by anyone, including a boy. After the text had been read orally, there would be exposition on it either by the reader or by another male. The preaching would be a commentary that either expounded the text or presented applications of its meaning. Preaching was directly connected to the reading of Scripture; there was no preaching without the reading of the text. Usually the sermon had a devotional character. Since anyone might be asked to preach, the preaching was more discussion than sermon, not so much persuasion as elaboration.

Jesus' Reinterpretation of Synagogue Preaching

This ancient Jewish liturgy provided Jesus with a regular and traditionally accepted format for his preaching (Luke 4:16). It also provided Paul with a place to preach in each new city he would visit (Acts 13:14-16). The reading and exposition of the Scriptures during public worship was the chief way that knowledge of the Law and Prophets was learned by the people. Thus, preaching had a supreme importance for Judaism. Though preaching had a significant role in Jewish worship, Jesus introduced a new concept into preaching. Preaching became the responsibility of all followers of Christ, in all places and at all times. For the Jews, preaching was a matter of safeguarding the Scriptures entrusted to them. Christ's command points toward a goal of spreading the Word, not guarding it.

Rick McDaniel

259 • TEACHING AND PREACHING IN THE SYNAGOGUE AND EARLY CHURCH

Preaching in the Jewish synagogue instructed members in faith and practice but also could be intended for indoctrination and proselytizing. Christianity first spread through the preaching of Paul and others who traveled from city to city, preaching Jesus and the Resurrection and calling Jews to conversion in Christ.

Preaching in the Synagogue

The most significant institution in Jewish life was the synagogue. Prior to and during the apostolic period, the synagogue was a developing institution. Synagogues were established in every town or village in Palestine and the Diaspora wherever Jews lived in sizable numbers. There was no central authority to maintain particular patterns of practice or belief. Jerusalem, Rome, and the other large cities had several synagogues. Acts 15:21 confirms the existence of such synagogues: "For Moses has been preached in every city from the earliest times and is read in the synagogues on every Sabbath."

Preaching occurred in the synagogues on a regular basis in relation to the reading of Scripture. Peter and Paul are recorded as preaching and teaching in the synagogues of the dispersed Jews. Preaching was not primarily a missionary activity in Judaism, but was the activity of instructing the people. The preaching in the synagogue was done by both priests and lay teachers. F. C. Grant (*Ancient Judaism and the New Testament* [New York: Macmillan, 1959], 45) described the practice of teaching as follows: "The preacher—who was really a teacher—sat (Matt. 5:1; Luke 4:20), and any likely visitor might be asked to give the sermon, homily, or exhortation (Luke 4:17; Acts 13:15)."

In addition to providing instruction in faith and life for members of the synagogue, the homily was also used for indoctrination and proselytizing purposes. Preaching was a practice of missionary enterprise of Judaism prior to the destruction of the temple in A.D. 70. It needs to be emphasized that this teaching practice of delivering a homily was for both believers and unbelievers. The synagogue service was one place for the unbeliever to learn of the Jewish religion, and it was used for this purpose. The service in the synagogue could and did serve multiple functions, including the spreading of different schools of thought within Judaism by way of traveling teachers who were propagandists, preachers, and lecturers.

It is important to recognize in the background of Christianity a number of synagogues that served as foci of different modes of thought. Missionary homilies, propaganda addresses, legal *halakic* discourses, and extremely loose, narrative, *haggadic*, instructive sermons were all characteristic of the synagogue at the time of Christian beginnings. Distinctions between preaching and teaching were not made.

This instructive activity was not confined to the synagogue. Both preaching and teaching occurred in the open air, a common practice in both Palestine and Babylonia. Courtyards, vineyards, the shade of buildings and walls, marketplaces, open fields, and

---

banks of rivers were used as sites of teaching-preaching.

Teaching and Preaching

No rigid distinction can be made between preaching and teaching in Judaism of the first century. This period of Judaism provided the immediate context and certainly the background of practices for the earliest church. There was a great difference within Judaism between the more popular *haggadic,* narrative style of homily or address and the strict *halakic* discourse. The popular address was given much more frequently in the synagogue service. This popular address or homily was considered a teaching practice whether it was oriented toward making proselytes, converts, or the edification of the congregation.

Neither preaching nor teaching as used in Judaism of the first century denote a distinct style or kind of activity with a distinct content. Both words refer to a variety of activities that took place as the Jewish congregation was exhorted, instructed, and edified. It cannot be claimed on the basis of existing evidence that preaching was a more spiritual, emotional, or vigorous activity than teaching, or that preaching was a missionary activity while teaching was for a local congregation. There is an interchangeability in the use of these words that corresponds remarkably to the interchangeability that is found in the New Testament.

The Preacher/*Darshan*

The most common word in Judaism for preacher was *darshan*. This person engaged in the activity *darash,* which meant "to inquire," "to seek after," and "to interpret." It also applied to the method of exegesis of the Pentateuch, which led to the interpretation of the Pentateuch. The *darshan* was an interpreter. The many uses of *darash* and its derivatives support the idea that the preacher was one who examined, questioned, taught, lectured, argued, and interpreted the law.

Daube has pointed out that the term *darshan* originally was used to describe that person who expounded the law, the teacher of the *halakah;* but this use lost its significance. It eventually came to refer to the teacher "who addressed the people in general, taught them the doctrines of religion and morality, confronted them in the grievous days that followed the destruction of the temple, and expounded texts of Scripture not with a view of their *halakic* or legal interpretation but to their *haggadic* or edifying possibilities" ("Rabbinic Methods of Interpretation and Hellenistic Rhetoric," *Hebrew Union College Annual,* 22:240).

The possible differences between the preaching activity in the early church and that conducted by the *darshan* needs to be noted. The possibility of new and distinctive patterns of activity and content in the early church exists. The Jewish *darshan,* for example, was not a post-Resurrection figure in that we do not find evidence of a direct continuity of his office in the early church. It is certain that he as a Jewish preacher did not have a *kerygma* in the sense of a particular body of content or tradition. He was primarily an interpreter and expositor of Scripture.

The activity of Jesus corresponds closely in many ways to that of the *darshan.* The similarity between the *darshan* and the post-Resurrection apostles is not as apparent. The style of teaching-preaching of the apostles is primarily that of delivering narrative, haggadic *midrash.* The *darshan* also taught and preached in this style, but is not noted for this in the same way he is noted for halachic discourse. The historical link between Jesus and the *darshan* is clear because the styles of teaching-preaching have great similarity.

It can also be argued that the *darshan* has close similarity to apostolic teaching-preaching in that both used the loose, narrative, *haggadic* style of communication. The distinctions are not as clear and rigid as C. H. Dodd and others have made them. There is a real possibility that early Christians used the modes of interpretation and retained many of the practices from Judaism to communicate their own post-Resurrection faith. The *darshan* was a teacher in early Judaism, and the early church was probably influenced to a considerable degree by his practices.

Teaching-Preaching in the Early Church

This aspect remains as a central feature of teaching-preaching in the earliest church. The multiple theological-Christological interests and commitments form the basis of teaching-preaching. Also in contrast to Dodd's theory is a view of the diversity, pluralism, and complexity of Jewish interpretative practices that form the background of the multiple contents of teaching-preaching.

From a theological-Christological basis, early teacher-preachers were free to use a variety of interpretive practices, modes of reasoning, and cultural linguistic carriers of meaning. Teacher-preachers apparently used the thought forms and modes of reasoning from a pluralistic Palestinian milieu to interpret Christian faith. Tradition, the Bible (Old Testament), and contemporary events were interpreted through a theological-Christological interest and commitment using the linguistic instruments surrounding the early church. It is obvious that early teacher-preachers made both past and present serve their theological commitments.

The style of teaching-preaching that the early church had was that of combining theological concerns, Scripture and tradition, and cultural carriers of meaning to interpret Christian faith to believers and unbelievers in a variety of locations. Teaching-preaching was more than a transmission of tradition. There was struggle and dynamism in the process of interpretation as those early Christians brought their intellect, their knowledge of Scripture and tradition, a variety of modes of reasoning, and cultural carriers of meaning to serve faith and the Lord of that faith in the communication of the good news of God's work in Jesus of Nazareth.

Teaching-preaching was the way of communicating Christian faith to believers and unbelievers in different contexts through the interpretation of tradition, and through the interpretation of the work, person, and sayings of Jesus. Teaching-preaching used a variety of methods, ideas, and practices from different sources to the end that those who heard would receive life in the kingdom, in Christ, in the post-Resurrection Christian community.

Robert C. Worley[17]

260 ◆ JESUS AT NAZARETH

In the account of the sermon Jesus delivered in his hometown, three necessary elements of preaching are evident. First, there is the liturgical element: Jesus' sermon was in the context of worship. Second, there is the exegetical aspect: Jesus interpreted a text. Third, there is the prophetic element: "Today this scripture has been fulfilled in your hearing." These three elements—worship, exegesis, and prophecy—have figured significantly in the history of preaching; they constitute the essential framework for the sermon.

Jesus Preaches in His Hometown

Jesus returned to Galilee in the power of the Spirit, and news about him spread through the whole countryside. He taught in their synagogues, and everyone praised him.

He went to Nazareth, where he had been brought up, and on the Sabbath day he went into the synagogue, as was his custom. And he stood up to read. The scroll of the prophet Isaiah was handed to him. Unrolling it, he found the place where it is written:

> The Spirit of the Lord is on me,
>   because he has anointed me
>   to preach good news to the poor.
> He has sent me to proclaim freedom for
>   the prisoners
>   and recovery of sight for the blind,
>   to release the oppressed,
>   to proclaim the year of the Lord's favor.

Then he rolled up the scroll, gave it back to the attendant and sat down. The eyes of everyone in the synagogue were fastened on him, and he began by saying to them, "Today this scripture is fulfilled in your hearing." (Luke 4:14-21)

261 ◆ THE *KERYGMA* OF THE EARLY CHURCH

The kerygma (preaching) is a summary of the preaching themes of the early church, based on the study of the sermons in the book of Acts. These themes, most visible in Peter's sermon on the day of Pentecost (Acts 2:14-41), lie at the heart of the gospel:

> *The prophecies are fulfilled, and the new age is inaugurated by the coming of Christ.*
> *He was born of the seed of David.*
> *He died according to the Scriptures, to deliver us out of the present evil age.*
> *He was buried.*
> *He rose on the third day according to the Scriptures.*
> *He is exalted at the right hand of God, as Son of God and Lord of the living and dead.*
> *He will come again as Judge and Savior of men and women.*

The Use of *Kerygma* in the Early Church

The Greek word *kerygma* means "that which is preached," stemming from the root *keryssein*, signifying "to preach." For the first century church kerygma characterized the central power of the gospel. The essence of earliest Christianity was contained in the kerygma's repeated proclamation.

The term _kerygma_ appears in the New Testament eight times: twice by Jesus making reference to Jonah's proclamation to Nineveh and six times referring to the apostolic preaching. The term most often has, as its object, the gospel, the glad tidings of the early church. While the word itself is not cited often, the kerygma (the gospel to which it refers) can be found throughout the Gospels, Acts, and the Epistles.

The message to which kerygma refers consisted of the basic evangelistic proclamations of the gospel that brought persons to faith in Jesus. It typically included elements enumerated as evidence of the truthfulness of the gospel. Certain events in the life of Jesus Christ were always present: first, that Jesus was the fulfillment of what was proclaimed by the prophets; second, Jesus Christ died on the cross and rose again; third, God has made Jesus Christ as Lord; fourth, Jesus would reign over a judgment to come; and finally, a call to repentance and an offer of forgiveness.

Whereas exhortation and _didache_ (teaching) had origins in the early church for instruction, the kerygma served solely as public announcement that Jesus is the Christ in whom salvation is to be found. Modern preaching has become more exhortative and teaching in nature. In contrast, the early church reserved the moments of proclamation for the kerygma in order that men and women might be won to faith.

Of primary importance to the kerygma was the one who proclaimed. The Greek word _keryx_ could be a town crier, an auctioneer, or a herald. Usually, the keryx would be someone given authority to announce that which was heralded. Also, the herald would draw public attention to the message. The keryx would bring an edict from another party sovereign over the subject matter. For the early church, the proclamation of the gospel in power was delivered by those worthy of its content.

Essentially, Christian faith did not exist until there was the kerygma, the message to be believed and embraced. Nearly all of the New Testament relates to and expands on the meaning of the kerygma.

Judith Wall Baker

262 • THE PREACHING OF PAUL

There appears to be a distinction in early Christian worship between the Jewish tradition (fixed forms, with a somewhat didactic preaching) and gentile worship (free worship with ecstatic utterances). Paul's preaching appears rational and exegetical, as do his remarks to the Corinthian community (1 Cor. 12-14). Paul's sermon preached in Athens (Acts 17:22-31) is a prime example of logic and coherence. It begins with a thesis statement and builds an argument from the premise that moves toward a logical conclusion. This sermon was a model for the more systematic and academic sermons that appeared in the Middle Ages. It also influenced Protestants, who were drawn to its pedagogical approach.

———— Paul's Sermon in Athens ————

Paul then stood up in the meeting of the Areopagus and said: "Men of Athens! I see that in every way you are very religious. For as I walked around and looked carefully at your objects of worship, I even found an altar with this inscription: TO AN UNKNOWN GOD. Now what you worship as something unknown I am going to proclaim to you.

"The God who made the world and everything in it is the Lord of heaven and earth and does not live in temples built by hands. And he is not served by human hands, as if he needed anything, because he himself gives all men life and breath and everything else. From one man he made every nation of men, that they should inhabit the whole earth; and he determined the times set for them and the exact places where they should live. God did this so that men would seek him and perhaps reach out for him and find him, though he is not far from each one of us. 'For in him we live and move and have our being.' As some of your own poets have said, 'We are his offspring.'

"Therefore since we are God's offspring, we should not think that the divine being is like gold or silver or stone—an image made by man's design and skill. In the past God overlooked such ignorance, but now he commands all people everywhere to repent. For he has set a day when he will judge the world with justice by the man he has appointed. He has given proof of this to all men by raising him from the dead." (Acts 17:22-31)

263 • LAY PREACHING IN THE EARLY CHURCH

Evidence collected about the early church suggests that most of the preaching in hamlets, villages, and rural areas was done by uneducated but devout lay people. The apostolic preaching, as well as the writings of the apostolic fathers of the second century that have been preserved, stand as exceptions to this overall trend.

—————— Informal Preaching ——————

For the greater part of the period from A.D. 30 to 230, after the close of the events in the New Testament, we know very little of Christian preaching. The reasons for this almost entire lack of sermons

The Rock of Salvation. The symbol of Christ as the rock is based on 1 Corinthians 10:14 "For they drank of that spiritual rock that followed them: and that rock was Christ." The rock is shown in several ways. When it stands alone, it represents the idea of Psalm 18:2: "The Lord is my Rock and my fortress." When the cross is on top of the rock, as above, the symbol refers to the words: "Let us make a joyful noise to the rock of our salvation" (Ps. 95:1). Other symbolic uses of the rock include a house built upon the rock (Matt. 7:24) and a church built upon the rock (Matt. 16:18). When the rock is pictured with four rivers flowing from it, the reference is to either the four Gospels or to the four rivers of paradise.

remaining from the first two centuries are several, the chief one being this: The preaching of the time was, in general, quite informal. The preacher did not make *logous,* discourses, but only *omilias,* homilies, that is conversations, talks. Even in the fourth century, there was still retained, by some out-of-the-way congregations, the practice of asking the preacher many questions and answering questions asked by him, so as to make the homily to some extent a conversation. And in this period it was *always* a mere familiar talk, which of course might rise into dignity and swell into passion, but only in an informal way. The general feeling appears also to have been that dependence on the promised blessing of the Paraclete forbade elaborate preparation of discourses. And this feeling would prevent many from writing out their discourses after they were spoken.

—————— Lay Preaching as the Rule ——————

But we must by no means imagine that there was but little preaching during the first two centuries because no sermons remain. In fact, preaching was then very general, almost universal, among the Christians. *Lay preaching* was not an exception, it was the rule. Like the first disciples, the Christians still went everywhere preaching the Word. The notion that the Christian minister corresponded to the Old Testament *priest* had not yet gained the ascendency. We find Irenaeus and Tertullian insisting that all Christians are priests. We learn from Eusebius (History VI.19) that Origen, *before* he was ordained a presbyter, went to Palestine and was invited by the bishops of Caesarea and Jerusalem to "expound the sacred Scriptures publicly in the church." The bishop of Alexandria, who was an enemy to Origen, condemned this, declaring it unheard of "that laymen should deliver discourses in the presence of the bishop." But the bishop of Jerusalem pronounced that notion, a great mistake, appealing to various examples. It was still common in some regions to invite laypersons who could edify the church, to do so; this even when sacerdotal feeling was growing strong.

In these first centuries, then, almost all the Christians preached. Thus, preaching was informal, and therefore unrecorded. Even of the presbyters at that time, few were educated or had much leisure for study. And, when some able and scholarly man became a Christian, however he might occupy himself with profound studies and the preparation of elaborate works, as did Justin or Clement of Alexandria, Irenaeus or Tertullian, when he stood up to preach, he would lay his studies aside and speak impromptu, with the greatest simplicity.

John A. Broadus[18]

264 ❖ MELITO OF SARDIS (D. 190)

Formerly it was thought that Christian rhetoric did not begin until the fourth and fifth centuries. The discovery, however, of a sermon by Melito, bishop of Sardis, known as "On the Passover" suggests that a tradition of skilled rhetoric and sermon construction had begun earlier. Melito's sermon carefully blends typology, analogy, and parallelism. Scholars now believe that two distinctive styles of preaching existed in the second century: the unstructured, informal homily of the lay person and the highly developed oration typified in "On the Passover."

The Importance of the Sermon

The sermon of Melito "On the Passover" is the work of the famous and influential bishop of Sardis who is known to have written voluminously but whose literary productions have been almost entirely lost. The discoveries have identified not only the sermon, but have also enabled scholars to correctly assign authorship to other ancient fragments wrongly assigned until now. It is an important discovery because it sheds new light on the content and style of Christian preaching in the second century and causes previously accepted theories on the subject to be reconsidered.

The Content of the Homily

The theme of the sermon is immediately announced to be the Passover as a prefiguration of the passion of Christ. The Passover in ancient Egypt was a temporal event, establishing the chosen people under the law. But it was also a timeless event because it was the prototype of the sacrifice of the True Lamb, establishing the church under grace. This dual nature of the Passover is a reflection of the dual nature of Christ, who suffered and died as a man but was raised as God, being by nature both God and man.

The sermon moves next to an elaborate and highly imaginative account of the story of the Passover; the destruction of the firstborn and the desolation of Egypt are related in vivid detail. Israel is protected from the death angel by the blood on the doors, which, in Melito's thorough typology, is not the blood of the sheep but the spirit of the slain Christ.

This typology continues: in an elaborate analogy the old dispensation under the law is likened to a poorly constructed and temporary pattern from which an artisan works; the finished work of beauty and perfection is the new dispensation under grace through the passion of Christ. The pattern rendered useless by the emergence of the finished perfection is discarded and replaced by the reality. Thus, the law is valueless, replaced by the gospel which it prefigured; the people of Israel are supplanted, replaced by the church they prefigured; the Passover with the sacrifice of the sheep, now useless, is replaced by the blood of Christ's passion which it prefigured. Old Jerusalem is replaced by eternal Jerusalem; the Passover lamb is replaced by the Lamb of God.

Turning then to humanity, Melito rehearses humankind's fall to depravity and the pervasive need for the sacrifice of Christ. This sacrifice is seen to be foreshadowed in the heroes of Israel, who in their actions were really prefigurations of Christ. He moves on to an elaborate denunciation of the Jews for their treatment of Jesus and concludes with a peroration in which Christ himself enumerates the details of his saving actions on behalf of humanity. A doxology to Christ closes the sermon.

Implications for Preaching

The homily brings to light a new episode in the struggle of Christian preaching to use rhetoric without being captured by it. A question asked by Yngve Brillioth in *Predikans Historia* is quite appropriate: "Was biblical realism to be submerged by this flood of rhetorical craftsmanship which, however exquisite in its kind, was surely . . . alien to the spirit of the gospels . . . ?" During the Middle Ages, particularly in sermons aimed more toward the clergy than laity, the battle was lost. Using all the cruel text-twisting of allegorical interpretation and all the elaborately detailed and intricately embellished ornamentation of scholastic rhetoric, the sermon's subject was of so little importance and the real intent of Scripture so ill-considered by the preacher that sermons were nothing at all save literary fabrications.

Historians have long maintained that the flirtation with rhetoric did not affect Christian preaching seriously until the time of Hippolytus; he has been stigmatized as the first to succumb and use Greek rhetoric with abandon in preaching. The third and fourth centuries have been characterized as the "oratorical period," and some tried to explain why the sermon remained largely unadorned until the Cappadocian Fathers, crowned by John Chrysostom, accomplished a proper wedding of the old "prophesying" and Asian rhetoric.

Melito's sermon sweeps away all such notions that preaching in the second century was still as simple and unstructured as 2 Clement has led us to believe. The question must seriously be faced whether elaborate rhetoric was in use, not only by Melito but by others, a generation earlier than we had thought. Not all of Melito's devices of rhetoric are noted here. His elaborate use of typology, analogy, and parallelism are, however, only pale reflections of what must be called an elegant and profuse application of rhetorical devices. One author even calls it "artificial." Melito was certainly—what some have said was not to be found until the third century—a "conscious orator," and in him the oratorical period may have been born quite early in Christian history. Melito's sermon "On the Passover" warrants his inclusion in works on the Fathers, perhaps as the earliest known Christian orator.

It may be possible to distinguish two kinds of preaching in the second century: the unstructured, unlearned, moralizing sermon that 2 Clement represents; and the kind of address later defined as "an oration delivered from the pulpit with full development and rhetorical effect." Melito represents the latter and may thus be the earliest known preacher of a "sermon." His theology is a gospel of grace, whereas 2 Clement promotes legalistic obedience.

R. C. White[19]

265 ✦ ORIGEN (185-254)

Origen was one of the earliest and most influential of the Greek preachers. He intertwined exegesis and preaching and created a sermon style that was essentially a running commentary of the text. This style dominated Christian preaching in the ancient church and continues to be used effectively today. In addition, Origen developed the allegorical method of exegesis, a method which is associated with the Alexandrian school of thought and the Eastern church. The allegorical interpretation of Scripture leads the listener to five possible meanings of the text: (1) the historical; (2) the doctrinal; (3) the prophetic; (4) the philosophical; and (5) the mystical sense.

A Teacher of Preaching and Teaching

The first period in Christian preaching is divided from the second by the work of Origen. He was truly an epoch-making man, in biblical learning, in ministerial education, and in homiletics. As to biblical learning, all Christian scholars in the next two centuries, and many in every subsequent century, drew largely from the vast stores of learning gathered in his great works. He was also the great *educator* among the early Christians. For nearly thirty years, beginning as a precocious youth of seventeen, he was chief catechist in Alexandria, or as we should say, theological professor, aided after a time by one of his distinguished pupils. And when banished from Alexandria, and living at Caesarea in Palestine, he taught as a private instructor, but with students from distant lands, and with great éclat, for about twenty years more. During a great part of this time, from youth to age, he also preached every day, while at the same time laboring over his varied and immense works, so large a portion of which have long ago perished. Origen was not only a teacher of preachers, but also a teacher of teachers. He had had predecessors in Alexandria, such as Clement and *his* teacher Pantaenus, but it was Origen who made the Alexandrian school the chief seat of Christian learning for many generations to come.

Allegorizing

In respect to methods of preaching Origen made history. As to interpretation of Scripture, he dignified and appeared to justify the practice of allegorizing. Yet, it would be a mistake to say Origen was the father of this practice. Origen's great master in this respect was Philo, the Alexandrian Jew, a contemporary of Jesus. Origen applied to the New Testament and to the Old Testament those methods of allegorizing by which Philo made the Old Testament teach Platonic and Stoic philosophy.

Celsus, the shrewd and vigorous unbeliever, made it an objection that the New Testament did not admit of allegorizing. Origen resented this as a slander, adducing several passages in which Paul himself had used allegory, and doubtless feeling all the more called on to show by his own allegorical interpretations that the Christian books _did_ have those deep allegorical meanings that the Jews claimed for their books, and the Greeks for theirs. Allegorizing had long been the rage at Alexandria. Porphyry pretended that Origen had only learned it from the Greek mysteries. Philo himself only carried out more fully and ably the method of Aristobulus, his predecessor by a century and a half. Egyptologists indicate that fifteen centuries before Christ, the Egyptian priests were disputing as to the true text and allegorizing the statements of their Book of the Dead, or Funeral Rites.

While Origen did not originate allegorizing, he did do much to recommend it by presenting the striking theory that as a human being is composed of body, soul, and spirit, so Scripture has a threefold sense—the grammatical, the moral, and the spiritual. He also promoted allegorizing by actually working out a spiritual sense for a great part of the Old and New Testaments. In this way he injured preaching. Those who held to a deep, esoteric sense, which only the few could understand, who, like the Gnostics, regarded themselves as a sort of spiritual aristocracy, would not only neglect to bring forth and apply the plain teachings of Scripture, but they habitually made light of these teachings and cared mainly for such hearers as could soar with them into the "misty mid-regions" of allegorizing. It is very well as a general principle that one should preach with some reference to the wants of the highly cultivated and should deal in profound thought, but it is the plain truths of Scripture that do the chief good, to the cultivated as well as the uncultivated. One who begins to regard him- or herself as distinctively a preacher for the intellectual or the learned will spoil his or her preaching.

At a later period, all Christians became accustomed to the methods of allegorizing, and it ceased for the most part to be an esoteric affair, becoming almost universal—with the exception of Chrysostom and his associates—in all the subsequent centuries until the Reformation.

The Form of Origen's Sermons

Origen did well, however, in teaching persons to bring out the grammatical and the moral sense. Early on a teacher of grammar and rhetoric, Origen had a facility with language, an exegetical sense, and his homilies and other works form the first examples of any painstaking _explanation_ of Scripture, or approach to accurate exegesis.

As to the _form_ of Christian discourses or sermons, Origen, following Melito of Sardis, was one of the first to give homiletical shape to a sermon—rather than presenting a string of loosely connected observations, dependent for their connection on accidental suggestion or emotional influences. He also was the first to preach sermon series on entire books of the Bible. This was a great advance and prepared the way for future improvements, yet the Christian sermon remained without unity of structure. Origen did not take the fundamental thought of the passage and treat every verse in relation to that; rather he took clause after clause as they came and remarked upon them in succession. Not till a century later was this fault corrected, and only partially then. In fact this lack of unity is still the commonest and gravest fault in ordinary attempts at expository preaching.

John A. Broadus[20]

266 ✦ BASIL THE GREAT AND GREGORY OF NAZIANZUS (FOURTH CENTURY)

Christianity changed considerably in the fourth century with the conversion of Constantine, who made Christianity legal and opened the door toward its accommodation with society. Worship developed rapidly through extensive building projects, the development of liturgies, the observance of the Christian year, creation of the lectionary, and the contributions of music and the arts. In this setting, preaching took on the characteristics of Roman rhetoric and became considerably more formal. Among the Greek Christians of the time, several stand out as exceptional preachers, especially Basil the Great, his brother Gregory of Nyssa, Gregory of Nazianzus—collectively called the Cappadocians—and John Chrysostom, who will be treated in the next entry.

Basil the Great (329–379)

Basil the Great possessed all possible advantages. His family was rich and of high social position in Pontus and, from his grandparents down, had been remarkable for piety. Two of his brothers became bishops, one of them famous (Gregory of Nyssa); and his older sister (Macrina), who powerfully influenced him, founded and presided over a monastery. His father, a distinguished rhetorician, gave him careful instruction from childhood. At school he surpassed all his fellow pupils. Then he studied at Constantinople, taught by Libanius, the most famous teacher of rhetoric in that age, with whom he formed a lasting friendship. Afterwards he went to Athens, where his fellow students included Julian (afterwards emperor and apostate), and Gregory Nazianzus, his early friend. Gregory tells us in a well-known funeral eulogium (Oration 43) that when he heard Basil was coming to Athens he gave the students so high an opinion of his abilities and eloquence that they consented, as a special distinction, to exempt Basil from the species of hazing to which new students were always subjected.

Thus he had every advantage—good breeding, and all pious and inspiring home influences, careful early training, then life in the great capital city (giving knowledge of the world) and afterward at the chief seat of learning in that age, Athens, with the ablest instructors and the most gifted fellow students. There his intellect disciplined, and his taste cultivated by the study of classic philosophy and oratory, and yet his Christian feeling ever warmed anew by the sympathy and example of his intelligent and devout kindred at home. He died when less than fifty years old, but his life was crowded with religious and literary labors.

———— Basil's Preaching ————

As a preacher, Basil shows greater skill in the construction of discourses than any Christian orator who had preceded him. He usually extemporized, but he knew how to put a sermon together, or to make it grow in a natural manner. The chief excellency of his preaching is in the treatment of moral subjects. He had a rare knowledge of human nature, and you may notice that among all the changes of preaching in all the ages, two branches of knowledge possess a universal and indestructible interest: deep knowledge of human nature, and deep knowledge of Scripture. Basil shows wonderful power in depicting the various virtues, and still more remarkable skill in tracing the growth and consequences of leading vices.

Basil's style has the faults of his age, but taking just one discourse at a time, you feel that you are dealing with a great mind, a noble character, a deeply devout and truly eloquent preacher.

——— Gregory of Nazianzus (329–389) ———

Gregory Nazianzus, the friend and fellow student of Basil, was doubtless at that time considered the most eloquent of all preachers until Chrysostom became known. Very ambitious and enjoying the finest educational opportunities, Gregory was especially a student of eloquence and was a man of imaginative and passionate nature. He was the first great hymn writer; and his hymns became exceedingly popular in the Greek church. Yet it has been justly said that his poetry is too oratorical, and his oratory too poetical. You may notice that few great preachers have written even a single good hymn, and no great hymn writer has been very eminent as a preacher, unless Gregory be the exception, or Ephraem the Syrian. So more generally as to oratory and poetry: The oratorical and the poetic temperament seem closely related, yet are remarkably distinct. An orator may derive very great benefit from studying poets, but many preachers are damaged by failing to understand the difference between the poet's office and their own. *Imagination* is the poet's mistress, his queen; for the orator she is the handmaid, highly useful, indeed absolutely needful, but only a handmaid. And *splendor of diction,* which for the poet is one chief end, is for the orator only a subordinate means.

But the very faults of Gregory's style, according to our taste, were high excellencies in the estimation of his contemporaries. His extravagant hyperboles, perpetual effort to strike, and high-wrought splendor of imagery and diction, were accounted the most magnificent eloquence, and perhaps did really recommend the truth to some of his hearers. Thus while patriarch of Constantinople, he preached five discourses (still extant), which are said to have done much in curing Arianism there, and which procured him the surname of *Theologos,* discourser on the deity of Christ.

John A. Broadus[21]

267 • JOHN CHRYSOSTOM (347–407)

John Chrysostom, known as the "golden orator," was a master communicator, certainly one of the two or three greatest preachers in the church's history. He was a follower of the Antiochian method of biblical exegesis. This tradition rejected the Platonic allegorizing of the Alexandrian school in favor of a concern for a grammatical, historical, theological method of interpretation.

Chrysostom's Educational Background

John, afterward surnamed Chrysostom ("golden-mouthed," so-named for his preaching), was younger by fifteen or twenty years than Basil and the Gregories. He was of a distinguished and wealthy family in Antioch and, under the devoted care of a widowed mother, received every possible educational advantage. The great teacher Libanius had now returned to his native Antioch and found in John a favorite pupil, whom he would have wished to make his successor as professor of rhetoric and kindred subjects. In the great city John saw the world and sharpened that penetrating knowledge of human nature for which he was remarkable. For a short time he practiced law, and Libanius warmly commended some of his speeches at the bar. But he turned away, weary and disgusted, from the thousand corruptions of society and government. After his mother's death, he went into retirement with several friends and spent several years in the close study of the Scriptures. Among other and greater results, it is said Chrysostom knew almost the whole Bible by heart. In these studies they were directed by Diodorus, the head of a neighboring monastery, and afterwards a bishop and author of long famous commentaries and other works.

Diodorus founded what then appeared to be a new school of biblical interpretation, a reaction from the well-known tendency of the older school of Alexandria. He shrank from allegorizing and held closely to "the literal and historical meaning of the text." His copious writings have perished, except a few fragments. But Diodorus lives forever in his theological pupil, Chrysostom. It is among the greatest distinctions of Chrysostom that his interpretation is almost entirely free from the wild allegorizing that had been nearly universal ever since Origen. It is a delightful contrast to turn from the other great preachers of the time (including Augustine), with their loose interpretations and fanciful spiritualizing, to the straightforward, careful, and usually sober interpretations of Chrysostom. His works are not only models of eloquence, but a treasury of exegesis. And for this the world is mainly indebted to Diodorus. Chrysostom had much native good sense, it is true, but so had Athanasius, Basil, and Augustine. But Chrysostom's early studies of Scripture were directed by a truly wise and able instructor; and his good sense enabled him to seize the just principles of interpretation set before him, to develop them still more ably, and to recommend them far more widely than the instructor himself.

Chrysostom's Preaching

Chrysostom long shrank from the work of preaching and the office of priest, the difficulties and responsibilities of which he had so impressively stated in his little work on the priesthood. He wrote this and other valuable works while holding minor offices in the church, but was ordained and began preaching only at the age of thirty-nine. He died at sixty, after three years of exile. Thus, his actual career as a preacher lasted only eighteen years, twelve years at Antioch and six at Constantinople. In these years he preached almost daily, leaving about one thousand sermons (many of them reported by others) that have descended to us.

We cannot fully discuss the characteristics of Chrysostom's preaching. It must be admitted that he is by no means always correct in his interpretations, particularly in the Old Testament, being ignorant of Hebrew, and often misled by the errors of the

The Crown. The crown bears a double meaning: it denotes Christ's kingly office (Luke 1:33) and expresses the eternal life of believers. Scripture makes mention of the crown of life (1 Pet. 5:4; Rev. 2:10; 3:11).

Septuagint. It must also be conceded that his style often wearies us by excessive copiousness, minute and long-drawn descriptions, multiplied comparisons, and piled-up imagery. But we must always remember that this did not look to excited throngs as it does to us. Under such circumstances a certain rhetorical exaggeration and exuberance seems natural, as a statue placed high upon a pillar must be bigger than life-size.

But admit what you please, criticize as you please, and the fact remains that Chrysostom has never had a superior, and it may be gravely doubted whether he has had an equal in the history of preaching. He does not, it is true, show such consummate art as the great Greek orator Demosthenes. But the finish and repose of high art is scarcely possible, and scarcely desirable, in addressing the preacher's heterogeneous audiences, comprising persons so different as to culture and interest in the subject. Demosthenes has everywhere a style as elegant and purely simple as the Venus de Medici or the Parthenon; Chrysostom approaches in exuberance of fancy, in multiplication of images and illustrations, and in curiously varied repetitions, to a Gothic cathedral. Demosthenes is like the Greek tragic drama, strictly conformed to the three unities; Chrysostom is more like the romantic drama. I cannot say like Shakespeare—the Shakespeare of preachers has not yet appeared. But why should one not someday appear? One who can touch every chord of human feeling, treat every interest of human life, draw illustration from every object and relation of the known universe, and use all to gain acceptance and obedience for the gospel of salvation? No preacher has ever come nearer to this than Chrysostom, perhaps none, on the whole, so near.

A Syrian Greek and a Christian Greek, Chrysostom, in no small measure, combines the Asiatic and the European, the ancient and the modern. The rich style and blazing passion of an Asiatic is united with the power of intellect and energy of will that mark Europeans; while the finish and simplicity of Greek art are not so much lacking as lost in the many-sidedness of Christian thought and Christian heart. His style certainly ranges the whole gamut of expression. While it is generally elevated, often magnificent, and sometimes extravagant, it occasionally becomes homely and rough as he lays bare human follies and vices. Chrysostom is undoubtedly the prince of *expository* preachers. And he has very

rarely been equaled in the treatment of *moral* subjects.

John A. Broadus[22]

268 ◆ Augustine (354–430)

Augustine represents the preaching of the Latin church, a style that may be traced from Tertullian through Cyprian to Ambrose, Augustine's spiritual father and mentor. The Latin style of preaching shows an acquaintance with classical literature, Latin rhetoric, and symbolism.

Augustine addresses the matter of homiletics in the fourth book of De Doctrina Christiana. *He basically argues that the sermon should be an exposition of the text. Concerning approach, he urges the speaker to appeal to intellect, feeling, and will (to teach, delight, and influence). He mentions three styles of preaching—the restrained, the moderate, and the grand. He advises against the grandiose style, however, because audiences will not tolerate it. Augustine makes a strong case for a restrained style in which the form of the sermon reflects the content.*

Augustine has written works of very high *literary* merit, apart from his theological and homiletical writings. His *Confessions* form one of the most unique and strangely impressive works in all literature—one of the books that everybody ought by all means to read. His *City of God* has been called a "prose epic" and is a combination of history, philosophy, and poetry that has a power and a charm all its own. His work on *Christian Teaching* is the first treatise on sacred rhetoric and homiletics.

Augustine's Sermons

But if we had nothing else from Augustine than his sermons, of which some 360 remain that are reckoned genuine, we should recognize him as a great preacher, as a richly gifted man, and should feel ourselves powerfully attracted and impressed by his genius, his mighty will, his passionate heart, and deeply earnest piety.

Augustine favored allegorizing, like every other great preacher of the age except Chrysostom. But his sermons are full of power. He carefully *explains* his text and *repeats* many times, in different ways, its substantial meaning. He deals much in dramatic question and answer, and in apostrophe; also in digression, the use of familiar phrases, and direct address to particular classes of persons present, using in general great and notable freedom. Yet freedom must be controlled, as in Augustine it commonly is controlled by sound judgment, right feeling, and good taste.

The chief peculiarity of Augustine's style is his fondness for, and skill in producing, pithy phrases. In the terse and vigorous Latin, these often have great power. The capacity for throwing off such phrases is mainly natural, but may be indefinitely cultivated. And it is a great element of power, especially in addressing the masses, if one can, after stating some truth, condense it into a single keen phrase that will penetrate the hearer's mind and stick.

John A. Broadus[23]

269 • BERNARD OF CLAIRVAUX (1090-1153)

The renewal of preaching in the medieval era is traced to the rise of the crusades, the monasteries, and the scholastics. Bernard combined the enthusiasm of crusade rhetoric with the ascetic lifestyle of the monk and reflected a scholastic influence through his struggle with Abelard. His fiery eloquence was powerful enough to make an impression even on those who did not understand his language. Unusually gifted, he was a master of the art of public speaking.

Bernard's Personality and Preaching Style

Bernard of Clairvaux, commonly called St. Bernard, a devoted monk and a fervently pious man, lived from 1090 to 1153 in France. Pale, meagre, attenuated through much fasting, looking almost as insubstantial as a spirit, he made an impression the moment he was seen. He possessed extraordinary talents, and though he made light of human learning, he at least did so only after acquiring it.

His sermons and other writings do not indicate a profound metaphysical thinker, like Augustine or Aquinas, but they present treasures of devout sentiment—pure, deep, and delightful—mysticism at its best. His style has an elegant simplicity and sweetness that is charming, and while many of his expressions are as striking as those of Augustine, they seem perfectly easy and natural. His speech and gesture are described as impressive in the highest degree. His power of persuasion was felt by high and low to be irresistible. Even his letters swayed popes and sovereigns.

The Last of the Fathers

Bernard is often called "the last of the Fathers." If we were asked who is the foremost preacher in the whole history of Latin Christianity, we should doubtless find the question narrowing itself to a choice between Augustine and Bernard. His sermons show more careful preparation than those of the early Latin Fathers. Anselm's principal works appeared before Bernard was born, and Abelard was his senior by a dozen years. Therefore, he felt to some extent the systematizing tendencies of the scholastic thought and method, which one can see in the orderly arrangement of his sermons, though they do not show formal divisions.

He greatly loved to preach, and we are told that he preached oftener than the rules of his order appointed, both to the monks and to the people. He was accustomed to put down thoughts and schemes of discourses as they occurred to him, and work them up as he had occasion to preach—a plan that many other preachers have found useful. His methods of sermonizing have considerable variety, and his manner of treatment is free. He was devoted to allegorizing, which was universal in that age.

Bernard wrote eighty-six sermons on the Song of Solomon. When the series was cut short by his death, he had just begun the third chapter. In his other sermons he quotes the Song of Solomon as often as Chrysostom quotes Job. Bernard was warmly praised by Luther, Melanchthon, and Calvin. I think that beyond any other medieval preacher, he will repay the student of the present day.

John A. Broadus[24]

270 • THOMAS AQUINAS (1224-1274)

An influence on preaching that originated from both the monasteries and the scholastic theology of the universities was the logic of Aristotle. As a result, sermon writers placed greater emphasis on coherence and clarity. This scholarly approach to preaching was developed in the great universities of the medieval period such as Paris and Oxford and spread to the Dominicans (Bernard), the Franciscans, and the Augustinian Anchorites. Consequently, a great many new handbooks on preaching were published along with collections of illustrations and outlines for sermons.

These works urged preachers to first find a theme and then allow the sermon to grow organically from that theme. The sermon was to be characterized by natural and logical divisions and subdivisions. Likewise, material was to be carefully grouped into supporting texts from the Bible, the writings of the Fathers, and illustrations. Readers could also find suggestions for appropriate gestures and humor.

Unfortunately these academic sermons lost touch with people's lives and failed to address their spiritual and moral needs in the way that the simpler sermons of the early church did. Thomas Aquinas, the greatest intellect of the thirteenth century, was an exception, for he had a way of presenting his vast learning with warmth and simplicity.

—— An Intelligent, Yet Practical Style ——

Thomas Aquinas, the Neapolitan count and Dominican friar, who died in 1274 at the age of fifty, is by common consent regarded as the greatest theologian of the Middle Ages and one of the greatest minds in the history of philosophy. It is surely an interesting fact that he was at the same time very popular as a preacher to the common people, being thus faithful to his Dominican vow.

Amid the immense and amazing mass of his works are many brief discourses, and treatises that were originally discourses, marked by clearness, simplicity, and practical point, and usually very short, many of them not requiring more than ten minutes, though these were doubtless expanded in preaching. He has also extended commentaries on perhaps half the books of Scripture, in which the method of exposition is strikingly like that of Matthew Henry's commentaries, leading us to believe that the exposition was, for the most part, first presented in the form of expository sermons.

Aquinas is not highly imaginative nor flowing in expression; the sentences are short, and everything runs into division and subdivision, usually by threes. But while there is no ornament and no swelling passion, he uses many familiar and lively comparisons, for explanation as well as for argument. It is pleasant to think of the fact that this great philosopher and author loved to preach, and that ordinary people loved to hear him. Like him, contemporary preachers would do well to combine philosophical and other profound studies with simple and practical preaching.

John A. Broadus[25]

271 • John Tauler (d. 1361)

In the late medieval era, a renewed concern for the inner life emerged. This new kind of mysticism affected the medieval sermon. Mystic John Tauler did not completely abandon the scholastic rules for preaching, but he did alter them freely. It may be said that he practiced a devotional style of preaching.

The content of his preaching reflected his contemplative strivings in the Christian faith, namely, union with God through various mystical stages, to complete absorption with God where all distinctions of reality cease to exist. His preaching was full of power, a glowing fire of God's love and drawing grace. The influence of Tauler's sermons can be seen in Thomas á Kempis's The Imitation of Christ. *This mystical style emerges frequently in church history, particularly in those times when people have grown weary of an intellectualized preaching.*

A Mystic Preaching Spiritual Renewal

Of the great mystics John Tauler, doubtless, is the foremost of his class in that age. Tauler lived on the Rhine in the fourteenth century, having been educated at the University of Paris, then the greatest of all seats of learning. In a time of great political and social evils, of protracted civil war, followed by a terrible struggle between the pope and the emperor, a time of frightful pestilence, a time of dissolute morals even among priests and monks and nuns, Tauler labored as a faithful priest.

After years thus spent, he was, at the age of fifty, lifted to what some call a higher life through the influence of a young layman, the head of a secret society which was trying to reform religion without leaving the church. It was after this renewal period that Tauler preached the sermons that were taken down by hearers and remain with us to this day.

We ought to study these mystical writings. They represent one side of human nature and minister to men and women in every age. Our age is intensely practical. Yet, many persons readily accept the idea of a higher spirituality. Do not most of us so neglect this aspect of Christianity in our studies and our preaching as to leave the natural thirst for it in some hearers ungratified, and thus prepare them to catch at, and delight in, such ideas and sentiments when presented in an extravagant and enthusiastic form? If we do not neglect the scriptural mysticism—as found in the writings of John and also of Paul—we shall see less readiness among people to accept a mysticism that is unscriptural.

Tauler did not, however, preach mere mystical raptures. He searchingly applied religious principle to the regulation of the inner and the outer life

The Peacock. The peacock symbol, which is found frequently in the catacombs and in Byzantine art, declares the Resurrection and immortality. The peacock is said to shed its feathers annually, and new feathers that grow are finer and more brilliant than before. Another legend proclaims peacock flesh to be incorruptible. So also Christ did not see corruption but was raised to new life on the third day. Similar symbolism was attributed to the phoenix, the legendary bird that was said to immolate itself and then rise from the ashes every year, again symbolizing the Resurrection.

and urged that ordinary duties be performed in a religious spirit.

John A. Broadus[26]

272 • THE REFORMERS: MARTIN LUTHER (1483–1546) AND JOHN CALVIN (1509–1564)

Martin Luther, like John Wycliffe, John Huss, and Girolamo Savonarola before him, may be classified as a preacher of "prophetic personality." For these preachers, preaching was an act of spiritual warfare. Luther's sermons are polemics against the abuses within the Roman church and the hardheartedness of many of its priests. Luther also began the

tradition of preaching an additional pedagogical sermon. In these catechistic sermons he taught the Ten Commandments, the Lord's Prayer, and doctrines of the Reformation. The tradition of featuring both catechetical and homiletical sermons in services became common in some Lutheran (and Reformed) churches, and this practice still continues in some churches today.

John Calvin did not preach in the popular style that Luther did. However, he influenced Reformed preaching more than Luther's style influenced Lutheran preaching. Calvin regarded the sermon as the central point of the liturgy; in fact, the liturgy itself was but the framework for the sermon. Dropping the readings of the liturgical calendar, he often chose to preach a series of sermons through a book of the Bible. To Calvin, a sermon was an exposition. Following the historical, theological, and grammatical approach, he eschewed all allegorizing and mystical interpretations in favor of a traditional exegesis which sought to reveal the actual meaning of Scripture.

Calvin and Luther

It would be difficult to find so marked a contrast between any two celebrated contemporaries in all the history of preaching as that between Luther and Calvin. Luther (1483–1546) was a broad-shouldered, broad-faced, burly German, overflowing with physical strength; Calvin (1509–1564) a feeble-looking little Frenchman, with shrunken cheeks and slender frame, and bowed with study and weakness. Luther had a powerful intellect but was also rich in sensibility, imagination, and swelling passion—a man juicy with humor, delighting in music, in children, in animals, in poetic sympathy with nature. In the disputation at Leipzig he stood up to speak with a bouquet in his hand. Every constituent of his character was rich to overflowing. With all this accords his prodigious and seemingly reckless extravagance, and even an occasional coarseness of language when excited.

Calvin, on the other hand, was practically destitute of imagination and humor, seeming in his public life and works to have been all intellect and will, though his letters show that he was not only a good hater, but also a warm friend. And yet, while so widely different, both of these men were *great preachers*. What had they in common to make them great preachers? Along with intellect they had force of character, an energetic nature and will. A great preacher is not a mere artist, and not a feeble suppliant; he is a conquering soul, a monarch, a born ruler of humankind. Calvin was far less winning than Luther, but he was even more than Luther an autocrat. Each of them had unbounded self-reliance, too, and yet at the same time each was full of humble reliance on God. This combination, self-confidence, such that if it existed alone, would vitiate character, yet checked and upborne by simple, humble, childlike faith in God, this makes a Christian hero, for word or for work. The statement could be easily misunderstood, but as meant it is true and important, that one must both believe in oneself and believe in God if one is to make a powerful impression on others.

This force of character in both Luther and Calvin gave great force to their utterances. Everybody repeats the saying about Luther that "his words were half battles." But of Calvin too it was said, and said by Beza who knew him so well, *Tot verba, tot pondera,* "Every word weighed a pound"—a phrase also used of Daniel Webster. It should be noticed too that both Luther and Calvin were drawn into much connection with practical affairs, and this tended to give them greater firmness and positiveness of character, to render their preaching more vigorous, as well as better suited to the common mind. Here is another valuable combination of what are commonly reckoned incongruous qualities—to be a thinker and student, and at the same time a person of practical sense and practical experience. Such were the great Reformers, and such a man was the apostle Paul.

Calvin: Theologian and Church-Builder, Expositor and Preacher

The vast reputation of Calvin as theologian and church-builder has overshadowed his great merits as an expositor and preacher. With the possible exception of Chrysostom, I think there is no commentator before our century whose exegesis is so generally satisfactory and so uniformly profitable as that of Calvin. His Latin, so clear and smooth and agreeable, is probably unsurpassed in literary excellence since the early centuries. All his extemporized sermons taken down in shorthand, as well as his writings, show not so much great copiousness as true command of language, his expression being, as a rule, singularly direct, simple, and forcible.

The extent of his preaching looks to us wonderful. While lecturing at Geneva to many hundreds of students (sometimes eight hundred), while practically a ruler of Geneva, and constant adviser of the Reformed in all Switzerland, France, and the Netherlands, England, and Scotland, and while composing his extensive and elaborate works, he would often preach every day. For example, the two hundred sermons on Deuteronomy, which are dated, were all delivered on week days in the course of little more than a year, and sometimes on four or five days in succession. It was so with the other great Reformers. In fact, Luther accuses one preacher of leading an "*idle* life; for he preaches but twice a week, and has a salary of two hundred dollars a year." Luther himself, with all his lecturing, immense correspondence, and voluminous authorship, often preached every day for a week, and on fast days two or three times.

Luther's Preaching

Luther had less sustained intensity than Calvin, but he had at times an overwhelming force, and his preaching possessed the rhetorical advantage of being everywhere pervaded by *one idea,* that of justification by faith, round which he reorganized all existing Christian thought and which gave a certain unity to all the overflowing variety of his illustration, sentiment, and expression.

Luther showed great realness, both in his personal grasp of Christian truth, and in his modes of presenting it. The conventional decorums he smashes, and with strong, rude, and sometimes even coarse expressions, with illustrations from almost every conceivable source, and with familiar address to the individual hearer he brings the truth very close to home. He gloried in being a preacher *to the people.* Thus, he says: "A true, pious and faithful preacher shall look to the children and servants, and to the poor, simple masses, who need instruction." "If one preaches to the coarse, hard populace, he must paint it for them, pound it, chew it, try all sorts of ways to soften them ever so little." He blamed Zwingli for interlarding his sermons with Greek, Hebrew, and Latin, and praised those who preached so that the average person could understand.

Luther's Personality

Luther is a notable example of intense *personality* in preaching. His was indeed an imperial personality, of rich endowments (in talent), varied sympathies, and manifold experiences. Those who heard him were not only listening to truth, but they *experienced the man.* Those who merely read his writings, in other lands and languages, experienced the man, were drawn to him, and thus drawn to the gospel.

With all his boldness, Luther often trembled at the responsibility of preaching. He says in one of his sermons,

> As soon as I learned from the Holy Scriptures how terror-filled and perilous a matter it was to preach publicly in the church of God . . . there was nothing I so much desired as silence. . . . Nor am I now kept in the ministry of the Word, but by an overruled obedience to a will above my own, that is the divine will; for as to my own will, it always shrank from it, nor is it fully reconciled unto it to this hour.

What Luther says of preaching must end with a paragraph from the *Table Talk,* which makes some good hits, though very oddly arranged.

> A good preacher should have these properties and virtues: first, to teach systematically; secondly, he should have a ready wit; thirdly, he should be elegant; fourthly, he should have a good voice; fifthly, a good memory; sixthly, he should know when to make an end; seventhly, he should be sure of his doctrine; eighthly, he should venture and engage body and blood, wealth and honor, in the Word; ninthly, he should suffer himself to be mocked and jeered of every one.

The expression, "he should know when to make an end," recalls a statement I have sometimes made to students, that public speaking may be summed up in these three things: First, have something to say; secondly, say it; third and lastly, quit.

John A. Broadus[27]

273 ✦ JOHN WESLEY (1703–1791) AND GEORGE WHITEFIELD (1714–1770)

In the mid-eighteenth century, John Wesley and George Whitefield became famous through their revivalistic preaching. Although based on a Scripture, it differed from Reformed preaching in that it was not exegetical and did not place as much emphasis on correct grammatical, historical, and theological contexts. Instead, Wesley and Whitefield developed topics and presented applications for their listeners. Sin, grace, and reconciliation with God were their favorite themes. Wesley united this message with a zeal for sanctification. This style of preaching was directed particularly toward the poor, resulting in a tremendous movement for social and political justice.

Toward the middle of the eighteenth century two men became known who have made illustrious the English preaching of their day. Whitefield and Wesley were both Oxford men and used their cultivation in that preaching to the masses that had been the glory of the Puritan period. Whitefield and Wesley began to preach to the human conscience, and thus felt no need of confining their discourse to the cultivated and refined. This preaching to the conscience must be seen as the reaction to an age of skepticism.

——— The Men behind the Preaching ———

The biographies of Whitefield are full of instruction. The sermons we have were mere preparations, which in free delivery were so filled out with the thoughts suggested in the course of living speech, and so transfigured and glorified by enkindled imagination, as to be utterly different from the dull, cold thing that here lies before us.

The sermons of Wesley require study and will reward it. As printed, they were commonly written out after frequent delivery. They are too condensed to have been spoken, in this form, to the colliers and the servant girls at five o'clock in the morning. But they must be in substance the same that he habitually preached, and they present a problem. Wesley had nothing of Whitefield's impassioned oratory. He spoke with simple earnestness and remained quiet while his hearers grew wild with excitement.

What was the secret? Where the hidden power? We can only say that it was undoubting faith and extraordinary force of character, together with a peculiarity seen also in some generals on the field of battle, that their most intense excitement makes little outward noise or show, yet subtly communicates itself to others. No one can repeatedly make others feel deeply who does not feel deeply; it is only a difference in the way of showing it. Of course, this subtle electricity resides in the soul of the speaker much more than in the recorded discourse. But read carefully these condensed and calm-looking sermons, and see if you do not feel the power of the man and find yourself sometimes strangely moved.

John A. Broadus[28]

⚜ ELEVEN ⚜

Styles of Preaching

Throughout the history of the church, preachers have developed different styles of proclaiming the Word. These styles of preaching are often related to the hermeneutics of the preacher. Broadly speaking, the preacher approaches the task of speaking with one of three starting points.

The first of these starting points is the Bible. The preacher approaches the text with the question, What does it say? Sermons that fall into this general category are evangelistic preaching, expository preaching, liturgical preaching, narrative preaching, proclamatory preaching, prophetic preaching, and textual preaching.

A second starting point may be that of a more systematized sort. It draws from creeds, catechesis, and Christian doctrines with the explicit intent of teaching the system of Christian faith. Such approaches to preaching include catechetical preaching and doctrinal preaching.

A third approach to preaching which does not neglect the Scriptures or Christian doctrines is a view of preaching that begins with human need as the starting point. Such types of preaching include African-American preaching, confessional preaching, contextual preaching, lay preaching, life situational preaching, progressive-emotive preaching, and seeker-sensitive preaching.

274 ◆ EVANGELISTIC PREACHING

Evangelistic preaching aims at producing a response. Specifically, by preaching of the gospel and emphasizing sinful condition of each person, the hearer recognizes the need for repentance and confession of Jesus Christ as Lord and Savior.

—————— Defining Evangelism ——————

The word *evangelism* is a recent term in Christianity, appearing formally during the nineteenth century. If, however, one understands that evangelism means proclaiming, announcing, or preaching the Good News, it is evident that examples of evangelism go far back in Judeo-Christian heritage.

In Hebrew the word most closely associated with evangelism is the word *basar.* Its root meaning is related to the act of bringing good news. It was most often used for announcements of successful military encounters. This kind of announcement of good news, then, had to do with military and political victories. That meaning is carried over into sections of the Old Testament where, as in the book of Psalms and in Isaiah, *basar* is used to proclaim the Lord's victory over his enemies.

In the Greek two words need to be considered as one moves toward an understanding of the word *evangelism.* The first is the word *euangelion.* This word is most often translated as "good news" or "gospel." The second word, found three times in the New Testament (Acts 21:8; Eph. 4:11; 2 Tim. 4:5), is the word *euangelistēs,* which is translated "evangelist" and means "one who brings good news." The word *evangelism* also has roots in the Latin word *evangelium,* the verb form of what is generally translated "bring good tidings" (Isa. 40:9 and Luke 2:10).

Evangelism then is the process of announcing, proclaiming, preaching, and sharing the good news, especially as understood in the salvation completed and fulfilled in Jesus Christ. The evangelist is the one who brings this good news to others.

—————— Evangelism and the Sermon ——————

When the sermon is an expression of evangelism, or, to put it another way, when the sermon becomes a witness to the gospel of Jesus Christ, three things take place. First, the sermon is a reflection and expression of the preacher's encounter and struggle with the Word of God written in Scripture and incarnate in Jesus Christ and of discoveries made as a result of his or her confrontation with the Good News. Evangelistic preaching requires the preacher to begin his or her preparation with an exegetical encounter with the text.

Second, the evangelistic sermon occurs when the preacher shares either directly or indirectly where the gospel touches his or her own life and/or experiences. One danger, however, is that, if conscious care is not taken, the sermon may become more an ego-centered discussion rather than a Christ-centered proclamation. At the same time, it is difficult, if not impossible, to announce the Good News if the Good News is not known. Therefore, the task of the evangelist is to find in his or her own life those moments of discovery and experience that can lead him or her to announce with boldness and certainty, "This is the Good News for me."

When the preacher shares openly how the gospel is good news for him or her, either directly or indirectly, it allows the listener to get a glimpse of the personal fire by which the message has been refined. The sermon, then, identifies the evangelist as a fellow traveler on the road of faith, enabling the preacher to proclaim the Word from the vantage point of one who has experienced the gospel's presence and working in his or her own life. This then becomes a part of the dialogic nature of the evangelistic sermon. The sermon becomes a reflection, not only of the struggle the preacher must undergo with the text, but also of the struggle which he or she must experience concerning the impact of the gospel upon his or her life. Instead of preaching "from afar," the evangelist proclaims "from within." It is this part of the process that helps develop and determine the integrity and credibility of the one who has the tremendous task of announcing the Good News, the Word of God, the gospel of Jesus Christ.

The third aspect of the evangelistic sermon occurs when the sermon is an extension of the activity of evangelism. Preaching an evangelistic sermon is the result of the preacher's sensitivity to what is happening to those to whom he or she ministers. It is the announcement of God's good news, often in the face of obvious "bad news." When a sermon is a witness to the gospel of Jesus Christ, the life of the preacher and the lives of the people touch. As when two live electric wires are brought together, a brilliant spark is produced where the gospel touches and illumines both pastor and people.

The Dialogic Nature of Evangelistic Preaching

The evangelistic sermon is dialogic, therefore, because it grows out of the preacher's dialogue with those to whom he or she speaks and witnesses. The preacher considers seriously the few chance words spoken at the church door that signal that all is not OK. He or she listens carefully to the voice of the stranger on the street who is hungry and has no place to go. The preacher pays attention as children compete to be first and the most important. He or she is sensitive to observations made about plays, movies, and soap operas.

The comment, "Pastor, you help me see that text in a new light," is music to the ears of the evangelist. It is indicative of a personal journey that the listener took as new insights were weighed in relationship to old discoveries. This journey can lead the hearer to serendipitous experiences to which he or she can respond.

The first dialogic step, then, is to engage the listener in a dialogue with the Word of God and in this way to discover a common understanding of the meaning of the text. The end result could be an opportunity for both the evangelist and the person who is sharing the witness to engage in further dialogue that will plumb the depth of God's Word for humankind.

The second step engages the listener in dialogue with himself, during which time the question *What does the text say?* becomes *What is the text saying to me?*

It is important to realize in evangelism that room must be allowed for the response to come as a result of the other person's wrestling and struggling. Evangelism does not come with easy answers, pat formulas, and clear-cut prescriptions. Discoveries can be shared, but there has to be personal involvement in and acceptance of the discovery in order for it to mean anything. That is why it is sometimes good not to draw all of the conclusions, to leave some ends open, and to leave room for some wonderment.

Lastly, the evangelistic sermon leads the listener to a dialogue with the world in which he or she lives. The listener begins to see the secular through the eyes of faith and in this way comes to grips with many of the questions, problems, and pressures he or she may be facing.

Evangelistic Preaching Invites Decision

The purpose of evangelism is to present the gospel in order to invite a response. The goal of preaching when using the sermon as an evangelistic tool is to preach for a decision. As a result of what has been shared in the sermon, the listener may ask, *What new alternatives were presented?* and *In what way or ways will I to respond to those alternatives?*

The evangelist is the proclaimer of the gospel in a world that not only denies but even attempts to smother the Good News. The sermon is but one way in which evangelism can happen. But preaching service is the one time the preacher has the largest number of people together at one time, all of whom are experiencing the difficulties of life. It is the one regular opportunity he or she has to assure those whose ears are open to hear and whose eyes are open to see that, in the person of Jesus Christ, God reaches out to them in love and compassion, forgiving their sins and calling them to a new life. The evangelist will be the one whose life has been enriched and enlightened by this discovery and whose purpose is to help others make that same discovery. The evangelist is also one who is engaged in a dialogue with the Word of God, with himself or herself, and with those he or she meets and the world in which they live. This being done, the gospel can be proclaimed and the invitation given: "The kingdom of God is near. Repent and believe the good news!" (Mark 1:15).

James L. Henderschedt[29]

275 • EXPOSITORY PREACHING

Expository preaching is based on the grammatical, historical, theological method. Such sermons may be drawn from a verse or a passage, or they may develop a biblical topic or Christian doctrine.

— The Nature of Expository Preaching —

The type of preaching that most effectively lays open the Bible so that men and women are confronted by its truth is expository. At its best, expository preaching is *the presentation of biblical truth, derived from and transmitted through a historical, grammatical, spirit-guided study of a passage in its context, which the Holy Spirit applies first to the*

life of the preacher and then through the preacher to his or her congregation.

The Role of Scripture. This definition has several parts. First of all, the substance of the expository sermon is derived from the Scriptures. The expositor realizes that although the Bible is a book like no other book, it is still a book. In fact, it is a collection of writings that can be studied like other literature. R. A. Montgomery, in his book *Expository Preaching* ([New York, 1939], 42), makes this point:

> The preacher undertakes the presentation of particular books (of the Bible) as some men [or women] would undertake the latest best seller. The preacher seeks to bring the message of definite units of God's word to [the congregation]. [The preacher] discovers the main theme or constituent parts of the book's message as they were in the mind of the writer. . . . His [or her] treatment of words, phrases, texts, portions is important not only for what they may say separately, but as they relate to the main theme of the writer and the end he [or she] had in view in writing this book.

In a larger sense, therefore, expository preaching is more a philosophy than a method. It is the answer to a basic question: Does the preacher subject his or her thought to the Scriptures, or does the preacher subject the Scriptures to his or her thought? Is the passage used like the national anthem at a football game—to get things started but not be heard again? Or is the text the essence of the sermon to be exposed to the people?

Although it is possible to preach an orthodox sermon without explaining a biblical passage, unfolding a portion of Scripture guards the preacher's thought against heresy. Doing this regularly forces the preacher to speak to the many issues of life dealt with in the Scriptures that he or she otherwise might easily overlook. Above all, the preacher speaks with an authority not his or her own, and the man or woman in the pew will have a better chance to hear God speak directly.

Methodology. A second important factor in the definition involves the means by which the biblical message is communicated to the congregation. The preacher transmits it on the same basis by which he or she received it. In the study of the passage, the expositor examines the grammar, history, and context. In the pulpit, the preacher must deal with enough of the language, background, and setting of the text so that an attentive listener is able to check the message from the Bible itself.

As a result, effective expository preaching will be occupied largely with the explanation of Scripture. A good expository sermon will reflect the passage, not only in its central message, but also in its development, purpose, and mood. As this takes place, people not only learn the Bible as they listen, but they also are stimulated to study the Scriptures for themselves.

Benefits. Expository preaching offers great benefits to the preacher. For one thing, it gives him or her truth to preach. Many ministers spend a frustrating part of their week "starting to get underway to begin" their sermon preparation. Only a genius can think up enough original material that is fresh and stimulating and that will keep the same audience interested one hundred times a year. The preacher who draws topics from his or her own mind and experience dabbles in a puddle. The preacher who expounds the Scripture does business in great waters.

Expository preaching provides the preacher with many types of sermons. He or she may expound a single verse (Alexander McLaren was outstanding in this respect). The preacher may expound a passage—this is what is usually considered expository preaching. In addition, he or she may trace a topic or doctrine through the Bible. To do this, the preacher finds the many places in which a topic or doctrine is dealt with. First, the preacher relates the topic to the particular passage in which it is found, then the different passages to each other. Biographical preaching may also be expository. Much of the Scripture comes to us in the form of history or biography. Genesis, for example, is almost entirely composed of biographical material.

Our definition tells us that expository preaching also helps develop the preacher into a mature Christian. When an expositor studies the Bible, the Holy Spirit probes the preacher's life. As a man or woman prepares sermons, God prepares the person. Alexander McLaren said that everything he was, he owed to the fact that day after day he studied the Scriptures. T. Forsyth understood this when he wrote, "The Bible is the supreme preacher to the preacher" (*Positive Preaching and the Modern Mind* [London: Hodder and Stoughton, 1909], 11).

Purpose. Finally, the basic purpose of expository preaching is the basic purpose of the Bible. It takes

place so that through it the Holy Spirit may change lives and destinies. Preaching and teaching, of course, are not the only means by which God builds up his people, but they are the major means. The effective expositor knows that God is not speaking to people today *about* the Bible as though it were a textbook in history or archaeology. The Holy Spirit speaks to people today *from* the Bible about themselves. The person in the pulpit or the people in the pew do not sit in judgment on Judas, or David, or Peter, or Solomon. Under the teaching of Scripture, they must judge themselves.

To carry out this purpose, the expositor must know not only the message but also the people to whom it will be delivered. The preacher must exegete both the Scriptures and the congregation. Imagine that Paul's letters to the Corinthians had gotten lost in the mail and had reached the Christians in Philippi instead. Those people would have been perplexed at what Paul wrote. The believers in Philippi lived in different situations from the Christians at Corinth. The letters of the New Testament, like the prophecies of the Old Testament, were addressed to specific people living in particular situations.

"Doctrines must be preached practically, and duties doctrinally," was the way our Protestant forebears put it. Perhaps this is the largest problem in what is called "expository preaching" today. The preacher lectures about the "there and then" as though God lived back in the "once upon a time," and he or she fails to bring the eternal truth to focus on the attitudes and actions of people in the "here and now." Application is not incidental to effective expository preaching; it is crucial.

In relating the Bible to experience, however, the expositor dares not twist the Scriptures to fit people's lives. Instead the preacher calls persons to bring themselves into subjection to the standards of the Bible. Christians must conform to the age to come, not to this present age. The application moves both ways. Biblical truth must be related to men's and women's lives; but on the other hand, their lives must be changed to be relevant to biblical faith.

Conclusion

F. B. Meyer, himself a gifted expositor, understood the awe with which a biblical preacher approaches his task. "[The preacher] is in a line of great succession. The reformers, the Puritans, the pastors of the

Pilgrim fathers were essentially expositors. They did not announce their own particular opinions, which might be matter of private interpretation or doubtful disposition; but, taking their stand on Scripture, drove home their message with irresistible effect with, 'Thus said the Lord!' " (*Expository Preaching: Plans and Methods* [Grand Rapids: Zondervan, 1954], 60)

The major problems of our society are ultimately spiritual. People always stand in desperate need of God. "They will not ask for help, unless they believe in Him, and they will not believe in Him unless they have heard of Him, and they will not hear of Him unless they get a preacher, and they will never have a preacher unless one is sent. But as the Scripture says the footsteps of those who bring Good News is a welcome sound. . . . So faith comes from what is preached, and what is preached comes from the Word of Christ" (Rom. 10:14-17, NJB).

Haddon W. Robinson[30]

276 • NARRATIVE PREACHING

In recent years, the paradigm shift from a rationalistic worldview to a world in motion has shifted attention in biblical studies and preaching away from propositional statements to story. Narrative preaching draws on the Scripture as story and seeks to communicate through the form of story.

The Importance of Story

Narrative preaching is story-formed preaching—preaching that takes seriously, in method and form, Clark Pinnock's suggestion that "the essence of the gospel . . . is the biblically narrated epic story of salvation through Jesus Christ" (*Tracking the Maze* [San Francisco: Harper & Row, 1990], 154). Flowing out of the recent trend in biblical studies, theology, and ethics to make narrative their guiding construct, many contemporary preachers have also made narrative their touchstone. As Edmund Steimle, Morris Niedenthal, and Charles Rice stated in their collaborative work on narrative preaching:

We are trying to find that formative image that could both articulate what preaching is and free people to do it. Is there an image adequate to shape the form, content, and style of preaching? If we had to say, in a word or two or in a picture, what preaching is and how it is done well, what would that phrase or picture be? . . . Let us consider the storyteller. . . . If

we were pressed to say what Christian faith and life are, we could hardly do better than *hearing, telling,* and *living* a story. And if asked for a short definition of preaching, could we do better than shared story? (*Preaching the Story* [Philadelphia: Fortress Press, 1979], 12–13, 15)

Narrative preaching is an emerging methodology, and the last word on how narrative preaching should be defined is yet to be written.

A better perspective from which to view narrative preaching is to look at the methodologies of some of its leading practitioners. What one learns, as Thomas Long notes, is that narrative preaching gives foremost attention to the "how" of preaching versus other preaching methods, which may evince greater concern with sermonic content or the preacher's own ethos (*The Witness of Preaching* [Louisville: Westminster/John Knox Press, 1989], 36). As Richard L. Eslinger points out in his book *A New Hearing: Living Options in Homiletic Method* (Nashville: Abingdon Press, 1988), a review of five narrative preachers (Charles Rice, Henry Mitchell, Eugene Lowery, Fred Craddock, and David Buttrick), preachers of this method intend to shape their sermons after the fashion of the gospel, which for them, with the exception of David Buttrick, is nothing less than narrative. For these preachers, the form of sermon is narrative not discursive, evocative not rationalistic, dynamic not static, inductive not deductive, and true to the shape of Scripture, not Aristotelian rhetoric or logic. For them, narrative preaching is narrative both in form and in method, utilizing all aspects of narrative technique (plot, character development, and so on) to bring to the listener's consciousness the interplay between his or her own story and the biblical story.

Critique

Narrative preaching is not without its critics, as the growing literature makes known this method's implications. Perhaps the most common critique leveled against narrative preaching is its failure to acknowledge the fact that, while the biblical witness is to the redemptive story of God's dealings with humanity through Christ, Scripture also contains poetry, proverbs, and extended didactic passages. Only David Buttrick, who advocates both the narrative technique in preaching and faithfulness to the biblical form of the passage being preached, deals with this issue. Thomas Long's critique of narrative preaching deals with the overemphasis on evaluating a sermon's effectiveness by whether the sermon evoked a religious experience rather than whether it communicated a propositional truth of Scripture. As Long notes, preachers favoring a more rationalistic preaching methodology have a point when they remind us that God's revelation may not always move us when we want to be moved, but nonetheless it is God's revelation (_The Witness of Preaching,_ 40–41).

Narrative preaching, however, has some very practical benefits. First, no other preaching methodology is as intent on forming sermons to the shape of Scripture. Second, narrative preaching integrates concern for the biblical story, the listener's story (concerns, needs, experiences), and the preacher's story in a way few other preaching methodologies can or do. Third, narrative preaching is able to evoke the experiential dimension of faith in the listener in a way that rationalistic and cognitive methodologies, such as expositional preaching, cannot. It is not without reason, then, that Jesus "never taught them without a story."

The Historical Context for Narrative Preaching's Emergence

The application of narrative preaching moves along two axes: theology and praxis. From a theological perspective, many preachers, such as Thomas Oden, Clark Pinnock, and others, point to the end of the twentieth century as a transition phase between modernity and postmodernity. Whereas the paradigms of modernity were, according to Oden, rationalism, secularism, and radical individualism, the paradigms of the postmodern era are or will be metaphor, tradition (_i.e._, shared story), and community (_Agenda for Theology_ [San Francisco: Harper and Row, 1979], 48–49). The problem this poses for preaching is that the assumptions of the old homiletic worked out against modernity's background no longer hold true. Richard Eslinger, commenting on the preaching of David Buttrick, notes:

> The old rational homiletics is obsolete. "For nearly three hundred years, preaching has been trapped in a rationalist bind," observes David Buttrick. But the conditions that made for its viability no longer stand. Every dimension of homiletics—biblical interpretation, hermeneutics, language, theology, the

liturgical context, and even human consciousness—has changed radically. (_A New Hearing,_ 133)

Whereas modern preaching has depended on reason, logic, and propositional truth, narrative preaching depends on the metaphor, image, and story—qualities more in tune with a postmodern world. The preacher who is sensitive to the shift in consciousness from a modern to a postmodern world will readily welcome the applied benefits of narrative preaching.

Jack Mercer

277 • PROPHETIC PREACHING

Prophetic preaching condemns particularities and affirms generalities. It points to those values and hopes that are consistent with the reign of God and calls people to live by those values.

The Aim of Prophetic Preaching

Prophetic preaching is a contextual interpretation of God's Word based on the belief that God loves us enough to disturb us. The gospel is not only "Blessed assurance, Jesus is mine," but also "Blessed disturbance, we are Christ's!" Indeed, the biblical narratives as a whole have to do with God moving in on the human scene and contradicting the way things are.

The late Rabbi Abraham Heschel described the function of the prophets as one of interference. The Scripture is in fact a story of loving interference and inquiry, bringing inconvenience in order to heal and hallow life. Burning bushes, whirlwinds, pillars of fire, Holy of Holies, the still small voice, prophetic woes, and "you have heard it said . . . but I tell you." Only because God loves us enough to inquire, to invade, and to disturb is there transforming power in the gospel.

Popular and cultural tradition tends to produce unloving critics and uncritical lovers. The genius of biblical tradition unites judgment and mercy on behalf of a healing wholeness. God's love is a disturbing influence and power; God's judgment is a renewing and recreating catharsis. Critical love in the biblical sense is neither agreement nor rejection. It rescues from illusion and idolatry, pointing to a new future. For this reason the community of faith must be encouraged _to expect_ a biblically and theologically informed disturbance as a dimension of the redemptive Word. Otherwise, the ethos of the Christian church inevitably begins to sound and look like the surrounding culture and thereby loses its authority to change life.

Prophetic Preaching's Context

The context for prophetic preaching is a theology that embraces all of life. If a congregation has a growing appreciation for the inclusiveness of Christian faith, then prophetic preaching will not seem an intrusion into so-called secular matters nor an abandonment of the biblical and historic gospel.

The preacher would do well in word and deed to lift up a gospel as concerned with principalities and powers as with prayers and piety, with structures and systems as with sermons and songs. More to the point, the preacher's calling requires him or her to connect all of these, so that the church's worship and the disciplines of individual piety point to the action of God in all of Creation.

Some ministers do this exceedingly well by emphasizing a theology of the Incarnation. Christ has touched everything and continues to do so because the Word has become flesh. Others focus on an Easter theology—that is, God is loose in the world and goes before people into every nook and cranny of Creation: on the road, in the breaking of bread, in daily toil. Whether the preacher centers on the Incarnation or on the suffering/sovereign, vulnerable/victorious Lord or on both, the results should be a context for faith and therefore for prophetic preaching in which political and economic issues are perceived as moral and ethical issues under the sovereignty of God.

Anyone who has served for any length of time in a pastorate can hardly fail to notice the close connection between the pastoral and the prophetic. Effective preaching always involves a relationship of trust between preacher and people, doubly so when it comes to prophetic preaching. If the preacher has moved *toward* the people faithfully as a shepherd, they may also allow the preacher to move toward them as prophets from whom they have already experienced care and concern. Lee S. Moorehead writes: "Since preaching is an audacious and almost arrogant business, we who engage in it ought to realize that we cannot be tolerated unless we speak out of lives of humble service" (*Freedom of the Pulpit* [Nashville: Abingdon Press, 1961], 74).

The pastoral and the prophetic belong together not only in the functioning of the ordained, but also in the covenant faith and life of the people of God. The prophetic ministry is not an elitist possession of the ordained, but the very meaning of being called into the covenant. To be called is to be sent, and it is for this reason that prophetic preaching and ministry are the function of *both* preacher and listener in relation to the world.

Another contextual dimension for prophetic preaching, and one of critical significance for the preacher, is the history of this particular people—their characteristics, their customs, their ethos, their *story* as a people. Any interpreter or translator who does not know his or her people in this sense cannot preach with incarnational love. *The* story needs to intersect *their* story. The primary task of the preacher is to learn the story of the people whom he or she seeks to serve. This, of course, means listening to many people. The process is a labor of love requiring time and patience, but it is also a means of understanding the larger context which belongs to prophetic preaching.

One other contextual issue deserves mention—the freedom of the pulpit. What does freedom of the pulpit mean to the preacher? To the people? What are its limits? The responsibilities of both clergy and laity? The issue of prophetic preaching is inevitably linked with a theology of the pulpit, suggesting a need for preacher and people to explore the preacher's freedom of the pulpit together. Done carefully, it could pave the way for a mutual set of expectations for preaching, and especially for attempts at prophetic utterances.

The Way of Prophetic Preaching

No one can assume the mantle of prophetic preaching for long without learning some lessons about the gospel, the church, oneself, and prophetic preaching. Prophetic preaching is more likely to be on firm ground when it condemns particularities and affirms generalities rather than vice versa. Clear biblical mandates exist to condemn starvation, exploitation, and dehumanization. Furthermore, it is possible to be quite specific concerning causes as well as consequences, assuming appropriate study and research of the issues has been done.

The preacher can and must point to those values and hopes that are consistent with the reign of God. For example, in the name of the gospel, the pulpit may challenge the ongoing buildup of weapons of mass destruction, the lack of serious effort to negotiate international disarmament, and a governmental stance that favors the affluent and increases the misery of the disadvantaged. In the name of God the preacher raises the humane question, challenges the moral ethos from a biblical and theological grounding, lifts up those values that appear to be consistent with the mind of Christ, and points to the judgment/love of God present in every situation. This is what is meant by affirming generalities.

However, it is more difficult and more questionable to identify the gospel or a Christian solution with a particular political or economic program, lest we legitimatize ideological stances. The preacher must be painstakingly careful about assuming the position of policymaker or suggesting that he or she possesses the "how to" expertise to restructure society. As Peter Berger has observed, "The idea that moral sensitivity somehow bestows the competence to make policy recommendations is delusional" ("The Class Struggle in American Religion," _Christian Century_ [Feb. 25, 1981]:196). The biblical foundation is more conducive to lifting up the purposes and priorities of the kingdom or of the mind of Christ than to detailing specifics of programs and policies.

Even the denouncing or calling into question of specific evils will likely require careful homework. Of course some forms of oppression are so blatant that this is not the case. Frequently, though, one faces the likelihood of choosing between two or more undesirable possibilities. If a large corporation employing thousands of people is polluting a lake with waste by-products, for example, the choice may be between a devastated environment and the loss of jobs for hundreds of families, with the accompanying social consequences. One of the worst habits of some prophetic preaching is the naïveté and lack of good hard research undergirding the attempt.

There will always be an element of ambiguity in any complex social issue—if not in relation to ends, then in relation to means, and not infrequently in connection with consequences themselves. Irreducible ambiguity should not retard the preacher's willingness to speak out from the pulpit, but the preacher's own calling and responsibility to the church requires him or her to be as well informed as possible. The facts, insofar as can be ascertained, are never all "in," but the preacher should proceed on as solidly factual a ground as possible before presuming to interpret the gospel in relation to a specific issue. The credibility of prophetic preaching depends on trust and caring relationships. It also depends on accuracy of information and knowledge so that the case is not prejudiced at the outset owing to ignorance and oversimplification.

The "Amos style" of prophetic preaching—that is, a stance from a righteous position as one of the basic prophetic approaches—has much to commend it. There are times when a preacher must take a stand and declare it without mincing words. To do less would be a complicity of silence.

Yet the efficacy of an _inquiring_ mode of prophetic preaching is also appropriate in certain situations. In an oversimplified sense, one could say that the God-human encounter in Scripture focuses on combinations of the _indicative_ and the _imperative_. The shape of the gospel at times is a form of the indicative, which represents proclamation, pronouncement, assertion: In the beginning God created. God is love. The reign of God is at hand. The imperative mode of divine-human confrontation is frequently a command or exhortation: Follow me. Go into the world. Love your enemies. This mode is the call to action of much of the biblical narratives.

As biblical scholars have shown, the indicative and imperative are expressed in a variety of ways, and in Paul's writing they have the closest connection—indeed, are inclusive of one another. Indicative statements may be used to exhort, thus carrying imperative force, and questions likewise may have an essentially imperative thrust.

The questioning, inquiring style has great promise in prophetic preaching. The inquisitive mode may be simply another shape to the indicative or the imperative, but it reaches out to the listener in a different way. The inquiring approach lends itself to a confessional style and to a mutual search rather than to dogmatic coercion. Also, there is less likelihood of misusing biblical texts than otherwise might be the case.

In Scripture God is the ultimate questioner. As Gerhard Ebeling put it in _The Nature of Faith_ (London: Collins, 1959), "When we speak of God, we are speaking of the radical question about where man is, the question which concerns him unconditionally." In the teachings of Jesus, more than 150 questions are addressed to his disciples. What does it profit you to gain the whole world . . . ? Why do you see the speck . . . ? Which of you by being anxious . . . ? False prophets, ancient and contemporary, offer simple answers and an ecclesiastical

The Butterfly. *One of the best symbols of not only the resurrection of Jesus, but also the resurrection of the believers. The three stages in the life of the butterfly represent the three stages of the Christian: First, the crawling larva represents the lowly condition of humanity; second, the chrysalis, lying in its shell in a lifeless condition, depicts the body in the grave; finally, the pupa bursts its outer shell, emerges, dries its wings, and soars heavenward with a beautiful new body. So the Lord raises the dead at the last day.*

happy hour as a substitute for worshiping the Holy One of Israel. Prophets of God raise penetrating and disturbing questions.

The inquiring style is conducive to growth for both preacher and listener. It appeals to imagining and to searching more deeply. And it suggests that, even in the name of God, preachers are frequently uncertain and befuddled like everyone else. There are countless problems in the preacher's own time in history that were neither present nor envisioned in any direct sense in biblical times—such as nuclear energy, genetic engineering, and environmental complexities arising from modern technology. While perhaps not knowing the answers to many of society's social ills and injustices, the preacher had better know the questions that lead and even drive humankind to watching and waiting in expectant ways for God's prompting toward greater clarity and certainty.

William K. McElvaney[31]

278 ✦ TEXTUAL PREACHING

Textual preaching is more than making a comment or two on a text. Textual preaching, in contrast to expository preaching, focuses on the thematic unity of a biblical passage, challenging the preacher to seek the text's central truth.

Textual Preaching versus Expository Preaching. Textual preaching is one of the most common and elementary sermon types, taking its main themes and divisions (or points) directly from the textual material. Like the expository sermon, the selected text may vary in length from a phrase to an entire biblical book. The textual approach, however, seeks to draw a unified subject from the biblical passage which will eventuate in supporting points for discussion and further understanding.

While an expository sermon seeks to have its entire thought content come from Scripture and tends towards continuous exposition in the natural order of ideas presented in the text, the textual sermon allows for greater freedom in the choice of external materials and development, as long as the unified theme and specific divisions come directly from the text. Textual sermons, then, are differentiated from expository sermons by the necessity of a unifying theme and that the only text divisions incorporated are those that support the theme.

The Textual Sermon's Design. The divisions, or points, drawn from the text can be elucidated in the natural order of their appearance. The textual thought units may be rearranged for effect or clarity, provided the preacher does not violate the proper understanding of the text. Certain elements of a text may be omitted at times, particularly if the text is lengthy and certain elements do not contribute to the overall theme. The contents of some textual divisions may overlap each other, forcing the preacher to clarify them and explain their particular emphases.

Advantages and Disadvantages. There are several advantages to textual preaching. First, it focuses the attention of preacher and hearer on one part of the Scripture. In so doing it removes the tendency to "proof text" and allows a single, significant Scripture text to stand on its own. Second, a rudimentary textual sermon is relatively easy to prepare, as carefully chosen texts, after study, will yield a theme and divisions. Third, if the textual preacher has prepared well, the hearer will be able to follow the movements of the sermon as they unfold. Fourth, such a sermon brings the hearer into the inner meanings of the Bible. Fifth, the textual preacher need not fear preaching from the well-worn or favorite texts, as each preacher brings fresh exposition and arrangement of ideas.

There are also disadvantages to this form of

preaching. One, not every text that makes for a good sermon lends itself to the textual approach. Two, a lengthy text or one rich in homiletic possibilities may contain more ideas than a preacher can present in one sermon. Three, a text may contain only one idea and not have divisions that could be artificially imposed upon it.

John D. Baker

279 • CATECHETICAL PREACHING

Catechetical preaching, or preaching sermons based on the consecutive "Lord's Days" of the Heidelberg Catechism, is a centuries-old tradition among Reformed churches and has historical roots in the Calvinistic reformation of sixteenth-century northern Europe.

Background

The Heidelberg Catechism was written in 1563 under the watchful eye of Elector Frederick III of the Palatinate. His hope was to create a simple ecumenical statement of doctrine which would unite the people of his realm in the spiritual direction set by the expanding Reformed movement. Zacharias Ursinus of the University of Heidelberg is credited with the theological substance of the catechism, though the name of Caspar Oleveanus, pastor of Heidelberg's Holy Spirit Church, is always mentioned as well. The latter may have provided some of the pastoral sensitivity and emotional warmth that gives the Heidelberg Catechism its broad impact and continuing relevance.

As early as 1566, Peiter Gabriel, a prominent pastor in Amsterdam, began using the Heidelberg Catechism as a substantive teaching tool in the afternoon service of worship added to each Sunday's observance. The practice of an additional worship service originated with several of the Reformers who were concerned about the spiritual immaturity and scriptural illiteracy in their communities. The second Sunday gathering was intended to be a doctrinal classroom, and the Heidelberg Catechism soon became the primary teaching material. In 1586, a Reformed synod in the Netherlands broadened this practice by legislating that each Sunday afternoon in the Reformed churches of the Low Countries, a sermon be preached from the catechism.

Not until the great Synod of Dordtrecht in 1618–1619, however, did the practice of "catechetical preaching" become fully institutionalized. From its origins, the Heidelberg Catechism had a clearly developed three-part structure: I—Human Misery; II—Deliverance; III—Gratitude. But with the fourth edition, editors added a secondary structure or division that featured fifty-two "Lord's Days." These smaller groupings of material were intended to provide topical segments for study spanning a full year's weekly congregational gatherings. The delegates at Dordtrecht declared that all Reformed churches were to have sermons explaining these Lord's Days in succession each Sunday afternoon. That practice has been enshrined in nearly every Reformed church order since the Synod of Dordtrecht and continues as a regular practice in many branches of the Reformed church today.

Method

What does it mean to preach from the Heidelberg Catechism? Because of the strong emphasis on expository preaching in the Reformed tradition, pastors have struggled with this perplexing issue for generations. Three related yet methodologically distinct approaches have resulted.

Catechism as Homiletic Text. Some pastors, following the original intent of the Synod of Dordtrecht and the subsequent traditions of the Reformed churches, have indeed prepared sermons structured according to the individual answers in the Heidelberg Catechism. Thus, if a Lord's Day contained three or four theological propositions in its explanation of some element of Christian doctrine or life, the sermon itself would have those propositions as its "points." For example, Lord's Day 17 reads as follows:

Question: How does Christ's resurrection benefit us?

Answer: First, by his resurrection he has overcome death, so that he might make us share in the righteousness he won for us by his death.

Second, by his power we too are already now resurrected to a new life.

Third, Christ's resurrection is a guarantee of our glorious resurrection.

A catechetical sermon using this approach would probably be preceded by the reading of a relevant Scripture passage (such as 1 Cor. 15 or 1 Pet. 1:3-9), but then would be developed as a three-point sermon expounding the three "benefits" of Christ's resurrection outlined in the text of the catechism. If one were to challenge this approach because the "text" of the sermon came from the catechism rather than from the Bible, the answer would be that the catechism is merely a distillation of biblical statements and ideas. With this in mind, each line of the catechism's 129 answers is footnoted to relevant scriptural passages.

Scripture Exposition. Most of the Lord's Days of the Heidelberg Catechism, however, are much more complex. Lord's Day 18, for instance, has four questions and answers, ranging in topics from the historical evidence of Christ's ascension to issues of Christology and the nature of Christ's present intercession and reign in heaven. The homiletic difficulties of trying to explain adequately all of these ideas in a single message have fostered a second approach to catechetical preaching. Here the preacher chooses a Scripture passage that seems to relate to many, if not most, of the theological propositions contained in a single Lord's Day. The preacher then prepares an expository sermon based on that biblical text, rather than directly on the catechism propositions themselves. Elements of the catechism are usually brought into the sermon as illustrative material or as summary statements of belief.

Doctrinal–Topical. A third method of catechetical preaching is essentially topical. The pastor extracts a single topic from the collection of ideas contained in a Lord's Day and then designs a sermon that develops that topic in ways both relevant to the congregation and consistent with the theological heritage of the denomination. The sermon doesn't pretend to be expository, though it may include exegesis of one or more Scripture passages. Nor does it necessarily follow the Heidelberg Catechism's development of a doctrinal statement. Instead, the primary emphasis is placed on sound homiletical development of the topic.

Changing Traditions

Although these latter styles of catechetical preaching are more prevalent today than is the first, the Synod of Dordtrecht clearly intended that preaching of the Heidelberg Catechism be in the form of teaching sermons that explain each of the theological propositions of a Lord's Day in rote succession. In fact, whereas pastors in the Christian Reformed Church in North America at one time attempted to

"hide" catechetical preaching behind exegetical or topical approaches, the Christian Reformed Synod of 1950 specifically mandated that the questions and answers of the catechism be read *before* the sermon. The synod's reasoning was clear: the Lord's Day must be stated as the doctrinal text on which the message is based and from which it receives its homiletic structure and development.

But traditions change, and many Reformed churches (including the Christian Reformed church) now encourage "confessional" preaching. Here the historic emphasis on using the creeds and confessions of denominational identity as teaching tools still remains, but now it is broadened to include other confessional statements beside the Heidelberg Catechism (such as the Belgic Confession of 1561 or the Canons of Dort, 1618–1619), or even some of the more contemporary expressions of faith. Few of these documents, however, are as succinct or as clearly didactic as the Heidelberg Catechism. For that reason, the changing tradition virtually requires a movement away from sermons that use the text of the confessional statements to structure the form and content of the messages themselves. Instead, the new practices invite more extensive use of the expository or topical methods of "catechism preaching."

The best of catechetical preaching today is a hybrid. It combines the traditional strength of the Reformed emphasis on teaching the broad range of theological insights enshrined in its historic confessions with the warmth and pastoral sensitivity of insightful topical proclamation.

Wayne Brouwer

280 • DOCTRINAL PREACHING

Doctrinal preaching teaches and builds up the body of faith through a deepened knowledge of God.

Introduction

By simplest definition, doctrine means something that is taught. In more formal usage, it has more precise and binding implications. It consists of "a principle, or the body of principles in a branch of knowledge or system of belief." There is an element of acceptance, authority, taking a position, recognition of a constraining or compelling point of reference. Doctrine sets the boundaries of belief and determines the direction and character of response to ideas, propositions, lifestyles, and philosophies encountered in the long stretch of human experience. In the formation of doctrine, there is a codification of interpretations, understandings, and convictions that supports and gives meaning to selected courses of action. It is a formulation that calls for affirmation, identification, loyalty, and propagation.

Some of the attitudes expressive of this sense of attachment and devotion are contained in such pronouncements as "thus saith the Lord," "here I stand," "we hold these truths to be self-evident," and "for me to live is Christ." For such expressions there is a before and an after. The "before" aspect is a compounding of assurances and promises issuing from the ageless struggle with basic values and fundamental truths in the history of humankind. The "after" aspect is indeterminate. The validity of the declaration is attested in the fulfillment of expectations generated by the initial, or altered, statement of faith.

It is important to recognize the potential for belief and unbelief, faith and non-faith, inherent in doctrinal statements. This is not a danger but a necessary alerting to the inevitability of taking sides, encouraging partisanship, and giving support to those contenders who are most confident that they hold the "keys to the kingdom," or that it is they "to whom the truth hath been delivered, once for all."

Deterrents to Doctrinal Preaching

Two potent deterrents to doctrinal preaching are the prevailing antiauthoritarian mood at the end of the twentieth century and the spirit of broad tolerance in matters of religious belief—the latter fostering a high level of individualized religious expression.

This individualistic temper tends to resist the authority of utterances emanating from the understandings of a historic body of believers. It appears to be congenial to the unilateral formulations of radical individualists for whom corporate deliverances are a stumbling block, and inspired consensus in the fundamentals of faith is an inconvenience. Thus emerges a proliferation of beliefs, a deluge of doctrines, and a pandemonium of claimants. Each claims to know what one should believe about God and what duty God requires. Each succeeds in releasing those forces that erode the foundations of

the church as the body of Christ. This is done in the name of religious freedom.

Antiauthoritarianism, in reaction to statements of faith, is a defense against encroachments of "traditionalist" religion. The latter is symbolized in those confessions of faith transmitted through the centuries from church fathers, councils, and the continuous stream of ecclesiastical traditions. The language is awe-inspiring, but the luminous moment of apprehension rarely occurs. Doctrine is looked upon simply as something to be memorized and recited only at pivotal points in worship.

The sources of doctrine increase with the broadening and deepening experiences of the faithful in the life of the church. Consider the words of Paul to Timothy (2 Tim. 3:14-17): "But as for you, continue in what you have learned and have become convinced of, because you know those from whom you learned it, and how from infancy you have known the holy Scriptures, which are able to make you wise for salvation through faith in Christ Jesus." And then comes the tutorial assurance that, 'All Scripture is God-breathed and is useful for teaching, rebuking, correcting and training in righteousness, so that the man of God may be thoroughly equipped for every good work." This admonition and assurance of Paul includes sound doctrine derived from searching the Scripture under the inspiration of the Holy Spirit. God's revelation of himself is a continuing revelation, made real and present in Jesus Christ.

Doctrinal preaching is not popular preaching. It does not lend itself to the histrionics and acrobatics that prove to be such useful aids in creating certain effects and stirring certain responses in our hearers. The efficacy of doctrinal preaching is enhanced by the seriousness with which minister and congregation attend to regular and systematic reading of the Scripture and studying the pilgrimage of faith and practice in the Christian community. They must become conversant with the genesis and refinements in the creeds, confessions, and social pronouncements of the church.

Doctrinal Preaching's Essential Nature

The arena of debate has been electric with contention over the relationship between doctrine and decision making in matters of war, peace, racism, sexuality, poverty, and hunger. Doctrinal preaching provides opportunity for instruction in the faith that clarifies both individual and collective responsibility to God's call.

In a sense, all preaching begins and ends in doctrine. The order of service and roles of participants reflect the understanding of the church about the sovereignty of God and the working of the Holy Spirit. All of these implications of doctrine are persistent reminders of how the whole structure is joined together and grows into the Lord's holy temple.

The force of doctrine is conditioned by an awareness that the worshiping community is called by God. The community has a covenant relationship based upon the gift of deliverance by God. Unbroken fidelity to God is necessary for the believer to be a continuous recipient of that gift. Doctrine becomes, and is, a delineation of the character of the giver, the substance of the gift, and the requirements of the respondent.

Teaching and preaching from the perspective of covenant is a process of "in-house" consciousness raising regarding the divine-human pledge. Erosion, diversion, and watering down the demands of the gospel, as conveyed in doctrine, lead to a comfortable intoning "Lord, Lord," without any conscious intention of becoming a true disciple. The preacher may feel the necessity to be on the frontier of broad human concerns, to delight, entertain, chide, or titillate the egos of the influential members of the church. He or she may neglect the "the more important matters of the law" or minimize, by silence or infrequent reference, the stern reminder that "straight is gate and narrow the path that lead to eternal life." In the wisdom of our predecessors, and by the working of the Holy Spirit, crucial concepts have been set forth regarding God's being, purposes, actions, and promises.

Within a cosmic context, the preacher seeks to lay hold on the truth about the existence and destiny of persons created in the image of God. As the scenario unfolds, there are glimpses of an abiding presence in terms of whose activity the whole drama has meaning. The church, as the unique manifestation of this presence, attempts to interpret, explain, and embody what has happened, what is happening, and what is yet to come. The codification of these understandings is refined and amplified as the community of believers seeks more diligently and responds more faithfully to the Maker of heaven and earth and all that is in them.

There is a measure of audacity in doctrinal preaching, just as there is the exercise of preference in the formulation of doctrine. No ecclesiastical body can lay claim to the exclusive understanding or articulation of God's Word and will.

In moments of greatest uncertainty, the preacher is aligned with Paul's assertion in 2 Corinthians 4:1-6, with comforting resort to the assurance that "we do not use deception, nor do we distort the word of God. On the contrary, by setting forth the truth plainly we commend ourselves to every man's conscience in the sight of God. . . . For we do not preach ourselves, but Jesus Christ as Lord, and ourselves as your servants for Jesus' sake" (vv. 2, 5).

The audacity of the preacher is rooted in the essentials of the faith and is sustained by his or her knowledge of how ideas of Creation, sin, redemption, resurrection, the Holy Spirit, the body of Christ, and eternal life inform and influence the behavior of the believer, and how these concepts affect the whole mission of the witnessing community. In an age when a high premium is placed upon diversity, pluralism, ethnicity, freedom of conscience, and personal autonomy, it is urgent that the "community of faith" have a clearer conception of what it believes and what it is called to be and to do. An open-ended stance is untenable for those who profess Jesus Christ as Lord and Savior. The doctrines are designed to confirm in the life of the church the certainty of its hope and to provide guidelines for a pilgrimage of faith. In this endeavor, the preacher does not lose heart as he or she recalls the admonition of Paul to Timothy (2 Tim. 4:1-4):

> In the presence of God and of Christ Jesus, who will judge the living and the dead, and in view of his appearing and his kingdom, I give you this charge: Preach the Word; be prepared in season and out of season; correct, rebuke and encourage—with great patience and careful instruction. For the time will come when men will not put up with sound doctrine. Instead, to suit their own desires, they will gather around them a great number of teachers to say what their itching ears want to hear. They will turn their ears away from the truth and turn aside to myths.

The scriptural sources of doctrines are overwhelmingly convincing. In essence, the whole Pentateuch resounds with: "Hear, O Israel," this is what God has done and this is what he requires of you. Paul's letters to the Corinthians are replete with doctrine.

Those who had "ears to hear" were convicted by the authority of his message.

The preacher would do well to remind himself or herself of the charge of God to Israel through Moses: "These commandments that I give you today are to be upon your hearts. Impress them on your children. Talk about them when you sit at home and when you walk along the road, when you lie down and when you get up. Tie them as symbols on your hands and bind them on your foreheads. Write them on the doorframes of your houses and on your gates" (Deut. 6:6-9). And the opening paragraph to the _Directory for the Worship of God_ provides:

> God binds together as a people those whom he has called to be his children through faith in Jesus Christ. This community of faith is the Church, whose life is sustained by the power of the Holy Spirit, not by the power of the people.
>
> Those within the Church are called by God to honor him. Acknowledging their own sin, they are the more to acknowledge the power and love of God in overcoming sin by the gift of Jesus Christ the Savior, and to offer their lives in thankful devotion in his service.
>
> God, having established the Church had also commissioned it to be the means by which his redemptive love may be extended to all humanity. The Church is, therefore, to declare the wonderful deeds of him who calls people out of darkness into his marvelous light, and who in his grace reaches out to pardon, redeem, and empower undeserving humanity, through Jesus Christ.

This is the subject matter of doctrine. God alone can give perceptiveness sufficient to understand and the power boldly to declare for the edification of all who have ears to hear.

Frank T. Wilson[32]

281 • AFRICAN-AMERICAN PREACHING

African-American preaching arises out of the cultural and religious experience of the oppressed. It reaches people in their dislocation and relocates them in God and in the promise of a brighter future.

"Telling the Story"

The proclamation of the Word of God, the "telling of the story" is essential to authentic African-American worship. There is a saying among some of African-American preachers that the brothers and sisters will forgive you for anything but _not preaching_. African-American folk expect the preacher to "tell the story." What does it mean to "tell the story?"

Biblical Emphasis. African-American preaching, almost without exception, is biblical. It takes the biblical message and the biblical stories and weaves them in such a way that the stories come alive and relate to the lives, needs, feelings, and existential situations of those gathered in the congregation. Each story is told in a way consistent with the biblical story, yet having relevance and application for African-American people. This storied preaching is rich with sharp words and vivid imagery for disillusioned and disinherited people. African-American preaching is filled with stories that set hearts aflame and spirits right to have faith that God is more than a match for the evil structures of oppression. This preaching supremely illustrates Jesus' power to overcome these structures through his death and resurrection.

Prophetic Rather than Pastoral. African-American preaching is characterized generally as prophetic rather than pastoral. The Old Testament and the prophetic literature are used as material for sermonizing rather than the more pastoral material of the Bible. In addition, the synoptic Gospels of Matthew, Mark, and Luke are used as the testimonies of those who knew the prophet Jesus and his revolutionary activities in and around Galilee as he struggled with the powerful Roman government and the religious establishment of his day.

One illustration of African-American preaching's prophetic edge is that on the Sunday morning on which the four African-American children were bombed to death at Sixteenth Street Baptist Church in Birmingham, a survey of the sermons preached in that city on that Sunday morning revealed that, almost without exception, the African-American preachers preached from the Old Testament. The white preachers _without exception_ preached from the New Testament. That was not a coincidence. African-American preaching tends to announce judgment on the nation, and to call into question the institutions in society in a prophetic fashion whereas white preaching tends to be of a pastoral nature. Part of the reason for this is that the Anglo-

American church has a different relationship to the establishment than the African-American Church.

Anglo-American Christianity is so inextricably bound to the American way of life that it sees God, country, and American flag as almost synonymous terms. The emphasis more often than not in Anglo-American preaching is personal behavior and the individual rather than the revolutionary ethic of Jesus and the prophetic judgment on the whole community. In addition, there is not the strict dichotomy in African-American preaching of the priestly and the prophetic, the sacred and the secular. The priestly and the prophetic coexist as part and parcel of the same reality. Even where there is the clear element of judgment and the prophetic message, the celebration of life is present.

Poetic in Style. Generally, African-American preaching is poetic rather than rigorously logical and stymied by rationality. As Hortense Spillers has pointed out in her analysis of the style of the African-American sermon in reference to Martin Luther King, there is considerable use of metaphors and a greater number of nouns, adjectives, and adjectival clauses rather than verbs and verb forms. These combine to create a picturesqueness and grandness of speech. The African-American preacher relies on imagery to carry the subject, much like the language of the Bible. In the following excerpt from a sermon preached in 1962 by J. H. Jackson, president of the National Baptist Convention, it is clear that the preacher is painting a picture on the canvas of the mind. Jackson addresses facing the future with God:

> But I say to you my friends, fear not your tomorrow, and shrink not from the task or the lot that is yet to come. The future belongs to God, and the last chapter in the story of human life will not be written by the blood-stained hands of godless men but by the God of history himself. The same hand that raised the curtain of creation and pushed back the floating worlds upon the broad sea of time and flashed forth the light of life that put an end to ancient chaos and darkness; the same hand that erected the highways of the skies and rolled the sun like a golden ball across the pavement of the dawn; the same God whose hand has guided the destinies of nations, fixed the time and seasons and superintended the whole order of time and eternity will at His appointed hour pull down the curtain of existence, and will Himself write the last paragraph in the last chapter of the last book of human life and cosmic destiny. (Warner R. Traynham, *Christian Faith in Black and White* [Wakefield, Mass.: Parameter Press, 1973])

Such poetry, vivid imagery, and word pictures can be heard again and again in African-American preaching. The African-American preacher is confident that preaching is primarily an effort at communication both to the mind and to the emotions.

Dialogue between Pastor and People. African-American preaching is dialogical; it is a cooperative effort between the pulpit and the pew. The dialogue does not take place *after* the sermon but *during* the sermon. Sometimes an unpoetic preacher can be brought to new life, brilliance, and lyrical power when there is cooperation in the pew, with the help, expectancy, encouragement, and enthusiasm of the congregation.

Part of the African-American preaching tradition has been the prayers of the lay people for the preacher and/or the expectancy about the sermon. These prayers reflect the same vivid imagery and poetry and imagination mentioned earlier. The following prayer is an example:

> And now, O Lord, this man of God,
> Who breaks the bread of life this morning—
> Shadow him in the hollow of Thy hand,
> And keep him out of the gunshot of the devil.
>
> Take him, Lord, this morning
> Wash him with hyssop inside and out,
> Hang him up and drain him dry of sin.
> Pin his ears to the wisdom post,
> And make his words sledge hammers of truth,
> Beat on the iron heart of sin,
> Put his eye to the telescope of eternity
> And let him look upon the paper walls of time.
> Lord, turpentine his imagination,
> Put perpetual motion in his arms,
> Fill him full of the dynamite of Thy power,
> Anoint him all over with the oil of Thy salvation,
> And set his tongue on fire.

The dialogical style of African-American preaching reaches back into the wombs of Africa engendering, a call-and-response style that elicits participation of all those gathered. This makes African-American preaching a uniquely creative and beautiful art.

Teaches and Inspires. African-American preaching is didactic as well as inspiring. It seeks to inform as well as inspire. It seeks to discern the action of God in history as it relates to the existential dilemma of the African-American person, lends healing to people's hurts, and proclaims a liberating word while not denying the reality of pain.

Some have accused African-American preaching and the African-American church of anti-intellectualism. What may be more accurate is that there is little tolerance for rarefied abstraction. The African-American preacher can discuss anything of philosophical and theological import as long as it is presented in such a way as to make sense of life and relate to the lives of the hearers. How an issue is presented is often more important than what the issue is. People such as Gardner C. Taylor, Howard Thurman, George Outen, Vernon John, and Martin Luther King, Jr. have proven that African-American preaching can contain intricate historical, political analyses while at the same time "feeding the flock."

Declares Rather than Suggests. African-American preaching is characterized as declarative rather than suggestive. Someone once said when the Roman Catholic priests speak, they say, "The church says . . ." When the Jewish rabbis speak, they say, "The Torah says . . ." But when the African-American preachers speak they say, "My God told me . . ."

There is little room in African-American preaching for equivocation and spurious sophistry. The moral issues of the nation are far too clear, the presence of evil too certain, to be tentative. A stand is taken on an issue. Even when logical argument is used to present the case, the force of the preaching does not depend on argument and logical persuasion, but rather on the ability of the African-American preacher to probe the depths of the issue, to guide the hearers to reach the same conclusion. But always it is declarative rather than suggestive, matter of fact rather than tentative. The African-American preacher is neither too timid nor hesitant to say, "Thus saith the Lord!"

Slow and Deliberate in Buildup. African-American preaching is characterized by a slow and deliberate buildup. The path the preacher takes may be winding with a few detours, but always he or she is expected to be heading someplace and to take time getting there. In fact, in many congregations the African-American preacher can hear some members of the congregation admonishing, "Take your time." He or she is expected to allow time for both the mind and the emotions to react in a natural process. The African-American preacher is deliberate with the material, and nobody has the sense that he or she is in a hurry, for there is no place more important and nothing more significant than what the preacher is doing: rightly dividing the Word of truth. It is more important to say fewer things and be heard and felt than to present many ideas that are merely words and concepts introduced.

The Dramatic Pause. The dramatic pause by many preachers is used as an effort to force the congregation both to reflect upon what has been said and to anticipate what is to follow. This leads to an antiphonal response and sometimes into a rhythmic, harmonious singsong. One can describe this pattern as the Four *R*s: rhetoric, repetition, rhythm, rest. This was heard often in the preaching of Martin Luther King, Jr., and thousands of other African-American preachers. Often it is the repetition of a single word or phrase in which the congregation picks up the cadence of the preacher and there is almost a refrain. Recall King's speech at Lincoln Memorial in Washington in 1963 in which he repeats, "I have a dream . . ." By repetition and amplification, the speech builds. There is rhetoric, repetition, rhythm, and rest. The congregation echoes and verifies the preacher's own words in such a way as to make them emphatic.

King was familiar with this technique, for he had learned it from his elders and had seen it work time and time again. He was a master at euphony, carefully selecting and using a combination of vowels and consonants so as to make his sounds and words pleasing. These need to be heard to be understood, for the most effective observer of this style and technique is the human ear.

Life Situational. African-American preaching is expected to relate to life and the life situations of the audience. When it does not, no matter how well-conceived or how well-constructed or how theologically sound, that sermon is considered a failure. Illustrations are often used—drawn from history, everyday experiences, African-American history and culture, and literature. Illustrations from biblical literature are shaped in such a way as to relate the experience to the lives of as many persons as possible.

The Element of Hope. There is always an element of hope and optimism in African-American preaching. No matter how dark or gloomy a picture has been painted, there is always a "but" or a "nevertheless" or an element in the climax of the sermon that suggests holding on, marching forward, going through, or overcoming.

This is illustrated in a sermon preached by Otis Moss in which he described drug addiction and its terrible effects on the minds of African-American family and the African-American community.

> The last time that I saw the man he was on his way home. His eyes were clear with sight and insight. The scars of dull and dirty needles had been washed from his body. He was no longer the vehicle of dope but the instrument of hope. The last time that I saw him he was on his way home. His children saw him walking and smiled to themselves and said, "That looks like *my* daddy." His wife looked out and saw him and said, "That's my husband." And I could hear the man describing what had happened to him. Can't you hear him saying, "I met a man named Jesus and I had an exchange with him. I gave him my sorrows, he gave me his joy; I gave him my confusion, he gave me his peace; I gave him my despair, he gave me his hope; I gave him my hatred, he gave me his love; I gave him my torn life, he gave me his purpose. I met a man—a man named Jesus."

African-American Preaching and African-American Theology

Authentic African-American preaching provides a gospel message to African-American people whose lives and very existence are threatened daily by the insidious tentacles of power and oppression. If preaching fails to speak to the condition of African-American people and offers no promise of life for the African-American person, then it is not gospel to them. It is simply lifeless rhetoric.

Preaching is at the heart of Christianity. Not rapping, not unintelligible gibberish, not "sound and fury signifying nothing," not hip anecdotes from *Playboy* magazine or comic vignettes from "Peanuts," not recovery groups (as helpful as those may be), but preaching in which the Word of God is declared with clarion sound and an impassioned heart that has been set on fire by inspiration and the experience of a God who calls the person to declare his Word. Such persons do not just preach sermons but preach that *event* in history and eternity by which God entered most fully and effectively into

human life. Preachers must be persons who preach the judgment and the grace of God with passion and preparation, with fervor and faith, with prophetic vision and priestly hearts.

As important as ritual is to symbolize the acts of the faith and experience with God; as important as music is to convey the gospel of hope and the beauty of God's holiness, in the Christian religion these can never be *substitutes* for the proclamation of the Word of God, the "foolishness of preaching," the "inescapable claim" upon us. Jesus did not neglect the blind and the lame, the deaf and the lepers, the poor and the broken-hearted, the captive and the bruised—his gospel of liberation, love, and freedom was a declaration of the rule of God breaking in upon the forces that hold humans captive. He did not separate a gospel of changing conditions in society from changing the individual. His gospel is always personal and social. He knew nothing of a religion that spoke to the heart and not the conditions in which men and women live. But his words in Matthew 10 are clear: "As you go, preach!"

The Jesus that African-American preaching must proclaim has to be able to walk the dark ghetto streets of the North and the hot, dusty fields of a sharecropper's farm in the South. The Jesus that African-American preaching proclaims is the Christ of faith who is relevant to the needs, feelings, and aspirations of African-American people. It is Jesus whose face and image one sees in the rat-bitten, mutilated faces of children, and his suffering one sees in the scars from dull and dirty needles in the body of a drug addict in a stinking, dirty alley. That is the Jesus who is not only the liberator and emancipator, but he is the bishop of the souls of African-American folk. It was this Jesus that African-Americans' forefathers and foremothers knew and sang about: "O fix me, Jesus, fix me."

It has been an understanding of, and an acquaintance with, this Jesus that has led African-American preachers to create new Christological categories and to declare him to be "A Stone rolling through Babylon," "Water in dry places," "Bread in a starving land," "The Rose of Sharon," and "The Bright and Morning Star." When one hears preaching in a church where these Christological categories cannot be used, one can be certain he or she is not worshiping in an African-American church.

William B. McClain[33]

282 • CONFESSIONAL PREACHING

Confessional preaching arises out of the situation of the preacher. It builds on a personal experience, a matter of struggle, a triumph. It thereby connects with the lives of the hearers and draws them into the Word of God for their own situations.

——— Background ———

Confessional preaching is defined by its most famous contemporary practitioner, John R. Claypool, as a willingness "to share out of my own light and my own darkness—to share the truths that are saving me and the places where I find the struggle still to be most acute" (_The Preaching Event_ [New York: Harper and Row, 1990], 89). Confessional preaching seeks to give the listener entree into the preacher's innermost struggles, conflicts, and joys as a means of finding the full range of salvation offered in Christ.

Claypool's first efforts in confessional preaching came out of one of his life's darkest moments—the loss of his eight-year-old daughter, Laura Lue, to acute leukemia. Through a series of confessional sermons, compiled in a book entitled _The Tracks of A Fellow Struggler,_ Claypool sought to make sense of God's dealings with humanity for his listeners. Out of the crucible of that experience, Claypool further refined his confessional preaching method in the Lyman Beecher Lectures on Preaching delivered at Yale and published under the title, _The Preaching Event_ (mentioned above).

An early example of confessional preaching may be seen in Paul's defense before King Agrippa in the twenty-sixth chapter of Acts. In his speech before Agrippa, Paul rests the validation of both his faith and ministry on his Damascus road experience. He seeks to win Agrippa to faith by giving testimony to his personal experience. Through the history of the church, others, like Paul, have used their personal experience as the starting point in their preaching—e.g., Augustine in his _Confessions_ and John Wesley by way of his Aldersgate experience. Yet it has been only in the last quarter of the twentieth century that confessional preaching (understood as more than an evangelistic testimony of how the preacher was converted) has increased in popularity.

In many ways confessional preaching's growing acceptance in the mid-seventies may be seen to arise out of the human potential movement in psychology and the lay renewal movement in the church. Robert Raines, one of the early popularizers of confessional preaching or "preaching from the inside out," as he describes preaching that starts with the preacher's own personal struggles, points to Carl Rogers, Fritz Perls, Erik Erikson, and others associated with the human potential movement of the mid-seventies as having influenced his preaching. Claypool acknowledges influence of the lay renewal movement and such proponents as Paul Tournier and Keith Miller, whose book _The Taste of New Wine_ called the laity to a new openness in sharing. Today Claypool sees echoes of the confessional style in the writings of Frederick Buechner, especially his three-volume spiritual autobiography (_The Sacred Journey, Now and Then,_ and _Telling Secrets_). His most confessional work, _Telling Secrets,_ is shaped by the recovery movement (Twelve Steps, Co-Dependency, etc.), which gives some indication that confessional preaching has shifted its locus from the human potential movement to its natural successor, the recovery movement.

——— Critique ———

Confessional preaching's greatest strength may be in allowing listeners to enter into the experience of the preacher to find resources for help in their own situations. When confessional preaching is overused or used exclusively, the following dangers are inherent: exalting the preacher above Christ; psychological exhibitionism; and ignoring the social implications of the gospel. As D. T. Niles said, however, the power of one beggar showing another where he has found bread is irrefutable. One has only to read the second chapter ("The Blessedness of Possessing Nothing") in A. W. Tozer's classic devotional work _The Pursuit of God_ (Harrisburg, Pa.: Christian Publications, 1948) to understand, by its absence, the power of confession. As spiritually moving as is Tozer's description of Abraham's offering up of Isaac to God, it is more gripping to know Tozer wrote the chapter out of his own spiritual struggle to turn his own daughter over to God—a fact Tozer does not reveal.

Cautioning the preacher to "hide behind the cross" is warranted. Yet, the cross behind which the

The Candlestick. The candlestick is the symbol of Christ and of his proclamation "I am the light of the world" (John 8:12). The Latin in the symbol above is John 1:5: "The light shines in the darkness, and the darkness did not overcome it." When two candles are used, they represent the human and divine nature; six candles represent the days of creation; when the cross is placed among the candles, the symbolism speaks of the day of redemption.

preacher hides would do well to be a cross that bears witness both to the preacher's truthful story of his or her own frailty and to the Christ who redeems that frailty. This is the cross that confessional preaching lifts up.

Jack Mercer

283 • Contextual Preaching

Contextual preaching declares the Word of God in the context of the social, political, moral, and economic life situations of the listeners. It hears and proclaims the Word for the immediate context of the congregation.

Preparation. In the preparation of a contextual sermon, exegesis and application are a single process. This premise is vital. Exegesis and application may never be regarded as two separate tasks. In order to preach in today's context, the text and congregation must be brought face to face in the preparation of the sermon. Then the text begins to speak. Both the text and the congregation's situation must therefore be fundamentally integrated. In the prepa-

ration, the preacher must listen to the text permeated with the exigencies and problems, the conceptual categories of the time. Thus, a creative *confrontation* is brought about, in which the text itself declares and expounds its message for a particular situation.

The preparation of a sermon cannot be reduced to a method, because when the text speaks, it is an event—a Word event. The preacher cannot manipulate this event according to his or her own designs. The exegetical method can, at most, remove existing obstacles so that the Word can speak intelligibly in the language of the age. Only a few principles relating to the movement from text to sermon can therefore be laid down.

The Congregation's Situation. The preacher must grasp, must *live,* the situation and context of his or her congregation. The preacher must be involved with the "grassroots" experiences, the feelings and thoughts of the members of the congregation. He or she must absorb their theology. If the preacher sits with the community, suffers with them, despairs and hopes with them, rebels with them against injustice and oppression, then he or she can relate the message of the Bible to their lives. This is the method of contextual preaching.

In order to translate the message into contemporary language, the preacher should be conversant with the art and literature of the time. Poetry, drama, novels and graphic art all represent and clarify contemporary conceptual categories. They reflect modern humanity. Modern philosophy, political trends, and ideas also express reality as experienced and understood by people today. Dialogue with other sciences enhances one's understanding of the mentality of contemporary society, for whom the gospel has to be formulated. It is in this reality, using these linguistic and conceptual structures, that the preacher must proclaim Jesus Christ as Lord.

The preacher must know the individual parishioners who make up the congregation, each with their own conceptual frameworks. He or she must share their particular world, their specific situation in history, and the innumerable problems of their existence. At this point the message of the text must be made concrete. In such encounter with the text, brought about by the preacher, God's Word *from Scripture* addresses the congregation in a unifying way. This implies that the preacher must approach the text humbly. This unity between text and present reality is always wrought by _God's speaking_ through his Word, entering every age, demythologizing, expounding, and changing the situation.

Exegesis. Exegesis must assist the preacher by spelling out the message of a text as formulated in a bygone age. In scientific exegesis the text is encountered by the preacher who is saturated with the realities of his or her own situation, a fact that cannot be denied. In exegesis the preacher has to fathom the historical situation of the text in order to expound its message accurately, at all times allowing the present situation to confront the text. Exegesis is continued into and accomplished in the sermon. No text must be the subject of preaching unless it has addressed the preacher himself or herself.

Meditation. The encounter between text and the congregation's situation takes place in the form of meditation. The text must be rendered concrete and contemporary in the mind of the preacher. This is why meditation is such an important element in the hermeneutic process. It builds a bridge between the text and the present.

Meditation is the process in which the text confronts the situation of the congregation, the word addresses it, and the text crystallizes in thoughts that are then expressed in the language of the listeners. In meditation the language of the text encounters contemporary language, bringing about confrontation and dialogue between the text and the present. This confrontation causes a merging of horizons—the preacher's and the text's. Meditation is the way along which exegesis proceeds to the sermon.

In a sense, we can make a distinction between scientific exegesis and meditation, but we cannot divorce them. Exegesis interacts with the ideas it unleashes about the message of next Sunday's text. Preaching demands _creativity_ and imagination. It is an act of _linguistic creation,_ but exegesis is the criterion for the ideas it releases. It is the criterion for the truth of these ideas, that is, whether they accord with the text. Every time the ideas stirred up by the text threaten to run wild, exegesis brings them to heel. Meditation, therefore, runs like a thread through the whole process of composing a sermon because meditation and the search for a relevant message are the same process.

Text as Subject. In the hermeneutic interaction between text and contemporary situation, the text begins to _address_ the preacher. The text as subject now addresses the preacher as object, interpreting the preacher and expounding his or her life and situation. This encounter between text and preacher is an opening up: the true word "penetrates even to dividing soul and spirit, joints and marrow" (Heb. 4:12). Thus, in meditation, the confrontation between text and present reality ultimately possesses and overcomes the preacher. In this sense the word passes _through_ him or her and then to the congregation.

When the preacher is addressed by God's Word, he or she consciously experiences the message for the age. The preacher is overpowered by the omnipotence of God's mighty Word, which erupts into his or her life and situation. This happens as the preacher wrestles dialogically with the Word, which confronts the preacher at every level of his or her existence. And so the preacher comes to understand the message for the congregation. After all, preaching is the word of one who, having understood, wants to bring others to a similar understanding _of_ the Word _through_ the word.

The preacher now begins to express the message of God's Word as experienced in his or her mind. It is inherent in human nature to articulate, and this articulation is a rephrasing. In other words, the preacher phrases the message in the idiom of the congregation. The text is made present and concrete by the translation of the message that illuminates the contextual situation.

In this process, the Word as Scripture gives birth to the living Word in the sermon, creating a similarity between the Word in Scripture and the proclaimed Word. This similarity does not imply replication or repetition, but a _resemblance_ (as the child resembles the mother). The continuity lies in the message, the Word event in the text, which brings forth a new Word—the once only Word rephrased. The similarity between the written and the proclaimed Word is therefore not an identity in the sense of mere duplication. Preaching that allows the Word to speak in present reality remains bound to the text with an umbilical cord. Thus, the Word of God is heard in the present situation—in a new, unique way.

In the final analysis, the text is made concrete by the *congregation,* the interpreting communion of saints who, guided by the Spirit, understand the message as a *body.* The sermon opens up perspectives for the congregation and stimulates them in a particular direction. When, under the guidance of the Holy Spirit, listeners go out into the world and live out God's message in their community, the text is finally actualized. Then the understanding of the message for our day is fulfilled and the intention of the text is accomplished.

Summary. In summary, we are confronted with the problem of bridging an *actuality gap*—a problem of articulation. To solve this problem, text and present reality must encounter one another in the mind of the preacher/interpreter. This demands that the preacher know both his or her own situation and the situation of the text. When text and present reality thus encounter one another, the word forges the link between the text and the present by addressing a message to the present situation (the mind, being, and context of the listening preacher).

H. J. C. Pieterse[34]

284 ♦ LIFE-SITUATIONAL PREACHING

Life-situational preaching has as its starting point the personal concerns of its audience. It seeks to bring the hearer into the Word of God by making connections between Scripture and the hurts and issues of life.

The Starting Point. Life-situational preaching arises from the problems of life and seeks to touch the listener at the point of his or her personal concerns. Harry Emerson Fosdick (1878–1969), pastor of New York's historic Riverside Church from 1926 to 1946, and closely associated with the development of life-situational preaching, called it "personal counseling on a group basis." Whereas expository preaching begins with the biblical text and seeks to apply it to life, and topical preaching begins with a subject and seeks to make it relevant to life, life-situational preaching begins with life itself and seeks, in the words of one life-situational preacher, "to find a need and meet it; find a hurt and heal it."

Fosdick summarized the method involved in life-situational preaching this way: "Start with a life issue, a real problem, personal or social, perplexing the mind or disturbing the conscience; face that

problem fairly, deal with it honestly, and throw such light on it from the spirit of Christ, that people will be able to think more clearly and live more nobly because of that sermon" (*Twenty Centuries of Great Preaching,* Vol. 9: *Fosdick to E. Stanley Jones,* 16). The aim of life-situational preaching, then, is to bring hope and healing to the listener in the midst of the problems of life.

The History and Future of Life-Situational Preaching. The roots of life-situational preaching are difficult to trace. In one sense, a case can be made that all the New Testament Epistles, especially those of Paul, addressing as they did the issues of the early church, are a form of life-situational preaching. Another perspective, however, is to see life-situational preaching emerging from the theological and existential context of its foremost popularizer, Harry Emerson Fosdick. Fosdick was a self-avowed theological liberal, influenced by such theologians as Walter Rauschenbush and Frederich Schliermacher, who took as their starting point the experiential and social dilemma of humanity rather than divine revelation. It is little wonder that Fosdick, champion of liberal theology at the turn of the century, would develop a preaching method that began with humanity's problems rather than with God's problem with humanity. Following a mental breakdown, Fosdick described the major impetus to his preaching as a desire to "get at folks—ordinary, everyday folks—and try to help them" (*Twenty Centuries of Great Preaching,* Vol. 9:7). The irony is that life-situational preaching, which began as a preaching method in the theologically liberal tradition, is now practiced most often in evangelical pulpits.

In their desire to reach an increasingly secularized world, evangelicals have focused their attention on the needs and hurts of humanity. The needs and hurts evangelical preachers address are typically of a personal rather than societal nature. Life-situational preaching is employed in one form or another by popular evangelical preachers as diverse as Robert Schuller and Bill Hybels. Echoes can also be heard in the preaching of Charles Swindoll. The strength of life-situational preaching, especially in regard to evangelism, is its ability to meet people at the place where life pinches and to bring to bear the resources of the gospel. Life-situational preaching takes seriously, in a way that many other methods of preaching do not, the hurts and needs of the people.

──── Critique ────

Focused on the problems of individuals, life-situational preaching is prone to excessive individualism, which ignores both the communal dimension of its listeners as the gathered church and the sometimes systemic nature of the problems individuals are facing. Furthermore, as Thomas Long has suggested, this method in preaching "overworks relevance" and thus disregards the gospel's prophetic message that some problems (sin, death, social inequities—to name just a few) will not be resolved this side of the kingdom of God (_The Witness of Preaching_ [Louisville: Westminster/John Knox Press, 1989], 34). Yet the most serious critique of life-situational preaching has been that this method ignores the Bible in favor of psychology and reduces "theology to anthropology" (_The Witness of Preaching_, 35). Harry Emerson Fosdick, toward whom all these critiques were leveled, at one time or another defended the life-situational method in preaching as follows: "The [life-situational] sermon is a mediation of the revelation of God in Christ . . . an opportunity so to mediate a knowledge of God and the saving power of Christ that lives can be transformed." A reading of Fosdick's sermons will quickly reveal that he succeeded in his defense of this preaching method. However, there has been only one Harry Emerson Fosdick.

The applicability of life-situational preaching for today is as a corrective to preaching which, in a desire to be faithful to the biblical revelation, forgets that it is to the needs of humanity that the biblical revelation is addressed. The life-situational method in preaching calls upon the preacher to take seriously the jagged edges of the listener's marriage, failed career, or children run amok. Life-situational preaching forces the preacher to consider as homiletic grist the day-to-day stuff of life that pinches at the preacher and his or her listeners as well. Life-situational preaching seeks to touch people where they are and, when done aright, where the Spirit of God wishes to be incarnate through the preached Word.

Jack Mercer

285 • PROGRESSIVE-EMOTIVE PREACHING

Progressive-emotive sermons are generally classified either by their relationship to source material (topical, textual, expository) or by the method of their argument (inductive, deductive, dialogic). The progressive-emotive sermon, however, is defined by its intended impact on the listener.

──── Preparation ────

Change in behavior, attitude, or understanding never occurs in a vacuum. It is produced by three things: psychological interaction with a variety of sensory experiences; a clear understanding of a preferred way of thinking, acting, or believing; and a viable means by which to move in that direction. The progressive-emotive sermon seeks to bring these three elements of motivation together.

There are several major decisions to make in developing the progressive-emotive sermon. The first is to select an extremely clear and precise idea of the psychological movement desired in the emotions and will of the listener. This idea must be specific enough to shape all the materials considered for inclusion in the sermon. For example, a sermon entitled "Putting Your Heart Back Together," based upon the letter to the church in Pergamum (Rev. 2:12-17), reads that passage as indicative of the manner in which people live with the dissonance of motives and values that splinter hearts and sap spiritual energies. Only when Christ, by his Spirit, restores singular unity to one's existence does a person find life in its fullest sense, both now and for the future. Using the metaphors of broken hearts, splintered lives, mixed motives, and the idea of putting one's heart back together, the sermon keeps its direction true and refuses to get sidetracked by exegetical details, word definitions, or excessive historical background. Historical and grammatical study help the preacher understand the passage more fully, but they don't necessarily communicate the meaning or intent of the scriptural text to others in the homiletic development itself.

The second decision to make in preparing the progressive-emotive sermon is that of choosing to read broadly, to observe minutely, and to experience life meaningfully. Since one apprehends reality through constant reception of images created by a multitude of sensory experiences, the progressive-emotive sermon draws from a vast array of ideas, pictures, stories, facts, statistics, and the like as the raw material of preaching. People are rarely moved by rational argument alone. Rather, they are taken along the path of a rational argument in a convincing manner only as they see it surrounded by familiar images that attract and pictures defined by colors and sounds that direct them away from other possible walks of life.

Thirdly, the progressive-emotive sermon relies heavily on gifted storytelling. The progressive-emotive sermon does not *use* illustrations; it is *itself* an illustration, a moving picture, a living metaphor. That doesn't mean that the progressive-emotive sermon is merely a lengthy narrative. It may be that, but it is often more a rapid succession of word-pictures, incidents, common experiences, and the like, which together shape a passageway along which listeners will be encouraged to move.

─────────── Construction ───────────

In a sense, the progressive-emotive sermon is constructed visually. It attempts to see reality through the eyes of the listener and engages him or her in a quest, illuminated by Scripture, toward a new identity, a deeper knowledge, or a changed behavior. Thus the idea of one path among many is always at the heart of the sermon. Sometimes the message marks progression down that path; sometimes it uncovers the glory shaping that path; and sometimes it stops at intersections where that path needs to be more clearly distinguished from other possible paths. But the outcome is always the same: movement in the inner life of the listener that produces outward changes in thought and action.

In order to achieve this, the structure of the progressive-emotive sermon depends more on the type of "moves" that David Buttrick identified in *Homiletic* (Philadelphia: Fortress Press, 1987) than it does on traditional "points" and subpoints. For instance, the short tale of Simeon's role in the Christmas story (Luke 2:21-35) might be shaped by the familiar idea of "Home for Christmas" and then carried along by a number of specific "moves": (1) We all like to be "home for Christmas." (2) But, surprisingly, Jesus, who stands at the heart of our celebrations, wasn't himself "home for Christmas." (3) Come to think of it: often, spiritually, neither are we! (4) Actually, Jesus, being away from home at that first Christmas, made it truly possible for Simeon to go home! (5) And in the restless homelessness of our lives, Jesus also gives us the opportunity to go "home for Christmas" in the truest spiritual sense.

The first "move" in this homiletic development serves as an introduction, identifying our existential place in the rush of the Christmas season. Then scriptural elements of the Simeon narrative are used as illuminated markers to guide the other "moves"

of the sermon: (2) Jesus' circumcision in the temple (2:21-24); (3) Simeon's words to Mary about the character of her child (2:33-35); (4) Simeon's words of praise to God (2:29-32); and (5) the spiritual journey of Simeon's life (2:25-27). As the message unfolds, the listener journeys toward a new experience in understanding and celebrating Christmas.

A similar approach is possible for theological ideas that seem, at first, static and unmoving. They also can be made dynamic within the lives of the listeners. For example, John's encounter with Jesus in Revelation 1 defines the manner in which the vision of the book ought to engage its readers. A progressive-emotive sermon might begin with an introduction that finds each person encountering the reality of the divine presence in in his or her life in some experiential way. What does that encounter do to the person? (1) It shakes (see John fall to the ground); (2) it shelters (sense how this stronger presence protects him from the powers of the world that placed him in exile on Patmos); (3) it shapes (feel the changing contours of John's perceptions); and (4) it sends (walk with John in his new mission).

The procedure may vary significantly with different scriptural texts or topical ideas, but these things are always necessary: keep the normative change of thought, perception, or behavior clear and central, shaping every element of the sermon's development; and design the moves as a logical sequence of steps aimed at discovering and journeying toward the intended passageway.

─────────── Tools ───────────

A number of tools seem particularly suitable to use in enhancing the contact between the progressive-emotive message and the listener. Often these are in some way extensions of the preacher, aspects of his or her communication style already in place through personality traits. Still, the progressive-emotive sermon draws heavily on the following tools:

Clear and Contemporary Language. For the most part, the progressive-emotive sermon contains short sentences and a vocabulary that is up-to-date without being trendy or shocking. Language in the sermon should never call attention to itself by being too academic, too vulgar, too theological, or anything of the kind; rather, it ought to serve as a vehicle by which the listener and the message are connected.

Sensory Speech. Verbs of seeing, hearing, feeling, tasting, touching, sensing, holding, experiencing, and the like, draw the listener in. The sermon talks in pictures; it visualizes experiences of life. It does not _explain_ but instead seeks to take the listener by the hand and _show_ him or her what is happening.

Threes. For some reason, most people feel most comfortable in communication with groupings of three: three similar repetitions of an idea, three supporting stories, three examples. One thought moves past too quickly, two thoughts leave one wishing for just a bit more, and four thoughts seem tedious. Three is not a number to tie oneself to slavishly, but invariably it produces a bridge of communication that is stronger than those built on fewer or greater connecting supports.

Spoken English. Spoken language precedes written language. Sermons need to be spoken aloud again and again before they are preached. If a sermon is prepared at the study desk and uttered for the first time in the pulpit it is rarely likely to carry with it the impact of a sermon that is prepared orally.

Manuscript. The volume of material needed for the journey of images and pictures in the progressive-emotive sermon suggest the writing of a full manuscript. Clarity, precision, and storytelling technique do not occur typically without reflection mined laboriously from the preacher's consciousness and refined in mental sweat at the creative fires of trial and selection.

Patterns of speech that arise from the preacher's mind without extensive preparation tend to become repetitious and stale. Over time, manuscripts, whether well read or memorized, give freshness and vitality to one's preaching.

Pace. Students of communication suggest that persons tend to be drawn toward and believe more readily the speech of a person who talks rapidly. Rapid speech engenders confidence and keeps pace with the listener's thoughts. Yet variety in pace is also needed to reflect the variety of pace in normal speech and thus avoid jarring the listener.

Adaptable. The progressive-emotive sermon may be expository or topical, inductive or deductive, but it is primarily designed as a means of communication. It stays in touch with the movements of the listener's heart and uses that psychological development as the normative force in shaping its thoughts and images.

Wayne Brouwer

TWELVE

Approaches to Preaching

Approaches to preaching are as numerous as preachers themselves. In this section, however, only those approaches that seem most helpful to today's preacher have been included. The section begins with an overview of two approaches to preaching used throughout the church's history to guide the preacher in his or her selection of biblical texts—lectionary preaching and lectio continua (preaching through a biblical book).

These two historical approaches to preaching are immediately followed by a more recent innovation, the involvement of the congregation through a study group in the preparation and evaluation of the sermon. This innovation is indicative of the trend in the modern church to regard the preacher less as an authority on Scripture and more as the gathered community's interpreter of the Bible.

The next three entries outline two of the most popular approaches to contemporary preaching—story-formed preaching and seeker-centered preaching. Although story-formed preaching is as ancient as the Bible itself, as the entry about Jewish storytelling makes clear, only recently has the storytelling art been intensively applied to sermon construction. The how of that art is developed in an article by a preacher who has discovered the revolutionary nature of preaching that is shaped by story. Yet, for all the popularity of story among modern preachers, both in the church and in seminary, a differing approach, seeker-centered preaching, is also gaining attention from contemporary preachers. In the article by Bill Hybels, one will be able to discern the seeker-centered approach to preaching from one who has helped develop what might be considered the modern successor to the revivalistic approach to evangelistic preaching.

Two other new approaches to preaching are described in this section. In both cases, it is not the approach that is new, but rather the people who are preaching. Today major shifts are occurring in both the Protestant and Roman Catholic world as those who have been silent for years bring both fresh voices and approaches to preaching. Two articles, one by a woman, and the other by a lay Roman Catholic, describe these shifts.

Finally, two entries have been included to help the preacher in his or her own preaching. The first article suggests ways in which the preacher may evaluate the sermon. The second entry is a sermon planner that may potentially help the preacher in organizing the biblical witness, outside materials, and his or her own personal contribution to faithfully proclaiming God's Word today.

286 ◆ INTERPRETATION AND PREACHING

This following article takes issue with the way sermons are customarily developed and delivered. The author argues that preaching should speak of Scripture, not about Scripture.

Since the time of the Protestant Scholastics, sermons have been designed according to a schema: *subtilitas intelligendi, subtilitas explicandi, subtilitas applicandi*—careful understanding, explication, and application. A text was exegeted, interpreted, and applied in what was often a tri-part sermon. Through the years the pattern modified. A preference for brief texts emerged, employing a single verse from Scripture or sometimes even a phrase. Where a brief text was not chosen, preachers reduced longer passages to a single topic, a theme that could be stated propositionally. As a result, "stock" homiletic design evolved: An *introduction* was followed by the *text,* which in turn was reduced to a propositional *topic,* which was developed in a series of *"points"* (often categorical), before the sermon ended in a *conclusion.* The system, set forth in homiletic texts, is still with us.

In these homiletic systems there is what might be called a "method of distillation" by which passages are reduced to single propositional "truths." Let us probe the method more deeply. Suppose, for example, a preacher has decided to preach a passage from the New Testament, Luke 7:2-10, the story of the centurion's slave. Remember the narrative: A centurion has a slave near death. He dispatches "elders of the Jews" to plead his case with Jesus. "He is worthy!" the elders exclaim, and tell how the man loves the country and has shelled out for the synagogue building fund. Jesus heads toward the centurion's house but is intercepted by folk who relay a message from the Roman captain: "Lord, I am not worthy," he insists, "but say the word and my 'boy' will be healed." We catch onto what he means by "say the word" when we hear him speak of his own authority to command: When I say "go," they go. Then Jesus turns to a crowd (which has appeared out of nowhere) and says in effect, "This is faith, and I haven't seen it in Israel." The passage concludes with a postscript reporting that the centurion's slave is now a picture of health.

Now, how does the preacher proceed? Usually he approaches the passage as if it were objectively there, a static construct from which he may get some*thing* to preach on. Either he will grab one of the verses: "Say the word," "I am not worthy," "he loves our nation, and he built us our synagogue," treating the verse as a topic, or he will distill some general theme from the passage; for example, "the intercession of friends," "the compassion of Jesus," "an example of humility." Notice, in either case the preacher treats the passage as if it were a still-life picture in which some*thing* may be found, object-like, to preach on. What has been ignored? The composition of the "picture," the narrative structure, the movement of the story, the whole question of what in fact the *passage* may want to preach. Above all, notice that the passage has been treated as a stopped, objective picture from which something may be taken out to preach on!

Suppose we venture a different sort of exercise. Let us propose questions that a preacher might ask of a passage, questions that may yield different results and that may indirectly suggest a different way of "biblical preaching."

1. What Is the Form? Obviously form tends to orient consciousness; it predetermines expectation. So, for example, if we begin a story, "Once upon a time there was a lady who lived in a house that seemed spun of gold . . . ," listeners will expect a fairy tale. On the other hand, if we start, "Did ya hear the one about the farmer's daughter . . . ," listeners will brace for a dirty joke. Notice! In each case not only is expectation formed but response may be anticipated; I will get ready to respond as I ought to a vulgar story. Of course, the listener may be crossed up (as is often the case in the New Testament). The story of the farmer's daughter could turn into a plea for agrarian reform, or what started as a fairy tale could continue, "and her name was Hilda Glockenspiel and she lived at 2400 Grand Concourse, Bronx, N.Y." But, at the outset, let's notice that form, particularly in an oral culture, can orient consciousness, can predispose a hermeneutic.

So, at first glance, our preacher will see that Luke 7:2-10 is a "miracle story." More, he may realize that miracle stories were designed to evoke a "wow!" from listeners. The wise preacher will guess that a turgid apologetic for miracles or, worse, any rational explanation of miracles may scuttle the sense of "wow" and, therefore, be homiletically inappropriate. If a passage wants to provoke amazement, it would seem homiletically respectful to aim at the effect.

2. What Is the Plot, Structure, or Shape? While passages may be distinguished by form, every form will have a particular structural design. So looking at Luke 7, we may exclaim "miracle," but still note that the story involves a sequence of episodes, designed dialogue, and so on.

With narrative material, we are pointing to an aged distinction between "story" and "plot," or perhaps as may be the case in Scripture between plot and "hi*story.*" For what we bump into in Scripture is not history but plots, systems of structured telling, sequences of juxtaposed episodes that can be analyzed with literary categories—time, space, character, point of view. The distinction between plot and history may provide a way out of the undue preoccupation with historicity that has deformed both exegesis and preaching for too many decades. While there may well be historical bases for biblical narratives (surely Jesus did heal), historical questions are secondary to the material at hand, which is, of course, plots. In Luke 7:2-10 we have a plotted story, and a preacher can quickly demark episodes: Jesus with the elders; Jesus and the centurion's friends; Jesus and the crowd. Plot can be distinguished, interactions of episodes noted, and the "logic" of the system considered. Of course, non-narrative material may also be plotted, insofar as all language involves structured speaking, a sequence of ideas, or images logically designed.

3. What Is the "Field of Concern?" "Field of Concern" is a clumsy term for a crucial matter. Biblical writers are often working with sources. In writing, they look at their source material through some sort of hermeneutic lens. As a result, pericopes have in them a hidden perspective, a lurking field of concern. To seize an example, Isaiah 56:3-8 deals with an exclusion of eunuchs and aliens from the temple. YHWH objects: "My house will be called a house of prayer for all nations." Now if a preacher approaches the passage asking, "What in the passage parallels my congregation's experience?" one may end chattering about homosexuals and unbelievers in the church. (The question of parallels is almost always fatal!) On the other hand, suppose our preacher seeks a field of concern in the passage: He may then happen on the broader issue of exclusiveness and inclusiveness among God's people and, as a result, reach for rather different examples than are found in the passage itself.

4. What Is the "Logic" of Movement? Earlier we noticed that the historical-critical method and rational homiletics view passages as "still-lifes," static systems from which some*thing* may be taken out to preach on. Now, let's admit that passages in their episodic sections are more like film-clips from motion pictures: passages display movement of thought, event, or image. No wonder they so resist distillation!

Preachers can learn to ask, "By what kind of 'logic' does the passage move? What logic orders its plotted language, its sequence of event, its lively conversational give-and-take?" "Logic of movement" is tricky, for it involves a subject matter, an author's perspective and purpose, as well as an "implied reader."

5. What Is the "Addressed World?" Parable scholars of late have been pushing the idea that parables may speak to "world constructs" that live in the minds of listeners. So, the parable of the workers and hours (Matt. 20:1-15) seems to presume that listeners have bought into a "just" Deuteronomic world in which meritorious labors are rewarded by a record-keeping God; whereas the similitude of the mustard seed may address a mentality that anticipates the salvation of the pagans through Israel's triumph. To cite a non-narrative passage, Romans 12:1-8 may counter a lust for spiritual worship with the earthy word *body*—"offer your bodies." When a speaker speaks or a writer writes, he has some notion of the mind-set of his audience, some reading of the audience's "world."

6. What Is the Passage Trying to Do? Is it possible that all biblical language is intentional, that it is performative? In the ancient world, spoken language was employed in more sophisticated ways than in our crumbling linear culture. First-century folk grasped language like a tool, choosing form and style and structure to shape purpose. Thus, biblical language is language designed to function in consciousness. Now we are not suggesting that we can probe passages for authorial intent. What we do suppose is that passages may be analyzed as to how they may have operated in the consciousness of an audience. We can ask, "What is the *language* trying to do?" So, for example, the little parable in Luke 17:7-10 sets up its hearers in a position of mastery, "Will anyone of you who has a servant . . . ," only to flip them into slavery by the last line, "We are unworthy servants. . . ."

Speaking of Scripture

Preaching should be a speaking *of* Scripture and not *about* Scripture. Referential language—"In today's gospel lesson . . . ," "In our text, we see that . . . ,"—can be avoided: We need never talk about a text ("then") and draw application ("now"). On the other hand, we cannot tumble back into the immediacy of Scripture, preaching a dramatic monologue or uninterpreted story (the "I, Nicodemus" type of sermon), hoping for subjective effect. Sermons should be designed to locate as action in hermeneutic consciousness where language and the images of human experience meet. If there are passages that cannot be preached without launched expeditions into historical background or lengthy critical excurses, they may not belong in the homiletic "canon" (not all Scripture may want to be preached!). If preaching is Word of God as Reformers insisted, we cannot preach about tests as if they were objects of rational inquiry.

Preaching should favor mobile structures, foregoing fixed topics and categorical development. What we encounter in Scripture is movement of thoughts or event or image by some "logic." So sermon structures ought to travel through congregational consciousness as a series of immediate thoughts, sequentially designed and imaged with technical skill as to assemble informing faith. While sermon structure will be plotted much as narrative, moving episodically (or by some other logic) and displaying various "points-of-view," sermons need not follow the sequence of a particular passage slavishly. Likewise, a sermon need not be bound by biblical form: The *how* and *why* of form is more important than the form itself. In other words, to preach a biblical narrative we do not need to adopt a story form. Clearly, a sermon on Luke 7 could be designed as a conversation moving about in the field of theological concern with only slight reference to the text; or it could move as a story in which theological implications keep opening up to consciousness. In preaching, deep structures and performative purposes take precedence over form.

Certainly, a preacher must seek to discern an implicit field of concern. The odd idea that preachers can move from text to sermon without recourse to theology by some exegetical magic or a leap of homiletic imagination is obvious nonsense. Theo-*logic* is required to understand the "whys" of episodic juxtaposition in plot, is required for a reading of deep structures, and is surely required if we wish to grasp the depth of implication in a field of concern. Moreover, if exegesis involves some translation of biblical imagery into theological meaning, homiletics involves a reverse procedure, namely, the retranslation of theological understandings into designed, imagistic language. A preacher must be poet, exegete, and theologian simply because sermon structures must be shaped so that the language of preaching "plays" in a theological field of concern.

The idea of an "addressed world" is tricky. Is there something perennial about the "worlds" which the gospel addresses because "structures of the life-world," as social constructs, are inevitably sinstruck? Clearly, a contemporary world in consciousness will be different from a first-century world because human consciousness *is* historical. If

a sermon is to work, will the preacher not have to evoke a world for it to address? In preaching the parable of the works and hours, must we not buy into a world where justice demands fair pay for righteous works before we can be jolted by the boss's harsh "Take your pay and go!" And can we be shaken by the centurion's "I am not worthy," until we have admired his virtues to the point of exclaiming, "Now that is what I call right living!"? The notion of an addressed world can determine homiletic strategy.

The crucial matter for homiletic theory is the idea of performative purpose. The question "What is the language doing?" may translate into a craftsman's query, "What must my sermon seek to do?" Homileticians always think strategy, for they attempt to form understandings by the movement of language in consciousness. True "biblical preaching" will want to be faithful not only to a message, but to an *intention*. The question "What is the passage trying to do?" may well mark the beginning of homiletical obedience. Sermons can no longer be a weekly leap into a "stock" pattern (three points and a poem, revisited), because every text may intend differently, require different designing, and beg to fulfill different purposes. Presumably a sermon on parable will function differently in consciousness than one on a doxological poem; a controversy-pronouncement sermon will move differently than one on mythy stories from Genesis. But sermons built as moving modules of language *can* function variously and be open to various intentional strategies.

David G. Buttrick[35]

287 ✦ PREACHING THROUGH THE LECTIONARY

Preaching through a series of given passages goes back to the Jewish tradition and to the tradition of the early church. In Christianity, the readings of the lectionary are ordered by the Christian year.

Definition. The word *lectionary* is based on the Latin word *lectus,* which means "read." From *lectus,* English speaking people have derived such words as *lectern,* a stand behind which one gives a lecture. A lectionary is simply an organized schedule of Scripture readings for use in Sunday worship.

The Hebrews organized their readings for worship in this way, and the early Christians, following the Jews' lead, organized Scripture for Sunday readings in a similar manner.

The Common Lectionary. In modern times, various denominations have developed their own lectionaries. In 1983, however, a *Common Lectionary,* the product of a number of denominations, was created for trial use, and in 1988 the accepted *Common Lectionary* was released. The *Revised Common Lectionary,* the fruit of research and reactions to the original, was completed in 1992 and released in 1993.

The structure of the *Common Lectionary* is very simple: (1) Scripture is organized into a three-year cycle of biblical readings (known as Years A, B, C); and (2) each set of Sunday readings has an Old Testament lesson, an Epistle, a Gospel, and a psalm.

Benefits. Many Protestant preachers who preach through various themes, develop series of messages, or preach through books of the Bible find lectionary preaching to be of value for the following reasons: First, the lectionary provides an opportunity to present the drama of salvation in keeping with the great festivals and seasons of the church year, namely, Advent, Christmas, Epiphany, Lent, Holy Week, Easter, and Pentecost. The cycle of themes offered by the lectionary has the added benefit of providing a yearly review of the whole of the Christian faith and life, and prevents a narrow focus on a single element of the faith.

Second, the lectionary provides opportunities to preach through books of Scripture, especially in the nonfestive seasons of ordinary time. Ordinary time occurs twice in the Christian calendar: first between Epiphany and Ash Wednesday and then between Pentecost and Advent. The lectionary organizes a considerable amount of biblical resources to help the pastor in developing sermon notes and themes for every Sunday.

Third, lectionary preaching organizes an effective way for the ministers of music and the arts to plan ahead for worship.

Finally, lectionary preaching establishes a sense of unity with the whole church. Consequently, pastors from different traditions within a particular town or area have developed weekly study groups where common preparation for sermons and worship can take place.

Robert E. Webber

288 • PREACHING *LECTIO CONTINUA*

Preaching through a biblical book, also known as lectio continua *(Latin, meaning to read continuously) is presented here from the Reformed perspective as a viable option to preaching through the lectionary or preaching topical sermons.*

The History of *Lectio Continua*. Almost five hundred years ago in the city of Zurich, Ulrich Zwingli, inspired by the preaching of early church fathers Augustine and John Chrysostom, preached through the Gospel of Matthew. Reformer John Calvin enthusiastically adopted Zwingli's *lectio continua* approach to preaching. During his long ministry in Geneva, Calvin followed this ancient liturgical practice, preaching through most of the Bible. After eighteen years of using the *lectio continua* method of preaching, I am confident that this approach has as much value for our congregations as it had for the congregations of Calvin and Zwingli. I'm also convinced, however, that it is important for the twentieth-century pastor to carefully adapt this Reformed tradition to today's culture.

Fewer Sermons. In the first place, I preach through a book of the Bible (or a major section of a book) in fewer sermons than most Reformers did. I rarely preach more than a dozen sermons on a book in a series.

It is important to remember that, because the Reformers often preached daily, they were able to accomplish in a month what might take today's minister a half year to complete. For today's congregation, a series of twenty-five sermons on a book like 1 Peter, for example—a series Calvin might have preached—is too much. It becomes the preacher's job to interpret the book, outlining its major divisions and themes, and then to decide which of those themes are most appropriate to the needs of the congregation. One congregation might benefit most from sermons on the more theological concerns of the first chapter of 1 Peter, while another might appreciate emphasis on the more practical moral concerns in the remaining chapters.

The first time I preached through 1 Peter, the congregation I was addressing had been long accustomed to a strong emphasis on Christian ethics and had little understanding of the basic affirmations of the faith. I therefore dwelt at greater length on the themes of saving faith in 1 Peter 1:3-9, the Christian hope in 1 Peter 1:13-21, the new birth in 1 Peter 1:22–2:3, and the spiritual worship of the royal priesthood in 1 Peter 2:4-10. In contrast, I covered 1 Peter 2:11–3:12, the long passage on rules for the Christian household, in a single sermon.

If I had been preaching to another congregation, my focus might have been altogether different. For example, I might have preached separate sermons on the Christian's duty to civil authority (1 Pet. 2:13-17), working for hard masters (1 Pet. 2:18-25), and husbands and wives as heirs to the grace of life (1 Pet. 3:1-7).

Planning sermons according to the _lectio continua_ approach, then, does not imply being insensitive to the needs of the congregation or plodding through a book three to six verses at a time without ever looking at the book as a whole. The approach has often been misused in this way, to be sure, but does not have to be. In fact, one of the greatest advantages of _lectio continua_ preaching is that it recognizes that there is more than one way of dividing the Word of Truth.

Organizing the Year. Christmas, Easter, and Pentecost are poles around which I organize my preaching. Since Reformed tradition emphasizes Christian feasts rather than liturgical seasons, I often do a short _lectio continua_ series for these feasts. For example, I have done four sermons on the nativity narrative in Matthew at Christmas and a series of six sermons on the servant songs of Isaiah at Easter. The use of the _lectio continua_ approach, then, does not mean one has to neglect the evangelical feasts.

In the course of a year I try to treat many different types of biblical literature. I always try to do a major series on a Gospel, a major series on another New Testament book, and a major series on an Old Testament book.

I have never been so bold as to try to preach through a whole Gospel in a single series. Instead I usually focus on a section of a Gospel—such as the ministry of Jesus in the Gospel of John, the Sermon on the Mount in Matthew, or the passion narrative in Luke. Also, I try not to let the Pauline Epistles overshadow the rest of the New Testament. Certainly one of the most positive discoveries of contemporary biblical research is the rich diversity in the various strands of biblical literature. All of the books have distinct messages that need to be heard.

One of the strengths of Reformed Christianity is its appreciation of the Old Testament. A minister needs to give much attention to the various genres of Old Testament literature. The insights of the historical books, the Prophets, and poetry all need to be explored.

Organizing a series on one of these books can be difficult. For example, how does one do a _lectio continua_ series on Jeremiah with its fifty-two chapters? Again, selection is essential to interpretation. With the aid of John Bright's commentary on Jeremiah, I selected the ten most important passages in the book—that is, the passages I thought had the most significance for my congregation, the most vivid and preachable chapters in the book.

I usually treat the historical books through personalities. I have done a major series on the Abraham cycle in Genesis and another on the David cycle in 1 and 2 Samuel. One time I did a short series of five sermons on Elijah. However, I've occasionally departed from this pattern. For example, after discovering Brevard Child's commentary on Exodus, I preached one whole summer on the Christian interpretation of that book.

Discipline and Adventure. For me _lectio continua_ preaching has been both a scholarly discipline and a spiritual adventure. It is the secret behind my enthusiasm for preaching.

Hughes Oliphant Old[36]

289 • Preaching That Involves the Congregation

Preachers can prepare their sermons with respect to the needs of their people by engaging a representative group of people in conversation on Sunday's text. Guidelines for group preparation and feedback are outlined below.

Method. A number of churches are offering Bible study on the texts their pastors intend to use in future sermons. Beginning ten days prior to the preaching of the sermon, the group meets to study the text. The preacher either leads the study or participates in the group, asking a layperson to lead. He or she listens closely to the questions and issues that

The Anchor. *The anchor is one of the oldest symbols of Jesus Christ, originating in the days of the catacombs. The imagery is borrowed from Hebrews 6:19: "We have this hope as an anchor for the soul, firm and secure." The anchor in the figure also represents the cross and is presented as a symbol of hope in many of the earliest Christian burial monuments.*

emerge from the group's discussion of the text. The minister listens for ideas and attitudes that will influence the development of the passage into a sermon. The preacher avoids explaining to the group the way he or she intends to treat the passage. The preacher is there to learn from the group, not to hint at a plan he or she has already developed for preparing the sermon.

In addition to congregational study of selected texts prior to the sermon's preparation, a sermon response group may also prove helpful. Members of this group should be chosen from a broad spectrum of the congregation and should meet at regular intervals—whether monthly, bimonthly, or quarterly—usually for about thirty minutes after the church service.

The pastor does not attend the sermon feedback discussion but instead asks that it be taped for him

or her. A lay leader can enable the group to move through the process in the time allotted. Michael Williams, in his helpful book *Preaching Peers* (Discipleship Resources, 1987), suggests the following questions for the listening group to discuss: (1) What words, images, or ideas in the sermon had meaning to you? (2) Was there a clear relationship between the Scripture text and the sermon? (3) Did the sermon and the rest of the worship service tie together? (4) Was the sermon consistent with the person you have experienced the preacher to be? (5) Did the sermon's delivery support or detract from its content? (6) What was the word of God for you in the sermon?

Using the Lectionary. The study groups and listening groups are especially fitting for lectionary preaching, since the lectionary leads the congregation through the church year. For example, the study of Advent texts prepares the group both for the sermon and for the general celebration of Advent. If study group members use material based on the lectionary in their church school classes, this enriches their teaching as well as their listening to the sermon.

When the preacher and congregation follow the lectionary, they move together through the seasons of the church year, preparing for and celebrating the central events of the Christian faith. This is a learning opportunity for all ages as the congregation reflects on the two great cycles of salvation: Advent—Christmas—Epiphany and Lent—Easter—Pentecost. The congregation may want to learn more about the origin of these celebrations, and about ways to make them more meaningful today. Developed by Hoyt Hickman and other leaders in the contemporary liturgical movement, the *Handbook of the Christian Year* (Nashville: Abingdon Press, 1986) is a comprehensive guide to an ecumenical series of services for the renewal and deepening of worship. The book offers background, services for Sundays and special days, and texts and pastoral commentary. It can help each congregation develop its own traditions and unique ways of celebrating the various seasons of the Christian year.

The lectionary gives a focus and discipline both to preaching and to the church's life. Unchanneled energy is easily dissipated, but energy channeled through the lectionary can enable Christians to relate their faith to the world in which they live, to relate preaching, worship, and the seasons of the church year, and more effectively to anticipate and celebrate the festivals of the Christian year.

Perry H. Biddle, Jr.[37]

290 • DEVELOPING THE ART OF STORYTELLING

Storytelling is an art that needs to be developed in today's churches. Storytellers succeed through using dialogue, developing action and plot, opening up the imagination, and learning how to tell the story well. The following entry is one pastor's account of the transforming power of story in his own preaching. Its original title, "Spinning Yarns," suggests the necessity of retaining the first-person perspective because the best stories are our stories—stories told from personal experience.

Spinning Yarns

Throughout his conquests, Alexander the Great read the _Iliad,_ a book that kindles martial zeal. He often placed his copy, annotated by Aristotle, under his pillow at night alongside his dagger. It's not stretching it to say this one story's effect on Alexander may have changed the course of history.

I confess I had been preaching for years before I realized that well-told stories wield this kind of power, that they can actually change people's lives. I happened onto that realization the hard way. My college degree was in accounting, and I've always felt at home with facts, analysis, and principles— the abstract and conceptual. I would have been embarrassed to simply _tell_ a Bible story in a sermon; that was for children. I thought adults needed a quick summary of the story followed by cogent lessons from it.

But then I became pastor of an inner-city church in Chicago. I began to notice my sermons had less impact than in my previous location, a college town. I wasn't shirking on preparation. I painstakingly studied and outlined each text. But my people too often had blank looks. So I set a goal to learn how to communicate to my people, none of whom were college graduates, and a few of whom couldn't read.

Other inner-city pastors emphasized oratory and delivery, so I bought a book on classical rhetoric and tried becoming a flame thrower. Blank looks became surprised looks.

Then I read _Triumphs of the Imagination,_ by Leland Ryken, which discusses the nature and value of fiction. Frankly, I hadn't read fiction in eight years. But Ryken argued that a story has power—in itself. Hearing one, we enter the experience of others, feel what they feel, learn firsthand.

So I tried recounting Bible stories in my sermons, accenting dialogue, building suspense. I began woodenly, then loosened up and found I actually enjoyed telling the stories. Best of all, my people now had interested looks. They were enjoying the stories, too.

Since then I've read many more books on storytelling and fiction writing. I've found the same principles these yarn spinners use to make characters appealing and to heighten suspense have aided my preaching.

Characterization

People love people. Many magazines exist solely because of this fact. We are inspired by others' accomplishments. We are curious about their secrets. We are attracted by their virtues and repelled by their flaws. For good or ill, we are never neutral about people.

Fiction writers know that, and they labor to create characters that will bond with the readers' interests. If we care about their character, we will keep reading their book.

God has filled his Book with fascinating people: Joab, a no-holds-barred pragmatist; Abigail, an unflappable crisis manager; Jonadab, a crafty schemer; or Jonathan, the greatest friend someone could have.

In order to spotlight characters in a Bible story or modern-day illustration, I must come to know them. Fiction writers spend days imagining their characters' habits, emotions, weaknesses, abilities, ambitions, and fears. As I prepare to tell a story, I take the time to ask myself, _Were these people extraverts or introverts? What was their relationship to God? Were they assertive or passive, impetuous or controlled, can-do or defeatist?_ Because people are complex, that sort of thinking takes time. But if I don't do it, I end up with cardboard figures that are indistinguishable from each other and boring.

One way to bring biblical characters alive in my mind is to find contemporary parallels. Recently Jeroboam took off his sandals and put on black wing tips for me. Here is the consummate one-minute manager, high on the list of corporate headhunters. He is ousted from management only to return to claim the presidential suite. Yet he compromises principles and loses out with God.

Another way to ensure the characters in my sermons are vital is to concentrate on the universal elements of their personalities: ambition, loss, romance, unfulfilled desires, success, stress, and so on. Last year I preached an expository series through the life of David, and I wrestled with the text where David feigns insanity. Then I spotted the common denominator—when facing a crisis, David was resourceful. The text sprang open.

I have also found that Bible characters are more interesting if I portray their possible thoughts and motivations. My listeners know the complexity of their own inner lives. They identify with the Bible character when they discover his or her personal struggles.

For example, I imagined Sarah's reaction when the Lord promised Abraham, "I will surely return to you about this time next year, and Sarah your wife will have a son," something like this:

"Sarah was speechless. Then came a sudden association, a memory sadly pushed to the back of her mind years ago: God had promised they would have offspring as numerous as the stars of the sky. She had never known what to think of that. And now, at this word from these strangers, she did think, *"After I am worn out and my master is old, will I now have this pleasure?"*

It's easy to slide into the rut of characterizing by adjectives only. Though adjectives are useful, especially when time is short, fiction writers use many means to make each person in the story vivid and memorable.

- *Dialogue.* We get to know others by overhearing what they say.
- *Actions.* Play-by-play is perhaps the easiest way to inject life into a sermon.
- *Thoughts.* "As water reflects a face, so a man's heart reflects the man" (Prov. 27:19).
- *What other characters say.* One person brings the best out of our character; another the worst. Together they give the whole picture, like a statue viewed from different angles.
- *Description of appearance.* We discern much about others just by looking at them.

Dialogue

Of those methods for enlivening a character, dialogue is perhaps the most powerful. Some fiction writers advise that dialogue should make up one-third of the novel.

Some of the most memorable words in the Bible come from dialogue. What preacher would want to do without Moses' answer to God at the burning bush: "O Lord, please send someone else to do it"? or Abraham's words to a curious Isaac as they climb a mountain of Moriah: "God himself will provide the lamb for the burnt offering, my son"?

I have found using dialogue in my sermon stories helps in several ways.

Dialogue Invites Immediacy. It beckons the listener to eavesdrop on each conversation. The storyteller gathers the listeners and the characters into the same room by using direct quotation rather than indirect. If I quote only indirectly, I put myself between the listeners and the scene: "Jesus then told Nicodemus that unless a man is born again . . ." However, when I quote directly, I let the character do the talking: "I tell you the truth, unless a man is born again . . ." A subtle change, but a noticeable improvement in immediacy.

Dialogue Heightens Emotion. Which has more drama: to say, "Elijah sat down under the broom tree and felt depressed," or "Elijah sat down under the broom tree and said, 'I have had enough, Lord. Take my life; I am no better than my ancestors'"?

Dialogue Reveals the Person. We learn much about Naomi through these few words: "Don't call me Naomi. Call me Mara, because the Almighty has made my life very bitter. I went away full, but the Lord has brought me back empty." In a sermon I could say, "Naomi had been through great hardship and felt self-pity and bitterness," but her own words reflect that truth much more powerfully.

Because my listeners intuitively gauge the character from his or her words, I am particularly careful how I paraphrase and deliver a Bible character's dialogue. Slang and regional accents can add humor and contemporaneity, but they can also mislead or distract when used indiscriminately.

Action and Plot

When we recount a Bible story in a message, we obviously do not write the plot, nor do we alter it. The same thing applies to illustrations from books, news events, or our own lives. But learning what makes for a good plot has attuned me to the crescendos and decrescendos of a story. I want to be like the pianist who interprets a song more sensitively because of his or her grasp of music theory and composition.

When I was a teenager, I bought a classical music album entitled *Fireworks,* a marrow-throbbing collection of zeniths from various pieces. We owned other classical music, but I got every last spark out of *Fireworks.* My tastes have matured; I now enjoy the quiet and subtle movements as much as the grand finales.

My storytelling has followed a similar path. At first I told stories like one long finale, trumpets blaring from beginning to end. But I've grown more sensitive to downs and ups. Now I reserve my highest intensity for the climax.

The key to understanding a story's plot, and where the climax falls, is identifying the conflict. Whenever I prepare to tell a story, I consider: What problems is this person trying to solve? What adversity is there to overcome?

I had told the story of Isaac's birth many times before I recognized and developed one of the subsidiary conflicts: Would Sarah ever laugh again? Would her life ever take on joy? This problem isn't verbalized until the end of the story. At the birth of Isaac, Sarah says, "God has brought me laughter, and everyone who hears about this will laugh with me." I decided to tell Sarah's story, basing it on the problem of her lack of joy.

Since conflict sparks interest, I usually begin my story with it. Normally I don't launch the story with an eloquent description of a person, landscape, or background events; I unload that cargo as the plot progresses. With Sarah's story, I had to establish from the start her lack of laughter, unstated in Genesis until the end. I imagined her reaction to someone else's celebration:

"A new mother giggled with her family and friends. Sarah smiled too, but she couldn't laugh; she hadn't really laughed in years. She was glad for the mother, but it was a hollow gladness and a Mona Lisa smile. Would Sarah ever laugh again?"

Sometimes, feeling pressure from the clock, I rush the beginning of the story to get to the climax and make my point. Taking time to establish the person's struggle is difficult for me, a get-to-the-point person. But by slighting the conflict, I defuse the climax, leaving myself with an emotional dud.

For example, the parting of the Red Sea is a moving climax, but only if you've been through Pharaoh's repeated refusals and the ominous charge of the Egyptian cavalry. So when I told the story during a series in Exodus, I didn't skip a single plague. The greater the struggles, the more powerful the victory.

Sensory Description

The doorways into the imagination are the five senses. By appealing to the senses, the storyteller takes the listener by the hand and leads him across the threshold into the scene. Notice how the following sensory-filled introduction involves you in Joseph's experience.

"Joseph's head pounded as he looked at the crowd of buyers and wondered, *Which one will be my master?* He wanted to get off his feet, blistered by the desert trek. Raucous, foreign tongues filled his ears, but he longed for the voice of Jacob."

During my sermon preparation I close my eyes, place myself in the scene, and use my imagination. What do I see? What do I hear? What do I touch, smell, taste? When I put myself into Elijah's place at the ravine of Kerith where he was fed by ravens, the brook didn't just run dry. Stones hurt the back of my cupped hands as I pressed them into the riverbed for the trickling water. In the message I won't use all these perceptions, just enough to satisfy a healthy imagination.

Of the five senses, sight is the most influential. Storytellers are like film makers, who search for meaningful, emotive images: David twirling his sling; Abraham lifting a knife over his son; Adam hiding in the bushes from God.

Lengthy descriptions slow a story, so whenever possible I embroider description with action. For instance, instead of saying, "Goliath's sword was heavy," I would say, "David strained to raise Goliath's sword over his head."

When we taste, touch, sniff, observe, and listen, we tell the story freshly even to those who have heard the story ninety-nine times before.

Delivery

Rushing a story is like gulping down a Sunday dinner. It takes time to set the mood, to expressively speak the dialogue. Our listeners will not get emotionally involved in thirty seconds, nor can we build suspense in that time. We need pauses . . . silence.

There are occasions to speak rapidly, to increase the sense of fast action. But in general, a hurried story says, "Just get the facts." A slower pace says, "Feel this; live this." I used to balk at spending a large amount of time on a story, because I wanted to get to the point. Now I realize the story gets the point across better than my factual, declarative statements.

By trial and error I've developed a storytelling style that works for me. I write out the story in my own words, then read as little as possible, because when eye contact is broken, the mood evaporates. And I tell the story without pausing for principles or application. I want people to experience the story itself in a powerful way first.

Telling a story well requires extra preparation, and when a story is long or I don't manage time well during the week, I read more during the sermon. And I've faced those dreaded moments in which I am a few feet from the pulpit, with solid eye contact, and can't remember what's next. But those blunders are forgotten when a story hits home.

Surprises

As I increased the amount of storytelling in my preaching, I didn't have to jettison principles and propositions. But instead of the traditional format of ideas, then illustrations, I first tell the story or paint the image, proceeding from known to unknown, concrete to abstract. This gives the listener a solid box for storing sometimes wispy principles.

Recently I preached on how we often push God to the side during the week and live for our own pursuits. But I began by telling of King Ahaz, who was charmed by a pagan altar he saw in Damascus and then carved a copy in Jerusalem. He took the liberty of moving the furniture in God's house, sliding his new altar into the center and the bronze altar to the side. Ahaz instructed the priests to sacrifice on his altar. At God's altar he would seek divine guidance.

Only then did I raise the question, "Aren't we like Ahaz if we devote time, energy, and thoughts to personal ambitions but seek God only when we can't pay the bills?" Weeks later a member confessed, "Pastor, that story showed me exactly what I was doing."

A second surprise to come out of my increased yarn spinning is that Bible stories have become my main resource for illustrations. The Bible is packed with stories—adventures, mysteries, romances. It has heroes, villains, suspense. I never had enough illustrations before. Now I'll often use Bible stories to open windows on a subject.

Through these stories, Bible events and characters are becoming symbols for my people, things by which they interpret their lives. Recently Mary told me, "I used to complain a lot: 'Why do I have to go shopping today?' 'I hate to clean the bathroom.' But when you preached on the desert wanderings, and I saw the Israelites grumbling all the time, I just couldn't complain any more. And if I catch myself complaining, it hurts me inside because I don't want to be like them."

As I tell stories, I am affected as deeply as the listeners. Some time ago I sat with my boys at bedtime reading the story of David and Goliath from a children's book. I came to David's famous line: "All those gathered here will know that it is not by sword or spear that the Lord saves; for the battle is the Lord's, and he will give all of you into our hands."

For the rest of the story I fought back tears . . . just reading a children's book.

I'm not given to tears, but pastoring in Chicago, toe to toe with Goliath, I identified deeply with David. Suddenly I was ready to fight again.

Craig Brian Larson[38]

291 ◆ JEWISH STORYTELLING

Christian storytelling is rooted in the ancient Jewish tradition of telling stories. In telling the story, its reality and power are made present to the hearers, so that by entering into the story they experience its significance and power to shape their perspectives and the living out of their own stories of faith.

The Old Testament Background of Jewish Storytelling

Jews have always loved a good story. The Old Testament itself embraces hundreds of stories of every kind, and, almost without exception, they are told well. Plots are carefully worked out, there are surprises and clever turns, there is a relish for description and for fine points of psychology and motivation.

The story of stories was the Exodus, Yahweh's liberation of Israel from Egypt. Many books of the Old Testament (and the New Testament, for that matter) recount or allude to this central event in Israel's constitution and self-understanding. The rescue from Egypt and the crossing of the Sea was the great saving act of God that made Israel a people. It was an event through which all subsequent acts of Yahweh would be understood and reflected on, and it would affect Israel's own response to God as his covenanted people.

The story of the Exodus and what Israel's response to such salvation should be was to be repeated from generation to generation with loving fidelity. No detail of the story was to be lost. "Only be careful, and watch yourselves closely so that you do not forget the things your eyes have seen or let them slip from your heart as long as you live. Teach them to your children and to their children after them" (Deut. 4:9). "In the future, when your son asks you, 'What is the meaning of the stipulations, decrees and laws the LORD our God has commanded you?' tell him: 'We were slaves of Pharaoh in Egypt, but the LORD brought us out of Egypt with a mighty hand. Before our eyes the LORD sent miraculous signs and wonders—great and terrible—upon Egypt and Pharaoh and his whole household'" (Deut. 6:20-22).

The Role of *Anamnesis:* The Remembered Story

Deuteronomy: A Biblical Paradigm of the Remembered Story. This retelling of the story constitutes one feature of *anamnesis* (Hebrew: *zikkaron,* "remembering"). There are many elements to *anamnesis.* The Exodus was not conceived of as only a past event. It was somehow an everlasting event that continued to operate in Israel's history, and each succeeding generation was called on to "witness" for itself this event as a living reality.

The book of Deuteronomy is the best Old Testament example of this reality. In an atmosphere of growing despair, the Deuteronomist preached reform and renewal to the people. The book says, in effect, that the covenant made in Sinai with Yahweh after the passage through the Sea never really took hold, that the promises of the covenant had not been fulfilled by Israel. Instead of asking the people to return to remembrance of the Exodus and to the fidelity that should have sprung from that experience of Yahweh, the author brings his hearers directly into the events themselves, saying that it is now happening in their midst, and that they must respond to an activity of God that is present, not past. The Deuteronomist takes his listeners up Mount Nebo in Moab, on the border of Canaan, side by side with Moses, looking down into the Promised Land and demanding a response.

The words he puts into the mouth of Moses are not necessarily meant to record Moses' preaching to the Hebrews of old. They are his own preaching to these people about their own lives, and he means to strike a response deep in their hearts to stories that he and his people really believed were the words of Moses. When the Deuteronomist has Moses speak to his people about being eyewitnesses to the Exodus, he also means for the people of his own time to see themselves as eyewitnesses of, and participants in, this saving event, since for him the redeeming power of Yahweh in the Exodus remains a present and urgent reality (Deut. 11:2-5, 7).

Present and Future Reality of the Remembered Story. Part of *anamnesis,* then, is not just a recollection of the past, but a drawing of past events into the present as still effective. As Johannes Betz puts it, *"Anamnesis* [in the biblical sense] means not only the subjective representation of something in the consciousness as an act of the remembering mind. It is also the objective effectiveness and presence of one reality in another, especially the effectiveness and presence of the salvific actions of God" ("Eucharist I," *Sacramentum Mundi* [New York: Herder & Herder, 1968], 2:264).

One sees something similar in Joshua 24. When Joshua meets the Hebrews in Shechem who had not been in captivity in Egypt, nor experienced the Exodus as Joshua and his people had, he draws them into the covenant by making them acknowledge that the Exodus is an event for them, too—not just a thing of the past that they must accept as part of their own history, but an ongoing event that they now profess to, and witness in, their own lives. They become, by free choice, the *dramatis personae* of the constitutive saving act whereby Israel draws its being as a people. "Far be it from us to forsake the LORD to serve other gods! It was the LORD our God himself who brought us and our fathers up out of Egypt, from that land of slavery, and performed those great signs before our eyes" (Josh. 24:16-17).

This pulling up of the past into the present takes on greater definition in Isaiah 40 and the following chapters. While bringing the people the message of consolation that there will be restoration after the terrible experience of the Exile, the author tells the people that they must not think about the Exodus as merely a remembrance of the past. No, they must realize that the power and reality of the Exodus is still present and working in their midst and is forging their restoration. The coming restoration is but an extension of the Exodus itself. "This is what the LORD says—he who made a way through the sea, a path through the mighty waters, who drew out the chariots and horses, the army and reinforcements together, and they lay there, never to rise again, extinguished, snuffed out like a wick: 'Forget the former things; do not dwell on the past. See, I am doing a new thing! Now it springs up; do you not perceive it? I am making a way in the desert and streams in the wasteland'" (Isa. 43:16-19). He is not telling the exiles to forget the Exodus—he is urging them to see the Exodus as still working in their present. Indeed, he goes on to describe the return and restoration precisely in terms appropriate to the Exodus.

The Incarnation of the Remembered Story. There is one final aspect of biblical *anamnesis,* the reenactment of the event, a bringing of the past into the present, not just in memory but also in ritual, a sort of reincarnating of the event in symbol—or better, allowing the event to continue its incarnation forward in space and time. "You shall observe this as a perpetual ordinance for yourselves and your descendants. Thus, you must observe this rite when you have entered the land that the Lord will give you as he promised. When your children ask you, 'What does this rite of yours mean?' you shall reply, 'This is the Passover sacrifice of the Lord [Yahweh], who passed over the houses of the Israelites in Egypt; when he struck down the Egyptians, he spared our houses'" (Exod. 12:24-26, NAB).

This ritual reenactment of the Exodus was gradually built on an earlier agricultural festival, which was then given a new meaning—the idea of "transignification," which is used in contemporary eucharistic theology. This ancient feast was called the *pesach* in Hebrew and originally, apparently, was an ancient celebration that marked the spring yeaning, or birthing, and in which a lamb was killed as a sacrificial act.

This ritual was taken over as a structure to celebrate all events of the Exodus, and the individual rites were modified and given new meaning such that their original meaning was lost from consciousness, and they became symbolic reenactments of different facets of the great story. They were made into an *anamnesis* of the Exodus. The word *pesach,* which seems to have meant "leaping" and which possibly referred to a liturgical dance, now was given the meaning of "leaping over," the "passing

over" by Yahweh of the houses of the Hebrews when he visited the firstborn of the Egyptians with death.

The killing of the lamb no longer was a yeaning sacrifice, but a symbolic substitution for the firstborn of the Hebrews, who were spared. Similar embodiments of the Exodus story were attached to the ancient symbols of the unleavened bread—"there was no time to make leavened bread in the flight from Egypt"—the bitter herbs, the wine, etc. Anyone familiar with the contemporary Passover service will instantly recall the questions "Why is this night different from every other night" and "The unleavened bread which we eat, what is its reason?"

The Passover service is called the *Haggadah,* "the prayerful recital," or the *Seder,* "the ritual order." The ritual is an *anamnesis, a zikkaron*. It involves not just a recital of a past event, the Exodus, but brings it into the present, symbolized through liturgical reenactment. We read in the *Haggadah,* "In each and every generation, it is a man's duty to regard himself as though he himself went forth out of Egypt. . . . Wherefore we thank him who performed all these miraculous deeds for our fathers, but also for us. He brought us forth out of bondage." At the raisings of the second cup, this is recited: "Blessed are you, Lord God, king of the universe, who redeemed us and redeemed our fathers from Egypt, and enabled us to reach this night whereupon to eat unleavened bread and bitter herbs."

Thus the saving will of God, prototypically incarnated in the Exodus, reached into the present day as an ongoing saving reality. What is more, it will reach into the future: "So also, God of our fathers, may you enable us to reach holidays and celebrations to come, when we partake again of the Passover offerings."

The Exodus reaches upward in history and expands its effect by further realizations in changing circumstances—the restoration after exile, the rebuilding of the cities in the Promised Land, liberation in any struggle or darkness. These are all the Exodus at work in the midst of Israel. By ritual reenactment of the event and by remembrance of it, the partakers of the Passover feast celebrate the continuance of Yahweh's saving grace.

Jesus' Use of *Anamnesis*/Remembered Story. In the New Testament, Jesus' passage from death to life in his passion and resurrection are not only frequently described by means of Old Testament paschal typology, they are explicitly called an exodus. In the Transfiguration scene, Moses and Elijah appeared in glory and spoke of [Jesus'] exodus, which he was about to fulfill in Jerusalem (see Luke 9:31). In the Last Supper, Jesus, of course, celebrates precisely the Passover service with the disciples. One by one he takes up the elements of the exodus-*anamnesis* and proclaims that his approaching passion, death, and resurrection are the renewed exodus, just as the return from exile was for Isaiah. As the earlier Hebrews transfigured an earlier rite, now Jesus takes the exodus-*anamnesis* and makes it his own story. The tale is not of what has happened; it is the story of what is now happening. He himself is the paschal lamb that is killed so that others might live. The wine is no longer the sign of the sprinkled blood to seal the Sinai covenant; it is his own blood in a new covenant.

This thanksgiving of *Haggadah,* or Eucharist, becomes for the covenanted people formed by Jesus' death and resurrection the celebration of the exodus from Egypt precisely as this grace from the Father was at work in Jesus, leading from bondage to freedom. But as the Jews celebrated the Exodus as a continuing event in their own time, so Christians celebrate the passion and death of Jesus not as a past reality, but as the Passover of Jesus, as a present reality, extending from Jesus to the believer through the power of Jesus' Spirit. Those who partake of this paschal banquet celebrate Jesus' exodus from death to life as working in their own lives, and they proclaim his death until he comes again in glory. They confess that it will reach its fulfillment even in the future when they sit with the Lord at the heavenly banquet.

William Fulco[39]

292 ✦ SEEKER-CENTERED PREACHING

Seeker-centered preaching is directed to people who have had little or no contact with the Christian faith. Ideas are presented in a way that the secular mind can grasp, using language and concepts from everyday life.

Speaking to the Secular Mind. Driving home from church the other day, I pulled behind a guy on his Harley-Davidson. I noticed a bumper sticker on the rear fender of his motorcycle, so I pulled closer. It read: SCREW GUILT.

After the shock wore off, I was struck by how different his world was from the one I'd just left—and even from the world a generation ago. *In my day, we felt guilty,* I thought. *Now, it's not only "I don't feel guilty," but "Screw guilt."* I find that unchurched people today, the ones we are called to reach, are increasingly secular.

There was a time when a person's word was a guarantee, when marriage was permanent, when ethics were assumed. Not so very long ago, heaven and hell were unquestioned, and caring for the poor was an obvious part of what it meant to be a decent person. Conspicuous consumption was frowned upon because it was conspicuous. The label "self-centered" was to be avoided at all costs, because it said something horrendous about your character.

The Need for a New Approach in Preaching. Today, all of that has changed. Not only is it different, but people can hardly remember what the former days were like.

We need a new approach. Many churches, however, still operate with the understanding that non-Christians are going to come through the doors, feel pretty much at home, understand the sovereignty of God and the redemptive work of Jesus Christ, and in one morning make a complete transition from a secular worldview.

Even twenty years ago, that was a reasonable hope. The secular world view wasn't that disconnected from God's agenda. A guy would hear the claims of Christ and say, "Well, that makes sense. I know I'm a sinner," or "I know I shouldn't drink so much," or "I really should be faithful to my wife."

Today, even though we're asking for the same thing—a commitment to Christ—in the perception of the secular person, we are asking for far more. The implications of becoming a Christian today are not just sobering; they're staggering.

Recently I preached on telling the truth, and afterward a man came up and said, "You don't understand what you're saying."

"What don't I understand?" I asked him.

"You're just up there doing what pastors are supposed to do—talk about truth. But my job requires my violating about five of the sins you just talked about. It's part of the job description; I can't be 'on the level' and keep the position. You're not asking me merely to adopt some value system; you're asking me to give up my salary and abandon my career."

As I was reminded that day, we preachers have our work cut out for us. The topics we choose, the way we present Scripture, the illustrations we use, the responses we ask for, all need to contribute to our goal of effectively presenting Christ to non-Christians.

For the past thirteen years, we've geared our ministry at Willow Creek to reach non-Christians. During that time I've learned a lot, sometimes the hard way, about what kind of preaching attracts them, keeps them coming back, and most important, leads them to take the momentous step of following Jesus Christ. Let me share some of those principles.

Developing Sensitivity to the Secular Mind. If we are going to speak with integrity to secular men and women, we need to work through two critical areas before we step into the pulpit.

The first is to understand the way they think. For most of us pastors, though, that is a challenge. The majority of my colleagues went to a Bible school or Christian college and on to seminary, and have worked in the church ever since. As a result, most have never been close friends with a non-Christian. They want to make their preaching connect with unchurched people, but they have never been close enough to them to gain an intimate understanding of how their minds work.

If we're serious about reaching the non-Christian, most of us are going to have to take some giant steps. I have suggested for many years that our pastors at Willow Creek find authentic interest areas in their lives—tennis, golf, jogging, sailing, mechanical work, whatever—and pursue these in a totally secular realm. Instead of joining a church league softball team, why not join a park district team? Instead of working out in the church gym, shoot baskets at the YMCA. On vacation, don't go to a Bible conference but to a state park, where the guy in the next campsite is going to bring over his six-pack and sit at your picnic table.

When I bring this up with fellow ministers, I often sense resistance. It cuts against everything we feel comfortable doing. And yet not knowing how non-Christians think undercuts our attempts to reach them. If we're going to stand on Sunday and accurately say, "Some of you may be questioning what I've just said. I can understand that because just this week I talked with someone about it," then on the Tuesday before we've got to drive to the Y and lift weights and run with non-Christians. We can't win them if we don't know how they think, and we

can't know how they think if we don't ever enter their world.

The second prerequisite to effective preaching to non-Christians is to *like them.* If we don't, it's going to bleed through our preaching. Listen closely to sermons on the radio or on television, and often you'll hear remarks about "those worldly secular people." Unintentionally, these speakers distance themselves from the non-Christian listener; it's us against them. I find myself wondering whether these preachers are convinced that lost people matter to God. It's not a merciful, "Let's tell them we love them," but a ticked off, "They're going to get what's coming to them." These preachers forfeit the opportunity to speak to non-Christians, because the unchurched person immediately senses, *They don't like me.*

What helps many pastors genuinely like non-Christians is the gift of evangelism. When you have that spiritual gift, it's easier for you to have a heart for non-Christians. Not every pastor claims evangelism as a gift. But I've seen many develop a heartfelt compassion for non-Christians by focusing on their needs. That takes away any intimidation they might feel around non-Christians, and it frees the pastor to minister.

When I was in youth ministry in the early seventies, kids wore their emotions on their sleeve. They'd come up crying, or mad, but I could readily recognize their need. When I started ministering to suburban adults, everybody was smooth. Everyone dressed nicely and had a nice-looking spouse, two nice-looking kids, a nice car, a nice home. I thought, *What do these people need church for? Everybody's getting along fine.*

The longer I worked with them, though, the more I realized, *These people have gaping holes in their lives. That pretty wife hasn't slept with her husband in three months. Those kids, if you could ever get close to them, are so mad at their dad they'd fill your ears. That home is mortgaged to the hilt, and that job that looks so sweet isn't all that secure. That guy who looks so confident is scared stiff inside.*

The appearance of sufficiency is a thin veneer, and underneath is a boatload of need that we, as pastors and teachers, are equipped and called to address in the power of the Holy Spirit. As we learn the way non-Christians think and as we develop a genuine love for them, we can speak the words of Christ in a way they will hear.

The Importance of the Sermon Title. Unchurched people today are the ultimate consumers. We may not like it, but for every sermon we preach, they're asking, "Am I interested in that subject or not?" If they aren't, it doesn't matter how effective our delivery is; their minds will check out.

Five years ago the book _Real Men Don't Eat Quiche_ came out, and immediately sales took off. Everyone was talking about it. As I was thinking about the amazing success of that book, I decided to preach a series entitled, "What Makes a Man a Man? What Makes a Woman a Woman?" Unchurched people heard the titles, and they came; attendance climbed 20 percent in just four weeks. The elders were saying, "This is incredible!"

When the series ended, I began one titled, "A Portrait of Jesus." We lost most of those newcomers. Interestingly, the elders said to me after that series, "Bill, those messages on the person and work of Christ related to unchurched people as well as any messages we've heard." In this case, the problem wasn't the content; the people who needed to hear this series most didnt come because of the _title._

Since then, I've put everything I can into creating effective titles. I'm not particularly clever, so sometimes I'll work for hours on the title alone. I do it because I know nonchurched people won't come, or come back, unless they can say, "Now _that's_ something I want to hear about." The title can't be just cute or catchy; it has to touch a genuine need or interest.

Here are some series titles I've had good response to:

- "God Has Feelings, Too." People said, "What? God has emotions?" And they came to find out what and how he feels.
- "Turning Houses into Homes." When I announced the series (in church the week before it started), I said, "Our area is setting national records for housing starts. As you drive around and see one of the hundreds of houses going up, ask yourself, _What's going to turn this house into a home?_ That's what we're going to talk about in the next four weeks." I could have used a thousand other titles, but this one seemed to touch a nerve.
- "Telling the Truth to Each Other"
- "Fanning the Flames of Marriage"
- "Endangered Character Qualities"
- "Alternatives to Christianity"

I always begin a new series the Sundays after Christmas and Easter to try to bring back first-time visitors. Last Christmas Eve we announced, "A lot of people are saying, 'Christianity is the right way,' or 'The New Age Movement is the right way,' or 'Something else is the right way.' We're going to talk about the alternatives to Christianity, showcase the competition, and let you decide. We'll make an honest comparison, and if it's not honest, you tell us."

That was an A+ title, as long as we dealt fairly with the opposing points of view. I could have called the series "The Danger of the Cults" or "Why Christianity Is the Only Sensible Religion," but those titles would have attracted only people who were already convinced. From the very first words people hear about our message, we need to communicate, "This is for you. This is something you'll want to hear."

Sometimes people who haven't heard me preach misunderstand this and say, "Yeah, it's easy to attract people if you tiptoe around tough biblical issues and don't get prophetic on areas of discipleship." My experience, though, has been that you can be absolutely prophetic with unchurched people. We all should be like Paul when he said in Acts 20, "I didn't shrink back from giving you the whole counsel of God. I didn't shrink back in terms of the content or the intensity" (author's paraphrase). But to do that with any group, we need to preach in a way they can understand. We need to start where they are and then bring them along.

For example, we have a lot of people attend who can't conceive of a God who would ever punish anybody. That wouldn't be loving. They need to understand God's holiness. So I've used the old illustration, "If I backed into the door of your new car out in the parking lot after the service, and we went to court, and the judge said, 'That's no problem; Bill didn't mean it,' you'd be up in arms. You'd want justice.

"If you went to Wrigley Field, and the Cubs' best pitcher threw a strike down the middle of the plate, and the ump said, 'Ball four,' and walked in a run, you'd be out there killing the ump, because you want justice."

A person hears that and says, "I guess you're right. I wouldn't want a God who isn't just."

Then I can go on to say, "Now before you say, 'Rah, rah for a just God,' let me tell you some of the implications. That means he metes out justice to _you._" You can be utterly biblical in every way, but to reach non-Christians, every topic has to start *where they are* and then bring them to a fuller Christian understanding.

I've also found it helpful, as many pastors have, to preach messages in a series. With the non-Christian, you want to break the pattern of absenteeism. Over the course of the series, he or she gets in the habit of coming to church and says, "This isn't so bad; it only takes an hour." You're trying to show him or her that this is not a painful experience; it's educational and sometimes even a little inspirational. Sometimes it's convicting, but in a thought-provoking rather than heavy-handed way. Pretty soon, a guy says, "Why don't I come, bring my wife, and stop for brunch afterward?"

I've found I can't stretch a series longer than four or five weeks, though, before people start saying, "Is there anything else you're ever thinking about?" And obviously, if I'm going to talk about money or other highly sensitive issues, the series may run only two weeks.

Making the Bible Important to the Secular Mind. Unchurched people don't give the Bible a fraction of the weight we believers do. They look at it as an occasionally useful collection of helpful suggestions, something like the *Farmer's Almanac*. They tend to think, *The Bible has some neat things to say once in a while, but we all know it's not the kind of thing I'm going to change my life radically to obey.*

If we simply quote the Bible and say, "That settles it. Now obey that," they're going to say, "What? I'm supposed to rebuild my life on some book that's thousands of years old? I don't do that for any other respected literary work of antiquity." It just doesn't make sense to them.

So almost every time I preach, I'm trying to build up the reliability of Scripture and increase their respect for it. I do that by explaining the wisdom of God behind it. When you show them how reasonable God is, that captivates the secular mind.

Most of them have written off Christians as people who believe in floods and angels and strange miracles. My goal is to explain, in a reasonably intelligent fashion, some matters that touch their lives. I hope when they leave they'll say, "Maybe there *is* something to the Bible and to the Christian life."

Consider 2 Corinthians 6:14, the verse that instructs us, "Do not be yoked together with unbelievers." Some teachers speaking on that passage will say, "The implications are obvious: Don't marry

a nonbeliever. The Bible says it, and we need to obey it." For the already convinced person, who puts great value on the inspiration and infallibility of Scripture, that might be enough. I don't think most church people buy it as much as we hope they will, but let's say they give us the indication that they do.

The secular guy, on the other hand, sits there and thinks, *That is about the most stupid and discriminatory thing I have ever heard. Why should I refuse to marry someone I love simply because her religion is a little different?* So one Sunday morning, I started by saying, "I'm going to read to you the most disliked sentence in all of Scripture for single people who are anxious to get married." Then I read 2 Corinthians 6:14.

"This is that awful verse," I said, "in which, under the inspiration of the Holy Spirit, Paul cuts down the field from hundreds of thousands of marriageable candidates to really only a handful. And almost every single person I know, upon first hearing it, hates that verse. What I want to do is spend the next thirty minutes telling you why I think God would write such an outrageous prescription."

During the rest of that message, I tried to show, using logic and their own experience, that this command makes terrific sense. We were in a construction program at the time, so I used this illustration: "What if I went out to the construction site, and I found one contractor, with his fifteen workers, busily constructing our building from one set of plans, and then I went to the other side of the building, and here is another contractor building his part of the building from a totally different set of blueprints? There'd be total chaos."

"Friends," I continued, "what happens in a marriage when you've got a husband who says, 'I'm going to build this marriage on this blueprint,' and a wife who says, 'I'm going to build it on *this* blueprint'? They collide, and usually the strongest wins—for a time. But then there's destruction.

"God wants his children to build solid, permanent relationships and he knows it's going to take a single set of plans. In order to build a solid building or a sound marriage, you need one set of blueprints."

Over time, I want gradually to increase their respect for Scripture, so that some day they won't have to ask all the why questions but will be able to say to themselves, *Because it's in the Book, that's why.*

Contemporizing the Sermon. I've found that the unchurched person thinks most Christians, and especially pastors, are woefully out of touch with reality. _They don't have a clue as to what's going on in the world,_ he thinks. An unchurched person who ventures into a church assumes whatever is spoken will not be relevant to his life.

That's why I select 60 to 70 percent of my illustrations from current events. I read _Time, Newsweek, U.S. News & World Report, Forbes,_ and usually _Business Week._ Every day I read the _Chicago Tribune_ (_USA Today_ when I travel), watch at least two TV news programs, and listen to an all-news radio station when I'm in the car. Why? Because when I can use a contemporary illustration, I build credibility. The unchurched person says, "He's in the same world I'm in. He's aware that Sean Connery and Roger Moore no longer play 007. He's not talking about something years ago; he's talking about something I care about today."

I sometimes joke that one of my goals in ministry is to complete however many years God gives me without ever using a Spurgeon illustration. Non-Christians (even most Christians today) don't know who Spurgeon was. And once unchurched people find out, they wonder why I'm wasting my time with him. They think, _We've got missiles flying in the Persian Gulf, a teetering stock market, and political turmoil, and he's spending time reading some dead Englishman? If he's got the time to do that, he's not living in the same world I am._

The second thing an up-to-date illustration does is put me and the listener on an even footing. He heard the same news report I did; he saw the same show. When I quote Augustine, he feels like I'm not playing in the same ballpark. But when I say, "On 'Nightline' two nights ago, Ted Koppel was talking with . . ." the guy says to himself, _I saw that! I wonder if he felt the same way about that as I did,_ and he stays with me. An illustration from current events includes the non-Christian listener; it puts him on an equal footing with everyone else in the audience.

I learned this principle from studying the parables of Jesus. I noticed him saying things like, "You all heard about those eighteen people killed in Siloam when the tower fell on them . . ." (Luke 13:4, paraphrase). As I charted Jesus' parables, I saw quickly that these "illustrations" weren't quotes from rabbinic authorities but stories of things average people saw every day.

When people feel that somebody is in their world and has been real with them, that's powerful. That's why I'll continue to use illustrations that are current.

The Secular Mind Resists Demand. When people walk into church these days, often they're thinking they'll get the party line again: Pray more, love more, serve more, give more. _They just want something more out of me,_ they think. _I wonder what it'll be today that I'm not doing enough of._

It's easy for us pastors unintentionally to foster that understanding. One pastor asked me for help with his preaching, and we talked about what responses he was asking for. I suggested, "list the messages you've preached in the last year, and write either "pray more," "love more," "serve more," or "give more" next to any message where that was the main thrust of the sermon."

He came back and said, "Bill, one of those was the thrust of every single sermon last year." He recognized the implications. If every time my son comes into the living room, I say, "Do this more; do that more," pretty soon he won't want to come in the living room. But if he comes in knowing there is going to be some warmth, acceptance, a little humor, and encouragement, then on the occasions I need to say, "We've got to straighten out something here," he can receive that.

Often the goal of a message can be _Understand this reality about God_ or _Enjoy this thing God has done._ Recently my Wednesday night message was taken from Romans 12:3-8, a passage about using spiritual gifts. I could have pushed people to serve more, I suppose, but that evening I said, "This is the most serving church I have ever seen. You people are using spiritual gifts beautifully. What Paul is telling the church at Rome to get on the stick and do, you people have gotten on the stick and done." Then I gave fifteen or twenty illustrations of ways people in the church are serving selflessly, for God's glory.

I closed, "I want to say I respect you as a church. You're an unbelievable group of servants that God is pleased with. Let's stand for closing prayer." Parishioners are people, too, and sometimes people need to be commended for what they are doing already. In the case of the non-Christian, we may commend them for honestly considering the claims of Christ, for being willing to listen to what we have to say and not immediately writing it off.

With the unchurched, though, our primary goal has been determined for us: We want them to accept the lordship of Jesus Christ. Let me suggest two key principles in asking non-Christians for a commitment.

Give Them Freedom of Choice. I've been surprised to learn you really can challenge unchurched people as much as you would anybody else—as long as at the moment of truth you give them absolute freedom of choice. At the end of an evangelistic message, I often say something like: "You've got a choice to make. I'm not going to make it for you. I'm not going to tell you that you have to make it in the next thirty seconds. But eventually you've got to make some decisions about the things we've talked about. As for me and my house, it's been decided, and we're glad we've made the decision. But you need to make that decision as God leads you." I'm taking the ball and tossing it in their court. Then it's *theirs* to do something with.

During one message recently, I made a strong, biblical case for team leadership. At the end I said, "I know many of you own businesses and that you're accountable to nobody. I think from what we've read in the Scriptures today, you would be the primary beneficiaries of following God's plan of team leadership so your blind spots don't cause your downfall.

"But," I said, "it's your life; it's your business; it's your family; it's your future. I trust that over time you'll give this thought and make the right decision. As for me, I've got elders, I've got board members, I've got an accountability group. I feel glad I have a team to accomplish what God has called me to do. Let's stand for prayer."

When you give a person complete freedom of choice, he goes away saying, "Doggone it, I wish he would have laid a trip on me, because then I could have gotten mad at him and written off the whole thing. But now I have to deal with it." Rather than letting people get away, giving them freedom of choice urges them to make that choice.

Give Them Time to Make a Decision. Suppose a guy came into my office and said, "I have a Mercedes-Benz in the parking lot. I'll sell it to you for $500 if you write me a check in the next fifteen seconds." I wouldn't do it. By most counts, I'd be a fool not to buy a Mercedes-Benz for $500. But if you make me decide in fifteen seconds, I'd refuse because I haven't had enough time to check it out. I'd have some natural questions: Is there really one in the lot? Do you have title to it? Does it have a motor?

But on Sunday we're tempted to tell people who've been living for twenty, thirty, or forty years under a totally secular worldview, "You've got just a couple minutes at the end of this service to make a decision that's going to determine your eternity. It's going to change your life, and you might lose your job, but come on down." The non-Christian is thinking, *Whoa! This is a big decision, and I've been thinking about this for only twenty minutes.* When I ask today's non-Christians for a commitment, I'm trying to persuade them about something that's going to alter radically everything they are. They say things like, "You mean marriage is permanent? You gotta be kidding—like I have to reconcile with that witch? No way!" or "You mean I have to get serious about child rearing and not just hire somebody to do it?" Everywhere the non-Christian turns, he's finding that I'm asking for far more than he was first interested in. He senses a spiritual need—that's what brought him to church—but he's going to need a lot of time to consider the implications.

Most of the conversions that happen at Willow Creek come after people have attended the church for six months or more. The secular person has to attend consistently for half a year and have the person who brought him witness to him the whole time. He needs that much time simply to kick the tires, look at the interior, and check the title before he can finally say, "I'll buy it."

It's interesting: I get criticized for this as much as for anything else in my ministry. People protest, "Bill, you had them in the palm of your hand and you let them get away!"

I've heard this enough times that now I usually respond with some questions. "Do you think people heard the truth while they were here?" I ask.

"Yes, they heard the truth."

"Do you think the Holy Spirit is alive and well?"

"Of course I believe that."

"Do you think Bill Hybels ever saved anybody?"

They quickly say, "Oh, no, no."

I say, "I think we're okay then. If they heard the

truth, and the Holy Spirit is alive and active, God will continue to work in their lives, and Bill Hybels isn't the only way he can accomplish his will for them."

Having said that, however, there is a time to close the sale. Not all the time, but sometimes, people need to be challenged. And when I do challenge people, I challenge them hard. Periodically I'll say, "Some of you are on the outside looking in. You've been around here for a long time and have enough information. I'd like to ask you, what is it that's holding you back from repenting of your sins and trusting Christ right now? Sometimes a delay can be catastrophic. It's time to deal with this."

But—and this is critical—when I do that, I _always_ make a qualification for the people who aren't to that point. I'll say, "Now for many of you, this is your first time here or you've been here only a few weeks. You don't have enough answers yet, so I'm not talking to you. You're in an investigation phase, and that's legitimate and needs to go on until you have the kind of information the rest of the people I'm talking to have already attained."

Conclusion. Trying to reach non-Christians isn't easy, and it's not getting easier. But what keeps me preaching are the times when, after many months, I do get through.

Not long ago a man said to me, "I came to your church, and nobody knew what really was going on in my life because I had 'em all fooled. But I knew, and when you started saying that in spite of all my sin I still mattered to God, something clicked in me. I committed myself to Christ, and I tell you, I'm different. My son and I haven't been getting along at all, but I decided to take two weeks off and take him to a baseball camp out west. He started opening up to me while we were out there. Thanks for telling me about Jesus."

For a preacher, such a joy far surpasses the ongoing challenge.

Bill Hybels[40]

293 • LAY PREACHING

Although there were many lay preachers in the early church, their style of preaching quickly fell into disuse as the pulpit became dominated by the ordained clergy. The new code of the Canon Law of the Roman church now allows lay people

**The Agnus Dei and Banner of Victory.** Symbols of the Lamb of God are of ancient origin. Numerous examples are found on primitive burial monuments, in paintings, wood carvings, embroideries, illuminated manuscripts, stained glass and mosaics. This powerful symbol, which is rooted in Isaiah 53:7, John 1:29, and Revelation 5:12, tells the story of sin and the sacrifice of the Lamb of Calvary.

to preach once again under special circumstances. This article summarizes the value of lay preaching in the Roman Catholic Church.

The Restoration of Lay Preaching in the Roman Catholic Church

With the advent of the new Code of Canon Law, the prohibition against lay preaching in church has been lifted. Much of the groundwork for this welcoming of lay preaching (and it _is_ a welcoming, for the laity may be allowed to preach not only when it is necessary, but in those cases where it would be advantageous) was laid in the dioceses of West Germany in the 1970s. There, in virtue of a special rescript that the German bishops requested of Rome, lay preaching was permitted in church and at Mass.

In presenting their request for the approval of lay

preaching, the German bishops were careful not to base their arguments on the fact that the number of priests was diminishing, although that was certainly true. Instead, they argued that, in virtue of baptism, all Christians are called to give witness to their faith and that such witness has its place in church and in the liturgy.

Expectations. What are the expectations of lay preaching? What is hoped for? A fresh presentation of the Word of God is what one expects from lay preaching. Lay preachers, speaking out of their experience, can show how the Word intersects with and interprets those human realities that priests, by their training and life-style, simply cannot or, for the most part, do not know at first hand. For example, who can better speak of Advent expectation in terms of the fear and hope of Mary waiting for the birth of the one she was to call Jesus, than a mother who has herself waited for the birth of her child? Who can better speak of trust in the Lord's providence than those who know themselves to be poor and powerless in ways that few, if any, priests will ever experience?

Suggestions for Lay Preaching. Lay preaching can have a place in the church's liturgy. On occasion, lay people could be invited to preach in place of the homily; on other occasions their preaching might well be a part of the homily itself. For example, a eucharistic homily might be structured in such a way that a non-ordained preacher, a member of the liturgical assembly, could be invited to respond to a homily, indicating in an expanded and perhaps more detailed way how the Word of God can be translated into Christian witness. Or perhaps the pastor and a member of the community could jointly build a homily in such a way that the non-ordained preacher would describe some real human situation, analogous to the situation underlying the scriptural text, to which the homily could then be addressed as God's saving word. Such shared preaching might well emerge on occasion from the kind of homily preparation group described in the American Bishops' document on the Sunday homily, "Fulfilled in Your Hearing: The Homily in the Sunday Assembly," *United States Catholic Conference* (1982), 36–38.

The Basic Issue for Lay Preachers. However homilies are structured, by whomever preaching is done, the basic issue is always a hermeneutical one: Is the Word of God being heard as a word that speaks meaningfully to the community here and now? In order for that to happen, the preacher must be able to deal responsibly and intelligently with texts which, because of the ancient and foreign cultural setting in which they were composed, are not always immediately intelligible, or, even if intelligible, not always recognized as pertinent to the present. But while training in accurate exegesis is an essential part of the preacher's preparation, along with a knowledge of the church's tradition of interpreting the Scriptures, such training and knowledge are not sufficient for effective preaching. Equally as important is the preacher's knowledge of the real conditions and situations that make up the life of the people who will hear the Word preached. It is out of this area of knowledge especially that the lay preacher might well be able to bring new life to God's Word, a Word that creates a community of believers, called to worship their God in spirit and in truth.

William Skudlarek[41]

294 ◆ WOMEN AS PREACHERS

In recent years most denominations are facing the question of ordaining women to ministry. The following article explains the new dimensions female preachers bring to worship.

The Emerging Role of Women in Preaching

Throughout history, the role of preaching in Christian worship has been very important. Because Christians celebrate the Incarnation, the Word becoming flesh, Christian worship has stressed the value of preaching alongside important ritual action. Especially in Protestantism, worship has been dominated by the sermon.

In recent years, as more and more women are able to fulfill their calling to ministry through ordination and pastoral ministry, more and more women are preaching. What does this mean for worship and spirituality? If Christian worshipers are hearing the Word preached by women, how does this change worship? Will preaching change as more and more women do it?

For years, arguments were made that women

should not be ordained. For most Protestant churches this meant that women should not preach. People were warned, "beware of the petticoat in the pulpit." Yet, by the mid-nineteenth century a few women had overcome custom and were engaged in a preaching ministry. In 1859 Catherine Booth summarized the popular arguments against "female ministry": when women indulge in the ambition or vanity associated with preaching they become unfeminine; the Bible specifically instructs women to be silent in the churches; women cannot convey the Word as Christ did because he was a man; women have natural nurturing skills, but public speaking is not a natural gift; home and family will suffer if women are preachers (it was especially onerous to imagine a pregnant preacher); the credibility of the church will deteriorate without respectable male leadership; and finally, women lack the vocal power or stamina for public speaking. In spite of these arguments, women claimed the right to preach. Antoinette Brown was ordained as pastor of a small Congregational church in upstate New York in 1853. At her ordination, the preacher (a male) stated that the church did not gather to give her the right to preach the gospel; if she did not have that right already there was nothing they could do. The church was challenged to recognize her calling.

Since that time more and more ecclesiastical bodies have recognized the call of women to preach. Although sometimes this recognition has limited her audiences or regulated her relationship to sacramental leadership, the number of women preaching and the number of parishioners hearing the gospel preached by women has increased dramatically. In 1922, one woman wrote:

Some brethren are very fearful that women preachers will feminize the church, apparently unaware that the masculine monopoly of the pulpit has already done that. . . . But while feminizing the church, the brethren fear that the preacher herself will become masculine. This was shown to be the stock argument against every advance step women have taken. It had been said that education would destroy their fine nature; that the vote would make them unwomanly, etc. Woman have always worked; men have raised no cry lest scrubbing and washing would make them unfeminine; it is only the more desirable lines of work that cause the brethren to entertain lively fears lest woman lose her femininity. (Madeline Southard, _The Woman's Pulpit 1_ [1922], 3)

The Impact of Women in Preaching

Women knew that preaching was important. Today, as more and more women attend seminary, they are enrolling in preaching classes and preparing for positions that call on their gifts as preachers. By any standard they are good. But as more and more women preach, they are stretching the church's understanding of preaching and reshaping the nature of preaching itself.

First of all, women preachers remind us again that the sermon is a unique form of personal communication. It involves a complex mixture of message and person. The preacher not only "delivers" God's message, he or she embodies it. This emphasizes the incarnational presuppositions behind all preaching. Dogmatics are helpful, but the truest statement of God's love for the world was not dogma but Jesus Christ. Christians know that the gospel is best shared personally. This is why reading a sermon, or listening to a tape, or even watching a preacher on television is not the same as experiencing the preaching moment. When women preach they remind us that sharing the gospel requires men and women "preaching."

Second, if good preaching intentionally draws upon personal experience, when women preach, the worshiping community benefits from experiences never shared in quite the same way by male preachers. Most obviously, women preachers use their experience of pregnancy, birth, and mothering to enrich their sermons. Similarly, when Third World Christians preach out of their experiences with political and economic oppression, one discovers new things about his or her faith. All preaching that is done by persons whose life experiences are qualitatively different from those whose voices have been heard for many centuries has new power and strength. Old standards of excellence are shaken and new understandings of "good preaching" take their place.

Third, preaching is relational. The bond between preacher and pew is basic and quite personal. Throughout the centuries, the fact that the preacher was always male perpetuated certain relational patterns. Many of these patterns leaned upon existing social structures (family) and biological realities (sexuality). When a woman preaches, all of these habits are broken. This is why a woman preacher is sometimes so upsetting. She cannot be a "father." Her presence creates different sexual dynamics.

Men and women find it impossible to relate to the preacher in the same way. Century-old patterns of worship and spirituality no longer have the same effect.

Fourth, these changes lead to issues surrounding language. Modern linguistic study has documented that women use language differently than men. Women use more adjectives and adverbs, modifying nouns and verbs and qualifying statements. Women may handle nuances and subtleties of color and emotion more deftly in language. While a man may say "red" the woman may choose to speak of "crimson" or "burgundy." A man may make an authoritative statement where a woman may more often qualify her statement with tag questions, "Isn't that true?" or "Don't you think?" Some think this weakens women's language, conveying the feeling that she is not sure. In preaching, however, this less authoritative style could be a blessing. After all, to speak about God and salvation is an awesome thing. When the woman preacher shares her journey and vulnerability she may speak more directly to the needs of average believers.

Women have also become self-conscious about the use of masculine words to speak of human experience and to name or address God. In exploring biblical materials, women see the injustice and distortions that have resulted from the use of masculine language forms not warranted by the biblical text. These are not cosmetic problems, because language both reflects and shapes human understanding. Women preachers work self-consciously to be sure that theology shapes the language they use, rather than letting prevailing language usage shape their theology.

Finally, the relationship of preaching to all of worship and spirituality is changing as more women become preachers. In some ecclesiastical traditions preaching never played a strong role. Within most of American Protestantism, however, ordained ministry has been dominated by preaching. Churches still need and want good preaching. Women recognize the importance of preaching, but women are also more willing to accept the limits of preaching. Many women who have spent years in education, music, art, and service occupations come to preaching ready to experiment. The line between sermon, song, action and prayer gets blurred. It is possible to share the power of God's Word in many ways. Old assumptions about Word and sacrament change.

All of these factors point out that worship is fundamental to the Christian church. Before there was theology or ecclesiastical structure, there was worship. Women have always worshipped, but women have not always taken on the public authority of preacher and worship leader. (1) When women preach, the church is reminded that every sermon should embody the faith. Preaching needs to be incarnational. (2) When women preach, the church benefits from experiences that have rarely been available to preachers in the past. Preaching needs to draw upon all of human experience. (3) When women preach, the church remembers that sharing the gospel involves social and sexual realities. Preaching needs to understand human communities and relationships. (4) When women preach, the church discovers that language is never gender neutral. Preaching needs to use language with great care. (5) When women preach, the church explores the place of preaching in all worship. Preaching needs to appreciate the many ways in which God's people can and do worship.

Choices for Women Who Preach

Any discussion of women and preaching cannot end without a comment about authority. Women who feel a call to ministry in the church today are confronted with a choice. They can seek to win equity in the existing systems that give only men opportunities to preach. This usually means accepting some of the unexamined assumptions about leadership and preaching that exist in today's church. This certainly means doing enough, according to current expectations, to be acceptable. Many women are doing this and everyone agrees, "They are doing what men have done for years with great success."

On the other hand, some women want to preach "as women." Drawing upon their feminine experiences, they approach the preaching task with new sensitivities and assumptions. They use language differently. They incorporate dialogue and participation. They seek to preach through many forms of worship and spirituality. "They are doing what women have done for years, but no one called it preaching."

By existing and emerging standards, women as

preachers are adding new dimensions to worship and spirituality.

Barbara Brown Zikmund[42]

295 ◆ EVALUATING PREACHING

Those who preach and desire effectiveness through the ministry of preaching need a way to measure how well they are communicating. Below are ten tests for evaluating one's preaching.

The Need for Sermon Evaluation

Authentic preaching is responsible to its place in the total Christian community. It belongs not only to the preacher, but also to the congregation. It reflects the memory and expectation of the people of God in times past and in times present. It is rooted in the Word and standing in the world. True preaching steps onto the bridge between the mundane and the majestic, between mud and stars, and, recognizing the awesome mystery of the preached Word, dares to speak for God.

The quality of mystery referred to by Jesus regarding new birth also applies to preaching: "The wind blows wherever it pleases. You hear its sound, but you cannot tell where it comes from or where it is going. So it is with everyone born of the Spirit" (John 3:8). Because the vital center of preaching, that interaction between Word and congregation, is fraught with mystery, it cannot be wholly captured and defined by any sort of measurement. It is therefore important to recognize the limitations of our tests in evaluating preaching.

Ten Tests

Is the Sermon Faithful to the Biblical Witness? Some sermons that begin with a lesson, employ biblical language, and quote verses fail to recognize God in the Old Testament and God in Christ in the New Testament as the chief actor. Other sermons employ biblical words but neglect biblical meanings. Such sermons are not truly biblical. Again, there are sermons without any biblical text and that use little biblical language and yet remain centered on the memories and expectations of the people of God, who are central to the witness of Scriptures. They, despite neglecting the Bible as the common language of the church, may be biblically faithful.

Has the Scripture Passage Been Allowed to Speak Its Own Message? Because of the limitations of time and circumstances related to preaching, not every facet of a text and not every possible interpretation can be addressed. A preacher is necessarily selective. It is essential, therefore, that the first step in preparing a sermon involves listening to the text. The text must speak its own witness to the issue it chooses to address. The preacher cannot assume he or she has clearer understanding of life and truth than the text. The preacher must resist imposing his or her ideas on the text. It is not the preacher's responsibility to defend the text or to make it relevant. The preacher must let the text speak.

Does the Sermon Address Some Ultimate and Urgent Need? True preaching is not offered to satisfy the need for a sermon or simply to retell old truths. It addresses some contemporary issue and need. This need may be part of the fabric of the human situation in all generations. Such an issue should be critically important and real. The preacher should ask, "What concern or problem is addressed?" "Is it ultimately important?" "Can it be expressed in concrete realism?" Preaching that is authentic does not seem "long ago and far away," but wrestles with vital issues relevant to the first century and to the twentieth century.

Is the Sermon Thoughtful and Informed? Irrational and intellectually dishonest preaching is not true preaching. The preacher dares not avoid the tests of reason. Many sermons, ignoring the discipline of an intellectual pursuit and questioning of facts, offer sweeping generalities that claim too much. No preacher knows everything that experts know about any given subject, but the preacher's thoughts should be clearly reasonable and the sermon information correct. It may be summed up this way: the sermon must be accurate, but not academic; rational, yet more than rational.

Does the Sermon Encourage the Spontaneous Flight of Mood and Feeling? In every important conversation and encounter there is feeling. True preaching does not flee from emotion but recognizes the heat and power that may weld the Word into one's very life. While true religious experience does not depend on how one "feels" about it, there is yet inherent in it both joy and tears. True preaching is not only emotional, but gives attention to the counsel of the apostle Paul: "Rejoice with those who rejoice; mourn with those who mourn." Ask of the sermon,

"Is it emotional?" Then ask, "Is it only emotional?"

Does the Preacher Offer Anything of Himself or Herself? To be authentically present in communication is to offer one's own witness, and all witness involves risk. True preaching dares to say what the preacher has seen, heard, felt, and known. Such witness involves risk. It is safer, but poorer, to offer preaching that only reports the hearsay and common talk of others.

Does the Sermon Faithfully Present Both Judgment and Grace? Preaching often tends to be almost wholly negative and judgmental. It begins with a description of the ills of society and proceeds to catalogue the sins of the people. This scolding, carping criticism of the world and all that is in it (including the church) has little to do with authentic good news. When sermons only moralize, only criticize, only sound the "ain't it awful" complaints of a preacher, only suggest what "ought to be" and "ought not to be," there is no authentic saving word.

Moreover, when a disregard for all values and moral claims allows the preacher to offer easily and cheaply the gift of grace, true preaching does not occur. The preacher must test the message and ask, "Does it offer both the claim and the promise? Both judgment and mercy?"

Is the Preaching Forthright, Candid, and Bold? There is an authority and confidence in true preaching that does not say "perhaps," "maybe," "it seems," or such. There is no uncertain sound about true preaching. Preaching of the gospel is proclamation with clarity and candor. Therefore, the preacher takes counsel—chiefly with one's own beliefs, slowly with one's own doubts—and lets timidity be replaced by boldness. Carlyle Marney counsels preachers, "You're not asked to be right, you're asked to be forthright."

Is the Preached Word Caring, Responsive, and Faithfully Dialogical? The first responsibility of a preacher is to listen: to listen to the witness of Scripture and tradition, and to listen to what is being said and shouted, moaned, cried, sighed, and jeered in all the experiences of the men and women one is called to serve. After listening, the preacher may dare to speak but faces the requirement that the preaching be dialogical. This is not to suggest a "talk back" session after the sermon. It means being part of a lived-out conversation. The preacher does not simply hand out answers and make pronouncements from "up there" but, knowing that God is in the midst, strives for the meeting of meaning between Word and world. True preaching does not swing the authoritative club to bring the congregation into submission. The prophetic word, when spoken, is offered through tears and with caring.

Is the Sermon for All the People? Many sermons are so parochial and nearsighted that they fail to have the breadth of witness that addresses every man and every woman. They speak only to the interests and needs of the local and immediate situation. Preaching that tends to be a private affair is not authentic preaching. Recognizing that "God so loved the world" and that the great commission is to "go into all the world," true preaching finds its point of contact in a local and concrete situation and yet remains fully conscious of God's children everywhere.

The Lay Person's Tests of Good Preaching

In conclusion, the three tests that are most frequently listed by lay persons as their criteria for evaluating preaching are: (1) Does the preacher offer anything of himself or herself? (This usually is expressed in such terms as, "Is the preacher sincere? Does the preacher really believe what is being said?") (2) "Is it faithful to the Scriptures?" (3) Is it related to some real-life need or concern? These three criteria are not new (nor are the others), but they have continuing merit in setting the standards for true preaching.

John Bergland[43]

296 • THE SERMON PLANNER

This practical outline provides a step-by-step plan for creating sermons that add to the worship experience.

How To Use the Sermon Planner

The purpose of the sermon planner is to provide the preacher with a simple and effective way of building the sermon.

The sermon planner organizes the process of asking the most basic questions about the text and orders the way the preacher thinks about the persons to whom the sermon is delivered. Sermons grow. They start as the pastor prayerfully reads, studies, thinks, and meditates over the text and the needs of the people.

Consequently a purpose of the sermon planner is to stimulate the preacher to think about the right kinds of questions that will result in an effective sermon.

In addition a feature that makes the sermon planner so indispensable for the busy preacher is that it provides a handy and portable reference space where developing thoughts may be written down. With the sermon planner the preacher doesn't lose those flashes of insights or the special words, phrases, illustrations, and stories that come to mind here and there during the week.

Here is how to use the sermon planner:

Step 1: Preliminary Preparation.
Step 2: Understanding the Biblical Text.
Step 3: Understanding the Congregation.
Step 4: Forming the Sermon.
Step 5: A Summary Outline.

Step 1: Preliminary Preparation. The preliminary planning gets sermon building off to the right start as it provides space to jot down the essential data from which the sermon will develop. Here are the questions that order those preliminary steps to sermon preparation:

Date _____   Sunday _____

Season of the Christian Year _____

1. What are the texts for worship?

    Old Testament _____

    Psalms _____

    Epistle _____

    Gospel _____

2. What is the text/topic/theme of this sermon?

    _____

    _____

3. What is the occasion for this sermon?

    _____

    _____

4. What are some preliminary impressions about the text?

    _____

    _____

    _____

_____

_____

5. What are some preliminary observations about the felt needs of the people?

    _____

    _____

    _____

Step 2: Understanding the Biblical Text. In the second step a series of questions organizes the thought process by which the text begins to reside within the preacher and form the preacher's message:

1. What is the life or faith issue addressed by the text?

    _____

2. What is the message of this text?

    _____

    _____

3. What is the historical setting of this passage?

    _____

    _____

    _____

4. What words or phrases help clarify the meaning of the text?

    _____

    _____

    _____

5. How is the story or idea of this text developed?

    _____

    _____

    _____

6. What other Scriptures clarify, expand, or illustrate the message of this text?

    _____

    _____

    _____

7. What does this text say to me?

    _____

    _____

    _____

Step 3: Understanding the Congregation. In the third step, a series of questions are designed to help the preacher look at the text and the growing message from the perspective of the pew. These questions encourage the preacher to develop a message that meets the needs of the people.

1. What felt needs of the people does this text address?

    _____

    _____

    _____

    _____

2. What current media communications (newsprint, TV, video, theater) address these issues?

    _____

    _____

    _____

    _____

3. How do I in my life make connection with this text?

    _____

    _____

    _____

    _____

4. What comments, illustrations, or stories will build bridges between this text and the people?

    _____

    _____

    _____

    _____

Step 4: Forming the Sermon. In the fourth step, the sermon planner provides questions and space for the preacher to summarize the basic outline of the sermon.

1. How can I summarize this message in one sentence?

    _____

    _____

2. What do I want my people to take home?

    _____

    _____

3. How should I introduce this message?

    _____

    _____

    _____

4. How should I develop the body of this message (points, movement of the story, outline)?

    _____

    _____

    _____

    _____

    _____

    _____

    _____

    _____

    _____

    _____

    _____

5. How should I conclude this message?

    _____

    _____

    _____

    _____

Step 5: A Summary Outline. In the final section, a summary outline, space is provided for the preacher to outline the sermon in final or near final form. No outline is provided to follow, as the purpose of the sermon planner is to help the preacher with the process of sermon preparation, allowing the final outline to be shaped according to the particular style of the preacher.

Robert E. Webber

297 ◆ BIBLIOGRAPHY ON PREACHING RESOURCES

──── General Works on Preaching ────

Bond, D. Stephenson. *Interactive Preaching.* St. Louis: CBP Press, 1991. Bond posits a new kind of dialogic sermon that is a "transformative" psychological event and is defined as "any sermon that draws its text, its interpretation of Scripture, from the relational experience between the story of Scripture and the life context of the listener." Demonstrates communications-theory dynamics for grounding sermons and preparing congregations and gives numerous examples of four types of interactive preaching. Source: Christian Church (Disciples of Christ).

Buttrick, David. _Homiletic: Moves and Structures._ Philadelphia: Fortress Press, 1987. Critically acclaimed as one of the best contemporary sources on "homiletic design and procedure—the making of sermons." The encyclopedic work covers every area of the subject with depth and detail. Part I: Words, Moves, Framework, Images, and Language. Part II: Hermeneutics, Homiletics, Structures, and Theology. Great reading lists and bibliographies.

————. _Preaching Jesus Christ._ Philadelphia: Fortress Press, 1988. Buttrick offers a homiletic theology based on proclamation of the life, message, death, and resurrection of Jesus Christ. He discusses relevant problems regarding preaching and Christology, posits a homiletic Christology: story and image, and exhorts readers to consider afresh preaching and the [ever] presence of Christ.

Craddock, Fred B. _As One without Authority._ Nashville: Abingdon Press, 1971. The author analyzes the current malaise in preaching and insists that an inductive movement in preaching is necessary (moving from the particulars of experience to general truth), which is more in tune with the experience of moderns. His methodological proposal addresses preaching and imagination, inductive movement and the unity, text and structure of the sermon. A sample of the sermon process is offered, along with a sermon.

————. _Preaching._ Nashville: Abingdon Press, 1985. Craddock's comprehensive and practical "textbook" on the subject, written for seminarians and clergy, which summarizes a professor and preacher's homiletical, historical, theological, and hermeneutical insights for sermon preparation and preaching. The lessons start with silence, move to study, continue with shaping the message into a sermon, and conclude with speaking the message.

Davis, H. Grady. _Design for Preaching._ Philadelphia: Fortress Press, 1958. An unusual book that reports the "surprising variety of forms that turn up in sermonic design, and how each reflects and affects the content." Selected topics: Substance and Form, Anatomy of an Idea, Text as Source, Expanding Thought, Functional Forms (Proclamation, Teaching, and Therapy), Organic Forms, Continuity, Tense and Mode, Process in Interpre-

tation, Forms of Development, and Writing for the Ear.

Forbes, James. _The Holy Spirit and Preaching._ Nashville: Abingdon Press, 1989. Forbes embarks on an "ecumenical conversation on Holy Spirit renewal and the empowerment of preaching," reminding readers that "preaching is an event in which the living word of God is proclaimed in the [anointing, Pentecostal] power of the Holy Spirit." The author focuses on a recovery of the dynamic in preaching that makes it "more than mere religious discourse." Topics include: The Anointing of Jesus, Preaching and the Holy Spirit's Anointing, Sermon Preparation and Preaching, and Spiritual Formation of Anointed Preachers.

Gonzalez, Justo, and Catherine Gonzalez. _Liberation Preaching._ Nashville: Abingdon Press, 1980. The oppressed are given an articulate voice through the authors, who alert readers to the hidden elements of bondage that keep modern preachers from hearing the liberation themes in the Scriptures and preaching the same from the pulpit. The concept, dynamics, methods, and forms of liberation preaching are explained in order that the empowerment of the gospel might be more appreciated by the powerful and fully appropriated by the powerless.

Greidanus, Sidney. _The Modern Preacher and the Ancient Text._ Grand Rapids: Eerdmans, 1988. Hermeneutics and homiletics are considered equally in a scholarly and practical presentation of biblical (expository) preaching that demonstrates a firm grasp on contemporary issues in both fields via comprehensive discussion of relevant topics such as: literary, historical, and theological interpretation; textual and thematic preaching and the form and relevance of the sermon; and preaching Hebrew narratives, prophetic literature, the Gospels, and the Epistles.

Keck, Leander. _The Bible in Pulpit._ Nashville: Abingdon Press, 1978. The renewal of biblical preaching is the key to church renewal and will only come as preachers "impart a Bible-shaped word in a Bible-like way." Keck argues for the rediscovery of the validity and necessity of historical critical exegesis as the key to unlock the Scriptures, and tackles important matters of interpretation that arise as a result of his argument. Three sermons demonstrate Keck's assertions.

Killinger, John. _Fundamentals of Preaching._ Philadelphia: Fortress Press, 1985. A professor/preacher presents his view of preaching in a concise, easily read volume that begins with the tradition of preaching, importance of the Bible, and the personal dimension; continues with a "how-to" section on sermon construction, introduction, endings, illustrations, styles, and delivery; and concludes with chapters on homily variety, planning, titling, and the person behind the sermon. Basic and comprehensive.

Leuking, Dean. *Preaching: The Art of Connecting God and People.* Waco, Tex: Word, 1985. The focus of Leuking's book is the invaluable and often overlooked resource for preaching in people; in their communities, churches, experiences, narrative histories, and in the daily work of ministry. He wishes to expose the "quality of faith, hope and love in the whole range of relationships between preacher and people." Beginning with biblical narratives, the author writes a compelling argument for discovering this treasure trove of material and mining its riches.

Long, Thomas G. *Preaching and the Literary Forms of the Bible.* Philadelphia: Fortress Press, 1989. Psalms, proverbs, narratives, parables, and epistles are differing literary forms from which varieties of sermons ought to emerge. The author's vision is for preaching that accounts for these uniquenesses and conveys them to its audience through the sermon. A methodology is presented that enables the reader to account for the literary form and dynamics of the biblical passage in the text-to-sermon process.

_____. *The Senses of Preaching.* Atlanta: John Knox Press, 1988. Four sections outline a thoughtful and controversial volume in which Long uses anecdotes to expose and expound the "eyes" (vitality), "voice" (nature of sermonizing), "ears" (involvement of listening), and "embodiment" (liturgical context) of preaching. His goal is that preaching becomes a "one-to-one" relationship between proclaimer and each participant, and that preachers know the full dimension of responsibility before they "take the witness stand."

_____. *The Witness of Preaching.* Louisville: Westminster/John Knox Press, 1989. A seminal text in homiletic study. Theological vision and practical helps for sermon creation are comprehensive. Long takes the reader from the significance of preaching to biblical witness in and exegesis for

preaching; to the basic and refined forms of the sermon; and to techniques for openings, closings, connections, images, and experiences in the sermon. Everything from desk to pulpit, and sage advice along the way.

_____, and Neely Dixon McCarter, eds. *Preaching In and Out of Season.* Louisville: Westminster/John Knox Press, 1990. Nine prominent preachers offer helpful advice to pastors who preach from the church and civic calendars. Chapter topics include: race relations, family, work, church and state, global witness, evangelism, ecumenism, stewardship, and thanksgiving. Introductory notes and sermon starters are offered for each topic.

Lowry, Eugene L. *Doing Time in the Pulpit.* Nashville: Abingdon Press, 1985. The relationship between narrative and preaching. "A sermon is an ordered form of moving time," Lowry asserts in a book that advocates ordering experience rather than ideas, time rather than space. Preaching must give precedence to verbs over nouns. In preparation, texts must be freed from the "ruts" of exegetical scholarship, then consciously wrestled with, then given time—the work of experience, the unconscious, and the reflections of others—before being further prepared and delivered. Theoretically and practically helpful.

_____. *How to Preach a Parable.* Nashville: Abingdon Press, 1989. Designs for narrative sermons that use latest research in the style and function of Jesus' stories. Includes introductory material on recent biblical scholarship with reference to narrative. The bulk is a compilation of sample sermons by Craddock, Keck, Willis, and the author; followed by "running commentaries" and "Narrative Capabilities, Techniques and Norms" in a workshop-style format.

Maestri, William F. *Grace upon Grace.* Staten Island, N.Y.: Alba House, 1988. A large book of sermon topics and scriptural reflections as biblical, liturgical homilies for Sundays and Holy Days for cycles A, B, and C, with accompanying readings. Material is concise, sophisticated, and relevant, though brief. For both personal devotion and public use.

Robinson, Haddon W. *Biblical Preaching.* Grand Rapids: Baker, 1980. The "classic" source for the modern study of expository preaching, "the communication of a biblical concept, derived from and transmitted through a historical, grammatical, and literary study of a passage in its context, which the Holy Spirit first applies to the personality and experience of the preacher, then through him to the listeners." Robinson invites the reader on a step-by-step journey through his method of developing and delivering such sermons.

Robinson, Wayne B. _Journeys toward Narrative Preaching._ New York: Pilgrim Press, 1990. Sources such as R. Thulin, Lucy Rose, Robert Hughes, E. Lowry, Michael Williams, and the author combine to advocate the use of the narrative sermon. Starting with retelling biblical narratives, they discuss the parameters of narrative preaching, narrative as plot, narrative quality of experience as a bridge to preaching, parables as models for narrative preaching, and preaching as story telling.

Skudlarek, William. _The Word in Worship._ Nashville: Abingdon Press, 1981. Preaching in a liturgical year should be biblically centered and culturally relevant. The lectionary may be used without sacrificing the latter, Skudlarek contends. He devotes a section to argue that a service of the "Word" combines homily and Eucharist. Also included are notes on preaching at baptisms, weddings, and funerals. Source: Roman Catholic.

Smith, Herbert F. _Sunday Homilies._ Staten Island, N.Y.: Alba House, 1989. A series of short, solid homilies for use during cycle A years with appropriate readings listed. May be used by novice laity and seasoned clergy alike. Source: Roman Catholic.

Troeger, Thomas H. _Imagining a Sermon._ Nashville: Abingdon Press, 1990. Color, sight, sound, smell, and touch are sermon imperatives for Troeger, who wants preachers to learn new skills of observation and presentation in order to capture the imaginative (not fictitious) spirit with homiletic artists and create powerful homilies that seize the heart and set the mind ablaze. The stimulus is out there and the skills are available, he contends. Troeger offers a number of ways extant in the world around us that may be employed to create sermons for "the mass media generation" or with "electronic noodles."

Van Seters, Arthur, ed. _Preaching as a Social Act._ Nashville: Abingdon Press, 1988. Eight well-known contributors (J. and C. Gonzalez, D. Wardlaw, Edwina Hunter, W. Brueggemann, R. Allen, T. Troeger, and the author) argue the theological and numerous practical imperatives for preaching with a societal dimension—both in shape and influence. Appreciation and transcendence of social context is argued in respect to clergy, church, and the larger community. Other topics: the social nature of the biblical text; the social function of preaching; preaching as an interface of worlds; and the social power of myth.

Wagley, Laurence A. _Preaching with the Small Congregation._ Nashville: Abingdon Press, 1989. Wagley believes that small churches demand unique preaching styles. Participatory and biblical narrative preaching are offered as prime examples in a situation where sermons/homilies are central to the worship of the community. Descriptive analysis of the cultural milieu of the small parish is valuable and undergirds his insightful assertions.

Webber, Christopher. _The Art of the Homily._ Harrisburg, Pa.: Morehouse, 1992. The volume is replete with exegetical commentary on Scripture texts for special occasion readings and homilies. A great variety of texts is used that spans the entire Bible. Notes on the significance of homilies for each occasion preface individual sections on baptism, marriage, and burial. Homilies are concise and pithy.

Wilson, Paul Scott. _Imagination of the Heart._ Nashville: Abingdon Press, 1988. A new guide to contemporary preaching that draws together theoretical streams in theology, linguistics, and hermeneutics. It also takes a practical look at both contemporary innovations and the process of sermon preparation throughout the week. Wilson argues for a thorough understanding of techniques in order to express imagination, and draws from Jesus and "fine preachers" as source material.

Lectionary Resources

Bayler, Lavon. _Fresh Winds of the Spirit,_ for Year A. New York: Pilgrim Press, 1986. For public worship and personal devotion, this volume and its companions (see following entries) include complete service entries that may be used by novice and veteran, laity and clergy alike. The aesthetic quality of the work is refreshing: vivid imagery, fresh expression, and unusual honesty. The music feature is helpful—appendix of related hymns, 300 new hymn texts with tune meters, and hymn indices arranged alphabetically, topically, and metrically. Other indices include Scripture references, themes, and key words. Source: United Church of Christ.

_____. *Whispers of God,* for Year B. New York: Pilgrim Press, 1987.

_____. *Refreshing Rains of the Living Word,* for Year C. New York: Pilgrim Press, 1988.

Borsch, Frederick H. *Introducing the Lessons of the Church Year.* New York: Seabury Press, 1978. This volume is a guide for lay readers and congregations that contains introductory notes on introductions to texts, rationale for Scripture reading in church, a variety of suggestions for lectors, and hints at using the lectionary. Borsch then provides explanatory notes on each Sunday's readings that may be used as introductions or short commentaries on each passage. Source: Episcopal.

Burger, C. W., M. A. Muller, and D. J. Smit. *Sermon Guides for Preaching in Easter, Ascension and Pentecost.* Grand Rapids: Eerdmans, 1988. Sermon guidelines from the authors for subjects in the title for cycles A, B, and C. Each item divided into four parts: bibliographical, exegetical, hermeneutical, and homiletical. Introductory notes. Ecumenical.

Bushong, Ann Brooke. *A Guide to the Lectionary.* New York: Seabury, 1978. Originally developed for use in church school curriculum, the book is a unique guide to the lectionary in table form that provides a synopsis of lessons and psalms appointed for Sundays in cycles A, B, and C, as well as for Holy Days. Format: Hymn, First Lesson, [Gradual] Psalm, Second Lesson, [Alleluia] Chant, and Gospel Reading. List of optional hymns at book end. Source: Church Army.

Consultation on Common Texts. *Common Lectionary.* New York: The Church Hymnal Corporation, 1981. "Common text" lectionary for Sundays and special observances with helpful indices of Scripture readings and psalms, tables of readings and psalms, and titles of Sundays and special days, plus a section of explanatory notes for all years and special days. Source: Ecumenical.

_____. *The Revised Common Lectionary.* Nashville: Abingdon Press, 1992. Like the previous edition, based on the three-year Gospel cycle. Changes include many alternate selections that coincide with Roman Catholic, Episcopal, and Lutheran lectionaries, new arrangement and focus on readings from the prophets, psalter revision, revisions based on the findings of the editors of the NRSV Bible, more emphasis on the role of women in the biblical story, reconciliation of calendars, Old Testament lessons more closely related to the Gospel, and sensitivity to context of passages that may appear to foster anti-Semitism. Watch for a host of new guides to preaching and teaching from the revised lectionary.

Craddock, Fred, John H. Hayes, and Carl R. Holladay. *Preaching the New Common Lectionary,* for Year B, Advent, Christmas, and Epiphany. Nashville: Abingdon Press, 1984. Designed to "stretch" preachers beyond preferences and to areas of the canon into which they might not normally venture and provide movement with integrity while encouraging more disciplined study and advanced preparation, this volume and its companions (see following entries) provide textual "starters" in the form of exegetical notes on Scriptures used in the A, B, and C cycles. Notes are concise and "meaty." Source: Ecumenical.

Craddock, Fred, John H. Hayes, Carl R. Holladay, and Gene M. Tucker. *Preaching the New Common Lectionary,* for Year B, after Pentecost. Nashville: Abingdon Press, 1985. This and the following volumes add contributor Gene Tucker.

_____. *Preaching the New Common Lectionary,* for Year C, Lent, Holy Week, and Easter. Nashville: Abingdon Press, 1985.

_____. *Preaching the New Common Lectionary,* for Year C, after Pentecost. Nashville: Abingdon Press, 1986.

Johnson, Lawrence. *The Word and Eucharist Handbook.* San Jose, Calif.: Resource Publications, 1986. Consideration of the Eucharist/Communion in its historical, theological, and liturgical aspects. Volumes takes the reader/planner through the liturgy from preparation and introduction to concluding rites. Comprehensive, easy to read and follow. Bibliographies.

Lectionary for the Christian People, for Cycle C. New York: Pueblo, 1988. Complete lectionary for Lutheran, Roman, and Episcopal communions. RSV Texts. Emended for American English, inclusive language, and archaic forms omission.

Laughlin, Paul A. *Lectionary Worship Aids.* Lima, Ohio: C.S.S. Publishing, 1987. A variety of paragraphs, sentences, prayers, and calls based on Scripture readings for Year B. Each Sunday's offering has (1) the theme, (2) an exegetical note for each of the three readings, (3) a responsive call to worship, (4) a collect, and (5) a prayer of confession. The "exegetical note" replaces hymn suggestions, which may make the volume more accessible to a wider audience. Source: Methodist.

Proclaim the Word: The Lectionary for Mass. Washington D.C.: U.S. Catholic Conference, 1982. This short volume expounds a theology of the "word" as it is reflected in the Lectionary. It is a basic text with a study guide at the back. Roman Catholic.

Ramshaw, Gail. *Richer Fare.* New York: Pueblo, 1990. Reflections on the Sunday readings for years A, B, and C, based on the Roman, Episcopal, and Lutheran calendars. Each entry in the anthology is a quote from ecclesiastical figures or literature from the ancient to modern eras and offers insight on the scriptural themes that transcends context and reaches a broad audience.

PART FIVE

Resources for Planning and Leading Worship

❧ THIRTEEN ❧

Being a Worship Leader

The articles of this section recognize the importance of strong servant leadership and adequate planning for most services of worship. They focus first on the character and skills necessary for leadership in worship, with specific suggestions from various traditions. The final chapter on planning worship covers each of the major traditions. It also provides some general comments on planning in the context of the year, planning for continuity, and using a team approach to plan worship. The final entry is a useful form for planning. It may be reproduced and modified for your own specific situation.

The entries in this chapter discuss qualities a worship leader needs for success besides technical proficiency in such areas as music. The first entry discusses personal preparation for worship, preparations that should precede and have priority over even planning the service itself. The most important of these is spending time with God. The next entry discusses a number of keys to being an effective worship leader, focusing on such things as the worship leader's spiritual walk, relationships with others, and his or her understanding of the role and power of music. The chapter concludes with a discussion of the philosophy of worship and is meant to help leaders develop their own approach to worship.

298 • PERSONAL PREPARATION FOR WORSHIP

A constant enemy of worship leaders is busyness, for it takes them away from the all-important time spent with God. Other aspects of personal preparation for worship leading include knowing the needs of the congregation one serves; beginning preparations for services early in the week, if not weeks ahead of time (by choosing sermon themes far in advance); and seeking input from others.

Exactly how does a worship leader prepare to lead the congregation each week in worship? If my experience is typical, many leaders spend most of their time preparing the various elements of worship—such as the sermon or congregational prayer—and give little attention to preparing themselves for that majestic privilege of ushering people into the presence of God.

What strange creatures we are! We meticulously groom ourselves to meet some human dignitary but will waltz unthinkingly into the presence of the Almighty.

The Busy-Servant Syndrome. For me, the first step in personal preparation for worship is recognizing that worship is the highest and most important activity to which God calls me. More times than I care to admit, I have slid into my study, surveyed the piles of work on my desk, and thought about all the people I should visit that week and about the sermons I have to prepare for Sunday. In the press of all this busyness, I quickly open my Bible to skim a few verses and bow my head in a brief prayer so that as soon as possible I can get to the "real business" at hand.

When I find myself falling into that pattern, I remind myself of something that happened a few years ago—a homely incident with my son that helped me to realize that I was often neglecting the "real business." I was reading the paper one evening when our four-year-old son wriggled onto my lap. I looked down and asked, "What do you want, Jim?" "Nothing," he said, but then he snuggled closer to me. I realized then—in a rush of parental joy—that he just wanted to be with me.

Personal worship is simply "lap time" with God. God rejoices when I come to him daily to enjoy his presence. How awesome to realize that you and I are ingredients in divine happiness—that our daily fellowship brings God real pleasure!

So quiet time with God must be a top priority each day. I know this with my head but not always with my heart. I have had to learn and relearn this lesson repeatedly. As a pastor, I must read the Bible not just professionally but devotionally. When I am caught up in the "busy servant syndrome," it is much too easy to overlook my daily walk *with* the Lord in favor of doing things *for* him.

Doing versus Being. Living in the tension between *doing* and *being,* I am tempted to fall prey to artistic urges, forgetting that God calls me to *be* someone in relationship to him before I attempt to *do* anything for him. I cannot effectively lead people into the presence of God in corporate worship on Sunday unless I have been in God's presence during the week in private worship. So my first and basic preparation for worship is remembering that unless I am quiet before God, my outward journey to help the world will prove only to be frantic action without the proper spiritual undergirding.

My life is most meaningful when I deliberately center it in God, observing the daily disciplines of Bible-reading, prayer, and meditation. Only then can I face my task in God's strength rather than my own. Lap time with God is crucial.

Knowing My Congregation. Another part of personal preparation involves knowing the people I minister to. I can hardly expect to lead the members of my congregation effectively before God's throne of grace if I don't know what their experiences of God are. Where are they hurting? Are they seeking God's help in their suffering? What are their anxieties and their expectations? I must be in touch with people's needs. Surely my pastoral prayers and sermons will not be helpful if I am oblivious to what is troubling individuals. Though I am a senior pastor with primary responsibility in preaching and leadership/administration, I am assigned hospital and pastoral calls each week by our pastor of visitation. In a sense, every contact with members of the congregation during the week helps prepare me personally to lead them in worship on the Lord's Day. If I am worship leader as well as preacher for that day, I make a list during the week of special needs that should be included in the pastoral prayer.

Beginning Early. My strategy is to plan sermon titles and themes at least three months in advance, allowing room for change as special needs arise in the life of the worshiping community. However, I do most of my intense studying the week preceding the Lord's Day so that my preaching will be fresh and contemporary.

To avoid disaster on the weekend, I must get started in serious study early in the week. Usually I try to spend either Tuesday or Wednesday in the library, where I devote my time strictly to sermon preparation, uninterrupted by telephone calls or visitors.

I've discovered that disciplined time management is important; without it, other tasks and concerns quickly cut into study time. Of course, sometimes those can't be prevented. All ministers have weeks when unexpected emergencies consume time they intended to spend on worship preparation. When that happens, I just try to do my best with the hours I have left and leave the results to God.

During my earlier years of ministry, I frequently allowed legitimate but nonessential matters to rob me of precious hours of study time. But I soon discovered that panic praying on Sunday morning does not make up for the lack of careful preparation during the week. Such prayers are similar to that of the young boy who knelt by his bed asking, "Dear God, if I get an 'F' on my science test tomorrow, please make it stand for 'fantastic'!" Can we actually expect God to be impressed with emergency prayers offered against the backdrop of poor time management?

Allowing for Input. I meet regularly to plan worship with a committee composed of an associate pastor, the choir director, the chairperson of our worship council, and a congregational member-at-large. Together, we carefully coordinate the sermon theme with music and Scripture, plan innovations within the liturgy of the day, and ensure that the service will allow appropriate congregational participation and response. The result is a more unified and interesting worship experience.

Of course, there will always be a degree of tension between structure and spirit. How can we balance form and freedom? Is it possible to follow a liturgy without stifling spontaneity? I believe it is, but I also admit to praying, "Lord, let something happen today that's not in the bulletin."

Final Preparations. My Saturday usually includes giving the completed sermon, or at least the essence and flow of it, to my wife, who is my most loving and exacting critic. She has saved me from many a pitfall by reminding me of how a sermon sounds to the person in the pew.

The importance I attach to Sunday worship determines how I spend Saturday night. My rule of thumb is that I take part in only those Saturday evening activities that permit me to awaken refreshed and ready to meet God in worship on Sunday morning. I arise early each Sunday to have time for devotions and for fine-tuning the sermon.

No matter how carefully I prepare, however, I know there will be times when I fail, when worship seems like an empty exercise. In this earthly arena we can at best _attempt_ to worship. Thanks be to God that he meets us more than halfway. Jesus promised, "But the hour is coming, and now is, when the true worshipers will worship the Father in spirit and truth, for such the Father seeks to worship him" (John 4:23, RSV).

Worship is the loftiest activity of which humans are capable. God is pleased when we prepare as adequately as possible for worship, for by our actions we are saying that meeting him is important—and it is!

Jay R. Weener[44]

299 • KEYS TO EFFECTIVE WORSHIP LEADERSHIP

Effective worship leading requires much more than just nailing down its technical aspects. As important as or more important than technical skills are the worship leader's relationship with God and with others, his or her spiritual walk, knowledge of Scripture, attitudes, lifestyle, self-discipline, and understanding of music.

Personal Qualities of the Effective Worship Leader

Maintaining a Strong Relationship with the Lord. The only way to be effective long-term as a worship leader is to maintain a close relationship with the Lord. If a person is not in constant pursuit of a close relationship with the Lord, continually allowing God to fill him or her, then that person will have nothing to give. There are some practical things that can help a worship leader through a few services, but beyond that they will be empty. Worship leaders need to be daily renewed and refreshed by Jesus, the Living Water. If they forgo this ongoing relationship with Jesus, they have really missed the fullness of God's calling on their life.

Anyone aspiring to be an effective worship leader must have as his or her main anchor point an ongoing relationship with the object of their worship, the almighty God. Other ideas and concepts will be discussed below to help aspiring worship leaders on their path to becoming the most effective leaders of worship they can be. However, maintaining a relationship with the Lord is foundational to it all.

Maintaining a Humble, Servant Attitude. Although musical abilities are important for a worship leader, ultimately the Lord does not need human talents—he wants hearts. All the abilities that people can muster are of very little eternal consequence. God is looking for a broken and contrite heart, one that is not self-centered but focused on him.

Jesus portrayed this humble, servant attitude. He told people that he did not come to be served but to serve. He taught that his followers should do the same. "If anyone wants to be first, he must be the very last, and the servant of all" (Mark 9:35).

In practical terms, worship leaders can be servants in many ways. Serving the Lord can be done by worshiping and obeying him in all that they do and say. Serving one's church can be done by constantly learning and growing in the things that will enable a person to better lead others in worship. Worship leaders can serve their pastor by honoring him or her in words and actions. It is a daily decision to be, like Jesus, humble servants.

Keeping a Levitical Heart. The main purpose of the Levites in the Old Testament was to be given wholly unto God (Num. 8:14-16). Anything else in their lives was of secondary importance. All that they did and said was consecrated unto God. Nothing outweighed their belonging to him.

This attitude of being given completely to the Lord also needs to permeate the life of every worship leader today. What God required of the Levites is the same as what he requires of those involved in the ministry of praise and worship today. He is not just looking for talented musicians. He wants _hearts_. The main purpose in the life of a worship leader is simply to _be_ to his glory (Eph. 1:12). A leader of worship should model for others this idea of existing for God's glory.

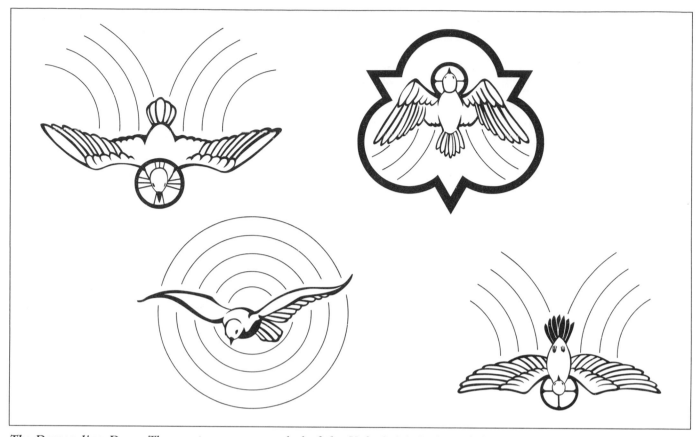

The Descending Dove. *The most common symbol of the Holy Spirit is that of the descending dove. This symbol is based on the account of Jesus' baptism in Mark 1:10 (NSRV): "And just as he was coming up out of the water, he saw the heavens torn apart and the Spirit descending like a dove on him." It is portrayed in many ways as shown above. Normally the dove is snow white in color and is shown with the three-rayed nimbus.*

Living a Life of Worship. A congregation can never fully enter into worship as God desires until that congregation learns to live out a lifestyle of praise and worship. The worship of the sanctuary is meaningless unless it is preceded by six days of worship as a way of life. The Sunday morning experience of worship should be the by-product of an entire week of worship unto the Lord.

This principle is obvious throughout Scripture. "I will extol the LORD *at all times*" (Ps. 34:1, emphasis mine). "From the rising of the sun to the place where it sets, the name of the LORD is to be praised" (Ps. 113:3). "Through Jesus, therefore, let us *continually* offer to God a sacrifice of praise—the fruit of lips that confess his name" (Heb. 13:15).

Christians must realize that worshiping God really is their reason for existing. "But you are a chosen people, a royal priesthood, a holy nation, a people belonging to God, *that you may declare the praises of him* who called you out of darkness into his wonderful light" (1 Peter 2:9). Effective worship leaders must teach this concept to their congregations, but more importantly, they must exemplify it.

Being Thankful to God. Christians should be models of thankfulness. They should cultivate thankfulness in their everyday interactions with people. More importantly, however, they need to cultivate continual thankfulness toward God. This is especially true for those who lead in worship.

God has forgiven and extended friendship to those who accept Jesus. Thankfulness should be a natural outgrowth of that relationship. Even beyond forgiveness and his constant companionship, God called us his children (1 John 3:1). With a realization of such great love, Christians should have a heart that overflows with thanksgiving. The main thing one must do is to simply make thanking God a habit. It is a choice to daily make giving thanks to the Lord a regular part of life.

It is necessary for people to mentally stop themselves from complaining or even being complacent. Instead, it is necessary to give thanks to God. A heart that is daily full of thanksgiving to the Lord will be much more effective in leading corporate worship.

Walking in God's Grace. Probably the most common cause of a feeling of inadequacy within worship leaders is the realization of their own failures. A common attitude is that, because of their sins and failings, they cannot stand before God and lead his people in worship. Of all the problems within the church today, the most prevalent is a failure to comprehend or fully believe the power of the gospel of Jesus.

There is no question that everyone has failed the Lord and will continue to do so. For this reason, God has made a way to find forgiveness and acceptance through Jesus' atoning work on Calvary. As people confess their sins with a desire to turn from them, the blood of Jesus truly does wash away those sins and the accompanying feeling of guilt. Grasping this seemingly simple concept would cause major changes within lives and ministries. When worship leaders understand that God's mercy can cover any failure, it will be easier for them to continually believe he can use them.

It is not a question of living a perfectly sinless life. If people had the power to do that, then Jesus died for no reason. The real issue is how sin is dealt with after it is committed. God's way is for people to turn to him in repentance and find grace and forgiveness.

Maintaining Self-Discipline. Self-discipline is not necessarily fun, but it is essential. Worship leaders must be willing to discipline themselves in many areas—prayer, the study of God's Word, musical practice time, preparation for leading, and others. This is often one of the most difficult things about being a worship leader. It requires less effort to procrastinate, be lazy, and be disorganized than it does to be organized, diligent, and disciplined.

Effective worship leaders will pray regularly for those whom they lead and minister to. They should pray regularly for their own sensitivity to the Holy Spirit. They must work diligently at music understanding, music performance, and music theory.

All of these areas require a truly committed attitude to be really effective. If worship leaders allow flesh, their mood, or even the attitudes of others to dictate the discipline in these areas, they will not be the leaders God has enabled them to be. Self-discipline is an absolutely essential element for the effective worship leader.

Knowing and Understanding God's Word. A major responsibility of any worship leader is to be a firm, solid Christian, who knows God through his Word. Putting all gifts, talents, and callings aside for a moment, this very basic foundation must be understood. God's Word is the only reliable source of truth. It must be the final authority in all one believes. The Bible has within it all that is necessary to know about walking through life. It teaches of God's unsurpassable love and grace. It declares the necessity of prayer and seeking God continually. It urges diligence in repentance and walking in holiness. Without a strong knowledge of and firm commitment to the truths that God has revealed in the Bible, no gift, no talent, no calling will ever bring about God's intended purposes.

Musical talents are an important commodity for a worship leader. But even more necessary is a thorough knowledge of God's Word. Knowing God through his Word is an essential element in being an effective leader of worship. Knowing the Lord through his Word needs to be an extremely high priority for all believers, but especially for worship leaders.

Accepting the Role of Being an Example. People have a need to be taught not only by words but also by actions. The "don't do as I do, do as I say" mentality must be removed from the thinking of the church. Worship leaders cannot just talk about worship being a way of life. People must see them live it out.

In his letter to the church at Philippi, the apostle Paul states, "Join with others in following my example, brothers, and take note of those who live according to the pattern we gave you" (Phil. 3:17). Effective worship leaders must be willing to accept this role also. Regardless of how worship leaders see their own position, others will look to them as examples. In every situation, they will be observed, and, therefore, their lives must be exemplary. They must not shun this responsibility but accept it.

Cultivating the Gifts That God Has Given You. God has given each one of his people certain gifts to use for his glory. "Now to each one the manifestation of the Spirit is given for the common good. All these are the work of one and the same Spirit, and he gives them to each one, just as he determines" (1 Cor. 12:7, 11).

The Lord gives gifts and then expects the recipients of the gifts to learn to use them to their fullest potential. Certainly he will lead and guide in their usage, but people must learn to work with the gifts to excel at them. It is very rare, even in Scripture, for the Lord to sovereignly give a "full-blown" gift to someone.

In practical terms, worship leaders need to use and work at the gifts God has bestowed on them for their position. Musical gifts must be cultivated. Songwriting skills should be honed. Public speaking skills should be enhanced. All of these things and more are necessary for one to become effective as a worship leader.

Keeping Priorities Straight. One of the most difficult things for people to do in any area of life is to decide what is the highest priority for the moment. Generally, this is because of the lack of defined priorities and goals within the life of an individual. When one has clearly established overall priorities, moment-by-moment decisions become easier.

Because of the potential busyness in the life of a worship leader, setting overall priorities is especially necessary. Therefore, it is essential for worship leaders to determine, understand, and implement biblical priorities in their lives and ministries. With these in place, they will find themselves directed more by God and his will than by the pleas of countless people and needs for time. Seeking the Lord for his priorities is an absolute for an effective leader of worship.

Using and/or Cultivating Administrative Abilities. The worship leader or minister of music is not ordinarily primarily an administrator. Musical leaders usually are most often enlisted for their artistic, musical, and creative abilities, not for their organizational prowess. In fact, they often have a disdain for administrative details. The worship leader with this type of thinking must change his or her attitude.

It is possible to develop organizational skills even if they do not come naturally. In endeavoring to do this, a person could take a class on administration at a local junior college. He or she could go to an organizational seminar. Administratively gifted friends can be a good resource for advice about a specific situation. Whatever course of action is followed, a worship leader cannot be truly effective without acquiring some degree of proficiency in administration and organization.

Caring for the Congregation. Since the first priority of a worship leader is to minister to the Lord, minis-

try to people sometimes seems difficult to grasp. However, if a worship leader sees only worshiping the Lord as valuable, he has missed half of his or her job title: Worship *leader*. Worship leaders have a responsibility to *lead* people in worship.

It is necessary for the effective worship leader to learn to not just "do ministry," but to minister to people. It is easy for leaders to miss this seemingly simple idea in much of what is referred to as "ministry." Caring for the congregation refers to seeing the needs of those being ministered to as more important than the needs of the minister(s). The Bible tells us to "do nothing out of selfish ambition or vain conceit, but in humility consider others better than yourselves" (Phil. 2:3). Caring for the congregation also means listening carefully to people's positive and negative comments. All of these are prerequisites to being effective as a worship leader.

— Building an Effective Worship Team —

Choosing Members of Your Worship Team. In adding members to a worship team, the first step is to pray. It is necessary to pray that the Lord will either raise up the right people within a congregation or send the right people to the congregation. Additionally, prayer for wisdom and sensitivity to the Holy Spirit is essential. The worship leader, who will make the final decision about who is to be a part of the team, should be careful to listen to the Holy Spirit.

It is also good to evaluate certain qualities in the lives of prospective candidates. Spiritual maturity should be the first quality to look for. Additionally, commitment to both the Lord and the church is necessary. A degree of musical proficiency is essential, too.

Finally, communication with prospective team members is imperative. Consistent, thorough communication, both written and verbal, addressing what is expected of each worship team member, needs to be implemented from the beginning.

Developing Unity. A worship team needs to be a group of friends who minister together. Friendship is a needed but neglected aspect of many worship teams. It is obvious from both Scripture and experience that negative attitudes within a congregation can be a hindrance to worship. The Bible teaches that God is building his people into a temple to offer up spiritual sacrifices, or worship (1 Peter 2:5). If the building is not built with right relationships, then the spiritual sacrifices offered in that temple will be lacking. This effect is magnified if poor relationships exist between the members of the worship team—a microcosm of the congregation as a whole. The main responsibility of the team is the area of worship. If there is constant discord within the team, then the praise and worship will suffer greatly. Great unity, however, can cause a positive overflow within the congregation.

Because of this, it is necessary to endeavor to build strong relationships among worship team members. God honors efforts to solidify the ties between his people. The Bible consistently encourages unity among believers. The worship leader should be the catalyst to building these relationships by continually caring for the members of the worship team.

Getting the Most from Rehearsals. In attempting to get the most from rehearsals, there are many practical considerations. The first of these is the frequency of the rehearsals. How often you rehearse must be determined by the situation; however, a once-a-week practice works best in most cases. The length of practice sessions should also be determined by the particular circumstances. A team of two musicians will probably not require as much time as a thirty-piece orchestra.

Additionally, what should be done at each rehearsal must be addressed. Many things should be considered: worship, prayer, introducing new songs, revising old songs, evaluations of previous services, teaching, discussion, practicing special music, etc. All of these can be done, although it is unnecessary to attempt to include all of them in each practice. Worship and prayer, however, should be a part of every practice session, though the amount of time dedicated to them will vary. In fact, using variety will help keep rehearsals from becoming boring and predictable.

—— Understanding the Role of Music ——

The Purposes for Music. Throughout the more than 800 references to music in Scripture, there are several reasons given for the use of music. One use is simply to praise and worship the Lord. Throughout the book of Psalms, God's people are entreated to "Praise the Lord!" and to "Sing unto the Lord!" Another use of music is to teach God's Word. "Let the word of Christ dwell in you richly as you teach and admonish one another with all wisdom, and as

you sing psalms, hymns and spiritual songs" (Col. 3:16). Music can also help to release God's power (Acts 16:25-26; 2 Chron. 20:1-22). Additionally, music is a means to tell of God's great works and, consequently, to stir up faith: "tell of his works with songs of joy" (Ps. 107:22). Music also helps to bring a unity within a corporate gathering and aids in the focusing of hearts and thoughts toward a central point, in this case Jesus. Understanding these purposes for music will enable a worship leader to be more effective.

Music as a Tool. Just as a craftsman carefully chooses the tool he uses for each specific task, so a worship leader can choose the instruments from among those on his or her worship team that best express the various "moods" of the Spirit of God. For example, a slow, intimate time of communing with the Lord would be better enhanced with soft strings or solo acoustic piano than with a blaring electric guitar solo or loud cymbal crashes. On the other hand, during a boisterous time of jubilant celebration, electric guitar and loud cymbals might be very appropriate. Obviously, these are extreme cases, but worship leaders need to learn even the subtle nuances of musical enhancement of worship. At times, this may even mean that worship leaders, if they lead with an instrument, must stop playing to allow a more fitting instrument to carry the music. Worship leaders who are willing to sit out themselves are better able to ask others to do the same. Using all of the instruments available to their fullest potential—but not overusing them—is the key.

The Power of Music. Music in and of itself is a powerful force. Even before adding the anointing of the Holy Spirit, there is an apparent force in music. Secular studies alone have proven that music will affect a person's mood, alter buying habits, help relieve pain, reduce or increase stress, make people work more efficiently, and even affect eating habits.

There are numerous scriptural references to the power of music (1 Sam. 10:5-6; 16:23; 2 Kings 3:15; etc.). God has apparently put an inherent quality in music that gives it some sort of sway over the unseen realm. This is true for both good and evil purposes.

An effective worship leader needs to begin to find through personal experience and the experiences of others how to use music to its fullest potential. In addition to instrumental sensitivity, a worship leader needs to find out how music relates to what the Lord is doing and then use it to accomplish his purposes. Seeking the Lord for his understanding of the power of music is the key.

Compiling a Solid Song Repertoire. The first thing to do in compiling a solid song repertoire is to examine the lyrics of old songs and potential new songs. It is best to examine the lyrics separately from the music. When checking the words, it is essential to be certain that they are consistent with Scripture, that they are within the experience and understanding of the congregation, and that they rhythmically fit the music.

When examining the music, it is good to be certain that the music is of good quality; that it is within the experience and understanding of the congregation, and that it enhances the words.

It is also good to check for overall variety within the song repertoire. Be sure that a variety of keys, rhythms and tempos, and styles of music is represented, and that there is variety within individual songs (e.g., men sing, women sing, soloist sings, etc.).

An effective worship leader must constantly be searching for new songs to enhance the repertoire.

The Path to Excellence

Being Loyal to Those in Authority over You. The most important characteristic a worship leader must pursue in relation to his or her pastor is loyalty. This is not a simple one-time verbal assent of loyalty, but a daily working out of that loyalty. Developing loyalty is not necessarily simple. It does not just happen; the worship leader must work at it (Heb. 13:17).

Pastors and worship leaders can have solid, fulfilling relationships, but those relationships must be seen from a biblical perspective. The pastor, just as the husband in a marriage relationship, is the one with ultimate authority. That does not mean he or she lords it over the worship leader, but it does mean that the pastor is in charge. He or she has ultimate responsibility for that particular congregation of people. The worship leader, just as the wife, must learn to be submissive. This is not always easy for a creative, artistic person, but it is essential to establish a trusting relationship between pastors and worship leaders. In addition, worship leaders who sow loyalty to their pastors will reap loyalty from their team members. Just as in a biblical marriage

relationship, cultivating loyalty in your relationship to your pastor is well worth the effort.

Sticking with It Even in the Not-So-Fun Times. Although leading worship can be a lot of fun, it is not always so. Difficult times are an integral part of being a worship leader. In any part of life, there will be trials. "A righteous man may have many troubles, but the LORD delivers him from them all" (Ps. 34:19). God is most interested in how people handle trials. Christians cannot base their walk with the Lord or even their service to him on how things seem to be going in life. There is only one standard by which to safely measure life—the Word of God. If worship leaders rely on good times, people's reactions, emotions, or anything but the strength of the Lord to carry them through, they will have ultimately missed God's best for them.

To be effective as a worship leader over the long term requires frequently recalling to mind the promises from Scripture that God will always love and sustain his people and never forsake them.

Ministering beyond Your Comfort Zone. Frequently, the Lord calls Christians to go beyond the comfort zones of their lives to allow him to "stretch" them. Staying where it is comfortable causes people to stagnate. Going beyond these areas can cause growth. The same is true for worship leaders. Continually doing the same comfortable things will not promote growth. It is only by going beyond those comfort areas that real development occurs.

Jesus said to "go and *make disciples* of all nations" (Matt. 28:19, emphasis mine). He did not say to do it only if it was comfortable. Ephesians 4:12 says that the role of leadership in the church is to equip the rest of the people for the work of the ministry. Sometimes it is easier for leaders to do the work themselves, but that is not God's best. Ministering beyond the normal area of comfort will cause growth and maturation in the worship leader and in those around him or her.

Preparing Yourself to Lead. The initial preparation needed for leading worship is the realization that there is only one way to come before the Lord: by the shed blood of Jesus (Heb. 10:19). One's own strength or goodness or even excellent musical abilities are not enough. Only Jesus' sacrifice on Calvary allows access to Almighty God.

Beyond this initial preparation is the preparation

for the specific service. This requires prayerful consideration of the theme and various aspects of the service, and then choosing songs, Scriptures, and other components of the service. All of this can be done prior to the service by asking for the Lord's guidance in all of the preparation.

Once the songs are chosen, diligent practice of the music performance is necessary. Consideration should be given to medleys, transitions, key changes, and similar matters.

Understanding the Dynamics of the Worship Service. Once preparation has been completed for a specific service, then it is time to lead. It is important to note that although all of the necessary preparation has been done, it is still absolutely imperative to remain open and attentive to the Holy Spirit while leading. A major change in plans is unusual if prayerful preparations have been made. However, changes can occur and preempt even the most carefully prepared song list.

In addition to this, other practical ideas can be helpful. Create a "flow" in worship by using medleys of songs (endeavoring to maintain concepts such as rhythm/tempo and lyric content), flowing from one right into another. Also, use simple chord progressions to allow the people to sing spontaneously unto the Lord.

Avoid progressing too quickly. Many of the people in the congregation have spent little or no time in preparation, and they are not mentally, physically, or spiritually prepared to enter the presence of the Lord. Finally, always keep your eyes on the Lord.

Desiring and Pursuing Excellence. God held nothing back when he created the earth. His creation was not a halfhearted effort but the absolute best it could be. The church needs to grasp the concept of excellence more fully, especially in the music department. Too often the attitude is, "It's good enough for church," or "The congregation will be singing along, so they won't notice the mistakes." This attitude is the complete opposite of God's attitude (Mark 7:37).

An effective worship leader really has no choice but to desire and pursue excellence. The standard of excellence is simply a part of the nature of God. The death blow needs to be struck to mediocrity within the church. If worship leaders can grasp and implement this attitude in their ministries, the blessing of God will be poured out to maintain it.

Praying toward that end and striving for excellence in all areas are the main keys.

Tom Kraeuter[45]

300 ✦ BUILDING A PHILOSOPHY OF WORSHIP

A philosophy of worship involves the way we approach worship and should include both a thorough analysis of and an explicit statement of our underlying presuppositions. Understanding our "worship worldview" (for example, the cultural background and formal training we bring to our task) will help us to understand why we worship the way we do. It is therefore important to articulate this worldview as clearly and precisely as possible (preferably in a written format). The examples given under the headings below are those of Vineyard churches. They can be used as is, or as a guide to creating one's own philosophy of worship.

The Elements of a Worship Philosophy

Values. Although values are unseen and often unarticulated, they are very influential. They are like the excavation within which the foundation of a building is placed. The foundation defines the location and the limits of the building. The deeper the foundation, the higher the building can rise. Values affect what we think and, consequently, what we do. Our values are an intrinsic part of us, although we seldom think about them in a conscious fashion. They determine the ideas, principles, and concepts a person or group can accept, assimilate, remember, and transmit. They are fallible and must be constantly revised and reviewed in the light of Scripture.

The following are values held at the Vineyard that we seek to instill in those to whom we minister: Worship is given solely for God's glory and honor (Deut. 5:6-10; Rom. 1:20-23). We are to be intimate and self-disclosing with God (Isa. 49:15-16; Eph. 4:13; Phil. 3:10). Nothing is done for effect or to manipulate God or people (cf. 1 Kings 18:26-29). We are committed to honesty and integrity (Eph. 4:15, 25; Col. 3:9). Although our worship may be emotional, we do not want to work up emotions. We want to "dial down" in worship and let our emotional responses flow out of our interaction with God (Rev. 1:17). We welcome the ministry of the Holy Spirit in whatever way he chooses to work among us (1 Thess. 5:19).

Priorities. Unlike values, priorities are seen. Priorities are not so much what is said, but what is done. Priorities grow out of values and may be likened to the pillars that sit along the edge of the value boundary. That is, they rise out of the foundation and hold the building together. Priorities are erected to give visible form to values. Priorities are the things that are most important in terms of action, visibility, and resources (time, energy, and money).

The following priorities control the philosophy of worship at Vineyard churches: Our worship is directed and focused upon God himself. We do not sing about God, but *to* him (Ps. 100:1; Rev. 5:9-10, 12-13). Worship is a twofold communication process: We worship God, and he touches us. Remember that the term for worship, *proskuneo* (pronounced pros-kyu-nay-o), literally means "to kiss." Worship is practiced as a lifestyle on both the corporate and individual levels (Col. 3:15-17). We set aside time to worship, like the early Christians did. (Pliny the Younger wrote to the emperor Trajan that the first-century Christians would frequently worship far into the night, singing for hours at a time.)

We invest money for musical instruments and sound equipment so that we will have quality in our worship (1 Chron. 25:1-6). We expend energy to rehearse, set up, and prepare for worship (spontaneity is best when it is undergirded with thorough preparation). We teach others how to worship so that they may experience intimacy with God (Col. 3:16). We feel free to integrate change as our worship grows and expands. We are careful, though, to maintain consistency between our values and our priorities when we do initiate change.

Practices. Practices are sometimes seen and sometimes not seen. They hang upon priorities. Practices may be likened to the fittings in a building—the wiring, the plumbing, the air-conditioning and heating systems, the furniture, etc. These components are so common that they become almost invisible as they flow through the structure. They become visible only at the point at which they produce the intended effect. Remember that practices are symbols that communicate values and priorities even though these values and priorities may never be articulated verbally. Therefore, it is vital to make a conscious effort to ensure that our practices do indeed communicate our values and priorities.

The following are practices that are found in the worship of Vineyard churches: We engage in practices that are biblically sanctioned, either implicitly or explicitly. We encourage the whole person to enter into worship through the use of the body (raising hands, kneeling, bowing), soul (reading of Scripture, singing, shouting, recalling God's works), spirit (Spirit to spirit, love, tongues). We worship whenever we gather in various groups and settings, even if the gatherings are spontaneous. We encourage an uninterrupted flow of worship; thus, we will sing many songs in succession without interjections from the worship leader. We worship in a contemporary musical style; this helps people to identify with what they are singing to God. We generally encourage moderate practices when we worship in corporate meetings so others are not distracted. We always seek to expand and deepen our present foundation. We seek new songs, new modes of expression, new experiences with God.

Four Basic Personality Types

In any given group, it is argued here, there are four basic personality types. Each responds to change in different ways. These must be taken into account when planning worship.

Radicals. These are people most open to and desirous of change. Typically, these people are radical in every area of their lives. When things become too settled, they usually leave to join another group.

Progressives. These individuals have some openness to change. They are often more stable in their lifestyles than "radicals" but have had a divergent past that continues to exercise an influence over their present views and practices.

Conservatives. These people are moderately resistant to change. They are the trustees of the traditions that are accepted in any given congregation.

Traditionalists. These individuals are least open to and desirous of change. Often their values, priorities, and practices are more in step with those of the past than with the present. These and the radicals will usually be the most difficult groups with which to work. The percentage of each personality type in relation to the whole group generally depends on the age of the group as a whole. Note that traditions are quickly and easily formed. Each personality group has its own function, value, and place in the life of the whole group.

Services

Like priorities, services are also seen. Services are structures that correspond with the particular rooms in a building—the living room, the dining room, the den, etc. Different services allow values and priorities to be further expressed in various ways. Services must accurately express our values and be appropriate to the context of a particular meeting (e.g., a full band versus an acoustic guitar).

The following services are part of the life of the Anaheim, California, Vineyard:

- Celebrations. These are often Sunday meetings but always include the various congregations from the church.
- Congregational meetings. These are gatherings of individuals who have shared interests or goals, such as youth groups, singles activities, etc.
- Kinships. These are small groups or home fellowships.
- Seminars. These provide the opportunity for further training and/or in-depth teaching on topics of interest to persons in the congregation.
- Other more spontaneous worship settings. These can range from spur-of-the-moment activities to beach barbecues, etc.

Implementing the Philosophy

First, give people time to learn new skills. Remember that everyone learns at a different pace. Consequently, introduce the right skill at the right time and be aware of the psychology of change: Change often results in unsettled responses, including fear, anger, insecurity, awkwardness, foolishness, feelings of being out of control, and vulnerability. Therefore, be as patient and understanding as possible. Respond lovingly with words of encouragement. Let people know that change is hard on the human psyche, and that they are doing well.

Second, reinforce the model, even after it is set. This is done through several means:

- Do it yourself. If you don't, they won't. Remember that Paul encouraged the Corinthians to follow him as he followed Christ (1 Cor. 11:1).
- Direct by not directing. Too much direction will stifle the people's initiative by making them feel controlled.
- Let them do it. People learn best in a context that allows them to make mistakes.

Do the reinforcing _before_ worship rather than _during_ it. By not interrupting the flow of worship, we push worship toward intimacy. Make any corrective comments short and to the point without being critical or manipulative and be especially wary of saying, "The Lord told me _____." Also, periodic seminars are very helpful to teach and teach again—to deepen understanding and recall ability.

John Wimber[46]

Developing Management Skills for Leading Worship

The entries in this chapter stress the management functions of worship leading. They encourage worship leaders to develop their managerial skills. Moreover, this section offers suggestions on building united worship teams, developing techniques of biblical leadership, planning, learning to serve others, and pursuing excellence.

---

301 • WORSHIP LEADERS LEAD PEOPLE

Worship leaders should make a priority of developing management skills, and not excuse themselves from this on the basis of their being artists. Rather, they are prophet-musicians in the church, a position that carries tremendous leadership responsibility.

I was startled one day to realize that worship leaders really don't lead worship. They lead people. This was new revelation for me. It meant that management skills were needed by worship leaders, too. Worship leaders, however, are not always happy to find this out. It may be revelation, but it's also hard work.

Rationalization by Artistic People. There are several problems inherent in building a team out of such a diverse group of people as "musicians." Having an artistic bent myself, I can readily identify with the rationalizations artists use to escape management responsibility. Perhaps the first of these is, "Artists are supposed to operate more by emotion and spirit, less by reason." That sounds logical, but it allows artists too much liberty to justify their moments of poor judgment or their impatience with details. It gives them freedom to remain impulsive and unpredictable—not good traits for a leader of others.

Even folklore suggests that the more artistic one is, the less likely he or she is to be responsible. I often used to comfort myself with this alibi while remaining generally sloppy, missing appointments, or being chronically late to meetings. Again, this myth needs to be dealt with in order to become a strong leader.

Another loophole artists use to avoid change is that they justify any disunity that may appear among them. The excuse? "Artists just have volatile personalities." In some circles denying the virgin birth of Jesus causes less trouble than the "proper" interpretation of a musical passage! Because of these and other "accepted" excuses for irresponsible behavior, it is no easy task to lead, let alone *manage* musicians.

Worship Leaders Are Prophet-Musicians. Some of these generally accepted rationalizations probably originate from a false identity among worship leaders. They don't have a clear opinion of who they are. The importance of their role has been downplayed or unrecognized for years. In my chats with worship leaders, pastors, and other church leaders, I have discovered that many think of worship leaders as only being musicians or "entertainers." But the Bible teaches that they function prophetically.

Rather than thinking of themselves as musicians first, worship leaders must see themselves as prophets, or at least as people who operate strongly in prophetic gifts. And prophets are men and women with tremendous responsibility.

Prophets are entirely different from worldly musicians. Prophets can make or break a church. Prophets are men and women of the Word who know the Scriptures and handle them rightly. They are leaders in their congregations. They have an awesome responsibility.

> Here is a trustworthy saying: If anyone sets his heart on being an overseer, he desires a noble task. Now the overseer must be above reproach, the husband of but one wife, temperate, self-controlled, respectable, hospitable, able to teach, not given to drunkenness, not violent but gentle, not quarrelsome, not a lover of money. He must manage his own family well and see that his children obey him with proper respect. (If anyone does not know how to manage his own family, how can he take care of God's church?) He must not be a recent convert, or he may become conceited and fall under the same judgment as the devil. (1 Tim. 3:1-6)

In this Scripture God describes the kind of people suited for leadership in the church. Prophetic worship leaders are far from being just "artists." Like all spiritual leaders, they set the lifestyle standards for the church and are to be examples of excellence. Everything the Bible teaches about leaders applies to the prophet-musician.

Worship leaders who think of themselves as "mere musicians" have a lot of identity-changing to do. Clearly, worship leaders must have the correct self-image. They cannot cast themselves in the role of entertainers. Called to a high honor and much responsibility, their ability to lead worship depends as much on their exemplary lives as on their musical skills.

As I conduct seminars around the nation, I see an increasing number of churches that are becoming aware of the responsible roles of their worship leaders. In these churches it is no easier to become a worship leader than it is to become an elder; these are also churches that honor their worship leaders and are blessed for doing so.

How to Become Creative and Organized. With the right self-image it becomes a little easier to want to get organized. One day the Lord spoke to me: "Just look at your desk!" he said. "It's disgusting!" I responded, "But Lord, I am the creative type. You know—artistic, musical, and all that." And he said, "Are you trying to suggest that _I'm_ not creative?" I responded, "No, sir, I would not want to suggest that. But it would take a miracle for me to keep my desk organized!"

Suddenly, I realized that I had just stumbled onto a key for personal discipline. I began that day to trust God for the change he would work in me and have kept a pretty neat desk ever since.

This seemingly insignificant lesson has helped me to realize that most change begins when we admit the obvious. Though we may see ourselves as not having been born with the gifts of organization and leadership, the skills involved _can_ be learned. If worship leaders lead people, then they must make a choice to develop the skills needed to manage, or pay the consequences in lack of teamwork and lowered effectiveness.

Add Leadership and Management Skills to Your Worship Anointing. You can always tell a leader: People follow him or her. Getting people to follow you into the Holy of Holies requires leadership skills. Once you have a following of people, you need to learn how to manage them: to organize, to plan, to direct, to train, to delegate, to evaluate. It's not an easy task. But the tools of leadership and good management will greatly increase the impact of your worship leading.

Nick Ittzes[47]

302 ◆ BUILDING A UNITED WORSHIP TEAM

A key to building a united worship team is to have a clearly defined statement. This entry suggests ways to go about developing such a statement, including planning a retreat for this purpose. Start beforehand by asking the right questions of your pastor. Determine what goals the team will have in your church, and work to define team values.

United purpose and action have tremendous power. I think about that when I fly on a jet plane. Air molecules are so tiny I can't see them. Yet if enough of them travel past the surfaces of a wing at one time, they can lift thousands of pounds off the ground! One of the first signs of good leadership is unity among the led. When there is heart-unity, we can reach any goal the Lord gives us.

Assuming we have godly people who have a call to lead worship, two important ingredients for building unity are (1) developing a clearly defined mission, with goals and objectives, strategies, and action plans; and (2) having a leader who practices the skills of team-building.

Clearly State Your Team Mission. Many worship teams develop serious problems of disunity as they increase in numbers. Very often that has less to do with disloyalty than with a missing sense of mission.

Joining a group that doesn't have a clear mission statement is like proposing marriage on a blind date. You are committed, but you don't know to what. Since everyone has his or her own perceptions of what a worship team ought to do, these perceptions proliferate as the group grows, and the seeds of disunity soon sprout like mushrooms after a cool rain.

On the other hand, if the worship team can clearly state its mission, objectives, philosophy of ministry, strategies, and action plans, those joining will more likely be people who are in agreement. They will probably spend most of their energies helping the group achieve its objectives instead of trying to change the group.

Better Stewardship of Resources. Churches are beginning to see the importance of defining their mission as a whole. But groups within the church also benefit from a specific statement of their particular mission. Can your worship team define its mission and how it will be accomplished? If it can, it is ready for better stewardship of its resources. It will invest itself consistently in doing things that help accomplish its mission, and there will be far less "wheel spinning" than if it has only a vague idea about supplying music for the church.

Give a Greater Sense of Value to Tasks. As groups age, they often lose the vigor and excitement of the early years. One of the reasons this happens is that every growing group has to deal with an increasing amount of "drudge work." Take the role of the music librarian, for instance. It has little inherent glamour. The music librarian is responsible for acquiring, cataloging, retrieving, and filing the music for your worship team. He or she has to secure performance rights. When the group is young, he or she is caught up in the excitement of it all. But as the group gets older, the person realizes that the job has become repetitive. If, at this point, the librarian does not see how his or her task is accomplishing a larger mission, he or she may find reasons to leave the post.

Ask the Right Questions. How can you define your worship team's mission? It begins with asking the right questions of the right people. Here is an outline of good procedures to follow:

1. Worship teams are accountable to their pastor; they cannot develop a vision indepen-

dent of the church they serve. Contact the pastor, and set up a time when you can meet to discuss both the church's vision and your team's role in accomplishing it. To help your pastor to prepare, you might ask him or her to read this article and the others in this section.

2. Meet with the pastor. Listen to her. Get her heart. Ask her how she sees the worship team fitting into the overall mission of the church.

3. Take your worship team on a weekend retreat. Spend time in prayer, informal talks, and group discussion regarding your mission statement. Write a preliminary draft.

4. Review your preliminary draft with the pastor.

5. Refine your statement of mission over a period of several weeks or even months, if necessary. Nothing is gained by hurrying.

6. After your mission statement is completed, refer to it often. Pray over it. Say it in church. Put it in your church handbook. Your mission statement will be the foundation from which you can discover God's long-range, medium-range, and short-range plans for your group.

How Are You Involved? What are some of the functions of a worship team? That will depend on your church. On your retreat, pool the ideas of your group based on the roles you have already filled as well as their dreams. Most of all, your team goal will be to make your distinctive contribution to the overall mission of your church.

Just to get your thinking started, you might consider the following:

1. Participate in the strategic planning meetings of the church. When the worship leader is intimately involved in the long-range, medium-range, and short-range planning of the church, he or she is better able to help move the church's vision forward through the incredible power of worship and music.

2. Prepare the people to receive the Word of God.

3. Prepare the people so that God's presence may manifest itself freely. Engage in consultation with the person who brings the Sunday message so that the worship time becomes a meaningful and coherent focus of the service.

4. Prophesy to the church through the Word and through music. As a team you do more than sing about God's glory: You impart it prophetically to the worshiping church.
5. Teach the church to sing. Because we are a spiritual priesthood of believers, all of us need to grow in our musical abilities for the sake of worship.
6. Develop the gifts of the church. Create opportunities for ministry.
7. Teach about worship and worship expressions such as dancing, clapping, kneeling, and so on.
8. Raise up additional worship leaders. Every ministry worth its salt disciples others.
9. Develop a worship awareness among the children and youth.
10. Meet with the pastor to plan services. Perhaps begin by working together on special services.
11. Serve as a resource for special evangelistic outreaches.
12. Sponsor seminars on worship for area churches.
13. Help raise up worship teams in other area churches.
14. Participate in evangelistic outreaches.
15. Develop worship leaders for house fellowships in your congregation.
16. Raise up specialized worship teams to visit shut-ins, nursing homes, hospitals, and jails.
17. Provide a library of resources for strengthening worship in the home.

As is evident just from this beginning list, there are endless possibilities for your team's involvement.

Define Your Values. Once your pastor and you have identified the goals your team is to have, you will then need to discuss your values as a team. By values we mean the standards of conduct and professionalism that will be required of worship leaders.

Your values must reflect the values of your church. For example, if your church is casual, your team would be out of place if everyone dressed in three-piece suits and formal gowns.

Most of your values will develop from applicable Scriptures regarding what spiritual leaders are to be like. In addition, you can learn a lot from attending gatherings for worship leaders and church leaders,

exchanging ideas with others who have a calling like yours.

A united worship team that shares a common vision can carry the church to the heights of communion with God. Commit yourself to learning how to build a team that is centered around a worthwhile mission.

Nick Ittzes[48]

303 ⬥ LEARNING BIBLICAL LEADERSHIP SKILLS

The Bible teaches that authority has its place in the church. It shows, however, that leaders should accomplish their goals through persuasion, not power; through support, not control; through open-mindedness, not closed-mindedness. The entry suggests ways of dealing with problems that arise and suggests ways to administer discipline.

Servant leadership is God's appointed method for managing the church. Unfortunately, most people who are thrust into leadership positions in the church have not been trained in biblical leadership skills. Many think that their position of leadership makes them the "boss" who hands down dictates. Others, who may realize how carnal that is, abdicate all leadership, and their group suffers from a lack of direction and discipline.

Neither kind of leadership pleases the Lord. God fully supports authority in the church. It is not a society of indistinguishable equals. Some people are to lead, others are to follow. But the tools of leadership are the issue. In this entry, we will look at some of the tools the Bible offers to help you fulfill your leadership role without violating your servant role.

The Person of the Leader. Jesus compared leadership to leaven in a loaf of bread. Yeast works quietly, in the background, without a lot of "hoopla." It's really a kind of infection, moving from cell to cell. But it takes good yeast to make good bread.

Similarly, if you are to infect your team with the right qualities, you must do it yourself. What you _are_ will always have more influence than what you _say_ and _do_. Therefore, your own character development must become the root out of which your leadership skills grow, lest you bear bad fruit.

Persuasion versus Power. One of the most important differences between carnal and biblical leading has to do with the overuse of power. Carnal leaders put far too much stock in their position. They think that their title, or even their obvious qualifications, should cause people to do as they are told.

That might work with immature Christians, but as they mature, people will begin to challenge that kind of leadership style. One of the most significant problems with the overuse of position, title, or power is that it fails to address the *heart* of the followers—the center of motivation and willing allegiance.

There is a proper use for authority and power, and we will deal with that later. But when leaders too often convey the attitude, "Do it because I said so," they will not capture the hearts of their followers. They will repel the strong and make hypocrites of the weak. This is why persuasion is the chief tool of the godly leader.

For instance, Paul writes to Timothy regarding the teaching role of the pastor. He says that pastors are to patiently instruct those who oppose them, so that God may give them repentance leading to knowledge of the truth (2 Tim. 2:25).

Top-Down Support versus Control. Another important aspect of biblical leadership is that it provides more support than it does control. Many leaders are driven by a desire to control others. They go far beyond training and try to determine all the details for their subordinates' work. Their subordinates have very little autonomy, and their ideas are generally rejected. But godly leadership equips people to develop their own gifts and their own creative ways of dealing with problems and opportunities. Godly leaders invest their own time to find other resources to help their subordinates succeed.

Maintain Open Leadership. Leaders do not have to have all the answers. God has all the answers. Yet leaders are often defensive about ideas and suggestions offered by those who work with or under them. Instead, all people ought to feel their leaders value their input and in fact seek it out. Leaders need to discern God's voice speaking through anyone he chooses. This calls for humility.

The main difference between valuable advice and criticism is timing. If you seek suggestions before you do something, it is valuable advice. If the suggestions come to you after you have done something, it is criticism. Choose to get valuable advice.

Deal with Issues Properly. Problems will arise in every group, no matter how saintly the people are.

There will be difficulties from the outside as well as from within. At this point, how you handle the problem will determine whether or not you are a team-builder.

Team-builders develop the ability to put problems "outside" the group. In other words, they approach every difficulty with the attitude, *we* have a problem.

For instance, suppose your piano player is unable to attend your practices on Thursday evenings. If you are a team-builder, you will not consider it the pianist's problem but something that your group needs to address and attempt to resolve. The piano player needs to feel that his or her schedule is important enough to the group that they will seek a way around it. Even if they fail, the piano player will not feel rejected.

You can always tell team-builders by their language. They uses phrases such as "*We* have a problem," "What can *we* do?" "What do *you* think?" "Do *you* have any ideas about worship this Sunday?" "Can *we* _____?" "What if *we* _____?"

Recruiting Team Players, not Soloists. Add new people to your group who will work well in teams. You need to be careful that you do not consider only their musical skills, anointing, or even their theological expertise. One can have all of those characteristics and still not make a good team player. If you inherit an egocentric "superstar," have a loving but frank conversation with him or her. Invite him to join the team indeed, or to resign and do occasional solos.

Apprenticing. One of the most successful worship leaders I know relies heavily on apprenticing. When people desire to join his worship team, they are invited to attend the practice sessions and just observe for several weeks. Then they are allowed to join in the practice. Finally, if they have been sufficiently integrated into the group, they are allowed to participate in leading worship on Sunday morning.

Consider the benefits that come from this approach: The worship team has the opportunity to get to know candidates and candidates get to know the heart of the worship team before they even have to think about playing their instrument or singing before them. They can see teamwork in action and can observe the values of the group. In addition, the lengthy trial period tends to wear out glory-seekers. It establishes the role of the worship leader as the one in charge. It also helps candidates to recognize the importance of their role. In the long range it increases the honor of the worship team in the eyes of the congregation by establishing a professional level of commitment. Finally, it tests the consistency of faithfulness of candidates before they are assigned to the team.

You should welcome any and all qualified candidates, but making it easy to join your team devalues the group and makes it less popular and less effective! Prayerfully consider developing an apprentice approach to your team-building.

Disciplining for Group Health. Before you even consider discipline, you must establish two things: (1) clearly defined limits (i.e., what is allowed and what is not); and (2) an atmosphere of love. With those things in place, you can exercise discipline when there are infractions.

First, there must be standards of performance. The group must have a clearly established commitment about such things as practice times, absences, tardiness, missing prayer times before services, and anything else that is important to the anointed functioning of the group. Then, if someone violates one of those standards, the leader should waste no time in properly reprimanding the offender.

If you allow the standards to be violated with impunity, the most committed members of the group will become demoralized. You will lose your best people and be left with the ones who have no standards at all, and they will reproduce after their own kind!

There are some simple steps to doing a proper reprimand: First, describe your perception of the problem without accusing. Your perception may be wrong, or there may be real extenuating circumstances. (*Example:* "John, it seems to me you have been thirty-five minutes late to the prayer time three Sundays in a row. Is that correct? Is something wrong?") If your perception was correct, and there were no serious, extenuating circumstances, describe how the behavior violates your team's standards. You don't need to act out anger; just be matter-of-fact. (*Example:* "John, you know that being late without good reason is contrary to your commitment to our team.")

Then explain the consequences. (*Example:* "It hurts us when you're late. Our prayer time is lacking your presence. It isn't fair to those who are on time. Frankly, I feel hurt and angry.") Explain that it is up

to John to be a team player and to support the group's standards. (*Example:* "John, it's up to you to decide whether or not you are going to be part of the team and really participate. No one can make you do that but you.")

Finally, explain what you will do if the improper behavior takes place again. It is helpful if such actions are established as a matter of policy. (*Example:* "If this happens again, I will recommend that you be placed on probation, which means you won't be able to participate in Sunday worship for six weeks.") End on a positive note. (*Example:* "But I really don't expect it to happen again. I know you love us and love the Lord. You are a tremendous asset to us with your skills on the synthesizer and your strengths in the Word.")

Conclusion. God has honored you highly by giving you authority to lead. Learn to do it well! Grow in your leadership skills day after day, and you will build a temple he will gladly inhabit.

Nick Ittzes[49]

304 • WORSHIP LEADERS AND PLANNING

Planning is a continuous process. Scripture encourages planning, and God promises success if we will invite him to be part of the process. This entry suggests that a retreat is an ideal time for long-range planning and offers suggestions for holding such an event. The entry also discusses planning weekly worship services.

In the book of Proverbs we read, "A sluggard does not plow in season; so at harvest time he looks but finds nothing" (Prov. 20:4). Sluggards are tragicomical figures. Can you imagine what kind of person would fail to plow, sow, weed, and feed, yet go out in the fall, surprised at not finding a harvest?

The sluggard fails to realize that today's decisions will determine tomorrow's results. He or she needs to learn that planning is a key to reaping a harvest. Worship leaders also need to plan. They are looking for a harvest of people who can enter into the presence of God unhindered, to bring him pleasure, and to be a channel for his power to be manifested in all the earth.

I know congregations in which there is a steady growth in worship life and power. They are blessed with growing numbers of people committed to worshiping the Lord. Their music is filled with life.

The Sevenfold Flame. *Next to the dove, the most common symbol of the Holy Spirit is the flame of fire. Based on the description of Acts 2:1-4, in which the Holy Spirit appeared as a flame of fire, this popular symbol is usually shown as a single flame or as the sevenfold flame seen here.*

People stand in line to become part of the worship team. They are able to field two, three, or more complete worship teams. Most of all, the power of God is evident in their times of worship, so much so that there are testimonies of physical and emotional healings occurring during the worship. Such power in worship comes, in part, from the dedication and the spiritual quality of the leaders and their people. But spirituality cannot be divorced from getting a plan from God for the worship life of the congregation.

God's Views on Planning

God more than allows us to plan, as if he were giving in to our weaknesses. With wonderful promises, he encourages us to plan. But he wants to be involved in the planning process. Our plans must be submitted to the Lord to succeed. Planning becomes carnal only if God is not invited to inspire and lead the process. But he promises that if we commit to him whatever we do, our plans will succeed (Prov. 16:3).

I have a friend who once stated proudly in his worship service, "We never publish a bulletin, and we never plan anything in advance because we want to be inspired by the Holy Ghost, and we don't want the devil to know in advance what we're going to do!" But that's not really a scriptural view. For God's inspiration can work flawlessly through the process of thinking, organizing, and planning.

The process by which Luke wrote his Gospel is a clear example of that. Luke did research as any historian would. Describing his strategy, Luke tells us he "carefully investigated" the stories about Jesus and wrote them down in an orderly fashion so Theophilus might be assured in his faith (Luke 1:1-4). Though Luke studied, researched, and in an orderly fashion recorded his findings, we receive his Gospel as "God-breathed" (2 Tim. 3:16), written by the Holy Spirit himself. Therefore, inspiration is not excluded by, or even limited by, the ordinary use of human intellect and planning.

Prosperity. When we plan, we open one of God's channels to prosper us: "The plans of the diligent lead to profit as surely as haste leads to poverty" (Prov. 21:5). This power-packed promise contains three main concepts: First, there must be plans. Second, there must be diligence. Third, our plans and diligence must help us avoid hasty "crisis management."

Unity from Planning. Planning has an amazing ability to unite people. This is especially true if they are allowed to contribute substantially to the process. Unless insensitive parents or other adults quash it, children have an unquenchable desire to *do*. "Let *me*, Mommy!" is the cry of just about any child I have ever known.

A worship team that lets its members have a vital share of the planning is responding to that God-ordained drive inside of people to create! It's unfortunate that in most churches the real doers have to live by the creed, "It's easier to get forgiveness than permission." Only the bold and perhaps slightly rebellious will be able to develop their potential. The submissive may have trouble flowering to their maximum under a rigid system.

Maximizing Group Gifts through Planning. Planning is essential to the stewardship of our gifts. For instance, let's suppose that your worship team is asked to minister at a large outdoor rally. If you plan ahead far enough, you will discover that your bass player has connections with the top supplier of sound systems in your five-state area. You further discover that if he has six weeks or more notice, he is able to arrange for a manufacturer's demo of its top-of-the-line product free of charge. You get $25,000 worth of public-address equipment for a weekend, and it doesn't cost you a cent! It takes planning ahead to benefit like that.

Some Basics about Planning

The exciting business of planning with the Holy Spirit is a big subject. To date, the best single resource I have seen to guide you through the process, short of retaining a professional consultant, is a book by Dr. R. Henry Migliore, titled *Strategic Planning for Ministry and Church Growth* (Tulsa: Honor Books, 1988).

Retreating Is Ideal. My favorite format to initiate planning is a retreat lasting at least a weekend, but preferably a whole week. The format should alternate between structured meetings during which the group works through a formal planning model (such as the one presented by Dr. Migliore) and relaxed times that give attendees opportunity for informal interchange, walks, prayer, meditation, and so on.

What should be involved? Your long-range plans for worship can include matters such as these:

1. Gradual upgrading of the sound system.
2. Upgrading of musical instruments.
3. Securing permission to perform copyrighted pieces.
4. Publishing a recording of your group.
5. Establishing and increasing funding for the purchase of music.
6. Plans to attend worship seminars and symposia.
7. Increasing congregational awareness of the importance of worship through special sermons, nights of worship, etc.
8. Increasing interest in worship leading as a ministry.
9. Involving young people more in worship and worship leading.

This list could go on almost indefinitely. What is included on such a list will depend greatly on your mission statement (discussed in a previous entry in this chapter).

Involve Everyone. Everyone who is involved in the worship life of the church—whether in a leadership role or as a selected representative of the congregation—ought to take part to some degree in the worship planning retreat. In addition, questionnaires can be distributed to the remainder of the congregation ahead of time, seeking responses about the worship life of the church.

Preparation for Planning

A good planning retreat requires much preparation. You must have attractive facilities, good food, and restful lodging. Even more, there must be spiritual preparation and practical homework.

Prayer, fasting, studying worship, and attending worship seminars and conferences are all important preparations for the retreat. If you are filled with the Word of God and godly advice about worship, your retreat will be very fruitful. Practical groundwork would include arranging for substitute worship leaders on the home front, as well as advertising the retreat to the congregation. It's important to let everyone know what you are doing, what your goals are, and why you are doing it. It would be very helpful if the pastor would support the idea of a worship leaders' retreat from the pulpit, explaining to people how such planning will benefit the whole congregation and the work of God in your community.

The Product of Planning. No planning program is complete until there is a written organizational plan encompassing all the items that are part of your planning model. I am convinced that writing a coherent statement about anything I am wanting to do helps me understand my task far better. Not only that, the written plan will help to keep you from "management by platitudes," in which vague statements of an undefined hope replace real goals.

Planning Is a Continuous Process. Part of your commitment as you begin planning is to decide that you will do planning continuously. This is necessary, first, because your written plan must be your working document—your written orders. Just as a contractor continually refers to blueprints, so you must continually check your progress against your written goals to see if you are on target.

Unlike those of the contractor, however, your

plans will continually change. You are not building with static materials on unmoving ground. Your materials and your ground are continually changing. If your plans are not adaptable to changing situations, they will be like Saul's armor to young David: Their weight will keep you from the battle.

And, unlike the contractor, you can never say your building is finished. So, if you are working with a seven-year plan, you can drop year one when it has ended, but you will have to add a new year seven. Every week you and your team ought to devote some prayerful time to check your progress against your plans. Every year, at least, you ought to update your long-range planning.

Finally, plans dealing with people must involve educated guesses. Most of us vastly overestimate what we can accomplish on the short term (although we tend to underestimate what we can do in the long haul). Consequently, you probably will need to adjust your plans to a less ambitious pace.

—— Planning for Worship Services ——

The concept of planning can be applied not only to overall goals for the worship team, but for the worship services as well. Each worship service can be a piece of the master plan. If your congregation is involved in strategic long-range planning, you have tremendous resources for planning your worship services, sermons included. For instance, one of the issues a church considers in planning is its strengths and weaknesses. Similarly, in your services you can encourage the strengths and prophesy solutions to the weaknesses!

Planning and Spontaneity. Planning does not exclude spontaneity. As with your longer-range planning, so in the services, you must retain flexibility. The Holy Spirit may not reveal all his plans to you because he wants to be able to use someone else in the congregation in a significant way. For example, I have ministered on several occasions with a worship team in which we sensed it was God's will to have a healing service; but we had no clue as to how the service would be conducted. But as we obeyed as much as we knew, the Lord gave his Word to someone in the congregation, revealing what else was to be done. And in every case, the service was a wonderful experience of his manifest presence.

Who Should Be Involved? As with large-scale planning, so planning the Sunday morning and other services needs to be open to all the people in the congregation. Ideally, they should be encouraged to call you or even to attend the planning session if they feel they have an insight from the Lord for the service. Of course, the pastor and other church leaders could make extremely valuable additions to the service planning.

Tools for Planning. How do you plan a worship service? Here is a simple outline that I have found to be effective:

1. Pray at your planning meeting.
2. Ask the preacher or teacher to tell the group what word he believes the Lord has given him.
3. Ask the others present to share any Scriptures, songs, hymns, prayers, insights, or perceptions they may have had that they feel relate to the service you are planning. If they have been going through some difficulty, encourage them to share that. Often what we experience is common to many others in the body.
4. Arrange the parts of the service for an orderly flow. For instance, if the Word deals with a need for deep repentance, starting the service with songs of rejoicing would be very odd. Such a sermon ought to pave the way for rejoicing, not the reverse.
5. In that regard, I also believe that *every* service ought to end on a note of victory unless the people remain unrepentant.

Plan to Plan. There is a great potential for blessing hidden in faithful, prayerful planning. You don't have to be an expert planner to start. As I said to a perfectionist friend of mine once, "I like my way of doing things better than your way of not doing things." Ask the Lord to help you, purchase a good book, attend a seminar on the subject, and start!

Nick Ittzes[50]

305 ✦ THE WORSHIP LEADER AS SERVANT

Servanthood is a powerful leadership tool. This is because, in serving others, the worship leader becomes like Jesus and walks the path that led to his glorification through obedience. Worship leaders serve God first, then their church's leadership, their worship team, and their congregation.

When his disciples began to vie with one another for positions, Jesus told them, "You know that the rulers of the Gentiles lord it over them, and their high officials exercise authority over them. Not so with you. Instead, whoever wants to become great among you must be your servant, and whoever wants to be first must be your slave—just as the Son of Man did not come to be served, but to serve, and to give his life as a ransom for many" (Matt. 20:25-28). In those few words, Jesus was stating a great leadership principle.

The Power of Servanthood

If you have learned to serve, you are bound for kingdom success. In fact, servanthood is such a powerful leadership tool that it works in any organization, whether church-related or not. There are at least two reasons why serving has such great power: It replicates the life of Jesus, and it puts us on the same path as Jesus.

Serving Replicates the Life of Jesus. Becoming more and more like Jesus is the essence of being Christians. And the more like him we become, the more we will be able to do his works. (See Jesus' complete sermon on this subject in John 13–16.)

A major part of becoming like him is becoming servants. Jesus commands us to follow him in servanthood. After he washed their feet, Jesus told his disciples, "You call me 'Teacher' and 'Lord,' and rightly so, for that is what I am. Now that I, your Lord and Teacher, have washed your feet, you also should wash one another's feet. I have set you an example that you should do as I have done for you. I tell you the truth, no servant is greater than his master, nor is a messenger greater than the one who sent him. Now that you know these things, you will be blessed if you do them" (John 13:13-17). The footwashing has significance beyond its obvious lesson in humility. In Jesus' day, washing the feet of guests was a common courtesy, much like helping someone off with his or her jacket would be in our time. It demonstrates that the leader is not above taking care of the ordinary needs of his staff.

Clearly, the servant-attitude on our part is an attitude that would please our Lord Jesus. Pleasing him is the roadway to kingdom power, for in the great miracle chapter, John 14, Jesus said, "Whoever has my commands and obeys them, he is the one who loves me. He who loves me will be loved by my Father, and I too will love him and show myself to him" (John 14:21). Our hearts' desire is to have God show himself to us in our worship services.

Obedient servant-leadership is surely an avenue for that to happen.

Serving Puts Us on the Same Path as Jesus. Another reason why serving has such great power is that it puts us on the same path that led to the glorification of Jesus. Jesus was exalted by God because he was first a servant. God commands us to

do nothing out of selfish ambition or vain conceit, but in humility consider others better than yourselves. Each of you should look not only to your own interests, but also to the interests of others.

Your attitude should be the same as that of Christ Jesus, who, being in very nature God, did not consider equality with God something to be grasped, but made himself nothing, taking the very nature of a servant, being made in human likeness. And being found in appearance as a man, he humbled himself and became obedient to death—even death on a cross!

Therefore God exalted him to the highest place and gave him the name that is above every name, that at the name of Jesus every knee should bow, in heaven and on earth and under the earth, and every tongue confess that Jesus Christ is Lord, to the glory of God the Father. (Phil. 2:3-11)

We Get Back What We Give

Imagine the power of a worship team that is composed of servants who desire nothing more than to glorify God and bless his church. In your role as leader, you can build such a team—not just by teaching on servanthood, but by being an example to the team.

Unfortunately, many people who come into leadership in the church think that leading is synonymous with throwing your weight around. But that destructive mentality must be replaced with obedient servanthood, in which we place God's will above all else and serve one another at every opportunity. Jesus promised, "Give, and it will be given to you. A good measure, pressed down, shaken together and running over, will be poured into your lap. For with the measure you use, it will be measured to you" (Luke 6:38). According to Jesus, therefore, if we give servanthood, we will receive servanthood back. We generate a giving people. Thus, the servant-leader is able to accomplish what the domineering leader can only long for—a serving people.

Targeting Your Serving

Let's now consider the target of your serving, and how to accomplish your servant-leadership.

The Worship Leader Serves God. It seems almost unnecessary to mention that you serve God. But we can lose sight of the basics because of our tendency to worship at the shrine of the extraordinary. The chief target of your ministrations is God. You are not the entertainer of a human audience. You are first and foremost a servant of the Most High God, to bring him pleasure. Then you can lead people where you have been. Your primary calling is to get close to the heart of God and to minister to him according to his desires.

You Serve the Church's Leadership. Worship leaders who try to enhance their own position at the expense of the other leaders in the church are clearly out of God's order. To use the incredible power of music and worship for selfish ends is utterly reprehensible. Rather, you will use your gifts to support the total ministry of the church. If that ministry is utterly unworthy of support and seems entirely unredeemable, then ask the Lord for a release to join another congregation.

Because music and worship have such a profound impact on the total life of the church, you can serve the other leaders by staying in close contact with them. Ideally, you should be involved in the top-level leadership of the church, where you can find out what the spiritual and strategic needs of the church are.

For example, let's suppose that the church is planning a missionary outreach to Mexico. If you are involved in planning, you can be seeking God for ways to prophesy life into that vision from your position as worship leader. God can give you creative ways to keep that vision before the saints.

You Serve Your Team. Serving your team means that you will see yourself as their supporter, equipping them to do their job well. Years ago, Larry Christenson said, "The sign of a successful leader is a successful staff" (*A Message to the Charismatic Movement* [Minneapolis: Bethany Fellowship, 1972]). Promoting, empowering, encouraging, training, equipping your team—these are the hallmarks of a professional leader. My church is singularly blessed to have as a worship leader one who runs a tight ship. Commitment is very high. But

his team knows that he will "go to bat" for them regarding their needs. Partly because of his commitment, our team has some of the finest sound equipment available today. They have a place of honor in our church and exert a positive influence at every age level and in every facet of our ministry.

A good leader will also "take the heat." You will shield your team from the many "well-meaning dragons" that come with their hundreds of mutually exclusive "suggestions" and complaints. You will see to it that your team is answerable to *you,* before other leaders in the church. You will be your team's advocate at church budget time; you will plead the team's cause to have money allocated for instruments, sound equipment, tuition, and expense payments so that your team can attend worship conferences and so forth.

You Serve the People. Finally, you are a servant to the congregation. Your purpose is to lead them into the manifest presence of God. You occupy a prophetic role and serve the congregation by leading and equipping them for true, spiritual worship. But if you are the servant-leader, you will be careful to lead the people with compassion and understanding. I have seen some musicians lead with a chip on their shoulder. They have an agenda. Their attitude is, "I'm going to teach you how to worship if it kills you." For example, I had a classmate in seminary who was very intellectual and deeply involved in liturgical worship. At graduation time, he asked for a call to a rural church somewhere in the Midwest. Since that seemed incongruous with his worship interest, the administration asked him why he would want such a call. His answer? "I want to teach those peasants how to really worship!" Needless to say, his request was declined.

As a servant-leader you will find out what your congregation's musical tastes, abilities, and worship skills are. Then, rather than looking at how much they are lacking, you will gratefully build on what they already have. You will stretch them without breaking them.

A New Standard for Leadership

This is an hour in which God is raising a new standard for leadership. The days of leadership by egomania are gone. God is looking for leaders whom he can trust to replicate the life and style of Jesus, for to such leaders he will gladly send people.

He is looking for churches that are safe for struggling Christians, where their leaders will care about the flock more than about themselves. If you will answer that call, you can take your place on the cutting edge of what God is doing today. Answer now, "Speak, LORD, for your servant is listening" (1 Sam. 3:9).

Nick Ittzes[51]

306 ✦ PURSUING EXCELLENCE

Excellence starts with a godly self-esteem, which worship leaders need to instill in their team members by helping them to understand who they are in Christ. Excellence is not something we arrive at, but something we continually pursue; it is a state of "being" more than a state of "doing."

Excellence has become a management buzzword. It may soon find itself on the list of "wonderful words to be used for management by clichés." Nowadays many people are climbing aboard the excellence bandwagon. But what does it really mean to pursue excellence? As worship leaders, can we define excellence so it is more than a noble-sounding sentiment? How can the worship leader develop a team that pursues excellence?

God Inside: Wellspring of Excellence. For the Christian, pursuing excellence is the inescapable consequence of his or her fellowship with the Christ who does "everything well" (Mark 7:37). This is so because everything we need for life and godliness has already been given us in Christ Jesus (2 Pet. 1:3), and we can access what has been given us by believing his "very great and precious promises" (2 Pet. 1:4). As a worship leader, therefore, your approach to excellence begins with creating grace-based, faith-energized people, for they always tend toward excellence.

Start Building a Godly Self-Esteem. As worship leader, your role will be to teach your team who they are in Christ. For if they have an unbiblical self-image, they will be hurt in at least five ways:

1. They will tend to ignore God's inspiration. Suffering from low self-esteem, they will think that any thought they have surely can't be worth much. You can imagine how that can rob a worship team of God's gifts.

2. They will tend to have a master-slave relationship with God rather than one of fellowship, love, and trust. They will be paralyzed by the fear of "doing something in the flesh," and won't budge unless God confirms their proposed action with supernatural events. They will fear innovation, although innovation is a sign of life.

3. They may suffer from a damaged internal guidance mechanism that torpedoes the things they do attempt. Somehow they will manage to inject a fatal flaw into their work.

4. People with low self-esteem often have difficulty receiving criticism or even suggestions from their leaders or peers. This is a serious leadership problem all over the world and is the silent killer of many a church and ministry.

5. Finally, people with low self-esteem tend to think they are failures if there is something they don't know. Therefore, they have difficulty in receiving expert help, too. They will stay away from training sessions, will resist attending conferences, and may not be willing to receive even their leader's correction.

Go for the Roots. When someone doesn't know who he or she is in Christ, he or she will produce bad fruit, setting "aside the grace of God" (Gal. 2:21). To start flailing away at the bad fruit may, in fact, create more bad fruit. If we don't deal with the roots, we will eventually cut our team off from Christ, for Paul also says, "Encourage one another and build each other up" (1 Thess. 5:11), and he proclaims a spiritual unity that grows out of God-given endurance and encouragement (Rom. 15:5).

The Foolishness of Preaching. Often I am asked, "Then, how can you deal with the consequences of a wrong self-understanding?" I can give no better answer than what Paul said in 1 Corinthians 1:21: "For since in the wisdom of God the world through its wisdom did not know him, God was pleased through the foolishness of what was preached to save those who believe." Every healthy Christian group includes nurture as part of its dynamic. I would encourage you to teach on the theme of who we really are according to the Word.

Spiritual Identity. Your team members must know who they are before they can exercise their gifts.

Nebuchadnezzar was the mightiest king of his day, but when God punished him, he forgot who he was and acted like a cow, not a king (Dan. 4:25-33). He was totally ineffective in his leadership role. Similarly, when Christians do not know who they are, the results may be bovine.

Excellence Is a Pursuit, Not an Achievement. In the pursuit of excellence, be careful not to substitute perfectionism. Perfectionists set absolute and usually quite arbitrary standards by which to judge themselves and others. Their standards may be so high that the result is a paralyzing inactivity. Because they dread failure, perfectionists often become expert procrastinators and blame-shifters.

On the other hand, those who are content to pursue excellence are unafraid to scale the heights. For them the chief issue is improvement. The perfectionists' standards are static. But those who pursue excellence impose no limits on their performance, and eventually will best the standards of the perfectionist. The gospel is clearly an invitation to pursue excellence. Character as well as the gifts of the Spirit are presented in terms of practice and improvement (1 Cor. 14:12; Phil. 3:14; 1 Tim. 4:15). One can talk about improvement only when something is imperfect. Those who pursue excellence are not undone by making mistakes.

——— **The Pursuit of Excellence** ———

Confrontation for the Grace-Based. Building excellence, then, begins with establishing people in grace, helping them achieve a biblical self-image, and unshackling them from the fear of failure. But it doesn't end there. Problems will still need to be confronted; however, our attitude as leaders must reflect the grace-based approach. Otherwise, we will revert to the old law system in which rules, reproaches, and shame are used to keep people in line.

The new covenant perspective sees confrontations as dealing with the conflict between flesh and spirit—between the old sinful nature and the renewed person in Christ (see Rom. 7:7-25). Thus, biblical confrontation comes from the position of an *ally,* working with Christian brothers and sisters to help them stand against their human tendency to sin.

Being before Doing. God's Word has in it the power to build us into channels of excellence. Therefore, as a leader you will want to focus on what Scripture says we are in Christ. With that as a foundation, the principles of the Law actually become promises of what God will work in us by his Spirit. Only in that context is it appropriate to discuss the parameters of excellence.

Before anything else, excellence must be *spiritual.* God is more interested in replicating his character in us than he is in getting us to do work for him. Joyce Meyer has said, "We are called human beings, not human doings" (*Counseling Psychology: Theories and Case Studies.* [Boston: Allyn and Bacon, 1975]). Consider, for example, 1 Corinthians 13:1, which introduces a concept repeated several times in the chapter, each time dealing with a different issue of performance without love: "If I speak in the tongues of men and of angels, but have not love, I am only a resounding gong or a clanging cymbal."

Even more pointed are Jesus' words of warning: "Not everyone who says to me, 'Lord, Lord,' will enter the kingdom of heaven, but only he who does the will of my Father who is in heaven. Many will say to me on that day, 'Lord, Lord, did we not prophesy in your name, and in your name drive out demons and perform many miracles?' Then I will tell them plainly, 'I never knew you. Away from me, you evildoers' " (Matt. 7:21-23).

Clearly, worship leaders must lead their teams into spiritual excellence. Godliness is to be preferred over musical skill if we can't have both.

Excellence in the Word. Closely linked with spiritual excellence is a deep commitment to accuracy, completeness, and honesty with regard to the Word of God. We have already said that worship leaders function in a prophetic role and that they must therefore be equipped with Scripture.

Excellence of the Externals. Although Jesus did not espouse glitz and glitter, we can also safely say he did not found the cult of mediocrity. Outward appearance does matter. External things, such as being on time, having your instrument clean, properly grooming your hair, are all signals to the observer that you mean business.

We are not talking about style here as much as a commitment to doing things well. A three-piece suit, for example, may be completely out of place in a church filled with baby boomers. But dirty clothes and their olfactory offenses are out of place among leaders in any setting.

Artistic Excellence. I have observed an ever-growing tendency toward musical excellence among worship teams. This trend result in the development of musical skills in the congregation, which is a worthy goal. Thus, learning at the congregational level is more "caught" than "taught."

Forbid Carnal Competitiveness. When we deal with artistic excellence, we have to be especially careful of the flesh. The Bible gives us wonderful, healthy advice on this issue: "Each one should test his own actions. Then he can take pride in himself, without comparing himself to somebody else" (Gal. 6:4). Aside from Scripture, _the primary yardstick for measuring excellence is each person's past performance._

Setting Goals for Excellence. We have now come full circle in the entries in this chapter. If excellence is to be more than a buzzword, then it requires our involvement in setting milestones for progress. That's what leadership does. It creates and fuels vision and mobilizes people to achieve more than they dreamed they ever could. My prayer for you is that the excellence of Christ in you and in your team will find increasing manifestation daily.

Nick Ittzes[52]

✎ FIFTEEN ✎

Leading Worship

═══

This chapter answers essential questions for worship leading such as: What are the desirable qualities of a worship leader? What spiritual preparations are needed for worship leading? Other entries give practical advice for worship leaders in the small but important areas of their work. Communication and leadership skills are also discussed, as well as worship leading in small churches.

═══

307 • WHAT IS WORSHIP LEADING?

What is worship leading? Why is it so important? The following article addresses the nature and importance of good worship leading. It attempts to dispel some misconceptions concerning the subject and offers helpful and practical tips.

Toward a Definition of Worship Leading: What Worship Leading Is Not

Worship leading is not just leading songs, choruses, or a song service. Someone fulfilling these roles is traditionally viewed as a worship leader. However, it would be more accurate to define someone in this role as a song leader or "music director."

In this model, a song leader or music director is an intermediary between musicians and other people. Usually his or her duties are to fill in time, to entertain, to prepare the crown for the sermon. Someone who travels with an evangelist or a convention or seminar speaker, whose purpose is to act as an introduction to the main speaker, would be a good example of a person filling this role. This person is song leading. Oftentimes, after every second or third song, he or she will say something like, "Oh everybody, let's stand up, and let's do this. Let's lift our hands to the Lord." The song leader's duty is to get the people ready for the speaker. The song choices are somewhat arbitrary: The purpose is to have the people sing a few gospel songs, hymns, or choruses.

I am not saying that song leading is bad. There is a place for this function, but it is not the same thing as worship leading. Worship leading is more than just "song leading."

Worship Leading Is Not Exhorting Others to Sing Songs, Even If Those Songs Are Worship Songs. This model casts the worship leader as the one who encourages the people toward praises, worship, and inspiration. Often, this is accomplished through mini-sermons, testimonies, or the "right" songs. The person in this role sets the mood for the people to worship. Basically, he or she becomes one who exhorts—a preacher before the preacher.

Worship Leading Is Not Worshiping God While Others Watch. I liken this to eating in front of hungry people. It is something like this: I have invited you over to my house for a banquet. I say, "Come to my house, we're going to have dinner around 7:00. We'll have a great time." Upon your arrival, you find us all sitting around the table, which is set for everyone, but the only plate with food on it is mine, and I start eating that food. I tell you how good it is. You can see by the expression on my face how good it is. I'm savoring every morsel. I might even tell you how good it is. "Boy, these sweet potatoes are good! And this turkey, it's wonderful! And these tamales, they're great!"

Whatever your favorite meal is, I'm eating it, and I'm telling you how delicious it is, and you can tell by looking at me that I'm enjoying every minute of it.

Oftentimes, you'll see worship leaders do this. Usually they do it without knowing that they're doing it. They simply don't understand their role, so they think, "I'm going to worship God because that is what I came here for." As a worship leader, however, you are also a servant. Your job is to draw people into worship.

Worship Leading Is Not Leading While Others Worship. This is similar to what I have just described, but somewhat different. It happens when the worship leader does not enter into worship when the people do. An analogy for this experience would be: We all come over to my house for dinner. The table is set for everyone. There is plenty of food for everyone, and everyone gets food but me. Someone says, "Hey, aren't you going to eat?" I say, "No, I'll eat later." I want to emphasize that as a worship leader you must have times with God apart from the time you spend leading worship. Just as pastors must spend time studying the Word of God and praying when they are not in the pulpit, worship leaders, too, must dedicate time to focus exclusively on God and their relationship with him.

Toward a Definition of Worship Leading: What Worship Leading Is

Worship leading is both worshiping God and drawing others into worship. Referring once again to the analogy of meals, worship leading is like all of us sitting down at the same banquet table and eating together. No one feels left out. I am encouraging you to eat, and you are encouraging me to eat. There is a sense of communion and fellowship.

Worship leading is like the role played by the usher at a wedding ceremony. He doesn't sit in his or her pew and yell to the back of the church to encourage the people to come and sit down. Neither does an usher go behind the people and push them to their seats. These are the functions that an exhorter fills. No, an escort or an usher goes to the people, makes an about-face, and escorts each individual to his or her seat. Similarly, the job of a worship leader is to find out where the people are, go to that place, make an about-face, and lead them into the presence of God.

At times, the people may be in front of me spiritually. This is like an usher coming in from the back of a church, walking up and meeting the people where they are, and then taking them to their seats. On the other hand, it is sometimes coming from the altar and going back to the people, making the about-face, and escorting them into God's presence. Below, we will discuss the tabernacle and the mercy seat of God or the Holy of Holies. We will compare worship leading with making a trek from the outer camp outside the gates, entering into his gates with praise and thanksgiving, and then going into the

Holy of Holies. As an escort the worship leader is juxtaposed between God and the people. His leadership is a sustained expression of where he feels God's Spirit is moving the people at the time.

Furthermore, having a sustained expression of worship to God without interruptions is what is going to do the people the most good. By stopping every three or four songs to encourage, you are no longer escorting the people, and you lose the value of the sustained worship experience.

The worship leader must be aware of the people, but he or she need not address or exhort them. Simply remind them that they are there to worship and draw them into the experience. If the songs are properly chosen, *they* will invite the people into worship. The worship leader's expectation is that the experience of worship is not merely a time-filler or a people-pumper but a sustained encounter of loving and responding to God without interruptions. Thus, a worship leader is someone who responds to God.

The Role of the Worship Leader

A Worship Leader Must Be Someone Who Worships. Before anyone can lead anything, he or she must master it for him- or herself. Thus, to be an effective worship leader the person must first become a worshiper. The psalmist wrote, "Glorify the LORD *with me; let us* exalt his name *together*" (Ps. 34:3, emphasis mine). The emphasized words are three expressions that indicate togetherness and the simultaneous expression of thanksgiving, praise, and worship to God. Therefore, it is important that a worship leader worship during the worship time.

A Worship Leader Must Be Someone Who Worships on a Continual Basis. On Monday nights, I led worship at a Bible study. On Tuesday nights, I led worship at a home group meeting. On Wednesday nights, I led worship for another class. On Thursday nights, I would fill in at another home group. On Friday nights, I would get together with friends who would ask me to bring a guitar and do some worship, etc., etc. After this went on for a while, I began to ask God why my heart was hurting, why I was drying up. When he told me that I wasn't worshiping, I didn't understand. I was leading worship Monday through Friday nights. He said that the problem was that I was leading worship, and not spending time being intimate only with him. He was pleased with what I was doing, but I needed to spend time coming back to the well when *I* was thirsty.

As I began to search the Scriptures, I found that they encouraged me to worship him on a continual basis. Heb. 13:15 says, "Through Jesus, therefore, let us continually offer to God a sacrifice of praise—the fruit of lips that confess his name." I was confused, though, because I was not paid in my job to sit around and worship God. I found, however, that I can worship him while I'm in the shower, driving down the street, washing dishes, mowing the lawn, playing with my kids, and so on. We all have times when we can worship God doing other things. As the psalmist wrote, "I will extol the LORD at all times; his praise will always be on my lips" (Ps. 34:1).

A worship leader must worship throughout the day because he or she is both a worshiper and a leader. By worshiping throughout the day, a worship leader models worship. By worshiping throughout the day, I nurture my own responsiveness to God. Then, when I'm leading worship in a home group and the Lord tells me to kneel, I do it.

Before coming to the Vineyard church, I went to a church where the basic philosophy of worship was different from that which I now hold. We were so into praise, and there was tremendous pressure to "worship" God. The whole idea was that if God inhabits the praises of his people—which he does—everyone should worship and praise him, for then the presence of God will come. The pastor would go around and physically lift up people's hands. It was a sincere effort. He thought this was the best way to do it. Practices similar to these are common in some sections of the church. However, this form of coercion rarely leads to "the sacrifice of praise" that the Scripture recommends.

A Worship Leader Must Be Someone Who Leads. How do you lead worship? The Holy Spirit, as counselor and as guide, directs the worship through the worship leader. The leader acts as a conduit through which the Holy Spirit can flow. The great part about it is that God uses ordinary people just like you and me. He directs the worship through the worship leader, and in turn the worship leader leads the people into the presence of God.

When Moses led the children of Israel, where did they go? Were they a people wandering aimlessly in the wilderness? No, God was directing them. God guided with a cloud by day, and a pillar of fire by night. Moses was called by God to lead the children of Israel, following the cloud or the pillar of fire, even when it appeared to go in an unexpected direction. In like manner, the worship leader is called to lead the people in the direction God is taking them.

All of this requires some planning, but the planning must be in accord with the leading of the Holy Spirit. Planning does not mean sitting down and deciding what song would be good to begin with, which song should be used to get people standing, what song would be good to liven up the mood, etc. Consideration should be given to some of the physical aspects, but this should not be the primary focus.

Planning means praying, and not just five minutes before you start. Once you have committed yourself to the job of leading worship, you have consecrated yourself to God. This may mean that some things in your life need to be changed.

In the Scriptures, we read about the call of the Levite. The tribe of Levi was a tribe separated unto God. Their inheritance was the Lord, not the land. Their job was to serve God in the temple and to serve his people. This is similar to a worship leader's calling today—a calling to be in communion with God and to serve the people. All of us need a more consecrated life, but as worship leaders, we need to be even more aware of our consecration. You must be led by the Holy Spirit.

Leadership means servanthood. We are not the spiritual head of the church or even of a small group—that is the pastor or other leader's role. Is this scene familiar to you?

"You know, Eddie, the pastor of my church just does not understand worship. I don't know what it is with him, but he wants me to do three songs, and that's it. He doesn't understand what's going on. I don't know what to do. I'm frustrated. Last Sunday, I went ahead and kept going. I did a half-hour of worship. He's talked to me three times and told me he doesn't want me to go that long, but I just went for it and did what God told me to do."

That is not right. You need to do what your pastor tells you with regard to worship. Submit to his authority, and show some respect. Pray for him. Yes, you may be right. Maybe he doesn't understand what is going on. You might be 100 percent correct. But right now your attitude is sowing seeds of rebellion, and you're getting into something that is not healthy for you, your pastor, or the church.

Pray for him, talk to him, and be his friend. Share

some of the things you have learned. He may feel threatened, but if you show respect, he may come to trust your judgment.

You must lead by keeping the spiritual needs of the people in mind. Sometimes I get comments from people that we need more songs of one type or another or that we haven't done a certain song in a long time. I listen to those requests, but I base my final decision on whether or not the particular request will enhance worship in this time and place.

A Worship Leader Must Be Someone Who Knows. The worship leader needs to know the present spiritual condition of the audience. Say, for example, you lead a small group, and there are twelve to fifteen people present. The worship at my church is something that I pray for regularly, if not constantly. I have committed myself to it. It is part of the job description. Nevertheless, it is not only important to hear from God, but also to listen to what people are saying or sharing during a small-group meeting. What are they talking about? What is God doing among the people? Have there been prophesies in the group? What has been the content of any recent teaching? What have the recent sermons been saying? Do these concerns have anything to do with worship? The Lord uses different means of showing us where the people are and where he wants to take them.

Therefore, talk to the people, relate to them, have contact with them. You cannot know where they are spiritually if you ignore them. If you arrive five minutes before a small-group meeting starts, and you leave immediately after it is over and never fellowship with the people or talk with them, how can you know their spiritual state? How can they know you and trust you as a leader and friend?

In summary, you need to know what the people's present spiritual condition is and where the people are going—what God's desire for them is.

Finally, a worship leader needs to know when God is present. Think about how you know you are in the presence of God. Have you ever walked into a service or small-group meeting late, when people have already been worshiping? What does it feel like? It's like, "God's here"—there is a sense of the presence of God. If God inhabits the praises of his people, then when we worship him, he is enthroned upon our praises.

In the Old Testament there are several illustrations of the awesomeness of the presence of God. In the

sixth chapter of Isaiah, we see the prophet trembling of the presence of God. The cloud had filled the place so heavily that he was weighed down with his unworthiness. But God touched him. This is how it is sometimes during worship. It does not only occur in a large crowd, but can happen in a small group where there are only eight to ten people worshiping God.

Do not use the corporate worship time to take care of your own needs. If you need repentance, repent before you start leading worship. If you need refreshment, get it before you start leading worship. If you need encouragement, get it before you start leading worship. This usually means going directly to the source—to God himself.

Intimacy with God and being in his presence are the key factors of worship. Healing and deliverance occur during worship. People experience the power of God or a miracle in their life during worship. Others get saved during worship.

Healing, deliverance, and salvation are all things that happened when Jesus walked into a city or entered a house. He walked in and announced the coming of the kingdom. Mary Magdalene repented at his feet. When he walked into a town, lepers were cleansed and demons fled. Why? Because Jesus was there. There is no difference between Jesus' physical body at that time and his spiritual presence in our worship today. We should expect the same miracles to happen to ourselves.

A Worship Leader Must Be Someone Who Serves. A worship leader must be someone who serves. First of all, serve God with all your heart, soul, and strength. You need to be committed to doing God's will and obeying him in all parts of your life.

The Scripture says, "Suppose one of you had a servant plowing or looking after the sheep. Would he say to the servant when he comes in from the field, 'Come along now and sit down to eat?' Would he not rather say, 'Prepare my supper, get yourself ready and wait on me while I eat and drink; after that you may eat and drink'? Would he thank the servant because he did what he was told to do? So you also, when you have done everything you were told to do, should say, 'We are unworthy servants; we have only done our duty' " (Luke 17:7-10).

Being a servant in the kingdom of God isn't all drudgery, but there is an aspect of humbleness and meekness that needs to be visible. But this is where real joy comes—in serving. The apostle Paul exhorts, "Do nothing out of selfish ambition or vain conceit, but in humility consider others better than yourselves. Each of you should look not only to your own interests, but also to the interests of others. Your attitude should be the same as that of Christ Jesus" (Phil. 2:3-5). Selfish ambition and vain conceit are things that cannot be a part of a worship leader's life.

One of the things that happens when you become a worship leader is that it becomes a part of your whole life—you eat, breathe, and think worship. Sermons suddenly will apply to worship leading. Scriptures that have not applied before to worship leading will now apply.

A Worship Leader Is Committed to Drawing Others into Worship. A worship leader is someone who serves the people by being sensitive to their needs. You serve God and you also serve the people by putting your own musical likes and dislikes aside to better focus the people's attention on the Lord. If you ever hear yourself saying, "I'm doing what God wants me to do; forget what the people want," your view is distorted. You are a servant to God, but you are also a servant to the people of God. Remember, the people belong to God and so do you. The call of the Levite was to the temple, to God, and to God's people.

Spiritual Preparation

Keep Your Heart Right before God. Psalm 27:8 (NASB) is one of my favorite Scriptures: "When Thou didst say, 'Seek My face,' my heart said to Thee, 'Thy face, O LORD, I shall seek.'" I think this Scripture sums up for me what worship is all about. It is God's invitation to his people: "Come, seek my face." The other side is our heartfelt response to God: "Yes, yes Lord, I will respond to your call to be closer, to be more intimate, to share with you what it is that I feel about you."

Psalm 51:10, 17 says, "Create in me a pure heart, O God, and renew a steadfast spirit within me. . . . The sacrifices of God are a broken spirit; a broken and contrite heart, O God, you will not despise."

God wants a broken and contrite heart. That is all he asks of us. Does that mean that you will always be acting as if your heart is broken? No, because God restores, renews, and refreshes. Don't get the meaning of a broken and contrite heart confused

with just being serious all the time. What it does mean is this: There is no place for secret sin in the life of a worship leader. You must regularly confess your sins to God.

Numbers 32:23 says that sooner or later your sin will find you out. Sins always come to the surface, and they do affect your ministry. Some people feel that if they are in sin, God will still use them. It is true that God might use you for the sake of the people. If he used a donkey (see Num. 22, the story of Balaam), he will use anyone for the sake of the people. Does this justify being in sin? No. God uses you for the sake of the people, but that doesn't mean that you are doing right before God.

Be Sensitive to God's Leading, and More Importantly, Obey. It is easy to hear God's voice, but it is hard to obey. Obeying means that you are willing to take responsibility for your actions. "The watchman opens the gate for him, and the sheep listen to his voice. He calls his own sheep by name and leads them out. When he has brought out all his own, he goes on ahead of them, and his sheep follow him because they know his voice. . . . My sheep listen to my voice; I know them, and they follow me" (John 10:3-4, 27). That last sentence encapsulates what is important as a worship leader. As you read this verse, replace "sheep" with "worship leader"—"My worship leader listens to my voice. I know him and he follows me." As a worship leader, you must listen to God's voice, know him, and allow him to know you—spend time with him, and obey God during worship and outside of worship.

Keep Motives and Ego in God's Hands. "Whoever exalts himself will be humbled, and whoever humbles himself will be exalted" (Matt. 23:12). Again, "Whatever you do, whether in word or deed, do it all in the name of the Lord Jesus, giving thanks to God the Father through him. . . . Whatever you do, work at it with all your heart" (Col. 3:17, 23). You can go wrong serving yourself. You can get into lots of trouble serving yourself, but you cannot go wrong serving God or serving people. Jesus Christ is the focus of attention, not you.

Seek God's Face; Pray. Why should we pray? One purpose is to receive direction and guidance. I cannot stress enough the importance of seeking direction. In the same way that a pastor prays for direction for what message to bring, the worship leader, no matter how big or small the group is, needs to be in prayer about what direction to take the people in worship.

Be Aware of What God Is Doing with the Group You Are Leading. This is done through prayer, and then by opening your eyes during worship and looking at what is going on. Here at the Vineyard we are taught to keep our eyes open and watch what is happening when we pray for someone, in order to recognize the signs that the Holy Spirit is doing something with that person. There are certain things that you look for, not only in the spiritual sense but also in the physical. One of the ways to tell what God is doing or not doing is by looking.

When I first came to the Vineyard, I only did songs of intimacy. I had come out of a celebration/praise type of church, and I was looking for an alternative style. What was missing in my worship life was intimacy. So, when I started leading worship, that was the direction I took. But I was leaving behind a whole group of people who had balance in their lives, and who enjoyed celebration. The celebration was necessary as a prelude to intimacy, as stretching and warm-up time is necessary to help someone run a race.

Prepare the Hearts of the People You Are Leading to Enter into God's Presence. We have talked about your own spiritual preparation for worship. There is also a spiritual preparation necessary for the people you are leading. Prepare their hearts. If the Lord is showing you that repentance is needed, go into repentance songs. If the Lord is showing you that celebration is needed, start off with celebration songs. Here are some examples (by theme) of songs to use for this purpose:

God's greatness. "Majesty," by Jack Hayford; "All Hail King Jesus," by Dave Moody.

Intimacy. "Glorify Thy Name," by Donna Adkins; "I Will Magnify," by Scott Palazzo; "I Worship You," by Carl Tuttle.

God's name. "Jesus, Name Above All Names," by Naida Hearn; "Glorify Thy Name," by Donna Adkins; "I Will Magnify," by Scott Palazzo; "You Are the Mighty King," by Eddie Espinosa.

Forgiveness. "Tender Mercy," by Peggy Wagner; "O Lord, Have Mercy on Me," by Carl Tuttle;

"Change My Heart, O God," by Eddie Espinosa; "It's Your Blood," by Michael Christ.

Unity and family togetherness. "Family Song," by Steve Hampton.

The most important thing to remember when choosing songs is that we need balance in selection. Also, we need to determine what songs are needed to help prepare people's hearts for worship. Don't decide according to your own experience. Ask God where the people are.

Sometimes we lead without any regard for the body. We must be aware of the spiritual level of the people and their circumstances. Then we can alternate between good singing and prayerful intercession.

Lead by Example. Keep in mind that we are never to manipulate people into doing something they don't want to do. For example, when people lift their hands just because someone is telling them to, they are doing that in outward gesture only, and not from the heart. Rather, the approach we take in worship is that body posture, movements, and expressions are, in general, outward signs of what is going on inside. When you bow down, you are showing reverence to God. When you lift your hands, you are submitting to God. When you kneel down, you give respect, homage, and honor to God. When you clap your hands, you express joy to God.

Here is how I encourage the outward expression of inward worship. I start singing a song that mentions lifting hands in its lyrics, for example, "I Lift My Hands" or "I Just Want to Praise You" by Arthur Tannous. It is difficult to sing something like that and not do it. But people still have a choice: If they want to lift their hands, they can. If they do not want to, that's all right.

The bottom line is that God doesn't care whether or not someone lifts his or her hands. God looks at the heart. The key element is choice. When God called Abraham to sacrifice Isaac, Abraham had a choice. He chose to obey willingly. Worship must be a voluntary response. Let God inspire so that it becomes the person's sacrifice of praise, not yours. It is not a matter of getting the whole group on its face before God so you can say, "Look what I did." Rather, it is the person's sacrifice of praise, her response, his free gift to God.

Approaches to Worship Leading

Below are three models of worship and suggestions for the development of worship songs through music:

The Psalm 95 Model—a Fourfold Worship:

1 Come, let us sing for joy to the LORD;
  let us shout aloud to the Rock of our
    salvation

2 Let us come before him with thanksgiving
  and extol him with music and song.

3 For the LORD is the great God,
  the great King above all gods.

4 In his hand are the depths of the earth
  and the mountain peaks belong to him.

5 The sea is his, for he made it,
  and his hands formed the dry land.

6 Come, let us bow down in worship,
  let us kneel before the LORD our Maker;

7 for he is our God
  and we are the people of his pasture,
    the flock under his care.

You can see that this passage contains elements of rejoicing (v. 1), thanksgiving (v. 2), praise (vv. 2-5), and reverence (vv. 6-7).

The Psalm 100 Model—a Journey into the Holy of Holies:

1 Shout for joy to the LORD, all the earth.

2 Worship the LORD with gladness;
  come before him with joyful songs.

3 Know that the LORD is God.
  It is he who made us, and we are his;
  we are his people, the sheep of his pasture.

4 Enter his gates with thanksgiving
  and his courts with praise;
  give thanks to him and praise his name.

5 For the LORD is good and his love endures
    forever;
  his faithfulness continues through all
    generations.

This passage seems to suggest a progression related to the way the Jews worshiped at the temple. The following is a guide to choosing songs according to this model of worship.

Worship Progression	Song Type to Use
Encampment outside the temple (vv. 1-3)	Fun songs
Entering his gates with thanksgiving (v. 4)	Gratitude songs
Entering his courts with praise (v. 4)	Praise songs, usually upbeat
Entering the Holy Place	Worship songs
Entering the Holy of Holies (the ark, mercy seat, God's presence)	Intimate songs

The relational approach to worship planning. Finally, here is a table that suggests songs to use in a progress of worship different from that above.

Stage	Types of Songs to Use
Invitation or call to worship	Songs that focus and remind us why we're together
Engagement	Songs that draw the congregation nearer to God
Exaltation	Songs that magnify and glorify God
Adoration	Love songs
Intimacy	Songs that speak of quiet time together

Eddie Espinosa[53]

308 • DEVELOPING COMMUNICATION SKILLS FOR LEADING WORSHIP

Three attitudes affect our communication with others: dignity, humility, and respect. Also important to our communication are five areas of confidence: in ourselves, in our relationship with the Lord, in our relationship with the people, in the importance of our ministry, and in the use of our tools.

A good worship leader must be a good communicator. Some people are born with a natural ability to communicate and lead, whereas others may have to work at it. This is an area that can be developed.

Foundational Attitudes

When considering the twofold relationship that has to be taking place when you are worship leading (i.e., communion with the Lord and with the people), the following three attitudes must become the foundation of all our thinking:

Dignity. The Oxford dictionary includes these definitions of dignity: "high or honorable office, rank, or title; high estimation; worth; proper stateliness; gravity." We are children of the King of kings, so hold your head up and don't apologize for your ministry. See yourself as a worthy minister and servant of your Lord.

Humility. We are children of the King of kings only because of what he has done for us, and we have no merit or right to this position in ourselves. Humility or meekness will ensure that dignity does not turn into pride.

Respect. To respect is to esteem and honor others. We must show great respect toward the Lord and his people when leading worship. It is possible that this respect is very much related to the attitudes of dignity and humility.

These three must become intertwined for there to be a solid foundation for good communication.

Confidence in Leadership

As the Lord develops the above three attitudes in our character, there then can come confidence to work as a worship leader. There are several areas of confidence that can be built up, and in so doing, our ability to communicate effectively will be improved:

Confidence in Yourself. Self-acceptance is a most important aspect of good communication with others.

Confidence in Your Relationship with the Lord. This may seem basic, but there are so many who do not know real assurance in their relationship with God. How can you lead others in a worship relationship with the Lord if you are lacking in this area? To do this, you must:

- maintain a repentant and righteous walk with God; and
- know how to hear from God. You must have confidence in this, or you will never be able to lead and bring direction.

One of the biggest questions people have when moving in the supernatural is, "The thing I feel to do or say—is it really God, or is it me—or possibly the devil?" Jesus said that his sheep would know his voice (John 10:27). This is a key in worship leading.

Confidence in Your Relationship with the People. This will never come about unless they know that you can be trusted and that you understand their needs and desires. It is not a matter of getting up in front with great confidence in yourself and God, and then forgetting the people. Pray and intercede for God's people. Develop a heart like a shepherd's. Respect them and be quick to put things right with anyone whom you may have offended.

Confidence in the Job That Has to Be Done. Many people are nervous and timid in leading because they do not know where they are going, how long they have to get there, or the direction in which they should travel. When you are worship leading, find out how much time you have and if the pastor feels that the meeting should be going in a particular direction. There is a wonderful sense of release that comes when you are not proceeding "in the dark"—you have heard from God or the pastor or both. There is such security in that. Know what you can and cannot do.

Confidence in the Use of Your Tools

- *Overhead projector or songbooks or hymnals.* Know how to turn on the projector and focus it. If you use songbooks or hymnals, know the number of each song.
- *Microphones.* Don't blow into the microphone, nervously poke it, or hide behind it. Learn how to operate this important piece of equipment. It really is one of your greatest friends because it gives your voice added strength and volume for leadership. Know how to adjust the microphone to your height.
- *Chorus/hymn list.* Have these in one file and keep it with you. This is an important tool because you should be able to lead a service or pull just a few songs right out of the file if your songs are correctly listed thematically and alphabetically.
- *Music.* The greater confidence you have in using and working with music and the musicians, the greater will be your ease in this area.

These may seem like simple points, but any lack in these areas will make you look like you do not know what you are doing and will, therefore, hinder your ability to communicate effectively. If you don't know what you are doing, then the people will not be at ease following you. It is a reasonably simple matter to take time with these practical considerations.

Communication is a fairly complex matter, and it is not within the scope of this entry to go into great detail on the art of communication. It is, however, a very important aspect of worship leading. One of the greatest keys we have found is seeking to be transparent and real in our relationship with God and his people. Many times you may have to minister to yourself and lead yourself as much as you are leading others in worship. In ministering to yourself and encouraging yourself, you will probably be touching others as well. The songs you use and the things you say will have added strength and relevance.

Mike and Viv Hibbert[54]

309 ◈ Practical Advice for Worship Leadership

Little things count. Improving oneself in the small but important practical aspects of worship leading can lead to greater effectiveness in that role. This entry gives practical instruction in a number of these areas, including visual presentation, oral delivery, movement and choreography, and content of services.

What does it take to lead worship well? As anyone who has prepared to step in front of a congregation for the first time knows, leading worship successfully takes more than courage or a mechanical awareness of what to do and when. Good worship leadership demands knowledge, ability, and preparation—and it begins with a good theology of worship.

In his classic piece "And Then What Must I Do?" Søren Kierkegaard chastens Protestant congregations for approaching worship with the same attitude with which they approach a concert or a play—as if they are the audience and the speakers (preacher, musicians, liturgists) are the actors. The churchgoers respond to the performance as critics—interested, bored, or deeply moved. Kierkegaard goes on to suggest that while worship might well be compared to a theater, the worshipers are actors, not critics. The worship leaders are prompters who help the congregation perform the act of worship.

The goal of worship leaders, then, is not to star in a great performance, but rather to become transparent prompters who help focus worship on God. How does that happen? By eliminating both the stumbling blocks and the theatrics that draw attention to the leader and away from God.

Visual Presentation

Good Grooming Is Essential. It may seem obvious, but the worship leader's visual presentation begins with grooming. One should certainly not have to be a fashion plate to lead worship, but basic cleanliness, modesty, and good taste are essential when setting a tone of reverence. Torn or unkempt clothes are obviously inappropriate, but in many contexts so is a too-expensive suit or party dress. Men and women will want to avoid suggestive clothing and garish jewelry, and women will want to keep makeup understated.

Consider the Style of the Worship Service. The formality of worship varies greatly from church to church. An effective worship leader will be aware of the culture, style, and formality of the service that he or she is called to lead. For the most part, the style of the service should determine the way in which the leader conducts himself or herself, not vice versa.

Good "Stage" Presence Takes Practice. Effective presence begins with good posture and attentiveness. Erect posture is both reverent and commanding and indicates to the worshipers that you are prepared to lead them.

Good eye contact encourages the congregation to listen carefully to what you are saying and invites them to participate fully in worship. When singing hymns or leading a responsive reading, you should lift your book so that your voice still projects and your eyes connect with the congregation.

If another leader is speaking, all attention should be fully directed to that person. If your attention wanders to your notes or you begin to gaze out at the crowd, the congregation will be distracted, too.

Gestures Need Not Be Loud to Be Effective. Often the smallest movement speaks volumes. If the congregation fails to rise to sing a hymn, for example, stand yourself. If they still don't respond, raise your hands to prompt them once more. Your role as a prompter is to help the congregation to worship God.

Oral Delivery

Oral delivery is one of the most criticized areas of leadership—and one of the easiest to change. We all know the frustration of trying to follow a speaker who talks too quietly or too quickly. These problems are heightened in sanctuaries that have poor acoustics.

Practice Diction. To improve your diction, try reading aloud privately or with a friendly "coach."

First, practice slowing down your speed until you are comfortable hearing yourself speak at a slower rate. Then pay attention to the consonants: Are you speaking each one distinctly? Many speakers make the mistake of dropping the consonants off the ends of words or of running two words together.

Once consonants feel comfortable to you, pay attention to the vowels. Each one requires your mouth to form a different shape. Practice saying phrases like "lips, teeth, tip of the tongue" to become aware of what you're doing and to make your mouth more flexible. It may feel strange, but it works!

Learn to Adjust Volume and Pitch. If you have a microphone in your sanctuary, practice using it before leading worship. Sometimes a quiet voice is most easily amplified by adjusting the microphone, but almost any voice can gain volume even without a mike.

The first step is to concentrate on how far the words need to go. Try getting your voice to reach the farthest corner of the sanctuary, the back row of the balcony. Then try breathing more deeply, using more of your lungs than in normal speech. A voice backed by diaphragm and lungs will carry many times farther than an everyday speaking voice.

However, sometimes being louder is not enough. Sometimes pitch needs to be adjusted as well. People with hearing problems lose their ability to hear higher notes first. If a worship leader has a very high-pitched voice, it may be difficult for some people to follow. With effort and time, a speaker can learn to lower his or her voice. One of the easiest ways to practice using the lower register is by singing. Instead of reading the soprano or tenor line of a song or hymn, try singing the alto or bass notes, or try dropping your voice an octave.

Use Appropriate Expression in Your Speaking and Reading. If you have ever listened to a great actor or storyteller, you know that interpretation can transform the written word into a powerful experience. Worship leaders must learn to use their voices to convey the Word in an expressive style that fits the content of the message.

How does that happen? Let's use the reading of Scripture as an example. To effectively read a portion of the Bible, the reader should begin by becoming familiar with the passage. Look over the passage for any questions of pronunciation. Then read it through a few more times, trying to decide what the central message or high point might be. Look for repetitions of words or phrases: the introduction of new characters, a shift in plot, a surprise conclusion. Determine what type of writing it is (history, poetry, prophecy, letter), and try to catch its tone. You might want to make a photocopy of the passage, jotting down notes to yourself about anything that catches your eye—words that you would like to emphasize.

Finally, practice reading the passage out loud. How does it sound to you? Are there other ways you could read it? Be careful not to overinterpret or get theatrical, but *do* use your best and most natural voice to get across the message of the Word.

Plan the Words That You Will Say Ahead of Time. Almost always, worship leadership entails preparing some of your own words as well as reading those of others. Your contribution may be as simple as introducing the prayer of confession or the Scripture lesson or as lengthy as offering the congregational prayer or preaching the sermon. Don't assume that you will remember what to say when you get to the lectern. Neatly type or write whatever you are going to say—prayer, announcement, invitation to confession, assurance of pardon, the creed, even the Lord's Prayer. Obviously, you know the creed and the Lord's Prayer by heart, but when you are under pressure up front, you always face the possibility that your mind will go blank. There is nothing wrong with that—as long as you have prepared for that contingency by having the words in front of you.

Also, make sure before the service that you have all the written materials that you need in place—at the lectern, at your chair, or in your hand. Usually these materials will include a Bible, a hymnal, and a bulletin (with your notes!).

——— Movement and Choreography ———

An often overlooked component of worship leadership is "choreography." The leader must know not only when he or she should stand, sit, or move but be able to help the congregation know their part as well. Once again, the leader is the prompter. The more confident the leader, the more comfortably the people will play their parts.

Plan Carefully before the Service. Go over it ahead of time, writing notes to yourself in the bulletin ("stand," "sit," "move to podium," etc.). Where do you need to be and when? Can you move to another position (e.g., behind the communion table or by the baptismal font) during a hymn, when it will be less distracting? Do the others involved in the service know their roles and positions? Are there some portions of the service that might be confusing to visitors and which, therefore, need some explanation?

Note ahead of time any misprints or confusing statements in the bulletin. Sometimes a hymn number is mistyped, or a change in the morning's order of worship isn't picked up in the bulletin. Decide if the problem warrants an oral explanation and determine when in the service it would be best to call the error to the congregation's attention.

Keep Choreographic Announcements Brief. Announcements are distracting. It is amazing how much you can convey just by your own movements. Without your saying a word, people will know they are expected to follow suit.

The only thing more distracting than too many announcements is a leader who doesn't know what he or she is doing. A poorly prepared leader makes people terribly uncomfortable and invites them to worry about the worship leader rather than focus on worship. So even if you don't know what you're supposed to do next, fake it. Look like you know. Someone has to lead—and in this case, it's you.

Content

What you say in worship is always more important than how you say it. A number of factors influence the content of prayers and the selection of the readings for worship.

All of the Elements of Worship Should Be Related. As you prepare to lead the service, ask yourself some of these questions: What else is going on in the service? What is the theme of the primary Scripture and sermon? Do these prayers and readings relate to and enhance the focus of worship for this service? In other words, do the pieces fit?

The Elements of the Service Should Have Theological Integrity. My preaching professor at seminary was a master at reading between the lines; he always pushed us to ask about the implications of what we

were saying. That's a good rule to keep in mind as we evaluate our prayers, litanies, sermons, and even introductions. What do our words say about God, and what do they imply about us? There are obvious extremes to be avoided—from Kahlil Gibran and New Age poetry to rigid fundamentalism and hellfire and brimstone. God cannot be so broadly or narrowly defined. Every time we pray, preach, and teach, we reveal our true theology.

Know What Belongs in Each Element of Worship. While there are no absolutes, the form and length of each element in the various liturgies is fairly standardized. The worship leader needs to be clear about what belongs and what doesn't. One seminarian I knew never got the hang of the pastoral prayer—she started with confession, moved to intercession and thanksgiving, returned to confession, and ended who-knows-where.

Use Appropriate Language. The language of worship should never offend. It can challenge, confront, even judge—but it must not abuse. Language both reflects and shapes the way we think, and, as worship leaders, it is important that we choose words that reflect the love of God for all people. Language that excludes people because of race, sex, physical limitations, or age displays our sinfulness and limitations rather than pointing to the embracing grace of God.

Great Rewards

Good worship leadership doesn't just happen. It begins with a good understanding of worship. It requires a great deal of thoughtfulness and practice. But, as you will discover, enabling and enhancing the congregation's worship of God is a tremendously rewarding endeavor.

Christine A. Chakoian[55]

310 ◆ LEADERSHIP WITH STYLE AND GRACE

This entry discusses use of body language (face, eyes, arms and hands, posture, movements); proper attire; movement and flow of a service; the role of silence; and a worship leader's relation to the rest of the assembly.

Body Language

Presiding well as a worship leader means using the body well. Presiding well means being comfortable with oneself in the public space to the extent that one doesn't call attention to one's uneasiness. It means looking like one knows what one is doing and speaking as if one means what one is saying. Presiding well means a certain honesty in expression: being who one is in the presence of God.

The Face. Some of us have faces that give us away; some of us have faces that conceal what we want to reveal. Live with the face you have, but be aware of it. A face that shows tension and strain (pursed lips, tight jaws, rigid head movements, tight neck muscles) calls out for attention and concern. Unfortunately, such faces draw attention to themselves and prohibit a "welcoming" greeting. Often such faces thinly mask a mind that is too concerned with trying to remember what's next in the order of service or what's next in a text. Such a face might loosen up when the worship leader begins actually attending to the assembly. Fear of one's own possible mistakes or fear of the assembly get in the way of effective worship leading.

The Eyes. The eyes have it! Eyes are meant for looking at people; for greeting them warmly; for offering sympathy, hope, congratulations. They can be wonderful windows into a person. They can also be glaring security gates that post "no entrance." They can stare blankly into space, giving the message, "no one's home."

People look away when they are afraid or intimidated. They look just over the heads of the group at the clock or the wall thinking that no one notices. But many do notice. In fact, within the assembled group are other sets of eyes waiting to make contact, waiting to be invited into human communion. Such eyes support and give assent; they empower the worship leader to lead from the heart.

The Arms and Hands. The arms of the worship leader reach out in greeting when they do so naturally. They gather the assembly together, including in their extension all who are present, never seeking to exclude by gestures made too small or by fingers that bend in. The hands look warm and human: a slight bend to them, not rigid and straight. The palms are raised heavenward while the arms gently gather those who worship. The movements of the arms and hands have a smoothness from one position to another, but a smoothness that does not call attention to itself.

Hands joined nervously in front of oneself merely transfer nervous energy down one arm and back up the other. Merely letting go of the hands allows nervous energy an exit. The worship leader is called at times to gesture in the name of the assembly. At those times the gestures are bold, but restrained, inviting the assembly into them, rather than warning all to keep their distance.

Sitting, Standing, Bowing, Kneeling. One can't be walking and bowing at the same time or walking and doing other things. Take time, use common sense, sit straight (if, for example, you are leading worship while playing piano), stand on both feet, don't roll. Bow or perform other actions for the benefit of the assembly—carefully and richly—and not merely for oneself. Point the entire body in the direction of the central activity, don't merely move the "head." That way, when one of the worshipers gets bored with the music and looks at the worship leader, the very way the worship leader is sitting or standing and attending to the music will call that worshiper back to worship.

Walking. This may not be an art, but there are better and worse ways of doing it. Public walking is a little slower than private walking, but good walking calls no attention to itself. "Be human and not overly religious" is my motto. On the other hand, I've seen people actually skip up the stairs of the sanctuary, taking two at a time on their way to lead worship. The action of worship demands more than this, and so does the assembly. I've seen people shift into place after several tries, sort of circling the area looking for the right place, and I've seen people cut corners so sharply you'd swear they had a sudden change of heart.

Appearance. If one is wearing a vestment while leading worship, he or she should make sure it is cleaned, pressed, and the proper length. Ordinary clothes offer their own problems: some clothes are judged by the assembly as inappropriate either because they are showy (a stunning evening gown or a formal ruffled shirt) or because they are too casual (e.g., shorts, sleeveless shirts, or blouses).

Movement and Flow. Every worship service has a high point, a focus, a central gesture; and every service has elements and gestures that lead to that point and others that move from there to conclusion. It is the worship leader and others who set the tempo and help the rest of the assembly experience the central focus of the service. This is accomplished by both voice and gesture, by tone and body reverence.

Silence. The advent of "new worship" seems to have signaled the end of silence. Silence gives the assembly time to center itself for prayer, time to take in the Word that is proclaimed, time to reflect on the preached Word, time to focus on an important gesture. Brief periods of silence (ten seconds or less) help establish the rhythm of the service; longer periods take on an important place in the service itself.

Deadly silence is silence that has no positive meaning for the assembly; it is the silence of musicians not being ready to play or the silence of someone taking public time for the private movement of books or candles, or the silence of someone fumbling to get ready for the next part of a service. Creative silence, on the other hand, is silence with a purpose; it is the silence that allows the assembly to breathe, to reflect, to pray.

While deadly silence encourages the feeling of boredom, creative silence pushes the service forward, but without the sense of rush. Time flies as the worshipers are caught up in the act of worship. Worship leaders, pastors, and others must learn the art of calling the assembly to quiet, of pacing the service through silence, of not wasting silence on movements that have no meaning for the assembly as such. They must also learn to treasure the assembly's quiet time so that they do not disturb it with a nervous word, lengthy explanation, or instruction.

Relation to the Worshipers. All of us who minister to the rest of the assembly remain part of that assembly even as we minister. As leaders of worship, we serve so that others might discover the presence of God in our midst. After all, the good news of the gospel comes through personalities and bodies, not automatically, not without working at it, but only when we are open to ourselves and to others, calling and inviting all of us to transparency and honesty before the Lord. Those who would lead worship must serve the assembly.

William Cieslak[56]

311 • LEADING WORSHIP IN A SMALLER CHURCH

Worship leaders at small churches can learn five principles from the life of a famous football coach to help them to better lead worship.

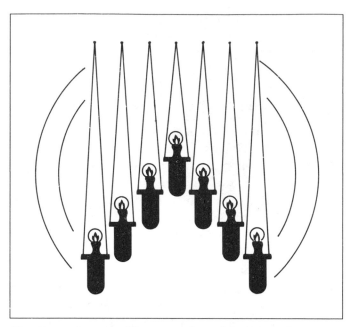

The Seven Lamps. The seven burning lamps is a common symbol of the Holy Spirit. This symbol is based on Revelation 4:5: "and in front of the throne burn seven flaming torches, which are the seven spirits of God."

If most of us had our "druthers," and we could choose between leading worship or being part of a worship team in a smaller church (75 to 100 members), or a larger church (500 to 600 or more), we would choose the larger. C'mon now, be honest! Fact is, though, many of the worship leaders and teams ministering today are serving in smaller churches.

Since 1975, I have helped build worship teams in five churches, mostly in southern California. Two of the churches grew quickly, having many musicians and creative people to work with. The other three grew quickly but had few musicians. All this is to say, I know how difficult it is to lead the people when you don't have the luxury and the pleasure of having a good solid rhythm section, an inspiring improvisational keyboard player, a tasteful guitar player, and a woodwind or string player.

If you are currently in a smaller church, there are some basic concepts to keep in mind that will help you to accomplish your goal as a worship leader (or team). Lest I be misunderstood, I am presupposing that you are squared away on all the heart issues concerning worship: what it is, why we do it, and so on.

At a memorial service for the late NFL Coach

George Allen, I was deeply moved and motivated by the impact that his life had on the lives of many great athletes. In twelve seasons of coaching pro teams, Coach Allen never had a losing season. But what was most impressive was that he accomplished that against great odds. His motto was "The Future Is Now," which to him meant that his focus was on winning now. That meant winning with players that everyone else thought were "over the hill," too old, and worn out, rather than building a team with a goal of winning in three to five years, the common practice for a coach starting with a new team. Coach Allen, a Christian, managed to accomplish his goals through the use of five essential principles. They are applicable to us and our goals for worship leading.

Leadership. The first principle is leadership. This may seem obvious, but sometimes this essential ingredient of worship leading is not there. The worship leader needs to lead. In the early days of our church, the Vineyard, the Lord led us in a direction away from the model of the "song leader" who functioned in many churches as a choir leader with the congregation as the choir. He or she called out the next number in the hymnal and directed it.

The Lord began showing us another way, which has become the general standard in Vineyard churches. We saw Vineyard worship leaders (and songwriters) Carl Tuttle and Eddie Espinosa stand up, start playing, worship the Lord, and not give a word of direction between songs. We learned to focus our attention on the Lord, and in our worship we learned that we could stand up, sit down, kneel, raise our hands, even sit on our hands as long as we were not drawing attention to ourselves.

Carl and Eddie were leading even though they did not say much. But in newer or younger churches where people are coming from a different style or from no church at all, they may not understand what's happening. It would then be important that some explanation be given as to what you are about to do and why.

Moreover, we have begun to experiment with different styles of worship; namely, the approaches of Graham Kendrick from England and Kevin Prosch from Kansas City, both of whom address the congregation from time to time during worship—an effort to bring praise, honor, and adoration to the King. Although you should avoid being a "cheerleader," don't be afraid to lead the people!

Passion. The second principle that characterized Coach Allen and his leadership style was passion. Passion refers to strong feeling or emotion. Coach Allen was passionate about his commitment to his players and his goal to make them winners.

Too often worship leading becomes routine, and it is difficult to maintain our passion for that commitment. When we first begin, it can be quite exhilarating, but after we have conquered the stage fright and have become accustomed to seeing and being seen up front, the exhilaration fades and the routine takes over. This can be especially true in smaller settings.

This leads to sloppiness and poor leadership and can deeply affect the worship of the people. They may do it, but they will do it in spite of you. Some people are naturally more passionate than others, but it is a quality that can be nurtured. It is the quality I most appreciated in songwriter and musician Keith Green. It is a quality that the apostle Paul encouraged in the church at Rome—"Never be lacking in zeal, but keep your spiritual fervor, serving the Lord" (Rom. 12:11). The Lord condemned the Laodiceans for lacking in it (Rev. 3:16), and it is the quality that characterized the life and faith of Caleb, who followed the Lord wholeheartedly (Num. 14:24). Don't draw back from expressing your love for Christ and your worship of him with passion, and your people will have the same passion for worship.

Enthusiasm. Third, Coach Allen was enthusiastic about his work. Enthusiasm is tricky. In my teaching on worship, and in modeling it over the years, I have been strictly against a "performance mode" for leaders and musicians. We have stressed, and I believe rightly so, that the preeminent requirement for a worship leader (or team) is humility, with a total focus on directing everyone's attention and heart toward the Lord.

It is sometimes difficult for professional musicians to become worship leaders because they have spent years developing performance skills and entertainment skills. As soon as they are in front of a group, these skills automatically take over. This is not necessarily bad, but it does not necessarily help people worship, either. They may enjoy themselves, and so forth, but are they worshiping?

On the other hand, because you are in front of the people to lead them, there is much to be said for warm smiles and enthusiasm in singing and playing.

Sometimes less-experienced leaders and teams have hearts to worship, but they are painfully shy, and this makes everyone uncomfortable and insecure. Sometimes we may not feel enthusiastic, especially in an early morning service, but it is our calling and our responsibility to lead the people, even if the audience is small. So "doing enthusiasm," like "doing good works," is something to consider. You must decide if you want to be effective. "Doing enthusiasm" can be a choice, and it can be a godly work. Try it—you'll like it. And so will your people.

Discipline. Fourth, Coach Allen was extremely disciplined. The card on his desk read, "Is what I'm doing—or about to do—getting me closer to my objective?" His objective was to win. Our objective is to worship and to lead others to worship the Lord. To reach our objectives, we must be disciplined. God highly values excellence. A passage of Scripture that has long been a favorite of mine is Exodus 35:30-36. It says that when it was time to build the tabernacle, God chose the finest master craftsmen and designers to do the work. He had "filled them with skill to do all kinds of work as craftsmen, designers, embroiderers in blue, purple and scarlet yarn and fine linen, and weavers" (v. 35). He had in mind to build a gloriously beautiful tabernacle that would express his own beauty, character, and creativity. The sight of it would draw the hearts of the people to him. I believe he desires the same from our music. If you have only a guitar or a piano, discipline yourself to play skillfully and creatively arrange the songs that you choose to fit your instrument. At my church the worship leader and I played guitar, piano, mandolin, and violin (switching off) for two years, until the Lord brought additional players. The worship leader worked very hard to program drums, bass, and strings into a sequencer. It had drawbacks, but it filled out the sound until live players came.

If you can't afford a sequencer, you can arrange the songs so they will work for you. But it takes work, time, and discipline. Let us not be lazy or negligent in perfecting our skills. Let us not depend on the old standby, "Well, the Lord will bless it anyway." No! Let us do it right. Let us honor him with our craft, or let us not do it at all.

Love. Finally, the principle that impelled Coach Allen to motivate others was love.

In his retirement years, after leaving the NFL, Allen took a job that raised people's eyebrows. He agreed to coach at Long Beach State. It was unheard of for a coach of his stature and age (seventy-two) to go from the NFL to a college that was not even a football school and to coach a bunch of kids who were not quality players.

Little by little, using all of these principles—leadership, passion, enthusiasm, and discipline—he accomplished what he (and many of his friends and former players) considered to be his greatest success. For the first time in years, and to the disbelief of almost everyone, Long Beach State had a winning season. How did he do it?

He practiced those principles, but there was one other principle. It was said that during the game halftimes, the main thing he told them was, "We've got to love one another!" What? In a halftime pep talk? Yes! Brothers and sisters, it always comes down to this, doesn't it? The bottom line is, we must love one another. We want to be successful and effective worship leaders (or teams), whether our church has 75 members or 600. We can if we take the time and care to practice these basic biblical leadership principles, and if we love one another.

Larry Myers[57]

312 ✦ GETTING THE MOST OUT OF REHEARSALS

Getting the most out of rehearsals starts with devoting time during practices to worship and prayer. Number three on the list of priorities below is learning new songs; other priorities for rehearsals include reviewing old songs, evaluating previous service(s), and working on special music.

Many churches ask for some practical ideas for their worship team rehearsals. Often, these practice sessions become mundane and boring. I don't necessarily have the final word on how to handle these sessions, but here are a few practical tips.

One of the major questions asked is, "How often should we get together as a team?" There are no right and wrong answers to this question, since there are so many variables involved. It must be determined by your situation. But once-a-week practice works best in most cases. It is difficult to work together musically in a given service if you are not very familiar with one another's abilities and musical styles. The ability to "flow" together as a team is made possible largely by working together often. Without this regular interaction it will be difficult, at best, to be "tight" musically.

The length of the practice session should also be determined by your particular circumstances. A team of two musicians will probably not require as much time for rehearsal as a thirty-piece orchestra. Remember, then, that as your team grows, your practices may need to be longer. Don't lock yourself into a certain practice length now and, if and when you change it, end up with disgruntled musicians. Let them know that there may come a time when your preparation sessions may have to change.

Another common question is, "What should we do at our rehearsals?" On the surface, the answer would seem obvious. However, by looking a little further, one can turn up some hidden ideas. Several are listed below, but keep in mind that all of these do not necessarily need to be a part of every practice. They can be intermixed and used at appropriate times to accomplish the necessary agenda.

Worship. This is an often overlooked part of the practice time. It is difficult to lead in worship on Sunday mornings as a team if we never worship together at any other time. Our job is not just to provide a musical background whereby others may worship—we are to be the leaders in worship. If our times of preparation consist only of "playing music" and not actually worshiping God ourselves, we are sending the wrong message to our musicians. We are telling them that the music aspect is more important than what is coming from the heart. Spending time in worship together as a team is vital.

Prayer. This, too, is frequently left out of many practice times. We should take time to pray for one another, for the congregation, for the pastor, and for other concerns. Pray and seek God's direction together for a particular service or series of services. All of these are important in building team unity.

As the leader, it is necessary to strike a balance in your own participation in the times of prayer. You should be an example for the others in prayer, but don't make it *your* time of prayer. Don't spend the entire time praying aloud and not allow the others to pray also. Encourage them to make their requests known to God (Phil. 4:6).

Learning New Music. Finally, we get to what everyone thinks practices are all about. Please keep in mind, though, that this is number three on the list.

When attempting to learn new songs, it is usually best to have music for all musicians. Some may be able to share, but asking twelve musicians to gather around one hand-scrawled 3″ x 5″ note card is a little too much.

Some teams prefer to have separate vocalist and instrumentalist sessions when learning new songs. This helps them learn vocal harmonies and various instrumental parts without interfering with one another. This, again, will depend upon your particular situation.

One important note on this: always try to learn a song thoroughly before using it corporately. This can save a great deal of embarrassment for everyone. At the same time, it should be understood that working on a given song for months without using it for a corporate service can be very frustrating to the worship team members.

Reviewing Old Songs. This is especially important if you add new people to your worship team. Most people simply assume that the new people know all the old music. Unfortunately, this is rarely the case. It is good to have a "working list" of songs and occasionally be certain that everyone on the team is familiar with all of these.

It is also worthwhile to sometimes take an old song and do a new musical arrangement for it. This can go a long way toward bringing new life to something old.

Evaluate Previous Service(s). This can be very helpful as long as you don't become scrupulous. Looking at what you did musically as well as considering the overall response can be beneficial for future reference. This is not so you can repeat something that worked but to evaluate why things happened as they did and what could have been done differently. This is not a time to be super-critical. Simply look at what happened for the purpose of learning. A great deal can be learned from sincere evaluation.

Introducing Special Music. These songs usually involve a bit more work than the praise and worship songs. This is, in part, because the special music is often more intricate, but also because the congregation will not be singing; they'll only be listening. Most churches will spend more time "polishing" their special music.

These ideas are not necessarily all-inclusive. There are probably numerous other practical suggestions that you know about or are presently using. Potentially all of these can be used in one form or another.

It is important to maintain the interest and the enthusiasm of your musicians on an ongoing basis. By doing this, you'll have a more contented and productive worship team.

Tom Kraeuter[58]

313 • HAND SIGNALS FOR WORSHIP LEADERS

The leader's communication with musicians is often vital to the flow of worship. Unfortunately, many worship leaders are

untrained in simple but effective hand signals that they can use to communicate. The hand signals here were developed by Shady Grove Church in Grand Prairie, Texas, and by Lamar Boschman.

If you have never used hand signals before, but would like to try them, please don't feel that you must use them all. Find the ones you are comfortable with and that work for your situation. Also, feel free to vary directions or make up your own. However you decide to use them, the important thing is to make sure the signals communicate clearly.

Lamar Boschman[59]

A. Song Directions

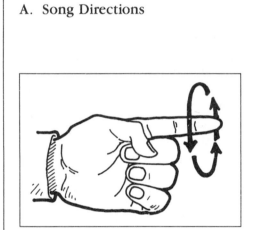

1. *Repeat chorus: Fist, with index finger sideways, slow circling motion.*

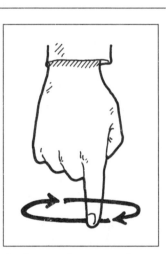

2. *Repeat last part (or last phrase): Fist, with index finger downward, circling motion.*

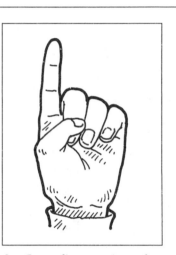

3. *Go to first section of song (may be chorus or ''A'' section): Fist, with index finger up.*

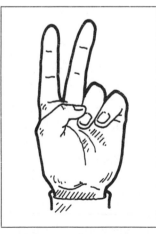

4. *Go to second section of song (may be verses or ''B'' section): Fist, with two fingers up.*

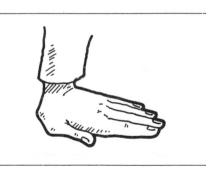

5. *Look out! A change is coming (or be ready to STOP): Hand extended flat, down low.*

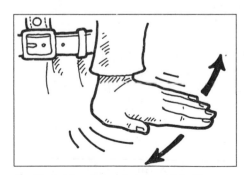

6. *Stop playing, sing a cappella: Hand extended flat (as in #5), with sideways back-and-forth motion.*

B. Tempo and Volume Changes

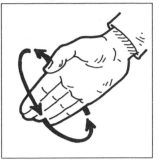

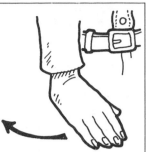

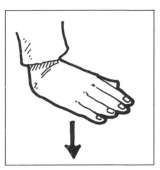

1. Speed up the tempo: Hand extended flat, with circling motion.

2. Slow down the tempo: Flat hand, moving slowly sideways.

3. Raise the volume: Fist extended, with an up-and-down motion.

4. Lower the volume: Hand extended flat, palm down, with a downward motion.

C. Keys

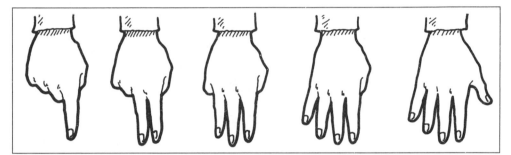

1. Key of C (no sharps or flats): Index finger and thumb in "C" shape.

2. Flat keys: Number of fingers pointing downward determines number of flats, and therefore the key. Thus: (1) one finger (one flat, key of F); (2) two fingers (two flats, B♭); (3) three fingers (three flats, E♭); (4) four fingers (four flats, A♭); (5) five fingers (five flats, D♭).

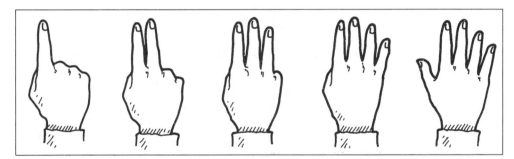

3. Sharp keys: Number of fingers pointing upward determines number of sharps, and therefore the key. Thus: (1) one finger (one sharp, key of G); (2) two fingers (two sharps, key of D); (2) three fingers (three sharps, A); (4) four fingers (four sharps, E); (5) five fingers (five sharps, B); f) six fingers (six sharps, F#).

D. Modulations

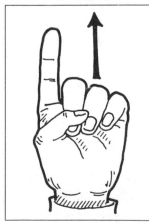

1. Modulation up a whole step: Fist with index finger up, upward motion.

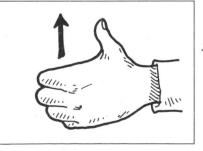

2. Modulation up one-half step: Fist with thumb up, upward motion.

❧ SIXTEEN ❧

Planning Worship

The following entries discuss different aspects of planning worship, which includes involving lay people, choosing songs, observing the church year, and enriching the flow of worship.

---

314 • PLANNING TRADITIONAL WORSHIP

Long-range and short-range planning are essential to worship services characterized by strength, order, and beauty. Pastors and church musicians are responsible for planning, but participation in music during worship should include adult and children's choirs and the congregation singing hymns, psalms, and anthems together.

In *Into His Presence: Perspectives on Reformed Worship* (Grand Rapids, Mich.: Christian Reformed Church Publications, 1985), James De Jong describes worship as a dialogue in which God's people *receive* God's greeting, pardon, instruction, and blessing, as well as *respond* in confession, thanksgiving, and praise. Many times the music in our services has blurred this view of Reformed worship. Howard Hageman tells of a worship service he attended in which the congregation had as much music to listen to as it did to sing, and the music had little or no relationship to actions of receiving and responding. Hageman then goes on to talk about "liturgical integrity" (*Liturgy and Music in Reformed Worship* [Fall/Winter 1983–84]: 4).

One way to avoid the kind of service Hageman describes is through careful planning. Long- and short-term planning helps worship leaders to integrate the ministry of Word and music and find ways of involving the congregation meaningfully in the service.

——— Responsibility for Planning ———

Who is responsible for planning worship services?

Since worship is the lifeblood of the church, pastors should realize that time devoted to worship planning is a necessary and vital part of their minis-try. To give choirs, instrumentalists, and soloists adequate time to prepare, pastors must plan their preaching schedules well ahead of time.

Involved in planning with the pastors are the church musicians—those in charge of proclaiming the gospel through music. Pastors and musicians, recognizing their roles as servants working for the glory of God and the edification of the congregation, together can make worship planning an enriching experience that results in God-pleasing, meaningful worship.

Pastors will use such planning sessions as opportunities to highlight the principles of Reformed worship. They will insist that contributions made by choirs and soloists should not be a source of poor theology, that "neither sentimentalism nor bombast are replacements for the nourishing word which builds and sustains faith" (Carl Schalk, *The Pastor and the Church Musicians: Thoughts on Aspects of a Common Ministry* [St. Louis, Mo.: Concordia Publishing House, 1984], 5).

In turn, the musicians will highlight the contribution of music. "The pastor needs the poetic aid of hymns as well as the exaltation of music to make the message come alive with splendor. The hallelujahs sound best when they are set to music and have an added dimension which the pastor himself could never give in any words. This understanding of the power of music to add a new dimension to the proclamation of the Word ought to draw pastor and church musician together in dialogue as nothing else can" (A. R. Kretzmann, "The Pastor and the Church Musician," *Church Music,* 2 [1970]: 8).

Since pastors and music directors usually have more flexible schedules during the summer, this is an ideal time to plan music for the year. Summer planning allows for more leisurely examination and purchase of music and gives accompanists and instrumentalists adequate preparation time. Such yearly summer planning also provides the groundwork for later seasonal and weekly planning sessions.

Planning Congregational Singing

Because hymns and psalms form an important part of the Christian life and faith, congregational singing is a vital part of worship. The goal of good singing is to involve the entire congregation in singing a sizable number of hymns and psalms with spiritual perception and musical artistry.

Select Opening and Closing Hymns. Use the topical index of the hymnal to select appropriate hymns to open and close the service. These will usually be hymns of praise and dedication that can be sung for several Sundays, but they need to be varied, preferably to reflect the seasons of the church year.

Select New (Unfamiliar) Hymns. The congregation's repertoire of hymns should be expanded. Every hymnbook includes some wonderful unknown hymns that should be introduced and sung regularly.

Plan New "Service Music." Service music includes doxologies, response to prayers, or musical settings of the creeds. Again, the congregation may need to learn this music, and the selections should be varied during the course of the year. Instead of using the traditional doxologies, consider singing doxological stanzas of hymns, such as the last stanza of "All Creatures of Our God and King."

Organize Hymn Sings. Hymn sings can be either designated sections of a worship service or full-fledged hymn festivals. Careful planning can make such hymn sings both educational and inspiring. The choice of hymns may be topical or seasonal, or may consist of "rehearsal" hymns to be sung in later worship services.

Planning Congregational Singing with Choir Participation

One way to escape the exclusive pattern of the choir performing while the congregation listens is to plan for joint singing. Such joint singing will clearly identify the choir as part of the congregation and may also encourage better congregational participation.

Hymn Concertatos. A hymn concertato is a hymn arranged for congregation, choir, organ, and various instruments. In many concertatos, choir and congregation sing alternate stanzas, or the choir sings a descant while the congregation sings the melody. Be sure to include an explanation in the bulletin, outlining the singing procedure for all participants.

Alternate-Stanza Singing. The singing of alternate stanzas is based on the ancient practice of antiphonal singing. Alternation can occur between choir and congregation or between segments of the congregation (e.g., men, women, and children).

Planning Adult Choir Music

The most important function of the choir is to provide strong and solid musical support for congregational singing, especially when new hymns are sung. The choir can also sing anthems and other more elaborate music.

Another important function of the choir is to lead the congregation in performing certain liturgical acts, such as a call to worship, a song of confession, or a musical meditation after the sermon. Through such "service music," people are encouraged to pray, confess, or meditate while the choir *formulates* the congregation's intention. Service music should not call undue attention to itself and must be clearly understood. (The words should probably be printed in the order of worship.) Some service music can be repeated in several services; other selections will be chosen for a particular service.

Summer is a good time to develop a schedule of choral music, balancing hymns or psalm settings that involve the congregation with anthems that will be sung by the choir alone. Music also should be ordered then to permit adequate rehearsal time later. The choir director and the pastor would do well to work together on the worship schedule.

Planning the Children's Choir Participation

The summer planning suggestions for the adult choir also pertain to the children's choir. Like the adult groups, the children's choir should be viewed not as a novelty but as an integral part of worship. John Calvin used children's choirs to teach the congregation the new settings for psalms, and such teaching continues to be legitimate today. A hymn such as "Infant Holy, Infant Lowly," for example, which may be new to the congregation, is easy for children to learn. Consider having the children sing such a song for the congregation, then inviting the congregation to join in. You'll find this "teaching method" is an excellent way of helping everyone, both children and adults, become familiar with a new hymn.

A beautiful contrast in sound can also be achieved by combining the children's and adult choirs. One example of an anthem arranged for such combining is "Like as a Father" (Cherubini, arr. by Austin Lovelace for children and adult choir, three-part canon, Choristers Guild, A156). Other anthems may be adapted for such use by assigning certain stanzas to each choir or to the combined choirs. This method works well for John Rutter's "All Things Bright and Beautiful" (one-part; Hinshaw Music, HMC-663).

Soloists

The same liturgical considerations that apply to choirs apply to soloists. Soloists should not convert the sanctuary into a recital hall; instead, their singing should remain an expression of the congregation's worship. Again, early planning, including careful communication with the soloist, is the key.

Periodic Planning

Yearly summer planning will greatly simplify the coordination of specific services, but periodic planning meetings are also necessary. The planning team (either a church staff or, in a smaller church, the pastor and the organist/choir director) should meet monthly to coordinate the services for the next several Sundays. They should discuss ways of introducing hymns (perhaps through a hymn-of-the-month program) and select hymns (including stanzas) for each service. If the choir is to sing, their selections should also be integrated meaningfully into the order of worship.

Using a preprinted weekly planning form is a good method of consolidating the necessary information. Such a form provides space for listing the hymns, anthems, call to worship, organist's service music, titles of instrumental music, soloists' selections, and participants' names and also leaves room for evaluating the music.

Since the best-laid plans may go awry, it is well for the pastor and the musicians to pray and consult briefly before each service. Only through such careful and prayerful planning will services evolve that reflect the strength, order, and beauty that should characterize our worship.

Does all this sound like too much work? First, remember that early, comprehensive planning is very efficient and will save time when planning for specific services. Second, as the poster on our choir room wall reminds us, keep in mind that "genuine praise is worthy sacrifice that truly honors God."

Wilma Vander Baan[60]

315 ◆ PLANNING CREATIVE WORSHIP

The communal nature of public worship is shaped and affirmed by liturgy, which is a script of a congregation's unfolding thought processes, social interaction, and psychological movement. Liturgy proceeds in stages of collective activities that can be both physical (outward) and psychological (inward); it helps a worshiping community gradually move into the presence of God.

Private devotions and public worship are quite different activities in the life of the Christian. While the former is shaped by individual preferences and tastes, the latter is built around a comprehensive public consciousness and identity. Liturgy is the tool by which this public consciousness is named and orchestrated in the rites of public worship.

Thus, the development of liturgy is more than merely a listing of things that will be done during an allotted period of time. It is instead a script of the unfolding of a community's thought processes, social interactions, and psychological movement. Liturgy sits in the director's chair, calling the mass of gathered individuals into a purposeful common ritual that will allow the congregation to commune with divinity, revisit heritage, reaffirm identity, refocus activity, and draw the cares and concerns of each participant into the healing graces of the whole.

Liturgical development often reflects the dominant features of the culture in which the church finds itself (e.g., the "parliamentary proceedings" of high church Anglicanism, the "town meeting agendas" of Congregationalism, and the "social rally" of African-Americanism). It may also imitate certain predominant psychological motifs within a theological tradition (e.g., the *"ordo salutis"* unfolded in historic Reformed worship, the "sacramental reception" of Roman Catholicism, or the "temple processional" of neo-Pentecostalism). But liturgy, within each of these types and the hundreds of others that exist, requires attention to the thought development of group identity to complete the psychological process inherent in the church's public worship of God.

That thought development involves at least four things: (1) plural speech; (2) an encounter or dialogue; (3) purpose; and (4) movement. The speech of public worship is plural because of its group character. An overemphasis on individual experience destroys what is at the very heart of a community's understanding of its identity. The dialogue or encounter frames liturgy's conversational interaction between God and his people. Purpose keeps each new worship experience focused and fresh, and movement plots its pace of development.

Psalm 100 graphically expresses these elements of liturgical development in what probably was a typical temple celebration of ancient Israel. It further unfolds the wavelike progression of group worship activities: series of similar worship rites collected in units that begin, pick up momentum, climax, and transition into a new focus of communal thought. They might be summarized from Psalm 100 as celebration (vv. 1-2), confession (v. 3), gift-giving (v. 4), and testimony (v. 5).

In the New Testament a casual reference to public worship activities occurs in Acts 2. Though incomplete as a basis for a full theology of worship, it nevertheless circumscribes worship in the early church in successive waves of group activities: learning, fellowship, sacraments, prayer, praise. A broader view of communal worship is shown in Revelation 4 and 5, where ever-widening ripples of praise flow outward in concentric circles from the throne of God in heaven, gaining strength and power until they become the warp and weft in the weave of the fabric of the universe.

Liturgical development serves the group mind best when it proceeds in stages of collected activities. These may be structured in terms of _physical_ movement:

1. We come, seeking God.
2. We worship, finding God.
3. We listen, understanding God.
4. We respond, reflecting God.
5. We disperse, praising God.

Or _psychological_ movement:

1. Worship: the desire of our hearts
2. Worship: the testimony of our voices
3. Worship: the unfolding of our spirits
4. Worship: the expression of our lives

Or even a combination of the two:

1. A time of preparation
2. A time of praise
3. A time of proclamation
4. A time of profession
5. A time of parting

The waves of worship may also find their orientation in God's activity toward his people:

1. God our Father draws us into his arms of love.
2. God our Father touches our lives with his grace.
3. God our Father guides our lives.
4. God our Father blesses us that we might be a blessing to others.

Or they might take their cue from the community's search for God:

1. We gather to worship the King.
2. We receive a word of encouragement from the King.
3. We give of ourselves to the King.
4. We boldly move on in life shaped and surrounded by the King's blessing.

In each liturgical development the titles describe the elements of worship activity that will occur within each of the successive "waves." Songs, prayers, Scripture readings, testimonies, gift-giving, responsive readings, confessions, greetings, teachings, blessings, sacramental celebrations, and the like become the building blocks of each successive "wave" of worship. Psychologically, these elements are arranged in such a way that they draw the communal mind-set of the group into a growing consensus of activity and then provide closure to each sectional movement.

The church's public worship of God requires careful planning if it is to draw the great variety of individual Christian experience into a common group activity that meaningfully moves the congregation through successive stages of its identity-formation and devotional expression. The "waves of worship'' are the stairs by which liturgy walks the worshiping community toward the throne of God.

Wayne Brouwer

316 ✦ PLANNING PRAISE-AND-WORSHIP-STYLE WORSHIP

Planning worship is sometimes problematic for leaders. Prayer is always the prelude to good planning; but the selection and ordering of songs for worship is also a spiritual activity. An effective leader compiles a master song list, allows a theme to influence his or her selections, anticipates the mood of the congregation, and takes into account the musical and lyrical content of each piece. When these preparations are carried out diligently, the leader will be able to lead the people gently into the presence of God.

Perhaps you've read the Scripture, ''No temptation hath overtaken you but such as is common to all worship leaders.'' When I open things up at worship seminars, the questions worship leaders ask are amazingly similar from coast to coast. And one of the questions I invariably am asked is, ''How do you plan for worship?''

When we think of planning a worship service, we immediately think of things like song titles, themes, musical keys, and tempo transitions. But that's only 10 percent of the worship leader's preparation. The bulk of the leader's preparation takes place on his or her knees.

Planning worship is much more than stringing a lineup of songs together. The only way to be able to plan a worship service is by sensitivity to the leading of the Holy Spirit, and the only way to gain that kind of sensitivity is by cultivating an intimate rela-

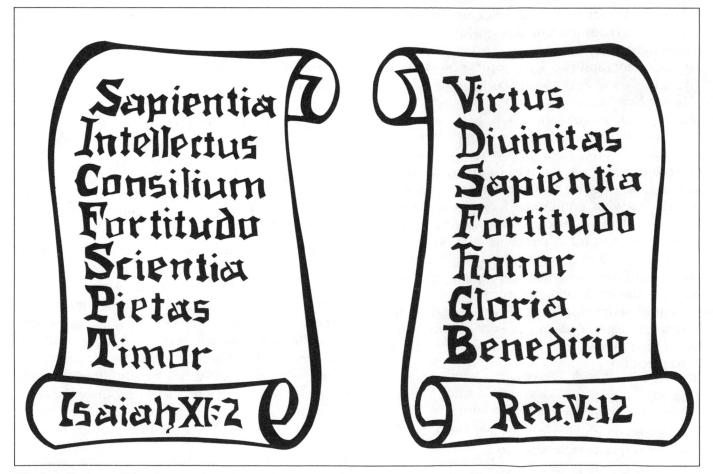

The Scroll. A scroll is often used to depict the seven gifts of the Holy Spirit. The Old Testament form (left) is found in Isaiah 11:2 (RSV): ''The Spirit of the LORD shall rest upon him, the spirit of wisdom and understanding, the spirit of counsel and might, the spirit of knowledge and the fear of the LORD.'' The New Testament form (right) is based on Revelation 5:12 (RSV): ''Worthy is the lamb who was slain, to receive power and wealth and wisdom and might and honor and glory and blessing.'' The New Testament scroll is found more often in Christian art than the Old Testament scroll.

tionship with the Lord. The first building block in service preparation is a personal commitment to daily devotional communion with the Lord—time spent in prayer and in the Scriptures. That's 90 percent of the leader's preparation.

But the purpose of this entry is to focus on the 10 percent. I believe that God, in his foreknowledge and infinite wisdom, is able to give us guidance for a worship service several days early. That gives us enough time to practice the new songs, rehearse the old ones, and get everything prepared well in advance.

In Defense of Planning. Before we get into the nitty-gritty of service planning, let me put in a plug for the concept of planning itself. Some people seem to feel that the most spiritual thing a worship leader can possibly do is come to the worship service without a list of songs, and depend completely upon the leading of the Holy Spirit for content as the service unfolds.

I see a couple of problems with that approach. It's easy to "freeze up" when you get before a group of people. If you don't have a list of songs in front of you, your mind can go blank, and suddenly you can't recall a single song your church knows. A lack of predetermined direction can also reduce the worship leader to "fishing"—"casting forth" a variety of songs in the hope that the people will "bite" at least one of them. Finally, when you fall back on a chorus that really worked last week and nothing happens this week, it's always safe to revert to the age-old words, "You may be seated as we turn the service over to the pastor."

Planning brings purpose to a service. It enables you to relax and lead with confidence, which in turn relaxes the congregation. The musicians can have their music before them, contributing to musical cohesiveness. Planning is one of the most spiritual things you'll do.

Sticking to the List. I have often been asked, "Do you find yourself sometimes discarding your song list during times of worship because of an unforeseen turn in the direction of the Spirit?" Let me answer by saying, first, that the Holy Spirit introduces many changes in our worship services that I do not anticipate. And thank God that he does! That's where the freshness is. And that's also where we worship leaders learn that blessed posture of complete dependence upon the Lord. If we knew exactly where the Holy Spirit was going to be taking

us every service, our worship would become "manmade" and would be directed through human manipulation. How refreshing when a prophecy or an exhortation or a Scripture reading directs the course of a service in an unplanned way.

Having said that, I'll answer the question more directly. I rarely find myself discarding my song list or adding a song that isn't on my list. Let me explain why. We're going along through the worship service according to plans and then suddenly someone leads out in a passionate prayer that directs our hearts in a very specific and unexpected way. My first thought is, "What song should I choose now?" Then I look down at my prepared list (and this has happened to me repeatedly) and I find that one of the songs on my list fits beautifully as a response to the prophetic prayer that just came. It is indeed the rare occasion when I find I need to move outside my prepared list to provide a song with a fitting response. Even though I didn't know on Tuesday what would be happening that Sunday, the Lord did, and he guided my planning on Tuesday.

A Master Song List. I maintain (with the help of a computer) what I call a "master song list." Since hymnals are already indexed with songs in assigned categories, my master song list contains mostly the short choruses and Scripture songs that are currently in our repertoire.

Songs are divided first of all into two main categories, _fast_ and _slow_. There are some medium-tempo songs that are great transition songs from fast to slow, but since they are relatively few in number, I assign them to either the fast or slow category. Under the fast and slow categories, I then arrange all the songs according to keys. Usually the first line of the song works best as the song title. Then, all the songs in the key of C are listed in alphabetical order, as are the songs in the key of D, etc. I will also note whether we sing a certain song in more than one key by placing the alternate key in parentheses after the song title.

I put all the fast songs on one sheet, all the slow songs on another, reduce them both down on a photocopier, paste the copies back to back, put protective plastic around them, and I have it: a master song list that slips into the cover of my Bible and sits up nicely on a music stand. It's my companion through every worship service I lead.

I finish off the master list with a couple of final touches. I'll add a column of communion songs, another column of Christmas songs, another of "openers," and yet another list that I dub "altar call." This last grouping is very helpful when planning the closing portions of a service.

About once a year, I update the master list. I'll delete the songs that have no more mileage left in them, and I'll add the new songs we've learned. This master song list then becomes my trusty companion (along with our hymnal) when I'm planning a worship service.

Choosing That First Song. Here's where we sweep away the mystical aura that surrounds service preparation. Some people think we wait until we hear an audible voice from heaven that says, "Start with 'This Is the Day.'"

Some worship leaders really wrestle with this area. They pray like this: "This is the day. I will enter his gates. This is the day. I will enter his gates. O God, what's your will? This is the day. I will enter his gates. Which song should I start the service with, Lord? This is the day. I will enter his gates. Speak, Lord, thy servant heareth. This is the day. I will enter his gates. O God!" And so they agonize. Meanwhile, God's up in heaven saying to himself, "I couldn't care less which song you start with. All I'm interested in is, whatever songs you sing, that you open your hearts to me." Can't you see it? God doesn't have a predetermined list in heaven that I have to figure out if we're going to have a Spirit-led worship service. Above all else, God wants communion with his people. He wants us to open our hearts to him no matter which songs the worship leader chooses.

I'd like to paint the backdrop for you of a hypothetical experiment. Suppose we got the five most anointed worship leaders in America today, took them aside, and said to each one, "We want you to fast and pray all day today, and come up with *the* list, come up with *the will of God* for this Sunday." Do you suppose they would supply us with identical lists? I think we'd find that all five lists would be very different. What's more, I think all five lists would "work" very well.

"But I thought we had to find the will of God for each service!" The will of God isn't a song list. The will of God is that we lower the self-protective barriers we erect in our hearts, allowing the Lord to melt every way in which we resist the gentle overtures of the Holy Spirit; the will of God is that we enter into the glorious intimacy of relationship that God intended from the start when he created man. The wise worship leader will build a service song list in such a way as to best achieve that goal.

Following a Theme. Some pastors will give their worship leader a theme for the worship service. If the pastor is preaching on the blood of Christ, every song is expected to mention the word *blood*. In my opinion, it's very possible to have a worship service that is clever in its following and expanding a given theme in preparation for the sermon, but in the end inspire a very uninspiring worship .

I am both the preacher (pastor) and worship leader at our church. And in all honesty, only occasionally do I pay attention to the theme of my sermon when I'm planning the worship service. Because the question for me is not, "Does every song point toward the sermon?" The question for me is, "Will this lineup of songs enable us to open our hearts to the Lord, so that we'll be prepared to hear whatever he has to say to us?" I would much rather have an enthusiastic praise service that ministers both to the Lord and to his people than have a worship service in which every song points to a certain theme.

So relax on the whole business of trying to get all the songs to line up according to one theme. (Special occasions such as Christmas are an obvious exception.)

The Moods of Worship. One of the first things I do is ask myself, "What kind of mood am I in? Am I in the mood to celebrate and rejoice this Sunday? Or do I feel more in a pensive, prayerful mood?" Sometimes my own moods point to the general mood the congregation when they come to the Sunday service. That in turn helps me determine the general direction of my song selection.

I have labeled what I see as eight "moods" or "flavors" of worship. Virtually all of our songs fall into one of the following categories: exaltation, intimacy, celebration, proclamation, warfare, prophetic, prayer, and special occasions (such as Christmas and Easter).

Before selecting songs, you may want to predict the general moods or flavors that you feel will characterize Sunday's worship service. Any one service will be confined to perhaps just two or three of the above moods, but over the course of time, a well-balanced menu of worship would mean the proper inclusion of all eight moods of worship.

The Process of Song Selection. Here's how I choose songs for Sunday morning worship. I scan through the index of the hymnal and choose a few hymns that I feel interested in singing. Then I scan through the "fast" side of the master song list and choose three or four songs that stand out to me. Turning to the "slow" side of the list, I then choose about three slow worship choruses.

This may sound like an "unspiritual" process I'm describing, but I sincerely trust the Lord to stir my heart as I go over the song titles, putting a desire within me to sing the songs that will best contribute to a flow of worship on Sunday.

Then I begin to arrange the song titles according to the best sequence. Several factors need to be considered:

The Key of Each Song. I try to position songs in such a way that the transition from the first key to the second key is smooth. For example, if one song is in the key of F and another in the key of G, I would consider singing the song that's in the key of F first, because it is easier to move up from the key of F to the key of G than it is to move down from G to F.

The "Mood" or Tempo of Each Song. Generally, I find myself drawn toward singing up-tempo, celebrative songs near the beginning of the service, moving into slower songs of intimacy and exaltation later in the service. (This is not a set formula—the Holy Spirit will lead you to invert that order at times.) Also, I tend to group the fast songs together, and then do the slower songs afterward.

The Lyrical Content of Each Song. For example, if the song is inviting us into God's presence with praise, obviously I would want to position that song at the top of my lineup.

The first three minutes of a worship service are often the most critical. Therefore, the first few songs you choose—along with the way you introduce them—are very important. Choose songs that invite participation, that get hands clapping, that focus minds on the reason we're gathered. Start with up-tempo songs that win the hearts of the children as well. Mobilize that royal priesthood of God's people into their holy calling of declaring his glorious praises! (See 1 Pet. 2:9.)

In planning the service's opening, I have to keep reminding myself of the true condition of many saints on Sunday morning. It's easy to assume that they've been feeding in the Word, getting renewed daily in the Holy Spirit, warding off every evil scheme of the devil, impacting their circle of friends with their vibrant witness—and now they've come with eager anticipation to join their voices with other holy saints in the corporate declaration of God's awesome praises. But I must remind myself that many people come to our services in a state of spiritual exhaustion. They've been living in the war zone, and many are fortunate to have made it to the service at all. The words and music I choose must reflect a sensitivity to where the people are, along with an eye toward the goal of where I want to bring them.

Once I have the songs listed in the order I want to sing them, I will then rehearse the entire worship service in my mind. I will imagine myself moving from one key to the next. Will that key transition work? Then I consider the "flow" of the moods from one song to the next. Is the progression of moods natural and inviting? Finally, I will picture where I want the people to have come by the end of the worship service. Perhaps it will be a place of high exaltation or loving adoration or bowing in humility and reverence. I will certainly want our hearts to have risen to new heights of faith as we have beheld through worship the glory of our risen Lord. The goal of the worship ministry is to stir up the holy passions of God's people. Will this list of songs in this particular order help us to move corporately toward that goal?

Planning an Exhortation. Now that my song list is intact, I need to plan for one other eventuality: what if, after leading with this wonderfully crafted list of songs, the people just don't enter in to worship? Maybe they're tired; maybe they had a fight on the way to church; maybe they're distracted; maybe they haven't prayed since last Sunday. Whatever the reason, one of the best tools I've discovered for inspiring a response in the congregation is that of exhortation.

Please understand, I'm not talking about a sermonette. I'm referring to about twenty to forty seconds of a brief, positive encouragement to participate, followed right away by a repeat of the song.

Exhortations are often most effective when planned ahead of time. You can choose your words carefully, making the most of the thirty seconds. As you spend time in the Word, ask God to place something meaningful in your heart so that when you share, others are edified. And usually the best weapon in a short exhortation is a Scripture. Read the Scripture, deliver a short and cheerful exhortation, and invite the people to join you in the song one more time.

Here is what *not* to do. Don't say, "What's wrong with you people this morning? Is anybody aware out there? It sounds like a funeral in here this morning!" Mr. Pew-warmer will say to himself, "You're right, I was out of it. But since you're going to be nasty about it, *see* if you can make me worship!" As we all know, nobody can force a person to worship. Worship is a willing response to the gentle promptings of the Holy Spirit.

Some worship leaders talk between every song, which breaks up the flow of the service. One or two short exhortations per service is usually adequate. Be the worship leader, not the preacher. Be encouraging, pleasant, enthused, inspiring. Let the warmth of Christ's love in your heart melt the resistance of cold hearts that may need fanning.

Planning New Songs. New songs play a critical role in the worship expression of a local church. If you're not learning new songs, you're stagnating. New songs force us to think. They expand our vocabulary of worship. And they bring with them a breeze of freshness. The new songs you choose to add to your repertoire will determine the future direction of your times of corporate worship.

Be picky, picky, picky. Look at the words and the style of the musical expression. Does the message add something to your church's breadth of communication? Does the musical style of the song add spice or depth?

Plan how and when you'll introduce new songs. I usually teach new songs near the beginning portions of a service. That way there's room for the worship service to "take off" afterward with a known song. But if I interrupt "high praise" with the teaching of a new song, the crescendo collapses immediately, and the new song gains the stigma of being a "dud."

Plan the reinforcement of new songs carefully. If we taught a song for the first time last week, it's important that we reinforce it this week, and possibly even the week after that. But then we'd better leave it alone for two or three weeks so folks don't get tired of it.

In summary, the worship leader's job in planning

is to craft a list of songs that will best help the congregation to open up to the Lord. Using tools such as short exhortations, the use of Scripture, and spiritual gifts, a worship leader has the awesome and wonderful privilege of leading people into the very presence of God.

Bob Sorge

317 ✦ PLANNING WORSHIP WITH THE LAITY

Because worship is a drama involving all the people, planning should involve not only the ministers, but also (and perhaps especially) the laity.

Worship, in the Christian tradition, is commonly understood as "the work of the people." This is, in fact, a literal meaning of the word "liturgy." By this is meant that worship is not intended to be a "spectator sport" but an activity involving everyone.

A timeworn but useful analogy by Søren Kierkegaard invites us to compare what happens in corporate worship with a drama. The problem comes when we see the congregation as the audience, the clergy and musicians as performers, and the Holy Spirit as the prompter. If this is the model, then our worship will involve the congregation passively at best.

Kierkegaard suggested we should change the roles. Worship for Christians is indeed like drama. Only it is God who is the audience, the clergy and musicians who are the prompters, and the members of the congregation who are the actors. Worship is what we all do in praising God—some of us have enabling functions, but the worship belongs to the whole people of God.

If we take this approach seriously, then we will involve lay people in the planning, preparing, and leading of corporate worship more than is customary.

What follows is a personal account of how one church has attempted to address this issue. This is, therefore, descriptive rather than prescriptive, and, it is hoped, suggestive of what might be done in other situations.

Laity Services

There was a time in most Protestant churches when we had what was known as "Laity Sunday" on an annual basis. One Sunday was given over to lay people to plan and to conduct public worship. It was a chance for the clergy to get "the view from the pew" and for a few people to get a better appreciation of what went into a Sunday service. In our church, Union Presbyterian Church of Schenectady, New York, there are about seventeen "laity Sundays" each year. These are very different from the old once-a-year version, but spring from some of the same values as well as new ones.

There are three different kinds of "laity Sunday" services in our planning: those designated simply "laity services," "family services," and "summer services." The "laity services" are the responsibility of assigned church groups—three Sundays a year are set aside in this category. The "family services" are planned by families of the church for those Sundays when the entire church family (including children) is present for the full service—these are set for special days such as the first Sunday in Lent or Pentecost, and the first Sunday after summer vacation concludes. The "summer services" are the ten Sundays in the summer—members of the worship department each select one to plan and recruit other lay people to help. (In addition, other special services, such as Christmas Eve and Easter Vigil, involve lay people in the planning).

— The Role of the Worship Department —

All of these services are the responsibility of the church's worship department. This group, comprised of three members of the session [the governing body of the Presbyterian church] and lay people at large, with musicians and the pastor, schedules the services and recruits the planners.

For the "laity services," groups of the church are formally invited to take responsibility for a service. When this process originated, the session set a good example by serving as the first group to plan and to lead a "laity service." The board of deacons and the trustees followed suit. Since then, groups such as the Membership and Evangelism, Christian Education, Mission, Support, and Worship Departments have planned services, as well as the senior choir, the high school choir, fellowship groups, church social teachers, and others.

The invitations are issued to these groups on a more-or-less rotating basis. By now, most of the groups have had several opportunities to plan and to lead services. Other groups, such as adult classes, have also been asked, or have volunteered, from time to time.

Each group usually selects a committee of its

members to plan the service, although more than the committee may take part in the service.

For the "family services," the pastors usually recruit families of the church at the suggestion of the Christian Education Department. A list is kept of those recruited to avoid undue repetition.

For the "summer services," the members of the Worship Department select one of the Sundays and recruit members of their own families, friends, or whomever they please. Sometimes people new to the church are included as a way of involving them early. Members who have had questions or concerns about worship are also involved at times to give them opportunities to express themselves.

The final responsibility of the Worship Department is to evaluate these services. Time is given at each department meeting following any of the services to discuss the effectiveness of the service and to note suggestions for future planners. Once a year, the department evaluates the whole process as it looks ahead to scheduling for the ensuing year.

— The Role of Laity in Planning —

At least one planning session is held for each service. Usually there are several lay people involved, and in the case of "family services," several children (grade-school age or older) are present. The pastor is also present, and for the optimum effect, so are the musicians.

The planning session begins with the group discussing the Scripture set in the lectionary for the Sunday in question. The texts are read aloud, and several translations are available around the table.

As the passages are read, lay people are encouraged to identify what speaks particularly to them—"What do you need to hear in that passage?" or "What would you want to hear in a sermon on that passage?" are good questions to ask.

Sometimes those passages set in the lectionary are not very useful, and the people find in them too little they can relate to or that seems timely. When this happens, there is freedom to let other passages come to mind.

The next step is to let a theme surface. Often this happens quickly, and some dimensions of the theme can be explored. When there are many ideas or concerns prompted by the Scripture selections, it may take longer to focus on a theme. But it is important to identify the theme so that the whole service can be built around it.

The preacher will want to invite the others to

make suggestions about the sermon. Personal insights about the Scriptures will be welcomed, as well as questions to be addressed by the sermon. This experience in the planning stage not only gives people ownership in the sermon, but allows them to grow as they talk about their faith with one another.

Hymns and other music are discussed in light of the theme. The musicians are often ready with suggestions because of advance planning. Sometimes lay people will have ideas about anthems or responses. Hymns can be selected by the group as a whole.

Prayers of the service are sorted out so that lay people may write or select their prayers. The pastor will want to be available to those writing prayers, but often little help is needed—prayers composed by lay people are often fresh and vital. The content and style of the service's prayers are discussed by the whole group at this point.

Other actions or visual aspects of the service are also explored. The use of banners, the manner of serving communion, processions, and countless other considerations may be given for the fullest participation of the congregation. It is the unique contribution of the lay people in planning to suggest what is meaningful to people in the pew.

It is important that the musicians have a comprehensive view of the year's worship experience as well as an understanding of the particular services. Awareness of the flow of the church year and the dynamics of each service is essential for musicians to make maximum contribution.

This means that the musicians, with the pastor, will do considerable advance planning for the whole year, noting those Sundays that will involve lay people in detailed planning. In the course of the advance planning, themes of the church year will be identified and the lectionary reviewed in its broad outlines. Some details of the lectionary will suggest specific pieces of music and should be noted in the advance planning.

When the actual planning meeting with the lay people occurs, the musicians will be prepared with resources to offer. It is good to have more to suggest than can be used, so some selections can be made.

If the musicians are participating in the planning process, new ideas will occur to them on the spot, and they will find their own creativity stimulated. Listening to what the lay people are saying, then, is an important role for the musician. The musician's purpose is to help the lay people give musical expression to the service they are designing.

The musicians are also teachers. They have an educational contribution to make in the planning so that all the others are better informed about the content and quality of church music and about the particular liturgical goals of the musicians. Something of the history and development of church music is often of interest to the lay people, as is the background of many of the hymns.

While the musicians are leaders in worship and have particular talents to bring, and while they are resource people to the planning meeting, they are mainly partners with the lay people and pastor in shaping the worship experience. It is this sense of partnership that is most important.

The pastor is the key person in this process. As "minister of the Word," the pastor has particular responsibility for the worship experience. But it is not an exclusive responsibility; rather, it is important in the planning stage for the pastor to include others in the fulfillment of that responsibility.

First, the pastor needs to listen to the people. Where are their needs for the gospel? What special insights of faith do they bring? How can they more fully participate in the acts of worship? These and other similar questions should be in the front of the pastor's mind during the planning.

Consider the sermon, for example. If the pastor is listening to the people about where they are and what they hunger to hear, the sermon will have a relevance beyond what is possible in one devised in isolation. Even specific illustrations will be suggested or quotes offered, and the sermon will have a vitality and authenticity not otherwise achieved. Children often have wonderful and quotable things to say in the planning sessions. At the very least, the preacher's pump is primed and creative thought is prompted.

Preachers who have not tried this will likely be somewhat threatened by this approach. But those who have experienced it are aware of the enormous benefits to be gained.

Another role the pastor plays in planning is that of teacher. Throughout this process over a period of years the pastor has an opportunity to teach about liturgy that is unparalleled. Each planning meeting is like a class in worship. Basic education about the theology and dynamics of worship takes place painlessly. Those doing the planning are eager students, as they would not otherwise be there.

This means that the pastor will have to be prepared and will have to do homework. The pastor is the resident theologian and, therefore, needs to study constantly. Teaching courses on worship in the church's education program will force solid study. One role of the pastor in the planning meeting is to be a teacher for worship. And the pastor will have to know more than anyone else to fulfill this responsibility.

Toward the end of the meeting, it is good to review the various responsibilities. Who will be reading Scripture, or writing what prayers, or leading what part of the service are some of the many details to be nailed down.

Then there will be follow-up conferences. If someone needs help with a prayer or guidance about which translation of Scripture to use or whatever, there will need to be opportunity for checking with each other. Any unresolved issues should have a definite way of being resolved.

Those who actually will lead worship should have a chance to practice. The pastor and musicians can be helpful in coaching. It is important to make sure the leaders feel comfortable to minimize distractions from the worship resulting from their nervousness or lack of preparation. More than that, the leaders should finish with a sense of having done a good job and with positive feelings about their participation in leading the service.

The overall effect of this process of lay involvement in planning and designing corporate worship at our church is that there are more people growing in their appreciation of the richness of worship. They have learned, not deductively because someone told them this is the way worship is supposed to be, but inductively because they have struggled with designing a service and discovered a new significance to worship.

The benefit to the pastor is that the sense of isolation is minimized. The pastor will be less inclined to be defensive about criticisms of worship or even the sermon because others are involved. Sometimes perpetual critics make excellent planners when they are given a chance to share their gifts in a positive and concrete way. A broad appreciation of worship from this kind of experience tends to give criticism a more helpful flavor.

This process also forces the pastor and musicians to be prepared. It requires study and work in advance and an openness to learn in the process. It is always educational for the professionals.

The participation of children in planning worship is essential. This need not happen every time, but it ought to happen some of the time. This prevents us from thinking what we can do "for" the children in worship and leads us to consider with them the purpose of our public worship. Children are potent interpreters and leaders, if we have the wisdom to listen and the grace to follow.

The purpose of all this is to praise God with all the fullness of the worshiping community. Worship belongs to the people, and it is appropriate that planning for worship include representatives of the whole family of faith.

Donald Wilson Stake[61]

318 • PLANNING WORSHIP WITH A WORSHIP DIRECTORY

Modern options for worship range from fixed liturgical practice at one end to "free church" liberty at the other. The directory approach, common among Presbyterians, falls in the middle. Modern directories are adaptations of the original directory of the church of Scotland (first published in 1645). In recent years many Presbyterian denominations have adopted new directories with the intent of using them to reform and renew worship. A directory not only guides worship, but also is useful as a teaching tool for pastors, leaders, and members.

A _Directory for Worship_ combines law with liturgical theology and gives practical guidance for planning and leading worship. The Presbyterian tradition's official texts deal with doctrine (the set of catechisms and confessions), government (the _Form of Government_ and _Rules of Discipline_), and liturgy (the _Directory for Worship_). Such documents are the constitution of a Presbyterian denomination. The liturgical standard or _Directory_ is found in the _Book of Order,_ with the governmental and disciplinary parts of the constitution. A _Directory_ is a strategy for ordering worship in a tradition that seeks to be evangelical, catholic, and Reformed.

--------- **Three Approaches** ---------

A directory approach may be contrasted conveniently with three other classic strategies for ordering worship. To the right of the spectrum is the prescribed liturgy such as the _Roman Sacramentary,_ the Episcopal _Book of Common Prayer,_ and the Lutheran books of worship. To the left is the

Free church tradition, which historically insists upon the local liberty to be governed by the Bible alone in ordering worship. The middle ground is represented by the Reformed churches, which have books for discretionary use by the pastor. A directory, such as that used among Presbyterians, is a fourth strategy, closely related to a discretionary liturgy. In fact, contemporary worship renewal displays more a continuum than a set of discrete alternatives among these strategies: Their characteristic features are blending together in the last quarter of the twentieth century.

American and Irish Presbyterians have repeatedly revised and rewritten their directories. The Church of Scotland, on the other hand, has never reworked the original directory (*The Directory for the Public Worship of God* or *Westminster Directory* of 1645). While other national traditions have also adopted the directory approach, the Presbyterians of the United States have maintained the model most consistently as their constitutional provision for worship.

Directory Contents. All directories for worship have dealt with these topics: the principles of worship, parts of the Sunday service, the sacraments of baptism and the Lord's Supper, pastoral ceremonies and ministries (weddings, burials, and visiting the sick), daily (family) worship, and special times of worship (fasting and thanksgiving). American Presbyterian directories a have added topics such as offerings (systematic giving), Sunday school (or "catechism"), and the prayer meeting (or "social worship"). The aim of the directory as a strategy has been to guide worship by the Word of God in Scripture, balancing liberty and liturgical tradition.

History of Directories. The notion of an abbreviated summary or outline of liturgical practices has a long history. The church orders of the ancient church (third to sixth century) described the practice of worshiping communities with varying detail. Many sixteenth and seventeenth century Puritans tackled the definition of essentials for evangelical church life and order. By the time of the Westminster Assembly in England (1640–49), various "directories" (such as that of Thomas Cartwright, 1574–90, reprinted 1644) expressed what the different parties favored in a reforming church order.

Scotland. The first generations of the reformed Church of Scotland, as well as the Reformed churches on the continent, adopted liturgical documents derived from the ministry of Calvin and other reformers. John Knox represents this extension into Scotland of the worship of the continental Reformed churches with the *Book of Common Order* (or "Psalm-Book"), which was printed continuously for Scotland from 1564 until 1644. But by the seventeenth century, English Puritanism and similar forces in the Church of Scotland demanded further reform in liturgy and polity.

The Westminster Directory. The *Directory of Worship* derived from the efforts of Puritans in England, and Scottish Presbyterians, to reform the British church at the Westminster Assembly of the 1640s. Westminster thus supplied Scotland with the first *Directory for Worship,* along with the doctrines (the *Westminster Confession of Faith* and *Catechisms*) characteristic of later Presbyterianism.

The Westminster divines sought a basic uniformity in doctrine, favored plainness of ceremony, and insisted on the freedom to obey Scripture and the Holy Spirit in worship. Disputes over liturgical customs necessitated measures of compromise between the Scots and the vocal minority of Independent Puritans. The *Directory for the Public Worship of God* proved both too radical for Puritans willing to tolerate a prayer book, and too restrictive for Separatists and many Independent Puritans. Though briefly enacted, the Assembly's *Directory for Worship* was virtually ignored in England.

Only the Church of Scotland replaced its liturgical book (the discretionary liturgy from Knox's book) with the new *Directory*. It became the distinctly Presbyterian liturgical strategy, adopted by the General Assembly along with a second document of 1647 known as the *Directory for Family Worship*. The ideal of liturgical unity in an English-speaking Reformed church resulted ironically in another new approach to liturgical order, alongside Free church liberty and the Anglican prayer book.

The *Westminster Directory* provided the order for the Sunday service and guidance for every part ("ordinance") of worship. An outline or schedule was given for each of the prayers. At least a full chapter from both the Old and New Testaments was to be read in every service. An eloquent treatise on the "plain style" preaching typical of Puritans and Scots provided edification for the pastors. Both baptism and the Lord's Supper were outlined with the ceremony, exhortations, and prayers in detail just short of a full wording.

The *Directory* demanded spiritual discipline and skill for the ministry of leading worship. The Bible was to be expounded through a continuous reading in public worship and was to be read systematically in family worship. The prayers were comprehensively outlined to guide the pastor through confession and petition for grace, intercessions, and thanksgiving. Considerable attention was given to marriage and visiting the sick, with an eye to civil law and pastoral theology. Other matters addressed included the Lord's Day, fast days and days of thanksgiving, burial (a civil event), and a brief mention of the singing of psalms. The *Directory for Family Worship* dealt with the daily worship of the church in its households.

The first *Directory* was a failure, both as a tool for guiding worship and as a means to reconcile different liturgical customs. The ideal of evangelical rigor in the worship of a comprehensively national church proved to be too demanding for the context in which it appeared. But it provided a precedent for later Presbyterians to pursue the same goals: guidance for worship that is broad enough to include diversity and hold a changing communion together, while excluding unacceptable deviations and providing specific helps for prayer and worship. The Presbyterian *Directory* bore fruit in later generations of liturgical renewal from the mid-nineteenth century through present efforts to revise resources and develop skills for worship.

Current Directories

The directory strategy currently is flourishing among American Presbyterians, as separate denominations shape their liturgical and doctrinal idiom. The largest denomination, the Presbyterian Church (USA), adopted a complex new directory in 1989 while it was also publishing a series of supplemental liturgical resources (1984–91). This latest directory was significantly influenced by the revisions of liturgical forms and books for voluntary use in worship. A new service book (projected for 1993) will share a partnership with the *Directory* in guiding worship. A similar relationship now exists in the Reformed Church in America (*Worship the Lord,* 1987). A service book for the Presbyterian Church (USA) will not have the constitutional authority of the *Directory,* but this option now clearly includes discre-

tionary liturgical book(s) for the use of those who plan and lead worship.

The Presbyterian Church (USA) *Directory for Worship* (1989) gives constitutional requirements for worship, but its role is shifting to primarily a teaching document. The change began in the 1960s, as a century of liturgical recovery and creativity once again inspired directories designed to guide reform of worship. This latest directory speaks more in permission and suggestion than as law or regulation; it is also by far the longest, most complex directory ever adopted.

Other Presbyterian denominations are revising and adopting new directories. The Cumberland and the Second Cumberland Presbyterian Church adopted in common a new directory in 1984. The Presbyterian Church in America reclaimed the nineteenth century tradition in its new directory of 1975. The Evangelical Presbyterian Church adopted in 1981 a directory based on the directories from the 1960s. In 1975, the directory of the Associate Reformed Presbyterian Church reduced its scope essentially to the sacraments, and acknowledged that many resources will be employed for assisting public worship. Both the Reformed Presbyterian and Orthodox Presbyterian Church are refining their directories from the 1940s to conform with their confessional priorities. An unofficial but general experiment seems in progress among American Presbyterians to discover how best to guide worship. Both the fracturing of the tradition and fresh ferment within it can be seen in the state of directories for worship in the United States.

Advantages and Disadvantages

The advantages and disadvantages of a directory approach tend to be the same features. Considerable authority is given to, and skill expected from, those who plan and lead worship. Principles and guidance must be translated into words, actions, and ceremonies. A directory can communicate the essentials of worship and define a denomination's liturgical tradition, while still encouraging local creativity. A directory (in contrast to a prescribed liturgy) may risk allowing poor liturgical discipline, because it requires self-discipline on the part of both leaders and worshipers. A directory can be a mirror of unity in the midst of diversity and also a tool for liturgical training.

The current generation of Presbyterian directories all tackle the educational task to a greater extent than previously. More of a background in theology of worship is given, as well as more practical guidance. These directories also assume the use of other resources in the manner of the Presbyterian Church (USA) service book, the official Reformed Church in America liturgy, or the relatively new tendency to borrow liturgical forms and texts of other denominations. Blending of strategies is taking place as one result of ecumenical sharing in scholarship and resources.

A directory approach expresses the truth of Christian worship that liturgy must be appropriated individually, and adapted to the local community. Many churches involved in liturgical renewal are struggling to move beyond the stage of preparation of new books to this deeper level. A directory for worship can be a teaching tool for ministers, leaders, and members. It can also affirm the nature of true liturgical unity within the variety of styles and missional requirements created by evangelization and change in denominations. A directory for worship is helpful when both training and resources are available, and pastors are committed to the ministry of leading and teaching worship. The directory strategy for ordering worship holds up the ideal of a comprehensive catholicity, combined with an evangelical fervor and Reformed obedience to the Word of God.

Stanley R. Hall

319 • PLANNING WORSHIP AROUND THE CHURCH YEAR

The church year provides a ready-made pattern for worship. The key seasons are Advent and Easter, which not only mark important events in the life of our Lord, but also inform the church's responses to these events in outward and inward worship. In addition, the church year puts the congregation in tune with a great body of Christian tradition that stretches across the world and back through the centuries.

The church year, also known as the Christian year or the liturgical year, not only has a venerable place in Christian tradition, but is an excellent framework around which to organize and plan worship over its course. In many churches today, the celebration of the Christian year is facilitated by the use of a three-year lectionary. This lectionary, indicating Old Testament, psalm, New Testament, and Gospel readings for each Sunday and festival, not only makes possi-

ble the regular systematic reading of substantial portions of the Scripture but provides a biblical framework for the planning of worship.

Cycles of the Year

The Easter Cycle. The church year is composed of two interlocking cycles. The first is the Easter cycle. This begins on Ash Wednesday, the first day of Lent (forty *weekdays* before Easter), and includes Lent, Holy Week, Easter, and the fifty days following Easter, concluding with the Day of Pentecost. Its principal theological theme is the atonement. Its center is Holy Week with its commemoration of the Triumphal Entry into Jerusalem on Palm Sunday, the Last Supper on Maundy Thursday, the Crucifixion on Good Friday, and the Resurrection on Easter Day. The fifty days following Easter, originally called the Pentecost, celebrate the new life in the risen Christ, and the Day of Pentecost celebrates the gift of the Spirit to the apostolic church. (Easter is the Sunday following the first full moon of spring, and the other dates are calculated from it.)

The Christmas Cycle. The second cycle is the Christmas cycle. Its theological theme is the Incarnation. The cycle begins with Advent, four Sundays before Christmas (the Sunday closest to November 30), leading into the celebration of Christmas on December 25. The twelve days of Christmas conclude with Epiphany on January 6 (Shakespeare's Twelfth Night), celebrating the manifestation of Christ. The three great events associated with Epiphany are the revelation of Christ to the magi through the star, the revelation of Christ through the dove and the voice at his baptism, and the revelation of Christ in his turning the water into wine at the wedding at Cana. Today, these are usually celebrated successively on the first three Sundays of the new year.

Sunday. The celebration of Sunday as the Lord's Day is the central building block of the Christian year. The weekly assembly of the people of God to hear God's Word, to offer their common prayers, and to celebrate the sacraments lies at the heart of Christian celebration. The biblical word *kyriake* (Lord's) occurs only in the phrases "the Lord's Day" and "the Lord's Supper." Sunday is preeminently the Christian day of worship. It is the first day, the day of the creation of light, in Genesis 1. It is the day of Christ's resurrection and the day of the gift of the Holy Spirit to the apostles on the Day of Pentecost. It is also the eschatological eighth day, the day that has a dawning but no evening, the eternal day of the heavenly Jerusalem. It is this weekly gathering for worship that gives meaning and form to the Christian year.

Seasons of the Year

Advent. The church year is generally considered to begin with Advent, although other days such as Christmas, Easter, the beginning of Lent, or even January 1 have sometimes been considered its beginning. The Advent season is almost archetypically a new year's festival. It combines joy with penitence, looking back with looking forward, remembrance with hope. It celebrates the coming of Christ—both his coming as a baby at Bethlehem and his coming again in glory "to judge the quick and the dead." The three great Advent figures are Isaiah, John the Baptist, and the Virgin Mary. The messianic prophecies of Isaiah have long been associated with Advent.

A traditional structure would begin with the eschatological Second Coming on the first Sunday. Isaiah 64:1 ("Oh, that you would rend the heavens and come down . . .") and Mark 13:35 ("Therefore keep watch because you do not know when the owner of the house will come back.") are typical themes. Bach's "Sleepers Wake" and Charles Wesley's "Lo! He Comes, with Clouds Descending" are typical Advent Sunday hymns. On the middle Sundays, the Baptist's preaching of the coming of the kingdom is the typical theme. "O Come, O Come, Emmanuel" is a hymn commonly sung here. On the fourth Sunday, our attention is turned toward Christmas. Luke's account of the annunciation to Mary and a hymn like _"I Know a Rose Tree Springing"_ move the theme toward the Incarnation. In North American culture, it is easy to lose sight of preparing for and looking forward to a festival and to be carried away by its anticipated celebration. Advent is intended to prepare us for Christmas, leading gently into it. _Promise of Glory_ (Catherine Nerney [Mahwah, N.J.: Paulist Press, n.d.]) contains a number of forms for Advent special services, as well as services for Christmas and Epiphany that keep the boundaries clear while recognizing the impossibility of refusing to live in our own culture.

In many churches, an Advent wreath—an evergreen wreath with four candles in it and sometimes a fifth in the center—is lighted during this season. One candle is lighted on the first Sunday of Advent, two on the second Sunday, and so on. If a fifth candle is used, it is lighted on Christmas. The candles symbolize the light of Christ shining in the darkness.

Christmas and Epiphany. The celebration of Christmas on December 25 and during the twelve days until Epiphany is the climax of the season. Christmas celebrates not just the birthday of the Christ child, but also the Incarnation. The prologue to John's Gospel, as well as the nativity account in Luke, are proper Christmas readings. John 1 is an appropriate reading and sermon text for one of the Sundays following Christmas. The season ends with the celebration of the baptism of Christ on the Sunday after Epiphany or (in some churches) of Christ's presentation in the temple on Candlemas (February 2). The baptism of Christ is an obvious occasion to make the principal service a baptismal service. The reading of the Gospel account of our Lord's baptism provides an occasion for a sermon on baptism as an introduction to the baptismal rite. Epiphany baptisms were the custom of many ancient churches of both East and West, and it is a tradition that can be profitably revived. If Candlemas is observed, the song of Simeon (Luke 2:29-32), with its reference to the light to enlighten the nations, serves as the pivot for a service of light and the refocusing of attention from looking back to Christmas to looking forward to the Crucifixion (Luke 2:34-35).

The baptism of Christ is celebrated on the first Sunday after Epiphany, and other manifestations of Christ on the following Sunday. The Lutheran and Episcopal versions of the three-year lectionary read the account of the Transfiguration on the Sunday before the beginning of Lent, using the references to the Passion and Resurrection in the accounts as a transition into the Easter cycle.

Lent. The Easter cycle celebrates the paschal mystery of the death and resurrection of Christ and the church's participation in it. The cycle begins with the first day of Lent, Ash Wednesday (a sort of Christian Yom Kippur), on which penitential liturgies reflect our confrontation with our own mortality and our sorrow for sin. Lent, however, is intended to be not a daily repetition of Ash Wednesday but a season of preparation for the joy of Easter. Baptism, the sacrament of the forgiveness of sins and participation in the resurrection of Christ, is the Easter sacrament par excellence, and Lent originated as a season of preparation for baptism. Its themes, therefore, are repentance, spiritual growth, and entering into union with Christ. The temptation of Christ in the wilderness is the traditional theme for the first Sunday in Lent ("Forty days and forty nights, thou wast fasting in the wild"). The most ancient readings for the Lenten season are the Gospel readings for the third, fourth, and fifth Sundays from Year A of the three-year lectionary. These readings are narratives of Jesus and the Samaritan woman, the healing of the man born blind, and the raising of Lazarus. The ancient Lenten lessons provided the texts for the instruction of candidates for Easter baptism and still serve as an introduction to the great theological themes to lead a congregation to renewal at Easter.

Lenten services can be planned to have a distinctive seasonal tone. The use of distinctive Lenten vestments or ornamentation of the church building, the choice of hymns, and the inclusion of penitential elements in the service are all ways of marking the season. Some churches refrain from using flowers during Lent; others use a single budding branch as a sign of spring and resurrection to come. Often, midweek evening services are a part of a congregation's Lenten plan.

Holy Week. Holy Week is central to the liturgical year. It begins on Palm Sunday. Traditionally, the celebration has had two distinct foci: the Triumphal Entry into Jerusalem, often expressed by a palm procession at the beginning and the distribution of palms to the congregation; and the Passion, marked by the reading of the Gospel account of the Crucifixion from one of the Synoptics and the singing of passion hymns and chorales. The movement from the joy of the Triumphal Entry to the solemnity of the Passion narrative is extremely powerful.

The contrast can be emphasized by gathering for the distribution of palms and the reading of the account of the Triumphal Entry in a place other than the church and proceeding to the church carrying palms. The hymns "All Glory, Laud and Honor" and "Ride On, Ride On in Majesty," are traditionally associated with the procession. The reading and preaching of the Passion, with appropriate music, then follows in the church.

Maundy Thursday is celebrated as the anniversary of the Last Supper. The celebration of the Eucharist with the reading of the account of the Supper are obvious ways of marking the day. In many places, John's account of the Last Supper is also read, and a symbolic footwashing takes place. The calendar ties the Last Supper to the events that followed it—the betrayal, trial, and Crucifixion—and the preacher should do likewise.

Good Friday is the church's solemn commemoration of the Crucifixion. John's account of the Crucifixion is the traditional reading. It was for this occasion that Bach composed his St. John's Passion. In some places, preaching on the Passion for three hours has become traditional. A more liturgical tradition links the reading and preaching of the Passion to devotions before the cross. An excellent modern interpretation of the traditional anthem, "The Reproaches," is contained in *From Ashes to Fire* (Nashville: Abingdon Press, 1979) and has been reprinted in many other service books.

Prayer vigils, either between the Maundy Thursday and Good Friday services, or from Good Friday until Easter sunrise, are often included in the planning. Increasingly, the ancient tradition of celebrating the Great Vigil of Easter between sunset Saturday and Easter sunrise is being revived. It was at this vigil that the catechumens were baptized, and it concluded with their reception of Holy Communion at the sunrise service on Easter.

The Easter Vigil. The Easter Vigil begins with a service of light at which the Paschal candle is lighted. This burns during worship throughout the fifty days from Easter to Pentecost and is a symbol of the season and our life in the risen Christ. It is also lighted at baptisms and funerals to continue the symbolism. The Word service contains a series of Old Testament readings. The congregation renews their baptismal vows, and baptisms (if there are any) take place. The Vigil concludes with the first service of Easter, traditionally a Communion service, including the reading of Matthew's account of the Resurrection.

Like the baptism of Christ, the Easter Vigil is a traditional time for baptisms. The Pauline baptismal theology of Romans 6 associates baptism so deeply with the death and resurrection of Christ that its celebration at this time has been a constant feature of Christian tradition. Lent is the time of preparation for baptism, the baptism itself is at Easter, and the fifty days of Easter are a period of rejoicing as the new Christians enter into the risen life.

Easter Season and Pentecost. *Alleluia!* is the great Easter word, and it is included in hymns and responses throughout the Easter season. The festal adornment of the church building and the joyful tone of the worship continue until Pentecost. The resurrection appearances and the life of the apostolic church as recorded in Acts are the customary Scripture readings and sermon themes. The Ascension is celebrated on the fortieth day after Easter (a Thursday) or the Sunday following, and the gift of the Holy Spirit (Acts 2) on the Day of Pentecost, which brings the season to a close. This is a part of the same Easter celebration, and services should be planned integrally for all eight Sundays. Frequently, the Easter character of services is lost after a week or two, so that Pentecost seems an unrelated celebration when it arrives. The early church called the Easter season "fifty days of rejoicing." It follows the forty days of Lent and provides balance.

Pentecost itself is appropriately observed in many churches as the day for confirmation. It is a celebration of the spread of the church throughout the world in the power of the Holy Spirit, and Christian unity, Christian missions, and evangelism are suitable Pentecost themes. Following the example of Acts 2, the Word is often proclaimed in as many languages as the congregation can muster among its people.

The Season after Pentecost. The season after Pentecost is the season of the life of the Christian church. We ourselves actually live in the season between Pentecost and the Second Advent. Some churches call it "ordinary time," but it is the time of our redemption. At the beginning of November, the parables of the kingdom become the Sunday readings, and post-Pentecost begins to look forward to Advent. It is not reasonable to plan the entire post-Pentecost season as a unit, because it would be too long, but this last part of the season can be so planned (e.g., the outline set forth in _Promise of Glory_). The last Sunday before Advent is often observed as a festival of the reign of Jesus Christ, which leads easily into the celebration of the _final_ Advent on the next Sunday as the climax to the series of readings about the kingdom of God. In this way, the years are bound together and the cycle begins again.

Using the Christian year as a basis for the planning of worship not only puts the congregation in tune with a great body of Christian tradition stretching all across the world and back through the centuries, but also assures a balanced, integrated, and biblically based plan, and frees the congregation from the whims and biases of the individual pastor.

Leonel L. Mitchell

320 • PLANNING THE FLOW OF WORSHIP

To enhance the flow of worship, a leader should working on acquiring necessary skills. Of particular importance is learning how to master the timing of worship. Well-planned transitions help the congregation to sense the intended purpose of each act of worship. Included here is a detailed outline of worship designed to go with Isaiah 6:1-8—Isaiah's encounter with God and the prophet's subsequent call to ministry.

An important aspect of the planning and leading of corporate worship is the creating of a sense of meaningful flow from the beginning of the service to the end. A flow of worship that effectively engages the attention of the worshiper and facilitates meaningful participation can be attributed to several factors.

First, it may appear that the control of this aspect of worship lies solely in the ability of the leaders to provide spoken and musical transitions with spontaneity and a masterful sense of timing. As important as these skills may be, there is more to it than that. The effective handling of transitions is contingent upon the structure provided by an order of service that progresses in a logical manner, facilitating the expression of thought and feeling. A matter of primary importance is sensitivity to the leading of the Holy Spirit in both the planning and the leading of worship. The mastery of timing is an essential part of all temporal art, including the drama of worship. For example, there are times when the Spirit would prompt a relaxing of the pace or the repetition of a song to provide a sense of resolution or closure. We want to avoid moving through the parts of a service as if they were items on an agenda to be completed within a fixed amount of time.

The primary focus of this entry is the creating of transitions against the underlying structure of the service. The need for emphasis on transitions can be seen more clearly if we consider a basic difference that exists between a worship service and a gathering of people for a drama presentation. In worship, everyone has lines to speak or sing, not just those on the platform. Words of introduction and transition help the people sense the intended purpose of each act of worship.

422 🞄 *Resources for Planning and Leading Worship*

To show how words can create meaningful connection for the parts of an established order of worship, several examples are offered here. The paradigm selected for the structure of the service is the written account of Isaiah's encounter with God at the time of his call (Isa. 6:1-8). God initiated the dialogue by revealing himself through worship (vv. 1-4). In contrast to God's holiness, Isaiah saw himself as one who needed cleansing from sin, and he confessed his unworthiness (v. 5). In response to his act of contrition, God pronounced forgiveness (vv. 6-7). After this opening dialogue (consisting of revelation, confession, and forgiveness), God spoke to the prophet, and Isaiah responded. The opening part of the dialogue serves as the basis for a Service of Entrance, and that which follows forms the basis for the Service of the Word. Although this model is usually associated with worship in so-called "liturgical churches," it may also structure worship that is freer in style.

Service of Entrance

Prelude Music. The service begins with an instrumental arrangement of congregational songs designed to (1) invite people to worship (e.g., "O Worship the King"); (2) express the corporate nature of the gathering and its need for the enabling power of the Holy Spirit (e.g., "Brethren, We Have Met to Worship," "Spirit of the Living God," and "Set My Spirit Free to Worship Thee"), and 3) draw attention to the object of our veneration (e.g., "Holy God, We Praise Your Name," "I Adore You," and "Fairest Lord Jesus"). An admonition, written or spoken, might be given to the worshipers to reflect on the words of the hymns listed as preludes (include the numbers of the hymns to be used an overhead projector).

Hymn of Adoration. In addition to labeling the hymn according to function (Hymn of Adoration), words of introduction help to facilitate the desired focus of attention, for example, for the hymn "Fairest Lord Jesus," we could say, "As we lift our hearts and voices in this song of adoration, may we see beyond the beauty of creation. Beauty was never intended to be an object of veneration, but he who creates and sustains is worthy of our praise."

Prayer of Adoration. The theme of the hymn is carried forward in prayer:

"Lord, God, you have spoken to us through your Son, Jesus, who is the radiance of your glory and the exact representation of your nature, who upholds all things by the word of his power. Truly, he is the Lord of creation, and we offer you, through him, all glory, honor, praise, and adoration. Give us eyes to see and ears to hear as you reveal yourself in all your splendor and glory, majesty, power, and redeeming love. Amen."

Corporate Prayer. Confession and forgiveness are highlighted in a prayer such as the following: "We are not, by our own nature, worthy of you, but through your Son, who died and rose again, we are made righteous in your sight. Thank you for the assurance that if we confess our sins, you are faithful and righteous to forgive our sins and cleanse us from all unrighteousness. Hear, O Lord, the confession of each heart before you now" (silence). (The act of confession can be intensified through singing. After a moment of silence, the worship leader could invite the people to continue in prayer, seeking personal cleansing as everyone sings "Create in Me a Clean Heart," or the first stanza of "Search Me, O God." The service of confession concludes with a responsive reading and a hymn of assurance.)

Leader:	Thank you, Lord, for your forgiveness. In Jesus' name,
People:	**Amen!**
Leader:	People of God, we are forgiven.
People:	**We are forgiven. Thanks be to God!**

Hymn of Assurance. Words of transition: "The truth that God has forgiven our sins must penetrate our hearts as well as our minds. As we sing of his marvelous grace, may each of us appropriate his forgiveness and receive rest for the soul." The desired outcome of confession is forgiveness, a sense of resolution (*denouement*). It is helpful to reinforce this through a hymn (such as "Grace Greater than Our Sin" that facilitates the internationalization of the truth that we are forgiven.

Greeting. Between the Service of Preparation and the Service of the Word, the historic salutation may be used or it could be substituted with a welcome, followed by an encouragement to greet one another.

Service of the Word

Preparing to Receive the Word. If a hymn that is directly related to text and sermon is not available, a general hymn on the theme of God's Word, such as "How Firm a Foundation," is appropriate. If a special musical selection precedes the sermon, it should be related to the message.

Sermon and Hymn of Response. An opportunity for response to the proclamation of the Word is an essential ingredient of worship. The pastor's introduction to the hymn at the close of the sermon is an effective means of assuring that the hymn's function as a vehicle of response will be understood.

Offering. Although the receiving of an offering in the free church tradition usually occurs earlier in the service, a case can be made for including it later. There it would serve as another means of responding to the proclamation of the Word. (In the paradigm from Isaiah, verses 1–4 are revelation, and most of the concluding verses are response.)

Service of the Table

An example of meaningful flow of worship is provided by the following excerpt from a Communion liturgy:

Leader: The Lord be with you.
People: And with your spirit.
Leader: Lift up your hearts.
People: We lift them up unto the Lord.
Leader: Let us give thanks unto the Lord our God.
People: It is meet and right to do so.
Leader: It is meet, right, and salutary, that we should at all times, and in all places, give thanks unto thee, O Lord, Holy Father, Almighty, Everlasting God. Therefore with angels and archangels, and with all the company of heaven, we laud and magnify thy glorious name, evermore praising thee and saying:

Leader and people (spoken or sung):

Holy, holy, holy, Lord God of Sabbaoth;
Heaven and earth are full of thy glory;
Hosanna in the highest.
Blessed is he that cometh in the name of the Lord;
Hosanna in the highest.

The above exchange of thoughts between the worship leader and congregation not only engages the worshipers in meaningful dialogue, but also creates a sense of eager anticipation that finds fulfillment in the heartfelt release of worship in the singing of "Holy, Holy, Holy."

Prior to the Words of Institution (1 Cor. 11:23–26), instruction such as the following could enrich the people's understanding of the breaking of bread as a symbolic act of worship:

As Christians in the early church broke bread and ate together, they did it "with glad and sincere hearts" (Acts 2:46). As we break bread from a common loaf, may we experience true joy and unity of spirit, as brothers and sisters in Christ. The common loaf from which we take and eat is a symbol of the unity we have in Christ. These lines from a first century hymn may help us to see an added dimension to the breaking of bread:

Leader: As grain, once scattered on the hillside, was in this broken bread made one,
People: So from all lands the church be gathered into thy Kingdom by thy Son.

(The *Didache*)

Another act of worship that can be a meaningful part of Communion is congregational worship in song during the distribution of the bread and cup (or as the people go forward to receive Communion). In addition to uniting the people, this provides a means of releasing joy and other emotions that are integral to meaningful worship. Songs of praise and adoration may be combined with traditional Communion hymns. As the service of Communion ends, the joining of hands could contribute to a sense of oneness as a song such as "One in the Bond of Love" is sung.

Dismissal. A good benediction provides more than a sense of closure to the service. Prefaced by remarks drawn from God's Word for the day, our going out into the world is given new meaning and purpose, for we are to be salt and light and extensions of his unconditional love for all humankind. Announcements pertaining to the work of ministry that continues through the days ahead may be included in the service of dismissal.

Things That Short-Circuit the Flow of Worship

A meaningful flow may be short-circuited by a number of factors, one being a lack of preparation with regard to logistics. All worship leaders (pastors, lay readers, musicians, and sound board operators)

should have a copy of the worship bulletin in advance of the service. The awkwardness of waiting for a microphone to be turned on can be avoided by noting when movement to the microphone is to occur. This is particularly helpful to less-experienced members of the ministry team.

Another factor that must be considered as an integral part of directing the flow of worship is the body language of the people on the platform. To avoid distracting the attention of worshipers from the significance of what is happening at each moment, all leaders must be attentive listeners.

A third factor is the thoughtful preparation of introductions to hymns, modulations, and other musical sequences. Without proper introductions and interludes, the worshipers cannot be expected to begin and continue confidently. The worship leader who rehearses musical transitions with the keyboard musician(s) will aid those who rely on their leadership.

Finally, an integral part of each of the above considerations is the matter of timing. A readiness or eagerness on the part of one who is about to move to the microphone could detract from the ministry in process, if that eagerness is expressed through body language. On the other hand, lethargic movements when the liturgical action calls for purposeful movement are, likewise, distracting. Audio cassettes and videotapes of services can be studied as means of assessing the effectiveness of our leadership. The senior pastor who values meaningful congregational participation in worship will need to provide opportunities for worship leaders to receive instruction in this important area of ministry. Effective leadership does not just happen. It is the result of prayer, study, planning, practice, and evaluation.

Ronald L. Sprunger

321 • THE WORSHIP PLANNER: TEAM MINISTRIES

As an introduction to the planning and evaluation chart that follows, this entry gives guidelines for developing a team of worship ministers, each charged with a specific duty in bringing about worship renewal.

The worship planner that follows is designed for use by a team of worship ministers. It is specifically designed to help the team (1) brainstorm; (2) develop the order of worship; and (3) evaluate worship.

The Nine-Pointed Star. The nine-pointed star symbolizes the nine fruits of the Spirit as expressed in Galatians 5:22: "Love, joy, peace, patience, kindness, generosity, faithfulness, gentleness and self-control." In the figure above, the Greek letter in each of the star points is the first letter of the fruit represented.

The worship planner may be used by a pastor, minister of music, or worship leader without the help of a larger committee of worship ministers. However, it is best to use the worship planner with a group of people who are serving the church as worship ministers.

A worship ministry is a group of people from the staff and congregation who encourage the continual improvement of worship through prayerful planning, thoughtful evaluation, and constant attention to the process whereby a worshiping community is formed. Follow the steps below to establish a planning ministry in the local church.

Step One: Establish a Core Group of People Committed to Worship Renewal. A church that is seeking renewal needs a core of godly people deeply committed to seeing worship come alive. The kind of worship we want in our church grows out of the spiritual life of the congregation and feeds back into that life. If many of the people in the church are spiritually dead, unconverted, or indifferent to the gospel, the task of worship renewal will be more difficult. Still, a small core of committed people who begin to pray for worship renewal, talk about it, and plan for it can have a significant effect on an entire congregation. This group should meet on a regular basis, weekly if possible, and certainly not less than once a month.

Step Two: Identify One Person Who Has the Calling for Worship Renewal. There needs to be one person in a leadership position who is committed to bringing the renewal of worship about. Worship renewal is not finding a few new gimmicks that will give people a religious high. Rather, worship renewal is a matter of content and spirit that requires considerate understanding and sensitive, wise leadership. In terms of understanding, worship renewal is rooted in a grasp of Old and New Testament teaching, understanding of historical development and theology, and a grasp of the arts (art, architecture, drama, liturgical dance, and especially music). No one person can know everything about all of these subjects, yet to make worship renewal a reality, there has to be one person who has some sensitivity to all these fields of study from which worship draws. This person may be the pastor, the music director, or a layperson. Whoever emerges as this leader must have a sense of calling to this ministry and the respect and cooperation of those who work for him or her on the worship committee.

Step Three: Establish a Team of Worship Ministers. A team of worship ministers has two basic responsibilities. The first is to plan everything related to worship—and the planning of worship is not limited to the order of worship itself. While that is certainly a central task of the worship ministers, other responsibilities include such matters as the worship environment, hospitality, music, drama, table matters, and technical concerns.

The second responsibility of the worship ministers is weekly evaluation. Each service must be evaluated, preferably within twenty-four hours. Planning worship is only half of the cycle. If worship is not evaluated on a regular basis, it will soon fall back into the old pattern, or else the new pattern will become established and lose its vitality. The committee must pay constant attention to worship through regular critical evaluation of all its parts.

Planning Team Size. The size of the committee of worship ministers will differ depending on the size and preferences of the congregation. Generally, in the smaller but growing church, a three-person ministry team is sufficient. In larger churches, the worship planning team may consist of four persons who administer four groups of people related to the ministry of worship (see below). The two configurations below are not absolute. A congregation should feel free to experiment with the development of a team of worship ministers to find a configuration that works for it. In any case, the worship planner remains effective in whatever shape is given to the worship ministry team.

The team of worship ministers in the growing church. In the smaller but growing church, the makeup of the team of worship ministers is generally no more than three persons. The minister of oversight, the minister of music and the arts, and the minister of housekeeping:

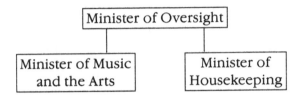

Minister of Oversight. Generally the pastor. Responsibilities include teaching worship, planning worship (with the other two ministers), and leading worship (or designating leadership).

Minister of Music and the Arts. Generally the person in charge of music. Responsibilities include oversight of all choirs and musical groups, the lay reader's group (Scripture readers, dramatists, dancers), and environmental art (seating, banners, flowers, etc.).

Minister of Housekeeping. Generally a person gifted in organizational skills. Responsibilities include supervision of the church bulletin, hospitality, preparation for the Communion, and technical matters.

The team of worship ministers in the larger church. In the larger church, the team of worship ministers is an expanded version of the same ministry in the smaller church. It includes a minister of oversight, a minister of leadership, a minister of music and the arts, and a minister of housekeeping in a capacity of leadership over the various ministries involved in worship.

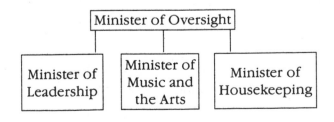

Minister of Oversight. This person coordinates the work of all the ministers of worship.

Minister of Leadership. This person coordinates all the work of the ministers of leadership. The minister of leadership may also fulfill the work of one or more of the following three ministries:

Teacher of Worship. Assumes responsibility to study worship, to teach a worship class, and provide educational input and resources for the other ministries listed below.

Planner of Worship. Actually plans the worship service, drawing on the input, expertise, and talent of the other ministries listed below.

Leader of Worship. Actually leads the congregation in worship.

Minister of Music and the Arts. This person coordinates music, drama, dance, and environmental art.

The Music Minister. Oversees all the musical groups in the church, such as choirs, soloists, cantors, and instrumental groups, and integrates their contributions to worship with the other ministries.

The Drama Minister. Oversees all groups related to communication, such as Scripture readers' group and drama group, and integrates their ministry into worship.

The Environment Minister. Oversees the setting of worship, such as the seating arrangement; the use of flowers, plants, and symbols of worship; and especially the visual symbols used during the seasons of the church year: banners, cloths, vestments. These matters are carefully related to the other ministries.

Minister of Housekeeping. This person coordinates all the ministries that surround and support the ministry of worship.

Bulletin Minister. Collects all the material necessary for the bulletin and coordinates the publication of the material.

Hospitality Minister. Provides directions for those who are called to create a hospitable environment for the worshiper through the work of greeting, ushering, coffee fellowship, and follow-up contacts.

Table Minister. Assumes responsibility for the demands related to the Table of the Lord, such as Communion ware, bread, wine, and tablecloths, as well as preparation and clean-up duties.

Technical Minister. Oversees the purchase, care, and use of microphones, recording equipment, and other technical matters related to worship.

Step Four: Evaluate Worship Weekly. The weekly evaluation of worship is indispensable to the process whereby a committee of worship ministers is enabled to bring about prayerful improvement of the spiritual impact of worship on the worshiping community. Each of the ministry areas may be evaluated by the entire committee of ministers in the beginning of each meeting of the worship ministers.

Robert E. Webber

322 • THE WORSHIP PLANNER

The following charts will be useful to worship committees in coming up with ideas for worship services, in planning services, and in evaluating services.

In the spaces below, jot down all comments that are necessary for this service:

Date _____

Season of the year _____

Sunday _____

Sunday morning _____

Sunday evening _____

Midweek theme _____

Other _____

Biblical texts _____

_____

_____

Theme _____

_____

_____

——————— **Step 1: Brainstorming** ———————

Music. (Organ, piano, guitar, synthesizer, band, orchestra, hymns, choruses, psalms, anthems, solo, other)

The Arts. (Scripture readers, drama group, dance, environmental art, seating, seasonal banners, cloths, vestments, visual symbols, other)

Housekeeping. (Bulletin, greeters, ushers, coffee fellowship, follow-up, Communion responsibilities, technical)

——————— **Step 2: Forming the Service** ———————

Select and order the material below in keeping with the style of worship desired.

Acts of Entrance: Coming into the Presence of God

The Gathering
(Informal singing, prelude, instrumental music, informal greetings, announcements, words of welcome, rehearsal of congregational music)

Opening Acts of Worship
(Entrance hymn, procession, greeting, invocation, acts of praise, confession and acts of pardon, opening prayer, the arts, other)

Order	Comments
_____	_____
_____	_____
_____	_____
_____	_____
_____	_____
_____	_____
_____	_____
_____	_____
_____	_____
_____	_____
_____	_____

The Service of the Word: Hearing God Speak

Scripture Readings
(Old Testament, Epistle, Gospel)

Responses
(psalms, choruses, canticles, hymns)

Response to the Word
(creed, hymn, talk-back sermon, invitation)

Prayer of the People, Passing of the Peace, Offering/Offertory, Other

Order	Comments
_____	_____
_____	_____
_____	_____
_____	_____
_____	_____
_____	_____
_____	_____
_____	_____

The Service of Thanksgiving

Thanks with Table
(Communion with lifting up of hearts, preface prayer, *Sanctus,* prayer of thanksgiving, words of institution, words of remembrance, proclamation of the mystery of faith, prayer for the Holy Spirit, invitation to receive bread and wine, manner of reception [sit, come forward], Communion song, anointing of oil, closing prayer)

Thanks without the Table
(songs of thanksgiving, prayer of thanks, Lord's Prayer)

Order	Comments
_____	_____
_____	_____
_____	_____
_____	_____
_____	_____
_____	_____
_____	_____
_____	_____

The Service of Dismissal

(announcements, benediction, Dismissal hymn, words of Dismissal)

Order	Comments
_____	_____
_____	_____
_____	_____
_____	_____
_____	_____
_____	_____
_____	_____
_____	_____
_____	_____
_____	_____

Step 3: Evaluating Worship

Go over each part of the service, evaluating strengths, weaknesses, and ways to improve.

The Spatial and Environmental Setting

Strengths	Weaknesses	Need for Improvement
————	————	————
————	————	————
————	————	————
————	————	————
————	————	————

Music and the Arts

Strengths	Weaknesses	Need for Improvement
————	————	————
————	————	————
————	————	————
————	————	————
————	————	————

The Order and Flow of Worship

Strengths	Weaknesses	Need for Improvement
————	————	————
————	————	————
————	————	————
————	————	————
————	————	————

323 ◆ BIBLIOGRAPHY ON RESOURCES FOR PLANNING AND LEADING WORSHIP

Worship Committee and Planning Guides

Baker, Thomas, and Frank Ferrone. *Liturgy Committee Basics.* Washington D.C.: Pastoral Press, 1985. Baker and Ferrone have authored a workbook outlining the effective functioning of a liturgy committee in Roman Catholic churches. They address the practical issues and the "hot potatoes," such as politics, membership, leadership, the agenda, and how to talk about liturgy. Writing is candid and clear. Ecumenical audience.

Cassa, Yvonne, and Joanne Sanders. *How to Form a Parish Liturgy Board.* Chicago: Liturgy Training Publications, 1987. A very practical workbook for getting and keeping together a worship committee/liturgy board. Part 1 subjects include: Formation, Model, Assessment, Job Description, Recruitment, and Training. Part 2 deals with Procedure, Budget, Agenda, and Evaluation. Roman Catholic/Ecumenical.

Cormier, Jay. *The Sower's Book.* Kansas City, Mo.: Sheed and Ward, 1989. A workbook and planning guide for homilists and preachers. The volume also acts as a journal of services, with evaluative tools to help the homilist reach his or her goals. Readings, themes, and reflections (commentary) are also included. Ecumenical.

DeJong, James A. *Into His Presence.* Kalamazoo, Mich.: Christian Reformed Church Publications, 1985. The workbook is designed as part of the Bible Way educational course for teaching the principles and practice of worship in the Reformed tradition. Definition, setting, roots, and preparation for worship are discussed along with preaching, reading, singing, prayer, and sacraments. Study guides for reflection are included at the end of each chapter. Christian Reformed church.

Dyck, Arlene Martin. *Worship Resources.* Newton, Kans.: Faith and Life Press, 1982. A basic volume on worship from a Mennonite perspective that helps worship leaders as they plan liturgy. There are general notes on the use of resources with the balance of the book; they discuss calls to worship, responsive readings, affirmations, and many other elements.

Engle, Paul E. *Worship Planbook.* Philadelphia: Great Commission, 1981. A worship tool that thematically and theocentrically matches hymns and psalms to Scripture readings under approximately thirty headings. It is a quick and handy guide that could be used in planning worship for an ecumenical audience.

Fleming, Austin. *Preparing for Liturgy.* Washington, D.C.: Pastoral Press, 1985. A theology and spirituality that includes both practical and pastoral reflections on a basic comprehension of liturgy, preparing liturgy (which is distinguished from planning liturgy), an understanding of traditional and contemporary styles, ministry/spirituality and liturgy connections, and benedictions. Roman Catholic.

Guilbert, Charles M. *Words of Our Worship.* New York: Church Hymnal Corporation, 1988. Comprehensive and concise dictionary of practical liturgical terminology. User-friendly and nonintimidating. Episcopal.

Hardin, Grady H. *The Leadership of Worship*. Nashville: Abingdon Press, 1980. A practical guide to planning and participating in worship. Chapter titles include The Planning Team, Spoken Words, Visible Words (body movement, gesture, space), Use of Things (vestments, furnishings, colors, texture) and Time, and The Work of the People (going into the world). For all audiences. Notes. United Methodist.

Hickman, Hoyt L. *Planning Worship Each Week*. Nashville: Discipleship Resources, 1988. A startlingly simple but amply practical introductory pamphlet on worship which, by itself, is enough to initiate persons to liturgical ministry. Help for worship leaders in planning, analyzing bulletins, marking hymnals to avoid redundancy, keeping a weekly worksheet, building on local traditions, and starting new ones. United Methodist.

Holland, James. *Modern Liturgy Planning Guide*. San Jose: Resource Publications, 1987. For every Sunday and major feast of all three cycles of the Roman lectionary. Idea starters for Sunday worship (programs, bulletins, children's liturgy, art and environment, and parish life), Scripture commentary for each reading, music suggestions, and a planning sheet.

Hovda, Robert W. *Strong, Loving, and Wise*. Collegeville, Minn.: Liturgical Press, 1976. Hovda's manual is already a popular "classic" study of the presider (spirit, planning, and preparation) and the act of presiding (environment, presence, and style) in the Roman Catholic tradition. His balanced presentation is practical, insightful, and full of the reflections of a parish priest and pastor. It is intended for all who preside. Ecumenical.

Huck, Gabe. *Liturgy with Style and Grace*. Chicago: Liturgy Training Publications, 1984. A good introduction to the Roman lectionary. The Rites and the Sacramentary are in one volume, suitable as a study guide for individuals or groups. Rather than being a source for complete liturgies, it is intended to provide a context in which to view practical problems. Roman Catholic.

Kavanaugh, Aiden. *Elements of Rite*. New York: Pueblo, 1982. A handbook of liturgical style that is at once a primer of rules for rite and a practical theology in clearest terms of liturgy. Though written for Roman Catholics, the volume is straightforwardly pointed on all subjects and valuable to all.

Langford, Thomas A. *The Worship Handbook*. Nashville: Discipleship Resources, 1984. For reform and renewal of worship, the book advocates change to biblical, simple balances of form and freedom that let worship be clear, logical, and progressive. The author urges leaders to avoid overly thematic, rationalistic, pragmatic, complex, or exclusively traditional formats. Material on service planning is complemented by chapters on children and movement in worship and on the environment of worship.

Thielen, Martin. *Getting Ready for Sunday*. Nashville: Broadman Press, 1989. A pragmatic primer on the practice of worship that includes some innovative service outlines from sources such as biblical texts, hymns, or elements of worship. Contains a service outline with explanations for the presence of each element, followed by sixty pages of completed orders of worship. Book concludes with a survey of contemporary trends. Baptist.

United Methodist Church. *Companion to the Book of Services*. Nashville: Abingdon Press, 1988. Introduction, commentary, and instructions for using the new United Methodist services. Volume is divided into five sections: Services of Word and Table, Calendar and Lectionary, Baptismal Covenant, A Service of Christian Marriage, and A Service of Death and Resurrection—with subheadings for each section. United Methodist.

Unruh, Wilfred J. *Planning Congregational Worship*. Newton, Kans.: Faith and Life Press, 1978. This pamphlet is one in a series intended to be a guide for a worship and arts committee as it plans liturgy. It has many practical suggestions and is written clearly and concisely in order that the widest possible audience be served. Though written from a Mennonite perspective, the material is valuable in all traditions.

Resources for Readers and Lectors

Lonergan, Ray. *A Well-Trained Tongue*. Chicago: Liturgy Training Publications, 1982. Lonergan's work is a preparation book for lectors that is full of communication techniques, methods of preparation, interpretation, and practical considerations (such as dress and movement). Appendices. Roman Catholic.

Marcheschi, Graziano, and Nancy S. Marcheschi, *Workbook for Lectors and Gospel Readers*. Chicago: Liturgy Training Publications, 1982. Corresponds to Cycle C and has introductory notes for lectors. Readings are printed with breathing marks, and both an outline of commentary and a complete commentary run alongside. Very helpful. Roman Catholic.

Resources for the Church Year

Adam, Adolf. *The Liturgical Year.* New York: Pueblo, 1981. A study of the church year as celebrated by contemporary Roman Catholics. Contains valuable historical information about the origins of celebrations.

From Ashes to Fire. Supplementary Worship Resources 6. Nashville: Abingdon Press, 1979. Contains services of worship for the season of Lent and Easter, providing access to traditional resources for Methodists and others in the Free church tradition. An excellent book and a good resource for those whose own service books lack such services. United Methodist.

McArthur, A. Allan. *The Evolution of the Christian Year.* London: SCM Press, 1953. A classic work by a minister of the Church of Scotland providing a history and rationale for the use of the Christian year, the restoration of which he was prompting in his own church. Its scholarship has been superseded on some points by studies such as Talley's *Origins of the Liturgical Year,* but it remains an excellent readable general introduction to the history of the church year.

Mitchell, Leonel L. *Planning the Church Year.* Harrisburg: Morehouse, 1991. A guide to the use of the Christian year for planning worship, based on the three-year lectionary used by many North American churches, including Roman Catholics, Episcopalians, Lutherans, Presbyterians, and Methodists. It is in the tradition of *The Book of Common Prayer.*

Pieper, Josef. *In Tune with the World.* Chicago: Franciscan Herald Press, 1975. A philosophical theology of festivity and the meaning of religious festival. What does it mean to celebrate a festival, and how does it differ from a mere historical commemoration?

Porter, H. Boone. *The Day of Light.* New York: Seabury, 1960 (reprinted Washington: Pastoral Press, 1987). A theological study of the meaning of Sunday in the Christian life.

The Promise of His Glory: For the Season from All Saints to Candlemas. Commended by the House of Bishops of the General Synod and the Church of England. Collegeville: Liturgical Press, 1991. Contains services for a variety of occasions in Advent, the Christmas, and Epiphany seasons, such as carol services, manger services, a feast of light, and the Week of Prayer for Christian Unity. The material can easily be adapted for use in other traditions.

Stevenson, Kenneth. *Jerusalem Revisited—The Liturgical Meaning of Holy Week.* Washington: Pastoral Press, 1988. A look at the origin and meaning of the celebration of the central work of the Christian year.

Talley, Thomas J. *The Origins of the Liturgical Year.* New York: Pueblo, 1986. A scholarly investigation of a number of problems concerning the origin of the church year, such as why Christmas is December 25.

Works Cited

Note: Some articles have been adapted or excerpted with permission of the publisher.

1 Excerpted from James Empereur, *Worship: Exploring the Sacred* (Washington, D.C.: Pastoral Press, 1987), 163–169.

2. B. J. Stonehouse, "It's Important to Be Open to Change," *Reformed Worship* 11 (Spring 1989): 14–15.

3. Thomas Howard, *The Liturgy Explained* (Wilton, Conn.: Morehouse-Barlow, 1981), 9–14.

4. Keith Watkins, *Thankful Praise: A Resource for Christian Worship* (St. Louis: Christian Board of Publication, 1987), 17–19.

5. Ruth C. Duck, "Creativity, Liturgical," in *The New Dictionary of Sacramental Worship*, ed. by Peter E. Fink (Collegeville, Minn.: Michael Glazier/Liturgical Press, 1990), 302.

6. Adapted from Melicent Huneycutt [Vergeer], "Worship in the Spirit: Charismatic and Neo-Pentecostal Worship in the Reformed Traditions," *Reformed Liturgy and Music* 21 (Spring 1987): 107–110.

7. Excerpted from Judson Cornwall, *Let Us Worship* (S. Plainfield, N.J.: Bridge Publishing, Inc., 1983), 143, 146, 150–151.

8. Watkins, *Thankful Praise,* 24–27.

9. Alexander Schmemann, *For the Life of the World* (Crestwood, N.Y.: St. Vladimirs Seminary Press, 1973), 26–27.

10. Barry Liesch, *People in the Presence of God* (Grand Rapids: Zondervan, 1988), 91–94.

11. Robert E. Webber, *Signs of Wonder* (Nashville: Abbott Martyn Press, 1992), 149–154.

12. LeRoy E. Kennell, *The Bible in Worship* (Newton, Kans.: Faith and Life Press, 1989), 71.

13. Jerry and Gail DuCharme, *Lector Becomes Proclaimer* (San Jose, Calif.: Resource Publications, 1985), 10–11.

14. James Wallace, *The Ministry of Lectors* (Collegeville, Minn.: Liturgical Press, 1981), 15–17.

15. Charlotte E. Arnold, *Group Readings for the Church* (Grand Rapids: Baker Book House, 1975), 9–10.

16. Hayim Goren Perelmuter, *Siblings: Rabbinic Judaism and Early Christianity at Their Beginnings* (New York: Paulist Press, 1989), 117–130.

17. Excerpted from Robert C. Worley, "Preaching and Teaching in the Primitive Church," *McCormick Quarterly* 20 (November 1966): 12–25.

18. Adapted from John A. Broadus, *Lectures on the History of Preaching* (New York: A. C. Armstrong, 1893), 43, 45–49.

19. R. C. White, "Melito of Sardis: Earliest Christian Orator?" *Lexington Theological Quarterly* 51, 2 (1967): 82–91.

20. Adapted from Broadus, *Lectures on the History of Preaching,* 51–57.

21. Ibid., 67–73.

22. Ibid., 73–79.

23. Ibid., 81–83.

24. Ibid., 97–100.

25. Ibid., 106–107.

26. Ibid., 110–112.

27. Ibid., 118–127.

28. Ibid., 221–223.

29. James L. Henderschedt, "The Sermon: A Tool for Evangelism," *Trinity Seminary Review* 7, 2 (Fall 1985): 23–29.

30. Excerpted from Haddon W. Robinson, "What Is Expository Preaching?" *Bibliotheca Sacra* 131, 521 (January 1974): 55–60.

31. William K. McElvaney, "Speaking Out from the Pulpit," *Christian Ministry* 13 (May 1982): 5–7.

32. Frank T. Wilson, "Doctrinal Preaching," *The Journal of the Interdenominational Theological Center* 9 (Spring 1982): 121–126.

33. William B. McClain, "The Soul of Black Worship," *The A.M.E. Quarterly Review* 93, 3 (October 1981): 11–29.

34. Excerpted from H. J. C. Pieterse, "Contextual Preaching: To Gerhard Ebeling on His Seventieth Birthday," *Journal of Theology for South Africa* 46 (March 1984): 4–10.

35. David G. Buttrick, "Interpretation and Preaching," *Interpretation,* 35 (1981): 46–58.

36. Hughes Oliphant Old, "Preaching by the Books Using the *Lectio Continua* Approach in Sermon Planning," *Reformed Worship* 8 (Summer 1988): 24–25.

37. Perry H. Biddle, Jr., "Breathing New Life with the Lectionary," *Christian Ministry* 19, 2 (1988): 3–4.

38. Craig Brian Larson, "Spinning Yarns," *Leadership* 4 (Summer 1987): 20–24.

39. Excerpted from William Fulco, "Jewish Storytelling and Anamnesis," *Modern Liturgy* 3, 8 (November–December 1976): 8–9.

40. Bill Hybels, "Speaking to the Secular Mind," *Leadership* 9 (Summer 1988): 28–34.

41. Excerpted from William Skudlarek, "Lay Preaching and the Laity," *Worship* 58 (November 1984): 500–506.

42. Barbara Brown Zikmund, "Women as Preachers: Adding New Dimensions to Worship," *Journal of Women and Religion* 3, 2 (Summer 1984): 12–16.

43. John Bergland, "Ten Tests for Preaching," *Duke Divinity School Review* (Winter 1976): 16–20.

44. Jay R. Weener, "Personal Preparation for Worship," *Reformed Worship* 8 (Summer 1988): 12–13.

45. Condensed from Tom Kraeuter, *Keys to Becoming an Effective Worship Leader* (n.p., 1992).

46. John Wimber, "Building a Worship Philosophy," in *Worship Leader's Training Manual* (Anaheim, Calif.: Worship Resource Center, Vineyard Ministries International, 1987), 33–39.

47. Nick Ittzes, "Worship Leaders Lead People," *Psalmist* (February–March 1989): 25–26.

48. _____, "Building a United Worship Team," *Psalmist* (April–May 1989): 25–26.

49. _____, "Learning Biblical Leadership Skills," *Psalmist* (June–July 1989): 25–27.

50. _____, "Worship Leaders and Planning," *Psalmist* (August–September 1989): 25–27.

51. _____, "The Worship Leader as Servant," *Psalmist* (October–November 1989): 28–30.

52. _____, "Pursuing Excellence," *Psalmist* (December 1989–January 1990): 18–19.

53. Eddie Espinosa, "Worship Leading," in *Worship Leader's Training Manual* (Anaheim, Calif.: Worship Resource Center, Vineyard Ministries International, 1987), 55–82.

54. Mike and Viv Hibbert, "Developing Communication Skills as a Worship Leader," *The Psalmist* (December 1987–January 1988): 18–19; reprinted from their book, *Music Ministry* (1982).

55. Christine A. Chakoian, "When You Lead Worship . . . ," *Reformed Worship* 21 (Fall 1991): 42–44.

56. William Cieslak, "At Home in the Sanctuary: Prayer Leadership with Style and Grace," *Modern Liturgy* 13, 1 (1986): 9–11.

57. Larry Myers, "Leading Worship in a Smaller Church," *Worship Update* 4, 1 (19): 3–4, 10.

58. Tom Kraeuter, "Getting the Most Out of Rehearsals," *Psalmist* (June–July 1989): 24.

59. Lamar Boschman, "Hand Signals for Worship Leaders," *Psalmist* (December 1988–January 1989): 14–15.

60. Wilma Vander Baan, "Planning Praise for the Parish," *Reformed Worship* 8 (Summer 1988): 7–9.

61. Donald Wilson Stake, "Planning for Worship," *Reformed Liturgy and Music* 18, 4 (Fall 1984): 170–173.

Index